ARCHAEOLOGIES OF COLONIALISM

The Joan Palevsky  Imprint in Classical Literature

In honor of beloved Virgil —

"O degli altri poeti onore e lume . . ."

— Dante, *Inferno*

ARCHAEOLOGIES OF COLONIALISM

*Consumption, Entanglement, and Violence
in Ancient Mediterranean France*

Michael Dietler

UNIVERSITY OF CALIFORNIA PRESS

Berkeley   Los Angeles   London

THE PUBLISHER GRATEFULLY ACKNOWLEDGES THE GENEROUS
SUPPORT OF THE CLASSICAL LITERATURE ENDOWMENT FUND
OF THE UNIVERSITY OF CALIFORNIA PRESS FOUNDATION,
WHICH WAS ESTABLISHED BY A MAJOR GIFT FROM
JOAN PALEVSKY.

University of California Press, one of the most distinguished university
presses in the United States, enriches lives around the world by advancing
scholarship in the humanities, social sciences, and natural sciences. Its
activities are supported by the UC Press Foundation and by philanthropic
contributions from individuals and institutions. For more information,
visit www.ucpress.edu.

University of California Press
Berkeley and Los Angeles, California

University of California Press, Ltd.
London, England

Library of Congress Cataloging-in-Publication Data

Dietler, Michael.
    Archaeologies of colonialism : consumption, entanglement, and violence
in ancient Mediterranean France / Michael Dietler.
        p. cm.
    Includes bibliographical references and index.
    ISBN 978-0-520-26551-6 (cloth : alk. paper)
        1. Social archaeology—Gaul.   2. Gaul—Colonization.
3. Gaul—Ethnic relations.   4. Colonization—Social aspects—Gaul—History.
5. Acculturation—Gaul—History.   6. Consumption (Economics)—Gaul—
History.   7. Violence—Gaul—History.   8. Gaul—Antiquities.
9. France—Antiquities.   10. Mediterranean Region—Antiquities.   I. Title.
DC62.D54 2010
909′.09822—dc22   2010005647

Manufactured in the United States of America
19 18 17 16 15 14 13 12 11 10
10 9 8 7 6 5 4 3 2 1

Cover illustration: Representation of the Gyptis legend, engraved by
C. Laplante. From F.P.G. Guizot, A Popular History of France from the Earliest
Times. Estes and Lauriat: Boston, 1869.

For
Ingrid Herbich
Dolores Dietler
Patrick Dietler
To whom I owe everything.

CONTENTS

ACKNOWLEDGMENTS

Having conducted research in France for nearly thirty years, I find it fitting that the final touches to this book should be made in Lutetia, capitol of the Parisii, as I return to France for a sojourn as director of the University of Chicago Center in Paris. Over all those years, I have accumulated many debts of gratitude to people and institutions. Let me begin by expressing my profound thanks to the Center for Advanced Study in the Behavioral Sciences at Stanford and to the Mellon Foundation for a memorable sabbatical fellowship during 2007–08 that enabled me to work the bulk of the manuscript into nearly final form. I would also like to thank the many colleagues at the CASBS whose engaged conversation aided my work, and particularly the members of the Imperialism, War, and Violence reading group: Don Brenneis, Gail Hershatter, Miles Kahler, Walter Scheidel, and Allan Stam. I also owe hearty thanks to the School for Advanced Research at Santa Fe, which provided me with another delightful sabbatical in 2002–03 during which I was able to rethink the original foolhardy attempt to compress multiple approaches to the colonial encounter into a single unreadable, gargantuan book. I am also extremely grateful to the Lichtstern Fund of the University of Chicago, the French Ministry of Culture, and the National Science Foundation for research funding. My thanks also to the École des Hautes Études en Science Sociale and the Université Paris I for sojourns as a visiting professor, and to Yale University, where I taught before coming to Chicago. Other institutions I would especially like to acknowledge include the Centre National de la Recherche Scientifique (CNRS) Unité Mixte de Recherche 154 at Montpellier-Lattes, the Centre Camille Jullian at Aix-en-Provence, and the CNRS Laboratoire de Céramologie in the Maison de l'Orient at Lyon.

There are many friends and colleagues in France whose work has provided much of the empirical foundation on which this book has been constructed and whose personal generosity has allowed me to participate in the archaeological exploration of the region. Michel Py, whose prodigious body of research has fundamentally transformed our understanding of the Iron Age in Mediterranean France, invited me to collaborate in the excavation project at Lattes in 1997; and this continuing experience, his friendship, and his collegial challenges have provided an invaluable grounding for thinking about the colonial encounter. Thanks are also due to Thierry Janin for the opportunity to continue collaborative research at Lattes up to the present, as well as for his friendship and intellectual engagement. The late Charles Lagrand, in addition to his generous friendship, provided a crucial introduction to the archaeology of Mediterranean France that I will always cherish. Jean-Paul Morel kindly opened the doors of the Centre Camille Jullian to me during the early years of my research and provided a stimulating body of scholarship on Phocaean colonialism that set a very high standard. Pierre Dupont provided my initial delightful introduction to French archaeology and culture, as well as access to the resources of the ceramic laboratory at Lyon. Andre Tchernia has been a dear friend for many years, as well as a primary guide to matters enological, ancient and modern. The list of other friends and colleagues in France, Spain, Germany, Britain, and the United States I would like to thank for various acts of generosity and stimulation is long (and undoubtedly incomplete): Natalia Alonso, Jean-Loup Amselle, Patrice Arcelin, Bettina Arnold, Guy Barruol, Michel Bats, Carme Belarte, Guy Bertucchi, Jean-Pierre Brun, Olivier Buchsenschutz, Ramon Buxó, Bruno Chaume, Jean Chausserie-Laprée, John Collis, Anick Coudart, Carole Crumley, Jean-Paul Demoule, Philippe Descola, Manfred Eggert, Jean-Luc Fiches, Eric Gailledrat, François Gantès, Dominique Garcia, Armelle Gardeisen, Pierre Garmy, Christian Goudineau, Michel Gras, Vincent Guichard, Antoinette Hesnard, Bruno Latour, Denis Lebeaupin, Pierre Lemonnier, Joan Lopez, Georges Marchand, Ian Morris, Gaël Piquès, Patrice Pomey, Matthieu Poux, Stéphanie Raux, Pierre Rouillard, Núria Rovira, Joan Sanmartí, Pierre Séjalon, Jean-Christophe Sourisseau, Henri Tréziny, Pol Trousset, Sander van der Leeuw, Peter van Dommelen, and Peter Wells.

The University of Chicago has proved a stimulating environment for thinking about colonialism, and among the friends and colleagues whose intellectual engagement I would like to especially acknowledge are Nadia Abu El-Haj, Arjun Appadurai, the late Barney Cohn, John and Jean Comaroff, Shannon Dawdy, Chris Faraone, Judy Farquhar, Jim Fernandez, Ray Fogelson, Jonathan Hall, Alan Kolata, Joe Masco, Nancy Munn, Stephan Palmié, Jamie Redfield, Marshall Sahlins, Adam Smith, Gil Stein, George Stocking, Rolf Trouillot, and Terry Turner. I would also like to thank the graduate students in my seminars on the Archaeology of Colonialism and Colonial Landscapes and those who have worked with me at Lattes, including especially Alison Kohn, Ben Luley, Will Meyer, Andreu Moya, Sébastien Munos, and André Rivalan.

Chapters 1 and 2 include large portions of an article published in *The Archaeology of Colonial Encounters* edited by Gil Stein, copyright © 2005 by the school for Advanced Research Press, Santa Fe. This material is reprinted by permission. Chapter 7 includes much material from a chapter in a volume entitled *The Archaeology of Food and Identity* edited by Kathryn Twiss, Center for Archaeological Investigations, Occasional Paper No. 34 © 2007 by the Board of Trustees, Southern Illinois University, and is also reprinted by permission I would also like to thank Blake Edgar of the University of California Press for expressing his early enthusiasm for the book and for shepherding it expertly through the publication process.

Finally, I would like to thank the three people to whom this book is dedicated. Ingrid Herbich has made enormous sacrifices over the years to see this work to completion, especially over the last couple of years of very intensive immersion in writing when she had to deal with a distracted zombie whose head was always about two thousand years away. Throughout, she has remained an ardent, understanding supporter and an active intellectual contributor. Quite simply, the book could never have been written without her, and it is fitting that it should be dedicated, with deep gratitude, to Ingrid. My parents, Dolores and Patrick Dietler, have also been constant, patient supporters who encouraged and enabled my long early years of research. They have also been a lifelong source of inspiration. The book is jointly dedicated to them as well.

Michael Dietler
Paris, October 2009

THE CUP OF GYPTIS
Introduction to a Colonial Encounter

From the people of Massalia, therefore, the Gauls learned a more civilized way
of life, their former barbarity being laid aside or softened; and by them they were
taught to cultivate their lands and to enclose their towns with walls. Then too, they
grew accustomed to live according to laws, and not by violence; then they learned
to prune the vine and plant the olive; and such a radiance was shed over both men
and things, that it was not Greece which seemed to have immigrated into Gaul, but
Gaul that seemed to have been transplanted into Greece.

JUSTIN XLIII.4

This statement summarizing the colonial encounter that constitutes the central focus of
this book was written during the reign of Augustus, the first Roman emperor, although
it purports to describe a process that began about six centuries earlier. It was written by a
historian named Gnaeus Pompeius Trogus, who, despite his Roman name and citizenship, was a son of the Vocontii, a powerful Gallic tribe[1] from what was by that time the
conquered Roman province of Gallia Narbonensis. This intriguing, if (as will be shown)
largely erroneous, evaluation of the effects of a protracted colonial encounter appeared
as the summation of a retelling of a legend about the foundation of the Greek colony of
Massalia on the coast of southern France nearly five hundred years before the Roman
conquest of the region and six hundred years before the reign of Augustus.[2]

The foundation tale is first known from a text written by Aristotle in the fourth century BCE, already more than two centuries after the event. The version of Pompeius
Trogus is more richly elaborated and contains some slight variations from that of
Aristotle.[3] According to this legend, rights to the territory of the settlement and friendly
relations between colonists and natives were secured originally through the marriage of
a wayfaring Greek trader, named Protis, to a native woman named Gyptis (the daughter
of Nannos, ruler of the local Segobrigai tribe). The Greek visitor was actually selected
by Gyptis from among a number of suitors at a feast by means of a ceremony in which
she offered a symbolic cup of drink to the man she chose as her husband (fig. 1.1). After
their marriage, Protis was given land on the coast by his new father-in-law to found
the colonial city that became Massalia and, eventually, modern Marseille. However,

FIGURE 1.1

A representation of the Gyptis legend from a nineteenth-century French history book (engraving by C. Laplante from Guizot 1869).

this generous welcome appears to have been short-lived, because the text of Pompeius Trogus goes on to describe how within a generation the natives became alarmed about the growing power of the colonial settlement and began to attack the Greeks. The passage then concludes, paradoxically, with the gushing statement about the civilizing influence of Greek colonialism that opens this chapter.

These observations about the consequences of the legendary cup offered by Gyptis mark the beginning of a long history of speculation, debate, and empirical study over a question that has continued to provoke the attention scholars to the present: what was the nature of the encounter between these seaborne intruders from distant Mediterranean city-states and the indigenous peoples of western Europe, and how did it affect the historical transformation of these societies? As will be shown, the answer to this question is one of great complexity and its implications extend far beyond the history of ancient Gaul or the Mediterranean. In many subtle ways, they lie at the heart of conceptions of modern European identity, contemporary colonial discourse, and scholarly debates about Euro-American colonialism.

This book is an attempt to address this ancient question from a new perspective. One may well ask why such an endeavor should be both necessary and of interest at this point in time. The reasons are several and complex, and explaining one of the principal ones will occupy the better part of the first two chapters. But, for the moment, let me begin by briefly noting that the past few decades have yielded an enormous amount of new archaeological data that have the potential to significantly transform our understanding of this encounter and to make it an exemplary case study for an archaeological contribution to the comparative anthropology of colonialism. However, although the book presents and synthesizes a range of impressive new data, this act of empirical documentation is not its ultimate goal. Indeed, a crucial aspect of the argument presented here is that the analysis of these data must be accompanied by a transformation of both our theoretical approaches to the study of colonialism and our understanding of the sociohistorical context of archaeological practice.

Hence, the book seeks to use this case to raise and engage a set of broader issues of major epistemological and theoretical significance for the anthropological and archaeological study of colonialism in general. More will be said about this later. But let me first point out that, as a prerequisite to the archaeological analysis undertaken in the book, it begins with an attempt to reframe the discussion by disentangling a complex recursive relationship that has developed between this ancient Mediterranean colonial encounter and modern European culture and colonialism. It seeks to demonstrate the curious historical process by which modern consciousness has been, in a sense, "colonized" by the ancient Greeks and Romans and how that colonized perspective has come to color the way archaeologists now understand ancient colonial encounters, including especially that seminal encounter represented by the tale of Gyptis.

In using the trope of colonization, I do not mean to imply that archaeology ever existed in a "precolonized" condition to which it can be returned through some sort of intellectual liberation struggle. As the first two chapters take pains to explain, the formation of archaeology as a professional practice was precisely a product of the broader colonization of European consciousness that I discuss there — archaeology was born already colonized, as it were. Moreover, archaeology often constituted an instrument, as well as a product, of colonialism: an alien technique for defining, constructing, controlling, and even appropriating the past of colonized peoples.[4] Nor do I imagine that we can really produce a completely "decolonized" discipline that is free from its history and political context. Both the study of postcolonial nations[5] and the sociological lessons of science studies[6] should have dispelled long ago that naive vision. What I am advocating is the necessity of striving for reflexive critical awareness as a crucial component of the analytical process, in the direction of Pierre Bourdieu's "participant objectivation"—one that places the analyst in the field of analysis and examines the conditions of possibility of disciplinary practice.[7] This approach is not conceived as a path toward some stable position of objectivity. That would be a chimerical fantasy. Rather, it is proposed as a necessary recurring phase in a continual dialectical process that opens new questions and enables new insights.

SETTING THE STAGE

Before explaining why the ancient colonial encounter in the western Mediterranean, and Mediterranean France in particular, has come to play such a pivotal role in modern European culture and colonial discourse (see chapter 2), and why this case matters to the comparative study of colonialism more generally, let me briefly introduce the main players in this historical drama and set the stage by situating them within an outline of the history of the encounter. That history is a long and complex one, and its debut actually predates the foundation of Massalia captured in the Gyptis legend by several centuries. It involved alien agents of multiple origins engaged in relationships of quite different kinds with a variety of indigenous societies over a period of more than a millennium.[8] This book explores the inception, unfolding, and consequences of that process in the Rhône basin of Mediterranean France.

The encounter in southern France actually took place at the tail end of a series of diasporic expansions of peoples from the eastern Mediterranean that began near the end of the ninth century BCE, over two hundred years before the foundation of Massalia (figs. 1.2 and 1.3). That process saw the establishment of various kinds of colonies in parallel streams. Traders and settlers from several independent city-states of the Syro-Palestinian coast, who are referred to collectively as "Phoenicians," dispersed along the southern shores of the Mediterranean. They established colonies in North Africa, Sicily, and Sardinia and moved rapidly all the way to southern Spain, where they began to establish settlements and trading centers in the eighth century BCE. By the sixth century BCE, Carthage, a large Phoenician colony in Tunisia, began to exert control over many of these formerly independent establishments and became an increasingly expansive center of power in the central and western Mediterranean. Meanwhile, Greeks from both the mainland and colonial cities along the Turkish coast moved westward along the northern shores of the Mediterranean and eastward into the Black Sea.[9] By the seventh century BCE, colonists from a variety of Greek cities had established new city-states along most of the coast of southern Italy, but they had not yet planted any colonies farther west in France or Spain.

In Mediterranean France, the encounter was initiated during the late seventh century BCE when a ship-based trade began bringing goods from Etruscan city-states in west-central Italy to the shores of southern France. These imported goods consisted mostly of wine, drinking ceramics, and a few small bronze basins. Shortly thereafter,

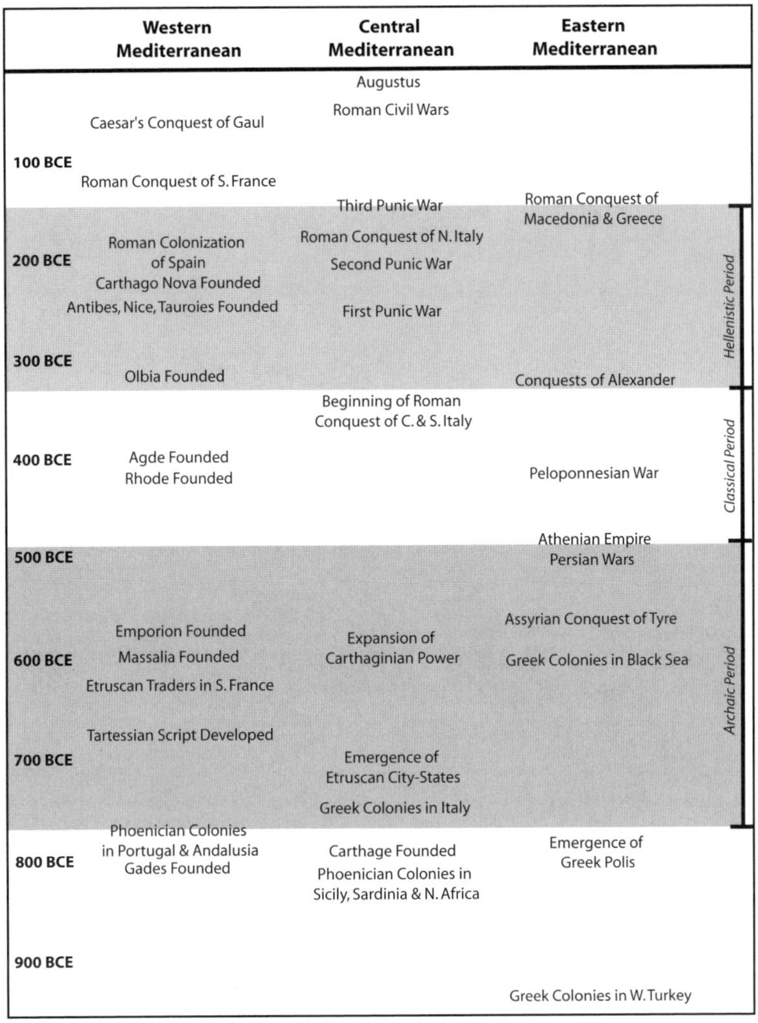

	Western Mediterranean	Central Mediterranean	Eastern Mediterranean	
		Augustus		
		Roman Civil Wars		
	Caesar's Conquest of Gaul			
100 BCE				
	Roman Conquest of S. France			
		Third Punic War	Roman Conquest of Macedonia & Greece	*Hellenistic Period*
	Roman Colonization	Roman Conquest of N. Italy		
200 BCE	of Spain	Second Punic War		
	Carthago Nova Founded			
	Antibes, Nice, Tauroies Founded	First Punic War		
300 BCE				
	Olbia Founded		Conquests of Alexander	
		Beginning of Roman Conquest of C. & S. Italy		*Classical Period*
400 BCE	Agde Founded			
	Rhode Founded		Peloponnesian War	
			Athenian Empire	
500 BCE			Persian Wars	
	Emporion Founded		Assyrian Conquest of Tyre	*Archaic Period*
600 BCE	Massalia Founded	Expansion of Carthaginian Power	Greek Colonies in Black Sea	
	Etruscan Traders in S. France			
	Tartessian Script Developed			
700 BCE		Emergence of Etruscan City-States		
		Greek Colonies in Italy		
	Phoenician Colonies in Portugal & Andalusia	Carthage Founded	Emergence of Greek Polis	
800 BCE	Gades Founded	Phoenician Colonies in Sicily, Sardinia & N. Africa		
900 BCE				
			Greek Colonies in W. Turkey	

FIGURE 1.2

Chronology of major events in ancient Mediterranean colonial history.

at approximately 600 BCE, Massalia was founded by settlers from the Greek city of Phocaea, on the coast of modern Turkey, as the first permanent colonial establishment in the region. This was followed within a few decades by the foundation of another Phocaean colony at Emporion (modern Ampurias), a voyage of about three hundred kilometers farther west on the Catalan coast of Spain. Both of these colonial establishments came to have important influences on the patterns of trade and exchange in the region, although the geographic extent and nature of those influences were quite different, as were the evolving characteristics of the colonial settlements themselves (see chapter 4). By the late sixth century BCE, some Greek and Etruscan objects were also finding their way over 500 kilometers north of Mediterranean France to sites of the so-called Western

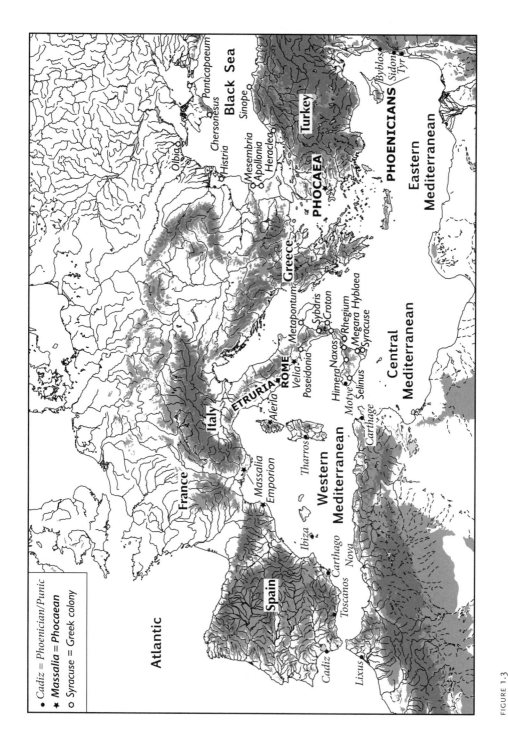

- *Cadiz* = Phoenician/Punic
- ★ *Massalia* = Phocaean
- ○ *Syracuse* = Greek colony

FIGURE 1.3

Map showing the homelands of the colonial agents operating in the western Mediterranean and some major Phoenician, Phocaean, and other Greek colonies.

Hallstatt zone in Burgundy, southwestern Germany, and Switzerland. This was a relatively short-lived phenomenon, however, as these imports largely disappeared from this northern zone by the end of the fifth century BCE.[10]

A few Phoenician objects had also begun to arrive in Mediterranean France from colonies in the south of Spain during the seventh century BCE. These became much more numerous during the sixth century BCE, but these were now mostly Iberian products (adapted from Phoenician and Punic models),[11] and their consumption was largely confined to the Emporitan sphere of influence in the western portion of Mediterranean France (that is, Roussillon and western Languedoc rather than the region around Massalia). It is uncertain whether Phoenician, Emporitan, or Iberian merchants (or all three) were trading these goods in the region.

Over the course of the next few centuries, Massalia also began to establish a number of very small subcolonies along the coast to both the west and east (at Agde, Hyères, Antibes, Nice, and other locations). However, it never managed to wrest a very large *chora* (or territory of direct political control and agricultural exploitation) from its indigenous neighbors. Indeed, it appears that Massalia's chora remained largely confined within a radius of about eight kilometers from the port for a period of nearly five hundred years. Massalian trade with indigenous peoples of southern France had a complex history over the centuries, but by the early fifth century BCE (or somewhat later in a few areas), it had largely replaced the earlier trade in Etruscan goods and Massalia remained the dominant source of imports in the lower Rhône basin for over three hundred years. Once again, wine amphorae dominated the repertoire of trade goods that were being consumed by indigenous peoples. These were accompanied by ceramic tablewares of several types and, eventually, by a few other kinds of objects.

The late second century BCE marked a dramatic change in the history of the evolving colonial situation. By the end of the third century BCE, armies of the rapidly expanding Roman Republic had already seized control of southern and eastern Spain from Carthaginian colonists and native Iberians during the Second Punic War. The provinces of Hispania Citerior and Hispania Ulterior were subsequently established, although it took nearly two hundred years for the interior of these provinces to be subdued. In southern France, at least twice during the first half of the second century BCE, Rome responded to calls for aid from its ally, Massalia, in conflicts with its indigenous neighbors. Around 125 BCE, following new appeals from Massalia for help in defending itself against the neighboring Salyes tribe, the Romans launched a rapid military conquest of Mediterranean France. This created a land bridge between their recently acquired possessions in Northern Italy and Spain. A permanent military base was established at Aquae Sextiae (Aix-en-Provence), just south of the Salyen capitol. Then, in 118 BCE, the consul Domitian founded the colony of Narbo Martius (modern Narbonne) on the coast of Languedoc, and a road, the Via Domitia, was established through southern France linking Italy and Spain.

Roman control of this region lasted for over half a millennium. However, the consolidation of Roman coercive and ideological control throughout Mediterranean France first required a series of further military campaigns to suppress occasional revolts, defeat incursions from the north, and subdue "pirates" along the coast, at the same time that Rome itself was experiencing a "social war" (in 90–88 BCE) and a violent civil war (in 49 BCE) with military conflicts that spilled over into southern France. This was accompanied by experimentation with the construction of an administrative infrastructure necessary to establish a hegemonic imperial order in this new Roman province that would eventually (in 27 BCE) be given the name Gallia Narbonensis by Augustus. Julius Caesar arrived in the region in 58 BCE as governor and immediately used Mediterranean France to launch yet another major campaign of conquest that brought the rest of Gaul (*Gallia Comata*, or "long-haired Gaul") under Roman control by 51 BCE. In 46 or 45 BCE, Caesar established at Narbonne the first of a series of colonial settlements populated by veterans of the Roman legions. Others of this type were established at Béziers, Arles, Orange, and Fréjus before 27 BCE; these sites witnessed, especially under the reign of Augustus, the gradual construction of monumental civic architecture in the Roman style (arenas, theaters, baths, arches, etc.) as well as the construction of networks of roads and aqueducts leading into these cities and the restructuring of space in agrarian hinterlands with cadastral systems.

Roman involvement in Mediterranean France differed radically in character from that of any of the earlier colonial agents. Rome was the first of the Mediterranean states to have the military and administrative capacity, and perhaps the imperial ambitions, to impose political control beyond a small territory immediately surrounding a port city. The cultural techniques of domination employed by the Romans were very effective. As will be discussed later, many of these served as inspiration for modern colonial practices, including the "investigative modalities"[12] deployed in places like British India and Africa. However, although the eventual social and cultural effects of Roman domination were profound, they were neither immediate nor uniform. Colonized peoples had a marked influence on the regionally distinctive development of colonial cultures and imperial practices, including, not least, the cultural and social transformation of the Roman metropole.[13] Nevertheless, to name only the most obvious of the eventual transformations that stemmed from this colonial situation, the Roman occupation resulted in the gradual extinction of indigenous languages throughout the region (and in the rest of Gaul, Spain, and Italy) and their replacement with creolized versions of Latin, as well as the dramatic restructuring of the landscape. This latter process included both the reorganization of rural landholdings and routes of communication, and the creation of public monuments and other structures, many of which are still visible on the landscape.

APPROACHING THE ENCOUNTER

While the broad sequence of historical events outlined here is well established and widely known, significantly less well developed is the crucial understanding of how those events resulted in the transformation of culture and consciousness and the emergence of new forms of economic and social relations. In other words, we still urgently need to investigate the operation of colonialism: the complex process by which alien colonists and native peoples became increasingly entangled in webs of new relations and through which there developed a gradual transformation of all parties to the encounter. In approaching the analysis of such a long and intricate colonial history with this goal in mind, no single strategy can serve to reveal the full complexity of the situation within the covers of one book. In fact, I would suggest that, as a general principle, developing an effective archaeology of colonialism that comes to terms with these issues requires a multiplicity of paths of entry, analytical trajectories, scalar shifts, and narrative structures in treating a given colonial situation. This book deploys a very particular strategy that forms part of a larger project of multiple analyses of the encounter from different directions, and it requires some prefatory explanation.

In treatments of this encounter, I have, so far, deployed two complementary modes of investigation, both of which involve a commitment to focused regional analysis within a broader comparative framework, but with different temporal orientations and data selection strategies. The first approach, which one might describe metaphorically as "horizontal," involves restricting the temporal scale of analysis in order to enable a detailed examination of short-term relational aspects of colonial encounters and entanglements throughout a region by means of a comprehensive exploration of contemporary archaeological data. This strategy was employed in a book examining the crucial initial phases of the encounter, during what is conventionally called the Early Iron Age, in the lower Rhône basin of France.[14] That work was intended as the foundational segment in a series of studies with different spatial, temporal, and thematic approaches. In contrast, the current book adopts a strategy that might best be characterized as "vertical." Still grounded in the analysis of a specific region (the same lower Rhône basin), it targets long-term colonial processes by focusing on historical transformations within selected domains of social life, such as the cross-cultural consumption of different forms of material culture, urban landscapes, economic practices, and forms of violence. This strategy serves as a way of illuminating the dynamic nature of colonialism and its entanglements by exploring exemplary strands in the fabric of the changing colonial situation over the course of nearly six centuries, from the first arrival of Etruscan merchants through the early phases of Roman colonization.

Another difference from the prior book is that, whereas that work attempted to deal with patterns derived from highly inclusive analysis of all of the hundreds of contemporary indigenous settlements and funerary sites within the region (using over a century of excavations of highly variable quality), the current work focuses primarily on a more limited number of representative sites where recent excavations have produced data of sufficient quality (in terms of context, quantification, and chronological precision) to yield nuanced interpretations of such things as subtle shifts in patterns of consumption or changes in inhabited space. The site of Lattes (ancient Lattara), on the coast of Languedoc, where I have been excavating for over a decade, plays an especially important role in this strategy because of the abundance and quality of the information generated by the large multinational archaeological project that has been ongoing there for over twenty-five years. But one cannot understand a complex historical process such as colonialism on the basis of one site alone: the data from Lattes become meaningful only within a regional context that is constructed from other excavations that offer possibilities for detailed comparison. This includes colonial settlements, especially Marseille.

Bringing the colonists into the field of analysis in a serious relational fashion is another departure from prior practice. Most other synthetic works have concentrated either on the history of indigenous societies (leaving Greeks, Etruscans, and Romans as a kind of unexamined external influence or force) or on Greek, Etruscan, and Roman history (with the indigenous world as a kind of inert framing background, environment, or resource).[15] Yet, if recent theoretical work emerging from studies of modern colonialism has taught us anything, it is that colonial encounters transform all parties involved. England did not simply export a stable version of English culture to its colonies; rather, English culture and identity emerged and were transformed as part of the colonial experience, every bit as much as did cultures and identities in colonized Ireland, India, or Africa.[16] The same was certainly true of ancient Greeks and Romans. Hence, what is necessary in the present case is a *symmetrical* analysis of the colonial situation: a relational examination of interconnections and transformations in, for example, both Massalia and the native settlements of southern France—one that does not privilege one or the other as an inherent historical agent or influence, or treat either as a black box that lies outside the field of analysis. Nor should one assume an inherent discreteness or stability in these categories.

Ideally, both works should be read in tandem to understand the strengths and silences, the potential and problems, of each approach. One thing that is common to both is a strong commitment to regionally focused analysis motivated by a self-conscious theoretical position concerning the requirements for developing an effective archaeology of colonialism. The logic of this position will become clearer later, but it can be briefly summarized as follows. As an anthropologist, I am concerned not simply with delineating macroscale structures of broad economic or political forces, but rather understanding local experience and situating local history in relation to larger historical structures. Colonialism is not a process that takes place, or can be explained, at the level of abstract structures, especially crudely economic ones. It is an active, historically contingent process of creative appropriation, manipulation, and transformation played out by individuals and social groups with a variety of competing interests and strategies of action embedded in local political relations, cultural perceptions, and cosmologies. In my view, sweeping evolutionary models of the political economy have little meaning or explanatory utility (or, indeed, verifiability) unless it can be shown how they relate to and, in fact, emerge out of the daily lives of particular peoples in particular localities. Clearly, this is not an easy feat. Yet the ability to deal with local practice, agency, and culture is one of the essential requirements for a serious archaeological contribution to the broader comparative study of colonialism.

I would suggest that one of the critical features of an appropriate strategy is commitment to the local: to detailed contextual analysis of particular regions. This book is designed to suggest one strategy for implementing an effective program of such regional analysis within a larger multiscalar framework. The "horizontal" and "vertical" approaches launched so far, although each is intended to stand on its own as a coherent analysis that produces distinctive kinds of insights, are also envisaged as creating the necessary regional foundational platform for future volumes that address the encounter from (1) the detailed microscale perspective of transformations of daily life within the different households and neighborhoods of a single settlement (Lattara) and (2) the macroscale of the broader history of colonial encounters in the western Mediterranean.

This book covers a temporal span of roughly six centuries, from the late seventh to the late first centuries BCE, and it explores the nature and consequences of interaction between indigenous peoples and Greek, Etruscan, and Roman foreigners. Analysis is focused particularly on the region of southern France designated here as the "lower Rhône basin"—that is, the area within a radius of about 150 kilometers of the colony of Massalia (fig. 1.4).

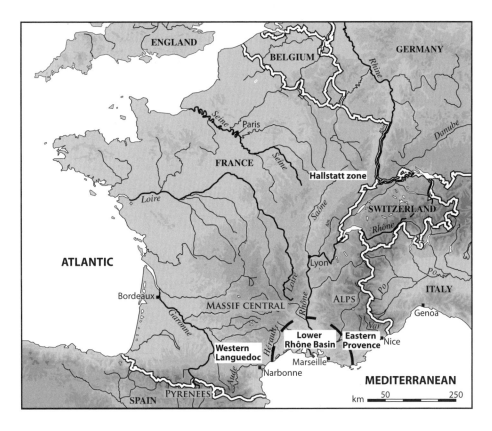

FIGURE I.4

Map showing the location of the lower Rhône basin region in relation to western Languedoc, eastern Provence, and the "Hallstatt zone," as well as to various modern European cities.

However, contemporary developments in neighboring areas are also considered where comparisons are relevant and useful—specifically, in other parts of Mediterranean France and in regions of temperate Europe to the north of the Rhône River corridor.

Why these temporal and spatial parameters? In previous work,[17] I chose to focus first on the latter part of what is conventionally called the Early Iron Age (roughly the mid–seventh to mid–fifth centuries BCE) because it constitutes the seminal stage in an encounter that, as noted, was to link indigenous and colonial societies in a complex, millennium-long history of entanglement and transformation (fig. 1.5).[18] Understanding this period in its own right, and in its fully historicized complexity, is a crucial prerequisite to any attempt to penetrate and comprehend subsequent historical developments in the continually transforming colonial situation. Yet, many current interpretations approach this period largely through backward extrapolation that produces a highly

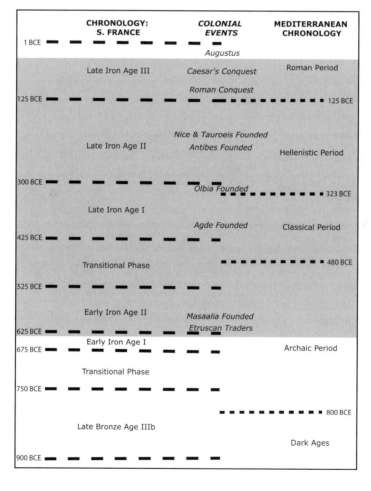

FIGURE 1.5

Chart of different chronology systems used in Mediterranean France. Shaded area represents the period covered in this book.

selective "Whig history" reading of this early period simply as an evolutionary stage in an inevitable colonial *telos*. Indeed, many scholars have treated the early encounter with Greeks and Etruscans as a kind of preparatory phase of "Hellenizing" preadaptation for an eventual and ineluctable process of "Romanization." I would argue that the situation needs a fresh critical treatment that transgresses and challenges some of the long-established interpretive orthodoxies that are endlessly repeated and embellished. These interpretive problems are due not to a paucity of relevant data, but rather to certain theoretical limitations and a resulting failure to pose some fundamental questions. The goal of this work is to operationalize a long-term historical analysis of colonialism that preserves a commitment to regional specificity and a fully historicized, contingent understanding of process.

Another feature of the strategy used in this book is a selective focus on tracing certain exemplary themes through the changing colonial situation. The book targets particularly processes centering on the body, such as the consumption of food, the inhabitation of space, and violence. The body is, after all, the basic nexus of colonialism—the target and agent of practices of control and the instrument of the embodiment and performance of identity.[19] The material dimension of the encounter is also a major focus of analysis in the book—both the fundamental role of material culture in processes of entanglement and transformation of consciousness and the crucial material conditions of engagement.

The areal focus on the region of the lower Rhône basin can be explained by the fact that, in terms of Mediterranean colonialism in ancient western Europe, this was for centuries a pivotal space — precisely the kind of region that Greg Dening, in his discussion of modern colonialism, referred to metaphorically as "the beach"[20] or that others have termed the "contact zone,"[21] the "tribal zone,"[22] or the "middle ground."[23] In other words, it is the zone of direct, sustained encounter between indigenous peoples and alien colonists, where mutually misunderstood cultural differences were worked through in political and economic practice, pidgins and creole languages, and, often, violence. This is the space, par excellence, for archaeologists to be able to perceive, for example, the complex intersecting webs of interest that Marshall Sahlins called "structures of the conjuncture,"[24] the creative accommodations of Richard White's "middle ground,"[25] or the "hybridity" of postcolonial scholars.[26] Yet, surprisingly, this region has been effectively ignored by nearly all the more ambitious works purporting to analyze the systemic impact of Mediterranean colonial activity in Iron Age Europe, and this point is especially true of Anglophone scholarship.[27] However, it is clear that this "contact zone" had important relationships with both Mediterranean colonists and the larger indigenous world to the north. Hence, it must form an essential part of any systemic understanding of the regional political economy of the colonial encounter in western Europe. Reciprocally, local researchers in southern France, who have done extensive and excellent research on such issues as Greek and Etruscan trade, have often been reluctant to relate their data to broader theoretical discussions of colonialism or to acknowledge the significance that a comparative anthropology of colonialism holds for their own research. This book attempts to show why such engagements in both directions are crucial to further progress in archaeological research and why that research is important to the broader understanding of colonialism. In fact, despite the highly focused temporal and geographic range of this work, I would suggest that the analysis of this particular regional colonial encounter has far-reaching implications and that it is necessarily of much more than local historical interest.

ARCHAEOLOGIES OF COLONIALISM

There are several good historical and anthropological reasons why the question I introduced with Trogus Pompeius's conclusion to the legend of Gyptis has generated such sustained interest and demands a fresh exploration, and these reasons lie behind my choice of the phrase "archaeologies of colonialism" as a title for the book. The title is intended to indicate the use of the term *archaeology* in both its traditional meaning and its metaphorical Foucaultian sense.[28] Indeed, one of the recurring themes of this book is that an intimate and ineluctably dialectical relationship exists between these two approaches to understanding colonialism in this context.

In brief, as hinted at earlier, I am proposing that by a curious historical process this particular *ancient* colonial encounter in the western Mediterranean had a profound influence on the cultural construction of *modern* European colonial ideologies and discourse, and that, reciprocally, this discourse has had a pervasive influence on modern scholars engaged in the archaeological exploration of that ancient colonial situation (and other cases as well). Hence, not only is there a particularly pronounced need for critical analytical scrutiny of ancient Greek and Roman colonialisms (because of the crucial role they have played in the foundational mythology and discursive constitution of "the West"), but it is impossible to evaluate and improve on current understandings of this particular ancient colonial encounter without simultaneously disarticulating the entangled strands of this relationship. As will be shown, the cultural foundations of modern colonialist discourse were largely grounded in interpretations and interpolations of the texts of the ancient Greek and Roman colonial powers. This process has resulted in a limited and doubly inflected view of the ancient encounter in which it is perceived through the prism of the highly partial impressions of ancient colonists further refracted through the lens of modern readers who have been formed by both a culture of admiration for Greco-Roman "civilization" (with a far from disinterested set of identifying attachments) and the distorting experience and motivations of modern imperial ventures. Hence, without a critical awareness of the complex referential loops involved in this process, archaeologists risk unconsciously imposing the attitudes and assumptions of ancient colonists, filtered and largely reconstituted through modern colonial ideology and practice and embodied as part of the Western intellectual habitus, back onto the ancient situation. Ironically, this would constitute a kind of second colonization of ancient Gaul, but one even more pervasive than the first in that all access to indigenous experience of the encounter would have been finally suppressed.

One can begin to circumvent this problem only by situating the discussion within a critical sociohistorical examination of the discursive role that the ancient encounter played in both the development of modern European culture and the institutional context in which the discipline of archaeology was formed. Despite the somewhat complicated strategy of argumentation this requires, it is hoped that the result will be of relevance not only to those concerned with the archaeology of the European Iron Age or with Greco-Roman colonial history, but also to anthropologists and postcolonial scholars interested more generally in the comparative understanding of colonialism (including the phenomenology of colonial and postcolonial discourses). Aside from this Foucaultian move, the title "archaeologies of colonialism" is also intended to indicate my interest in demonstrating the possibilities for a significant archaeological contribution to that broader theoretical project, as well as indicating the necessity of multiple intersecting approaches to the analysis of colonial situations.

COLONIALISM, COLONIZATION, IMPERIALISM

Up to this point, the word *colonialism* has been brandished quite freely without really defining what I mean by the term or showing how it might differ from other related terms such as *imperialism* and *colonization*. Moreover, I have yet to explain why this phenomenon called colonialism should be a useful focus of anthropological research attention, why archaeology has something to contribute to this endeavor, and why I have seen fit to apply this rubric to ancient encounters in Mediterranean France. None of these issues is self-evidently transparent, despite the fact that they are often treated as if they were.

As with *culture*, colonialism has become one of those ubiquitous concepts in anthropology and history (not to mention such fields as political science, geography, cultural studies, and postcolonial studies) about which there is general consensus regarding its importance yet little agreement about its precise definition. A perusal of the extensive relevant literature reveals a wide variety of ways in which the term *colonialism* is used and in the ways its meaning is seen to intersect with those equally protean concepts, imperialism and colonization.

Edward Said, for example, defined *colonialism* as the "implanting of settlements on a distant territory," while *imperialism* consists of "the practice, the theory and the attitudes of a dominating metropolitan center ruling a distant territory."[29] Others (Webster's dictionary, for example) would call the process of implanting settlements "colonization" and reserve the term *colonialism* for a major part of what Said included under imperialism. Alternatively, David Fieldhouse used *imperialism* as an umbrella term covering the entire range of relations between a dominant power and subject societies. He saw colonization and colonialism as two alternative outcomes of imperialism, as two forms of the domination of subject peoples: the former involves a situation in which the dominant group is a large resident population in the subject territory, whereas the latter involves control exerted by a small alien group.[30] Others, in contrast, would label these latter two forms of domination colonialism and imperialism, respectively.[31] Robert Young, in yet another variation, sees colonization and domination as two forms of colonialism: the former directed toward the acquisition of living space for settlers and the latter toward the extraction of wealth. In contrast to colonialism, which he sees as a pragmatic, ad hoc, and often chaotic process carried out by private interests on the peripheries without central control, imperialism is held to be a state-directed practice of power driven by a coherent ideology and a theory of centralized control.[32] Some Marxist traditions would define colonialism as the conquest and direct control of other people's land and see it as simply a stage in the history of imperialism, defined itself as an advanced (or terminal) stage in the global expansion of the capitalist mode of production.[33] Others see the distinction between imperialism and colonialism as a matter of conflicting perspectives on the same phenomenon of expansion and domination, with the former representing the view of the colonizer and the latter the perspective of the colonized.[34] Alternatively, Jürgen Osterhammel defined colonization as "a *process* of territorial acquisition" and colonialism as "a *system* of domination."[35] More specifically, colonialism is "a relationship of domination between an indigenous (or forcibly imported) majority and a minority of foreign invaders."[36] For Osterhammel, it is possible to have both colonies without colonialism and colonialism without colonies (Moses Finley dogmatically espoused the opposite opinion[37]). Moreover, according to Osterhammel's definition, imperialism differs from colonialism largely as a matter of scale: it is "the concept that comprises all forces and activities contributing to the construction and maintenance of *transcolonial empires*."[38] Hence, it is also possible to have colonial empires without imperialism (if they are not *transcolonial*). Finally, for Enseng Ho, colonialism consists of "the occupation of territory by foreign settlers, soldiers or administrators," and it involves the notions of possession and property. Imperialism is a different form of domination that is a relationship of influence rather than possession. It is the projection of power across space, including the boundaries of nominally sovereign states, by a variety of means, such as economic penetration and manipulation, clientship, political alliances, and intimidating performances of military muscle.[39] The permutations of these overlapping and interdigitating definitions are endless, and they have a long history extending well beyond the influential modern foundational texts of Hobson and Lenin.[40]

I raise this issue of terminology not out of a pedantic concern to impose a semantic orthodoxy, nor to indulge the kind of typological fetish for which we archaeologists are renowned. Indeed, I find the typological-normative mode of analysis to be a rather unproductive approach to understanding colonialism. Rather, than creating a set of prepackaged, all-encompassing concepts to which particular cases can be assigned as a stand-in for analysis, I favor a flexible analytical use of categories as devices for provoking questions by focusing critical attention on the similarities and differences exposed by the act of making comparative distinctions. But, aside from my belief that some self-conscious reflection on the meaning of the central analytical concepts one deploys is a minimum requirement of scholarship, I raise the issue of terminology here because it serves as a striking initial example of the subtle complexities of the problematic relationship between ancient and modern colonial situations already noted. This is because most of our modern analytical vocabulary for treating such phenomena derives precisely from this ancient Mediterranean colonial encounter, as did a good part of the operational vocabulary of modern colonialism. For example, the terms *colonization, colonialism, colonial,* and *colony* all derive from the Latin word *colonia,* while *imperialism* and *empire* stem from the Latin *imperium, civilization* from the Latin *civilis,* and so forth. However, the meanings of these words have been significantly transformed as they have been applied over the centuries to a variety of modern contexts and processes. Reapplying them uncritically to the seminal ancient context poses the danger of importing modern meanings back to the past and implicitly rendering the ancient cases simply as variants, or prototypes, of the modern. As we shall see in chapter 2, this was precisely the ideological proposition responsible for the original application of these ancient words to modern situations. But Roman "colonies" were not the same thing as nineteenth-century French or British colonies, and it is an analytically crucial move to recognize and make explicit that what has been terminologically constructed as metonymy is actually metaphor. Nor were either of these kinds of "colonies" the same as what modern scholars now almost universally persist in calling "colonies" in the ancient Greek context, despite the fact that the Greeks themselves used the terms *apoikia* and *emporion* for their "colonial" settlements. For example, the relationship of relative dependency/autonomy between colony and mother-city was radically different in the Roman and Greek cases, as were the political contexts and functions of foundation.[41]

As postcolonial critics have been instrumental in emphasizing, this is not a trivial problem. Robert Young, for example, has noted that "all perspectives on colonialism share and have to deal with a common discursive medium which was also that of colonialism itself: the language used to enact, enforce, describe or analyse colonialism is not transparent, innocent, ahistorical or simply instrumental."[42] As he further emphasized, a failure to challenge the way that colonialism has involved (in addition to its military and economic instruments of control) a permeation of knowledge risks attempting to understand colonialism through its own discursive products.

Circumventing the problems posed by this terminological palimpsest is not easy, but it is clearly quite important. The strategy frequently employed by cultural anthropologists to signal cultural and historical distinctiveness — that is, using indigenous terms in place of translating them into subsuming "etic" analytical categories — has, by and large, been precluded in the current case precisely because those terms have already been co-opted and integrated into our popular and analytical discourses with interpolated semantic content. My own inclination would be to simply abandon this vocabulary altogether and substitute a less compromised and entangled set of analytical terms. However, the idea of inventing and imposing on the reader a new lexicon to deal with ancient cases that avoids any Greco-Roman terms that have been incorporated into modern discourse seems a cumbersome and quixotic endeavor at best—the intellectual equivalent of spitting into the wind. Furthermore, that might risk seeming to deny, a priori, possible points of genuine similarity between ancient and modern cases. Rather, in the absence of any readily viable alternative path around the treacherous discursive landscape that lies before us, I would suggest that we are condemned to continue grappling pragmatically with the terms current in the disciplines of colonial analysis, with the crucial stipulation that we must maintain an ever-vigilant self-conscious wariness of the traps of implicit fusion and the dangers of anachronism. The complex roles that invocations of ancient Greece and Rome have played in the construction of modern European culture and colonialism (discussed in chapter 2) render this an especially delicate task in the present case. But I would suggest that the solution to this problem lies more in a critical awareness of the kind that the Foucaultian style "archaeology" of colonialism offered in this book is designed to impart than in simply tinkering with linguistic reform. Whatever imperfect vocabulary one ultimately decides to employ, vigilant attention must be paid to differences as well as similarities in the colonial contexts and processes that are clustered semantically.

In the face of this terminological heterogeneity, let me at least be clear and consistent in my own use of these terms. The word *imperialism* is used in this book to indicate an ideology or discourse that motivates and legitimizes practices of expansionary domination by one society over another, whatever those practices might entail (e.g. military conquest, economic dependency). In other words, one can have imperialism without an empire. I use the term *colonization* to indicate the expansionary act of imposing political sovereignty over foreign territory and people, and *founding colonies* to denote the act of establishing new settlements in alien lands. *Colony*, as used here, encompasses the Greek term *apoikia* and the Latin *colonia* (both originally implied the founding of a settlement in foreign territory, but with quite different relations of dependency within different structurations of the political economy).[43] I use *colonial province* to designate a subject territory that is the product of colonization.

Finally, by *colonialism*, I mean the projects and practices of control marshaled in interactions between societies linked in asymmetrical relations of power and the processes of social and cultural transformation resulting from those practices. Hence, colonization is, ultimately, solidified or maintained through colonialism, but colonialism can also operate without the formal subjugation of foreign territories that colonization implies. Or it may precede an eventual colonization. The nature and effectiveness of such practices defined as colonialism, and their potential permutations, may be extremely variable from one colonial context to another, ranging from such things as trade, to missionary activities, to warfare and raiding, to political administration, to education. Similarly, the processes of transformation are highly variable, and they always entail a host of unintended consequences for both indigenous peoples and alien colonists. Both parties eventually become something other than they were because of these processes of entanglement and their unintended consequences.

This definition of *colonialism* is sufficiently broad that it cannot be considered a precise typological category used to demarcate a uniform process or reified transhistorical phenomenon explicable within a single "theory of colonialism." Indeed, I am in agreement with the growing body of scholars who voice skepticism that such a project is possible.[44] Rather, colonialism, in the sense used here, is a pragmatically general and inherently plural analytical rubric employed to focus critical attention and facilitate the comparative analysis of a wide range of practices and strategies by which peoples try to make subjects of other peoples in a variety of disparate historical situations, and the complex transformations occasioned by those practices, in the effort to better understand both the differences and the similarities in these processes through history.

Why is this a worthwhile endeavor, and how can archaeology contribute to this research project? The answer to the first question is, I think, fairly easy. The kinds of practices clustered under the label of colonialism have been implicated frequently as some of the most significant forces in world history. It has been estimated that, by the early decades of the twentieth century, one-half of the surface of the Earth's continents was under some form of colonial domination, and about two-fifths of the population of the world (more than six hundred million people) were living under colonial rule.[45] Moreover, other regions (such as Latin America) had suffered long periods of transformative colonial domination in previous centuries before finally ridding themselves of European control during the eighteenth and nineteenth centuries. Following the rapid collapse of all the European empires in the face of indigenous resistance during the middle decades of the twentieth century, the term *postcolonial* has become a popular rubric for the contemporary world situation. However, few scholars would seriously contend that it is possible to understand the current state of affairs, including the various emergent forms of cultural and economic "neocolonialism," without reference to the historical legacy of colonialism. This is precisely the gist of the field of postcolonial studies. Moreover, it is highly questionable to what extent the internal situations of nations such as the United States, Canada, Australia, New Zealand, and several Latin American examples can seriously be called postcolonial—especially from the perspective of descendents of the aboriginal peoples of these lands.[46] And a glance at the recent projects of violent military expansion and domination by several regional and international powers might reasonably lead one to the conclusion that the situation is still resolutely pre-postcolonial in a number of parts of the world. This colonial legacy, of course, extends much deeper than these recent Euro-American manifestations. Indeed, two thousand years ago, perhaps half the world's population lived under the sovereignty of two immense empires (Roman and Chinese), and one could reasonably make the case that a good part of at least the past five thousand years of human history consists of an incessant series of colonial encounters. And it is not unreasonable to argue that something more than superficial understanding of the present requires a comparative exploration of the broad range of strategies and practices employed in the effort to exert control over other societies around the world and throughout history and the myriad repercussions of those practices.

The discipline of archaeology can contribute to this project in several ways. In the first place, it can aid understanding of the expansion of the Euro-American capitalist "world-system" that, from the sixteenth century on, has been responsible for the most extensive implementation of colonialism in world history.[47] It can do this by exposing and combating the tyranny of the text: by furnishing kinds of evidence that are qualitatively different from and independent of the colonial texts that constitute the vast bulk of evidence available to historians. Because most colonial powers were literate and many subjects of colonial domination were not (at least originally), the textual evidence for such encounters tends to be highly partial, in both senses of the term. This is manifestly not to deny that, by reading against the grain, it is possible to use these sources to reconstruct a vision of indigenous culture and the colonial process which differs from that of the colonial observers. Marshall Sahlins, for example, makes a compelling argument in favor of this possibility while, at the same time, demonstrating the complexity of the endeavor and the stringent requirements for source criticism.[48] Ethnohistorical information recorded by anthropologists provides a rich complementary source of data, although one that has its own interpretive problems of temporal depth, situated interests, memory, translation, and transformations of consciousness stemming from the colonial situation.

What archaeology offers is access to the *material dimension* of the encounter and to the processes of daily life through which the colonial situation was experienced and worked out by ordinary people. This is by no means a straightforward or unmediated window of access to an indigenous perception of the colonial situation. Archaeologists practice an interpretive discipline having many serious problems with data and epistemology that limit the range and quality of the information they can generate. But archaeology does provide at least a potential means of interrogating the "silencing of the past."[49] In any historical analysis, it is always crucial to ask, "Whose stories get told?" "Whose voices get heard?" and "Whose do not?" This point is especially true for colonial situations, which involve both asymmetries of power and asymmetries in access to the instruments of historical recording. The voice of "the subaltern" may indeed be epistemologically very difficult to hear,[50] especially when analysis is focused in the domain of texts; but the subaltern does live in and act on the material world. Hence, recovering the material record of the lives of those whose voices have not been recorded, imperfect as it may be, does offer at least a potential challenge to the colonizer's view of the world and the silences it imposes.

But more than simply providing an alternative kind of evidence, the archaeological focus on the material dimension of colonialism is crucial for another reason. After decades of neglect, a new appreciation has been emerging in recent years among cultural anthropologists, historians, and postcolonial scholars of the profound significance of material culture in the playing out of colonial strategies and processes.[51] It is increasingly recognized that material objects have been simultaneously an important tool of colonial strategies of engagement and control, a catalyst of desire and the inclination to tolerate alien intrusions, and a vector of myriad unintended forms of entanglement and cultural transformation. Of course, one must be careful not to fetishize material culture in such a way that relations between people become mystified as relations between objects and people. To do so, as will be shown later, amounts to swallowing one of colonialism's frequent ideological conceits. A recent book on archaeology and colonialism falls prey to precisely this trap by actually defining colonialism as "a particular grip that material culture gets on the bodies and minds of people" and claiming that "colonialism is crucially a relationship with material culture,"[52] thereby displacing agency, obscuring important relations of power between people, and ultimately hindering understanding of the more subtle and complex role that material culture plays in colonial processes. Nevertheless, without succumbing to such a seductively reductive position, it is crucial to recognize the profound significance of material culture in the working out of colonial strategies and processes. These features are discussed more fully in chapter 3, but it is easy to imagine why they promise fruitful possibilities for synergistic collaboration in the investigation of recent colonial history between archaeologists and scholars of colonialism from other fields. The former have long been specialists in the interpretation of material culture. As Arjun Appadurai has noted, the material world constitutes "the first principles and the last resort of archaeologists."[53] By necessity, they have been forced to develop continually methods to systematically examine the material remains of human life, analytical skills to recognize and evaluate material patterns, and interpretive theory to understand the properties, significance, and roles of material culture.

But an equally important contribution of archaeology to the study of colonialism derives from the fact that it is the primary (and in many cases the only) conduit to ancient, precapitalist colonial encounters, for which relevant contemporary texts are far more limited or absent. As noted earlier, understanding colonialism in the encounters generated by the historically recent development and expansion of the Euro-American capitalist system requires that they be set in comparative perspective through examination of the historical dynamics of other contexts. It is especially necessary, I would claim, to examine the many colonial situations that predate Euro-American capitalist expansion in order to ascertain both the singular and more widely shared features of this recent set of phenomena that has generated most of our anthropological theory on colonialism. This world of ancient colonial encounters made accessible by archaeology is crucial to the project of "provincializing" the modern European experience and its hegemonic role in the production of theory.[54] Unfortunately, to date, few of the social anthropologists, historians, or postcolonial scholars who have advocated such a comparative analytical project seem to be aware of the archaeological literature on colonialism or the contribution that archaeology has to offer. For example, a recent volume dedicated specifically to the task of challenging the Eurocentric slant of colonial studies by expanding the comparative field and "refiguring imperial terrains" failed to exploit the vast terrain of premodern cases made available by archaeology.[55] Despite the rapid growth of archaeological studies of colonialism,[56] the disciplines have not yet been brought adequately into conversation with each other.

It is also true that archaeology has an indispensable role to play in resolving debates in the realm of modern colonialism that otherwise risk degenerating into supposition and speculative history. Perhaps the most obvious example is the dispute between scholars who see the existence of a modern world system as an intrinsically new phenomenon that developed in Europe during the sixteenth century, such as Fernand Braudel and Immanuel Wallerstein, and those who see it as simply a late stage in an inexorable continuous expansionary process of a system that actually began over four millennia ago, such as Andre Gunder Frank.[57] Without recourse to archaeological data, such questions could be the subject only of surmises. As Frank's multiple missteps in his attempt to use archaeological data in support of his hypothesis indicate, this should not be done naively. But collaboration between specialists from different disciplines has the potential to yield productive results.[58]

The role of archaeology in illuminating the silences and silencing of colonial history is even more crucial in ancient contexts. This fact should be obvious in situations without texts — where there is no writing at all, archaeology is the only tool we have. But this role must be appreciated equally in situations where some preserved textual evidence is available. In general, the range of documents in ancient contexts is considerably more limited than in modern colonial situations. Hence, both the silences (due to accidents of preservation and discursive conventions) and the potential silencing of other voices (due to the privileging of more narrowly restricted points of view) are considerably greater.

Archaeological studies of colonialism should also serve to counter an occasional tendency toward temporal myopia among cultural anthropologists, historians, and postcolonial scholars, for whom modern Euro-American colonialism sometimes seems the only object on the horizon. While the huge geographic extent of capitalist expansion is undeniable, it is well to recall that, for example, the Roman empire lasted far longer than any modern empire and, in many ways, its colonial practices had even more profound cultural and social consequences than more recent examples. For instance, no modern empire managed to produce the same scale of language death and linguistic replacement as Rome did in its western provinces. Moreover, one frequently cringes to hear certain technologies of control or aspects of colonial practice naively attributed to a unique origin in the logic of capitalism when they were, in fact, a feature of much earlier colonial systems. As later discussion will show, the nineteenth-century European colonial administrators who were responsible for devising and implementing these practices were far more intimately familiar with the history of Greek and Roman colonialism than are most current scholars of colonialism and postcoloniality, and they were acutely aware of the prior origin of the practices they were trying to replicate or adapt. In this vein, it is also relevant to note that the late twentieth century is by no means the first experience of a "postcolonial" moment in world history. The ancient world had many such episodes. Ironically, for reasons that will become clear in chapter 2, these have often been referred to as "dark ages."

My point here is that scholars of modern colonialism need to contextualize their studies of colonial practice and ideology within a much longer and broader historical framework. This is necessary both in order to be able to recognize those aspects of modern colonialism that are genuinely unique and because, for the colonial agents they are studying, past forms of colonialism were often very much an integral part of their present consciousness. Colonial practices and strategies were not invented from whole cloth; they were part of a complex dialectical relationship between present and past (or, more precisely, an imagined past). Archaeology has an important role in furnishing that deeper context for a larger comparative understanding of colonialism, and, for reasons that will become clear in the next chapter, the case of ancient Mediterranean colonialism is particularly relevant in that regard.

Finally, having earlier voiced at some length my concerns with analytical vocabulary, why do I feel it appropriate to include the case of ancient Mediterranean France under the rubric of colonialism? Do the forms of interaction that we find, for instance, in the early phases of this encounter, represented by Etruscan and Massalian trade with indigenous peoples and the foundation of a few diasporic settlements, necessarily imply the existence of asymmetrical relations of power that the term *colonialism* entails? The nearly universal assumption in the archaeological literature to date would be that they do (although classical scholars generally eschew the term *colonialism*, with its negative moral connotations, in connection with Greek ventures in favor of what they perceive to be the more neutral term *colonization*[59]). However, my own view is that this is actually a complicated, but crucial, question that must be subjected to empirical investigation, and the reasons underlying this common a priori assumption itself need to be examined carefully.

As later chapters will show, there are good grounds to doubt the existence of effective domination or significant colonization (in the sense defined earlier) on a regional level during much of the period covered here. The Etruscan and Massalian relationships with native peoples were certainly radically different from the later Roman colonial occupation and from nineteenth-century European imperial ventures. Nevertheless, I would insist that it is crucial to include the early periods of encounter in the analysis of the history of colonialism in the region, even if relations during these early stages did not involve power asymmetries sufficient to merit the term *colonialism*. They did involve projects and contests of *attempted* control on both sides — including the seizure of a very small extraurban territory (*chora*) under direct Massalian control, the establishment of several colonial outposts along the coast, and periodic violence. But more important, they constitute the initial phases of engagement between alien Mediterranean states and indigenous societies that, whatever the original configuration of relations of power, created the conditions that drew all the parties into a process that eventually resulted in a clearly asymmetrical colonial situation. That colonial situation did not suddenly appear fully formed: it emerged out of a complex prior history. As Nicholas Thomas has warned for recent historical colonial contexts, "Although the ultimately exploitative character of the global economy can hardly be overlooked, an analysis which makes dominance and extraction central to intersocietal exchange from its beginnings will frequently misconstrue power relations which did not, in fact, initially entail the subordination of native people."[60] It is a serious analytical error to assume that asymmetrical relations or structures of power that ultimately appeared in later periods were an inevitable feature of the first stages of the encounter rather than a product of a subsequent complex history of interaction and entanglement.

The interest of the early phases of the encounter in Mediterranean France is precisely that they offer the opportunity to explore the ways in which the exchange of material objects entangled foreigners and natives in relationships that, even in the absence of initial domination, established the conditions for other, often unanticipated, kinds of colonial relations to develop. That highly contingent history of entanglement and transformation must be analyzed in a new way, such that it may be coherently understood as a process, but without falsely imbuing it with a telos. In other words, the goal is to make it understandable without making it seem inevitable. Hence, a detailed study of the initial phases and the subsequent unfolding of encounters, which does not simply extrapolate backward from its better-known historical sequel, must be an essential focus of any discussion of the history of colonialism in the region.

The following two chapters explain in more detail the strategy devised to undertake this analysis and its theoretical foundations. They do so by first contextualizing the project through a metaphorical "archaeology" of the relationship between ancient and modern colonialisms of the kind introduced earlier. This prepares the stage for a brief discussion of archaeological investigation of the colonial encounter in Iron Age France, a critical review of the major interpretive perspectives that have guided research, and (in chapter 3) an explanation of the rather different approach that directs the analysis that unfolds in the rest of the book.

GYPTIS TROPES

Before proceeding to that discussion, I would like to return briefly to the legend of the cup of Gyptis with which this chapter began, both because it cannot be left standing as a commentary without some critical intervention and because it serves as a useful way of highlighting in a preliminary fashion some of the salient themes of this book.

The legend as a whole is quite clearly a Massalian version of a rather typical colonial charter myth offering a moral justification for the establishment of a settlement on land that belonged to others. The land rights acquired through a wedding gift in this case may be compared, for example, to the proverbial twenty-four dollars paid to Native Americans for the island of Manhattan (but nicely exhibiting a contrasting precapitalist mentality with regard to land tenure on the part of the Greeks). Pompeius Trogus took care to emphasize in two different places within a short span of text that the land of Massalia was *freely given* to the colonists.[61] However, the subtext of the tale suggests that relations were more hostile than would be expected from the smooth and cordial insertion into native affinal networks and officially sanctioned possession of the land that the story portrays. Indeed, Comanus, the son of the purported land donor, Nannos, is described as having mounted an attack against the city because of fears that the Massalians "who seemed at present mere tenants would one day become masters of the country." The danger was purportedly conveyed to Comanus in a fable: "One day a pregnant dog begged a shepherd to give her a spot to lay down. Having obtained this, she then asked further permission to raise her young there. Finally, once her pups had grown up, supported by her domestic garrison, she claimed ownership of the place." The fears revealed in this metaphor of colonialism and the resulting hostility are portrayed by the Greeks as arising from native jealousy over the benign progress of the colony, but this should be treated with some skepticism.[62]

In fact, despite the elements of plausible local detail (e.g., personal and ethnic names are of the appropriate Celtic linguistic heritage), the events of the tale cannot be accepted as necessarily having any historical accuracy. Ancient Greeks were fond of speculating about the origins of things, and colonial foundations were a frequent subject of etiological mythologizing. These tales usually combine what would today be distinguished analytically as mythic, legendary, and historical elements in various combinations, but they tend to follow a predictable patterned sequence of cultural metaphors that Carol Dougherty identified as purification, riddling, and marriage.[63] The marriage metaphor, involving union with a local woman or nymph, she saw as a way of euphemizing violence and representing the civilizing, domesticating, and controlling ideology of the Greek relationship with natives and their land in colonial discourse, one in which "the power relationship between men and women which Greek marriage implies is then used to negotiate the terms of interaction between Greek colonists and local populations."[64] It provided an analogical trope for understanding the founding of colonies as a productive, harmonious union of opposites, but one with an implicit, axiomatic cultural understanding of the "natural" balance of power and authority.

Hence, the historical veracity of the events in the tale must be regarded as dubious. Nevertheless, it may be rehabilitated for present purposes as a useful trope hinting at a number of social processes that are likely to have had considerable importance in the historical development of the colonial encounter. For example, the probability of intermarriage between colonists and natives is a very real one, which is likely to have had significant social and cultural consequences for both sides. Moreover, for reasons that will become clear later, the fact that relations between Greeks and natives are portrayed as having been established through the offering of drink in the context of a feast presages one of the previously overlooked, but fundamental, keys to comprehending the cultural and social logic of colonial interaction in this instance.

Finally, although chapter 2 shows that the ultimate message of the tale (about the gradual absorption of "civilization" by "barbarians") represents a dominant tendency in past interpretative perspectives, somewhat paradoxically, the tale may also be used to introduce the gist of the alternative approach advocated in this book. In my view, the fact that relations between indigenes and colonists are portrayed as having been instigated through the active choice of the native woman, Gyptis, underlines the necessity of focusing seriously on the role of agency by indigenous peoples in the process. Colonial interaction is not a simple process of diffusion between an active donor and a passive receptor. Nor is it a simple playing out of structurally determined roles. Consumption of alien cultural elements is an active, motivated, creative process. Moreover, the portrayal of the formation of social relations between natives and colonists in the context of a traditional native institution (regardless of whether the suitors' feast is an accurate rendition of an indigenous custom) emphasizes that colonial interaction must be looked at from the standpoint of the social and cultural logic of indigenous societies with their proper cultural institutions and complex histories. To be sure, from the moment of the encounter, these histories unfolded as part of a newly configured "global" Euro-Mediterranean history, but they were not *determined* by events and structures in the domain of the colonial powers. Rather, both parties, natives and colonists, were linked in complex networks of interaction driven by different logics of social action and interest. This book seeks to explore new ways of understanding the colonial encounter in the lower Rhône basin as a process of entanglement and transformation of particular peoples at the conjuncture of local and global histories. Hence, it follows a strategy with three primary dictates: (1) a commitment to multiscalar analysis firmly grounded in a particular region, (2) the targeted examination of long-term historical transformations within selected domains of social life, and (3) a simultaneous symmetrical analysis of transformations in indigenous and colonial societies, with both viewed as dynamic agents and products of the encounter. All of this, of course, depends first on a critical sociohistorical contextualization of both the object of analysis and the analytical project, and this endeavor is tackled in the next chapter.

2

ARCHAEOLOGIES OF COLONIALISM

All our religion, almost all our law, almost all our arts, almost all that sets us above
savages has come to us from the shores of the Mediterranean.

DR. JOHNSON, IN BOSWELL 1887, VOL. 3:36.456

All civilized nations, in all that concerns the activity of the intellect, are colonies
of Hellas.

J. A. SYMONDS 1880:401

The continent of Europe has been our modern Hellas. . . . And surely we may
without self-flattery claim that in the high civilization which Europe has inherited
and passed on to her kindred across the oceans, is a Hellenism which the
barbarian rejects but still longs to understand and assimilate.

G. MURRAY 1953:52–53

Although the racial ancestry of the English was Nordic, their cultural ancestry is
predominantly Mediterranean.

D. S. FOX 1978:2

Perhaps the most intriguing and consequential case of "invented traditions" in European
history involved a sweeping "colonization" of modern consciousness by the ancient Greco-
Roman world. This process was launched several centuries ago, and its evolving manifestations have been a pervasive feature of European cultures ever since. The passages cited
above are illustrative of this curious cultural conquest of the present by the past, although
hundreds of other examples easily could have been substituted to make the point. More
important in the present context, however, is to examine the nature of, and reasons for,
the historical development of this referential and reverential engagement with the ancient
"classical" world and, especially, to reveal its connection to the intimate and problematic
relationship between ancient and modern colonialisms that I posited in chapter 1.

This issue is of particular concern in dealing with the colonial encounter in the ancient western Mediterranean. That is because this encounter constitutes the seminal episode in the colonial process through which the indigenous peoples of the territories that would eventually spawn the dominant colonial powers of the modern world—France, England, Spain, Portugal, Germany—first became entangled with the Greco-Roman world that later would come to play such an obsessional role in the collective ancestral imagination of these imperial nations. Hence, it is a moment of pregnant significance for modern discourses of imperialism and anti-imperialism. The urgency of a critical archaeological reanalysis of this encounter is clear, as are the desirability and difficulty of situating that analysis from a position that attempts to unsettle the encounter from its discursively embedded context.

This modern infatuation with ancient Greece and Rome stems from a particular moment in European history, the so-called Renaissance of the fifteenth century, when a new myth of European cultural ancestry was constructed. Not coincidentally, this was a period that also witnessed the first phase of modern European colonization beyond the Mediterranean.[1] In this chapter, I first examine the ways in which the development and embellishment of this ancestral myth was linked both to the construction of a field of "cultural capital" (in the sense of Pierre Bourdieu[2]) marshaled in processes of class differentiation within European societies and to the production of an imperialist discourse providing an ideological engine (or at least a rationalization) for European colonialism abroad. I then show how both of these closely interrelated features have subtly conditioned and constrained the interpretive perspectives of archaeologists engaged in the study of ancient Mediterranean colonialism and explain why it is so critical to reflexively challenge our intellectual habitus, to the extent that this is possible. This discussion serves as the foundation for presenting, in chapter 3, an approach to the colonial encounter that points the way toward circumventing some of these vexing problems.

The Renaissance was not so much a "rebirth" as an invention, a self-conscious attempt to link the present directly to a long dead and poorly understood period of the past by negating a millennium of intervening history and a wide variety of other cultural influences. As Michel-Rolph Trouillot has noted, "we need not take the naïve history of the West at face value: Greece did not beget Europe. Rather, Europe claimed Greece."[3] The movement began in Italy, and, not surprisingly, it was actually ancient Rome, rather than Greece, that provided the initial ancestral "golden age" and Roman culture that was the first focus of adulation and emulation. The alluring imperial legacy of Rome, with its widespread traces throughout western Europe, assured that this movement rapidly spread to other nations as well, including especially France, Spain, and England.[4] Liberally reinterpreted visions of Roman culture inspired facsimiles and established the canons of taste in everything from architecture to literature, art, political philosophy, furniture and clothing styles, and even gardens.[5] Some of these borrowings were deliberately historicist, while others were based on supposed timeless universal aesthetic principles that the classical world was believed to have distilled and codified. Latin was expanded and transformed from its monastic role as the language of the church to attain an even more elevated status as the universal language of secular rational intellectual discourse; and the works of Roman poets, orators, and historians were studied as stylistic models and sources of moral and philosophical inspiration. The lingering aura of prestige that Latin acquired during this time is reflected in the fact that most universities in the United States, thousands of years and miles away from any connection to ancient Rome, have Latin mottoes on their crests.

A widespread fascination with the ancient Greeks did not develop until several centuries after the debut of the Renaissance. This movement, in which the Greeks were lifted from insignificant obscurity to the level of a pan-European cultural obsession, and genealogically transformed from a part of the decadent oriental world to the quintessential occidental ancestor, stemmed largely from a romantic humanist vision developed in Germany during the eighteenth century and popularized by a scholar named Johann Joachim Winckelmann.[6] This romantic aesthetic fixation on the Greeks originated partly as a reaction against the rationalist Enlightenment tradition of "Augustan" neoclassicism that had become particularly associated with France. Although Winckelmann could never bring himself to actually visit Greece, he became convinced through his reading and observation of art that "Good taste . . . had its origin under the skies of Greece,"[7] that ancient Greek culture represented the pinnacle of human development in the quest for universal standards of absolute beauty and truth. For Winckelmann, emulation of Greek culture, or what he rather imperfectly imagined it to be, was almost a moral obligation. This version of passionate philhellenism, which Joachim Wohlleben has aptly labeled "Graecolatry" and "Graecomania,"[8] was adopted by Goethe, Schiller, Schlegel, and other influential German writers and intellectuals who came to believe that becoming Hellenized was the only possible path for someone seeking personal development (Bildung). Hence Goethe's famous dictum: "Let each man be a Greek in his way! But let him be one." This virulent strain of Grecomania soon infected France, England, and other countries as well,[9] leading to Shelley's famous battle cry of Romantic Hellenism in its waning days: "We are all Greeks."[10]

By the nineteenth century, the Greek colonization of modern European (and Euro-American) culture was at its apogee. Political philosophy, art, architecture, and education were permeated by appeals to the ancient Greeks.[11] Would-be Greek temples such as La Madeleine in Paris, the Altes Museum in Berlin, the British Museum in London, the Field Museum in Chicago, or the "Parthenon" in Nashville are impressive architectural testaments to the ideal of a monument thought to be expressive of "high culture" on both sides of the Atlantic during the nineteenth and early twentieth centuries (fig. 2.1). However, the kind of Hellenism that informed European life after the early nineteenth

FIGURE 2.1

La Madeleine, one of the most literal invocations of Greco-Roman architecture that compose the vast neoclassical landscape of Paris (compare the Maison Carrée of fig. 2.2). Commissioned in 1806 by Napoléon I as a temple to the glory of the army and now a Catholic church.

century was quite different from the Romantic Hellenism of Winckelmann and Shelley. As Susan Marchand has noted for Germany, the earlier Grecophiles

> borrowed their ideals—self-cultivation, disinterested contemplation of the beautiful, good and true, admiration of the ancients—from aristocratic models; but the incorporation of nineteenth-century philhellenism into the founding of Prussia's new research universities, secondary schools, museums, and art academies after 1810 universalized these values and in effect imposed them on generations of middle-class Germans. . . . As the century progressed, philhellenism became more and more the conventionalized predilection of the educated middle class *(Bildungsbürgertum)*, inextricably linked to the academy and state bureaucracy.[12]

Rome by no means disappeared as a cultural ancestor in the face of this rampant Grecolatry. It still remained a powerful source of inspiration in terms of legal, institutional, and architectural models, and the legacy of its imperial conquests continued to provide a standard of reference and ambition for modern European nations.[13] But the relationship between the Greek and Roman legacies was the subject of a broad range of complex, and often contradictory, interpretations. The characteristics of the two civilizations were often contrasted, with the Greeks dominating a hierarchy of cultural superiority and the Romans getting the nod for military and administrative prowess. However, the best aspects of Rome itself were often considered to be a product of its own Hellenization. As the classicist Gilbert Murray succinctly summarized this view, "Roman civilization, as it became more perfect, became more Hellenic."[14] Given that Rome (or at least its ruling elite) had been heavily influenced by Greek art, architecture, philosophy, and science, it was often seen to have been carrying out a historic mission as a middleman in bringing the superior moral and intellectual enlightenment of Greek civilization to the "barbarians" it incorporated into the empire. Hence, the European myth of cultural ancestry in the nineteenth century enshrined both Greece and Rome as hallowed progenitors with complementary characteristics and roles.

The same processes of institutional embedding that Marchand noted for nineteenth-century Germany were in operation in England and France as well, albeit with certain variations appropriate to the different political histories and educational systems of these nations. In all three countries, a knowledge of and a cultivated appreciation for the "classics" became a powerful form of "cultural capital," in the sense of Bourdieu,[15] by which members of the ruling class (now essentially the wealthy bourgeoisie) were able to assert and embody their cultural and moral superiority. Access to this specialized cultural competence was acquired in the universities and the institutions of secondary education that were available only to the privileged and that formed the elite class of each country: the English "public school" and the tellingly named German *Gymnasium* and French *lycée*.[16] The curricula of these schools tended to be heavily dominated by the study of the ancient Greek and Latin languages and ancient Greek and Roman literature and history, as contact with these idolized former civilizations was thought to have powerful transformative effects in the development of character and taste.[17] As Alain Gérard has remarked, the lycée student of the late nineteenth century was "a little citizen of the ancient classical world" who learned the history of his own country only as a brief episode in the history of Rome.[18]

Likewise, as James Bowen noted for England, the public schools were designed to fashion an elite ruling class that included both a remnant of the traditional aristocracy and a wealthy and powerful segment of the bourgeoisie. Their mission was to impart the traits of aristocracy to those who had not inherited them and to enhance the patina of superiority for those who had. "In the nineteenth century that had been the task of Hellenism; its content provided the appropriate ideology, while its vehicle, the Greek language, served an essential mystifying function, since the express purpose of arcane learning is to exercise domination over the uninitiated."[19] Appropriately, this classical education was designed primarily to instill "mental discipline and the cultivation of taste" rather than to produce pathbreaking original scholarship.[20] As Lawrence James noted, for the Victorian public schoolboy, in training to learn to rule an empire, "Intelligence mattered less than the acquisition of 'character,' and intellectual activity was largely restricted to otiose and repetitive exercises in the languages of two former imperial powers, Greece and Rome."[21] The public schools took their lead in this obsessive focus on classical education from Oxford and Cambridge, the prestige universities of Victorian England, which the public schools were designed to service. Classics dominated the curricula of these universities and admission to them depended on having acquired the proper training in Greek and Latin.

To a certain extent, the hierarchical vision of the relationship between Greek and Roman culture noted earlier also came to reflect and reinforce finer class distinctions within the English bourgeoisie. At least a smattering of Latin was diffused more widely through the middle class via the grammar schools, whereas Greek continued to be the preserve of "expensively and extensively educated males" of the public schools.[22] Moreover, while a romanticized familiarity with Roman history (including especially the Roman colonization of Britain) and a reverence for Latin were more widely diffused through popular literature, the Hellenists tended to affect an Olympian disdain for things Roman. For them, Latin was a practical language appropriate for conquest and administration, while Greek was an inspired language appropriate for intellectual discourse and literature. In brief, knowledge of Greek was a prime source of cultural capital in the cultivation of diacritical "distinction" of the kind analyzed by Bourdieu.[23] The fashionable practice of the "grand tour" visit to the Mediterranean became, from the eighteenth century on, another important element in developing the cultural capital of classical cultivation, one that was available only to those wealthy enough to undertake such an expensive voyage to see the landscape and statuary of their classical "ancestors."[24] As even that archetypically insular Englishman, Dr. Johnson, noted, "A man who has not been to Italy is always conscious of an inferiority."[25]

The barriers to social mobility for those who were not in a position to acquire this cultural competence (that is, to become Romanized and, especially, Hellenized) were more than simply social conventions. They were also increasingly institutional. In France, Germany, and England during the nineteenth century a knowledge of Greek and Latin was not only necessary to enter university, but the entrance examinations for the civil service all began to require a strong competence in these ancient languages.[26] This feature also assured that politicians and upper-level administrators of the empires controlled by these countries all had in common the feature of having been steeped in the classics. From Bismark to Gladstone, Napoléon III, and the graduates of the École Coloniale, they shared an exclusive common bond of tastes, values, and implicit cultural references lodged in esoteric access to an idolized and idealized ancient culture. The British prime minister, William Gladstone, for example, who wrote an influential book on Homeric Greece,[27] expressed a sentiment common to his class in opining that "the state of Athens at its climax, that is of human nature at its climax."[28] Similarly, the French emperor Napoléon III devoted his energies to writing a two-volume history of Julius Caesar and financing archaeological excavations to document major events in Caesar's conquest of Gaul.[29]

This classical training and taste constituted a far more exclusive point of transnational elite commonalty than, for example, Christian religious beliefs and familiarity with the Bible (something that was shared with the lower classes). Even if many upper-class schoolboys managed to acquire only a veneer of classical learning, their education provided them with (1) a conviction that the cultural ancestry of their own country lay in ancient Greece and Rome, (2) a belief in the inherent attractiveness and superiority of Greek "civilization" in an absolute, universal hierarchy of cultures, and (3) an assurance that the personal cultivation of Hellenized tastes that their schooling imparted was a sign of their own superiority and an appropriate diacritical mark of their class and its destiny to lead others.

Clearly, the legacy of the classics was not simply one of personal cultivation and the pursuit of truth and beauty. From Athens to Alexander, to Caesar, to Augustus, it was also seen as a legacy of colonization and imperialism. This legacy was interpreted by each of the modern European states that saw itself as the legitimate heir to Greco-Roman civilization as a mandate to continue an inherited mission to "civilize" the "barbarian" world and as an ideological model for its own imperial practices.

An institutionalized infatuation with the ancient "classical" world was by no means confined to the European powers, it also had an influential role in those colonies that were settled by large, dominant European populations, such as the United States.[30] The political center of the United States, Washington, DC, for example, is clearly a would-be neoacropolis on the Potomac. The Supreme Court building, the Capitol, the White House, the Treasury Building, and the Lincoln and Jefferson memorials, among many others, are all an architectural homage to ancient Greece and Rome. Moreover, the same is true of most state capitol buildings, city halls, and courthouses throughout the country. But the influence is not confined to buildings with political functions; it is also evident in myriad banks, churches, libraries, museums, and other forms of monumental public architecture. It is also quite widespread in the domestic architecture of the wealthy and powerful classes in the United States (for example, most obviously, the plantation manors of the South).

This pervasive phenomenon is partly due to the influence of contemporary European models. For instance, American universities during the great period of educational expansion in the late nineteenth century were heavily influenced by German universities under the Hellenocentric model established by Wilhelm von Humboldt in Prussia at the beginning of the nineteenth century. But Greco-Roman influences were evident at an even earlier period. At Yale University, for example, the study of classics was a mandatory requirement for the bachelor of arts degree for 230 years until the requirement was finally dropped only in 1931; and PhD degrees are still awarded in Latin (although few of those involved in the ceremony are now able to understand what is being read). These early American appropriations of Rome and Greece were to a large extent the result of a self-conscious attempt by what might be called the "classical class" of the former colonies, including notably Thomas Jefferson, to fashion an independent national taste

FIGURE 2.2

The Maison Carrée Roman temple at Nîmes: the model for Thomas Jefferson's Virginia state capitol.

that would express and inspire a sense of historical destiny for the new republic. Jefferson quite explicitly saw the newly independent United States as a new Greece developing in the wilderness of America, and he turned directly to ancient Athens and, especially, the Roman Republic for appropriate architectural models.[31] His design for the state capitol in Virginia was based directly on the Maison Carrée, a well-preserved Roman temple in Nîmes (a building, in the lower Rhône basin of France, that is a material manifestation of the colonial encounter treated in this book; see fig. 2.2). Similarly, his designs for the University of Virginia and his home, Monticello, were modeled on the Pantheon in Rome.[32]

Also under Jefferson's influence, a national land ordinance was enacted by Congress in 1785 in order to survey and register the new western territory colonized by the country, thereby rendering it "legible" to the state.[33] It instituted a system that was a radical departure from previous practice but that, once again, harkened back to ancient Rome. In the square-grid uniformity of its design, it imposed a highly regularized abstract system of territorial division on the landscape over vast regions in a manner that, not accidentally, resembled the ancient Roman practice of cadastration by which the landscape of colonized territories was restructured. This system, in fact, had a marked role in producing the colonial landscape of Mediterranean France in which Jefferson's beloved Maison Carrée was located.[34]

As this last example suggests, the multifarious roles that Greco-Roman colonialism played in the development of the discourse of modern imperialism and the practices of modern colonialism are difficult to overestimate. This involved both implicit assumptions and explicit use of the past as a symbolic resource in constructing imperial rhetoric and colonial practices. At the most basic level, it involved an axiomatic absorption of the fundamental Greco-Roman hierarchical dichotomization of the world into "civilized" societies and "barbarians," a perspective that would have far-reaching effects in the development of modern imperialism (and, as we shall see, in archaeological interpretive models). But the specific manifestations of the ideological relationship between ancient and modern colonialisms were both varied and pervasive.

Initially, from the fifteenth through the seventeenth centuries, Rome was the nearly exclusive source of imperial models. As Anthony Pagden has noted:

> It was, above all, Rome which provided the ideologues of the colonial systems of Spain, Britain and France with the language and political models they required, for the *Imperium romanum* has always had a unique place in the political imagination of western Europe. Not only was it believed to have been the largest and most powerful political community on earth, it had also been endowed by a succession of writers with a distinct, sometimes divinely inspired, purpose.[35]

Of course, the Italians also shared in this project: Machiavelli's influential writings, for example, are permeated by advocacy of colonization on Roman models.[36] In fact, all the European empires made continual symbolic and discursive reference to the Roman Empire.[37] However, this Roman legacy, known mostly through the ancient texts of writers, the remnants of its monuments, and, eventually, the remnants of its material culture provided by archaeologists for the museums of the imperial capitols of Europe, was interpreted in an astonishing variety of ways.

For example, Patricia Seed has convincingly demonstrated that, from the fifteenth through the seventeenth centuries, the major European colonial powers all explicitly based their "ceremonies of possession" in the New World, by which they claimed sovereignty over land and peoples, on their understandings of ancient Roman practices. However, these understandings were radically different in character. The Portuguese, for example, attributed a Roman origin to their practice of planting stone pillars and constantly used the Roman Empire as a standard to measure their own accomplishments. The French, who felt themselves to be the most direct heirs of the Roman civilizing mission, preferred elaborate processional rituals (also putatively based on Roman models) through which the natives purportedly expressed their eager consent to receive the benefits of French rule. The English, in contrast, eschewed formal ceremonies but quoted Virgil and Herodotus to justify their claiming possession of the land by surveying and erecting barriers and fences, practices that might be likened to the implantation of Roman cadasters. "Despite manifold dissimilarities on multiple grounds, Portugal, England, France, and Spain all proclaimed Roman expansion as their central political metaphor. Yet each of the four powers invoking Rome constructed entirely different ideas about what the 'Roman Empire' had been."[38]

Greek colonization and imperial politics were also gradually incorporated into imperialist discourse and became particularly influential in Victorian England. Many of the English of this period liked to see themselves more as enlightened modern Athenians than as Romans, and compared the British Empire to the Athenian Empire of the fifth century BCE, an analogy bolstered more by the common reliance on sea power than any other dubious similarity.[39] The Athenian Empire was also the analogy of choice for Prussians of the early nineteenth century, although with somewhat different criteria of identity.[40] But the Romans retained a very powerful role in imperialist discourse despite competition from the Greeks. This was especially true in France, although the numerous books comparing the British and Roman empires[41] attest the allure of this legacy in England as well. Roman precedents and analogies also permeated debates in the British Parliament and in newspaper editorials.[42] Moreover, Rome provided a practical source of models for the practices and vocabulary of both Enlightenment and high modernist colonialism. Such technologies of control as the Roman colonial census, taxation, and cadastral land restructuration practices, as well as ethnographic surveys, all had their derivatives in, for example, British India, Africa, and Ireland.[43] Greek and Roman colonial models were, in fact, both contrasted and combined in a variety of complex ways. The English classicist Gilbert Murray's opinion that "at home England is Greek, in the Empire she is Roman"[44] exemplifies some of these analogical complexities and paradoxes.

While the United States has generally preferred to see itself alternatively as a modern Athens or a descendant of the Roman Republic,[45] analogies from abroad have tended more toward the Roman Empire, and usually toward its less flattering characteristics. Italian scholar Guglielmo Ferrero viewed American society (with its philanthropic customs and legal practices) positively as a more direct descendant of ancient Rome than European societies corrupted by intervening influences.[46] Murray's perception in the midst of the Cold War was that "there is waiting across the Atlantic a greater Rome which may at best establish a true world Peace, and will at the worst maintain in an ocean of barbarism a large and enduring island of true Hellenic life."[47] Much depends on the particular modern traits and the particular period of antiquity seized on in order to construct an analogy.

Whatever the relative Greek/Roman emphasis, what is strikingly clear is that ancient Greek and Roman versions of colonialism were seen as axiomatic points of reference for modern situations. As Richard Livingstone noted, "These ages, with which we have spiritual affinities and which have anticipated our problems, have a special interest and instructiveness for us. They are our *Doppelgänger*. We recognize our faces in theirs."[48] This was no less true in the matter of colonialism than in other aspects of life. Examples illustrating the pervasive and symbolically powerful operation of such analogies are innumerable, beginning most obviously with the adapted terms of supreme rulership for the new "empires"—*empéreur* for the Napoléons, *Kaiser* (Caesar) for the Prussian Wilhelm, "Empress of India" for Victoria, *czar* (Caesar) for the Russian court.

At the laying of the foundation of the Castle in Capetown in 1666, Dutch colonists accompanied the ritual with an oration in which the conquests of Alexander, Augustus, and Caesar were invoked to symbolically situate this modern colonial endeavor firmly

FIGURE 2.3
The Arc de Triomphe in Paris, commissioned by Napoléon Bonaparte in 1806.

within a tradition stemming from ancient Greece and Rome.[49] A notorious later South African colonist, Cecil Rhodes, even proposed erecting replicas of Doric temples at Capetown and Kimberly, although one of his favorite sayings was "Remember always that you are a Roman."[50]

In France, modern imitations of triumphal arches built by the Romans to celebrate victories in their wars of conquest are found in cities ranging from Paris, to Lyon, to Marseille; and these were erected by governments as diverse as those of Louis XIV, to Napoléon I, to the Third Republic (fig. 2.3). Indeed, the recently constructed Grande Arche de la Defense in Paris is a modernist interpretation of this tradition. According to Hautecoeur, Napoléon I insisted that public monuments "ought always to be in the style of the Romans. His empire ought to be the continuation of that Empire which spread from Egypt to the British Isles."[51] To further this project of symbolic association, Napoléon had himself portrayed in Roman garb in a bronze statue atop a monumental column in the center of the Place Vendôme imitating precisely the Roman emperor Trajan's Column at Rome (fig. 2.4). Moreover, the heroic portraits of Napoléon in laurel crown and other Roman imperial imagery by Ingres and David and the innumerable statues and drawings of Napoléon that display him as a Roman emperor or god attest to the pervasive character of this iconography.

FIGURE 2.4
Statue of Napoléon Bonaparte as a Roman emperor atop the column in the Place Vendôme, Paris, imitating Trajan's Column at Rome.

A major aspect of this invocation of the ancient empires, especially from the nineteenth century on, was the representation of modern colonialism as the continuation of a civilizing mission that had been inherited from one's cultural ancestors.[52] Colonization could thus be portrayed almost as an unavoidable altruistic duty imposed by history, as in the French colonial doctrine of the *mission civilisatrice*. The English equivalent was the famous "white man's burden" poetically encapsulated by Kipling at the end of the nineteenth century, which Gilbert Murray would refer to half a century later as "the fine work of the better colonial governments in performing their 'sacred trust.'"[53] As Kipling's phrase suggests, this hierarchical classification of cultures was frequently undergirded by racist ideology, a prime example being Sir Francis Galton's scientistic scalar classification of the natural intellectual ability of various regional, national, and racial groups, in which "the negro" ranked several grades below "the Englishman" and ancient Athenians topped even the English.[54]

The classical connection in this ideology of bringing civilization to the barbarians was often quite explicit. For instance, the colonial governor of Kenya, Sir Philip Mitchell, began an influential document analyzing *The Agrarian Problem in Kenya* by comparing the "primitive condition" of Africans to the inhabitants of pre-Roman Britain and arguing for the comparable civilizing influence of English colonists.[55] Another influential British colonial administrator, Lord Lugard, wrote, "As Roman imperialism laid the foundations of modern civilisation, and led the wild barbarians of these islands along the path of progress, so in Africa today we are repaying the debt, and bringing to the dark places of the earth, the abode of barbarism and cruelty, the torch of culture and progress, while ministering to the material needs of our civilisation."[56]

Similarly, the French emperor, Napoléon III, in the history of Julius Caesar that he wrote, used the Roman conquest of Gaul as both a moral lesson about the benefits of colonialism and a statement of France's claim as inheritor of the Roman civilizing mission. He portrayed the conquest as an ultimately beneficial, if temporarily painful, victory of Roman "civilization" over "barbarism." In writing about the final crushing defeat by Caesar of the Gallic leader Vercingetorix, he observed that "we must not lament his defeat. Let us admire the ardent and sincere love of this Gallic chief for the independence of his country, but let us not forget that it is due to the triumph of the Roman armies that we owe our civilization; our institutions, our customs, our language, all of this comes to us from the conquest."[57] While admitting that Roman domination was accomplished "across streams of blood, it is true," he concluded that it "led these peoples to a better future."[58]

I do not mean to imply in this brief and necessarily schematic discussion that the invocation of the classical past was a homogeneous phenomenon. On the contrary, it was richly riddled with complexities, contradictions, and controversies. As I suggested earlier, the character of the Greek and Roman legacy evolved considerably from its early manifestations at the beginning of the Renaissance through the Enlightenment, to the Romantic humanism of the eighteenth century, to its bourgeois bureaucratic incarnation in the nineteenth and twentieth centuries. Moreover, within each of these periods, Greek and Roman precedents were selectively marshaled to argue all sides of a given philosophical or political issue. They were invoked both as a self-satisfied endorsement of the status quo and as a critical appeal for reform (as, for example, in the famous debate between the "Ancients and Moderns" in France).[59] And in terms of its political context, as Marchand notes, "Over the course of a century and more, German philhellenism moved from left, to liberal, to right, and from the fetish of young outsiders to the credo of aged academics."[60] Nor can the invocation of the Greco-Roman past be reduced simply to a cynical manipulation to rationalize imperial ambition and greed. In fact, Roman and Greek precedents were often invoked to criticize current imperial policies and practices as much as to justify them.[61] The excesses of Roman colonialism, for example, which were seen to have been responsible for the collapse of the Empire, were often invoked to warn against the corrupting dangers of current imperial hybris and brutality.[62] But what was common to all sides of these debates was a fundamental implicit acceptance of the direct relevance of ancient Greco-Roman colonialism to modern cases, and the assumption of a common "Western" cultural heritage in the civilizations of ancient Greece and Rome. There was, in other words, a shared discourse that implicitly defined the terms of discussion by shaping the boundary between the taken for granted and the unthinkable, by structuring the submerged intellectual landscape of axioms and assumptions. As Richard Jenkyns has noted astutely in this matter, "It is a sign that an idea is pervasive when it is accepted by both sides of a debate."[63]

The overtly hegemonic grip of the classics on European culture has gradually diminished in the wake of the sundering of the Victorian world produced by the catastrophic trauma of World War I. Indeed, is has been said that Hellenism died on the battlefields of Flanders.[64] Rather, I would suggest that, although it was perhaps mortally wounded, that death has been a long and slow affair. It is true that "classics" departments now occupy more the intellectual periphery than the center of European and American universities; but they still vastly outnumber those dedicated to the study of any other ancient culture, and no university feels complete without one (contrast this situation with, for example, departments of Celtic studies). Moreover, the privileged status of classical scholarship within academia persisted more strongly in some countries than it did in the Anglophone world—the prime examples being Germany and France, where it was only the revolutionary decades of the 1960s and 1970s that marked a major watershed of reform.[65] Even in the Anglophone academic world, our common operational vocabulary and specialist jargons are still permeated by terms (*colloquium, symposium, syllabus, anthropology, archaeology, et cetera*) that derive from and subtly reinforce an implicit hierarchy of valuation in which terms of Greek or Roman origin (or sometimes hybrids of the two for neologisms) have greater symbolic capital than their Anglo-Saxon analogs. Even if some individuals no longer know the original meaning of many of the terms they use, there is a tacit understanding that, for example, a "colloquium" sounds more elevated than a "talk" and that "catachresis" sounds more analytically incisive than "misuse of words."

What is more, although the field has been changing rapidly, within many classics departments there are still deeply entrenched conservative Hellenist and Romanist perspectives (involving hierarchical assumptions about ancient cultures) and disciplinary practices that have influenced and constrained the exploration of the classical past in subtle and not-so-subtle ways.[66] Finally, while it is clear that cultural capital within the academy, and in society at large, no longer is linked to an ability to read Greek; nevertheless, the myth of cultural ancestry created in the Renaissance and the hierarchies of cultural superiority engendered by this tradition have persisted as a profoundly embedded implicit part of popular consciousness.

As recently as the 1950s, on the eve of decolonization, a famous English classicist could deliver a series of popular lectures on British and French radio proclaiming, "Yet I feel strongly that the Western Community, with all its faults and vulgarities, and with all that it still has to learn from certain Eastern nations, is nevertheless, by virtue of its Hellenic and Christian heritage, called upon to lead the world."[67] Concluding with three purported aspirations of the "old Hellenistic world," he went on to say, "The last of the three aspirations is the hellenization of a barbarous world. It is here that, if only the great Third War is averted, the next generation may find its most persistent conflict and its best hope. It must use all its strength, all its wisdom, to see that the main drift of the world is Hellenic and not barbarous."[68]

Richard Livingstone noted in 1935 that "Hellenism is a far more powerful force today than when the classics held an undisputed sway in higher education."[69] This observation was somewhat pathetically wishful in the sense he intended it, but it contains an unanticipated truth. That is because, although an overt concern with the classics is now the preoccupation of only a relatively small body of academic specialists, many of the tenets of the Renaissance, Romantic, and Victorian engagements with the Greeks and Romans have been absorbed subtly, as implicit unarticulated attitudes, into the consciousness of people who know and care little about ancient history. They have become an axiomatic part of a popular habitus that operates at the level of unquestioned assumptions about the "natural" order of things. Christian Goudineau's (admittedly informal) recent survey shows, for example, how persistent, even among well-educated French people in the postcolonial era, have been the ideology of the colonial civilizing mission and the cultural hierarchy of "civilization" and "barbarians" that informed Napoléon III's interpretation of the Roman conquest of Gaul. Over 85 percent of those he interviewed considered the Roman conquest of Gaul to have been "beneficial," and almost 60 percent thought of it as "a model to reproduce." Almost 70 percent of those who considered it positively did so because it was responsible for bringing "civilization."[70]

Given this deeply embedded colonization of modern European and American consciousness by the classical world, what implications does it have for the central problem addressed in this book? The answer is both complex and subtle, and it can best be revealed in greater detail in the following discussion of the history of research on this ancient colonial situation. But one of the most obvious points that can be made at this stage is that archaeologists, and the discipline of archaeology, have also been formed within this broader discursive field. Indeed, archaeology (particularly the archaeology that deals with this episode of colonialism) developed as a professional discipline largely as a result of the antiquarian desires stimulated by this infatuation with the ancient classical world, and it has been frequently implicated in the concomitant process of modern colonialism.[71] The museums of northern Europe and North America are now filled with treasures of Greek and Roman sculpture, architecture, bronzework, and ceramics as a result of the acquisitive urge that motivated the development of archaeology as a means of bringing back the tangible relics of an ancestral past; and the archaeology of Rome, for example, was born of Napoléon's conquest of Italy and his obsession with its colonial legacy.[72] These objects, in turn, have formed the basis for the development of connoisseurship, one of the forms of "distinction"[73] that became an important element of the cultural capital of cultivated tastes.

However, this does not mean that all archaeologists are unreflexive products of a uniform, all-pervasive hegemonic discourse or that archaeology as a discipline has been a static instrument of such a discourse in any simple, straightforward way. Susanne Marchand has demonstrated, for example, how the professionalization and institutionalization of German classical archaeology eventually undermined the ideals of the romantic Hellenism that spawned it and how it eventually challenged the dominance of philology, to which it was originally viewed as a handmaiden. What she also clearly shows, however, is that an understanding of the practice of archaeology requires that it be situated within the evolving cultural history of its institutional landscape.[74]

In the current case, I have suggested that the intimate entanglement of ancient and modern colonial situations presents some severe challenges to archaeologists attempting to reexamine and understand the ancient case. Fusions of vocabulary, for example, have sometimes led to the imposition of anachronistic motivations and structures stemming from modern colonialism onto the past, as in the treatment of trade in the ancient Mediterranean in terms that derive from the competitive nationalist colonial projects of the nineteenth century[75] or, as I argue later, in the application of world-system models. Does this mean that the analysis of ancient colonialism should strive for a kind of intellectual quarantine and avoid all reference to modern analogies or theoretical insights derived from modern colonial situations? Clearly not. Such a position would not only render archaeological interpretation impossible (all our inferences depend ultimately on some form of analogical reasoning, whether implicit or explicit), but it would also negate both the very project of a comparative analysis of colonialism and the possibility of an archaeological contribution to that endeavor that I have been advocating.

The keys to a productive engagement between ancient and modern colonialisms include, first, basing comparative analysis on common theoretical issues rather than on a purported common genealogy. In other words, we must abandon the naive ideological construction of European ancestry as a basis for anything but an urgent "archaeology" of modern colonial discourse—it cannot serve as the criterion of relevance for selecting comparative cases. Second, regardless of the criteria of relevance, it is essential to avoid uncritically imposing one case on another and thereby eliding differences. One must employ multiple sources of comparison and pay as much attention to *contrasts* as to commonalties: the dialectic between these features will provide a heuristically fertile strategy for illuminating the historical particularities of each case. Moreover, as the previous discussion should have made clear, what is crucial is the constant questioning of our implicit assumptions and their discursive bases, because these have a great influence in conditioning research goals, interpretation, and evaluation of knowledge claims. Such assumptions may, for example, preclude the asking of certain questions, and they may create uneven standards of plausibility for competing interpretations. I am not advocating that this be carried to the level of "epistemological hypochondria"[76] that was common in much recent postmodern criticism, but the dangers obvious in the palimpsest of colonialisms revealed earlier should require a high degree of vigilance in the present case. It is crucial to remain rigorously self-conscious of our own situation in the history of colonialism and of the discursive fields that structure our intellectual landscape of implicit tenets and teleologies.

REINTERPRETING THE ENCOUNTER IN MEDITERRANEAN FRANCE

The problem of the nature and consequences of the encounter between ancient Mediterranean city-states and the indigenous societies of Iron Age Europe is, as noted earlier, an old and enduring theme. The topic was first broached, albeit in somewhat sporadic and anecdotal fashion, by ancient Greek historians and geographers who tended to portray the situation as a process of either tension and conflict or beneficial diffusion of superior civilization to inferior "barbarians." Both of these themes are clearly evident in the text of Pompeius Trogus discussed earlier. Similarly, Strabo saw the Greeks as having initiated a process of pacifying and civilizing that was being continued by the Romans in his time.[77] For their part, the inhabitants of Massalia actually left very few impressions of the neighbors in the hinterland of their city, particularly during the early centuries of the encounter; nor did they pass much information on to other Greeks. Hence, we are left with the few passages about the legend of Gyptis cited in the first chapter to complement various scraps of more general ethnographic description from later centuries when, first, "Celtic" peoples brought themselves forcefully to the attention of Greeks and Romans by invading their territory and, later, the Roman Republic began aggressively to turn its economic and political attention northward.[78] In fact, almost all of the more detailed textual information we have dates to this later period when Roman trade and imperialism were dominant factors encouraging ethnographic enquiry.[79] Although it might be due simply to the selective hand of document survival, this curious lack of information from Massalia may well indicate, as Arnaldo Momigliano suggested, that Massalians never penetrated very far beyond the coast of Gaul and had only a superficial interest in the culture of their neighbors, being content to remain in a state of willful ethnocentric ignorance.[80] Presumably, this would have been less true of the merchants who were attempting to ply their wares at native settlements along the coast than it was of the class of Massalians who composed literary and scientific texts (see chapters 4 and 5). What one can say is that this pattern of ignorance about the interior is a point of contrast with Greek colonists on the Black Sea, who were much better informed about their indigenous neighbors.[81]

We know nothing of Etruscan views of the natives with whom they traded, as their non-Indo-European language is still undeciphered, and no long narrative texts have been preserved. Indeed, as with the indigenous peoples of Gaul, textual information about Etruscans is largely from Greek and Roman sources. It is telling that modern scholars do not even refer to them by their own ethnonym—*Rasenna*—but rather by a Roman name. It bears reiterating that Mediterranean history that is dependent on texts is history seen through Greek and Roman eyes and filtered through Greek and Roman cultural dispositions, prejudices, and cosmologies.[82] One can only imagine how radically different our picture of the ancient Mediterranean would be if we had to rely entirely on Etruscan, or Phoenician, or Celtic, or Iberian texts.

In any event, until the nineteenth century, those Greek and Roman texts that survived into the modern period served as the sole basis for apprehending the encounter between Iron Age peoples of western Europe and Mediterranean colonists.[83] Not surprisingly, post-Renaissance excursions into antiquity tended to mimic the attitudes and assumptions of the ancient sources, with both sets of authors sharing a common colonial gaze. By the nineteenth century, the growth of antiquarian interest, now infused with Romantic Hellenism, had stimulated an increasingly voluminous literature of speculation, analysis, debate, and synthesis, as well as a sustained series of archaeological explorations seeking to connect the ancient texts to the material remains of the encounter. To understand the present state of research in this domain, and to appreciate the various interpretive challenges and frontiers faced by current scholars, it is necessary to examine critically, if briefly, a few themes and trends in the history of this body of scholarship in light of the previous "archaeology" of the significant role that this ancient colonial encounter played in the construction of European discourses of national and class identities.

In the first place, it is important to point out that the study of this colonial encounter has been pursued by scholars from a variety of different intellectual backgrounds. At the most basic level, there are differences in theoretical orientations and methodology stemming from the national academic traditions (French, German, Swiss, Spanish, Italian, British, and American) of scholars engaged in this research. Aside from presenting certain difficulties in assessing the comparability of excavation data, these divergent traditions involve epistemological differences concerning legitimate sources of interpretive analogies and evaluation of the relative plausibility of inferences. For example, with a few notable exceptions,[84] German scholars have been especially reluctant to admit the relevance of ethnographic comparative data or anthropological theory, while these have been fundamental for Anglo-American scholars. Perhaps even more important, however, is that the subject straddles the border between two long established academic disciplines: it has been approached from the perspectives of both classical archaeology/ancient history and prehistoric (or, as it is known in France, "protohistoric") archaeology. Practitioners of the former have tended to focus primarily on the colonies of the Mediterranean states themselves, and only secondarily on relations with the indigenous peoples surrounding these colonies, and then usually only insofar as they were seen to have some economic or political impact on the colonists. Perhaps not surprisingly (especially as textual information from classical sources tends to be granted a privileged authority), until recently, such analyses have usually emphasized a view of the diffusion of "civilized" customs among "barbarians" as a natural and inevitable outcome of contact. This "Hellenization" perspective is one with which Pompeius Trogus or Strabo would have been quite comfortable but that an anthropologist must obviously find inadequate.

Prehistoric archaeologists, in contrast, have focused primarily on the "barbarian" end of the relationship. They have been more interested in the internal development of indigenous societies, and an interest in contacts with Mediterranean civilizations grew originally out of a concern with dating: Greek and Etruscan trade objects and borrowed motifs and techniques were useful in linking indigenous sites to much more refined Mediterranean chronologies that were grounded in historical records.[85] However, this utilitarian approach to alien objects soon stimulated an interest in the significance for native societies of the cultural contacts represented by their presence at indigenous sites. As early as 1913, for example, the seminal synthesizer of French archaeology, Joseph Déchelette, identified as a "problem of great importance for the protohistory of the western regions [of Europe]" the question "What was the role of Massalian influences in the development of Celtic culture?"[86] Of course, the inverse question was not posed, for reasons that should now be clear. Moreover, because of the previously described hierarchies of cultural capital institutionalized within the academy, prehistorians have been heavily influenced in their interpretations of the significance of the imported objects they used for dating by the Hellenocentric European intellectual tradition that flourished during the period during which archaeology began to take shape as a discipline. Indeed, most French Iron Age archaeologists ("protohistorians") still receive their primary academic training in classical archaeology programs, given that, until very recently, there were almost no university faculty positions specifically for protohistorians or programs in regional protohistory. Moreover, career trajectories in the field are still heavily dominated by the weight of the prestigious École Française de Rome and École Française d'Athènes.

The result is that, with some notable exceptions, until the late 1980s scholars working in Mediterranean France, both classicists and protohistorians, tended to gravitate toward "Hellenization" as both an explanation of social and cultural change and a subject of study. Similarly, archaeologists working in the more northerly Hallstatt region have tended to emphasize the role of Mediterranean trade as a prime mover in the development of marked social stratification and political centralization in the area, often with a comparable Hellenization perspective. But, as will be argued later, even as scholars have turned toward approaches based on anthropologically derived models (such as center-periphery or world-systems analysis), there has been a tendency to replicate many of the same implicit assumptions underlying the Hellenization approach. Let us briefly review some of the major perspectives guiding research before moving on to explore ways of circumventing some of the problems that have plagued analysis of the encounter.

HELLENIZATION AND ROMANIZATION

As noted, for many decades, the dominant interpretive framework for the Greek colonial situation in the western Mediterranean was the Hellenization concept.[87] In brief, this was the idea that a desire for Greek objects, and Greek culture in general, was a natural and inevitable result of contact. For scholars steeped in the adulation of the ancient Greeks and the prestige accorded a knowledge of the classics within academe, the superiority of Greek culture was self-evident, and they assumed that barbarians would recognize this preeminence as well and automatically wish to emulate it whenever they had the privilege of being exposed to Greeks or Greek objects. Greek material culture was attributed with an almost magical power to instill desire and provoke cultural transformations. The focus of research, therefore, was more to chart the clumsy progress of an ineluctable phenomenon. Studies were generally content to measure the "degree" of Hellenization during different periods of the Iron Age by equating the different forms of borrowing with different depths of cultural assimilation, without really grappling with the potential social functions or ramifications of adopted techniques, objects, and practices in native systems. There was a failure to ask why a desire for alien Greek goods might exist *at all* and what the meaning and consequences of such consumption might be in terms of indigenous culture, identity, and social life. The assumption was that, like water, high culture flows downhill.

I need not dwell at length on the severe limitations and dangers of this perspective, as these should be obvious from the previous discussion. Moreover, it has been progressively abandoned, at least in overt form, since Jean-Paul Morel's critique in the early 1980s.[88] In addition to some strong theoretical arguments against the idea, the empirical evidence of archaeology has increasingly demonstrated that Greek culture was not passively emulated in a blanket fashion but, rather, consumed in a highly selective and creative manner—and, as will be shown, ignored or rejected with equal selectivity. Hence, archaeologists have gradually sought new interpretive approaches, although many of the underlying tenets of the old framework have persisted in the form of implicit assumptions.

"Romanization" is a similar concept that has frequently been deployed to explain transformations of culture and identity among colonized subjects of the Roman Empire, not least in Gaul. Given that such transformations have generally been more obviously profound and have involved many mimetic adaptations of Roman practices, this concept has enjoyed a more robust life as an overt interpretive perspective, although not without a great deal of critical discussion.[89] The origins of this concept lie in the same process of the construction of European ancestry and imperial ideology discussed earlier, and the term was coined at the height of the British Empire to describe a purported process of complete assimilation to Roman imperial culture and identity by the natives of England.[90] A number of scholars have advocated abandoning the term, and even those who still argue for retaining it use it in a far more nuanced way than was common a couple of decades ago. But lingering assumptions about inevitability and the unidirectional flow of cultural influence continue to haunt the interpretive landscape.

In response to growing unease about both of these related approaches, some scholars have turned to both anthropology and postcolonial studies, the fields most concerned with the effects of colonialism on the daily lives of colonized peoples in the modern world, for new theoretical insights. But within anthropology itself, there has been an evolution in approaches to the problem of colonial contact and cultural transformation that is important to understand for those engaging in cross-disciplinary consumption of interpretive models.

ACCULTURATION THEORY

Most of the early anthropological work on colonial encounters until the 1960s can be grouped under the heading of "Acculturation Theory." This was a largely American program of research that attempted to systematize knowledge on a cross-cultural comparative basis about changes in the culture of small-scale societies as they came into contact with politically and economically dominant Euro-American states and to categorize cultural responses to contact.[91] This research program was especially concerned to establish uniform definitions of concepts and comprehensive typologies of contact situations and responses. Although research carried out under this program produced many valuable insights that are still useful, the acculturation perspective as a theoretical approach is now considered to be seriously flawed for several reasons.

One of the most salient problems was that the models developed tended to use the transfer of "culture traits" (often meaning material culture objects or techniques) as a measure of cultural change, which implies a rather static conception of the nature of culture. In fact, this stems from the vision of non-Western societies prevalent during this period, which was rooted in the functionalist paradigm of anthropology. It tended to view what were called "primitive" or "traditional" societies as organically bounded units possessing stable, unchanging cultures. Change was something introduced by contact with dynamic Western colonial societies. In the ironic phrase of Eric Wolf, these were "the people without history."[92] The history they would acquire was simply one of structurally predetermined reactions to Western contact, and the possible outcomes were generally limited to various forms of assimilation (acculturation) or destruction (deculturation). Moreover, despite occasional programmatic statements to the contrary, and some interest in individual psychology and the process of innovation, contact was usually seen to occur between "autonomous cultural systems"[93] with little role allotted to individual agency or resistance. Cultural transfers were assumed to be largely a passive phenomenon operating in a unidirectional flow from more to less complex societies (that is, from "the West to the rest"), and the crucial power relations involved in contact situations were neglected. Finally, the project as a whole was tainted by its frequent association with capitalist "development" projects and the demands to produce strategies for "successful acculturation."[94] It is hardly surprising that many scholars working in the ancient Mediterranean turned first to acculturation as a potential interpretive framework, as many of its underlying principles bear a distinct resemblance to Hellenization and Romanization models. Consequently, the acculturation approach replicates, rather than circumvents, many of the problems outlined earlier.

During the 1960s and 1970s, various versions of what may be called "world-systems" or "core-periphery" theory were developed by economic historians and economists as a way of conceptualizing colonial and postcolonial relations of power as a coherent global system. They arose largely out of a conjuncture of what was originally called "dependency theory"[95] (that is, Marxian critiques of modernist development economics) and Althusserian structural Marxist analyses of the expansion of capitalism through the "articulation of modes of production." Despite some important differences, these approaches share the use of macroscale models of regional structural dependency that emphasize an exploitative global division of labor maintained by counterflows of raw materials and finished goods. They seek to explain particularly the development of a system that allows postcolonial maintenance of economic domination in the face of apparent political autonomy between nation states. One major point of disagreement among the seminal theorists is that Fernand Braudel and Immanuel Wallerstein view the modern world system as a fundamentally new phenomenon associated with the emergence of European capitalism in the late fifteenth century, whereas Andre Gunder Frank sees it as the result of an ineluctable process of expansion of a system that began over five millennia ago.[96]

During the 1970s, world-systems analysis had a significant influence among anthropologists, particularly those operating within the American political economy and European structural Marxist paradigms. In fact, within anthropology as a whole, the world-systems perspective had the beneficial effect of making scholars explicitly deal with the fact that the "traditional" rural peoples they were studying were not pristine, isolated societies and that many of the practices they observed could be understood only in relation to the history of incorporation within the larger international relations of power conceptualized as the world system. This provoked a healthy shift toward a new focus on the economic and political history of the peoples studied by anthropologists. However, by the mid-1980s, both internal and external critiques of orthodox world-systems theory had already weakened its appeal and altered its application.[97] Despite this waning influence, during the late 1980s and 1990s, world-systems models became increasingly popular in the analysis of the ancient world by archaeologists and other scholars.[98]

Such models have also become influential in discussions of the Greco-Etruscan colonial encounter with Iron Age Europe, especially among archaeologists focusing on the Western Hallstatt societies.[99] These studies situate Early Iron Age Hallstatt political relations within a broad Mediterranean-centered world system in which Hallstatt chiefs expanded their power by monopolizing a role as intermediaries in a huge Mediterranean-oriented system geared toward draining raw materials from temperate Europe through Massalia. The apparent collapse of the Hallstatt political structure in the mid–fifth century BCE is held to be the result of shifts in this system resulting in changes in control of access to Mediterranean prestige goods. However, a growing number of scholars have also been voicing serious objections and caveats concerning the applicability of these models to Greek and other Mediterranean colonial situations.[100] Not least among the many empirical objections to such applications (aside from a surprising neglect of the societies of Mediterranean France in the middle of this supposed system) is the fact that there is little evidence for the existence of trade of a kind that could have supported systemic regional relations of dependency between Hallstatt societies and the Mediterranean at this early date. But there are basic theoretical objections as well.

As noted, the archaeological attraction to world-systems models arose at a time when interest in them had declined rapidly in cultural anthropology and when they had been largely superseded by more culturally sensitive, less reductionist and mechanistic ways of situating local histories in larger global structures and flows. Unfortunately, archaeological applications of world-systems models, even when applied to situations of less dubious relevance than Greek colonialism in western Europe, often suffer from a magnification of problems inherent in the original versions of world-systems theory that inspired them—in particular, an aspiration to construct what Marshall Sahlins has aptly lampooned as "a physics of the world-historical forces" that obscures historical and cultural variation.[101] Such models tend toward reductionist structural determinism in which explanation resides solely at the level of economic macrostructures of power and the mechanistic articulation of modes of production. When considerations of agency are allowed to intrude in such models, this is usually confined to the "core" societies, which are seen as a kind of historical juggernaut. History is determined at the core, and the peripheries simply react. Hence, in addition to a neglect of the operation of culture as a historical force, there is an inability to account for local choice and resistance, to explain the astonishing variety of locally grounded experiences of colonial situations for both colonized and colonizers, or to understand the ways in which the larger system may be transformed by its interaction with peoples on the so-called periphery.[102]

What is even more to the point in light of the earlier discussion in this chapter, the very use of the analytical concepts of "center" (or core) and "periphery" poses some alarming dangers in that it all too easily melds the physical and the metaphysical into a reified landscape of hierarchical binary difference. In other words, it risks reproducing a set of linkages among binary oppositions (center/periphery, civilization/barbarism, dynamic/static, modern/premodern, etc.) that were fundamental to colonialist ideology and then smuggling them into a stable geography of power that cartographically inscribes and naturalizes these metaphysical constructs. As a number of postcolonial theorists have pointed out, the unintended consequence of the very process of applying a center-periphery model to recent history is that it serves to reproduce and perpetuate a hegemonic project in which Europe was able to define itself as the center, as the cultural and economic engine of world history.[103] The subsequent uncritical projection of this concept into the distant past serves to further naturalize this image by validating the etiological and teleological mythology of European ancestry. The radical move that is necessary to break out of this trap is to deconstruct the very idea of a center and to dismantle the entrenched binary categories that undergird the center-periphery concept.

This warning is even more urgent in the archaeological cases where center-periphery models have been applied to ancient situations—and most particularly in the ancient Mediterranean, for reasons that should be abundantly clear by now. One must ask, for example, on what basis the precarious colonial settlement of Massalia is defined as the center (or part of the center) and the indigenous societies of Gaul as the periphery? In fact, there is little evidence to indicate that Massalia fit any of the economic or political criteria that characterize the center in a modern world-system model. Rather, this definition hinges on the various other linked hierarchical binarisms that furnish the implicit subtext of the model—the same set of binarisms that informed the recursive relationship between ancient and modern colonial ideologies. In other words, Massalia is the center because it was "Greek" (whatever that might mean in the sixth century BCE), and indigenous peoples of the region were "barbarians" (the Greek Other)—by definition the denizens of the periphery of the Greek worldview. Hence, one can assume that Massalia served roughly the same core structural role as modern Europe and correspondingly assume the economic evidence that does not exist.

THE HISTORICAL ANTHROPOLOGY OF COLONIALISM AND POSTCOLONIAL STUDIES

Although they have yet to make a broad impact in Mediterranean France, recent developments in the intertwined fields of the historical anthropology of colonialism and postcolonial studies have been transforming the comparative analysis of colonialism more broadly in recent years and offer some potentially productive points of engagement.[104] Scholars working through these perspectives by no means ignore the global structures of economic and political power in which colonial encounters unfolded or reject wholesale the numerous insights of world-systems analysis in this domain. Rather, they seek to improve on previous work by countering the mechanistic, reductionist tendencies noted earlier through finding more flexible and sensitive ways of situating local histories within global processes. In the first place, they pay serious attention to culture as both a historical product and agent. Moreover, they explore the role of indigenous agency and resistance, but in a way that, at least in their more mature forms, avoids naive romanticization of these features. The emphasis is on understanding local experience of colonial encounters and subtle transformations of culture, consciousness, and identity. Finally, there is a recognition that these encounters transform all parties engaged in them and that studies must be symmetrical in including local peoples, colonists, and distant metropoles in the field of analysis.

Differences distinguish these two loosely rubricated approaches, but there are many points of overlap, dialogue, and fusion as well. One focus of prominent mutual concern is the issue of boundaries, identity, and the nature of colonial societies. Many previous perspectives have tended to represent colonialism in terms of a relationship between distinct binary categories: colonists and natives, colonizer and colonized, center and periphery, and so on. This was equally true of many of the early anticolonial theorists such as Aimé Césaire, Franz Fanon, and Albert Memmi, who tended to portray colonial relations in terms of a starkly Manichean opposition between colonizers and colonized.[105] In contrast, postcolonial scholars (although counting Fanon, in particular, as a seminal influence) have tended to emphasize, and to celebrate, mixture and complexity. Three slightly different analytical terms have generally dominated discussion of these issues in the postcolonial literature: "hybridity,"[106] "creolization,"[107] and (among francophone scholars) "métissage."[108] These are metaphors rooted in biological concepts that were extended to language and then to culture generally.[109] Moreover, they are positive inversions of what were formerly derogatory terms of colonial racial discourse that viewed mixing as a threat to purity.[110] In the case of hybridity, which has become very important to considerations of agency in postcolonial theory, Mikhail Bakhtin was responsible for developing the concept as a linguistic model,[111] and Hommi Bhabha was responsible for popularizing it as a concept for the analysis of colonial culture.[112] Following the usage of Bhabha, postcolonial scholars generally employ the term to refer to what Bakhtin distinguished as an intentional, strategic, politically contestatory form of hybridization, as opposed to an unconscious "organic hybridization" that leads almost imperceptibly toward fusion.[113] The latter process is what generally falls under the rubric of creolization and métissage (although métissage is used variably to cover both processes).

These concepts have been employed to explain the emergence of new syncretic, and often synergistic, social and cultural forms out of the complex melding of situations of colonization, as well as to break down some of the essentialisms of the politics of ethnicity in postcolonial contexts. Moreover, they are intended to invert the previous analytical emphasis on the flow of goods and influences from dominant colonizers to the dominated. Instead, they emphasize the creative, and sometimes subversive, appropriation and domestication of alien objects and practices—with multiple paths, diversions, ruptures, ambivalencies, and rejections. In that sense, the analytical perspective of this book is clearly in sympathy with the goals and gist of postcolonial scholarship, and it is obviously informed by developments in that domain. However, as Aimé Césaire said of Surrealism, "in it I have found more of a confirmation than a revelation."[114] Moreover, I am not an uncritical consumer of postcolonial theory, and I have some reservations about certain elements, including, especially, the application of the terms *creolization, métissage,* or *hybridity* to the colonial encounter in Iron Age France.[115]

My own approach, in fact, grows out of the conjuncture of the historical anthropology of colonialism[116] and the largely humanities-based field of "colonial discourse analysis" that eventually emerged as postcolonial studies.[117] As noted, a good deal of theoretical fusion between these two approaches has clearly occurred in recent years; but, at the same time, each retains some distinctive elements. Postcolonial studies is by no means a unified field. It is a heterogeneous arena of debate rife with disputes and tensions concerning everything from the definition of "postcolonial" and the meaning of the presence/absence of a hyphen in *post-colonial/postcolonial*,[118] to the problem of agency, to the ambivalent relationships to Marxism and postmodernism.[119] However, a few common intellectual ancestors are variably invoked, including especially Fanon and Foucault. Moreover, given its disciplinary origins, the primary evidentiary domain of such studies has been discourse, and especially discourse located in texts. With some exceptions,[120] the emphasis on discourse has resulted in a certain neglect of the material dimension of colonialism. Anthropology, in contrast, has been far more engaged with the material conditions of colonial situations and the nondiscursive aspects of daily life, while developing very similar concerns with indigenous agency, cultural appropriations, transformations of consciousness, and the like. Understanding the power dynamics and historical operation of colonial discourse is clearly important (as the first two chapters, in particular, attest), but an anthropological exploration of the localized material context of colonial encounters is equally crucial.

To return to explaining my ambivalence about the postcolonial concepts of hybridity and creolization, I am, in the first place, generally wary of the use of biological metaphors to understand cultural processes (and especially biological metaphors that are the discursive products of colonial ideologies of race). This seems to me a particularly dubious move, given the current alarming trend toward the biologizing (indeed, the geneticizing) of social and cultural features in Western popular and scientific discourse. But I have more particular objections in the context of ancient Mediterranean France, as well. To be sure, the concept of hybridity has been heuristically employed to conceptualize colonial processes in some situations in the ancient Mediterranean, such as the case of Punic colonies in Sardinia.[121] Moreover, it is certainly of potential relevance to the period of Roman colonization of the western Mediterranean. But I am less convinced that the concepts of hybridity, in particular, and creolization and métissage, more generally, are very helpful in illuminating the early encounter in Mediterranean France, except perhaps within the urban sphere of Greek colonies such as Massalia and Emporion. For one thing, if, as Amselle[122] quite reasonably claims, métissage is originary and an omnipresent process in all cultures (see chapter 3), then one has to explain what is distinctive about it in colonial contexts and how it helps us to explain the history of specific colonial situations. Simply labeling something as hybridity does not, in and of itself, perform any analytical work. Moreover, *hybridity* has a very specific meaning within colonial contexts; and to the extent that one automatically interprets the appropriation of alien goods or practices as an inherent sign of hybridity, one risks committing the same kind of error as that of previous scholars uncritically accepting such evidence as inherent signs of acculturation or structural dependency. Or, to put it another way, if archaeologists naively assume that every colonial situation can be reduced to a process of hybridity, then the term loses its specific analytical content and ceases to explain anything. It loses its power to inform us about the diversity of the processes clustered under the rubric of colonialism—the myriad ways that people try to make subjects of others in distinct historical circumstances.[123] Such use of *hybridity* can tend to represent colonialism as an entirely cultural issue, thereby obscuring the process of entanglement in complex relations of economic and political power that colonial situations entail.[124]

As explained in the following chapter, in the context under consideration here, I prefer to approach assimilated objects and practices first as a phenomenon of consumption, with careful attention paid to contextual data that can lead to an understanding of the specific local logic and meanings of these goods and practices and the ramifications of their consumption. This is why I prefer to use the term *entanglement* to describe the process that unfolded in Iron Age Mediterranean France, reserving the terms *creolization* and *hybridity*, insofar as they may be useful at all, for the quite different kinds of situations and cultural transformations, lodged in very different asymmetries of power, that developed later in the history of the encounter following Roman colonization. As I have noted, postcolonial theory has been especially concerned with the analysis of discourse, to the general neglect of the material dimension of colonialism. In using the term *entanglement*, I want to signal my interest in pursuing the complex webs of economic, political, social, and cultural linkages that can result, often inadvertently, from the consumption of alien material culture—features that, I believe, have been more intensively researched and effectively theorized in the historical anthropology of colonialism and the anthropology of consumption.

As Nicholas Dirks has argued for modern colonialism, "It is tempting but wrong to ascribe either intentionality or systematicity to a congeries of activities and a conjunction of outcomes that, though related and at times coordinated, were usually diffuse, disorganized, and even contradictory."[125] This caveat is even more apt in the context of the ancient western Mediterranean. In order to understand how structures of colonial dependency and domination may have been created gradually, often in the absence of coercive instruments of power, we must seek to understand the historical complexities of the role of material objects in this process. This means that we must first understand how and why some practices and goods were absorbed into the everyday lives of people, while others were rejected or turned into arenas of contest, and how those objects or practices triggered a process of cultural entanglement and transformation.

3

CONSUMPTION, ENTANGLEMENT, AND COLONIALISM

Developing the theoretical tools to accomplish the goals outlined in the previous chapters, and to enable a productive archaeological contribution to the comparative understanding of colonialism, requires coming to grips with the issue of agency in both indigenous and colonial societies and abandoning the kinds of teleological assumptions of inevitability that have been shown to underlie many of the approaches discussed previously. Progress in understanding the colonial experience and its unfolding consequences in the specific contexts examined here depends on recognizing that intercultural consumption of objects or practices, the process that instigated the initial entanglement of the colonial encounter, is not a phenomenon that takes place at the level of cultures, social formations, or other abstract structures. Nor is it a process of passive diffusion. It is an active process of creative appropriation, transformation, and manipulation played out by individuals and social groups with a variety of competing interests and strategies of action embedded in local political relations and cultural perceptions. People use alien contacts and goods for their own strategic political agendas and they give new meanings to borrowed cultural elements. Foreign objects are of interest not for what they represent in the society of origin but for their perceived use and meaning in the context of consumption. Hence, the colonial encounter must be very locally contextualized in the intersection of the different social and cultural logics of interaction of the specific parties involved. This is the level at which agency is potentially discernible in the archaeological analysis of colonialism, and at which its operation is historically crucial.

COLONIALISM AND AGENCY

In invoking the concept of agency, I am decidedly not talking about an attempt to introduce a notion of Cartesian individualism into archaeology. Rather, the aim is a more nuanced relational understanding of human subjectivity and consciousness in which the conditions for consequential action, and its motivation, are displaced from transhistorical metastructures (particularly crudely economic ones) to socially situated positions and culturally constructed dispositions that are locally contextualized. In other words, I wish to avoid both the Scylla of individual autonomy and the Charybdis of forms of reductionist historical determinism in which agency is attributed solely to macrostructures of economic or political power.

Local agency is, obviously, not something to be treated naively in colonial encounters. The concept often has been myopically exaggerated and overly romanticized in ways that effectively deny the genuine coercive and discursive power of colonial agents, institutions, and structured environments in many situations. But, on the other extreme, the kind of analysis that sees every practice, action, or institution as an effect of, or a reaction to, colonial domination is lapsing into a dangerous kind of macrofunctionalism in which all aspects of indigenous life are reductively explained simply by their supposed hegemonic or counterhegemonic functions within an overarching colonial system.[1] Aside from doubts about the coherent systematicity of many colonial situations voiced earlier, I would add that such a perspective is powerless to provide insights into the specific cultural forms and meanings that motivate and structure daily life in indigenous and colonial societies; in effect, it furthers the ideological projection of colonial domination by negating, a priori, the possibility of consequential action or voice by those subjected to colonialism. Choices, desires, and actions are clearly conditioned by broader structures of the political economy, but they arise from particular cultural systems of categories and dispositions, particular positions within social fields, and particular sets of practices. Moreover, they always have significant unintended consequences that continually alter the broader structures of power in a recursive dialectical fashion. It is precisely this *situated agency* and the dynamic unfolding of *unintended consequences* that should be the focus of analysis in colonial encounters if we hope to expose and understand the crucial contradictions and contingencies of colonial situations and processes.

One of the main points of this study is to understand how both indigenous societies and alien Mediterranean states, through the operation of the disparate (and often contradictory) desires, interests, and practices of their diverse groups, categories, and classes of members, gradually became entangled in broader fields of power relations and were transformed in the process. Such an understanding of the colonial encounter can emerge only from a consideration of multiple points of agency, their structuring contexts, and the consequences of action at a variety of scales.

TOWARD AN ARCHAEOLOGY OF CONSUMPTION

The key question, of course, is how one can effectively operationalize this notion of agency in archaeological contexts. Several solutions are possible, but in the current case (as in many others), I would suggest that a focus on the process of consumption provides a particularly promising means of penetrating this issue. As shown in subsequent chapters, this was an encounter that, before the Roman conquest (and for some time after), was articulated primarily through the consumption of objects and practices across cultural and political frontiers. It was a distinctive type of "consuming colonialism" that took place under political conditions that were radically different from the later forms of colonialism that accompanied Roman colonization, although processes of consumption were instrumental in that case as well. Hence, it is crucial to place at the center of discussion a basic question that has been largely ignored: one must ask seriously why indigenous societies of Iron Age Mediterranean France, especially in the early phases of the encounter, would have had *any interest at all* in Etruscan and Massalian goods or practices? To what social conditions and opportunities and to what cultural values and dispositions was the consumption of alien goods a response? The answer to these questions demands that we look much more carefully at the particular *things* that were actually consumed and the *ways* they were consumed; that is, we must examine the specific properties and contexts of these objects and practices and try to understand the social and cultural logic of the desire for them and the social, economic, and political roles that their consumption played. It is also, of course, necessary to examine the counterphenomenon—that is, what might be called the logic of indifference or rejection. It is necessary to understand what goods and practices were available for appropriation but were ignored or refused, and why this particular pattern of selective consumption emerged from a range of possibilities. In brief, we must find a way to discern and explain the *choices* that were made. Finally, one must also address the equally crucial question of the consequences of consumption: what were the immediate and long-term social and cultural ramifications of the selective incorporation of these specific alien goods and practices?

CONSUMPTION, MATERIAL CULTURE, AND COLONIALISM

Following years of neglect, consumption has become an increasingly prominent focus of analytical interest within anthropology and the social sciences in general over the past couple of decades.[2] This attention corresponds with both a renewed theoretical interest in material culture within cultural anthropology[3] and a growing awareness of the significance of material culture and consumption in colonial processes by scholars of colonialism and postcoloniality.[4] However, the nature of these new approaches to consumption and colonialism, as well as their relevance to the current case, require some discussion—not least a few initial caveats.

In the first place, let me make clear that I am not talking about consumption simply as the final stage in a purely economic process (as in neoclassical microeconomic theory), but rather in the sense that it has come to be understood within anthropology—as a symbolic activity deeply embedded in social relations and cultural conceptions. However, it must be acknowledged that an exclusive focus on consumption, particularly as exemplified in some of the more semiotically oriented forms of analysis stemming from the early work of Baudrillard, may risk decoupling it from those more traditional, but still important, domains of analysis: production and exchange. This move would be particularly dangerous in a colonial context, where the issue of exploitation and the political context of the articulation of production and consumption should be ever-present concerns. Hence, an abstract treatment of consumption as the circulation of pure signs that is divorced from consideration of the relations of power in which they are embedded, or that ignores the crucial material dimension of the objects being consumed, is manifestly not the goal pursued here.

A further danger that must be acknowledged is that much of the theoretical work on consumption has been developed to understand the particular characteristics of modern and, especially, postmodern capitalist consumption (the so-called "consumer society"). For example, a great deal of attention has focused on a hypothesized major transformation in which consumption has supposedly replaced production as a primary basis for identity construction in post-Fordist Western societies.[5] Similarly, analysts of "globalization" have focused on the role of consumption in the historically specific configurations of local/global relations and processes that have emerged recently in the postcolonial, late capitalist cultural economy, with its peculiar conjunctures of electronic mass mediation, mass migrations, and global capital flows, that have created, arguably, new forms of diasporic communities and radically new transnational spaces of imagination and identity.[6] Clearly, these theoretical models cannot simply be universalized across all cultures and histories, and especially not as a substitute for the empirical investigation of particular historical contexts. Having criticized the archaeological application of world-systems models, I have no desire to replace one anachronism with another. As noted earlier, one must always be attentive to contrasts as well as commonalties in juxtaposing cases or theoretical programs from different historical or geographic contexts—differences are, in fact, often more revealing than similarities.

Hence, I would suggest that, while the uncritical imposition of theoretical models from the literature on capitalist consumption or globalization studies risks obscuring the historical distinctiveness of ancient cases, a judicious critical engagement with this body of research (presupposing an eye toward contrasts) can prove heuristically fruitful. In any case, the basic insights of such studies, illuminating the fact that consumption is *never* simply a satisfaction of utilitarian needs or an epiphenomenon of production, but rather a process of symbolic construction of identity and political relations, are certainly relevant to the past. Moreover, contrary to assumptions of much neoclassical economic theory, anthropological studies of consumption have shown that demand can never be understood as a simple or automatic response to the availability of goods, and especially not in colonial situations. Consumption is always a culturally specific phenomenon and demand is always socially constructed and historically changing. These features offer, therefore, a good potential starting point for launching an exploration of the role of material culture in colonialism and the operation of agency and contingency in colonial encounters.

The approach to colonialism and consumption proposed here requires consideration of a few key concepts. Let us begin with culture. This is important because, not only is consumption structured by cultural categories and dispositions, but "culture is constructed through consumption."[7] This statement implies two things. In the first place, objects "materialize" cultural order—they render abstract cultural categories visible and durable, they aid the negotiation of social interaction in various ways, and they structure perception of the social world.[8] The systems of objects that people construct through consumption serve both to inculcate personal identity and to enable people to locate others within social fields through the perception of embodied tastes and various indexical forms of symbolic capital.[9] Despite somewhat hyperbolic claims by some scholars about recent revolutionary transformation of such practices, this is by no means something unique to capitalist consumer societies, although it clearly operates in quite different ways in different contexts. But more than simply reproducing static systems of cultural categories, consumption constructs culture in a more dynamic sense; and this is especially relevant to the issue of cross-cultural consumption and colonialism.[10] In effect, consumption is a process of structured improvisation that continually materializes cultural order by also dealing with alien objects and practices through either transformative appropriation and assimilation or rejection.

To accept this perspective implies an understanding of culture that differs fundamentally from the one held by many scholars of ancient Mediterranean colonial encounters, as well as from the older "acculturation" paradigm that guided earlier analysis of colonialism and "culture contact" in American anthropology. Rather than viewing culture as simply an inheritance from the past, it is important to recognize that it is also a kind of eternal project.[11] In other words, culture is not a fixed, static, homogeneous system of shared beliefs, rules, and traits, but rather sets of embodied categorical perceptions, analogical understandings, and values that structure ways of reasoning, solving problems, and acting on opportunities. The operation of culture is always a creative process of structured improvisation. Among those problems/opportunities to be resolved is the ever-present one of dealing with exogenous peoples and objects. This process involves both the selective domestication (or "indigenization") of formerly foreign goods, practices, and tastes and the rejection of others. Such selective incorporation operates according to a specific cultural logic, but it also has a continual transformative effect in the reproduction of culture. Moreover, this process does not occur through the actions of reified cultures coming into contact, but rather through the often contradictory actions of individual human beings and social groups located differentially within complex relational fields of power and interest.

This process of selective appropriation and indigenization is not something that is unique to colonial situations. It happens everywhere and continuously, given that societies have never existed in a state of isolation and people must always negotiate their lives in relation to external conditions. This is what Jean-Loup Amselle, following Ricouer's observation that "selfhood" is constructed in a permanent relation with alterity, means in talking about "originary syncretism."[12] Cultures are inherently relational in nature: they have always been both products of fusion and in a ceaseless process of construction through fusion. The distinctive feature of colonial contexts is that the particular configurations of colonial relations of power have a marked influence on the nature and structure of the process. Moreover, precisely because of the significance of consumption to the construction of culture, material culture has repeatedly been used as a tool of colonialism.

Perceiving culture in this way means deconstructing the entrenched Western dichotomy between tradition and change (and the linked dichotomy between static and dynamic societies). It also means understanding that the adoption of foreign goods and practices does not result in "deculturation," nor does it render cultures inauthentic or incoherent. As Marshall Sahlins has noted, "Anthropologists have known at least since the work of Boas and his students that cultures are generally foreign in origin and local in pattern."[13] Moreover, cultural continuity usually consists of the distinctive ways that cultures change.[14] Hence, cross-cultural consumption is a continual process of selective appropriation and creative assimilation according to local logics that is also a way of continually reconstructing culture.

This is not to deny that such consumption has significant consequences in terms of altering the conditions of cultural reproduction. It certainly does. Indeed, focusing on the role of consumption in the process of colonial entanglement is intended to underline precisely this feature. But these effects are often subtle and gradual, and they frequently will not be perceived by the participants as marking a cultural discontinuity (although there will sometimes be generational or gender differences in such perceptions). What *is* potentially perceived by native peoples as marked rupture or discontinuity is *colonization* and the forms of colonialism that follow it—that is, the sudden loss of control over the process of cultural reproduction and the imposition of techniques of repression and discipline.

In the case of the ancient Mediterranean, this kind of cultural continuity and authenticity in the face of assimilation of exogenous objects and practices has been tacitly accepted for Greeks. But the consumption of Greek objects by "barbarians" is treated in a very different way. For example, Greeks are allowed an "Orientalizing" period, when innumerable borrowed objects, tastes, and practices from the Near East and Egypt transformed Greek culture, without any perception of disjuncture or inauthenticity, because this was assumed to be a creative process of selection and adaptation. However, the consumption of Greek objects by, for example, the natives of Gaul usually has been seen as a clumsy attempt to imitate Greek culture, an incoherent aping of alien customs that has no indigenous cultural logic or authenticity. But both of these processes of consumption are actually quite similar and deserve to be subjected to a symmetrical analysis that shows how cultural dispositions guide consumption and how consumption continually constructs culture in all contexts. Moreover, it is important to recognize that situations of colonial consumption involve appropriations by both sides and have transformative effects for both sides. Even in the context of powerful empires, the experience of colonialism has profound cultural and social ramifications not only in colonial outposts, but also in distant metropoles.[15]

Given the discussion in chapter 2, it is not surprising that one can see parallel assumptions to those noted here operating in the case of Western societies and their colonial Others (repeating the false dichotomy between "dynamic" societies and those locked in conditions of static "tradition"). For example, Euro-American societies are allowed any number of invented traditions (the Renaissance, for example) and indigenizations of foreign objects and practices (pasta and tomatoes in Italian cuisine, tea in England, or the decoration of American homes with African baskets, Indonesian cloth, Persian rugs, and Japanese furniture, for example). Yet these features provoke no sentiment of cultural crisis or inauthenticity in popular consciousness. However, similar kinds of adaptations of European or American objects or practices in places like Africa are often seen as somehow flawed mimesis of "the West" rather than creative, and indeed subversive, appropriations. Jean and John Comaroff have used the revealing example of a Tswana chief in South Africa of the 1860s, who had a Western-style suit made for himself out of leopard skin, to show that, rather than simply imitating Western goods in a curious way that did not quite get it right, he was creatively playing on symbols of power from two domains to create an object that doubled its impact.[16]

As the case of the Tswana chief underlines, it is important to recognize that (contrary to the beliefs and desires of many agents of colonialism) when objects cross cultural frontiers, they rarely arrive with the same meanings and practices associated with them in their context of origin. Commodity chains in such situations traverse different regimes of value. To use one of the most prominent contemporary examples, if one thinks of the consumption of Coca-Cola, a bottle of this beverage consumed in rural East Africa does not have the same meaning as an identical one consumed in Chicago. In Chicago it is a fairly banal and ubiquitous drink enjoyed daily, especially by the young, and it is often associated with fast food consumption. However, in the countryside of western Kenya among the Luo people (during the period when I was engaged in ethnographic research there), Coca-Cola was a prized luxury drink. When consumed, it usually was reserved for distinguished visitors and sometimes incorporated into ceremonial commensality (in a pattern reminiscent of the use of imported French wine in bourgeois homes in Chicago, where it would be unthinkable to use Coca-Cola in a similar way). Hence, the presence of bottles of Coca-Cola in rural Kenya is not a sign of the "Americanization" of Africa, but rather of the "Africanization" of Coca-Cola.[17] Moreover, it would be wrong to assume that one can measure a purported process, or relative degree, of "Americanization/ acculturation" by simply counting the quantity of Coke bottles consumed in an area (as has been done frequently with Greek ceramics on indigenous sites in Iron Age Europe). Rather, it is crucial to understand the specific contexts of consumption in order to recognize its meaning and significance. The same would be true in Paris, Potsdam, or Pisa, where the consumption of Coca-Cola follows different patterns and signifies something quite different than in either Chicago or western Kenya. After all, it is reported that in Russia Coca-Cola is employed to remove wrinkles, in Haiti it is believed to revive the dead, and in Barbados it is said to transform copper into silver.[18] Moreover, Coca-Cola is sometimes valued precisely for its foreign origin (indeed, sometimes for its indexical relationship to an imagined concept of America), while in other contexts it comes to be seen as a thoroughly local drink without any aura of the exotic.

Let me make very clear that I am not implying that the consumption of Coca-Cola in Africa is a benign activity without potentially serious economic and cultural consequences. In some contexts, imported soft drinks can come to replace native beverages, which can have implications for both nutrition and relations of economic dependency.[19] Nor am I denying that the availability of Coca-Cola in Africa is driven by strategies of corporate executives seeking global market penetration and is enabled by a massive international infrastructure of production and distribution. I am also not advocating naively a romanticized vision of unfettered indigenous agency in which consumption becomes an autonomous form of liberating resistance. As I have taken pains to emphasize repeatedly, there are always both intended and unintended consequences in consuming alien goods, and these consequences ought precisely to be the focus of analysis in understanding the entangling operation of consumption and the subtle transformation of consciousness and identity. But this is not a simple homogeneous, or homogenizing, process of the "cocacolonization"[20] of passive peripheral subjects. Whatever the hegemonic schemes of Coca-Cola executives for global market domination, demand for this beverage in western Kenya, or Chicago, or Paris, is a product of local desires and tastes generated according to local cultural conceptions and social practices. In order to be desired and used, exotic goods must always be imbued with culturally relevant meaning locally and incorporated into local social relationships. And these processes of redefinition and reorientation must be contextualized and understood if we are to comprehend the transformative effects of cross-cultural consumption.

In invoking the Coca-Cola-example, it is also important to point out the differences between this corporate capitalist commodity and, for example, ancient Etruscan and Massalian wine. All three items are forms of drink exported as a commodity in distinctive durable transport containers. But the similarities are limited. One of the most salient differences is that the Etruscan and Massalian economies were not driven by the capitalist logic of constant expansion and capital accumulation, necessitating a continual search for increasing market share and new consumer markets. There were no attempts to stimulate demand and brand loyalty through such practices as advertising, consumer research, and bulk discount purchasing. Nor were producers and consumers linked directly by the logic of an overarching abstract price-making market in which production output and prices were geared closely to calculation of fluctuating supply and demand. Indeed, this would have been extremely difficult to calculate given that, as will be discussed in later chapters, money was not involved in articulating the trade; exchanges with consumers were on the basis of barter. Another salient difference is that, in the case of Etruscan and Massalian wine, the trade itself was in the form of small-scale merchant-sailors plying the coastal waters with mixed cargoes and looking for propitious places to make favorable exchanges. Producers were not directing networks of distribution, and (with a few exceptions) there was probably little knowledge, or concern, by producers about precisely where their goods were being consumed. Conditions of transport and mechanisms of distribution were very different, and the commodity chains linking agents of production, distribution, and consumption were far more fragmentary and disjointed in terms of knowledge and control. Finally, this ancient trade took place under conditions radically different from the political, military, and economic dominance exercised by the United States in the post–World War II period. Neither the Etruscan nor Greek city-states occupied a role in Gaul even remotely similar to American imperial power and mass-mediated omnipresence in the current world situation. Far from making the example of Coca-Cola irrelevant, however, these differences can help us to think about the distinctive characteristics of ancient consumption. At the same time, the example serves to emphasize the universal importance of consumption as a domain of social practice and the necessity of discerning the specific cultural and social logic of desire for alien goods. If these latter issues are crucial in understanding the cross-cultural consumption of a global commodity like Coca-Cola, how much more so must this be in understanding consumption in the ancient Mediterranean?

The previous discussion must also lead us to introduce the subject of the significance of material culture in strategies of colonialism, something that has gained increasing recognition among anthropologists in recent years. As Nicholas Thomas noted, "Material cultures and technologies are central to the transformative work of colonialism."[21] Given the importance of consumption in constructing culture and social relationships, it should not be surprising that goods have not only been appropriated and indigenized, they have also been used by both parties in exchanges to attempt to control the other— "making subjects by means of objects."[22] This involved not only attempts to create novel desires for new goods, but also attempts to get people to use imported objects in particular ways, as well as the belief that the use of particular objects or technologies would inherently induce certain kinds of desired behavior. For example, it is clear that clothing played a very important instrumental role in the strategies of European missionaries to "colonize the consciousness" of indigenous peoples in various parts of the world. Christian missionaries in the Pacific tried to use clothing as a means of transforming Samoan and Tahitian moral consciousness and instilling new concepts of work discipline, temporality, and gender relations.[23] Similarly, among the Tswana in South Africa, both clothing and architecture served as vehicles for attempts by missionaries to inculcate European concepts of domesticity and bodily discipline; and they became sites of struggle as the Tswana used these new material forms as an expressive language to structure identity in new ways and contest colonial categories and aesthetics.[24] As this case suggests, such strategies to use material objects as vectors of control always have unintended consequences for all the parties concerned.

A further paradoxical point needs to be emphasized at this stage: far from being signs of "acculturation," imported objects or practices can become salient symbolic markers of the boundaries of identity between consumers and the society of origin. This can be true even in the case of the adoption of what Appadurai distinguishes as "hard cultural forms" that "come with a set of links between value, meaning, and embodied practice that are difficult to break and hard to transform."[25] The "indigenization" of the English game of cricket in India and the adoption of American baseball in Japan are classic cases in point.[26] In both cases, the games/rituals are played with the same implements and costumes under the same rules in constructed spaces of the same form. Yet, because of such things as the spirit motivating play, the behavior expected of players, and the social origin and position of the players, the games have come to be seen as profoundly different in each cultural context. These shared sports become privileged sites for the revelation and reification of cultural boundaries, and potential arenas of conflict and the contestation of values.

To cite a highly relevant ancient example, Greek, Etruscan, and Roman versions of the wine-drinking ritual, the *symposion* (or Roman *convivium*), represent an analogous situation (fig. 3.1). Greeks developed their version of the symposion from older Near Eastern feasting practices, and this was subsequently adopted by Etruscans and Romans.[27] However, each version differed slightly, but in symbolically significant ways, from the others. Disapproving Greek references to the presence of wives at Etruscan symposia, a practice unthinkable to Greeks,[28] should alert us to the nature of the differentiation being evoked through this practice. Like Etruscans, Romans also allowed wives to join their husbands—but not to recline with them (they had to remain seated in chairs). For Greeks, the symposion was a resolutely male affair at which the only women present were *hetaerai* (courtesans) providing entertainment for the men—one would never find "proper" women attending.[29] Cicero offered strikingly revelatory evidence of the cultural dissonance in this common drinking ritual in recounting an episode in which Romans joining a symposion in the house of a Greek suggested that the host's daughter join them, provoking a brawl during which one of the Romans was killed.[30] Aside from these gender issues, other practices also subtly marked boundaries. Greeks and Romans used rooms of slightly different shapes and sizes (the Roman *triclinium* versus the Greek *andron*), involving different arrangements of the couches for reclining. There were also differences in the symbolic role of the crater and the ways of mixing water and wine. Finally, while the Greek spatial arrangement of symposiasts tended to emphasize egalitarian relations among the men present, the Roman arrangement marked clear hierarchies between men and women, between adults and youth, and between the status of the adult men. Ironically, after some time under Roman imperial rule, the Greeks eventually ended up adopting a transformed version of their own exported practice from the Romans.[31]

There are, of course, clear differences between the cases of baseball, cricket, and the symposion as well. In the first two, where the adoptions took place following military conquest and occupation, these practices may be viewed as a form of what Homi Bhabha has defined as "mimicry."[32] This term, which has become a key concept in postcolonial studies, describes a process of inherently incomplete mimesis of the cultural practices,

An Etruscan version of the symposium showing husbands and wives drinking together: a mural from the Tomb of the Leopards at Tarquinia (early fifth century BCE).

institutions, and even values of the colonizer that can become a threatening challenge to colonial hegemony precisely because such mimicry is always perilously close to mockery and parody. It thus embodies the ambivalent relationship between colonizer and colonized and exposes the limits of control. In the Etruscan/Greek case, the adoption of symposion practices took place under political conditions that were radically different— there was no process of colonization, and Etruscans did not constitute a colonized population. Hence, the explanation for the adoption must be sought in the cultural and social logic of Etruscan consumption of the exotic and the specific nature of their relationship to Greek colonies in southern Italy. Nevertheless, cross-cultural consumption of objects and practices is inherently an act of appropriation, which is subversive in effect if not in intent, and this explains why in all three cases these shared practices served as focal points for the revelatory definition of cultural boundaries and distinct identities.

The issue of boundaries is, in fact, subject that demands some clarification, especially in the light of the discussion of postcolonial theory in the last chapter. In speaking of cross-cultural consumption and the persistence of culture as it is constructed through consumption, I emphasize that I am not invoking the old reified organic model of culture as a homogeneous entity with rigid boundaries. Rather, the processual understanding of culture outlined earlier implies a great deal of fluidity and socially differentiated embodiment of cultural categories, dispositions, and tastes. Moreover, it is clear that, from an analytical perspective, social and cultural boundaries do not necessarily involve spatial discreteness or segregation. Rather, they are symbolically constituted and contextually defined and invoked, often with variable indexical attributes. Yet, for individuals, such boundaries have great affective importance and are often seen as clear and distinct, and group identities are often perceived in ways that make them seem essentialized and stable, even as they are rapidly changing. In colonial contexts, such boundaries may be more distinctly perceived (in either emic or etic terms) at certain periods in the history of an encounter than at others, they may be very differently perceived by different parties in the encounter, and they may undergo significant transformations. Hence, the term *cross-cultural*, as used here, implies a sense of difference (in terms of categorical perceptions, dispositions to action, etc.) but not necessarily separation or discreteness. The boundaries in such processes are always subject to definition within specific contexts and they are always an evolving relational phenomenon.

Furthermore, in treating cross-cultural consumption, it is important to reiterate that one must not impute motives or agency to cultures or societies: action occurs at the level of individuals and social groups. Consequently, colonialism in action transgresses boundaries and borders in complex ways. It produces alliances that traverse ethnic and political boundaries as it aligns structural oppositions within colonial and indigenous societies in new configurations of interest. This is what Sahlins called "structures of the conjuncture."[33]

THE LOGIC OF DEMAND, INDIFFERENCE, AND REJECTION

Demand is another concept that requires some discussion. I am not using the term here in the sense that it has acquired in neoclassical microeconomic theory, as an undifferentiated psychological response to the availability of goods used in the quantitative calculation of marginal utility. Rather, I use the word as a general term to designate the desire for certain objects stemming from a particular cultural and social logic. Demand is a product of the variable interplay of embodied categories and tastes, strategic decisions about the potential deployment of goods in particular social roles, creative analogical interpretations of new instrumental or social uses, semiotic understandings about the relationship among goods in "systems of objects" (in the sense of Baudrillard), and other such factors. It is important to reiterate that demand is not a uniform property or product of cultures. It is socially situated and constructed; that is, it varies among classes and categories of people as a result of the interplay of the factors noted above in the internal politics of social life. This is clear in, for example, Pierre Bourdieu's analysis of the differential distribution of tastes and cultural capital across social fields within late twentieth-century French society,[34] but it is equally crucial to remember in analyzing situations of cross-cultural consumption in small-scale precapitalist societies. Demand for foreign goods and practices may vary according to social position or category, and the differences may be generated largely by the relational dynamics among social groups or fields. Obviously, in archaeological contexts we will usually not be able to discern the relative operation of all these factors in great detail. But we can distinguish demand as a selective force structuring consumption within a specific world of options and attempt to discern as completely as possible the logic of patterns of choices made—not in terms of marginal utility, but in terms of socially situated interests and cultural categories and dispositions.[35]

As noted earlier, demand is never an automatic response to the availability of goods, and especially not in colonial situations. Historical accounts of early colonial encounters in various parts of the world during the period of European expansion demonstrate that, to the general surprise of European merchants, their goods were not inherently irresistible to indigenous societies. These peoples were usually very selective in both the goods they were willing to accept and to give in exchanges with colonial agents, and they sometimes refused to interact at all. Thus, for example, early English attempts to engage the Native American tribes of New England in the fur trade were a failure because these peoples were not interested in the various goods the colonists had to offer. It was only when the English finally discovered the native demand for *wampum* shell beads that they were able to begin an exchange relationship, and they were then forced to manufacture this native valuable in order to have something to offer in exchange for furs.[36] Similarly, Europeans first attempting to trade for pigs (to provision their ships) in the Marquesas reported great difficulties in persuading the local people to part with them. The Marquesans valued their pigs (which were important for ceremonial feasts) far more than the iron axes and hatchets the Europeans were willing to offer in exchange. They could only be induced to give up pigs in return for sheep (regarded as a special kind of pig) and birds (the feathers of which were used in ceremonial regalia), and the Europeans were unwilling to part with these items.[37]

To cite another illuminating example raised by Marshall Sahlins, in the early days of the Sino-British encounter, British diplomats/merchants were vexed and perplexed by the fact that the Chinese failed to be impressed by, or to covet, the European guns and gadgets they were offering. He attributed the astonishment of the British to the fact that they held a culturally embedded assumption of a natural functional relationship between technology and cultural sophistication that the Chinese did not share.[38] As the British Sinologist Thomas Taylor Meadows wrote, the Chinese had an inability "to draw conclusions as to the state of foreign countries from an inspection of the articles . . . manufactured in them."[39] This deeply entrenched Euro-American assumption that people perceive immediately and "naturally" the superiority of a culture by perusal of its objects and technology, and that this should stimulate an automatic desire for those objects and their parent culture, is one that has both plagued modern American "development" strategies abroad and has been transferred by scholars to their investigations of encounters in the ancient Mediterranean. In the latter case, our venerated ancestors, the Greeks, stand in for modern Europeans and Americans. It is this assumption that lies behind the attribution of quasi-miraculous transformative effects of mere contact with Greek goods, while the Greek gaze on "barbarian" objects has no effect, except perhaps provoking disdain.

But why should we assume that native peoples of Gaul shared this culturally specific assumption? Why should they have seen the reflections of a "superior civilization" in the bottom of a ceramic drinking cup? We must think realistically about what trade between Greeks and natives really involved during the sixth century BCE. What did indigenous peoples of Gaul actually perceive when a small group of Massalian traders (as we shall see, quite probably a rather motley crew) pulled their boat up on the shore with a cargo of wine and ceramics? What they surely did not experience is rapturous visions of the Parthenon, Praxiteles, and Plato—that is, all the things that suffuse our modern Western sensibilities metonymically as we gaze admiringly at an Attic vase under glass in a museum. Aside from the fact that none of the trio above actually existed yet in the sixth century BCE, it is highly unlikely that anyone in a village in the Rhône valley would have known about them if they had existed—or even necessarily cared. Nor would they have had a conception of "Greeks" or "Greek culture" that linked Massalian sailors to Athenian philosophers, and that joined Achilles, Aristotle, and Alexander to sixth century BCE wine amphorae in a Hellenic historical epic. These people lived long before Winckelmann, and it is a grotesque anachronism to impose our own Hellenophilic conceptions and aesthetic perceptions on people of the past. We cannot assume that our own heightened valuation of Attic and Massalian ceramics as indexical signs of a panoramic "Greek culture" could have had any meaning for the natives of southern France or could have played any role in their demand for these goods. Nor can we assume that their consumption of such goods is any indication of a native admiration for Greek culture. We must try to understand indigenous demand on its own terms, divorced from our own historically constructed preconceptions about Greek culture and our own culturally specific assumptions about a natural functional relationship between technology and cultural sophistication.

As is shown in detail in subsequent chapters, indigenous demand in Early Iron Age France was every bit as specific and selective as the ethnographic examples cited above: it was largely confined to a desire for wine and drinking paraphernalia, from whatever sources it came. Which brings us to other kinds of assumptions about the "naturalness" of demand. Although an appetite for certain kinds of goods, such as imported alcohol, might appear straightforwardly "natural" and self-evident, closer analysis shows that this is not at all the case. This subject is treated in much greater detail in chapter 7,[40] but for the moment, suffice it to point out that there are numerous examples of societies (both ancient and modern) refusing the importation of various forms of alcohol.[41] Moreover, as Sidney Mintz has demonstrated with his analysis of the historical development of the apparently equally "natural" craving for sweetness and sugar in modern England,[42] demand is always an artificial product of particular sociohistorical circumstances and the meaning of goods arises out of their use in social relationships.

I have suggested previously that the specific properties of objects and practices must be examined very carefully in evaluating the nature and meaning of demand for them. How this can be done productively is shown in much greater detail in chapter 7. For the moment, let me simply note that one can begin the process by making a few distinctions: for example, whether the goods consumed are of a singular or a standardized character.[43] That is, is one dealing with more or less unique items valued for their distinctive, individual traits (even as they form a common functional class of objects)—such as art paintings or haute couture in Paris, or Kula valuables in the Trobriands, or bronze wine-mixing vessels in Hallstatt Burgundy? Or is one dealing with items that constitute a common repetitive series produced in standardized, redundant form that are viewed as units and valued mostly in their quantitative abundance—such as bottles of Coca-Cola in Chicago or amphorae of wine in ancient Mediterranean France? For archaeological cases, especially, it must be emphasized that one cannot assume either singularity or standardization in the context of consumption based simply on the characteristics of objects in their context of production. For example, beer mugs that were mass produced in Germany may have been valued for their singularity in the interior of colonial Africa if they circulated in very limited quantities. Moreover, finished goods in one context may be viewed simply as raw material in another, as with the Native American practices of chopping up European copper kettles to make their own jewelry and other implements[44] or modifying gun barrels for use as flutes and tent stakes.[45] This question must be sorted out empirically by careful analysis of the context of consumption, in the manner I have outlined elsewhere,[46] to determine how rare or common such goods actually were and how they were treated.

This issue can provide a very useful first clue to penetrating the nature of demand for objects in situations of cross-cultural consumption. For example, Marshall Sahlins offers the illustrative contrast between eighteenth-century Hawaiian chiefs and Kawakiutl chiefs of the northwest coast of North America. On the one hand, the Hawaiian chiefs monopolized trade with British and American trading ships and had a very precisely targeted demand for highly distinctive, singular, fashionable adornments and domestic furnishings that they could use to distinguish themselves from their fellow aristocratic rivals through personal possession and hoarding. Kwakiutl chiefs, on the other hand, sought standardized items in exchanges with fur traders (such as Hudson's Bay blankets) that they could accumulate by the thousands in preparation for giving them away at potlatches.[47] Hence, both the nature of the goods desired (singular versus standardized) and the practices of consumption (possessive hoarding versus distribution) were quite different in the two cases, although both were marshaled in strategies geared toward maintaining political power. One can also cite cases in which singular objects were distributed as gifts and standardized objects were hoarded. The key in trying to understand the nature of demand and the meaning of consumption in specific cases is to try to use contextual clues in the archaeological record to sort out the social and cultural logic of the process.

As noted earlier, the question of what might be called "negative" demand is also very important to consider. That is, what things did people *not* consume, and why? Of course, before engaging this question, one must first assure that the selective pattern of consumption being analyzed is not simply a product of lack of availability—choices are made from among the possible (although the impossible can also be desired). But having satisfactorily established the range of availability, as well as having taken appropriate measures to assure that one is not simply dealing with patterns resulting from differential preservation of goods in the archaeological record, one is then faced with the task of differentiating between indifference and rejection. In some cases, goods or practices may be rejected as an act of contestation or political resistance. Such acts may become particularly salient in colonial situations that Ranajit Guha characterizes as "dominance without hegemony."[48] In such contexts, asymmetries of coercive power are marked, but ideological struggles over identity and authority are continual. These contestations can take many forms, but very often they are materialized in the process of consumption. In such cases, some goods and practices come to be invested with especially strong value as indexical signs of reified identities or social boundaries, and such things as "revitalization movements" may occur that focus on the rejection of materialized signs of colonial domination (for example, Gandhi's rejection of English clothing). Such rejection may be as much lodged in the logic of internal relational struggles between classes, groups, or categories of people within a society as directed at external forces of domination, or they may be aimed at both. However, in many other cases, it would be a mistake to impute conscious resistance. In many encounters, particularly those without oppressive asymmetries of power, there may simply be indifference to objects that do not fit within culturally structured categories, tastes, or dispositions and for which there is no perceived utilitarian or social use for such objects. For example, the Marquesans described earlier were not trying to resist colonialism or contest European values. They were simply not terribly interested in the foreigners or what they were offering. These patterns can, of course, change quickly in response to a variety of factors; and they can shift in various directions (such as from indifference, to avid consumption, to rejection).

Among other things, such "negative demand" patterns can highlight by contrast the specific focus of attraction for things that were selected. In the case of Mediterranean France, the list of objects and practices that met with indifference is a very long one (clothing, jewelry, weapons, religion, etc.), much longer than the small number of appropriations. But this issue is well illustrated by brief consideration of the history of the adoption of coinage and writing. Both of these processes show centuries of indifference followed by rapid appropriation under specific historical circumstances.[49] In the case of writing, it might be objected that native peoples were simply unaware of the practice rather than uninterested, and that the adoption came once they were exposed to writing. This was clearly not the case. In the first place, people in close proximity to Massalia would certainly have seen writing being used. But even those farther away along the coast would have seen merchants writing accounts. At Lattes, for example, there are multiple Etruscan graffiti on ceramics from the early phase of the settlement in the sixth century BCE, and there are many Greek graffiti from the mid–fifth century BCE on.[50]

There is even a lead tablet inscribed in Greek—the kind of device used by Greeks and others for recording contracts and letters—that was found in fifth century BCE levels, much like the fifth century BCE example with Greek and Etruscan writing found at Pech Maho in Western Languedoc (see chapter 5).[51] Yet there is no contemporary evidence of the use of writing to record the Celtic language; that is not found at Lattes until the late third century BCE, and this pattern holds throughout the Rhône basin. As Michel Bats has pointed out, the intensity of archaeological activity in the region and the chronological coherence of the evidence found precludes the absence of earlier finds being attributed to problems of recovery.[52]

Only two scripts had a major impact in Mediterranean France before the Roman period: Greek and Iberian.[53] The Greek alphabet found favor only in the lower Rhône basin, and the script employed was the Ionian version used at Massalia. As Celtic was the language represented with this script, it is called "Gallo-Greek."[54] The earliest evidence of Gallo-Greek dates to the end of the third century BCE (about four centuries after the debut of the colonial encounter), and the latest examples in Mediterranean France date to the end of the first century BCE. In Roussillon and western Languedoc, despite the nearby presence of Greek Emporion for over two hundred years, it was the Iberian alphabet that served as the adopted model for the first use of writing in the mid–fourth century BCE. This script was first developed by indigenous peoples in southern Spain during the seventh century BCE as an adapted version of the Phoenician alphabet.[55] In this region it was used to record both the Iberian and Celtic languages (and a few rare instances of possible Ligurian[56]). The Ligurian speakers along the coast of eastern Provence never chose to adopt any writing system before the Roman conquest.

In comparison to Greek and Etruscan, the range of functions served by both Gallo-Greek and Iberian writing appears to have been extremely limited, as were the media to which they were applied (fig. 3.2). As Michel Bats has pointed out, the first use of writing in both contexts was for purposes of asserting individual identity: that is marking personal property (especially pottery) with one's name.[57] This practice was developed further in a more ostentatious fashion in the Gallo-Greek context by monumental inscriptions on stones, of both funerary and votive character. Legends on coins are another, more mobile, kind of ostentatious display of identity through writing, whether of individual leaders or groups. There is also, of course, a political dimension to public declarations of identity of this kind that is different from marking property. In contrast to the Gallo-Greek situation, the Iberians also apparently employed writing to serve as a tool in the economic sphere. This is seen in the various lead tablets containing lists of names and numerical information or brief texts (still undecipherable) that are also found farther south in Spain.[58] A series of over sixty Iberian graffiti engraved on rock walls in association with engraved drawings in the high plateau of the Cerdagne in Roussillon also attests to the use of this script for probable ritual purposes.[59] Many questions remain to be answered about the use of writing, such as the degree of literacy among

30247

FIGURE 3.2

Gallo-Greek graffiti on a Campanian cup from Lattes: late second century BCE (UFRAL).

indigenous peoples and its association with status or role, and the details of the process of adoption and adaptation. However, it is undoubtedly significant that the first interest in the practice occurred, as subsequent chapters show, at the same time as other signs of social transformations during the third century BCE, such as the appearance of courtyard style houses, ritual sites with collections of heroic warrior statues, an increase in conflict between Massalia and its neighbors, and the emergence of powerful political confederations.

Coins are another element of alien material culture towards which indigenous peoples exhibited a general indifference for centuries, and the monetization of the indigenous economy did not occur until after the Roman conquest. Massalia was the first source of coinage in the western Mediterranean, and it began to mint coins during the last quarter of the sixth century BCE. It was followed in this practice by two other Greek colonies in Spain, Emporion and Rhode, in the fifth and third centuries BCE, respectively.[60] Among indigenous societies of Mediterranean France, isolated hoards of Massalian and other alien coins are found on scattered settlements of the lower Rhône basin from the fifth century BCE on,[61] including a few early Etruscan coins from Populonia.[62] The earliest coins minted by indigenous societies of the western Mediterranean were actually fifth-century BCE imitations of Massalian silver *oboles* by the neighboring tribe in the territory that would eventually be that of the Salyes.[63] However, these were extremely rare and sporadic in their production. Most indigenous coin series of Mediterranean France began only in the second and first centuries BCE.[64] What is more, the distribution of Massalian coins was largely confined to the lower Rhône Basin until the end of the third century BCE, and there is no quantitatively significant evidence of monetary circulation in Mediterranean France as a whole until the second century BCE. Furthermore, it is only on settlements dating to the first century BCE, that coinage (then mostly bronze) is found distributed widely enough and in quantities large enough to begin considering the possible development of a monetary economy in the indigenous domain.[65]

Coins were not made originally for purposes of trade; they were a form of special-purpose valuable produced for a limited range of (largely political) practical and symbolic functions, including making state payments (for example, for military operations and building projects), collecting taxes and tribute, and affirming the power of a polity to define standards of value.[66] The range of uses to which they were put once in circulation was undoubtedly much larger than the specialized functions that motivated their production, and this eventually included trade (at least for large transactions). For example, the lead tablet from the settlement of Pech Maho, in western Languedoc, mentions a transaction in which coins constituted part of a large payment for a ship.[67] However, as the small quantities and limited distributions of coins suggest, during most of the Iron Age, most exchanges in the western Mediterranean were transacted through barter (direct exchange of goods and services), and local societies of the region were aware of the idea of coinage without seeing any need to mint or use coins for centuries. It may be that for most of this period the use of coins was confined to transactions between merchant traders and exchanges between traders and producers at Massalia and Italy, and their function in the indigenous world was limited to certain kinds of transactions with foreign traders.[68] That is, they may have served as an occasional means of temporarily bridging different regimes of value, but they had little significance for native peoples beyond this specific function as a highly specialized token for acquiring external goods from foreign traders.

One of the few striking transformations of daily life in the Rhône basin that is associated chronologically with the initial period of Roman colonization is the rapid monetization of the economy during the first century BCE. The case of Lattes has been particularly well documented and analyzed.[69] At Lattes, despite the discovery of a few impressive hoards (fig. 3.3), coins remain very rare in domestic contexts until the first century BCE. Then, they suddenly become numerous in most domestic units. The range of types in use during the first century BCE is quite diverse, but the overwhelming majority consists of Massalian small bronze coins with a charging bull.[70] It is also worth noting that Lattes did not figure in the mix of types in use because, unlike a number of other indigenous societies, the town never produced its own coinage. Comparative ethnographic and historical analysis suggests that this sudden incorporation of coinage into the daily lives of Lattarians was probably linked to the imposition of Roman taxes, something that would have had a variety of unintended consequences, including the potential disruption of spheres of exchange and regimes of value (and their attendant political structures), changes in the economics of gender relations, and the stimulation of markets.[71]

FIGURE 3.3

A hoard of 104 Massalian silver obole coins from Lattes in the course of excavation, found in house 52101. The coins were originally contained in an indigenous CNT urn. Scale in centimeters (UFRAL).

As noted, consumption of foreign goods entails both intended and unintended consequences, which must be a major focus of analysis. I describe these consequences, in general, as a process of *entanglement* that links societies together in colonial relationships in a variety of new ways (cultural, political, and economic).[72] This highly contingent process has a wide variety of possible transformative effects, depending on the specific nature and history of entanglement.

4

SOCIAL, CULTURAL, AND POLITICAL LANDSCAPES

When traders peddling Etruscan goods first anchored their small ships along the shores of southern France in the late seventh century BCE, they encountered a diverse and dynamic indigenous world composed of exotic peoples whose languages and customs they did not understand. A few decades later, colonists from a Phocaean homeland at the other end of the Mediterranean claimed a space on the north shore of a small harbor on the rugged Provençal coast and began to build homes within the tiny and precarious new settlement of Massalia. By moving here, on the far western edge of the world known to Greeks, they were inserting themselves into a complex social and cultural landscape that they would have comprehended dimly, at best, and to which they initially would have been of marginal significance. The misunderstanding would, of course, have been mutual. Local people would undoubtedly have regarded these foreigners with a mix of suspicion, curiosity, and pragmatic self-interest structured by their own ethnocentric cultural conceptions of the world and of proper standards of behavior.

Yet, the very vulnerability of Massalia, especially in its early days, and the exigencies of sailors trying to induce local peoples along the coast to engage in exchanges, would have forced colonists and traders gradually to develop some conceptions, however flawed and ethnocentrically translated, of the tastes, customs, and identities of local peoples. There would also be obvious advantages in attempting to forge stable relationships of various types that would channel interaction and enable communication. For local peoples, as the selective consumption of some Etruscan and Massalian goods gradually became established practices and as desire for these alien objects grew, they would also have developed a working understanding, in their own terms, of the curious behavior and interests of the alien merchants who brought these goods from somewhere beyond the horizon of their local worlds. Over time, the effects of these exchanges produced, for all parties, various forms of economic, social, and political entanglements and transformations of culture, consciousness, and identity that far exceeded anything imagined at the beginning.

But how do we understand the social and cultural logic of these encounters and the process of entanglement and transformation? The previous chapters have set out in some detail both the challenges presented by this question and a strategy toward a potential solution. To begin with, it is imperative that we start by attempting to construct a more realistic sense of what these encounters were actually like to the people who experienced them, one that is forcefully wrenched free of the tacit assumptions inherited from the Hellenocentric tradition of post-Renaissance Europe discussed in chapter 2. For example, we must seriously consider what the inhabitants of a place like Lattara, a port town on the coast of Languedoc, would have experienced when observing a motley crew of foreign sailors arriving in their port with a small boatload of exotic goods to peddle. Decidedly not the irresistible aura of "civilization" or the self-evidently miraculous wonders of "Greek culture." Rather, they were presented with a few tired, dirty, and incomprehensible men who behaved in curiously inappropriate ways and who were trying to induce them to give away their possessions in exchange for some odd-looking pots and other curious things. Why would the inhabitants of Lattes who met these foreigners on the beach have had any interest in bartering for these strange objects? What, precisely, did they see in some of these alien goods that would make them potentially useful in their daily lives and that would thereby make them desirable and give them value? What were these foreign traders seeking that would compel them to undertake dangerous voyages along the margins of a strange and mysterious "barbarian" world where they might be met with indifference or hostility?[1] And what kinds of relationships developed as a result of these engagements?

These are the kinds of questions that arise from an approach grounded in the anthropology of consumption. Grappling with them requires a careful, nuanced consideration of the identities and interests of all the parties involved, one that moves beyond sweeping models of contact between cultures or broad ethnic categories to consider locally relevant social categories and groups and socially situated interests and their complex intersections and conflicts.

IDENTITIES

Let us begin with the vexing but fundamental issue of identity. And let us begin that discussion with a caveat about terminology. At one level, it is possible—and indeed pragmatically unavoidable—for certain kinds of discussion to employ the crudely Manichean terminology of *colonists* (Greeks, Etruscans, and Romans) and *natives* (or *indigenes*).

In fact, these categories have usually served as the standard terms of reference in prior analyses. However, these terms really are viable only as a kind of loose rhetorical shorthand, as imprecise generic indexical gestures toward broad populations. They cannot be assumed to have had any necessary significance in terms of emic categories of identity for the people involved, and they should not be reified as constituting "groups" with uniform collective characteristics, interests, or powers of agency (lest we end up simply reimposing colonial binarisms such as "civilization/barbarians" under new labels). What is more, while they might have had greater enduring relevance in some microregions, and some currency for the initial stages of the encounter more generally, over the course of the long history of the colonial situation, the definition and boundaries of these categories become inherently more blurred, unstable, and difficult.

For example, one might imagine that for the inhabitants of the hills immediately surrounding the colonial city of Massalia (at a town such as Les Baou de Saint-Marcel, for instance), the distinction between native and colonist might have remained a salient category of identity for many generations, as stories of the appropriation of territory and tales of conflict became inscribed in collective memory. But, by the time that the "indigenous" settlement of Lattara was founded on the coast of Languedoc in the late sixth century BCE, the "colonial" city of Massalia had already been in existence for a couple of generations about 120 kilometers farther east along the Provençal coast—it was a well-established feature of the regional landscape. To the extent that they were even aware of the precise location of Massalia, there is no reason to assume that the people of Lattara viewed Massalians as not being native peoples of the region. To be sure, these merchants and sailors were foreigners who spoke a strange language, dressed in odd-looking clothes, and had some bizarre, even disgusting, customs. But they were not necessarily more alien than others with whom they interacted. As we shall see, Mediterranean France was a region of multiple languages (Iberian, Ligurian, various Celtic dialects) and ethnic affiliations. Hence, for the residents of Lattara, it is quite conceivable that Massalians represented nothing more than another "indigenous" neighboring group of the region, whom they experienced primarily in the form of merchant-sailors during the periodic arrival of ships at their port.

It is also clear that, after several generations, Massalians would have come to view themselves as permanent residents of the region who "belonged" there, on "their territory." Indeed, like settler colonists in many modern contexts, they would have been faced with the ambivalent challenge of constructing a new sense of indigeneity or belonging while simultaneously perpetuating a sense of privilege and superiority through cultural ties to a distant homeland. They would not exactly have become "natives" in the strict sense—after all, many of them (especially the conservative privileged class) maintained etiological legends about the founding of the colony by Protis and sentimental ties to their Phocaean origins across the Mediterranean. But many of the "indigenous" towns may have had comparable legends (true or not) about being founded by people who came originally from somewhere else (as is common, for example, in many current

African societies). It is also probable that, over time, "indigenous" people may have begun residing at Massalia, and Massalian traders, craftsmen, exiles, escaped slaves, and others at native settlements, further complicating issues of identity.[2] Especially for the immediate neighbors of Massalia, it is likely that they had been used to visiting the city, and perhaps even living and working there, and may have had daughters or nieces who had married Massalian colonists, freedmen, or *metic* traders. Hence, the local distinction between colonist and native may have been one that was marked in certain contexts, effaced in others, and dissolved in new hybrid identities in yet others. Moreover, it should also be remembered that, as a port city, a good part of the population of Massalia probably consisted of noncitizen foreigners of various kinds from other parts of the Mediterranean (traders, immigrants, slaves, former slaves, etc.). In Athens, it is estimated that *metics* (resident foreigners) represented as much as half of the free population, although the proportion was undoubtedly lower in some other cities.[3] Finally, when Roman armies took control of the region in the second century BCE, it is probable that Massalians saw themselves as long-established natives of their territory and the Romans as foreign colonizers (although, initially at least, sympathetic ones who were allies).

These themes will be discussed in more detail later, but I broach them here in preliminary fashion to caution immediately against imbuing the problematic terms *colonists* and *natives*, when pragmatism dictates their reluctant usage, with undue significance as an index of identity or fixed social categories. Ideally, I would prefer to dispense with these terms altogether, but I have found that the discussion of patterns in the regional archaeological record becomes so cumbersome and confusing without them that they are an unavoidable narrative vice. Hence, they will be employed in this book always with implicit "scare quotes" as crude indexical markers of discursive convenience in referring, respectively, to people coming originally from elsewhere in the Mediterranean (and those broadly descended from them) and to people (and their descendants) who were already living in the region when these foreigners arrived. That the people clustered loosely under these vague categories experienced processes of cultural transformation that involved fusions, appropriations, and identity mutations of various kinds is obvious: the goal of this book is precisely to understand when, how, and why this happened, and what consequences it entailed.

LINGUASCAPES

That said, what can we discern in more precise and useful terms of the landscape of ethnic and social identities in the region? At the broadest level, it is clear that speakers of at least three language groups can be identified among the indigenous peoples of Mediterranean France: Celtic, Iberian, and Ligurian. These names all derive from terms used by ancient Greek and Roman authors to describe, more on the basis of geography than language, different populations among the inhabitants of the western Mediterranean. They were reemployed by modern philologists to designate language groups that were constructed on the basis of comparative linguistic studies. Once again, this manifestly does *not* mean that ancient speakers of one of the constituent languages of these groups would have been aware of such connections or would have derived any sense of common identity from such groupings.

Celtic languages, which are still spoken in parts of Ireland, Scotland, Wales, and Brittany, belong to the Indo-European family. They were widely spoken over large areas of Europe (including most of Gaul) during the first millennium BCE. Iberian languages do not belong to the Indo-European family. Although formerly spoken over much of southern and eastern Spain and the southwestern part of Mediterranean France, as a result of Roman colonization and colonialism they are now extinct and still largely incomprehensible. Because it is extinct and known only from toponyms and ethnonyms, Ligurian is even less well understood and its affiliation is uncertain, although most scholars seem to agree on a tentative placement within the Indo-European family.[4]

It is tempting to equate the Greco-Roman use of the terms *Celtic*, *Iberian*, and *Ligurian* with the identification of these language communities, especially as there is a very rough correspondence between the areas (sometimes) designated by these terms and clusters of linguistic evidence. However, one must be wary of projecting modern redefinitions of these terms onto ancient writers. For instance, it is clear that the term *Celt* was intended primarily as a geographic designation, meaning simply the inhabitants of a certain region that the Greeks chose to call Keltike. Strabo, writing in the first century CE, proposed that the term *Celts* was originally the name of a people of Mediterranean France well known to the Massalians and that it was subsequently projected by the Greeks onto all the inhabitants of interior Gaul.[5] Hence, it is quite possible that these original "Celts" in the neighborhood of Massalia actually may have spoken what we would now classify as a Ligurian language.

As a general summary of an extremely complex situation, suffice it to say that, although far from consistent, the term *Ligurian* is most often associated in ancient texts with peoples occupying the area from Marseille eastward into Etruscan territory in Italy—that is, the area with the greatest density of toponyms indicating use of what is now called the Ligurian language (fig. 4.1).[6] For example, Hecataeus of Miletus, writing in the early fifth century BCE, noted that Massalia was a Phocaean *polis* located in Liguria (Lygustike) near to Keltike and that Monoikos (Monaco) was a Ligurian town.[7] Herodotus also noted that the Ligurians lived near Massalia.[8] In contrast, the term *Iberian* is used most consistently to designate peoples on the far western end of the region considered here, on the coast and hinterland of western Languedoc and Roussillon (and, especially, Spain). This is also the region with evidence of Iberian language use and where the Iberian alphabet was adopted by indigenous peoples (including some Celtic speakers). The term *Iberian* was clearly not an indigenous ethnonym for these peoples; Greek texts, in fact, speak of two Iberias, one in Spain and the other "near the Persians," with the name of the Spanish version linked to the river Ebro (Iber).[9] Moreover, Strabo explicitly stated that Iberia was a geographic designation invented by the Greeks that had undergone frequent redefinition by Greek and Roman authors.[10] Celtic speakers were

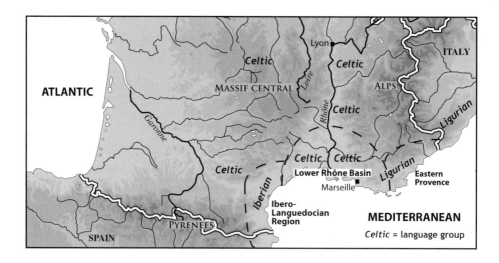

FIGURE 4.1

Map of the distribution of major Iron Age archaeological/material culture regions (dashed lines) and language groups in Mediterranean France.

clearly a majority component of the peoples inhabiting the lower Rhône basin and the interior regions of western Languedoc and the rest of France. Their presence in Mediterranean France during the last few centuries BCE is abundantly clear from linguistic evidence (toponyms, Gallo-Greek inscriptions, coin legends, etc.). For example, at Glanum, about sixty-eight kilometers northwest of Marseille, the names preserved on stelae of the period after the Roman conquest (Bimmos, Elusku, Litumaros, Sigotoutiorix, etc.) are clearly Celtic, as is the name of the god Glanis after which the site is named.[11] Some textual evidence, such as the Gyptis legend, also suggests that Celtic speakers were already in the region when Greeks arrived at the beginning of the sixth century BCE.[12] One hypothesis proposed by J. Untermann using linguistic data (including the disappearance of Iberian names in later inscriptions written in Latin) even suggests that the general population of western Languedoc and Roussillon was also largely Celtic speaking and that Iberians were a specialized urban group of literate merchants originally from Spain who controlled trade and other economic transactions until the Roman conquest.[13]

Textual indications of boundaries between zones are variable. For example, the eastern boundary of the Iberians is sometimes stated to extend all the way to the Rhône River and sometimes only to the Hérault River. The latter indication has tantalized archaeologists because the Hérault valley developed in the Iron Age into a remarkably clear and persistent material culture boundary that is also reflected in the mutually exclusive distribution of adopted Iberian and Gallo-Greek alphabets.[14] For the Ligurian language zone, some authors have also pointed to a potential boundary marker in the fact that the distribution of Gallo-Greek writing does not extend east of Marseille.[15] However, the situation is further complicated by the use, in late texts (that is, post–third century BCE), of the compound term *Celto-Ligurian*. For example, Strabo remarked that, although a people known as the Salyes (or Salluvii in Roman texts), who lived north of Marseille near Aix-en-Provence, were called Ligurian in early Greek texts, later writers called them Celto-Ligurian.[16]

The traditional archaeological interpretation of these data was that they reflect invasions of Celtic-speaking peoples from the north into Mediterranean France during the fourth and third centuries BCE (the period of Celtic incursions into Italy, Greece, and other areas) and the subsequent imposition of Celtic control over indigenous Ligurian populations.[17] However, given that recent archaeological evidence everywhere shows a very gradual and continuous evolution of domestic material culture, scholars are now nearly unanimous in rejecting the idea of major movements of people into the region during this period.[18] Hence, the term *Celto-Ligurian* is now most often interpreted as signaling a political alliance between groups with cultural or linguistic differences.

Two conclusions about Celtic speakers of the Mediterranean region are evident: (1) they did not share very much in the material culture complex of their fellow Celtic speakers to the north in continental Europe (aside from a few imported weapons and broaches), and (2) there was nothing particularly distinctive about their material culture vis-à-vis their near neighbors speaking different languages. Neither of these conclusions should be especially startling for scholars familiar with the ethnographic record. There is no *necessary* reason for linguistic boundaries to be particularly marked in material terms or for significant material boundaries to correspond to linguistic ones.[19] Moreover, these patterns suggest that for most Celtic, Ligurian, and Iberian speakers, language was not an especially salient focus of ethnic identity *on a large scale*; although it may have been invoked as a prominent marker of distinction in local contexts. In other words, it is simply not credible that all speakers of Celtic languages felt (or even recognized) some kind of unitary identity. However, a particular Celtic-speaking community in the lower Rhône basin may have considered language as a salient cultural element that marked them as having a distinctive identity from the neighboring village. More productive than continuing to pursue the strategy of trying to match language groups or ambiguous broad Greek-derived ethnic designations to the material evidence is, perhaps, to ask what sociohistorical processes produced the regional material culture distinctions and boundaries that we find and what their social and cultural significance was. The evolving nature of the colonial situation in each area is clearly an important component in understanding these issues.

There were also (at least) three intrusive languages that became part of the colonial linguistic mix. Etruscans spoke a non-Indo-European language that was unrelated to other languages spoken in Italy at the time, which were of the Indo-European family (such as Latin, Umbrian, and Oscan). It eventually became extinct as a result of Roman expansion. Etruscans were literate: by the beginning of the seventh century BCE, they had developed their own alphabet based on that of the Greek colonists they encountered in southern Italy. Although a vocabulary of a few hundred words and several grammatical aspects are understood by modern scholars, the language cannot be fully translated. We know the names of many Etruscan objects, places, and persons. But we cannot really understand texts in any consequential way, and, in fact, very few longer texts have been preserved.[20] The Phocaean colonists who settled at Massalia spoke an Ionian Greek dialect that was common to the region of Turkey from which they came, and they wrote with a characteristic Ionian script. Latin was the language of the Roman merchants who frequented Mediterranean France in the second century BCE and the Roman conquerors who invaded the region near the end of the century. In a way that Greek never had, it gradually replaced native languages of the region during the course of the first few centuries CE in all the subject communities of the province.

Although there is no compelling proof, one can also reasonably surmise that various pidgin versions of some of these languages may have emerged locally, especially in port contexts, as a response to the needs of barter across cultural boundaries. In the case of the western part of Mediterranean France, it is tempting to speculate that this development may have resulted in the fairly broad spread of some pidginized version of Iberian as a regional "vehicular" trade language, much like Kiswahili in East Africa and Bobangi/Lingala, Kituba, and Sango in Central Africa, leading eventually to the spread of the Iberian script as well.[21]

REGIONAL MATERIAL CULTURE DIFFERENTIATION

In shifting from language to material culture, what recent archaeological data make clear is that the region of Mediterranean France as a whole had been undergoing a gradual process of differentiation in microregional material culture patterns since the Late Bronze Age.[22] Although not without subtle local differences, during the Late Bronze Age IIIb period (roughly 900–750 BCE), most of this region was characterized by a relative similarity in funerary practices, range of settlement types, ceramic styles, and other such things. However, the transition to the Early Iron Age, from the mid–eighth century BCE on, is marked by growing concatenations of regionally distinctive material culture patterns with new emerging boundaries that would persist for centuries (fig. 4.1). Very broadly, a zone encompassing Roussillon and western Languedoc can be distinguished from a zone in the lower Rhône basin (encompassing the land on both sides of the Rhône—that is, eastern Languedoc and western Provence), with the border between the two zones falling quite distinctly in the Hérault valley. The Rhône basin zone can also be distinguished, somewhat less dramatically, from a zone along the Côte-d'Azur and its hinterland in the Alpes-Maritimes, with a less distinctive boundary falling east of the eventual emplacement of Marseille. As a convenient shorthand, these three zones may be referred to as the Ibero-Languedocian region, the lower Rhône basin, and eastern Provence, respectively.

To be sure, there are local differences within each of these zones, but the range of variation became much less within each zone than it was between them, particularly after the seventh century BCE. For example, to the east of the Hérault valley, the early part of the Early Iron Age (Early Iron Age 1 period, roughly 675–625 BCE) in the lower Rhône basin was characterized by inhumation (and some cremation) burials under small tumuli on both sides of the Rhône and similar pottery repertoires and styles (albeit with a longer persistence of Late Bronze Age modes on the Provençal side). However, to the west of the Hérault, in the Ibero-Languedocian zone, one sees the emergence of what is called the Grand-Bassin I (or Mailhac 2) material culture complex, characterized by large cremation cemeteries and pottery styles that are quite distinctive from the "Suspendian" style and its derivatives that one finds in eastern Languedoc.[23]

The reasons for the emergence of these material culture zones and their boundaries at this time are not entirely clear, although growing population and decreasing mobility of settlements may have played a role.[24] Nor is their meaning in social and cultural terms entirely understood (more will be said about this later). What is clear, however, is that Etruscans and Greeks who first arrived in this area near the end of the seventh century BCE encountered societies that had been undergoing these processes of change for over a century. In other words, these were not transformations that were produced by colonial encounters, but rather dynamic situations that formed the context for interaction between colonists and natives. Furthermore, as will be explained in subsequent chapters, the colonial encounters played out according to the regional patterns already established in the prior century. At least until the period of Roman colonization, the encounters appear to have reinforced, rather than disrupted, the existing regional distinctions and boundaries.

A salient example of this is the process of "Iberization" or "Iberism" that came to define the Ibero-Languedocian zone.[25] These terms are used to describe a process responsible for the perceived amplification of the "Iberian character" of the societies of the littoral zone of Roussillon and western Languedoc over the course of the Iron Age. This complex phenomenon is indexed by two main features: (1) the adoption of the Iberian script and (2) the development and spread of a ceramic ware usually designated as "Ibero-Languedocian." The concept of "Iberization" is problematic because the term has been used variously to indicate the process of formation of a local Iberian culture (a kind of in situ ethnogenesis), or the diffusion through trade of elements of such a culture formed elsewhere, or the actual displacement of local populations by Iberian immigrants.[26] What is clear is that, both in the larger context of Spain and within the western Languedoc-Roussillon region, "Iberization" was by no means a homogeneous phenomenon: there was a great deal of local variation. But what is important for present purposes is that this process marks a continuing contrast with what was occurring in the Rhône basin, and there was a resilient boundary along the Hérault River valley. Moreover, there is general agreement that this transformation is associated in some important way with the development of colonial trade relations in which Ibero-Punic goods played a significant role.[27]

THE INDIGENOUS ETHNIC AND POLITICAL LANDSCAPE: BEYOND CELTS, IBERIANS, AND LIGURIANS

The identification and understanding of ethnic groups has been a continuing subject of research and debate among scholars working in Mediterranean France for over a century, and it has figured prominently in the interpretation of the patterns noted in the previous section. This interest in ethnicity stems not only from the general archaeo-logical preoccupation with this subject, which has a long and checkered history,[28] but also from the unusually rich and tantalizing array of apparently complementary evidence available for the Iron Age in this region. Moreover, although the search for ethnic groups in the archaeological record is notoriously fraught with methodological problems and political dangers, this is an issue that must be seriously addressed by any study of an evolving colonial situation precisely because colonial relations are so often implicated in the process of ethnogenesis and the transformation of identity.[29]

Ethnicity, in the sense that it is generally understood by anthropologists, is a social relationship and a form of classification rather than an inherent property of a group.[30] It is a simultaneous sense of belonging and exclusion, one that defines affective affiliation to a social collectivity and boundaries that exclude others. The criteria that may be mobilized as symbolic markers of belonging and exclusion are highly variable and mutable, and they are developed through interaction with others rather than through introverted isolation. Various cultural practices or beliefs may become salient signs of difference, but only selective cultural differences are held to be relevant. Nor do cultural similarities necessarily obviate a sense of distinctiveness between those who hold many things in common. The scale of collective identification can also be quite variable, but most of what one would call "ethnic groups" tend to hold an ideology of common origins (often a myth of fictive kinship), have a commonly recognized group name (or *ethnonym*), share a collective memory of a common history (again, perhaps fictive), and have an attachment to some indexical cultural features (often, but not necessarily, some combination of language, religion, cuisine, or dress). There is also usually some attachment to a place in the landscape, either a territory of residence or a distant homeland (perhaps mythical), and one frequently finds an ideological preference for group endogamy, although this is not necessarily observed in practice. The groups defined in this way are not primordial essences, although this frequently becomes part of the common ideology. Rather, they emerge, mutate, and disappear in response to particular social and historical circumstances. But once a sense of ethnicity develops, it becomes a highly charged affective force that can exercise a kind of historical agency in a way that purely instrumentalist explanations of ethnicity fail to explain.

As noted, colonialism has frequently been implicated as a major factor in the transformation of ethnicity and in the process of ethnogenesis (that is, the emergence of new ethnic groups). This latter process can occur in a variety of ways, including, perhaps most commonly, when categories and boundaries of group membership imposed by colonial administrations on subject peoples begin to produce a realignment of identity or the coalescence of common identity among a number of formerly distinct communities. Examples of this phenomenon are innumerable, but one can cite the case of the Abaluhya of western Kenya, a new "tribe" composed of about eighteen smaller groups speaking Bantu languages, some mutually unintelligible. The Abaluhyia as an ethnic entity is largely a creation of the British colonial period (the name dates to around 1930), but the sense of ethnic identity that emerged out of colonial systems of classification and administration has been reinforced in the postcolonial era by competition with other tribal groups in the politics of the Kenyan state.[31] The various "investigative modalities" and techniques of control employed by colonial states (such as cartography, census taking, language classification and standardization, compilation and recording of tribal history, and structures of indirect rule) often have a profound role in such processes of ethnogenesis.[32] In other cases, disparate refugee populations fleeing slave raiding or warfare have banded together and emerged as a coherent new ethnic group. Examples include the various Maroon societies of the Americas and the Native American Seminole and Ojibwas.[33] In still other contexts, resistance to colonial wars of conquest, or to the escalating warfare radiating out from frontiers of colonization (such as the Iroquois expansion or the Zulu Difaquane), can result in the emergence of new ethnic solidarities out of strategic alliances and common threats.[34] This can involve the formation of new, larger ethnic states with powerful (sometimes predatory) military capabilities, or the violent dispersal of a former ethnic group into diasporic segments that later merge with other groups to form new ethnic identities, as with the demise of the Native American Jumano and the later emergence of the Kiowa.[35]

In brief, the role of colonialism in the transformation of ethnic identity is complex, and it operates through a variety of different processes that depend on the nature of the encounter and of the parties involved. What is clear, however, is that not only the scale and composition of groups can be transformed, but the very forms of ethnic affiliation can be radically altered. Given this general theoretical perspective, what can we say about such possible processes in Mediterranean France?

As noted, archaeologists in this region are fortunate in having an unusually rich assortment of evidence at their disposal: in addition to the usual kinds of material culture data, there is a wealth of potentially exploitable textual and linguistic information. The texts consist of descriptions of indigenous peoples recorded by contemporary Greek and Roman authors, often including references to specific named groups.[36] The linguistic information derives from the study of personal and group names recorded in those texts; but also from toponyms and from inscriptions made by indigenous peoples using scripts adopted from different colonial societies. However, the interpretation of this information is far from straightforward, and one must bear in mind a number of caveats in attempting to coordinate and understand these sources of evidence.

A major danger lies with the nature of the texts: they are all expressions of alien colonial perspectives on indigenous peoples, and they are subject to distortion and error through both ignorance and ethnocentric prejudice. Furthermore, few of the texts we have about Mediterranean France were written by people who had actually visited the region (Polybius, Posidonius, and Caesar are notable exceptions), and the works tended to be compiled from other (sometimes unacknowledged) sources ranging widely in date. Moreover, the authors were not bilingual anthropologists trained in modern ethnographic methods of participant observation; their accounts can be more readily compared to the observations of early European traders, travelers, and colonial administrators in Africa, with their problematic tendencies toward generalization from limited experience and knowledge. A further difficulty is ambiguity in the rubrics used by ancient authors to classify indigenous peoples. The Greek concept of *ethnos* and the Roman *gentes* and their relationship to language, geography, and identity were already complicated in Greece and Rome.[37] When applied in the context of the "barbarian" West, it is often difficult to discern whether the names attached to peoples correspond to indigenous ethnonyms or whether they are rubrics applied to alien Greco-Roman perceptions of linguistic, geographic, cultural, or political units. This difficulty is compounded by the fact that different authors sometimes offer contradictory information and individuals were often inconsistent in their usage. Some of this ambiguity is undoubtedly also a reflection of an important temporal dimension of complexity involving both continual changes in the configuration of ethnic, political, and linguistic entities and changing knowledge of that situation by colonial observers. As the earlier discussion suggests, a final difficulty stems from the inherent complexity of the phenomenon of ethnicity and its relationship to colonial encounters: the colonial situation itself has a central role in creating, fracturing, and freezing cultural identities and political communities. From the moment of the encounter, ethnicity ceases to be intelligible outside the dynamic of the colonial situation.

With these somewhat daunting caveats in mind, what then can be discerned of the changing ethnic and political landscape of Mediterranean France during the Iron Age? In the first place, among the many names of indigenous groups recorded by Greek and Roman authors, a rough hierarchy can be established. At the broadest level of inclusion are the three recurrent classificatory rubrics discussed earlier: Celts, Iberians, and Ligurians. The textual, toponymic, and coin legend data also present us with a much larger number of peoples with names associated with smaller and more precisely localized territories (fig. 4.2).[38] Many of these, particularly groups named on coins, have a much more likely chance of representing genuine foci of indigenous identity and of being meaningful native ethnonyms. Among the assortment of such group names, some, such as the Samnagenses identified on coins from the lower Rhône basin, are difficult to link to a specific place.[39] However, it is often possible to locate the corresponding territory and settlements fairly precisely (at least in their final state at the time of the Roman conquest) because of a combination of names on local coins and the perseverance of toponyms. For example, Nemausus was the town of the Namasates, and these names were both preserved in the modern city of Nîmes and appear on the first coins minted by indigenous societies in eastern Languedoc (as NEMAY and NAMASAT) in the late second century BCE.[40] However, it should be remembered that the bureaucratic division of the landscape of Gallia Narbonensis under Roman administration into *civitates* territories, based on Roman perceptions of these indigenous groupings and Roman conceptions of *gentes*,[41] froze into homogeneous static form what was undoubtedly a momentary state in a fluid process of continual transformation of heterogeneous systems of identity and

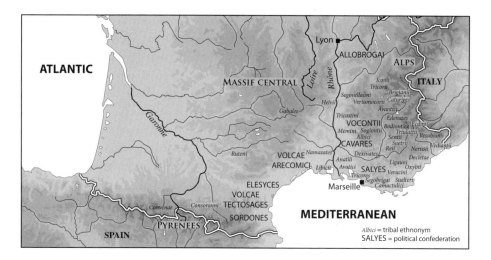

FIGURE 4.2

Approximate location of groups with known ethnonyms and major political confederations in Iron Age Mediterranean France (not all names are contemporary, although most date to the last two centuries BCE: information especially from Barruol 1975). As indicated, many more names are known for Provence than for Languedoc.

political relations. It was also undoubtedly responsible for a number of cases of ethnogenesis. Before Roman control, there is no reason to expect a uniform model of ethnic identity or territorial definition, nor a stable one.

As Marshall Sahlins has noted, the definition and nature of solidarity can vary according to political structure. For example, where allegiance to a chief or king is the basis of community (what he called "hierarchical solidarity"), the relations of common people to each other may be mediated less by similarity in culture and kinship (as in the case of acephalous groups) than by submission to a common authority.[42] Parker Shipton found that, in East Africa and perhaps more generally, societies with territorially defined chiefdoms and political hierarchy tend to be found in areas with lower population density and abundant land, whereas those organized by segmentary lineages are in areas of higher population density and greater land shortages.[43] The broader point here is that most regional social landscapes are complex mosaics of differently organized communities, and within pre-Roman Mediterranean France there is good reason to expect considerable temporal and spatial diversity in political structures and corresponding forms of group identity.

A few of the group names that were recorded in Greek texts appear very early and then disappear from the historical record, such as the Segobrigai noted in the legend of the founding of Massalia and the Elesyces of western Languedoc.[44] However, most of these group names appear for the first time in texts of the second century BCE and later. Among all these names, a few are applied to fairly broad areas (for example, the Sordones of Roussillon; the Elesyces and Volcae Tectosages of western Languedoc; the

Volcae Arecomici of eastern Languedoc; the Cavares, Vocontii, and Salyes of Provence), and they appear to encompass multiple smaller named groups. These are generally interpreted as political confederations of smaller "tribal" or ethnic units. At least some of these political confederations may have included peoples speaking different languages, as the term *Celto-Ligurian* applied to the Salyes may indicate. The nature, structure, and duration of such political alliances (such as asymmetrical patron-client networks, loose associations of equal partners through cross-cutting religious institutions, temporary ad hoc military alliances for a specific conflict, etc.) are not always clear, but these features were probably variable. In the cases where a name is applied in both this broader regional confederation sense and in a more precise fashion to a particular local group (for example, with the Cavares in the Vaucluse and the Salyes near Aix-en-Provence), one may suspect a patron-client arrangement with the named group dominating a larger confederation of clients that Greco-Roman authors called by the same name. In the case of the Volcae Arecomici of eastern Languedoc, Strabo was unusually precise in noting that their principal city was Nemausus (Nîmes), which exercised authority over a confederation of twenty-four towns that contributed to its expenses.[45] But this describes the situation well after the Roman conquest, and there is no mention of the Volcae Arecomici in texts dating before the first century BCE.[46]

In general, we can be fairly confident in accepting that at least six (and perhaps more) major political confederations encompassing multiple smaller ethnic groups existed within different areas of Mediterranean France in the period around, or after, the Roman conquest of the region in the late second century BCE (fig. 4.2). Four of these were in the lower Rhône basin: the Volcae Arecomici, Salyes, Vocontii, and Cavares. But how long had these existed, and in what forms? Were they a recent phenomenon, or did they have a longer history? There is no definitive answer to this question, but the evidence available tends to indicate that these large regional political confederations were a relatively late feature of the political landscape, at least in the Rhône area. Within the Rhône basin there is little evidence of large-scale centralized political organization or marked social hierarchy of any kind before the second or late third centuries BCE at the earliest. Instead, the settlement and burial data from the Early Iron Age and a good deal of the Late Iron Age argue generally for small-scale, relatively autonomous polities of a more egalitarian nature, although some of the individual villages and towns may have had more centralized forms of administration.[47] There are no convincing indications of the formation of hierarchical social classes, marked social distinctions, or institutionalized hierarchies of power until perhaps the third or second century BCE, when there are various signs of significant social transformations.[48] Some scholars, notably Patrice Arcelin, have used the absence of such evidence to argue for the existence of a warrior aristocracy living away from the towns at rural estates: the seats of power would be located in these small rural sites and not in the densely occupied towns of farmers.[49] But this interpretation seems to derive mostly from a desire to have an ancient aristocracy comparable to that in the Iron Age societies in the northern parts of Gaul. It is unsupported by any convincing evidence; none of these supposed aristocratic residences, for example, has yet been identified.

In brief, this was a political landscape divided into a large number of micropolities centered around small, but densely occupied, defended settlements that Michel Py has called "oppidum-cités." During the second century BCE, there were about a dozen of these towns in Eastern Languedoc spaced less than fifteen kilometers apart on average, controlling potential territories generally less than about fifteen kilometers in diameter.[50] In the Hérault valley, such sites were even closer together.[51] This is by no means a unanimous interpretation. Some scholars prefer to see larger-scale centralized structures existing much earlier, but the evidence for this interpretation is very weak.

Nîmes and the Volcae Arecomici present the obvious test case because they appear to offer the most plausible potential support for the idea of early regional centralized political power due to the unusually large size of the city and the comments of Strabo and Pliny about a confederation of twenty-four subject towns (oppida ignobilia) of the Volcae Arecomici ruled by the "metropole" of Nîmes.[52] But Strabo and Pliny were describing the situation as it existed in the early first century CE, after more than a century of Roman provincial administration, and particularly after the efforts that Augustus had taken to augment the prestige, power, and privileges of Nîmes under his scheme to remodel the institutions and networks of provincial centers.[53] Those advocating early political centralization have argued that the Romans simply sanctioned officially a hierarchical regional power structure that existed long before; but this view should be treated with a good deal of skepticism.[54] Instead, Roman administrative practices transformed a prior confederation of relatively autonomous polities led by Nîmes into a centralized hierarchical structure of power dominated by Nîmes, within a set of juridically defined provincial territories and identities that resulted in a process of ethnogenesis.

Nîmes was founded in the late sixth century BCE, and some scholars have suggested that it had developed into a major trade center already by the mid–fifth century BCE and that it had become a preeminent political force in its region by the fourth century BCE.[55] The idea of its early importance is based on the relatively large quantity of imported ceramics found in the very limited excavations undertaken in some early levels and the unusually large area (fifteen to twenty hectares) of the settlement by the mid–fifth century BCE. However, the evidence indicates that this area was not densely settled and had a more rural than urban character, with dispersed groups of wattle-and-daub houses separated by agricultural fields.[56] This was at a time when several other sites in the eventual territory of Nîmes (such as Le Marduel and Lattes), although much smaller in area, already had stone ramparts enclosing dense occupations. Around 400 BCE, Nîmes was surrounded by a rampart and ditch system that may have enclosed an area of between thirty-two and forty-four hectares of land, although the traces are not entirely clear. A settlement of about twenty to twenty-five hectares emerged on the lower slopes of the hill, rather than the top.[57] This was unusual in terms of both its very large size and its position (most contemporary defended sites were on hilltops and less than a quarter of this size). Unfortunately, excavations of fourth- and third-century BCE levels are in-sufficient to offer much reliable detail about the urban structure or economic situation of the town at that time, but the highly unusual size of the settlement and its extensive fortifications do argue for a certain importance within its regional context already in this period. However, this does not necessarily indicate the existence of the same structure of regional political dominance described by Strabo. As Michel Py has suggested, Nîmes at this time may well have developed into an influential regional center for trade, pilgrim-age, and political gatherings for the leaders of neighboring village and town polities, but without having the power or authority to exercise sovereignty over the region.[58]

During the first half of the second century BCE a series of important transforma-tive projects were undertaken at Nîmes, including reconstruction of the southern de-fenses and a peripheral road inside the fortification, the replacement of the former stone tower on the Mont Cavalier with an ostentatious new one twenty meters tall, the gradual spread of houses over the slopes of the northern hills, and the opening of new land to intensive cultivation.[59] Shortly after the Roman conquest of 125 BCE, the Via Domitia (a Roman road from the Alps to the Pyrenees) was built to pass near the town. By the end of the century, the settlement extended over an area of thirty to thirty-five hectares, mak-ing Nîmes a city of unrivaled size in all of Mediterranean France, except for Massalia and Glanum (and perhaps Arles).[60] During the late second century BCE, Nîmes also became the first settlement in Eastern Languedoc to mint its own coins, and these were stamped with the name of the town, in Greek letters.[61] This was clearly an act of political symbolism. While these features, again, argue for the growing size and self-conscious political importance of the town, they are not a clear indication of dominant sovereignty over the region of the kind described by Strabo. For example, at Lattes (which was almost certainly one of the twenty-four towns noted by Strabo and Pliny), when the use of coin-age became common in the town during the first century BCE, coins of Nîmes, though present, were not particularly numerous—no more so, in fact, than other indigenous coins and far less so than those from Massalia.[62] Hence, before the conquest, one can perhaps better interpret Nîmes as an increasingly large and powerful city at the center of a coalescing regional confederation of smaller defended towns with their own civic in-stitutions and identities: what Strabo and Pliny would identify collectively (in a later, sig-nificantly transformed state) as the Volcae Arecomici. Some of these towns would have been linked to Nîmes by patron-client relations of various types, with mutual military obligations and some confederative political offices. They would have served as the base for the later regional political structure, but with important transformations linked to Roman administrative practices from Pompey through Augustus that fixed boundaries, codified legal statuses and identities, granted new rights, and defined formal political of-fices and structures.[63] At some point in the late first century BCE, Nîmes was given the status of *colonia Latina,* and its sovereignty over the twenty-four *oppida ignobilia* was offi-cially ordained.[64] These Roman colonial practices effectively resulted in the ethnogenesis of the Volcae Arecomici out of a formerly fluid coalition of different polities and ethnic groups.[65] It is worth noting in this regard that coins with the legend Volcae Arecomici (AR/VOLC or VOLC/AREC) are written in the Latin script and date to 70 BCE at the earliest, a good two generations after the Roman conquest and after the first emissions of coins at Nîmes (which were marked, in Greek script, with the name of the town and its people rather than this later ethnic entity).[66]

On the other side of the Rhône was the "Celto-Ligurian" confederation headed by the Salyes (or Salluvii) that became a major threat to Massalia in the second century BCE. According to Strabo's description, taken from the early first-century BCE text of Posidonius, this confederation, which extended all the way to Antibes, was composed of ten sections that raised a joint military force of infantry and cavalry.[67] Although he did not specify, these sections are presumably the smaller, relatively autonomous ethnic groups of this region that are named in other sources.[68] The name of the Salyes, the group that lived around Aix-en-Provence, was applied to the whole federation, presumably because they were a dominant force within the ten. This federation appears to have been a relatively effective military force: Strabo mentioned that the Romans were able to defeat them only after a prolonged conflict (see chapter 5).[69]

The principal city of the Salyes is thought to be the site now known as Entremont, although its ancient name is not known.[70] Entremont was not founded until the beginning of the second century BCE, and there is no settlement in the immediate vicinity that would be an obvious candidate for the center of an earlier regional political hierarchy (although Saint-Blaise and Glanum offer tantalizing possibilities as sites of importance that have a much deeper past and are only thirty-nine and fifty-eight kilometers distant, respectively). Moreover, at only 3.5 hectares at the period of its greatest expansion, Entremont was dwarfed by Nîmes and by another settlement in the Salyen territory: Glanum. It clearly did not have the same demographic importance. The original settlement of about 0.9 hectare was located on the highest section of a plateau overlooking the Arc River valley and was densely occupied and protected by a stone rampart. After about a generation, the town expanded over a larger section of the plateau to the east and north about 150–140 BCE, and a new rampart was constructed to encompass an area roughly four times the size of the original settlement. Excavations have revealed two episodes of Roman military action against the town, at about 130–120 BCE and 100 BCE, after which the site was abandoned. Hence, the entire history of the settlement lasted less than a century, or roughly three generations. Unlike Nîmes, there was no subsequent occupation on the site, with the result that archaeological exploration has been much easier and more complete.[71]

In terms of its size, organization, and architecture, Entremont was, in many ways, a fairly typical fortified town of the Rhône basin. There was little differentiation between houses in terms of size or the repertoire of objects found within houses, and the impression is of a typical agricultural town with a relatively homogeneous population. The architecture of the new area settled in the second period is similar to that of the first except that the rooms are generally larger and they are grouped into houses with two to five communicating rooms. Some houses also show traces of a second floor. The difference in the size of dwellings between the two zones, given that the older section continued to be occupied after the new parts of the settlement were built, has been used to argue for social differentiation at the site. This distinction was not marked by ostentation in the elaboration of dwellings, but simply by their size.[72]

Despite its general similarity to other towns of the region, Entremont does have a few noteworthy distinctive features. Most important of these is that, in a pattern that seems to be almost exclusively Provençal (and perhaps even more exclusively Salyen), Entremont was one of the few indigenous settlements to have monumental public buildings of a ritual nature *inside* the settlement (see chapter 8). The size and location of the "sanctuary" of the first period is not known, as the building has been identified by carved stone columns and lintels incorporated into later buildings. For the second period, a large hypostyle room open to the street has been identified. Above it was a large second story room with a pseudo *opus signinum* floor (see chapter 8), plastered walls, and about twenty skulls that show traces of having been affixed to the walls. Outside in the street, the remains of a number of life-size painted limestone statues of male warriors, women, and severed heads have been found that probably belonged to another adjacent public building that has not yet been identified. Whether these were representations of gods, ancestors, or living local persons of importance is not certain, although François Salviat, the main authority on this statuary, prefers the latter possibility.[73] If this interpretation is accepted, then it would argue for the emergence of some form of social hierarchy, or at least a new way of marking status. The unusual public buildings, with their displays of statuary and mounted human heads, would certainly seem to imply some sort of ritual function, perhaps as centers for public political or religious meetings.

According to Livy, the Salyes were led by a "king" *(Salluviorum regem)* named Teutomalius (or Toutomotulus) who fled up the Rhône valley to the Allobrogai after Sextius's victory over the Salyes.[74] Whether the term *regem* in this context can actually be taken to indicate what one would properly classify as a king in the anthropological sense, or whether it is simply a generic term for a ruler or leader of some unspecified kind is not clear. But it does seem to suggest some form of centralized authority vested in a particular person. Aside from this, there is little more that one can say about the nature of the Salyes confederation, except that it seems to have been short-lived. There are no textual references to the Salyes earlier than the second century BCE, and, unlike Nîmes and the Volcae Arecomici, there are few plausible traces of an earlier settlement hierarchy in the area of Aix-en-Provence that might imply the gradual development of a regional center of power.[75] The description by Polybius of the attack in 154 BCE by the Oxybii and the Decietae against Nice and Antibes while Massalia was being simultaneously besieged seems to imply some coordination, but perhaps not the same degree as that later indicated by Strabo.[76] Moreover, the confederation was disrupted by Roman military intervention in a way that did not foster the subsequent crystallization of a centralized provincial administration based on the former center of power. Strabo mentioned that, in contrast to the Volcae Arecomici and the Vocontii who were ranked as autonomous entities by the Roman administration, the tribes of the Salyes federation were put under the authority of *praetors* who were sent to Narbonensis.[77] Moreover, some of their territory was undoubtedly part of that ceded to the control of Massalia by the Romans at this time. Finally, unlike the Vocontii and the Volcae Arecomici, the term *Salyes* seems to have largely passed out of the literary record after the early first-century CE texts of Strabo and Livy.

The Vocontii, the people of Pompeius Trogus (whose account opened this book), were another major confederation occupying a very large area located to the north of the Salyes, in the Vaucluse and parts of surrounding departments. Barruol includes the Avantici, Sebaginni, Sogiontii, and Vertamocorii among the secondary tribes of the Vocontii confederation.[78] The earliest mention of the name Vocontii is in texts of the first centuries BCE and CE, although Livy connected the name to the much earlier passage of Hannibal through the region in the late third century BCE.[79] Little is recorded about them in these early descriptions except their geographical location and the extent of their territory. However, they concluded a treaty of friendship with the Romans in the early years of the conquest that (despite a later revolt put down by Pompey) spared them the fate of the Salyes and allowed them to maintain many of their traditional institutions, and the Vocontii were granted the status of a *civitas foederata* with autonomy from the imposition of tribute and Roman law, a status shared only by Massalia within Provence.[80] They had two main urban centers at Vasio Vocontiorum (modern Vaison-la-Romaine) and Lucus Augusti (Luc-en-Diois). Vaison was established gradually, beginning around 40–30 BCE, as the Vocontian elite moved out of a hillfort on the other side of the Ouvèze river and built villas near the river that served as the focal point for the emergence of a wealthy town with Roman-style architecture and monumental public buildings, but with a decidedly un-Roman street plan.[81] The town never had a defensive city wall; and by the second century CE it had sprawled over an estimated sixty to seventy hectares, much of which remains under the modern town and unexcavated. Unfortunately, little is known about the earlier hillfort settlement because it is largely covered by the medieval town, although ceramics dating from the sixth to the first centuries BCE have been found during road construction.[82] Lucus Augusti and the town that later eclipsed it in importance as a Vocontian center, Dea Augusta (Die), are less well explored archaeologically than Vaison.

Positioned between the Vocontii to the east, the Volcae Arecomici to the west, and the Salyes to the south was the last of the major confederations of the lower Rhône basin: the Cavares. Their territory, according to Strabo, covered a large area of the Rhône valley plain east of the river, running from the Isère River in the North to the Durance River in the South.[83] Once again, the name Cavares is not mentioned in texts earlier than the late first century BCE, although peoples of this territory described simply as Celts are recorded to have resisted Hannibal's passage in 218 BCE. Strabo considered this confederation to be very powerful. It was dominated by the Cavares proper and included the client tribes of the Memini, Tricastini, and Segovellauni.[84] Barruol noted that the Cavares were apparently not among the peoples who fought battles against the Romans in the wars of conquest from 125 to 121 BCE: their name does not appear either on the list of conquered peoples of the Triumphal Acts or in the texts describing the various battles. He also speculated that they may have been allies of Massalia from a relatively early date.[85]

In brief, the emergence of these larger regional confederations in the second century BCE (or perhaps a little earlier in some cases) was very probably linked to the evolving colonial situation, but they took on the specific form that was described in classical texts of the first century BCE as a result of developments after the Roman conquest. Moreover, within these emerging confederations, ethnic affiliation was much more likely to have resided at the level of the microregional groups with ethnonyms noted earlier; and the confederations did not include all of the smaller ethnic groups in the region, some of which remained independent.[86] It was only after being subsumed within the Roman imperial administration that these political confederations began, in some cases, to take on ethnic significance. Similarly, before the period of the larger confederations, the scale of ethnic affiliation was likely to have been at the microregional, or even town or village level, although shifting political and military alliances were undoubtedly forged between such groups as circumstances dictated. The lower Rhône basin was a social landscape composed of villages and towns of a few hundred to a few thousand people each, undoubtedly with local affinal links of marriage recruitment between many settlements. Intertown religious connections, kinship ideologies, exchange friendships established between influential individuals, and patronage networks may also have provided cross-cutting ties that could be mobilized for political and military alliances of an ad hoc or more enduring nature. This is the situation that most likely characterized the indigenous world of the Rhône basin at the moment of the encounter, and the one that persisted, with shifting transformations, over more than four centuries. By the late third or second century BCE, one begins to see the emergence of several larger regional political confederations that would confront militarily both the Massalians and the Romans and that, once subjugated within the Roman provincial administration, would form the basis of Roman territorial divisions and ethnic classifications linked to processes of colonial ethnogenesis.

ETRUSCANS

Information about the "Etruscan" sailors and merchants who first brought wine to the shores of Mediterranean France in the late seventh century BCE is elusive. For one thing, we cannot be sure that all of the people transporting Etruscan wine were actually from Etruria. As the later discussion of the nature of trade argues, we have no reason to assume that trading ships were manned by ethnically homogeneous crews or that the origin of the objects traded necessarily is linked to the identity of the traders who were peddling them. But assuming that at least a number of these traders were from Etruria (and there is *some* evidence to support this idea), what can we say about them?

In the first place, *Etruscan* is not an endogenous ethnonym: it is an alien Roman term used to designate collectively the inhabitants of a number of large independent city-states in the Tuscan region of central Italy who referred to themselves as Rasenna and who were called Tyrrhenoi by Greeks. As noted earlier, the inhabitants of these cities spoke a non-Indo-European language that gradually disappeared in favor of Latin after Tuscany was eventually subsumed within the expanding Roman sphere of control. Although the Etruscans had developed their own script by the seventh century BCE, based on the alphabet of Greek colonists in Italy, we do not have access to textual descriptions of their encounters in the western Mediterranean; none have been preserved (if any were ever written), and they would be largely untranslatable if they existed.[87] Greek texts are also silent on this theme. Hence, the conclusion that there was an Etruscan presence in this region rests on arguments made from archaeological data. This is a relatively recent interpretation that is still subject to skepticism from a few scholars, although it has been greatly strengthened by mounting recent evidence.[88]

Etruscan goods were exported to several parts of the western Mediterranean, including Sardinia, Sicily, Carthage, and Emporion; but southern France was by far the greatest external consumer of Etruscan goods.[89] This market for imported Etruscan material was a relatively brief phenomenon in southern France, lasting only a little more than a century in most of the region and disappearing almost completely by the early fourth century BCE. It was also largely a coastal phenomenon: no sites more than about thirty kilometers from the coast have significant quantities of Etruscan material, although small quantities of wine made it to a few settlements of the Rhône basin garrigues, such as Plan-de-la-Tour and Le Marduel, and to the interior regions of the Hérault and Aude valleys, as far as fifty kilometers or so from the sea; and individual objects were sometimes passed along through indigenous exchange networks over much longer distances.[90] Furthermore, the range of goods consumed in southern France was quite selectively limited, consisting overwhelmingly of wine (transported in a limited subset of Etruscan amphora types).[91] This was originally accompanied by much smaller quantities of *bucchero nero* kantharos drinking cups and wine pitchers, but these ceased to be imported after about 525 BCE (fig. 4.3).[92] The earliest imports, appearing even before the wine, included a scattering of other drinking ceramics produced in Etruria (including some Greek-style wares such as the Etrusco-Corinthian series).[93] A small quantity of ceramic mortars has also been found at some sites.[94] In addition, a small number of bronze objects, including especially shallow basins with decorated rims and small bronze discs, has been recovered from a scattering of (especially) funerary contexts: these objects circulated by indigenous exchange networks more widely than the wine, with a few even reaching the Alpine region.[95]

As noted, the bulk of Etruscan trade in Mediterranean France was heavily concentrated in the coastal region, but even more precisely, in the coastal region of the lower

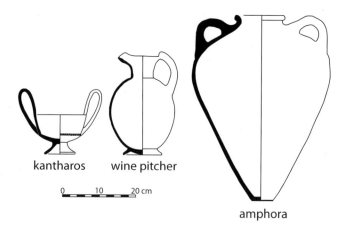

kantharos   wine pitcher

0   10   20 cm

amphora

FIGURE 4.3

Etruscan *bucchero nero kantharos* (drinking cup) and wine pitcher, next to an Etruscan amphora (drawings after Py 1993b).

Rhône basin, essentially the zone between Marseille and the Hérault River. Beyond this area, Etruscan objects are much less common, and very rare west of the Aude basin.[96] The first traces of exchanges date to the mid– to late seventh century BCE, roughly a generation before the foundation of Massalia; and it was only during the latter part of this period, with the emergence of the first consumption of wine in France, that the quantity of goods exchanged became sufficient to qualify as trade. Before that, the Etruscan objects consist of a few scattered ceramic drinking cups and a few small bronze vessels. This trade expanded in the early sixth century BCE, perhaps, as Michel Bats has suggested, with the aid of Massalian merchants trafficking Etruscan wine, which was satisfying most of the demand at Massalia during that period as well.[97] But the importation of Etruscan wine began to wane sharply in the last quarter of the sixth century BCE, and this source was replaced by the rapid expansion of Massalia's own wine exports. Only in eastern Languedoc did Etruscan imports remain numerically significant after 500 BCE, and, except for a small trickle, they largely disappeared from that region by the mid–fifth century BCE. Very small amounts of Etruscan wine did continue to be consumed until the mid–fourth century BCE, but after about 475 BCE the quantity of amphorae found in Mediterranean France is truly miniscule in comparison to Massalian amphorae.[98]

The archaeological data suggest that, unlike the Phocaeans who followed them, the Etruscan presence in France consisted largely of a ship-based "floater" trade without the founding of permanent colonial settlements. None of the hundreds of archaeological sites of Mediterranean France excavated to date bears even a remote resemblance to an Etruscan town or city: the types of architecture, urban settlement organization, domestic practices, and funerary practices characteristic of Etruria are simply not reproduced in this region (as they clearly were, for example, in the Etruscan expansion into northern

Italy).[99] Nor are any such Etruscan colonies mentioned in Greek texts. There was no Etruscan equivalent of a Massalia, or even an Emporion, Agde, or Olbia.

However, alongside the floater trade, there seems to have developed the elements of a "trade diaspora" with small enclaves of Etruscan traders residing at some indigenous settlements.[100] Such enclaves have been suggested for a few sites, most notably Saint-Blaise in Provence and Lattes in eastern Languedoc.[101] Recent excavations at Lattes offer the only material evidence strongly supporting such a proposition to date (other claims are based simply on elevated percentages of Etruscan ceramics), but it seems unlikely that this was a completely isolated case.

At Lattes, the evidence from ongoing excavations is increasingly compelling, although the data are still ambiguous in terms of the precise scale of an Etruscan presence at the site: the potential scenarios range from a small enclave of traders living near the port, to multiple dispersed households in a mixed ethnic settlement, to the less likely, but still possible, idea that Lattes was founded as an Etruscan colony. Excavations in an area (zone 27) along the interior of the rampart just west of the main gate of the town leading to the port have uncovered traces of two houses from the earliest levels at the site (dating to the late sixth century BCE) that were unusual for both the region and the period, in terms of dimensions, construction techniques, and contents (fig. 4.4).[102] These large multiroom houses had walls consisting of a stone foundation with a mud-brick elevation plastered with a thin coating of clay mixed with straw that was then coated with a chalk-based layer that gave the walls a white color. Other evidence indicates that some walls probably had a painted decoration of orange bands as well. Traces of wooden doorframes have also been preserved. The objects found in these houses consisted almost exclusively of large quantities of Etruscan ceramics (over 90 percent of all the ceramics present): many wine amphorae along with smaller amounts of cooking vessels and tableware. Some of the Etruscan cooking pots have graffiti in Etruscan letters engraved on their rims or bases, adding to the already unusually large collection of Etruscan graffiti from the site (fig. 4.5).[103] The large dominance of Etruscan amphorae (over 80 percent of the ceramics and 99 percent of the amphorae), many of them crushed in place in concentrated groups, and the paucity of domestic debris (such as animal bones) suggest that several of the rooms served in large measure as a storehouse for wine (fig. 4.6).[104] These houses were destroyed by a large fire around 475 BCE (and covered by a thick rubble level), after which Etruscan imports dropped precipitously at the site and in the region in general. It is important to point out that Etruscan graffiti and Etruscan cooking ceramics are virtually unknown elsewhere in the region, aside from a few mortars. Giovanni Colonna has even suggested that one of the names among the graffiti (ucial) is that of a native woman written in Etruscan letters, perhaps the local wife of a resident Etruscan trader.[105] Given all these features, the presence of Etruscans residing at the site on a relatively full-term basis is a reasonable interpretation.

Contemporary Etruscan ceramics, especially amphorae, were found at the base of a number of hasty sondages opened by Henri Prades during the 1960s and 1970s at

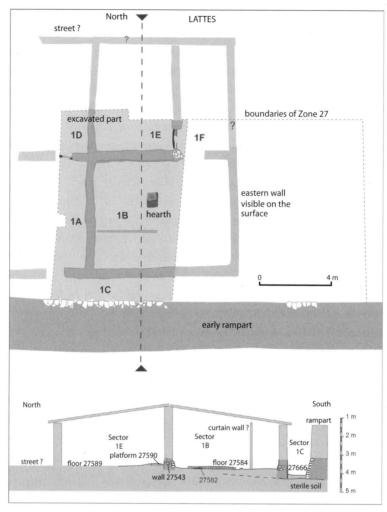

FIGURE 4.4

Plan and reconstructed elevation of a probable Etruscan merchant's house of the late sixth century BCE at Lattes, zone 27 (after Lebeaupin and Séjalon 2008).

various locations around the site,[106] but at present it is impossible to determine if these represent a larger resident Etruscan population at Lattes or simply goods from the Etruscan merchants of zone 27 consumed in indigenous homes. The fact that the ceramic assemblages from these sondages show a more mixed character, with larger percentages of indigenous CNT ware[107] (*céramique non tournée*, discussed more fully in chapter 7) and Massalian products, points toward the latter conclusion, although the stratigraphic integrity of the finds is questionable. Meticulous excavations in zone 1 (over a hundred meters away, along the eastern rampart) are currently nearing the early fifth century BCE levels and should be able to resolve this issue with greater precision. Until then it is impossible to know how extensive the enclave was, but an Etruscan presence does seem confirmed. The marked regional pattern of a strong persistence of Etruscan wine imports at the

FIGURE 4.5
Etruscan graffiti on the base of a *bucchero nero* vase from Lattes, zone 27, 450–425 BCE (UFRAL).

FIGURE 4.6
Etruscan amphorae in the storeroom of the Etruscan merchant's house at Lattes, zone 27, against the rampart (UFRAL).

site after their dramatic decline in Provence suggests the stubborn maintenance of an independent commodity chain linking eastern Languedoc to southern Etruria.[108] The demonstration of such an independent connection is highlighted by considering that, during the early fifth century BCE, 99 percent of the amphorae in zone 27 of Lattes were Etruscan while a mere forty-four kilometers to the east at Espeyran, 95 percent of the amphorae were Massalian.[109] Combined with the domestic data at Lattes, the conclusion that an enclave of Etruscan merchants lived at the site and anchored these continuing trade relations seems the most plausible explanation. Although it is possible that this may have been the only enclave situation of this kind in the region, additional examples may yet be discovered as more extensive excavations proceed in the deeper levels of other coastal sites (these levels at Lattes lie under several meters of later stratigraphy and below the water table). The broader significance of such resident merchants is discussed in the following chapter, but one can at least offer here the observation that the presence of these resident foreigners at Lattes is an indication that trade had already shifted by the late sixth century BCE (at least at one site) from something probably conducted outside the town, as a periodic boundary-market phenomenon, to a routinized aspect of town life incorporated within the walls of the settlement.

Given that at least some of the goods imported from Etruria were brought by Etruscan merchants and some Etruscans were living at native sites in France, what does this actually mean in terms of the cultural identity and social position and interests of these foreigners? In the first place, "Etruscans" should not be thought of as a homogeneous ethnic, cultural, or political group. Quite the opposite: each city-state was fiercely independent politically and had its own identity, resources, and interests. Moreover, the cities were often in conflict with each other and had their own complex histories of ascent and decline in their fortunes and territories.[110] At least three main geographic zones can be discerned for the original Etruscan region before the sixth century BCE expansion into the Po valley and Campania, including the metal rich area of northern Etruria (from the Arno to the Ombrone rivers), the inland zone of the Apennine mountains (especially along the Tiber valley), and the southern coastal zone (from the Fiora to the Tiber rivers) (fig. 4.7). The northern zone contained most of the metal resources of Etruria (iron, lead, copper, tin, silver) and was an exporter of metal.[111] In contrast, the southern zone had relatively minimal sources of metal ore, but the cities of this area (Caere and Vulci in particular) appear to have been the main source of most of the Etruscan wine and *bucchero nero* pottery exported to southern France.[112] Hence, the cities of different zones of Etruria had different interests in terms of resources that would have been desirable to import, and in terms of products they had available for exchange. Populonia (in the northern zone), for example, would have had little interest in importing iron, whereas demand for iron at Caere would have been strong.

More than this, it was not cities that conducted trade but merchants, and it is a mistake to construct a model of commerce with cities as actors pursuing collective civic political or import-and-export interests (except in a few cases for essential *import* products such as grain). Instead, one must imagine a set of relatively independent maritime traders who, by virtue of specialized knowledge of disparate markets, were able to make connections between areas with complementary sets of demands and goods to exchange. But their interest was to make a profit for themselves or for the wealthy people who sponsored them, not to serve the needs of particular Etruscan cities. They would

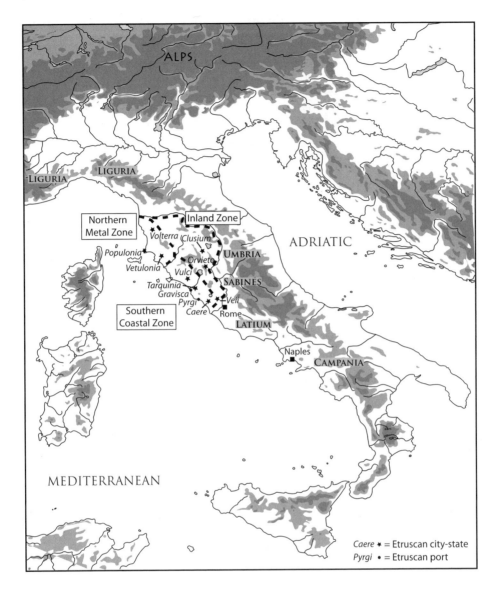

FIGURE 4.7

Map of the regions of Etruria showing some of the principal Etruscan city-states and ports.

undoubtedly trade goods from any town to any other town, depending simply on their knowledge of the landscape of demand in Etruria and southern France. This could involve both fairly direct voyages and exchanges (perhaps, for example, between Vulci and Lattara, brokered by resident merchants), as well as coastal port hopping with constant partial exchanges that would involve offloading some cargo and taking on new goods in each context, according to the local conditions of demand and availability. And this could be carried out by both full-time and part-time traders.

FIGURE 4.8
Etruscan tumulus graves, cemetery of Caere, Italy.

The status and identity of these traders are discussed in more detail, in the discussion of the nature of trade in the following chapter, but for the moment let us simply note that, by the time the trade with southern France had begun, Etruscan cities were highly stratified hierarchical societies.[113] The precise nature of the social structure of particular cities is often obscure, as interpretation rests heavily on archaeological funerary data. However, in general, the late seventh and sixth centuries BCE are seen by many scholars to be marked by a transition from what Bruno D'Agostino has called "gentilicial" to "timocratic" forms of organization.[114] That is, there was a gradual shift from a system with power vested in large kinship groups or clans (Latin *gentes*) with marked internal disparities in wealth between aristocratic elites, recruited clients, and slaves (with economic power correlated with land ownership) toward a system in which the *gentes* still held considerable sway in defining social status, but economic power was increasingly atomized to family households and based on personal wealth derived from specialized agriculture and trade. This is sometimes described (somewhat anachronistically) as the rise of a middle class of *nouveaux riches*. The status of the wealthy classes in general was marked by, among other things, lavishly opulent consumption patterns; but one sees a shift from the construction of enormous, richly furnished tumulus burial structures of up to forty to fifty meters diameter (fig. 4.8) toward other forms of burial with smaller, simpler, more uniform, and more regularly organized structures, such as the streets lined with "*a dado*" cubical tombs of Caere (fig. 4.9). These shifts occurred somewhat differently and at different times within the various regions of Etruria, but they are generally a product of the sixth century BCE.

FIGURE 4.9
Etruscan *a dada* graves, cemetery of Caere, Italy.

Several observations of relevance to the discussion of southern France can be derived from this picture of Etruscan society. In the first place, it is highly unlikely that
the sailors and merchants who peddled shiploads of wine along the shores of southern
France included members of the wealthy Etruscan elites under either system. Wealthy
and socially distinguished Etruscans undoubtedly profited from this trade discretely by
selling the produce of their estates to merchants and financing trading voyages, but,
for reasons that will be discussed in the next chapter, they would not themselves have
deigned to descend to the level of becoming traders: and they would not have been the
agents of contact with native peoples of southern France. Hence, we should not expect
to find anything like Etruscan aristocrats residing at a foreign port such as Lattes. These
would most likely have been individuals who were socially marginal (although economically important) in both contexts.

A second feature to emerge from consideration of Etruscan societies of this period, is
that the flourishing of trade in France corresponds temporally to significant transformations in Etruscan social relations: the rise of the timocratic "middle class" noted earlier.
Given its relatively modest scale, it would be severely overstating the case to claim that
the Etruscan wine trade to France was directly responsible for the increasing wealth of
this rising class or the fortunes of cities such as Caere and Vulci. But it undoubtedly

formed part of a set of economic practices that were linked to the creation of new wealth through trade of agricultural goods from landed estates (such as wine), raw materials (such as metals), and manufactured objects, albeit through the mediation of a useful but socially marginal group of professional traders. Hence, the encounter between Etruscans and the indigenous peoples of France should not be seen as one in which elements of a stable or homogeneous Etruscan culture were imported to Gaul and set off a series of imitative transformations. Rather, Etruscans and Gauls were both agents from societies in the midst of significant social and cultural transformations, and the encounter had a role in shaping the direction of those transformations for both parties. More will be said about this later, but let us now move on to a discussion of the next foreigners to arrive on the scene.

MASSALIA

In an event romanticized in the famous legend of Gyptis and Protis, the colonial settlement of Massalia (modern Marseille) was founded about 600 BCE on the north shore of the "Lacydon," an inlet in the rocky Provençal coast. Massalia was the first permanent colonial settlement in Mediterranean France, and the first Greek colony beyond Italy in the western Mediterranean. It also became, within a few generations, by far the largest and most important colonial settlement in the region until the Roman conquest five centuries later. However, it was still rather small in comparison to Etruscan cities and the Greek colonies in southern Italy, many of which were five to ten times as large. Moreover, Rome at the time of Augustus was over 35 times the size of Massalia's maximum of fifty hectares.[115]

Although it has often been assumed that Masalia's location was selected because of its proximity to the Rhône River and its potential as a route to resources such as Cornish tin and slaves from the deep interior of Gaul,[116] this is implausible for a number of reasons.[117] How, for example, would Phocaean traders have known that tin resources can be found over a thousand kilometers to the north when it is unlikely that the inhabitants of the Rhône basin were aware of this? And how would they have imagined making this long overland voyage through unknown and potentially hostile indigenous societies who populated the intervening regions? Far more likely is that Massalia was seen as a step on the coastal route to rich metal resources farther west in Spain, including the legendary wealth of Tartessos and Huelva with which Phocaeans were frequently associated.[118] Not only was Massalia located on perhaps the best natural harbor in Mediterranean France, but it was also one of the last such harbors before the coast turns into a flat sandy beach with little relief that runs from the Rhône delta all the way to the Pyrenees. This vast expanse of beaches, flanked by saline lagoons and a broad, flat coastal plain, would actually have posed more of a hazard to ships than the rocky Provençal coast. This is because it provided no natural shelter from the frequent storm winds and currents and because it provided few readily distinguishable landmarks for navigation, both of which were extremely important to the kind of ship voyages practiced at that time.[119] Strabo, for example, remarked on this fact explicitly when he noted that the Massalians set up light towers in the Rhône delta in the Roman period (when they finally were given control of the area by the Romans) because the mouths of the river were dangerous for ships to try to enter given the swift currents, the constant silting up, and the "lowness of the country, so that in foul weather one cannot descry the land even when close to it."[120] It is equally suggestive that when Massalia founded a series of subcolonies in subsequent centuries, these were spread along the coast to the east and west of the city rather than up the Rhône valley.

Ancient texts are unanimous in describing the first settlers as Greeks from the city of Phocaea on the Ionian coast of Turkey.[121] These texts all date to long after the foundation, however, and it is possible that the colony was originally founded by groups of settlers from several parts of Ionia and attained an increasingly specific Phocaean identity only later, especially after an influx of new colonists in the late sixth and early fifth centuries BCE following the fall of Phocaea to Persian forces.[122] Within a few decades, another, much smaller Phocaean colony, Emporion, was established farther west on the Catalonian coast of Spain. In subsequent centuries, Massalia also established a series of small colonial outposts of its own along the coast of Mediterranean France.

In contrast to the central Mediterranean, where a wide variety of mother cities sent out settlers, colonial activity in the western Mediterranean was largely a Phocaean affair, and it was rather late. Massalia was founded about 170 years after the first Greek colony in the Central Mediterranean (Pithekoussai, on the island of Ischia), and at least 100 to 125 years after the coast of southern Italy had already been densely peppered with Greek colonies. Phocaeans were not significant participants in this earlier phase of establishing colonies, and they were largely absent from the central Mediterranean (with the exceptions of Alalia, on Corsica, and Velia, in Campania, both of which were also late foundations of the sixth century BCE). For this and other reasons, it is important to avoid simply viewing the case of Massalia from the perspective of Greek colonies in southern Italy or imposing models from that region farther west. Unlike Massalia, colonial ventures in Italy began when the institution of the polis was still in the early stages of development. Moreover, Massilia and other Phocaean colonies in the west were much smaller than Greek colonies in Italy and they were much less densely concentrated in the region. They also had a very different balance of power with native peoples, and their political context did not involve anything remotely similar to the violent history of warfare and destruction between rival Greek colonies that characterized southern Italy.

But what does it mean to say that the settlers of Massalia and Emporion were "Phocaeans" or that Phocaeans were "Greeks"? In the first place, the term *Phocaean* certainly does not imply a stable, unified culture or a uniform sense of collective identity, and the term *Greek* even less so. As Jonathan Hall has pointed out, it is useful to distinguish between *Greek*, as an analytic indexical term designating people who came from the Greek mainland or from colonial settlements deriving from that area, and *Hellene*, as a term used to designate individuals who felt an emic sense of identity and community with other "Hellenes."[123] The disparate peoples whom we choose to call Greeks did not necessarily always have a sense of being Hellenes. When that sense of common Hellenic identity developed, it was a product of specific historical circumstances that emerged at a particular moment, and it was transformed through time as a result of a variety of factors, prominent among them the experience of colonial encounters with other cultures. As Hall points out, the term *Hellene* first was used to refer simply to the people living in a small region south of Thessaly, and it emerged as a broader ethnic term within the Greek world only in the sixth century BCE, largely as a result of a political strategy by Thessalians to promote their own hegemony within Central Greece by excluding others living in the area from a place in a genealogical definition of common identity. As he further argues, it was in the Classical period (specifically, the fifth century BCE) that the definition of Hellene shifted from an ethnic to a cultural one, and this definition owed a great deal to the newly emergent contrastive definition of the "barbarian" resulting from encounters in various parts of the Mediterranean to which Greeks had emigrated, and particularly to the Persian War, in a process that was heavily influenced by Athens and an Athenocentric doctrine of Panhellenism.[124]

Hence, one must emphasize that Phocaean settlers did not arrive in southern France as bearers of a collective, stable Hellenic identity and a common Panhellenic culture. These things emerged, to the extent that they did, over the course of the colonial encounter and as a result of the colonial experience. Moreover, it is important to point out that, even given the eventual construction of some affective sense of common bonds of "Hellenicity" based on privileging a few selected cultural criteria, there were enormous cultural and social differences within the Greek world formed by complex local histories. Moreover, Greek cities were politically autonomous and frequently at war with each other. Hellenicity would have been only situationally relevant and not even equally shared by different social groups and classes within individual Greek cities. Local distinctions were generally far more important than appeals to a transcendent Panhellenism. It is important to look at developments locally in order to understand how particular Greek identities actually developed in different colonial contexts. The contrast between Massalia and Emporion is instructive in this vein. But before undertaking that comparison, let us also consider the meaning of being "Phocaean," something both of these cities had in common.

The city of Phocaea is located near Izmir, on the coast of Turkey. Although excavations were begun at the site as early as 1913, they have been intermittent and limited in extent.[125] Hence, a good deal more is actually known about Massalia than about its mother city. However, what is known is that Phocaea was the northernmost of a band of Ionian-speaking Greek cities along the Turkish coast. Ionians spoke a dialect of Greek that was shared by Euboeans and Athenians, among others, and that distinguished them from speakers of the Doric (for example, Corinth, Syracuse) and Aeolian (Thessaly, Cyme) dialects.

It appears that Phocaea was founded near the end of the ninth century BCE as part of the first wave of Greek colonial expansion from the mainland, and the Phocaeans developed a reputation as being the first great adventurous sea voyagers among the Greeks. Herodotus, for example, in noting their exploits, recounted an expedition to the metal-rich kingdom of Tartessos, in the Guadalquivir region of southern Spain.[126] If correct, this must have been before the end of the sixth century BCE, when Tartessos disappeared.[127] It is possible that early exploratory voyages by Phocaean traders seeking routes to Spanish metal resources may have established the geographic knowledge that led eventually to the establishment of colonial settlements such as Massalia and Emporion, although archaeological evidence for such a "precolonial" phase of exploration is, understandably, rather slim.[128] Despite their early trade voyages, Phocaeans were somewhat late arrivals to the practice of founding colonies, beginning only in the late seventh century BCE, and going first toward the Black Sea and then (in the sixth century BCE) primarily to the western Mediterranean. Phocaea fell under Lydian control in the mid–sixth century BCE, and was subsequently conquered by the Persian armies of Cyrus the Great in 545 BCE. This latter event resulted in the diasporic exile of a large number of Phocaean citizens, many of whom, according to ancient texts, settled at Alalia (on Corsica), and Velia (in Campania). Some may also have settled at Massalia, although the texts are ambiguous about this, and the subject remains a matter of discussion among modern scholars.[129] It would certainly help to explain the remarkably rapid increase in the size of Massalia during the mid–sixth century BCE, as well as clarifying a discrepancy in the date given for the foundation of Massalia by certain texts that link the origins of Massalia to the capture of Phocaea by the Persians.[130] In any case, from this point on, although the city of Phocaea continued to exist, the mother city was replaced by Massalia as the most important "Phocaean" city.

Greek colonies often retained (or created) certain sentimental and cultural ties to the mother city, but they were generally autonomous politically and economically.[131] Massalia was no exception in this regard. Moreover, its evolving identity, social institutions, and culture were shaped by the local colonial context into which it had inserted itself as much as by kinship with a distant Phocaean homeland. This was, in fact, true of all the Phocaean colonies, each of which shared certain practices with Phocaea, but each of which also developed into a quite distinctive city. As Jean-Paul Morel said of Velia, it was a Phocaean city, but one in Magna Graecia (hence certain peculiarities, such as its links to Naples and Athens); and it was also a city of Magna Graecia, but a Phocaean one (hence its singularity in Italy). Moreover, as he further noted, many aspects of its spiritual and material culture were oriented less toward Magna Graecia proper than toward the very local context of southern Campania.[132]

Massalians continued to speak an Ionian dialect, to write with an Ionian script, and to use conservatively Ionian naming practices.[133] They also maintained certain religious traditions characteristic of Ionia, such as an emphasis on the cults of Ephesian Artemis and Delphinian Apollo.[134] Massalia even came to the aid of Phocaea on occasion, as when

Massalian envoys pleaded with the Roman Senate to spare Phocaea from destruction after it had participated in an anti-Roman insurrection in 130 BCE.[135] But one can also point to many aspects that show local transformations resulting in distinctively Massalian practices. For example, many of the earliest coins of Massalia were clearly modeled after Phocaean prototypes, with images based on shared religious elements. However, other types showing a peculiarly Massalian iconography also emerged quickly and became dominant. Moreover, by the mid–fifth century BCE, Massalia was producing coins based on a new metric unit that diverged significantly from Phocaean practices and corresponded more to the standards common in southern Italy.[136]

One should also emphasize that, on a general theoretical level, there is nothing natural about the persistence of cultural signs, practices, and beliefs in colonial societies. When one sees conservative elements, those need to be explained every bit as much as does change. They require a good deal of symbolic work to maintain and they are the result of political strategies played out within particular structures of social relations. One can perhaps best illustrate this feature by a brief comparison of the two colonies of Massalia and Emporion.

Both were founded by Phocaeans within a few decades of each other, about three hundred kilometers apart along the western Mediterranean coast. The initial settlement at Massalia was over an area of about twelve hectares on the western tip of the triangular spur of land it would eventually occupy on the northern shore of its harbor. However, the city grew relatively quickly to become a much larger settlement of over fifty hectares with an eventual population of fifteen thousand to twenty thousand (see chapter 8).[137] Emporion, on the other hand, first occupied a small island called the *Palaiapolis*, before expanding to the adjacent mainland (to a site now called the *Neapolis*).[138] However, the settlement remained very small: it never exceeded about five hectares in size (until after the Roman conquest when a new Roman town was constructed alongside the Greek town), and the population probably did not exceed about 1,500 (fig. 4.10).[139]

Recent excavations have shown that, in contrast to Massalia, the Palaiapolis (under the current village of San Martí d'Empúries) was occupied by an indigenous settlement before the arrival of Phocaean settlers.[140] Ancient texts further indicate that the Greek population was essentially surrounded by a large native settlement of 105 hectares that was initially separated from them by a common wall, and that the two communities eventually became a creolized polity with a common constitution and a hybrid legal system.[141] Strabo noted that such arrangements were, in fact, fairly common in colonial situations;[142] other authors have described, for example, mixed populations of "Helleno-Scythians" near the Black Sea and mixtures of Greeks and Pelasgians in Chalcidice.[143] Although the location of the initial adjacent indigenous settlement of native "Indiketans" remains elusive, both texts and modern excavations (especially of cemeteries) have tended to confirm the small and dependent nature of the colony and to suggest an intimate process of coexistence with the indigenous peoples of a type quite different than at Massalia.[144] For example, when surrounding native peoples adopted the practice of

FIGURE 4.10

The excavated remains of the Neapolis of Emporion, Spain.

writing, those around Massalia appropriated the Greek script, whereas those around Emporion adopted the Iberian script.[145] Moreover, the history of Massalia is peppered with accounts of hostilities between Massalia and its neighbors, many of which were serious enough to request outside aid from Rome.[146] Although the silence of texts is hardly proof, no such accounts of outbreaks of violence exist in the case of Emporion and it is difficult to imagine that, had they occurred, this tiny, precarious town could have survived the kind of attacks that the much larger Massalia found threatening to its existence.

Finally, in contrast to the situation described here for Emporion, Massalia had a reputation in antiquity for extreme cultural conservatism and a constitution that preserved Ionian laws and a rather archaic, closed form of aristocratic government.[147] Massalia was ruled by an aristocratic assembly of six hundred men, called *Timouchoi*, who held office for life. The immediate business of government was conducted by an elected council of fifteen of these men, and these fifteen were, in turn, presided over by three men at the top of the pyramid of power. Eligibility for a Timouchos to become one of these three depended on being the descendant of a family that had been citizens for three generations.[148] Obviously, given the generational stipulation, this was a system constructed well after the city was founded in a moment of self-conscious creation of an aristocratic structure with archaizing tendencies (but before the mid–fourth century BCE when Aristotle was commenting on it). This conservatism is one of the main reasons that prominent Roman families sent their sons to Massalia for an education rather than to the more cosmopolitan Athens, and it was remarked on admiringly by numerous Roman authors, including especially Cicero.[149]

One gets a sense of Massalians (or rather, the aristocratic ruling class of Massalia) trying very hard to self-consciously maintain (or construct) certain elements of a nostalgic, static vision of Phocaean culture and identity in a diasporic colonial context long after Phocaea itself had been dramatically transformed. This is much like outposts of the British Empire that developed versions of Englishness that were both performatively hyper-English and out of touch with contemporary developments in the metropole.[150] As Livy noted in a rather curious gratuitous cultural defense of the Hellenic character of colonial Greek cities in general:

> If the native temperament of the Massilians could have yielded to the influence of their soil they would have been long ago barbarized by the wild untamed tribes all round them, but we are given to understand that they are held in as much honor as though they were living in the heart of Greece. They have preserved their language, their dress, their personal habits, but above all, they have maintained their laws and customs and their open, straightforward character, untainted by any contact with their neighbors.[151]

Actually, the evidence for substantial and continual contact with Massalia's neighbors is overwhelming, so this conservatism was precisely a reaction to such contact. As Strabo noted, in contrast to Massalia, situations with a mixture of both "barbarian" and Greek laws had evolved in many other cases.[152] Hence, the danger of "going native" is clearly one recognized by many ancient Greeks, often with a certain anxiety. They were clearly not as confident of the unidirectional and inevitable flow of "civilizing" influences as modern scholars who accepted so easily the concept of Hellenization as a way of understanding colonial encounters. It is quite possible that such cultural transformations among colonial Greeks are what lie behind the inability to recognize several of the Greek colonies of the western Mediterranean that were mentioned in ancient texts but have never been identified archaeologically (Rhodanousia in France and Mainake, Hemeroskopeion, and Alonis in Spain). This fear is one that was perceived as a threat in many modern colonial contexts as well and occasionally, as in the case of the English in Ireland and the infamous Statutes of Kilkenny, provoked desperate legislative action to prohibit the adoption of local customs and intermarriage. Massalia certainly seems to have reacted against this tendency in a way that Emporion did not, although this is not necessarily evident in the architectural and material culture traces of the settlements.

It should also be pointed out that this view of the conservative character of Massalia that is derived from certain texts applies primarily to the wealthy aristocratic class who controlled its public institutions and not necessarily to the rest of the city's inhabitants. Nor does it apply to all aspects of Massalian culture. A few texts, especially by other Greeks, offer a rather different vision of the city. For example, Athenaeus described with scorn Massalian men wearing the same kind of highly decorated robes and long tunics as Iberians, and he considered them to have become very effeminate and spoiled by luxury. He even noted in connection with these features that there was a common saying, "May you sail to Massalia," that would be roughly equivalent to "going to the dogs."[153] Such texts offer hints of another face of the city that is out of line with the image of conservative aristocratic Hellenic virtue so admired by Romans.[154] As Arnaldo Momigliano has pointed out, Varro indicated that Massalia in his time (the first century BCE) was a trilingual city, with Greek, Celtic, and Latin being the presumed languages. He also noted that at least one Massalian in the service of the Ptolemies in the second century BCE had a Celtic name (Cinto).[155] But a clearer view of the rest of the denizens of the city (the ordinary citizens, slaves, metics, transient foreigners, and others who are largely invisible in the texts) depends on archaeology.

It is important to recognize that preindustrial cities, even small towns of a few thousand inhabitants, almost invariably experienced negative rates of natural population growth, with deaths exceeding births. This fact stems from, among other factors, increased levels of mortality resulting from conditions facilitating the spread of infectious diseases and the prevalence of certain density-dependent endemic "urban diseases" (such as tuberculosis) that are relatively rare in low-density rural settings. Hence, migration was essential just to maintain the population at the same level, and especially to grow.[156] Massalia certainly would not have been immune from this trend, especially considering the problems posed by malaria and tuberculosis in the ancient Greek world[157] and the fact that Massalia was surrounded by swampy ground. One can safely presume the need for a constant influx of migrants to sustain the growth that it witnessed over the centuries. These immigrants would most probably have included, in addition to Phocaean emigrants and slaves, a sizable number of foreign merchants (perhaps from Etruria, the Greek colonies in southern Italy, and beyond) as well as local Gauls, Ligurians, and Iberians.

COLONIAL GENDER RELATIONS: INTERMARRIAGE, COURTESANS, AND PROSTITUTES

One other obvious question raised by the tale of the foundation of the city is the degree of intermarriage between Massalians and local peoples, or of other forms of intergender relationships between colonists and native peoples. If one puts any credence in the symbolism of the story of Gyptis and Protis, then Massalia was founded on the basis of intermarriage between a Greek man and a native woman. But how common was this practice in daily life? Is there more to it than simply an anecdotal version of a common etiological trope typical of Greek colonial foundation stories?[158] Did the Phocaean colonists bring women with them from the homeland, or were they entirely dependent on securing wives and sexual partners from local peoples once they arrived? If they did bring wives, was the Massalian community entirely endogamous, or did native women play a role in becoming wives and mistresses—and what was the extent of their presence?

These questions are difficult to answer, due not only to the inherent problems in addressing such issues with archaeological data, but also to the paucity of textual evidence and of good household archaeological data at Marseille (see chapter 8).[159] The tale of the secret attack against the city by Comanus that was foiled by a native Ligurian woman who informed her Massalian lover of the plot may be an indication that such relationships were more than simply a formulaic part of foundation myths, and that such relationships took other forms than marriage. But few other textual references shed much light on this question. Strabo noted that when the Phocaeans stopped at Ephesus on their way to settle Massalia, a priestess named Aristarcha joined them on the command of the goddess Artemis, but there is no information about other women accompanying the colonists.[160]

These textual anecdotes certainly suggest that native women may have had some role in the domestic sphere of the Greek city and as intermediaries between Massalia and its neighbors. However, it is not clear precisely what forms these roles took or what the incentives might have been for the women to take up such roles. The possibilities range from wives to courtesans and prostitutes, to domestic servants and slaves. In the case of slaves, the question of incentives for the women is not relevant as this was not a situation of choice. It should be noted that we have no evidence of any kind for the presence of local Gauls as household slaves at Massalia, although this does not preclude the possibility. In other cases, the incentives may have been political alliances with, for example, daughters given in marriage regardless of their own desires. However, other possibilities exist as well for women who may have desired to extract themselves from restrictions in their own societies or who were ostracized or forced to flee for various reasons. From the comparative literature on colonial encounters, one can imagine, for example, something like the *signores* of the Senegambian and Guinean coast in Africa. These were women of slave and creole descent who established unions of convenience (as wives or concubines) with French and Portuguese traders. Some of them developed into wealthy traders in their own right, acquiring a degree of status and independence that was not possible in their natal context.[161]

We know that Greek cities, especially port cities, had many brothels *(porneion)* and prostitutes of various kinds. Indeed, the famous lawmaker Solon is reputed to have founded the first state-owned brothel of Athens, with slaves providing the sexual services.[162] In contrast to common prostitutes *(pornai)* who worked the streets and brothels, there was also a class of independent courtesans called *hetaerai*, some of whom became wealthy, famous, and influential. As Sarah Pomeroy has noted, they were "the only women in Athens who exercised independent control over considerable sums of money."[163] Unlike proper, virtuous wives *(gynaekes)*, hetaerai were permitted to attend symposia (indeed the emergence of the category is linked to the development of the symposion), and they often had cultivated skills in music, dance, and educated conversation. They wore special clothes and paid taxes, and they were usually foreigners or ex-slaves.[164] Apollodorus summed up the Athenian male perspective on the need for women in a court case, stating that "Hetaerai we keep for pleasure, concubines *(pallakai)* for attending day-by-day to the body and wives for producing heirs, and for standing trusty guard on our property."[165] That Massalia had such a range of roles for women, especially foreign women in the various categories of prostitutes, concubines, and courtesans, is very likely. However, we can only speculate about the possible participation of local women of the Rhône basin, as there is no evidence aside, perhaps, from the anecdote about the Ligurian woman warning her lover of an attack. But what about intermarriage?

Evidence concerning the significance of intermarriage in Greek colonies in general is scanty and ambiguous, and scholarly opinions vary widely on this issue. Herodotus's observation that the colonists at Miletus had married local Carian women rather than take along spouses has often been interpreted as an indication that this was a common practice. However, the passage also describes how the Greeks killed the fathers, husbands, and sons of the women before forcing them to marry, resulting in an oath passed on to their daughters that they would not eat with their husbands or call them by their names. This can hardly have been a model for a sustainable source of marriage partners.[166] In general, texts are of little help because women are rarely mentioned at all in accounts of colonial settlement. Several archaeological attempts have been made to detect native women in, for example, the burial evidence at Pithekoussai, focusing especially on aspects of dress such as non-Greek fibulae; and the predominant view is that initial colonists were usually male and intermarriage with local women played a major demographic role in Greek colonial foundations in general.[167] However, Tamar Hodos cast serious doubt on the use of such clothing objects in detecting marriages with Sikel women in Sicily given the problems of distinguishing trade items.[168] Moreover, A. J. Graham has offered a highly skeptical evaluation of the prevailing idea that Greek women were not included among colonial emigrants. It should be emphasized that his skepticism is directed specifically at this issue of the absence of Greek women among founding colonial settlers, not about whether Greek colonists ever married native women. As he readily admitted, numerous examples show that Greeks did not object in principle to intermarriage (Demosthenes' grandfather was married to a Scythian, for instance) and various texts suggest that the practice occurred on a significant scale in many instances (at Cyrene, Samothrace, Chalcidice, etc.).[169] It is probable that these intermarriages often had cultural effects given that, when they are mentioned at all, it is often in the context of etiological explanations of the peculiar customs of women in a given city. At Cyrene, for instance, Herodotus described the women as worshipping the Egyptian god Isis and practicing a prohibition against eating beef, the same dietary exclusion practiced by the neighboring nomadic tribes. The women of the nearby Greek colony of Barca ate neither beef nor pork.[170]

But what can we say about Marseille in particular? Aside from the anecdotal textual references already noted, Philippe Boissinot has pointed to some possible clues to the presence of native women in the material culture found in a few domestic contexts.[171] For example, about 18 percent of the table and cooking ware in the early levels at

Marseille (first quarter of the sixth century BCE) consists of local CNT wares, and this includes nearly all the cooking pots.[172] For reasons that are explained in chapter 7, this may be particularly revelatory. Boissinot also noted a mud-brick house at the Saint-Laurent church site dating to the beginning of the sixth century BCE that had an indigenous bronze bracelet and a CNT urn mixed in with Etruscan and Greek ceramics. But these are highly ambiguous proxies for the identity of household residents. He also noted second to first-century BCE dedications from a Greek sanctuary at Acapte near the colony of Olbia that are written in Greek, yet about 9 percent of the names are of Celtic origin, and some are children of Gauls who bear Greek names and vice versa.[173] Unfortunately, little other useful onomastic evidence has so far come to light, and the burial data have little to add to these few meager indications: one cremation grave at the Saint-Barbe cemetery had two iron La Tène fibulae and another had two unidentifiable fibulae, but this is hardly sufficient to identify alien spouses.[174] We also have no evidence that would indicate flows of partners in the other sense—that is, marriages between native men and Massalian women, either in Massalia or at native settlements. There is certainly no inherent reason to exclude the possibility of such intermarriage, at least once the colony achieved a certain population base. Indeed, these marriages may have been strategically desirable for the creation of political alliances. But empirical evidence is simply lacking.

One of the few texts that does specifically mention women colonists is Herodotus's account of the flight of large numbers of men, women, and children from Phocaea during the Persian siege of the city in 545 BCE. These refugee colonists are said to have gone to Alalia on Corsica, before shifting to Velia in Italy after losing the naval battle of Alalia.[175] But it is possible that, as Strabo's account of these events indicates,[176] some may have settled at Massalia as well, especially given the evidence for rapid demographic expansion of the city around this time. If so, then there may have been an influx of Phocaean families into a city where most (or many, or some?) of the initial wives may have been of Ligurian or Celtic origin. In brief, we are probably justified in assuming that intermarriage occurred at Massalia, but without being able to evaluate its precise demographic significance. To what extent such intermarriage may have produced cultural transformations is equally uncertain. On the basis of the present archaeological data, such effects appear to have been subtle, if any; but current evidence is very meager and this is an important question to pursue as excavations continue.

MASSALIAN CHORA, COLONIES, AND MERCHANT ENCLAVES

The extent and nature of the *chora* of the colonial city—that is, the extraurban zone under its direct political control—has been a subject of considerable research and debate.[177] This was the zone on which the colonists would have depended for at least an important part of their subsistence and which would serve as a buffer against the periodic hostility of their neighbors. Given that wine served for many centuries as the primary commodity that articulated interaction with its neighbors, Massalia also became dependent on its chora for the vineyards that enabled it to sustain its relations with indigenous peoples.

How one goes about investigating the establishment and evolution of such a territory is by no means self-evident.[178] To begin with, there are various ways for a colony to exert control over a territory wrested from native peoples, and these may involve very different kinds of boundaries or borders. Such possibilities include, for instance, forcibly ejecting indigenous peoples beyond a certain perimeter, conquering an area and ruling over native settlements left in place as clients, or inserting itself into native political contests as an ally and using some native groups to expel or subdue others and defend Massalian interests. The archaeological detection of the extent of an area of sovereignty in the latter two cases will be considerably more difficult than in the former. In defining colonial territories there is also the problem of confusing different spaces (economic, cultural, political) of dependence, "influence," and mere contact that will necessarily extend well beyond the chora proper and will not necessarily overlap in a coherent fashion.

Despite the interpretive difficulties, the weight of current opinion supports a reconstruction of the extent of the Massalian chora proper that is far smaller than that proposed by earlier scholars.[179] Until at least the late third century BCE (and probably a century later), it appears to have been largely confined within a radius of less than about eight kilometers from the city, in the area of the small basin of the Huveaune valley that was ringed by arid mountains dotted with native settlements (fig. 4.11). It was not until nearly five hundred years after its foundation that Massalia was able to expand its territory beyond this zone to some of the larger, more fertile plains (such as those of Aubagne and Marignane) and the Rhône delta; and the fate of its territory during the last couple of centuries BCE appears to have been intimately linked to the expanding power of Rome. Massalian control of the mouth of the Rhône, for instance, seems to have occurred only at the end of the second century BCE when, according to Strabo, it was granted by the Roman general Marius after the defeat of the Ambrones and Teutones, when the Massalians were allowed to set up light towers and collected tolls.[180] Ironically, Roman activity in southern France may well have first enabled Massalia to acquire a larger chora, and then taken it away.[181] After its ill-fated support of the losing side in the Roman Civil War in 49 BCE, it appears that Massalia's territory was again reduced, perhaps to its former meager extent in the Huveaune valley.

It has often been suggested that a small chora was typical of Phocaean colonies which, stereotypically, are considered to have had a commercial rather than an agrarian orientation: that is, to be *emporia* rather than *apoikiai*.[182] However, François Villard disputed this in the case of Massalia, stating that its ability to sustain a successful trading community grew out of its strength as a normal Greek polis with a balanced agrarian and fishing base.[183] Henri Tréziny's analysis also shows that, in terms of *relative* size of city to territory, Massalia's chora was not significantly smaller that other Greek colonies in southern Italy.[184]

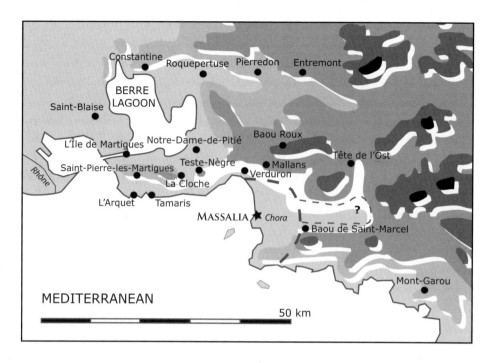

FIGURE 4.11

Map showing the probable extent of Massalia's *chora* (dashed line) until the second century BCE and the location of some of the major surrounding indigenous settlements (not all are contemporary). A possible extension up the Huveaune valley to the east during the third century BCE is indicated by the small dashed line.

Population estimates are notoriously problematic, but Michel Bats and Michel Py have offered tentative figures of about fifteen thousand to twenty thousand inhabitants for Marseille at the time of the Roman siege in 49 BCE.[185] That would be a population density of about three hundred to four hundred people per hectare (or thirty to forty per square kilometer). Using average consumption figures suggested by Michel Gras of six hectoliters per person per year,[186] one can estimate rather crudely that, in addition to other foods, such a population would require about 90,000 to 120,000 hectoliters of grain per year. Estimating ancient agricultural production figures is a guessing game with considerable problems, as ancient seed-to-yield and yield–per–land area ratios are not really known; and local variables such as soil fertility, labor intensity, and cropping, fallowing and manuring practices would all be important sources of variation.[187] Nevertheless, with an emphatic caveat about the highly speculative nature of the calculations offered here, it seems useful to at least attempt a crude estimate. Using an average yield figure of about two to eight hectoliters per hectare,[188] to feed the city would necessitate a minimum of about 11,250 to 45,000 hectares of good agricultural land for the lower population figure, or 15,000 to 60,000 hectares for the higher population figure. Of course, this amount should be doubled to account for biennial fallowing. Hence, even

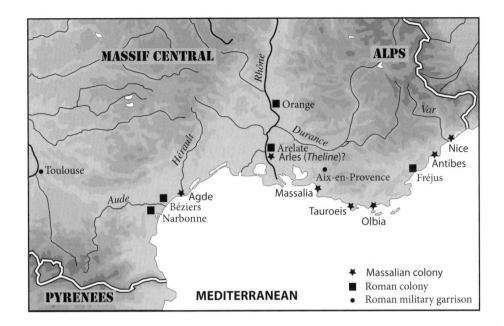

FIGURE 4.12

Map of Massalian colonies and later Roman colonies and military garrisons in Mediterranean France.

employing the most productive figure for the smaller population would require 22,500 hectares of good agricultural land; and this would, of course, be in addition to the land devoted to olive and vine cultivation and grazing for livestock. The area of the small chora generally attributed to Massalia before the late third century BCE would appear to be less than a third of this size and clearly insufficient to meet these demands. Moreover, Strabo described the land of Massalia as being planted with vines and olive trees, but generally too poor for grain.[189] Hence, the colony would have almost certainly been dependent on indigenous peoples to maintain its grain supply.

However, a consideration of the Massalian chora is impossible without also taking into account the sea. Not only was it a rich source of protein (from fish) but a convenient communication route that allowed Massalians to expand the range of the trading network that engaged with native peoples. It also enabled them to establish a series of secondary colonial satellites to both the east and west along the coast of Mediterranean France (fig. 4.12).[190] These were of two potential types: actual colonial settlements and small trading posts, including especially small diasporic enclaves of resident traders at indigenous settlements. For the former, various Greek and Roman authors mentioned a number of such colonial settlements by name;[191] in addition to the fact that many have preserved corrupted versions of their original Greek name, several have been positively identified by archaeological research. The earliest of these was Agathe (modern Agde), founded at the end of the fifth century BCE on the remains of a previously indigenous town at the mouth of the Hérault River (without any clear archaeological traces of violence).[192] Olbia was founded about 325 BCE near modern Hyères on a site without any traces of prior occupation.[193] These are the only two for which foundation dates have been clearly established by archaeological excavations. Although the dates are considerably less certain, it was probably during the late third century BCE that Antipolis was founded at Antibes, and during the late third or early second century BCE that Nikaia was founded at Nice.[194] Both were established immediately adjacent to indigenous hillforts that had existed since the sixth century BCE, but almost nothing is known archaeologically about the Greek colonies that lie under the modern cities that preserve their names. A colony called Tauroeis was also founded near the end of the third century BCE, probably at the site of Le Brusc, near Six-Fours-les-Plages.[195] The name Rhodanousia was also mentioned, but its location is disputed, as is that of another colony called Theline (perhaps Arles?) mentioned by only one author, but not by Pseudo-Scymnus or Strabo in their lists of Massalian colonies.

The functions of the Massalian colonies were probably somewhat mixed.[196] Strabo emphasized their essentially defensive character, stating that they were established as strongholds to defend against the indigenous peoples, and especially to keep the sea lanes clear.[197] However, it is not clear to what extent this is an accurate reflection of the goal of their foundation or whether it reflects subsequent relations and functions that had developed by Strabo's time. In any case, the Provençal colonies were clearly not defending Massalian landholdings because it appears that it was only through Roman intervention that these settlements acquired narrow strips of land that were not under native control. The defensive character of some colonies would seem to be supported by lack of significant resources of trading interest around a site such as Antibes and the impressive fortifications and highly uniform layout of a settlement like Olbia (see chapter 8).[198] However, it is less clear in a case like Agde, which was at the mouth of a river leading to important metal resources and which, in contrast to the Provençal colonies, appears to have had a more developed chora.[199] Agde was also the only one of these subcolonies to develop its own ceramic industries for trade to the natives of the region, and none appears to have been a producer of wine. All of the colonies were quite small in comparison to Massalia. Agde and Olbia, which are the best explored and documented of these sites, covered areas of about 4.25 and 2.5 hectares, respectively.[200]

A Greek presence of the second kind noted above has also been suggested for a number of sites in Mediterranean France: small diasporic communities of Greek traders resident at indigenous settlements. The list of such possibilities includes Agde, Arles, Beziers, Espeyran, Lattes, La Monedière, Pech Maho, and Saint-Blaise.[201] In the case of Agde and Arles, these are sites at which full-fledged Greek or Roman colonies later developed; and Agde, La Monédière, Espeyran, and Béziers have all been claimed as settlements actually founded by Greeks, although these interpretations are disputed by most other scholars.[202]

In most cases the archaeological demonstration of the hypothesis of resident Greeks is less than clear; and even the more generally accepted cases of early Agde and Arles present some interpretive enigmas. At Arles, for example, recent excavations suggest that it was originally a fairly typical indigenous village from the mid–seventh to the late sixth centuries BCE. It may have attracted a Greek trading community during the late sixth century BCE that perhaps grew to become the Massalian colony of Theline named in several texts before evolving into a hybrid settlement in the fourth century and eventually being taken over and established as the first Roman colony (called Arelate) in the lower Rhône Basin in the mid-first century BCE (see chapter 5).[203]

At Agde, the evidence for an early Greek merchant presence in the sixth century BCE, before the foundation of an actual colony at the end of the fifth century BCE, consists essentially of a rampart constructed of mud brick on a base of basalt blocks.[204] At the nearby indigenous settlement of La Monédière, were found several late sixth century BCE apsidal form houses of mud brick on a stone foundation. These are similar to one from the early sixth century BCE found at Marseille (Esplanade de la Tourette) and at various Ionian cities, leading to the suggestion of a small enclave of Greek merchants.[205]

At Lattes, evidence for resident Etruscan merchants seems increasingly compelling, for the reasons outlined earlier. But the presence of Massalian merchants has also been claimed for later centuries. This interpretation is tied to the general abundance of imported goods (amphorae and tableware) at the site, in combination with finds of Greek graffiti on ceramics and Greek inscriptions on a recently discovered lead tablet. The graffiti include alphabet primers, showing individuals practicing writing Greek letters: presumably either the children of merchants or local residents learning to write Greek.[206] The lead tablet was found in a level securely dated to the fifth century BCE in the same area as the earlier Etruscan houses.[207] Although identification of a specific dwelling of a Greek merchant has not yet been possible to the same degree of plausibility as the Etruscan case, perhaps the best candidate is house 1 of block 3. This four-room structure of the late third century BCE is contained within an otherwise typical linear block. But, at 150 square meters, it is much larger than most other contemporary houses and it is of eccentric form in comparison to the other four-room structures known at Lattes (see chapter 8). Furthermore, one of the rooms has a type of floor consisting of lime concrete with inset stones, a technique resembling the Greek *opus signinum* style that is extremely rare before the first century BCE outside Marseille, Ampurias, and Olbia.[208] It is also perhaps significant that this house is built on top of an earlier structure with a room having an unusual arrangement of benches lining three walls that resembles a Greek *andron* or Roman *tryclinium* (the room for symposia).[209]

The claim for an early presence of Greek merchants at Saint-Blaise is based largely on the unusual quantity of imports: over 40 percent of the ceramic assemblage consisted of amphorae during the latter half of the sixth century BCE, and more than 20 percent consisted of imported fineware (mostly drinking cups).[210] However, this interpretation is also founded on the presence of houses of an apsidal form with mud-brick walls that resemble those from La Monédière, Marseille, and various Ionian cities.[211] For the second century BCE, it is the construction of an impressive rampart of carefully tailored limestone blocks built in a typically Greek style (and with Greek-letter quarry marks) that suggests a Massalian presence at the site.[212] This, however, may have been simply a product of Greek masons being engaged to construct the rampart, in a move that had more to do with political relations than traders.

MASSALIAN INTERESTS, AGENTS, AND PRODUCTION

As discussed in greater detail in chapter 7, the articulation of Massalia's trade with native societies depended for centuries primarily on two related products: wine and ceramics designed for its consumption. Excavations have revealed that over the centuries, Massalian merchants used several types of amphorae to transport the wine of the city's vineyards.[213] Excavations at the site of Saint-Jean du Désert have further revealed traces of such a vineyard in relatively close proximity to the city dating probably to the third to first centuries BCE.[214] The vast majority of the wine produced by Massalia was consumed in Mediterranean France, but small quantities of these amphorae have also been found at a few late Hallstatt and early La Tène sites (in temperate France, Switzerland, and southern Germany) as well as in other areas of the western Mediterranean.[215]

Massalian production of its own ceramic fineware began within a generation after the founding of the colony. This initially involved two series of wares known as "Colonial Cream-ware" and "Gray-Monochrome" that were simultaneously consumed at Massalia and its subcolonies, traded to the native peoples of the region, and quickly imitated in indigenous workshops (see chapter 7).[216] Pottery production took place at several different locations of the city at different times, as kiln wasters and/or kilns have been identified at the rue Nègrel, the rue Leca, the Centre Bourse, and the Butte des Carmes.[217]

These provided the bulk of Massalian exports (in addition to ships and military hardware mentioned in texts for markets outside the region), but what was the nature of demand within the city, the things being sought from indigenous peoples? As noted earlier, grain was undoubtedly at the top of the list of essential items. But the lower Rhône basin was a rich source of timber and pitch needed for ships, house construction, fuel, and coating amphorae. Salt, fish, coral, flax, purple dye, and various aromatic and medicinal plants have also been proposed as resources sought by both Massalians and Etruscans from peoples of the littoral. To this one might add stone, including basalt for grindstones[218] and the limestone blocks of which the city wall of Massalia was constructed. The Rhône basin was devoid of metal resources, but rich sources of copper and other metals were available farther west in the Ibero-Languedocian zone, and several shipwrecks from the fourth century BCE and later have been found with metal ingots of various kinds (see chapter 5).

Another probable native contribution to the economy of Massalia is labor. Of course, this would require the Greeks to find a means to induce local people to work for them. But once such connections had been made and practices of remuneration had been established, this would have provided a very useful pool of exploitable labor. Especially, but by no mean exclusively, in the early phase of the colony when the Greek population of the city was still small, seasonal workers would have been crucial in the planting and harvesting of Massalian vineyards and olive groves. Moreover, construction projects in the rapidly growing city (houses, public buildings, defensive walls, harbor facilities, etc.) would have benefited considerably from a willing native labor force. The precise contribution of local peoples to the work force of the city in different domains (domestic service, agricultural work, construction, shipbuilding, craft production, and other such things) is uncertain. The available evidence indicates that some participation occurred, but it is insufficient to evaluate the relative importance of native labor in comparison to slaves, metics, and Massalian citizens.

It is clear that combinations of both slave and free labor were employed commonly by Mediterranean states in Antiquity, although the relationship between these forms of labor, and their relative economic advantages, varied considerably through time according to particular circumstances.[219] Unfortunately, we do not know the size (or origin) of the slave labor force of Massalia for any period, although we can be quite sure that it existed. If other Greek cities can be taken as a rough proxy, then the contribution of slave labor to the economy was likely to have been significant, especially in the household, craft, and agricultural domains. However, most experts are agreed in seeing slavery as far less important in Greek agricultural work than it became in the Roman context, and especially so outside Athens and Syracuse.[220]

But even with a substantial slave population, the hiring of seasonal or sporadic casual free laborers would have been crucial for tasks that required concentrated pooling of extra labor at regular intervals, such as grain, vineyard, and olive harvests, or for ad hoc tasks, such as construction projects. As Ellen Wood noted, in ancient Greek texts the word for "harvester" is virtually synonymous with "hired man," implying that wage labor, rather than slave labor, was typical for harvesting.[221] Indeed, even in Roman agriculture, there was a constant need for hiring seasonal free labor.[222] This free labor could have derived from either marginal Massalian smallholders or landless peasants, or from nearby indigenous settlements. However, it is questionable that Massalia throughout much of its history had a large enough population of landless individuals to provide a reliable body of workers who depended on casual labor for their livelihood. Moreover, given the Greek disdain for those who worked as hired laborers for others *(misthotoi)*,[223] it is likely that local natives would have provided a more amenable target for labor recruitment than Greek smallholders.

Strabo, in fact, made parenthetical reference to indigenous people working as hired labor for a Massalian man: both men and women were hired together to perform ditch digging on his land. The incident was related to Posidonius during a visit to Massalia by his host, Charmoleon, to illustrate the "barbaric courage" of Celtic women, one of whom gave birth while digging and returned immediately to work.[224] But, for our purposes, this is mainly of interest in that it attests the practice of indigenous hired labor in Massalian fields at least by the second century BC, although it tells us nothing about the method of compensation (for example, work feast, payment in kind, or coinage?). Unfortunately, it is one of the few pieces of solid information, textual or otherwise, that we have concerning such practices; but it does demonstrate the willingness of native peoples to perform agricultural work for Massalian landowners and, by its tone, it seems a good indication of the unexceptional nature of such arrangements.

We also know that local peoples were recruited as mercenaries for protection of the city against other hostile native groups and other colonial powers (see chapter 6). This kind of arrangement for peace and protection could also easily take on the character of a kind of "protection racket," where native groups extracted gifts from Massalia for promises not to attack the settlement: this may well have been the situation behind the tale of the native leader Catamandua who was persuaded by a goddess in a dream to lift his siege and make peace with Massalia near the beginning of the fourth century BCE.[225] It is also possible that native tribes saw alliances with Massalia as a way of recruiting convenient outside military help in their struggles with other local groups, which would provide a rationale for the willingness to enter such relationships.

ROMAN COLONIZATION AND COLONIALISM: THE FIRST HUNDRED YEARS

Roman involvement in southern France actually began a couple of generations before the military conquest that brought the region within the sphere of Roman political control in 125 BCE. Initially, this included both sporadic state-directed actions stemming from a political alliance with Massalia and, in the informal sphere, Roman and Latin merchants *(negociatores)* trading wine produced in southern Italy. This trade, involving primarily the so-called Greco-Italic amphorae and black-gloss Campanian tableware, soon overturned Massalia's more than three centuries of primacy as the main source of wine in southern France.

Colonization, however, followed soon after these early trade and political contacts. As noted above, Rome and Massalia had a long-standing relationship of alliance that was formalized as early as the beginning of the fourth century BCE in a treaty granting Massalian citizens *aequum ius* ("equal rights") and other privileges when in Rome. This relationship involved mutual services over the years, principally between Massalia's navy and Rome's army, and included intelligence passed to Rome about Hannibal's passage through the region during the Second Punic War. In 182 BCE, Rome cooperated in a naval venture attempting to rid the Ligurian coast of troublesome pirates.[226] Massalia again appealed to the Roman Senate in 154 BCE for help in defending itself and two of its colonies, Antipolis and Nikaia, against attacks by two Ligurian tribes, the

Oxybii and the Decietae. After the Roman legates sent to investigate the situation were attacked, Rome responded by sending troops commanded by the Consul Quintus Opimius, which quickly vanquished the two tribes and gave Massalia some of the territory of the defeated Ligurians before returning home.[227] Another conflict broke out around 125 BCE, this time with the Salyes. Once again, Roman troops moved in to help, under the command of a consul, M. Fulvius Flaccus.[228] However, this time, after defeating the Salyes, the Romans expanded the operation by launching campaigns of conquest against a number of other Ligurian- and Celtic-speaking peoples that succeeded within about three years in seizing at least tentative control of all of Mediterranean France and the Rhône valley east of the river up to Vienne. Massalia and its colonial outposts were then left as independent Greek enclaves in the midst of a new Roman province.

The reasons for this imperial venture are complex, and they have provoked a good deal of debate. However, one obvious feature is that Mediterranean France provided a convenient land bridge between Rome's new provinces in Spain and its territories in northern Italy. It can hardly be coincidental that one of the first acts undertaken after the conquest was the construction of a road, the Via Domitia, that traversed the province from the Italy to Spain.

Conquering a territory militarily is one thing, but ruling it is quite another. The latter requires the production of consent, or at least grudging acquiescence, among the indigenous population. This is the problem that faced Roman administrators toward the end of the second century BCE as they set about trying to consolidate their act of colonization through practices of colonialism. The strategies and tactics that were gradually developed relied on a combination of coercive force and cultural techniques of domination, and they were ultimately effective in producing profound transformations of culture and consciousness. However, the eventual results do not justify retroactively imbuing this process with undue coherence, monolithic intentionality and agency, or teleological directionality. One must be wary, for example, of taking at face value the later Roman discourse concerning a mission to spread civilization *(humanitas)* or the idea of its ineluctable destiny to rule the world (articulated, for example, in Vergil's Aeneid) that became so influential in later European colonial ideology. In fact, while attempting to establish a system of provincial control in Mediterranean France, Rome itself was hardly a stable entity exporting an established model of colonial administration and Roman identity. Rather, it was in a state of constant flux and self-redefinition in which its colonial experience played a major role in its own emerging identity. Hence, if one wishes to continue to employ the problematic term *Romanization*, then it is perhaps best reserved for the process of self-definition that was occurring within Rome itself—a process that was obviously linked to the broader colonial world in which it had become entangled and to developments in the provinces.

During the early first century BCE, the center of the rapidly growing colonial empire, the city of Rome, was a chaotic sprawling mess populated by an extremely heterogeneous, highly stratified, and often unruly population. The population of Rome quintupled during the last two centuries BCE, and the city's more than one million inhabitants included a great many people of foreign origin from the far-flung provinces it had conquered, including fortune-seeking immigrants, merchants, slaves, and freed former slaves. Overpopulation, food shortages, and poverty created tensions that erupted periodically in riots. All the while, ambitious politicians and generals from the Roman upper class engaged in political intrigues that undermined the crumbling structure of the Republic and that sometimes erupted into major rebellions (as with the Social War in Italy from 90 to 88 BCE) or open civil war. Moreover, these violent upheavals frequently spilled over into the provinces, as with the revolt of the former governor of Spain, Sertorius, from 80 to 72 BCE and the civil wars between Caesar and Pompey from 49 to 45 BCE and between Octavian and Antony from 44 to 31 BCE. At the time of the final demise of the Republic and the formal establishment of the Empire *(Principate)* by Augustus in 27 BCE, it was not even certain that Rome, rather than the large and equally cosmopolitan city of Alexandria, would be its capital. It took an ambitious ideological project of symbolic manipulation by Augustus to construct Rome as the center of empire in the popular imagination.[229] Moreover, the inhabitants of the rest of Italy beyond the walls of the metropole were working through the construction of Roman identity at roughly the same time as the inhabitants of southern France. Although all of Italy had been conquered since the early third century BCE, Roman citizenship had been granted to the diverse inhabitants of the peninsula only after the Social War of 90–88 BCE, and the shift to a consciousness of being "Roman" (rather than Etruscan, Oscan, Sabine, etc.) was something still being constructed during the first century BCE.

Under these conditions, it is hardly surprising that, as in the case of imperial England,[230] the ruling elite of Rome had as much interest in controlling the restless population in its own city and hinterland as that of its conquered provinces abroad, and that the practices for attempting both were intimately linked. Those practices also took a long time to work out, and they were not always initially successful, nor even necessarily directed primarily by the interests of the state. For example, Cicero's defense of the abusively corrupt governor of the province of southern France, Fonteius, against charges brought by its inhabitants in 70 BCE demonstrates the way in which administration was at first left largely to the devices of ambitious individuals of the Roman upper class who often used office ruthlessly as a means to obtain personal wealth and clients that could be deployed in political struggles back in Rome.[231] Oppressive taxation and other heavy-handed measures by provincial magistrates gave rise to several revolts that had to be put down by the army, including a major rebellion by the Allobrogai of the Rhône valley in 62–61 BCE.[232] Yet, cultural transformations and a kind of hegemonic political control did gradually emerge out of the often contradictory interests and actions of a variety of individuals.

So what were the diverse interests of the major players in Rome and its province in Mediterranean France and the practices they worked out that shaped the emergence of new cultural forms? Those varied over time as the situation evolved, and it is useful to divide the history of the province into three successive moments, at least for the period that concerns this book. The first is the phase of initial conquest and experimentation (from the late second century to near the mid–first century BCE), the second is the reign of Caesar as governor of Gaul and then effective head of the Roman state, and the third is the reign of Augustus as Emperor.

During the initial period, the intervention of the Roman state in southern France was somewhat limited, aside from military actions. This was a time during which the very definition of a colonial province *(provincia)* was still being worked out. Originally this term, meaning "appointment," signified simply the sphere of operations assigned to a Roman magistrate. Only gradually did it come to have the sense of a territorial division of the Roman Empire with fixed and clearly defined boundaries.[233] Moreover, the imposition of the status of provincia did not automatically produce a homogeneous political or social space within its bounds: such provinces usually contained cities and towns with a variety of different statuses, rights, obligations, and forms of government. These might include *coloniae* composed of Roman citizens, semiautonomous *civitates foederatee* (federate cities) that had negotiated treaties with Rome specifying their rights, *civitates liberae* (free cities) that were exempt from the reign of the colonial governor, the rare *civitates liberae et immunes* that were also immune from taxation, various other forms of *municipia* (cities that had their own types of government), and villages that might be under the administrative control of a city. Furthermore, the duties, privileges, constraints, and mission of the magistrates who governed these provinces also gradually emerged out of a series of laws tailored to the circumstances of individual colonial situations, the changing needs of the metropolitan center, and the correction of abuses by various magistrates.

In the case of southern France, a Roman military garrison was first established at Aix-en-Provence (Aquae Sextiae) soon after the defeat of the Salluvii (or Salyes), which later (at a still uncertain date) became a Latin colony (fig. 4.12). Another military garrison was established at Tolosa (Toulouse).[234] However, the initial conquest had to be followed by a series of further military actions to subdue rebellions and to defend against incursions from other foreign invaders. These campaigns were directed by a variety of different commanders who were sometimes in competition with each other, and they included disasters as well as successes. Most serious of these was the invasion of two Germanic tribes, the Cimbri and Teutones, who entered Gaul around 108 BCE after passing through northern Italy and defeating a Roman army there. They inflicted at least two other humiliating defeats on Roman armies in Gaul before they were finally beaten decisively in 102 BCE by the Roman general Marius, who had undertaken a major reformation of the Roman army to make it a yet more effective instrument of war. Meanwhile, a simultaneous revolt of the Volcae Tectosages in western Languedoc resulted in the capture of the garrison at *Tolosa* and the defeat of another Roman army sent out to liberate it in 107 BCE. The fort was finally re-taken the following year by another general (Q. Servilius Caepio), who was subsequently crushed by the Cimbri. Revolts by other groups also flared up periodically and had to be put down. The most serious of these included rebellions of the Salluvii in 90 BCE,[235] the Vocontii at an uncertain date before 70 BCE,[236] and the Allobrogai in 62–61 BCE.[237] However, the revolt of the Allobrogai marks the end of major violent resistance against Roman domination in Mediterranean France. Things remained calm even during Caesar's subsequent wars against the Gauls farther north, when many southern Gauls actually joined his army.

For the early phase of provincial administration, the main actions of the state in the nonmilitary domain included, first, the beginning of construction of the Via Domitia by the consul Domitian very soon after the conquest, followed by the foundation in 118 BCE of the Roman colony of Narbo Martius (modern Narbonne) near the coast in western Languedoc. This became the effective administrative capital of the province. But for over half a century, Narbo, populated by settlers from Italy (primarily from Umbria, Picenum, Latium, and Campania), remained the only major concentration of nonmilitary Roman colonists in the region.[238] Early Roman colonialism also entailed the confiscation and redistribution of land in some areas, especially around Narbonne and Béziers. There, a new system was imposed of spatial division of the landscape according to an abstract grid pattern—the cadastral system—and use rights were shifted from indigenous peoples to Roman colonists.[239] Cadastral systems were eventually implanted in several other areas as well (for example, around Orange), but probably not before the middle of the century; and much of the province was unaffected by such expulsions, land transfers, and boundary transformations. It appears that, contrary to what had happened in Italy several decades earlier, there had still been no attempt to impose any other form of social integration, such as broad-scale granting of *Ius Latii* (Latin rights), in southern France as late as Pompey's administrative reform decrees or Cicero's comments in the *Pro Fonteio* in 70 BCE.[240] For most of the inhabitants of the province, the extraction of taxes was probably the most pervasive intrusion of the Roman state into their daily lives, and one with perhaps the unintended consequence of a rapid monetization of indigenous settlements.[241]

Returning to the issue of the main actors and situated interests in the historical context outlined here, the concerns of the Roman state, in the form of the Senate, were primarily limited to two things for nearly all its provinces: the maintenance of order and the collection of taxes. The Roman state never sought to intervene directly in the management of the economy at home or abroad: there was no effort to control the production or distribution of goods, no state factories, no state merchant fleets, or other such things.[242] Taxes, however, were crucial. The Roman elite relied essentially on taxes from the provinces to finance the measures used to maintain social control within Rome itself, as well as to sustain the armies that kept the provinces under control. For example, they relied on taxes in kind to supply the massive importation of wheat necessary to maintain the public distribution of this fundamental component of the diet for more than two hundred thousand people in the city receiving free rations.[243] Yet, there was no common system for collecting taxes throughout the conquered lands, but rather a hodge-podge of different practices worked out according to local conditions and traditions in the roughly forty provinces that eventually constituted the empire. Moreover, much of this relied on subcontracting the collection of taxes to private companies, the *societates publicanorum*, given that the Roman provincial bureaucracy remained extremely light. Generally, the magistrate put in command of a province by the Senate had one junior magistrate responsible for financial matters (a *quaestor*), a small advisory council, and a tiny staff of minor officials to rule over a large territory.[244] Most administrative functions were actually left to the cities within the province, according to the systems they had worked out.

The magistrate who governed the province received his instructions from the Roman Senate. But the individuals who were appointed to these temporary posts also saw them as a means to serve their private interests that had little to do with the goals of the metropole or the local people. Hence, there was a constant tension between the exploitation of the province for personal wealth and power and the needs of the state to fund the military and the state treasury and to pacify the provincial population. This tension, which was certainly not unique to southern France, is evident in the constant series of court proceedings brought in Rome against former governors for corruption and extortion, and in the laws passed by the Senate in an effort to control the powers of provincial magistrates. Provincial governors of consular or praetorian rank generally had the power of *imperium*, which included the power to command an army.[245] They were also forbidden by law from leaving the province during their command, but this did not prevent frequent military adventurism; and control of armies by provincial governors posed a constant risk to Roman central rule (as in the case of Caesar crossing the Rubicon). One of the ways in which Augustus eventually managed to alleviate this problem was to have laws passed that assured that the power to command an army was granted by the emperor rather than inhering in the authority vested in a provincial governorship.

Roman armies garrisoned in the province needed to be paid, fed, and provisioned with equipment, all of which was an expensive proposition. They also needed secure accommodation and good roads for rapid deployment. They also needed to be supplemented with new recruits. Much of this burden fell on the cities of the province in which the troops were stationed.

Beyond the army and the administration, a handy list of different categories of Romans who were also operating in the province at that time was provided by Cicero in his defense of Fonteius: *negotiatores, colonii, publicani, aratores, pecuarii* (these were categories of people who were not unhappy enough to offer testimony against the former governor).[246]

The publicani were private contractors who were in charge of collecting taxes for the state. They were organized into wealthy and powerful private companies, called *societates publicanorum*, that bid for the lucrative franchises to collect taxes, including especially the *stipendium* demanded for maintenance of the army and various transit duties *(portoria)* on goods traded.[247] Raising the expected tax sum was normally the responsibility of local communities, by whatever system was appropriate in the area. But the publicani were responsible for enforcing collection from the communities, or they could intervene directly in some cases, especially in the case of portoria. Their profit derived from keeping a percentage of the taxes that was set by the contract under which they operated. However, as Andrew Lintott noted, although theoretically strictly regulated, in practice it was difficult to supervise and enforce the contracts in the field.[248] The power of the publicani in the realm of taxes was curtailed somewhat by Augustus, who initiated reforms that placed government officials in charge of more closely supervising taxation. In addition to taxes, these companies were also essential for a variety of other services required by the provincial government, such as the operation of mines and the construction of public works; and these were also orchestrated through bidding for contracts to operate such concessions. The societates publicanorum were controlled by wealthy members of the Roman upper classes, especially the equestrian order, but the staff in the field usually consisted of slaves.

The next phase of colonialism began with the arrival of Julius Caesar as governor of the region in 58 BCE. He immediately used Mediterranean France as a base to launch a major war of conquest that brought the rest of Gaul to the north (*Gallia Comata*, or "long-haired Gaul") under Roman control by 51 BCE. Caesar's army in this venture included at least one legion (Legio V Alaudae) raised from Mediterranean Gaul as well as various auxiliary units from the region.[249] Loyal soldiers in his campaigns were often rewarded with Roman citizenship and other forms of patronage. In 46 or 45 BCE, Caesar established at Narbo and at Arelate (Arles) the first of a series of colonial settlements populated by veterans of the Roman legions. Several others of this type followed during the period between Caesar's murder in 44 BCE and the imperial reign of Augustus that began in 27 BCE. These included especially Béziers (Baeterrae), with veterans of Legio VII, Orange (Aurasio), and Fréjus (Forum Julii), with veterans of Legio VIII, all founded probably between 36 and 33 BCE.[250] These colonies of veterans were useful because they removed potentially troublesome former soldiers a safe distance from the volatile political scene in Rome where they might otherwise have been mobilized as client militias. However, they also had an impact on the regions into which they were inserted, given that these veterans tried to reproduce the accoutrements of Roman urban life they had known in Italy (fig. 4.13). Caesar was also most probably responsible for the introduction of Roman law into southern France. Most current scholars date this event to 46–45 BCE, although some texts suggest that it might have been as late as 43–40 BCE.[251] This system entailed a new hierarchical classification of urban settlements with important effects. A very few major cities, such as Massalia and Voconces, were given the status of nominal political equality to Rome and allowed an autonomous administration. About thirty others were give the status of "Latin" towns *(oppida Latina)* and about twelve were noted as "colonies." Below these were designations such as the twenty-four oppida attributed to the orbit of Nîmes (Nemausus) that had "subordinate Latin rights."[252]

However, in general, Caesar's approach to administration of the province had been relatively unobtrusive. Augustus, in contrast, immediately undertook an ambitious program of administrative reform that had far-reaching effects. This included centralized restructuring of the provincial taxation system and military command, the division of

FIGURE 4.13
Reconstruction of the Roman colony of Narbo Martius, modern Narbonne (courtesy of Editions Errance; watercolor by Jean-Claude Golvin, from Coulon and Golvin 2002).

FIGURE 4.14
The Roman style arena at Nîmes.

provincial land into *civitates* territories centered on native towns based on administrative understanding of ethnic divisions, the founding of additional settler colonies, and other moves. Both colonies and native urban centers began to see the construction of monumental civic architecture in the Roman style (arenas, theaters, baths, arches, etc.; see fig. 4.14) as well as the construction of networks of roads and aqueducts leading into these cities and the restructuring of space in agrarian hinterlands with cadastral systems.

5

TRADE AND TRADERS

As should be clear from the previous chapter, throughout most of the period covered in this book, trade, interspersed with episodes of violence, was the principal form of inter-action between indigenous peoples of the region and Etruscans and Greeks. But even after the Roman military intrusion into the region in the late second century BCE, trade continued to be a major element of colonial relations and a significant factor in the history of the colonial situation. Hence, a consideration of the nature of trade and traders is a crucial aspect of the attempt to understand the interests and practices that entangled the parties to these exchanges in new relations.

BARTER

Cross-cultural trade in Mediterranean France remained for centuries almost entirely in the form of barter. Coinage, although employed for various purposes within Greek settlements, was little used in indigenous contexts until the first century BCE, and there were few low value coins in circulation before that period that could have served the needs of small-scale exchanges. Nor is there evidence of other forms of special purpose money (such as standardized metal bars or ingots, shells, etc.). Some objects could have come to serve as commonly accepted abstract *standards of value* invoked in negotiating exchanges. Given their ubiquity and their standardized size, amphorae of wine are a likely candidate. But it is unlikely that these actually functioned frequently as a *medium of exchange* for other goods or an intermediary *store of value* in conducting transactions between merchants and local consumers. For one thing, they flowed in one direction only: Greek merchants would have had little interest in receiving back amphorae of wine in exchange for other goods they were peddling. So wine would not have served the same range of functions as coins or general purpose money. In brief, exchanges would have relied on traders and consumers finding some way of negotiating to reconcile their competing systems of value and to agree over the relative valuation of particular items that were to change hands in particular contexts.

The initial attempts at such exchanges were undoubtedly subject to a wide variety of misunderstandings (such as gift vs. commodity expectations), inadvertent breaches of etiquette, and conflict. But increasing habituation to such interactions would have resulted in the working out of systems of communication (perhaps with the development of pidgin or trade languages) and cultural interpretation that would smooth the process. The presence of resident traders at some indigenous settlements serving as cultural brokers would greatly aid this process, not least through the formation of social relationships that could anchor networks of exchange, stabilize flows of goods, and enable the extension of credit. Individual exchanges would always have involved negotiations over the relative value of the specific items involved, but these would increasingly be carried out within the framework of mutually accepted sets of practices and understandings of value and commensurability.[1]

Merchant ventures in the ancient Mediterranean were full of risks from weather, pirates, and uncertainty about supply and demand conditions because of slow information flows. As Neville Morley noted, several strategies were used to counteract these risks. One was to carry very mixed cargoes in the hope that something in the ship would always be saleable in one location or another. Alternatively, one could "cultivate a regular route, building up knowledge of the preferences of customers, perhaps establishing relationships with those customers and perhaps specializing in particular goods which would always find a market."[2] It appears that Etruscan and Massalian merchants (or, rather, those peddling Etruscan and Massalian goods) turned fairly quickly toward the second strategy. The cargoes of most ships during the first few centuries of the encounter focused quickly on wine and a limited range of drinking ceramics. They usually had "mixed" cargoes, but only in the sense that the wine and ceramics were from a variety of origins. Functionally, this was an extremely narrowly targeted range of goods, and this pattern is reflected on consumption sites.

Once objects traversed cultural frontiers at the various liminal points of exchange along the coast, they would, of course, have been reinserted into local systems of value and networks of exchange (for example, within indigenous societies or within the Massalian world) and redeployed with different meanings in consumption practices that both were structured by local cultural conceptions and structured local social and political relations. Objects that could not be used in this way would have had no value, and it is ultimately these local arenas of consumption that would create patterns of desire or indifference for foreign goods. Moreover, the very possibility of adding value by stepping outside local systems of valuation to exchange goods or services for items that can subsequently be reintegrated and redeployed in local arenas of consumption at a higher level is one of the primary attractions that draw people to engage in exchanges with foreigners. However, over time, such exchanges can have unintended consequences in terms of transforming local conceptions and structures of value. A prime example is the gradual disintegration of the moral barriers to certain kinds of conversions within "spheres of exchange" or "transactional spheres" and their associated structures of power relations, as happened in a variety of modern colonial contexts.[3]

SHIPWRECKS AND THE NATURE OF MARITIME TRADE AND TRADERS

Another basic observation is that the cross-cultural trade we are analyzing in Mediterranean France depended on the sea. Except for direct exchanges between Massalia and the neighbors in its immediate hinterland, imported goods arrived at their points of exchange primarily by maritime transport. Hence, it is important to ask what the nature of this trade was and who the agents that operated it were. The bad fortune of some of these ancient traders has been the good fortune of archaeologists in that it has produced a substantial quantity of shipwrecks. Combined with some information from ancient texts and archaeological data from consumption sites, these shipwrecks can tell us a great deal about such questions.

Shipwrecks offer crucial data about the size and cargo capacity of trading ships, the specific composition of cargoes, and the pattern of trading activity. Somewhat more ambiguously, they also offer clues about the possible origin of ships and identity of traders. Recent finds of very well-preserved ships in the ancient port of Marseille, at the Place Jules-Verne and Centre Bourse sites, provide additional information about shipbuilding techniques and vessel performance characteristics. In all, more than seventy shipwrecks have been investigated in the western Mediterranean with dates extending from the sixth century BCE through the Roman period. Hence, they also allow the reconstruction of the historical development of all these features over many centuries. Of course, the nature and quality of the evidence are highly variable, ranging from scatters of broken amphorae to well-preserved ships with cargo still in place.[4]

Because of preservation factors, the vast majority of all the shipwrecks found are located along the rocky Provençal coast, whereas the flat sandy coast of Languedoc and Roussillon has yielded relatively few (fig. 5.1). This is true despite the fact that, for reasons explained earlier, the latter area would have presented more severe difficulties and dangers for navigation. The evidence is also skewed chronologically, with at least seventeen identifiable shipwrecks dating from the sixth through the third centuries BCE and over fifty dating from the Roman period. Among all these, the bay of Marseille (which had a dangerous entry in antiquity) has yielded twenty-seven shipwrecks, of

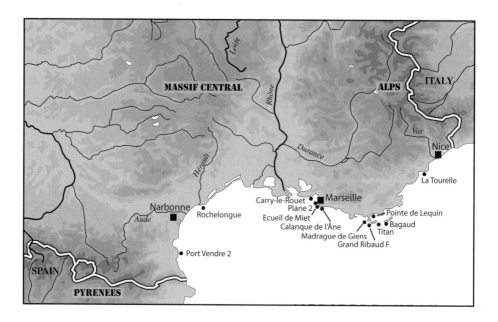

FIGURE 5.1
Location of shipwrecks mentioned in the text.

which four date to the sixth through the fourth centuries BCE, six date to the late third and early second centuries BCE, and seventeen date from the mid–second to mid–first centuries BCE.[5] One can add another dozen finds of scuttled ships (not, strictly speaking, shipwrecks) to this total from the excavations of the harbor's edge at Jules Verne and the Bourse.

A few ships show a relatively homogeneous cargo. For example, the sixth-century BCE wreck of the Ecueil de Miet, interpreted as an Etruscan ship bound for Massalia, was loaded with perhaps about one hundred Etruscan amphorae as well as *bucchero nero kantharoi*.[6] The recent discovery near Hyères of the early fifth-century BCE Grand Ribaud F shipwreck also showed a homogeneous cargo of Etruscan amphorae (all type Py 4), Etruscan bronze basins, and a few fineware ceramics, although in this case the number of amphorae is thought to number between eight hundred and one thousand.[7] However, the majority of ships before the Roman period had much more mixed cargoes. For example, the late fifth-century BCE wreck of Plane 2 (near Marseille) had a cargo of about fifty mixed Italo-Greek, Massalian, and especially Punic amphorae, an assortment of Attic fineware ceramics and at least sixty copper ingots.[8] Even the Grand Ribaud F shipwreck contained small quantities of Massalian and other Greek amphorae mixed with common ware, although, given that they were all clustered in the rear of the ship, these are interpreted as ship's supplies and equipment rather than cargo.[9]

These cargoes were mixed in the sense that they reflect a range of production locations, but they were actually remarkably homogeneous in the functional classes of objects involved: wine and tableware ceramics constitute the overwhelming bulk of the material found on ships bound for indigenous sites in Mediterranean France, especially for the early centuries of the trade. In other words, they were geographically heterogeneous, but targeted to specific regional patterns of demand. However, shipwrecks such as Plane 2 highlight other items that offer material evidence of the kinds of goods sought by Massalian, Etruscan, and, later, Roman consumers. Unfortunately, most wrecks with this kind of material date to the second century BCE and later, and we have relatively few direct indications for earlier periods. However, based on the quantities of Etruscan amphorae found at Marseille, one can assume that much of the Etruscan wine from sixth-century BCE wrecks may have been destined for Massalian consumers as much as native Gauls. This is also probably true for the largely East-Greek wine, the several thousand Ionian cups, several hundred Attic cups, the dozens of lamps, the several bronze and clay statuettes, and the variety of other ceramic material from the late sixth-century BCE Pointe de Lequin 1A shipwreck found near Hyères.[10] The early sixth-century BCE Rochelongue shipwreck (near Agde) is an interesting case in that it is one of the few found along the Languedoc coast. But more important, it contained about eight hundred kilograms of copper ingots, a few ingots of tin, and about 1,700 bronze objects of diverse indigenous Early Iron Age types (Iberian, Atlantic, Central European, Italic) that appear to have been destined for recycling at Massalia or in Etruria.[11] The latter collection resembles in many ways the seventh- and sixth-century BCE "Launacian hoards" found at a variety of terrestrial locations throughout Languedoc from Montpellier and the Tarn River,[12] and probably represents one of these scrap collections that had been traded to a maritime merchant in exchange for wine. As Michel Py has suggested, the disappearance of these hoards from Languedoc during the course of the sixth-century BCE may well be linked to the emerging role of maritime trade as a primary magnet attracting these objects for removal to Greek or Etruscan markets.[13]

Among the ships from later centuries, metals and building materials are salient finds, although wine, tableware, and foodstuffs of various kinds are the most common goods. For example, a second-century BCE shipwreck from Carry-le-Rouet, about seventeen kilometers west of Marseille, was loaded with twenty-four large blocks of limestone (each weighing about one metric ton) from the quarry of Ponteau-Lavera, near Martigues.[14] These blocks had engraved Greek letters that match precisely those found on the pink limestone rampart of Massalia from the Hellenistic period.[15] An early first-century BCE wreck off the island of Bagaud, near Hyères, had a cargo of iron ingots and also contained one tin ingot with a stamp indicating a group of Celts organized around a Greek named Herakleides for the commercial exploitation of tin. This ship is located well east of Marseille, presumably indicating that it was headed farther east.[16] Another ship of the early first century BCE found near La Tourelle de la Fourmigue (near Antibes) had a number of sculptural metal furniture attachments and other cast bronze ornaments, many with Greek assembly-code letters. These are interpreted as luxury objects made in a Greek workshop and headed for a wealthy provincial Roman household.[17] A ship found near Marseille at the Calanque de l'Âne was filled with ceramic roof tiles. This actually dates to the late first century CE, roughly a century after the period covered in this book, but it illustrates the kinds of building materials that were increasingly traded in the Roman period.[18] The mid-first-century CE wreck of Port Vendres II (off the coast of Roussillon) had a cargo of wine, oil, *garum*, and ingots of copper, lead, and tin that illustrate the varied exploitation of Spanish resources during the Roman imperial epoch.[19]

It is important to emphasize that the pattern of heterogeneous cargoes on pre-Roman ships is not unusual: it is mirrored by other finds in the western and central Mediterranean.[20] For example, the fourth-century BCE wreck of El Sec, off Majorca, carried (along with a *lebes* and other central Mediterranean bronze objects, several pithoi, and Attic ceramics) a cargo of twenty-nine different types of amphorae: Corinthian, Greco-Italic, Samian, Chian, Punic, Ibizan, and other types.[21] Similarly, the early sixth-century BCE Giglio shipwreck off the coast of Tuscany carried a mixed cargo of Etruscan, Greek, and Phoenician amphorae, and an equally diverse range of fineware ceramics (including some Greek lamps), lead and copper ingots, and other items; and the late sixth-century BCE Gela shipwreck off the southern coast of Sicily had a mix of various kinds of Greek amphorae (Chian, Lesbian, Corinthian, Attic SOS) and Punic amphorae, in addition to other ceramics.[22]

This information about cargoes suggests something important about the general nature of trade in the western Mediterranean during the pre-Roman period. It was, for the most part, predominantly a small-scale enterprise carried out by merchants moving back and forth along the coasts of the western Mediterranean in quite small ships: a form of trade called "*cabotage.*"[23] These merchants carried heterogeneous lots of cargo—that is, heterogeneous in terms of origin, but focused within a narrowly restricted range of functional classes of goods targeted toward regional patterns of demand. These goods were acquired either piecemeal at successive ports along the way or at ports that were major redistribution centers, where goods coming from various regions were reloaded for secondary export. They traded their goods and took on new materials at various ports and beachheads along their routes according to demand.[24]

The aggregate data from shipwrecks of the western Mediterranean clearly indicate that the cargo capacity of ships of the sixth to third centuries BCE was generally quite small: it rarely exceeded about five metric tons. Such ships usually carried cargoes of less than a hundred amphorae, and more often about fifty. However, shipwrecks such as those of El Sec, with 474 amphorae, and Grand Ribaud F, with 800 to 1,000 amphorae, indicate that some ships with a significantly larger capacity were operating as well by the fifth century BCE. The Grand Ribaud wreck, in particular, offers evidence of the emergence of a parallel trade by larger ships with monofocal cargoes that probably operated directly between major ports and production centers. However, the shipwreck evidence strongly suggests that most of the imports found on indigenous consumption sites in southern France reached their destinations through the work of small coastal trading ships. This conclusion is reinforced by the location of the major indigenous trading

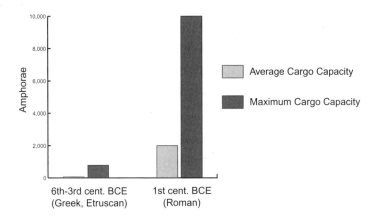

FIGURE 5.2

Estimated pre-Roman and Roman period cargo capacities of shipwrecks along the coast of Mediterranean France.

FIGURE 5.3

Excavation of the Roman shipwreck of the Madrague de Giens, near Hyères, France, filled with Roman Dressel 1 wine amphorae (courtesy of the Centre Camille Jullian: Université Aix-Marseille/CNRS).

centers along rivers or coastal lagoons (described later). These were places that would have been inaccessible to large deep-sea freight ships and could only have been served by small ships or boats.

Even the Grand Ribaud ship is small in comparison to the huge increase in scale during the Roman period: from the second century BCE on, ships carried cargoes of up to ten thousand amphorae of wine, weighing four hundred to five hundred metric tons, and even the average cargo was over two thousand amphorae (figs. 5.2 and 5.3).[25] These ships, associated especially with the massive influx of Roman wine in Dressel 1 amphorae into Gaul (see chapter 7), mark a clear shift in the nature of trade in the second century BCE with new possibilities at the upper end for a large-scale monofocal commerce in which both the profits and risks of single trade voyages would have been greatly magnified.[26] This is not to say that small-scale local cabotage trade disappeared. It continued to serve a role in the redistribution of goods out of major ports along the French coast, as it did elsewhere. The "Titan" shipwreck of the first century BCE, off the Île du Levant near Hyères, for example, contained a cargo of about seven hundred amphorae filled with garum (and, in one case, almonds), but also tiles and grindstones, along with ceramics and a few other items.[27] Moreover, most trade throughout the Mediterranean continued to be conducted in medium sized ships of sixty to eighty metric tons.[28] But the relative scale of the direct long-distance port-to-port trade, and the overall balance, had clearly shifted dramatically. The shipwreck data and terrestrial amphora finds also indicate a major increase in the volume of trade during this period. As was noted earlier, the number of shipwrecks found off the French coast from the Roman period is nearly three times the number for the five previous centuries. Moreover, this pattern is mirrored in the rest of the Mediterranean, where over 220 shipwrecks of merchant vessels are known for the Republican period alone, indicating a rapid acceleration of trade in the mid second century BCE.[29]

TRADERS

But who were the traders who conducted this trade, what was their social position, and what were their interests? These are important questions given that these merchants were the first and principal agents of contact with indigenous peoples of the region for about five centuries. In discussing these traders, a useful general distinction derived from Greek texts should be introduced here: a distinction between *emporoi*, who were specialists relying on interstate maritime trade for their livelihood, and *naukleroi*, who were the owners of the ships in which emporoi sailed. Naukleroi did sometimes act as emporoi as well (how often is not clear), but emporoi generally sailed in ships owned by others. Emporoi also generally did not produce the goods they were trading, but rather purchased them from producers with the aid of loans. The emporoi generally owned the goods in the ship rather than acting as agents for others, at least from the sixth century BCE on, although Benadetto Bravo has argued for the significance and persistence of traders who were dependent agents of wealthy landowners.[30]

In the case of wine, perhaps the most important commodity in the colonial history of southern France, the general practice in Greek contexts was that producers were not involved in maritime export. They would consume some wine from their vineyards themselves, and they might sell it in their city, at the agora or in taverns. However, wine destined for export was most often purchased by merchants who came to the estate and, after tasting, emptied the *pithoi* in which it had been fermented and transported the liquid to a port, where the wine was put into amphorae and loaded onto ships.[31] This process also seems to have been the norm in the Roman Republic and Empire. Cato, for example, described the sale of wine to traders and their practice of transporting it to the port in leather wineskins.[32] Several bas-reliefs and paintings also show the transport of wine in huge bags made of ox hide, called *culleus,* that were placed in a wagon.[33] The stoppers of the Dressel 1 and Dressel 2/4 amphorae that were widely traded in Gaul often bear the names of these merchants.[34] There were, to be sure, a few domains that engaged in the long-distance trade of their wines as well, such as the Sestii of the Cosa region during the first century BCE. But this was not the usual practice.

These categories of emporoi and naukleroi, and the division of labor they evoke, are derived from Greek contexts, and especially from Athenian ones. Nevertheless, there is good reason to believe that they form a reliable basis for approaching pre-Roman maritime trade in the western Mediterranean more generally, albeit with some local variations. Moreover, the basic pattern remained similar in the Roman Republic and early Empire. A ship's crew would, of course, also have included a number of common seamen (pilots, sailors, oarsmen, etc.). They are rarely mentioned in texts in any detail, except in casual references to the presence of *nautes.*[35] Hence, we know little of their identity. But, judging from the occasional matter-of-fact substitution of references to slaves when referring to the crew of a ship,[36] it is reasonable to conclude that these seamen would usually have been predominantly slaves, with perhaps the addition of some free men poor enough to be willing to hire themselves out for such activities. Benedetto Bravo has suggested that ships often transported several merchants, each with his own load of cargo. The crew would normally be overseen by a captain or guardian (called *diopos, nauphylax,* or *neouros*), either a slave or a hired free man, who was appointed by the ship owner *(naukleros)* to keep the peace and inventory the cargo to make sure none of the merchants appropriated the goods of others when they debarked at various ports.[37]

Three other basic observations can be made in response to the questions posed earlier. The first is that the merchants and crews of trading ships were not necessarily ethnically homogeneous, nor was trade necessarily organized along ethnonationalist lines. The second is that these emporoi, who were agents of contact and intercultural brokers, were certainly not the aristocrats of Etruscan, Greek, and Roman societies, but usually foreigners of humble means. The third is that, contrary to common implicit assumptions, there is no reasonable basis for excluding indigenous peoples of the western Mediterranean from consideration as having developed a place among the ranks of traders. Indeed, there is good reason to conclude the opposite. Let us explore each of these observations in greater detail.

The discussion of colonial trade in the ancient western Mediterranean has usually been couched axiomatically in terms of a "Massalian trade," an "Etruscan trade," and a "Phoenician/Punic trade" in competition with each other.[38] But this framing of the issue is an anachronistic projection of modernist conceptions of nationalist mercantilism and pervasive state control of the economy.[39] A more realistic scenario would envision a heterogeneous mixture of private emporoi, naukleroi, and sailors from various cities (including Greeks from the Central and Eastern Mediterranean, and indigenous Iberians, Ligurians, and Gauls) plying the coastal waters in, as already noted, small ships with cargoes and crews of mixed origins. There is little reason to imagine that merchant ships "flew the flag," so to speak, or that cities tried to impose ethnonationalist monopolies on trade. Greek cities had neither state commercial fleets nor state trade policies. At most they had concerns about attracting a few key imports and customs revenues.[40] When they intervened militarily in such matters, it was to suppress the activities of pirates who created insecurity and disrupted the normal flow of vital trade goods, not to impose nationalistic commercial monopolies.

Abundant textual evidence makes it clear that, in most Greek cities, trade was a private affair generally left happily in the hands of foreigners, either resident aliens (called *metics*) or transient foreigners (called *xenoi*).[41] Aside from trying to assure the importation of a few essential items, especially grain and precious metals for the treasury (and, to a certain extent, timber and slaves), the state took little direct interest in trade except to tax merchants on imports and exports, to invest in harbor infrastructure and a market space for exchanges (an *emporion*), and to provide legal mechanisms for settling disputes in which traders were involved.[42] The state was not very concerned about the ethnic identities of traders, as long as customs revenues were flowing and a sufficient number of traders could be attracted to the port to assure an influx of crucial supplies for the citizens.[43] As C. M. Reed has argued, in classical Athens, both the emporoi and naukleroi who were responsible for the substantial trade that flowed through the port were not only predominantly foreigners, but mostly nonresident *xenoi*.[44] In fourth-century BCE Athens, Phoenician traders from Cyprus were granted permission to acquire land to build a temple for their use when in the port, as Egyptian merchants had done earlier.[45] Moreover, it is clear from archaeological evidence that Phoenicians had a similar presence at Pyrgi (the port of the Etruscan city of Caere), where a gold tablet was found in a temple with a dedication written in Phoenician to the god Astarte.[46] Similarly it is quite probable that Etruscan traders were resident at Massalia, and vice versa.[47] Etruscan graffiti have, in any case, been uncovered in the excavations of the ancient port area of Marseille, and concentrations of Etruscan cooking ware and tableware have been found in some neighborhoods of the city.[48] In the early sixth-century BCE levels at the Îlot de la Cathédrale zone, for example, about 25 percent of the fineware ceramics were Etruscan (in contrast to the usual 3 percent in other contemporary areas), leading Jean-Cristophe Sourisseau to suggest an "Etruscan quarter" or at least an area regularly frequented by Etruscans.[49]

It is important to emphasize that Greek, Etruscan, and Phoenician cities should not be viewed as competing collective national entities. Each city acted independently, and individual Greek cities could be allied with individual Etruscan cities while being enemies with other Greek or Etruscan cities (see chapter 6). Moreover, there is no reason to assume that these political alliances and hostilities had much, if any, effect on the largely foreign merchants who were flowing in and out of ports with their trade goods. For example, there is no clear reason to imagine that the much-invoked naval battle of Alalia,[50] off Corsica (fought by Etruscans and Carthaginians against Phocaeans around 540 BCE, ostensibly to suppress Phocaean piracy), had much effect on the activities of merchants and consumers, except perhaps to reduce the risks of piracy. In fact, the evidence of the late sixth-century BCE shipwreck of Pointe de Lequin 1A, with its cargo of material from the Central and Eastern Mediterranean, points clearly in the opposite direction by demonstrating not an isolation of Massalia after the battle, but rather the continuing flow of Greek goods through Etruscan waters, something further confirmed by the increasing quantities of Attic pottery consumed at Massalia.[51]

What is more, one should not assume that ship crews were necessarily ethnically homogeneous, or that the origin of cargoes is necessarily an indicator of the identity of merchants or ship owners. Greek merchants could happily transport and sell Etruscan or Phoenician amphorae, and vice versa. In addition to its wildly diverse mix of amphorae, the El Sec shipwreck described earlier also had fifteen Punic graffiti and twenty-four Greek graffiti on Attic vases that make the ethnic identification of the ship very difficult, if such a thing even has meaning.[52] The Grand Ribaud F shipwreck, with its large cargo of Etruscan amphorae, had a shipboard equipment of ceramics of Massalian and Greek origin with numerous graffiti, some of which indicate a probable Latin merchant with an Etruscanized name.[53] Most probably, patterns such as these are an indication of the generally heterogeneous identity of the ship's crew and traders.[54] This complex heterogeneity of trading activity is also indicated by a lead tablet dating to roughly 475–450 BCE found at the indigenous port settlement of Pech Maho in western Languedoc. On one side it has a Greek inscription recording the purchase of boats from Emporion (and perhaps elsewhere as well) by a merchant named Kyprios, with all the witnesses to the sale bearing Iberian names. On the other side is an older Etruscan inscription with the names of Etruscan and Latin merchants involved in some commercial transaction at Massalia.[55] This points toward the open nature of ports such as Massalia, Emporion, and Pech Maho (and probably Lattes and other native ports), with a diverse mix of merchants and sailors of varied origins and allegiances engaging in trade in ships owned by naukleroi of equally diverse origins. This complexity is well illustrated by a court case in Athens that reveals a ship owned by foreigners from Halicarnassus, used by two emporoi from Phasalis (a city in Bythnia, on the southern coast of Turkey), for a trading voyage funded with money loaned jointly by an Athenian and a Eubeoan, which brought Mendaean wine to the Black Sea and came back to Athens without its return cargo of salted fish, wine from Kos, and other sundry goods (wool, goat skins) that was purportedly lost at sea. Others on board included slaves of the ship owner from Halicarnassus, a pilot named Erasicles (of unspecified, but probably Athenian, origin), and a few passengers of mixed origins.[56] This is not to say that ethnic affiliations played no role in trade: family and ethnic ties were undoubtedly very important in establishing networks and mobilizing social resources that could help merchants to acquire information about market opportunities, credit, and the like. But cooperation in commercial ventures was clearly not constrained narrowly by ethnic boundaries.

As noted before, the sailors and merchants who plied their goods along the coast of southern France were decidedly not drawn from the ranks of the Etruscan, Massalian, or Roman aristocracies or wealthy citizen families. Members of those classes certainly profited discreetly from such ventures by owning ships, loaning money for ships and cargo, or selling goods from their estates to traders, but they were not the ones to sail off and haggle with "barbarians." The general Greek attitude toward emporoi was decidedly disdainful and suspicious.[57] No upstanding citizen would wish to be mistaken for a merchant. These individuals were considered by Plato to be in many ways less than slaves, as they were free men who voluntarily made themselves like slaves by doing menial tasks for the lure of money, when the only honorable source of wealth was landed property. At the same time, maritime traders were likened to migratory birds because of their unstable residence and constant circulation between cities. They were seen as individualistic adventurers without roots, and men who were more interested in personal gain than in the communal good. These features made them morally dubious and dangerous. Trade itself, including exchanges in the local market by retail sellers *(kapeloi)*, was seen as an inherently unsavory activity, although it was also recognized to be essential for the city. It is for this reason that trade was generally left in the hands of foreigners. The good citizens of the cities were dependent on these foreigners to service their desires, and willing to profit from their activities, but they were generally not willing to engage in the unseemly work of trading.

Historical schemes of the development of Mediterranean trade have often posited a shift from an ancient phase, in which aristocrats did, in fact, set sail with their *hetairoi* (companions or entourage) on voyages that combined gift exchanges and raiding, to a later phase, in which trade became a specialized activity dominated by professional merchants who were disdained by the aristocrats. This is the distinction made, for example, by Alfonso Mele between his *prexis* versus *emporic* forms of trade.[58] However, the idea of aristocratic trade is largely derived from selective interpretation of Homeric texts, which are almost entirely a reflection of the ideology of the noble class, along with some passages from Hesiod.[59] The economic and social importance of such voyaging aristocrats and their trading/raiding, and the chronological duration of such activity, have been the subject of considerable debate.[60] However, to the extent that this is not simply a mythical conception of a prior "golden age" constructed to highlight, through contrast, the unsavory reputation of contemporary traders, it would, in any case, have had little to do with the patterns of encounter we see in southern France. Whatever interpretation one might wish to give to the scattered handful of isolated ceramic drinking cups found in Mediterranean France dating to the mid–seventh century BCE, I am in agreement with Michel Gras in concluding that the Etruscan amphorae consumed from the late seventh century BCE on at sites such as La Liquière, Lattes, and Massalia were already the product of a thoroughly "emporic" form of trade that had little to do with wandering aristocrats of

Homeric legend.[61] Indeed, S. C. Humphreys has suggested that the earliest traders were not aristocrats but "probably landless men, detached from their own community, often no doubt combining piracy with trade."[62] C. M. Reed's analysis of ancient maritime trade also concludes that professional traders were already operating in the Greek world in the eighth century BCE, although perhaps more commonly as agents of wealthy patrons than as independent entrepreneurs. He sees the period from the late seventh century BCE to about 475 BCE as one marked by the growing dominance of independent traders, the pattern that was characteristic of the classical period, when "inter-regional trade by sea in the Greek world was largely in the hands of poorer men of low status."[63] That is not to say that some men did not become wealthy by becoming traders, but becoming a trader would certainly not be the career choice of an already wealthy man.

As in the earlier Greek situation, the Roman state never had a merchant fleet, and it relied on private merchants and ship owners for the importation of crucial resources.[64] The disdainful Greek attitude toward emporoi was also largely shared by upper class Romans, who referred to such merchants as *mercatores* (or *negotiatores* under the Empire), while ship owners were called *navicularii*.[65] Aside from social sanctions against engaging in such activities, men of the senatorial class were even prohibited by law from owning seagoing ships under both the Republic and the Empire. However, as John D'Arms pointed out, this law, established in 219–218 BCE, appears to have lost much of its force by the late Republic. Moreover, it was quite permissible to sell the produce of one's agricultural estate (the prime source of respectable wealth) to shippers. Furthermore, merchants could, in practice, transform a fortune made through commerce into respectable wealth by investing it in land, and the de facto possibilities of men of the *equites* class to legitimately include trade (maritime loans, ship ownership, etc.) within the range of activities that constituted their business affairs *(negotia)* was not as limited as upper-class ideology implied.[66] Some merchants also managed to buy their own ships: the cost of a large ship was roughly comparable to the price of a small agricultural estate. Some slaves and freedmen were also established in business by being provided with a ship by an owner or patron.[67]

Roman trade was, in fact, frequently organized through large commercial partnerships that were called *societates privatae* or, for government contracts and concessions, *societates publicanorum*. These partnerships distributed capital and risk among a broad group of men that could include individuals of very different social standing (wealthy *equites*, slaves, freedmen, and clients). The participation of upper-class individuals, especially senators, in such commercial ventures was generally discretely camouflaged behind the more public role of men of lesser status. These were not permanent limited-liability, capital-accumulating corporations in the modern sense, but rather shorter-term multiple partnerships with some attributes of corporations.[68]

Roman traders were active not only along the coast of Mediterranean France, but they also penetrated inland after the conquest of Gallia Narbonensis and used the province as a base for trading with the unconquered part of Gaul (Gallia Comata) to the north.

Diodorus Siculus, writing in the first century BCE, commented on the cupidity of these merchants in trading wine to Gauls in exchange for slaves, at the astonishing rate of one amphora per slave.[69] As the Romans improved river transport systems by establishing haulage tracks and other infrastructure, merchants became very active on the rivers. The first century CE saw the development of a number of wealthy and powerful brotherhoods or guilds (collegio) of river boatmen (nautae), or rather boat owners, as these men would rarely have participated themselves in the actual transport of cargo. These associations, such as the Nautae Condeates et Arecarii of Lugdunum (Lyon) and the Nautae Atricae et Arecarii of Arles, were especially active along the Rhône and Saône rivers, which had developed into a major trade artery. They were far more numerous in Gaul than anywhere else in the Empire.[70]

The indigenous peoples of the western Mediterranean have been almost unanimously ignored in discussions of maritime trade. It is sometimes allowed that they may have controlled trade routes to the interior once ships had brought goods to their shores, although recognition of even this role has been slowly and grudgingly admitted.[71] But agency on the seas has been considered the exclusive domain of Greeks, Etruscans, Phoenicians, and Romans.[72] In many ways this is curious, because there is certainly evidence to suggest that indigenous peoples were active and proficient sailors. The Ligurians of the Provençal region were, for example, considered highly troublesome as pirates by Massalians and Romans. These two states, with their powerful fleets, had great difficulty trying to control these pirates, which would seem to be an indication that Ligurians were capable seamen. Moreover, one campaign in 181 BCE involved the capture of thirty-two Ligurian pirate ships, which would also suggest that these vessels were quite numerous.[73] Given the close connections between trade and piracy in the ancient Mediterranean (discussed later), it is curious that the possibility of indigenous participation in maritime trade has not been entertained. This is even more astonishing in view of an explicit observation by Polybius, in connection with Hannibal's passage through southern France in the late third century BCE, that the Carthaginian army was able to obtain a large number of boats to cross the Rhône because "many of the inhabitants of the Rhône valley are engaged in sea-borne trade."[74] Diodorus went even further in noting that the Ligurians were not only pirates but fearless sailors who "as traders . . . sail over the Sardinian and Lybian seas."[75]

To be sure, evidence of fishing practices from indigenous sites in southern France shows a strong preference for fish from coastal lagoons and a significant development of deep-sea fishing only near the beginning of the first century CE.[76] But deep-sea fishing has certainly been attested in the region since the Neolithic,[77] and this Iron Age pattern may simply reflect a cultural preference rather than an inability to perform deep-sea fishing (some remains of deep sea fish are present at Lattes from at least the beginning of the third century BCE, albeit in minute quantities[78]).

Finally, another piece of suggestive evidence is that when a script was adapted to write the local languages in western Languedoc and Roussillon, it was the Iberian script rather than the Greek script of Emporion that was chosen. This may well be an indication of the importance of Iberian traders operating in the region (perhaps with resident enclaves at some settlements[79]), with Iberian possibly having become something like a vehicular trade language. In any case, it is difficult to imagine that the inhabitants of Lattara, for instance, would have invested in the construction of the substantial port facilities found there[80] yet simply have waited passively for goods to arrive. It is impossible to judge with any precision the degree of participation of native peoples in the maritime trade that brought wine and other goods to their settlements, but it seems untenable to exclude them a priori from the ranks of ship crews and merchants engaged in such voyages simply because they were not Greeks. It would be surprising if they were not at least involved in cabotage along the shores of the region, especially given their advantages in dealing with other local peoples in terms of linguistic and cultural competence, and perhaps even kinship connections.

TRADE ENCLAVES AND DIASPORAS

As noted in the previous chapter, the presence of at least a few trade enclaves of foreign merchants (Etruscan and Greek) residing at indigenous settlements during the early phases of the encounter in Mediterranean France is increasingly supported by archaeological evidence. This shift from a purely ship-based "floater" trade to a situation augmented by the establishment of a trade diaspora has some significant implications.

As William Fitzhugh noted, a floater trade can even be practiced by sailors who are not full-time merchants—for example by fishermen who occasionally dabble in trading.[81] With a floater trade, access to imports by local people may be sporadic and unpredictable. But ships frequently develop a habit of returning to the same locations because of a well-protected port or anchorage or because of the presence of a local group with a reputation for hospitality and an interest in trading. This can even result in a shift in local population towards such a regularly frequented trade site even without the presence of resident alien traders, as in the case of Basque merchants in Labrador.[82] In fact, it is often more advantageous for local people to not allow foreign merchants to settle on their land. As Grumet noted in the case of the Tsimshian fur trade along the northwest coast of America, "time works against the trader."[83] Merchants sitting in a ship at anchor, with limited supplies of food and water, are at a disadvantage in negotiating with people on land who can afford to wait. Both sides have options: those on land can stall until a ship's provisions are nearly exhausted and play on the fear that another ship may arrive with competing goods, while the ship can threaten to sail off and trade elsewhere (if it has some knowledge of likely prospects at other locations). But these established loci of trade benefit both sides, local people because they can control trade in imports toward the interior and have privileged access to the arrival of ships, and merchants because they have the assurance of a place where they know exchanges can be made easily with a receptive consumer community ready with goods to exchange. As the volume of trade increases, competition between coastal settlements for access to such trade can sometimes even provoke hostilities between rivals (as happened with the Tsimshian case noted earlier), and this can be a reason for some local settlements to tolerate the installation of resident foreign traders within their community. This assures a permanent link to an external trade network that they can control.

The potential development of such trade diaspora situations depends on the level of competition between local groups for imported goods, the nature of the local societies involved, and the level of competition between merchants. But these are not normally a feature of the first phase of the encounter. Rather, they are a possible result of the acceleration of trade.

As Philip Curtin has shown through cross-cultural historical analysis, these trade diasporas can be highly variable in form.[84] But such a diaspora normally implies a more structured network than a floater trade. This is because the resident merchants are specialists in a single type of economic activity, whereas the host group constitutes a complete society, with a full range of economic roles and social statuses. Hence, the resident traders are completely dependent on their long-distance relations for their existence: it is the regular influx of exotic goods that enables the continued toleration of their presence in the community. Similarly, the relations of power between resident traders and hosts is highly variable, but always asymmetrical.[85] Often, these merchants are treated as a pariah group—that is, with disdain, suspicion, and exploitation. In other cases, they find ways to integrate better, often by marriage with local women. Alternatively, many strive to maintain ethnic distinctiveness, and sometimes even to carve out a kind of autonomy as self-governing communities with their own coercive power. But their situation is always precarious. It is usually up to them to learn something of the language, customs, and trade practices of their indigenous hosts and to serve as a kind of intercultural broker.

One can imagine that much of the earliest material from Etruria found in southern France was the result of a tentative and sporadic floater trade that gradually increased in volume and regularity as knowledge of the region increased. This would include the eleven earliest "Greek-type" ceramics (most, actually, of Etruscan manufacture) found at several coastal sites of the region that are dated to the mid– to late seventh century BC,[86] as well as much of the Etruscan amphorae and *bucchero nero* drinking ceramics found at sites (such as La Liquière) dating to the late seventh century BCE and later.[87] As noted before, we now have good evidence that at least one native settlement (Lattes) had allowed Etruscan traders to live within the town by the late sixth century BCE, and this practice may have happened even earlier elsewhere (St. Blaise, for example?). Once resident traders had been accepted at certain ports, they would have anchored a diasporic social network that would have facilitated the stabilization and concentration of trade relations, although a floater trade serving other coastal sites undoubtedly persisted alongside the trade diaspora. Local inhabitants of these towns with resident alien merchants would have acquired privileged access to a predictable supply of desired imports, and merchant sailors would have benefited by a knowledge of the location of certain ports that would provide reliable and hospitable markets for exchanges mediated by Etruscan or Massalian (or Iberian, etc.) brokers who had established personal relationships with local patrons, had developed a working knowledge of local customs, tastes, and language, and could store imports and exports on site and enact exchanges even when ships were not present. As noted, this latter feature would be especially important in reducing the time pressures on trading ships, as they would not have to wait for locals to arrive individually with goods to trade and would be less subject to being kept waiting (with dwindling provisions) by locals trying to drive the bargaining price down.

One should not imagine these resident merchants anachronistically as trade representatives of Etruscan or Massalian export firms or shipping lines, but rather as independent operators who mediated exchanges with both sides, but who had kinship, friendship, religious, or other connections with certain emporoi operating out of Etruria or Massalia that assured the return of ships and a flow of goods. Hence, the interests of local people, resident merchants, and ship-based merchants would all be somewhat different in these transactions, although entangled by social relationships of various kinds. As noted earlier, these resident emporoi would certainly not have been Etruscan or Massalian aristocrats, but more likely members of the kind of marginal groups who typically handled trade in Greek and Etruscan ports.

INDIGENOUS EMPORIA OR COLONIAL TRADING POSTS

Recent excavations have raised the possibility that a series of similarly situated settlements located along rivers in several parallel valleys leading inland from the coast of the lower Rhône basin may have played a specialized role in trade networks as either native emporia or colonial trading posts, and it is precisely at these sites that the presence of alien merchant enclaves has been suggested. The distinction between the two is subtle: the native emporia would be places of exchange under the control of local people that were open to a range of merchants of diverse origins, whereas the trading posts (comptoirs) would be exclusive outlets set up by a particular group of foreign traders for the exchange of their merchandise. In practice, this distinction is not always possible to discern, and there could easily be frequent shifts in the nature of individual sites. One can imagine, for example, a small trading post set up by a group of foreign merchants that soon attracted a native settlement to grow around it until the trading post became subsumed within the town. This seems to be what occurred in a number of cases with Phoenician establishments in southern Spain during the sixth century BCE.[88] On one hand, such growing settlements might gradually welcome a diversity of other merchants such that one would have the development of an emporion situation. On the other hand, one might have native settlements that were open to receiving foreign traders but that initially attracted only a limited group, in which case the pattern of imports might resemble that supposedly characterizing the more monopolistic arrangement imagined under the trading post scenario, but for different reasons. As knowledge of such a market grew, it might also attract a growing diversity of traders, yielding a pattern expected of an emporion. Finally, one might well have an emporion situation with an open diversity of foreign traders, but where the range of goods imported was reduced or shifted because of changes in other segments of commodity chains (such as a decline in production of some exports), resulting in an impression of monopolistic control of access that is misleading.

Although not impossible, the idea of intentionally monopolistic trading posts controlled by particular city-states in the ancient western Mediterranean seems an anachronistic projection based on analogies with situations such as European colonial outposts in West Africa under conditions of nationalist mercantile capitalism. Emporion and Massalia, the cases of foreign implantations in the region for which one has the most information, were clearly based on the open emporia model. That these emporia would subsequently try to establish monopolistic trading posts, or have the ability or desire to enforce the imposition of trade monopolies, seems unlikely. As explained earlier, this runs counter to the pattern of state noninvolvement in the activities of merchants that was prevalent in the ancient Mediterranean. On the other hand, the idea that small groups or networks of merchants established special privileged relationships with particular local communities and were secretive about sharing with other traders information concerning the location of markets and the tastes, customs, resources, and standards of value of trade partners is far more plausible. Attempts at microlevel competitive exclusivity through stealth and manipulation of relationships is much more likely than coercive state intervention in regional markets.

Whatever the precise arrangements of these native emporia or colonial outposts, they are presumed to have formed a secondary network of trading markets between the major colonial emporia, and to have been locations at which enclaves of foreign merchants may have resided (fig. 5.4). In the Rhône basin, the most extensively excavated of these sites is Lattes (ancient *Lattara*), located between two ancient branches of the Lez River that winds down from the hills north of Montpellier. Lattes is located where these river branches flowed into the Pérols coastal lagoon that connects to the Mediterranean. Thirty kilometers to the east is the site of Cailar, on the Vistre about seventeen kilometers upstream from the sea. Another seventeen kilometers farther east is Espeyran, on the western bank of a branch of the Rhône (the Petit Rhône) and about twenty-five kilometers from the sea. Another sixteen kilometers farther east is Arles, on the east bank of the main branch of the Rhône and about twenty-five kilometers inland from the sea (or forty-three kilometers if one follows the course of the river).[89] Another thirty-seven kilometers farther southeast, and only thirty-five kilometers northwest of Marseilles, is Saint-Blaise, located in the midst of several coastal lagoons.

Similar claims have been made for a few other sites farther west in Mediterranean France, including La Monédière and Agde (forty-five kilometers west of Lattes, on the Hérault River)[90] and Béziers (on the Orb River),[91] all of which have been suggested as

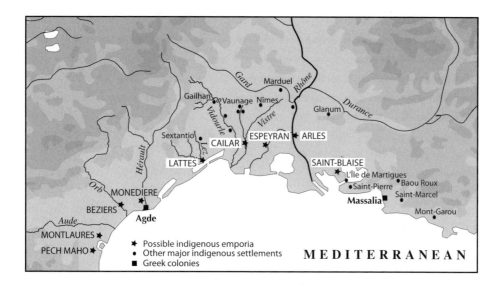

FIGURE 5.4
Map showing the locations of possible indigenous emporia settlements of the lower Rhône basin in relation to some other major indigenous settlements and Greek colonial sites. Suggested indigenous emporia of western Languedoc are also indicated.

being either Greek colonial outposts or indigenous emporia with a Greek presence, as well as Montlaurés (in the Aude valley near the site of the future Roman colony at Narbonne) and Pech Maho (on the banks of the Berre River leading into a coastal lagoon of the Aude valley).[92] The coast of Spain has also produced a number of convincing candidates, including especially the site of La Picola (Santa Pola), in Alicante.[93]

For those in the Rhône basin, what primarily distinguishes these sites from other indigenous settlements is the exceptionally large quantity, in proportional terms, of amphorae and other imported ceramics (although there are interesting differences between sites on the two sides of the Rhône). At Espeyran, for instance, about 60 percent of the ceramic assemblage consists of wine amphorae (of which 90 percent are Massalian). Similar figures at Cailar and Lattes (see below) are not only vastly higher than surrounding settlements, but the percentages of amphorae are greater than those found at Greek sites such as Marseille and Olbia. This and a few other features have led to the suggestion that these sites served as local centers for cross-cultural exchanges and gateways to their hinterlands, and that at least some may have attracted resident alien merchants or even been founded by such merchants, although the role of foreign traders has been a subject of continuing debate. For example, Guy Barruol saw Espeyran as a Greek settlement and even identified it as "Rhodanousia," the name of a colony mentioned in texts that has never been located precisely.[94] This interpretation has been contradicted by other scholars who noted that all of the domestic cooking ware found there is typical of other indigenous settlements of the area and that there is nothing distinctively Greek about the site (inscriptions or architecture, for example) except the elevated levels of amphorae and imported tableware ceramics.[95] Similar controversies about the Greek versus indigenous character of emporia have raged over interpretation of the sites of Béziers, La Monédière, and Arles.[96] Let us review briefly the data for the proposed emporia of the lower Rhône area, moving west to east.

At Lattes, founded around 525 BCE, amphorae also constitute as much as 50 percent or more of the total ceramic assemblage for many periods, whereas at contemporary sites toward the interior the percentages of amphorae are less than half that at Lattes (see chapter 7). There are also substantial dock facilities that date to at least the second and first centuries BCE.[97] As discussed earlier, the presence of Etruscan merchants has been convincingly demonstrated there during the early fifth century BCE, and the later presence of Greek merchants is suspected on the basis of various Greek inscriptions and one unusual house. What is important to note is that Lattes, at least from the fifth century BCE on, was not simply a functionally specialized trading center, but rather a normal fortified town of over three hectares size with a port where an unusual amount of trade was concentrated. Aside from the large quantity of imports and its relatively early rampart, Lattes is in most other ways a fairly typical indigenous settlement with an agro-pastoral subsistence base and a substantial population. On present evidence, it appears to have been an indigenous town that attracted a small enclave of foreign merchants to settle there, but the alternative possibility of an Etruscan trading post that subsequently attracted an indigenous town to grow around it cannot be entirely ruled out until more excavation of the earliest levels has been undertaken.

Cailar is located between the Vistre and Rhône rivers, just upstream from their confluence. It is near the point where the valleys formed by those rivers, the Vaunage and Nîmes basins, open onto the coastal plain and it is close to a former immense coastal lagoon that existed during the Iron Age but has subsequently been drained. Excavations at Cailar, which began only in 2000, are still in progress and only a preliminary analysis has been published.[98] The earliest levels excavated to date are of the mid–fifth century BCE, but surface finds extend the chronology back to the end of the sixth century BCE. Surface finds are not viable for quantitative analysis, but the in situ material from the period of about 450 to 350 BCE shows an extremely elevated proportion of amphorae (about 70 percent of all ceramics on average), of which 99 percent are Massalian. Roughly 10 percent of the ceramics are local CNT cooking items and tablewares, and the rest consist of imported tablewares (predominantly painted Cream-ware and Attic), dolia, and other cooking ware. In contrast, for contemporary settlements of the Vaunage basin, only about fifteen kilometers farther inland, amphorae constitute less than 20 percent of the ceramic assemblage and other ceramics are consistently composed of over 80 percent CNT.[99] Five blocks of finely dressed limestone were also found as reused elements in a context of the beginning of the fourth century BCE, meaning that they originally were part of one or more buildings of the fifth century or earlier. These are of a technique that is highly unusual in the region, outside Marseille, before the second century BCE. Other features of the excavation that have yet to be published, such as the presence of weapons and crania in ritual contexts, point to the highly unusual nature of this site over several centuries, but seem to place it firmly within the indigenous world.

Espeyran is located near the banks of a branch of the Rhône (the Petit Rhône) on a small peninsula of low-lying land jutting into a coastal marsh about four kilometers south of the village of Saint-Gilles. It has been subjected to only a few small exploratory excavations over a total area of about twenty-five square meters, but these have revealed an occupation dating from the late sixth century BCE until the Roman period. No domestic structures have been uncovered in the early levels of occupation, and the settlement organization is unknown. However, post holes were located at the base level in two excavation trenches, and debris of daub architecture and clay hearths was also recovered. After the mid fifth century BCE, mud-brick construction is found. An unusual feature is the very low percentage of indigenous pottery found at the site (only about 19 percent), even in the very earliest levels. This indigenous pottery includes both bowl and urn forms typical for the region, a number of large storage jars (dolia), and two very unusual wheel-made sherds of an urn. Imported pottery is, correspondingly, quite abundant, particularly Massalian amphorae. These constitute over 90 percent of the amphora material from the early levels and over 55 percent of the total ceramic assemblage. Amphorae of all types (Massalian, Etruscan, Ionian, and Punic) represent consistently between 55 and 65 percent of the ceramics from the founding of the site in the late sixth century through the early fourth century BCE. Other imports include Attic drinking cups, substantial quantities of Cream-ware and Gray-monochrome-ware, and a few Massalian mortars. The imported finewares constitute 25 to 28 percent of the total ceramic assemblage for the same period.[100]

Arles (ancient *Arelate*, a name of Celtic origin) is located on the east bank of the main branch of the Rhône. It was chosen as the site for one of the earliest colonies of Roman military veterans founded in the region by Caesar (the Colonia Iulia Paterna Arelatensium Sextanorum), but has a long history before that extending back to the sixth century BCE. Excavations have been hampered by the existence of the modern city and numerous Roman ruins on the site of the ancient town, and they have been largely limited to a few projects enabled by construction work, particularly the Jardin d'Hiver parking garage. The detailed results of these excavations have not been fully published, but the preliminary reports show a site with some unusual characteristics that have placed it at the center of arguments about the identification of Massalian trading posts or colonies and native emporia.[101] The pre-Roman site was mentioned in some ancient texts in contradictory ways. Strabo and Caesar, writing after the conquest, mentioned it as both an important trade center and as a place capable of building ships of war for Caesar to defeat the fleet of Massalia during the Roman Civil War.[102] Avienus noted that Arelate was called Theline when the Greeks lived there, yet it was not mentioned as a Greek town by Polybius in writing about the Rhône delta in the second century BCE, nor was it mentioned in lists of Massalian colonies by Pseudo-Scymnus or Strabo.[103]

Excavations in several locations have revealed a complex history for the site, with traces of a first indigenous occupation during the first half of the sixth century BCE for which the ceramics consisted of 93 percent local CNT cooking and table wares along with small quantities of Etruscan amphorae and Ionian drinking cups. Around 530 BCE, the first traces of houses with stone foundations are found. Then at the beginning of the fifth century BCE a block of large rectangular rooms centered around a courtyard was built in a previously unoccupied area (the Jardin d'Hiver) and was bordered by a rectangular grid of streets. This architectural phase persisted until about 375 BCE, during which time 17 percent of all ceramics are amphorae, another 40 percent are colonial Cream-ware (or over 70 percent of all tableware), 5 to 7 percent are Attic (including a large component of lamps), and both native CNT and Gray-monochrome wares are relatively rare in comparison to surrounding sites. Patrice Arcelin has estimated that the town expanded dramatically at this time to an area of about thirty hectares, although given the extremely limited extent of excavations this statement must be viewed with some caution.[104] During the third quarter of the fourth century BCE, the internal organization of the block began to be radically broken up by subdividing the rooms and courtyard, creating several smaller houses of four to five rooms, and from around 400 BCE until the block was abandoned suddenly around 180 BCE the quantity of local CNT wares jumped to 35 to 40 percent of the ceramics. Based on the ceramic profile, some purported similarities of the architectural structure of the Jardin d'Hiver to several Greek colonial sites (including early fourth-century BCE Massalia), and some possible traces of monumental buildings (chalk plaster and some fourth-century BCE roof tiles at the Cryptoportiques site), all of which contrast sharply with nearby settlements, Patrice Arcelin has interpreted the appearance of this block as part of a large Massalian colonial implantation alongside a previously indigenous site. As he sees it, this would have been originally a Massalian emporion established around 540–530 BCE that then became a full blown *apoikia* in the early fifth century BCE, populated in part by refugees from Phocaea after its defeat by the Persians. Nevertheless, he also pointed to differences in various features between the excavations at the Cryptoportiques and Jardin d'Hiver sites as indicative of a growing indigenous population as well, beginning in the fourth century BCE. He concluded that Arles may have developed into a hybrid colonial city along the lines of Emporion: this is when the Greek name of Theline would have changed (or perhaps reverted) to the Celtic name of Arelate. After major disruptions and reconstruction around 180 BCE, the imports shifted radically from Massalian to Italian, and this is seen as a sign of the early importance of Arles as a center for Italian merchants operating in the Rhône area before the conquest.[105] This interpretation of an unusual site, although not implausible, requires much more extensive excavation and publication before it can be accepted as more than an interesting hypothesis. For the moment, one can say simply that Arles is a site that differs in significant ways from many surrounding settlements. By its position and some other features, it resembles the series of native emporia to the west of the Rhône. However, it differs from them in that, although the percentage of Massalian imports is equally high during the fifth century BCE, at Arles they consist predominantly of Colonial Cream-ware table ceramics whereas at the Languedocian sites wine amphorae are overwhelmingly dominant. This means that the nature of trade is fundamentally different: in comparison to the Languedocian emporia, either the Arlesians consumed far less of the wine they were importing and passed more of it on to other settlements in their hinterland, or they imported far less wine than tableware.

Saint-Blaise differs from the other sites in that it is not the gateway to a river valley, but rather is located in the midst of several coastal lagoons at the base of the Rhône delta. As Patrice Arcelin has argued, the fact that indigenous CNT wares constitute as much as 88 percent of the ceramics at the end of the seventh century BCE and continued as the majority component of the ceramic assemblage throughout the sixth century BCE would seem to contradict earlier suggestions that the site was founded as an Etruscan or Massalian trading center.[106] It is possible that foreign merchants may have resided at the site, but only as a small enclave within a native settlement. The question is whether Saint-Blaise was an indigenous trading center serving as a gateway for wine and ceramics flowing to sites of the interior, or simply a fairly typical coastal site using its resources (salt, for example) to acquire and consume a large amount of imported goods.

In summary, excavations have revealed a series of settlements with unusual quantities of amphorae and/or imported tableware spaced fairly regularly along the coastal plain between Massalia and the Hérault River, most of which are located in river valleys at places that would have favored their control of access to the interior. In a pattern that is consistent over several centuries, these sites generally have very large quantities of imported ceramics in proportions that are radically different from contemporary indigenous settlements farther toward the interior. It is these sites that have raised suggestions of resident Greek and Etruscan merchants and specialized roles as native emporia or colonial trading posts. But in order to judge the plausibility of these interpretations it is also crucial to ascertain whether they have significantly larger quantities of these imports than other sites along or near the coast, or whether the pattern one sees is simply a generalized feature of all coastal sites, with a more intensive consumption zone along the coast and a gradual fall-off toward the interior. In this regard, there seem to be significant differences between the situations in eastern Languedoc and Provence. The difference in the relative weight of amphorae versus tableware among sites on the two sides of the Rhône is fairly clear, with the Languedocian sites having a dominant emphasis on amphorae. But Arles and Saint-Blaise also appear to be much less distinctive in comparison to other Provençal coastal sites in terms of their pattern of imports than are Lattes, Cailar, and Espeyran in comparison to other Languedocian coastal sites. At the Provençal site of Mont Garou, for example, the levels of the early sixth century BCE show only about 3 percent amphorae and 6 percent imported tableware, but this rose to about 24 percent amphorae and 26 percent imported tableware by the mid–fifth century BCE, which is comparable to Saint-Blaise (although Saint-Blaise achieved these figures about a century earlier).

The eastern Languedocian sites show a much greater degree of separation in import figures from other coastal sites, and one that continued for a long period of time. Moreover, they show a quite different relationship between coastal and hinterland consumption patterns than during the previous period before they were founded: the quantities of amphorae at the late seventh and early sixth century BCE coastal sites of La Rallongue and Tonnerre I (about 8 to 10 percent of all ceramics) are not only far less than the later emporia (Lattes, Cailar, and Espyran), but they are almost identical to the contemporary interior site of La Liquière.[107] Hence, these special emporia settlements clearly had privileged access to the trade networks that linked Massalia and southern Etruria to the indigenous world of the Rhône basin. In seems clear that most, if not all, of these sites were indigenous settlements that attracted foreign merchants to trade, and sometimes to reside, there. Compelling evidence to support the hypothesis that some of them were actually founded by Massalian or Etruscan merchants as trading posts or emporia is, so far, lacking, although this remains a possibility that cannot yet be excluded. But the precise identity of the founders is of far less importance than the role these sites served in the networks of trade that articulated the colonial encounter. They were clearly primary spaces of direct encounter: the places where regular exchange took place between local peoples and foreign merchants arriving by ship. They were the places where barter was negotiated between peoples with different systems of value, different customs, and different languages: where mutual misunderstandings were worked out and creative experiments with the consumption of foreign objects and practices were transacted.

A question remains as to whether these sites were primarily gateway sites that acted as middlemen in servicing demand for wine in the interior and drawing goods from the hinterland to supply the demands of maritime traders, or were they primarily privileged consumers of alien goods taking advantage of connections to external trade networks and providing most of the goods sought by traders from their own production, with only a small flow of goods being traded farther inland? This may have varied according to the individual site. Lattes, for example, would seem to fall more in the consumer category. There are few resources upriver on the Lez that would not be more plentiful on the coastal plain, and the sites of the interior show very small quantities of imported goods. Some wine and ceramics were passed along through exchange channels, but one does not get the sense of Lattes having a major effect on mobilizing export production much beyond the lower reaches of the Lez. Cailar, on the other hand, was geographically connected to settlements of the Vaunage and Nîmes basins, both of which were areas with rich agricultural potential. The quantities of imports at sites in these two areas were certainly less than at Cailar but still substantial.

One thing is clear: however much wine and other goods were being traded to the interior, all of these coastal emporia were consuming a lot more of it than they were passing on. Moreover, at the beginning of the fourth century BCE, there was a sharp decline in imports on hinterland sites, yet the quantities of amphorae remained high and relatively constant at Espeyran and Lattes until the middle of the third century BCE (see chapter 7).[108] This implies that trade links to the interior declined further in importance during the fourth century BCE and the vast majority of the consumption of Massalian wine was taking place at these sites of direct encounter, at least in eastern Languedoc. In other words, these coastal sites became primarily consumption centers, and the significance of any redistributive gateway function declined to the status of an afterthought. Whether this reflects a decline in demand for imported wine at sites of the interior or a growing unwillingness by coastal peoples to allocate wine to trade rather than consumption is unclear, but the latter seems more likely.

Whatever these sites were providing to traders in exchange for wine, it was certainly not metals. Farther west, the Hérault valley provides a route to very rich copper resources of the interior, and Agde would have been well situated to exploit a role as a gateway to these. But none of the sites in the lower Rhône basin had metal ores in their hinterlands. Their ability to trade would more likely have been based on providing agricultural goods (especially grain and animal products), forest products (timber, pitch), and products of the lagoons (salt, salted fish). Most of these emporia sites were located in zones that would have provided access to a diverse range of environments with potential for producing abundant resources of this type, and their locations would have allowed them to expand the zone of exploitation by tapping into rich agricultural areas upriver.

PIRACY AND TRADE

Piracy—that is, the violent seizure of property on the seas—is a practice that cannot pass without mention in a discussion of trade for several reasons: it was endemic throughout the ancient Mediterranean, it had an impact on trade, and the same individuals often practiced both activities. Pirate was not a label of self-ascription but an epithet applied by others. Greeks used the word *leistes* and, later (from the mid–third century BCE), *peirates*, and Romans employed the words *praedo* and *pirata* to cover the same category.[109] Philip de Souza traces the concept of piracy (although not the practice) to the eighth century BCE, when it was first distinguished from other forms of violence that were viewed more favorably (that is, state-sanctioned maritime warfare and raiding). But the distinction was often not that clear; much depended on the point of view of the observer. Hence, evidence for piracy comes exclusively from ancient texts, because there is nothing that would distinguish it materially as an activity distinct from other kinds of warfare and trade.

As noted, piracy appears to have been an endemic practice from at least the eighth century BCE through the Roman period—that is, throughout the entire history of colonial encounters treated in this book.[110] Some areas and peoples (for example, Cretans, Illyrians, and Cilicians) developed a particular reputation for piracy, but the accusation was quite widely distributed. Piracy was attributed as a common activity to the early Greek colonists in Italy, while Etruscan pirates were also considered to be a problem for these same Greeks.[111] Phocaeans in general had a reputation as pirates, and the battle of Alalia was purportedly launched by Etruscan and Carthaginian allies to suppress the troublesome piracy of the Phocaeans settled on Corsica.[112] But Phocaeans also complained vociferously about the piracy of others. Massalia, for example, both complained about and struggled against the notorious piracy of Ligurians along the Provençal coast and established subcolonies there in an effort to suppress them. This was a struggle in which the Romans also became engaged, with variable success.[113]

The slave trade was also partly fed by pirates, and this became a more important source during the Hellenistic era (that is from the late third century BCE on). However, it was probably not a major contributor to the overall supply of slaves.[114] Ransoming of wealthy captives and the capture of cargo that could be traded were probably far more significant contributions to the profits of piracy. In any case, piracy added to the substantial natural risks that merchants endured from bad weather and navigational hazards. When it periodically rose to the level of presenting a serious disruption to the flow of vital trade goods to Greek, Etruscan, or Roman cities, states attempted to suppress piracy by military force. But it is worth emphasizing again that this was not an effort to impose commercial monopolies. Rather, it was designed to improve conditions of security for all merchants and assure the regular flow of vital goods that cities came to depend on.

In the case of Mediterranean France, the Ligurian peoples to the east of Massalia were singled out by ancient texts, as mentioned earlier, for exhibiting an especially troublesome level of piracy, at least from the early second century BCE on. Strabo, for example, noted that the Ligurians made raids by both land and sea, and even Roman armies had trouble passing through their territory.[115] Peoples to the west of Massalia were not described in similar terms. This should not be taken to indicate the absence of piracy in this area, but more probably a lesser degree of such activity that was insufficient to cause major alarm among merchants and provoke a military response, although the multiple destruction levels at L'Île de Martigues may be related to the suppression of piracy in this area (see the following chapter).

6

A HISTORY OF VIOLENCE

Violence is a crucial subject of analysis in any colonial encounter. That is not to say that it is an inevitable feature of colonialism or even necessarily the most important. But colonial situations do frequently involve aggressive action (or at least the threat of such action), and they often provoke or alter various forms of collective homicidal conflict. Transformations in the extent and nature of collective violence among societies in the area radiating out from the boundaries of an intrusive state are a common feature of many colonial situations, both ancient and modern.[1] This is particularly marked in the case of territorial empires (such as the Roman expansion into the western Mediterranean), where organized violence is fundamental to the process of colonization and the attempt to establish sovereignty, but it can also be a feature of other kinds of colonial situations. Such violence can be a direct implement of colonialism, or a form of resistance to colonialism. But it can also be an indirect, often unintended, consequence of other colonial processes and relationships that develop. The growth of powerful, aggressive indigenous states and an increase in regional violence in the hinterland of European trading colonies in West Africa during the sixteenth to nineteenth centuries is a prime example,[2] as is the devastating expansion of Iroquois warfare on the margins of the European fur trade in eighteenth-century North America.[3]

Hence, although this topic rarely has been subjected to more than cursory examination in prior works on Mediterranean France, it is important to consider what the evidence indicates about such potential processes in the lower Rhône basin over the several centuries of the changing colonial situation. It is crucial to inquire about the nature, extent, and consequences of violence by and against Massalians, Etruscans, and Romans in relations with their indigenous neighbors and with other colonial agents. But it is also crucial to examine changing patterns of violence among indigenous societies. In other words, one must attempt an assessment of the shifting regional landscape of intersocietal violence by examining the phenomenon from a variety of scales and angles. This is not an easy issue to resolve because much of the evidence is circumstantial and ambiguous, but it cannot continue to be ignored.

Cultural anthropologists and archaeologists have turned increasing attention toward the examination of warfare as a social phenomenon over the past couple of decades, after many years of relative neglect.[4] In this, they lagged somewhat behind scholars of ancient and modern history, for whom the subject has long exercised an attraction.[5] However, despite the recent proliferation of work on this theme, the evidentiary problems for archaeologists in detecting warfare and, especially, in evaluating its extent and nature remain formidable. In general, three main sources of evidence are potentially available in the present case, and each of these has its own utility and interpretive problems. The first of these sources consists of ancient texts, including specific descriptions of episodes of conflict and more general discussions of modes of warfare. Unfortunately, such texts are written entirely from the Greek and Roman perspective, with all of the obvious interpretive problems this fact poses. Nevertheless, these documents do present useful (if patchy) information that must be judiciously analyzed, often by reading against the grain. The second source consists of material evidence of conflict in archaeological contexts, including such things as weapons, traces of destruction at settlements, and graphic representations of warfare. The third source consists of physical evidence of violence to individual bodies, in the form of skeletal evidence of trauma. Unfortunately, evidence of the last type is largely lacking in the current case due to the prevalence of cremation as the primary form of funerary treatment after the sixth century BCE and a general absence of appropriate analysis of the little skeletal evidence that does exist.

EPISODES AND THEATERS OF CONFLICT

Textual descriptions of episodes of conflict between colonists and natives in southern France are relatively few, and of variable quality, but they date from the earliest period of the foundation of Massalia and are scattered over subsequent centuries. The account by Pompeius Trogus of the foundation of the colony begins almost immediately by mentioning the great exploits of the Massalians in defending themselves against the "fierce Gauls" and in attacking those who had menaced them, and it later notes that the neighboring Ligurians became jealous of the city and "harassed the Greeks with continual war" which was repelled and matched by unspecified Massalian conquests.[6] He further described two specific incidents of war. The first took place during the early history of the city, when Comanus, the son of Nannos (the local leader who was supposed to have granted settlement rights to the Phocaeans), devised a stealthy strategy to attack the city when he assumed power after his father's death. According to the plan, a number of men would infiltrate the city on a feast day and would throw open the gates to the raiding warriors at night once the Massalians were sleeping off the effects of their drinking. The plan was foiled by a Ligurian woman who had a relationship with a Massalian youth whom she informed of the plot in order to induce him to flee. He, in turn, informed the magistrates and the plan was defeated, after which seven thousand of the Ligurians were reportedly killed.[7] The second incident occurred almost two centuries later, just before the attack on Rome by Gauls in the early fourth century BCE. By that time, Pompeius Trogus mentions that Massalia had already fought several other battles against Gauls and Ligurians, as well as a naval battle against Carthaginians.[8] In this event, the city was saved from an attack led by a man named Catamandus when he reportedly lifted the siege spontaneously and made peace after having a dream about the Greek goddess Minerva.[9] The accuracy of the historical detail of these accounts is uncertain, and not particularly important. But they do at least demonstrate a persistent discourse of apprehension by Massalians about the danger posed by their indigenous neighbors and about the relative fragility of their own situation—disaster in each case was, after all, narrowly averted by chance events or divine intervention.

Other sources recount several specific incidents of conflict with Massalia's indigenous neighbors dating to the second century BCE. Livy noted that, in 181 BCE, Massalia pleaded for help from Rome in its struggle to subdue Ligurian pirates and was rewarded by a Roman campaign that managed to capture thirty-two Ligurian ships and to subdue the inhabitants of the Albegna region, with a reported fifteen thousand Ligurians killed in the battle.[10] Polybius reported that, in 154 BCE, Massalia, which "had long suffered from the incursions of the Ligurians," again appealed to Rome when the city was "entirely hemmed in" and its subcolonies at Antibes and Nice were also besieged. A Roman army marched on the offending Oxybii and Decietae tribes and defeated them, after which Opimius, the Roman commander, sold many of the captives into slavery, gave some of their territory to Massalia, and forced them to give hostages to Massalia.[11] Finally, in 125 BCE, Massalia appealed to Rome again for help in beating off an attack by the neighboring Salyes. This was the incident that precipitated the Roman military colonization of Mediterranean France as a whole. The victorious Roman general, Sextius, both established a Roman garrison at Aix-en-Provence and turned over to Massalia some captured land along the Provençal coast. But as Strabo noted, even he was not able to push the natives back more than eight to twelve stadia (roughly between 1.25 and 2.2 kilometers).[12] After this point, Rome, rather than Massalia, became the main agent of conflict with indigenous peoples of the region.

These latter reports, obviously, cannot be taken uncritically at face value either. One must question, among other things, how the figures about casualties were obtained and how accurate they might be. But what these accounts do indicate fairly clearly is that Massalia's relations with its immediate neighbors were by no means always peaceful.

They involved a certain amount of at least periodic mutual violence and the perception of a recurrent threat. This conclusion would seem to be supported by the rapid construction and reconstruction of a substantial stone rampart around the growing city. Further support may be derived from Strabo's account of the foundation of Massalia's small subcolonies along the coast, which are described as "strongholds" against the barbarians who lived around the Rhône River and against the Salyes and the Ligurians living in the Alps.[13] What these reports also indicate is that, despite the occasional rhetorical flourishes touting Massalian military valor, the colony was never a powerful military force, at least on land, and it was never able to wrest a sizeable area away from indigenous control by force. Indeed, the textual evidence indicates that it was only multiple Roman interventions in the second century BCE that granted Massalia even a moderately significant territory. Most of the episodes of conflict described represent Massalian defensive actions rather than wars of conquest, and the repeated appeals to Rome late in its history indicate how precarious the city was at that time.[14]

It is also clear that native societies of the region were capable of mobilizing quite effective military forces for both aggression and defense, at least in the Provençal hinterland of Massalia. The evidence for this is less clear in eastern Languedoc, where texts provide little evidence of effective or prolonged resistance to Roman incursions. This may be simply a problem of lacunae in sources, but it could also be a reflection of the longer experience of direct conflict with Massalia in Provence provoking a more militarily powerful indigenous response (discussed later). In any case, this military prowess was particularly marked by the second century BCE with the emergence of regional alliances, such as the Salyen confederation. According to Strabo, this confederation consisted of ten groups that provided a joint military force of infantry and cavalry. These forces not only were more than a match for Massalian military resources, but as Strabo further noted, the Ligurians of the Côte d'Azur made the coastal roads impassible even for large Roman armies until, after eighty years of warfare, Rome finally succeeded in pushing them back from the road, but initially only for a distance of twelve stadia.[15]

Just as clearly, however, relations with native societies were not entirely or continually hostile.[16] Aside from the archaeological evidence of extensive trade relations persisting over centuries, other textual reports indicate that Massalia also had allies among indigenous peoples, such as the Celts who acted as guides for Roman cavalry in their attempts to intercept Hannibal during his passage through southern France, and whom Polybius described as "in the service of the Massalians as mercenaries."[17] Caesar, in his account of the siege of Massalia during the Roman Civil War in 49 BCE, also noted that the Massalians called on the support of the Albici, "a barbarian tribe, who lived in the mountains above Massilia and had rendered allegiance to them ever since the remote past."[18]

Hence, Massalia had a checkered history of relations with local polities characterized by periodic episodes of violence with some groups but also by the establishment of political and military alliances and networks of economic exchange partners. Maintenance of such relations, and peaceful conditions more generally, undoubtedly required frequent flows of political gifts to allies, mercenaries, and potential enemies. These situations may have fluctuated over time, but there is little to indicate a growing Massalian capacity for colonization or military domination of large areas of Mediterranean France. Quite the contrary: Massalia's continued presence and prosperity in the region necessarily depended more on the creation of consent than on coercion, although it certainly was involved in periodic violent engagements. That, of course, changed dramatically in the late second century BCE with the arrival of Rome.

Roman armies increased the scale of violence significantly. They were able to inflict a series of decisive defeats on various native societies throughout the region and to suppress several incursions and major revolts that broke out during the late second and first centuries BCE: by the Allobrogai and Arvernians between 122 and 121 BCE, the Cimbri and Teutones between 113 and 102 BCE, the Volcae Tectosages between 106 and 104 BCE, the Salyes in 90 BCE, the Volcae Tectosages (again) and Vocontii in 77–72 BCE, and the Allobrogai (again) in 66 and 62–61 BCE, to name only the major episodes that attracted the notice of historians. Although complete pacification took over sixty years, Rome eventually was able to impose regional sovereignty. By the mid–first century BCE, Julius Caesar was able to expand Roman military colonization throughout the rest of Gaul through a war of conquest that lasted about eight years and during which perhaps a million Gauls were killed and another million taken prisoner and made into slaves.[19] As noted earlier, during Caesar's wars with the rest of Gaul, the peoples of Mediterranean France offered no further resistance and did not join in the revolts that took place farther north. Rather, many joined the Roman side. In part, Roman military success was due to tactical and organizational reforms, especially those instituted by the Roman general Marius around the time of the invasions of southern France by the Cimbri and Teutones near the end of the second century BCE. Among other innovations, Marius opened army recruitment to the landless lower classes and made them a paid, well-trained professional fighting force enlisted for long periods of service, in contrast to the prior temporary citizen armies raised to meet crises.[20] Greek armies, in contrast, were generally composed of part-time, self-equipped amateur warriors who had little training and heavy competing demands on their time from agricultural duties. Moreover, most Greek cities relied increasingly on mercenaries from the late fourth century BCE on.[21] But even more important was the sheer difference in the scale of manpower that Roman armies were able to mobilize and sustain in the field in comparison to what Massalia could muster.

Aside from the fact of the broad regional nature of Roman military projection, the radically different scale of Roman violence is also indicated by the numbers of soldiers and casualties reported. Although these figures must always be treated with great caution, a crude comparison can be suggestive. Remember that the account of the defeat of Comanus in his attack on Massalia mentions seven thousand native dead, and Massalia had to call on the Romans to put down native piracy in 181 BCE, with a casualty figure given of fifteen thousand Ligurians.[22] However, the Roman army was capable of sustaining the loss of a reported eighty thousand troops in a defeat by the Cimbri and Teutones at Arausio (modern Orange) in 105 BCE,[23] yet still able to come back within three years with a force capable of inflicting a defeat on the Teutones and Ambrones near Aix-en-Provence in which at least a hundred thousand enemy troops were estimated to have been killed and captured.[24] And this was only one front in the extensive Roman landscape of war around the Mediterranean. It is important to recall that the entire population of Massalia at its greatest extent in the mid–first century BCE is estimated to have been no more than about twenty-thousand people (citizens and noncitizens).[25] This would mean that, under normal demographic conditions, fewer than six thousand adult males would have been available to act as a military force even in defensive emergencies that would require full mobilization; and the number available to serve in a standing army for offensive campaigns of any significant duration would have been far smaller. Moreover, these population figures would have been considerably less in earlier centuries. In contrast, Rome was a city with a population approaching one million people by the time of the late Republic and also had the vast demographic resources of its provinces in Italy and elsewhere to call on.[26] Even if these casualty figures are wildly inflated, the order of magnitude difference is, I think, valid and significant. Massalia's ability to establish control though inflicting violence, even on a small regional scale, was meager in comparison to Rome's.

To further contextualize this transformation of the situation, it should be reiterated that Roman colonization in southern France was a late phase in a process of military aggression and territorial expansion that had begun in Italy during the fourth century BCE and had expanded throughout the western and central Mediterranean by the third century BCE, bringing Rome into conflict with Carthaginians, Greeks, Iberians, Gauls, Etruscans, and various other Italian peoples (not to mention its expansion into the eastern Mediterranean and beyond). By the time Roman armies moved into France, they had already annexed northern Italy and Spain and were in the process of undertaking the conquest and pacification of indigenous Iberians and Celts in Spain and Portugal that would take almost two centuries to complete. Hence, aside from the manpower issues, the violence inflicted by Rome must be viewed as operating on a vastly different geographic and organizational scale than any previous colonial venture in France.

Returning to the consideration of Massalia, as noted earlier, its episodes of conflict were not limited to its indigenous neighbors, but also extended occasionally to other foreign operators in the region. These were almost exclusively in the context of naval battles, and it was on the sea, rather than the land, that Massalia was able to project its power somewhat more widely; although Massalia's reputation as a naval power may be somewhat overblown.[27] Specific recorded incidents of this kind are less frequent, but a few have been reported. Sometime between about 540 and 535 BCE, Massalia participated in a naval battle off the coast of Corsica near the recently established Phocaean colony of Alalia that supposedly pitted 60 Phocaean ships against a combined Etruscan and Carthaginian fleet of 120 ships. The results of the battle, said by Herodotus to have been won by the Greeks but at the cost of having most of their fleet destroyed, are much debated by historians. However, the ultimate effect was the Phocaean abandonment of Corsica, which puts the report of victory in a skeptical light. The cause of the conflict was reported to be the aggressive piracy of the Alalia Phocaeans that had become troublesome to several of their neighbors.[28] Thucydides, writing at the end of the fifth century BCE, also mentioned a naval victory of Phocaeans over Carthaginians "while they were founding Marseille," without specifying where this took place.[29] This is most probably a somewhat anachronistic reference to the battle of Alalia rather than an indication of a recurrent early conflict with Carthage. However, there are other references to naval battles pitting Massalians against Carthaginians, including during the Second Punic War as allies of the Romans and an earlier battle near Artemision.[30] Strabo also mentioned that the Massalian citadel housed large quantities of the fruits of their victories in naval battles.[31] The major report of a Massalian land battle against a foreign colonial power was during the Roman Civil War of 49 BCE when Massalia entered the war on the losing side by supporting Pompey. The city was besieged and captured by the forces of Julius Caesar, resulting in the confiscation of its fleet and some territory, but it was treated rather leniently and was left as an independent city within a Roman province.[32]

Little is known about possible Etruscan violence in southern France, as there are no textual records and no archaeological indications of such conflict. The sole potentially relevant example is the burning and destruction near the beginning of the fifth century BCE of what is interpreted to have been the house of Etruscan merchants residing at the port town of Lattes, in Languedoc.[33] But this isolated episode can tell us little about violence by or against Etruscans more generally. Most probably Etruscan merchants were not in a position to embark on military ventures of any great consequence, and their presence in Mediterranean France was at the sufferance of local peoples. The Etruscan domain of historically known military action was much closer to home, and what has been recorded are references to Etruscan conflicts with Gauls in northern Italy and participation in numerous battles against other colonial powers in the Central Mediterranean. The latter include the naval battle of Alalia noted earlier. After an earlier period of expansion, the fifth century BCE marked a period of declining Etruscan military fortunes and power. In the early fifth century BCE, an Etruscan force was defeated by a combined army of Latins and Greeks at Aricia, in Italy, and shortly thereafter, in 474 BCE,[34] an Etruscan fleet suffered a serious defeat against the Greek fleets of Syracuse and Cumae near Naples.[35] Etruscans also later allied with Athenians in a disastrous attack on Syracuse in 415 BCE.[36]

The latter two episodes, in particular, marked the beginning of a sharp decline from the height of territorial control by Etruscan cities that eventually resulted in Roman domination. Livy noted that Etruscans had earlier expanded from the original twelve city-states in Tuscany to plant an additional twelve colonies across the Apennines and control most of the Po valley up to the Alps, but then gradually ceded the Po to migrating Celtic tribes. This picture is confirmed in general terms by archaeological evidence.[37]

Moreover, the fourth and third centuries BCE witnessed a series of largely unsuccessful struggles by various Etruscan cities against both Celtic and Roman expansion. At the beginning of the fourth century BCE the Etruscan city of Chiusi was attacked by the same army of north Italian Gauls that later sacked Rome,[38] while Strabo mentions another battle in which Etruscans from Cerveteri defeated the same Gauls as they moved back north.[39] Rome, after recovering from its defeat by the Gauls, began to expand gradually northward, bringing it into sequential conflict with the Etruscan cities, beginning first with the conquest of Veii and followed by a particularly brutal war that saw the defeat of Tarquinia and Cerveteri in the mid–fourth century BCE.[40] In subsequent wars, Etruscan cities were sometimes allied with Gauls against Rome and sometimes with Rome against Gauls. But by the middle of the third century BCE, Rome was in effective control of most of Etruria. The divisions between Etruscan cities and between internal factions and classes within the cities played a major role in their vulnerability to relentless Roman expansion, a pattern that would be repeated in many of Rome's other conquests in Gaul.[41]

Consideration of these episodes and webs of conflict is useful in situating the history of colonial violence in Mediterranean France within a larger regional geopolitical framework. It becomes clear, for example, that Massalia's power to intervene militarily in its hinterland was rather limited in comparison to the later Roman situation, but also in comparison to the military power of Etruscan cities within Italy (though not in France). This remained true for centuries, despite Massalian efforts to establish a few small strategic colonial settlements along the coast. Hence, Massalia could neither dominate nor ignore its neighbors. Rather, its survival and prosperity depended on engaging with indigenous peoples in a complex, ever shifting set of relationships that involved variable permutations of exchange, alliance, and violence.

Simultaneously, Massalia was involved, from the beginning, in broader networks of alliance and conflict among the colonial powers of the central and western Mediterranean, albeit as a relatively minor player. Its fleet allowed it to project a modest amount of power at sea that it clearly lacked on land. But the fact that Rome allowed Massalia to continue as an independent Greek city after its conquest of southern France, and after the defeat of Massalia in the Roman Civil War, is a clear sign of the limitations of Massalian power. It is certainly not a result simply of the longstanding alliance of friendship between the two cities—this would have counted for little had Rome seen Massalia as anything more than an insignificant threat to its own hegemony in the region.

Perhaps an equally salient message from this analysis is that the history of recurrent conflict between shifting alliances of Greeks, Etruscans, Carthaginians, Gauls, and Romans in the broader Mediterranean, although it did not have a direct impact on the native societies of southern France until the late second century BCE, did affect the fortunes, interests, and power of the colonial agents who operated in the region. The history of local violence was not determined by those broader conflicts, but it must be read in conjunction with developments in that sphere of action.

Moving beyond the question of violence by, against, and among colonial agents, what can one say about the prevalence and nature of warfare among indigenous societies and how this was affected by colonial encounters? For example, was warfare a common feature of life in the region before the arrival of Etruscans and Greeks, or was it something that developed (or diminished) after contact? Did the experience of the encounter change the patterns and meaning of conflict among indigenous societies over time, and, if so, how?

We have virtually no textual information about specific episodes of violence among native societies of southern France, and relatively little about such events among other Celtic, Iberian, or Ligurian peoples. Understandably, this seems to have been of far less interest to Greeks and Romans than conflicts in which they were directly involved. Hence, we are left to try to infer patterns and practices from other kinds of information.

Greek and Roman texts do provide some rather general clues to the military practices and proclivities of Gauls, conceived broadly, although these tend to be mostly late and not always helpfully specific in terms of geography. This is an important fact to bear in mind, because there were enormous differences among Gallic/Celtic societies over both time and space. The inhabitants of Mediterranean France, in particular, were quite different from peoples speaking related languages farther north in terms of sociopolitical organization, settlement patterns, and other features that would have had an important bearing on the patterns and prevalence of warfare.[42] Hence, for example, the descriptions by Julius Caesar of the large armies and battle practices of the Celtic states of central and northern France that he faced in his conquest of that area may be quite misleading if applied uncritically to the lower Rhône basin where settlements and polities were vastly smaller than in the zone of the "oppida" towns covering dozens to hundreds of hectares.[43] There was, for example, probably no town in the lower Rhône basin (including Massalia) capable of raising on its own the seven thousand warriors mentioned as casualties in the account of Commanos's attack against Massalia in the sixth century BCE. Similar problems arise in using later descriptions to model earlier practices. For example, it is clear that chariot warfare of the kind that was last attested among continental Gauls in descriptions of the Battle of Telemon in 225 BCE[44] had largely disappeared from continental Europe by the time of Caesar's conquest in the first century BCE, although it was still practiced in Britain.[45] Moreover, archaeological evidence of chariots has yet to be found in the lower Rhône basin during any period, although it is abundant in the Champagne and other regions to the north.[46] Similarly, the practice of taking the heads of vanquished foes described by Polybius and Posidonius may be something quite specific to the third to first centuries BCE, and perhaps only to certain groups of Gauls during this period,[47] although a case can be made for the episodic appearance of culturally specific manifestations of this practice at other periods and places in European prehistory.[48] Finally, one must be wary of ethnic stereotypes and recurrent "barbarian" topoi that are a common feature of Greek and Roman texts. Strabo's characteristic assertion that "[t]he whole race which is now called both 'Gallic' and 'Galatic' is war-mad, and both high-spirited and quick for battle"[49] is an obvious example of an essentializing statement that generalizes unacceptably over time and space. War is a product of specific sociohistorical circumstances, not the psychological proclivities of cultures, nations, or "races."

What, then, can we say specifically and reliably about indigenous patterns of warfare in Mediterranean France? To answer this question we must rely heavily on the archaeological evidence of weapons, fortifications, and graphic representations.

WEAPONS, WALLS, AND WARFARE

It is clear from the objects included in burials dating from the seventh century BCE and earlier that weapons (especially swords) played some symbolic role in the ritual marking of status in Mediterranean France well before the colonial encounter, albeit perhaps a relatively minor one. Weapons are, in fact, rather rare in graves of both the Late Bronze Age and the Early Iron Age in the lower Rhône basin. Where they are found, these consist of a few swords (primarily the long *Gündlingen* type, in bronze or iron) and an even smaller scattering of daggers, spears, and arrowheads included in small tumulus burials in both eastern Languedoc and Provence. In eastern Languedoc, for example, weapons are found in only 4.3 percent of Early Iron Age burials,[50] and less than a couple of dozen swords have been identified among all the hundreds of Early Iron Age burials excavated throughout the lower Rhône basin. Moreover, some cemeteries have no graves with weapons at all and no cemetery has more than a few examples.[51] This pattern is consistent for graves dating to both before and shortly after the first encounters with Etruscans and Massalians.

These statements about regional patterns might be questioned in terms of representativeness, given the radical disparities in percentages of graves excavated and published in different areas and cemeteries.[52] However, as noted, in eastern Languedoc, a region with a much more completely excavated and published funerary record than Provence, the estimate for tumuli with weapons is just slightly above 4 percent. Moreover, individual cemeteries that have been extensively excavated show exactly the same paucity of weapons. For example, the cemetery of Cazevieille, in eastern Languedoc, yielded only three graves with swords and one with a spear out of ninety tumuli excavated.[53] Similarly, at Saint-Martin-de-Londres, also in eastern Languedoc, only one sword, one spear, and one knife were found in nineteen excavated tumuli. Arrowheads are even more rare, and most cemeteries have yet to yield even a single grave with any kind of weapon. Pottery and bracelets (bronze and iron) are vastly more common as grave inclusions than any form of weapon or even cutting implement.

The veracity and interest of this pattern are further emphasized by its stark contrast with the neighboring region of western Languedoc. There, the number of graves with weapons (usually swords and spears) shifted dramatically from a comparable 1 percent during the precolonial late eighth and seventh centuries BCE to about 40 percent during the sixth century BCE.[54] In essence, weapons became a standard male accompaniment in funerary contexts, and this pattern continued in this region until the end of the first century BCE.[55] At cemeteries such as Couffoulens, the weapons were placed on the funeral pyre with the body and intentionally destroyed by bending before inclusion in graves—perhaps a further symbolic statement of the association between weapons and identity.[56] This practice marks a clear and dramatic transformation in the symbolic (and perhaps practical) significance of weapons in western Languedoc that did not occur contemporaneously in the Rhône basin. Michel Py has suggested that this pattern of warrior identity symbolism may be linked to the multiple levels of destruction found at settlements such as Mailhac and Pech Maho, and seen as evidence of an increase in interpolity warfare in western Languedoc.[57] It is perhaps also significant that Herodotus listed the Elesyces people of western Languedoc among the mercenaries recruited by Carthaginians in the early fifth century BCE,[58] whereas references to mercenaries from other parts of Mediterranean France do not appear until a couple of centuries later. In any case, it is clear that there was no comparable fluorescence of weapon symbolism in the Rhône basin during most of the Iron Age.

To what extent this pattern can be taken to represent a relative lack of importance of warfare or raiding in daily life in the Rhône basin is difficult to determine when considered in isolation. For one thing, there is an ambiguous relationship between the symbolism of weaponry and the prevalence of violence.[59] Furthermore, the symbolic salience of weapons may shift between different ritual domains. For example, for the late third century BCE in the Picardie region of northern France, not a single warrior grave has been identified, yet the sanctuaries are overflowing with weapons.[60] A similar phenomenon may be indicated by the excavations currently underway at the settlement of Le Cailar in eastern Languedoc, which have yielded the unusual discovery of abundant weaponry in association with crania in a third century BCE context.[61] Hence, interpretive caution is clearly warranted.

Nevertheless, what can be said is that although weapons were important enough symbolically to figure among the range of objects used occasionally in funerary contexts in the lower Rhône basin before and during the early phase of the encounter, they were clearly not a part of the standard repertoire of symbols of male status, at least in the domain of funerary ritual[62] (unlike, for instance, in western Languedoc in the sixth century BCE or the Champagne region during the fifth century BCE[63]). With the intriguing exception of Le Cailar, nor have large numbers of them been found in other ritual contexts or on settlements, where they are, in fact, even more rare.

Weapons also do not seem to have been consistently associated in funerary contexts in the lower Rhône basin with particularly ostentatious displays of wealth or ritual elaboration, as one might expect, for example, in the case of the formation of an institutionalized warrior elite. Consideration of the patterns of association of grave objects, treatment of the body, size and structure of funerary monuments, and other aspects of burial practices, indicates that weapons do not appear to be indexical of status or role in any clearly discernable way.[64] They are not consistently associated in any recognizable pattern of status iconography with such things as unusually large or architecturally complex funerary monuments, with particular modes of body treatment, with ostentatious assemblages of funerary goods, or with particular classes of objects, such as Greek or Etruscan imports, although this does occur occasionally.[65] For example, in some cases, a grave with a weapon constitutes the largest tumulus of its group and contains the largest assortment of other metal objects (for instance, at four of the groups within the cemetery of Cazevieille); but in other cases, weapon graves are among the smallest and poorest tumuli of their group (for instance, at Ravin des Arcs).[66] The Tumulus 1 de l'Agnel at Pertuis (in Provence) is unusual in this respect. It is one of the very rare graves in the lower Rhône basin to contain body armor (a bronze chest plate), and this is associated with part of a dagger or sword blade and scabbard fragment, an iron spear butt, two imported Etruscan bronze vessels (a wine pitcher and a basin), and a number of other metal and ceramic items. The fact that this unusually rich grave was that of a seven- to ten-year-old child (despite the adult-sized armor) indicates that the weaponry was clearly not a testament to the military prowess of the deceased. It may, however, have been indexical of a form of prestige that the child's family possessed or wished to claim.[67] In eastern Languedoc, weapons are found exclusively in adult graves. Again, these are not consistently the richest burials, and very few of the graves that contain Etruscan bronze basins or Greek and Etruscan ceramics have weapons.[68]

In brief, weapons do not appear to have been a common part of the symbolic "social skin"[69] of inhabitants of the lower Rhône basin before the colonial encounter, and they did not become so for centuries after. Nor were weapons a consistent marker of elevated status in any recognizable way as part of a widespread set of indexical objects in the region. The Tumulus 1 de l'Agnel, the cemetery of Cazevieille, and a few other cemeteries do point to some potential significance in a few local contexts for the possession of weapons and their association with other forms of goods used in other contexts of status competition. Hence, the arts of violence may have constituted one arena, among several, for the acquisition of symbolic capital, but there is little indication of a heavily armed population or the prevalence of warfare as a way of life in the lower Rhône basin during the first few centuries of the encounter. This does not square well with the stereotypic image of "war mad Gauls" of Greek and Roman texts. Moreover, it should make us cautious in interpreting statements such as those of Pompeius Trogus about the "fierce" Gauls and Ligurians in Massalia's hinterland who "harassed the Greeks with continual war," or those of Strabo about the native men of Narbonensis being "fighters rather than farmers,"[70] or Avienus's description of the Elesyces people of western Languedoc as "fierce,"[71] as an indication of a general pattern of endemic conflict among indigenous societies. Attacks against Massalia may have been a specific collective response to the actions of the colonists rather than a product of generally belligerent conditions.

Ambiguous as these data may be, several other types of evidence also point to the conclusion that it is highly unlikely that the mobilization of substantial armies or large-scale warfare was a common feature of the precolonial and early colonial political landscapes in this region during either the Late Bronze Age or Early Iron Age. In the first place, most settlements of this period throughout Mediterranean France were small, unfortified agropastoral villages, hamlets, and farmsteads. Few of these would have had a total population beyond a few hundred to a couple of thousand people. As discussed in chapter 4, there is also little indication of political centralization or territorial hierarchies extending over broad areas until perhaps the second century BCE or later. Finally, nor is there evidence for significant episodes of widespread settlement destruction until the second and first centuries BCE, and that evidence is concentrated in the area immediately surrounding Massalia (discussed later).[72]

On the other hand, sporadic intervillage livestock raiding, feuds, and the like, are a distinct possibility. The majority of settlements were located on elevated positions (hilltops, plateaus, etc.) that were presumably chosen for the obvious natural protection they afforded. This kind of low-level recurring hostility would certainly have provided a periodic arena for the acquisition of status through prowess in the arts of violence, although most likely as simply one of several competing (or complementary) forms of symbolic capital (such as oratorical skill, commensal politics, magical/religious expertise, genealogical position). The idea of the formation of a "warrior aristocracy" of the type described by Kristian Kristiansen elsewhere in Bronze Age Europe[73] seems highly unlikely in this context.

What changes in this situation can we detect as a result of the colonial encounter? As noted, at least until the end of the sixth century BCE, the scarcity of weapons in graves continued throughout the lower Rhône region. After that period, the general funerary rite shifted to cremation in flat graves, which can present certain problems for identifying grave goods, or even graves. But the rarity of weapons continued in those graves that have been found and on settlements.

However, let us also consider in more detail the evidence of the history of fortifications alluded to here. Massive defensive ramparts that have left archaeological traces were extremely rare throughout Mediterranean France during the period immediately preceding the colonial encounter. One cannot rule out the possible presence of wooden palisades surrounding settlements, although these have yet to be detected. Aside from a few sites with impressive ditches (such as Carsac in western Languedoc[74]), the Late Bronze Age settlements at Le Baou Roux[75] (in Provence), La Jouffe[76] (at Montmirat in eastern Languedoc), and Le Cros[77] (in western Languedoc) are among the very few examples known with genuine ramparts during this early period. However, concomitant with the beginning of the encounter, a few sites show evidence of the construction of massive stone (or in some cases stone and mud-brick) ramparts. The earliest of these in the Rhône basin are all along the coast and in close proximity to Massalia, which is certainly suggestive of some relationship to the evolving colonial situation;[78] although, the pattern in western Languedoc was rather different.

FIGURE 6.1
Rampart with round towers at Nages, eastern Languedoc.

It is important to emphasize that, although many settlements of this early phase of the encounter were located on plateau spurs, hilltops, or the upper slopes of hills that offered some degree of natural defensive protection, relatively few actually took advantage of the extra measure of security (and the symbolic statement) afforded by a substantial rampart. This general absence of Early Iron Age fortifications is underlined by the fact that most of these same sites that continued to be occupied into the Late Iron Age, or were reoccupied at that time, did construct stone ramparts during this later period (such as Le Pègue, Roque-de-Fabrègues, and Mont Garou).[79] Indeed, by the fourth century BCE, there were hundreds of settlements with fortifications, and massive ramparts had become a standard feature of the urban landscape throughout the region (fig. 6.1; see also chapter 8). This included both larger towns and small sites of less than one hectare: the mountainous Ligurian hinterland of the Côte d'Azur, for example, is dotted with over six hundred tiny sites with impressive fortifications, most of them less than half a hectare in size.[80]

Closer examination of the proliferation of defensive ramparts on indigenous sites is instructive, as the pattern suggests responses to some of the questions posed earlier. It should go without saying that this phenomenon can in no way be attributed to some vague social evolutionary telos: large-scale fortified settlements were constructed in the region already during the Neolithic, and the practice of building ramparts appeared and disappeared over the centuries in response to specific historical conditions.

On present evidence, only three Iron Age settlements in the entire Rhône basin were fortified before the mid–sixth century BCE. All of these fortifications were in Provence and in close proximity to Massalia. During the century that followed, an additional dozen or so fortified sites are known in the lower Rhône basin. The locations of these settlements with ramparts had become more dispersed on both sides of the Rhône (although still predominantly in Provence), and they are not clustered in close proximity to each other. However, they were still, with a few exceptions, relatively close to the coast.

Saint-Blaise, located on a plateau overlooking a coastal lagoon near Martigues, was the earliest site with a stone rampart, and the only one dated with some certainty before the foundation of Massalia in 600 BCE. The earliest rampart there (of several reconstructed versions) is dated to the last quarter of the seventh century BCE, and this was replaced by a thicker wall with round bastions during the second quarter of the sixth century BCE. Tamaris, a settlement on a small spur of land jutting into the sea a few kilometers southeast of Saint-Blaise, has a rampart protecting its landward side that dates to the first half of the sixth century BCE.[81] Les Baou de Saint-Marcel, only seven kilometers east of Marseille overlooking the Massalian chora in the Huveaune valley, is a crescent-shaped promontory fort enclosed by a rampart on the north and east sides. The eastern rampart dates to the early sixth century BCE with subsequent modifications for reinforcement during the second quarter of the century, and the northern rampart dates to the second quarter of the sixth century BCE with a complete reconstruction near the end of the century.[82]

During the last quarter of the sixth and early fifth centuries BCE, fortifications appeared at several other sites, predominantly along the littoral but with a few examples in the interior country as well. Lattes, on the edge of a coastal lagoon south of Montpellier, is unusual among these in being a lowland settlement. On present evidence, the first rampart there is contemporary with the foundation of the site around 525 BCE, although there are tantalizing indications of a slightly earlier rampart found at the base of a well excavated in the middle of the site.[83] Other sites in eastern Languedoc include Les Gardies, Le Marduel, Roquecourbe, and Plan de la Tour. The latter three are sites of the inland garrigues zone rather than the coast, but still within fifty kilometers of the sea. Sites east of the Rhône with ramparts from this period are more numerous. They include Saint-Blaise and Les Baou de Saint-Marcel near Marseille, which continued their use of fortifications, as well as new constructions at Saint-Pierre-les-Martigues, L'Île de Martigues, Glanum,[84] Le Baou des Noirs, Le Mourre Pela,[85] Montjean, and Maravielle farther east along the Côte d'Azur. The fortifications at Le Baou des Noirs may possibly be earlier than the others, perhaps even as early as the initial rampart at Saint-Blaise, but this dating is uncertain.[86] In addition, the site of Soyons in the Ardèche, overlooking the Rhône near Valence, has a rampart that may date to the end of the sixth century BCE (a possible rare exception to the general Rhône basin pattern of early ramparts being generally a coastal, or near-hinterland, phenomenon).[87]

By way of comparison, stone ramparts also began to appear during the late seventh and sixth centuries BCE at several sites in the western part of Mediterranean France, although there the pattern was reversed. Pech Maho[88] is a coastal site, but La Cité at Carcasonne,[89] Le Cayla de Mailhac,[90] La Crau at Caunes,[91] and Puech Crochu are all settlements of the interior. The settlement of Carsac at Carcassonne also had a substantial defensive system since the Late Bronze Age, but one quite different in nature, consisting of a system of trenches. Another, less elaborate Late Bronze Age or Early Iron Age defensive trench has been found at the site of La Moulinasse at Salles d'Aude.[92]

During the late fifth and beginning of the fourth centuries BCE, fortifications appeared at a number of other sites in the Rhône basin, including Le Mont Garou in Provence and Roque-de-Fabrègues, Nîmes (Mont Cavalier), and Saint-Vincent de Gaujac in eastern Languedoc. And the rest of the fourth century BCE marks a period of rapidly increasing construction of fortifications on sites of the interior, a trend that established them as a standard feature of the Late Iron Age urban landscape throughout the region. From this period on, newly founded settlements were automatically built with a rampart and previously unfortified sites, such as Le Pègue in the northern part of the region (130 kilometers north of Marseille), were enclosed by a defensive wall.

What can be inferred from these innovations in techniques of marking settlement boundaries about the issue of concern here? The lingering hypothesis from the Hellenization tradition of interpretation—that indigenous ramparts were simply one manifestation of a general emulation of Greek or Etruscan practices—can be quickly dismissed on both theoretical and empirical grounds (see chapter 8). Among other things, the early ramparts are quite varied in form and construction techniques, and those closest to Massalia were initially the least similar to the Massalian form.[93]

The obvious question of interest here is to what extent the spread of fortifications may be a result of transformations of the extent and nature of intercommunity violence. In fact, it is perhaps the clearest sign of increasing insecurity in the region, and one stemming from the colonial situation radiating from Massalia. The issue is complicated because the appearance of fortifications is not inherently a sign of increasing violence, nor is their absence necessarily a sign of the lack of a need for defense. Defense involves the cultural solution of a particular set of perceived security problems, and many solutions to similar problems are possible.[94] The addition of massive ramparts to the means by which settlements assure, or display, their security may result from changes in various factors, including changes in the relationships of the social groups engaging in hostilities or changes in the tactics of warfare. For example, groups organized along similar economic and social principles and with interlinking exchange or genealogical relationships may have cultural conventions or political agreements regulating the extent, seasonality, nature, and locus of raiding and warfare; and these may make the construction of fortifications unnecessary. Moreover, in small-scale polities of the type that existed during the Early Iron Age in the lower Rhône basin, warfare is rarely a matter of extended campaigns by large armies; defense against surprise attacks by small parties is the major concern. This may be accomplished without constructing physical barriers by using the natural environment in locating settlements and farmlands (e.g. utilizing hilltops, swamps, rivers, forests, and other natural barriers) or by employing the social environment as a warning system (for example, lineage or friendship networks over large territories may provide security from surprise raids by outsiders over large areas). Thus, the appearance of ramparts may signal a change in the social landscape, such that conventions governing warfare among social groups have broken down, lineage territories have reduced in size or lineages have segmented, or new groups have appeared on the landscape that do not respect the same conventions of warfare. Alternatively, fortifications may reflect a change in the pattern or tactics and weaponry of warfare—for example, a shift from a system based primarily on blood feuds to one based on raiding for cattle or slaves, or a new emphasis on projectiles in combat. Finally, for ramparts, the function of serving as a utilitarian defensive barrier may, in many cases, be less important than their value as a symbolic statement about territorial legitimacy, group prestige, or the materialization of spatialized notions of social inclusion and exclusion, the domestic and the wild, and so forth.[95] However, given that most ramparts did not completely surround settlements, but simply blocked off the most vulnerable terrain and used features of natural relief such as cliffs to protect the rest (see chapter 8), defense seems to have been a far more significant concern than display in the initial construction of fortifications. Although subsequent labor was sometimes invested in the construction of increasingly ostentatious towers (as at Nîmes), little effort was exerted in building structures in areas where their value would have been limited to simple visibility (for example, along the edge of cliffs). In other words, it would be difficult to argue that these were intended primarily as politicosymbolic statements rather than motivated by security concerns. In any case, what the appearance of these fortifications in the Lower Rhône basin does indicate, at a minimum, is that certain groups of people decided, for undoubtedly a variety of somewhat different reasons in different areas, to invest a considerable amount of communal labor in the monumental demarcation of protective settlement boundaries. Fortunately, there are other sources of evidence that allow a more nuanced consideration of the possible role of changing patterns of violence in the appearance of ramparts.

EVIDENCE OF DESTRUCTION OF BUILDINGS AND FORTIFICATIONS

Archaeological evidence of violent destruction of settlements comes in the form of levels indicating widespread fire and demolition of buildings and fortifications. Obviously, not all episodes of fire are necessarily the result of violence, and some interpretive caution is warranted: densely packed towns where people were cooking on open fires under flammable roofs would have been particularly susceptible to occasional disasters. Sometimes this epistemological difficulty is eased by the presence of objects that are a clear indication of military action, such as numerous spear points or stone catapult balls, associated with such evidence of destruction. In some cases periods of abandonment may follow levels of destruction, although, again, settlements are abandoned for reasons other than warfare. Many individual cases remain ambiguous, but broader patterns may offer some clues, as they appear to do in this instance.

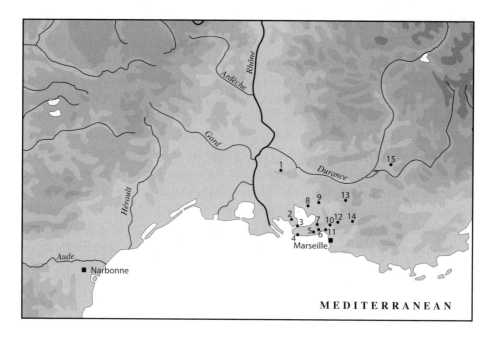

FIGURE 6.2

Lower Rhône basin settlements with evidence of major destruction episodes: (1) Glanum, (2) Saint-Blaise, (3) l'Île de Martigues, (4) L'Arquet, (5) La Cloche, (6) Teste-Nègre, (7) Notre-Dame-de-Pitié, (8) Coudounéu, (9) Roquepertuse, (10) Le Griffon, (11) Le Verduron, (12) Baou Roux, (13) Entremont, (14) Tête de l'Ost, and (15) Buffe Arnaud. Note the contrast between eastern Languedoc and Provence.

The vast majority of evidence of large-scale destruction of this type comes from Provence, and even more precisely, from a zone within a radius of about forty kilometers of Marseille (fig. 6.2). This is not a product of uneven sampling, because the number of excavations is comparable on both sides of the Rhône. Although it is usually impossible to date such episodes with sufficient precision to link them with specific historical events, most occurred from the beginning of the second through the early first centuries BCE, and a number are roughly associated with the period of Roman military activity in the region in the late second and early first centuries BCE.[96] Saint-Blaise, for example, despite its impressive Greek-style rampart of massive limestone blocks, was destroyed militarily around 130–120 BCE and had only a small-scale reoccupation of the site around 70–30 BCE. Over sixty large spherical stone catapult balls were found there, of a type very similar to those found in slightly later destruction levels at Entremont (early first century BCE) and Glanum (also around 90 BCE), and about a century earlier at Roquepertuse (around 200 BCE).[97] Le Baou-Roux and Tête-de-l'Ost are other Provençal sites with evidence of major destruction dating to the last quarter of the second century BCE.[98] Buffe Arnaud, a site located about sixty-eight kilometers northeast of Marseille near the rugged gorges of the Verdon River about fifteen kilometers upstream from its confluent with the Durance, also met a fiery end sometime during the second half of the second century BCE during a battle that involved the use of catapult darts. At the moment of its demise, every available pot was stocked with grain, a feature interpreted as preparations against a siege.[99] In view of its somewhat remote location, the idea of Massalian involvement seems implausible during a period when the city had to call on Rome to aid in its own defense, but a Roman attack is quite possible.

This is not to say that these late second- and early first-century BCE destructive events were inflicted exclusively by Roman armies: some may have involved conflicts between indigenous polities settling scores or have been the result of Massalian aggression. But a large number fall within the context of a period of regional warfare that was precipitated by the conflict between the Salyes and Massalia and was resolved through a Roman campaign of conquest and suppression of subsequent revolts. Some other sites, such as Les Baou de Saint-Marcel, seven kilometers east of Massalia, were abandoned around this time without evident traces of violent destruction but perhaps for reasons related to this period of unrest.[100] La Cloche, located twelve kilometers north of Marseille, was destroyed about 50 BCE, seemingly by a Roman army, and perhaps in connection with Caesar's siege of Massalia during the Roman Civil War. This might indicate an alliance with Massalia during this conflict, given that it falls at a period when native opposition to Rome had been quiet for several decades.[101]

A number of sites of the region also show evidence of warfare around the beginning of the second century BCE. The unusual site of Le Verduron (also known as Le Pain-du-Sucre) was littered with iron spear points and catapult darts from a battle that occurred probably near the beginning of the second century BCE.[102] This very small, compact site was located only nine kilometers north of Massalia on heights directly overlooking the bay of Marseille. A number of other sites were also destroyed around this time, including Roquepertuse (twice), L'Île at Martigues, Teste-Nègre,[103] La Borie-du-Loup, Notre-Dame-de-Pitié,[104] and Le Griffon.[105] One neighborhood of Arles (the Jardin d'Hiver) was also destroyed and abandoned around 180 BCE, and the presence of an iron catapult dart in the decomposed wall may be an indication of military action, although flooding of the Rhône is also a possible explanation.[106]

Some earlier episodes of destruction before the second century BCE are revealed by excavations as well. Again, within the Rhône basin, these are almost entirely in Provence rather than eastern Languedoc. The highly unusual site of Coudounèu, which is located about five kilometers north of the Berre lagoon and appears to be a fortified farm granary more that a settlement, was destroyed by fire near the end of the fifth century BCE less than fifty years after its founding, although without specific indications of a military attack.[107] Perhaps the most impressive case is the site of L'Île at Martigues, in which the entire village was destroyed three times by fire. The first of these was about 440–430 BCE, shortly after it was founded. The site was quickly reoccupied, but entirely destroyed again around 360 BCE. While it is possible that the first fire was accidental, the second episode is marked by finds of about thirty "Olympus-type" spear heads scattered throughout the site and the complete destruction of all of the roughly one hundred-dred houses within the rampart. The site was again reoccupied and expanded, but after a century and a half without incident, it was destroyed once again and abandoned around 200 BCE.[108] The excavator attributes the first two of these attacks to Massalia and the last to Rome, although, aside from the spear heads, there is no evidence linking the events to a specific aggressor. This might be related to Massalia's various attempts to suppress "pirates" along the coast (assuming the residents of this island fortress were engaging in activities that Massalia viewed as piracy), but it is also possible that this violence was the handiwork of such pirates. L'Arquet, another site directly on the coast about eight kilometers south of Martigues was also destroyed by fire around 400 BCE (that is, between the first two episodes at L'Île) and subsequently rebuilt.

What makes this history of repeated destruction even more interesting (and suggests that the piracy hypothesis may have some merit) is the stark contrast with the terrestrial hilltop settlement of Saint-Pierre-les-Martigues, located midway between these two coastal sites, which, after a brief reorganization of the site near the end of the sixth century BCE, shows a long sequence of continuous occupation throughout the entire Late Iron Age without any traces of violent destruction.[109] The cases of L'Île and L'Arquet are not entirely exceptional, however. Roquepertuse, located about twenty-eight kilometers north of Marseille, also shows a history of multiple episodes of fire and destruction (in the late fifth, late third, and early second centuries BCE). The episode near the end of the third century shows extensive burning associated with, as noted earlier, fragments of catapult balls that are a clear indication of a military assault. Again, the assailant is uncertain, but Massalia is suspected because of the technique of using large catapults.[110]

Comparable evidence of significant destruction is, so far, missing in eastern Languedoc. That this absence is not simply a product of insufficient excavation is shown by the fact that several sites in the western Languedoc-Roussillon region (such as Mailhac, Pech Maho, and Le Moulin at Peyrac-de-Mer) show major destruction episodes despite this region having been subjected to much less systematic archaeological exploration than eastern Languedoc. The important port site of Pech Maho, for example was abandoned during the last quarter of the third century BCE after a destruction level that involved dismantling of the rampart, destroyed homes, horse skeletons in the streets, a collective cremation pyre, and catapult balls.[111] Nothing of this kind has appeared between the Hérault and the Rhône rivers. The presumed Etruscan merchants' house at Lattes was destroyed by fire around 475 BCE in an incident that also saw the subsequent rebuilding of the adjacent rampart.[112] But there is not yet enough evidence from other parts of the site to know whether this was an isolated accident, a case of aggression by inhabitants of the town against a small community of resident foreigners, or an external attack on the settlement as a whole. Other burned rooms have been found from later periods at Lattes, but these are clearly isolated cases of house fires without wider consequences.[113] Similar evidence of scattered individual house and granary fires has been found spread over several centuries at sites such as Le Marduel, Gailhan, Mauressip, and Roque-de-Fabrègues, but these do not appear to be connected to any signs of major military violence. Various sites were abandoned at different points, including a number in the early third century BCE (for example, Gailhan, Roque-de-Viou, and Roquecourbe). But abandonment can happen for many reasons and, again, these do not appear to be in connection with episodes of violent destruction. In fact, several of these cases (for instance, at Mont Cavalier-Nîmes and Beaucaire) seem to be connected to the growth of settlements on the plain below these hilltop towns, which would seem to work against the idea of fears of violence. Moreover, during the second century BCE, when violence seems to have reached a peak in Provence, eastern Languedoc was in the midst of a resurgence of small rural settlements on the plain after a notable decline during the fourth century BCE.[114] Ancient texts also present a stark contrast with Provence in the matter of violence, as they are completely silent on such matters in eastern Languedoc until the first century BCE, aside from mentioning the passage of Hannibal's army through the region on his way to Italy in the late third century BCE. In particular, they do not mention any of the kinds of battles with Roman armies that were recorded in Provence in the late second century BCE. Nor are there any traces of the destruction levels associated with this conquest that one finds in abundance in Provence.

This does not mean that the region was entirely peaceful. Monumental stone fortifications had become as much a part of the standard urban landscape there as they had in Provence, and a number of sites (most prominently, Nages) exerted great effort in expanding their ramparts to protect a growing settlement. But the scale of warfare appears to have been much smaller and less destructive, perhaps because local societies lacked the resources necessary to sustain the kind of sieges that could defeat the defensive obstacle presented by these ramparts. One can imagine periodic raids, skirmishes, feuds, cattle raids, destruction of crops, and the like, but major military campaigns capable of taking and destroying fortified cities do not seem to have been part of the landscape of violence in this part of the Rhône basin. It is also reasonable to suspect that opposition to the Roman invasion was far less organized or effective than it was in Provence and that it was easily swept aside or resolved through treaties.

In connection with this chronology and geography of the earliest evidence of destruction in Provence, it is worth noting again that Massalia's founding of sub-colonies along the coast began around the beginning of the fourth century BCE. To the west, Agde was founded about 400 BCE; and to the east, Olbia was founded around the end of the fourth century BCE. This was followed by Antibes, probably in the third century BCE, and then Nice and Tauroeis at the end of the third century BCE (see chapter 4). Strabo noted that these Massalian outposts had primarily a military function, and excavations at Olbia, which can best be described as a compact fortress, certainly seem to confirm this idea (although the case of Agde is rather different). But this military function was directed toward protecting the sea lanes from pirates rather than establishing an inland territory. All of these colonies were ports, and it is clear from both texts and archaeological evidence that neither Olbia nor any of the subsequent

Massalian colonies along the Côte d'Azur managed to wrest any significant territory from the natives of the Ligurian coast until after the Roman conquest. It is tempting to suggest that this founding of colonies is related to a growing series of conflicts with Massalia's neighbors reflected in the archaeological evidence of episodes of destruction, and that these conflicts reached an especially high level toward the end of the third century BCE with the formation of several regional political alliances among indigenous societies, leading to a particularly violent second century BCE that drew Rome into the conflict. The period from the fourth century to the beginning of the second century BCE is also a period that saw the establishment of a number of new fortified settlements on the immediate periphery of Massalia's chora (Verduron, Teste-Nègre, Notre-Dame-de-Pitié, Le Griffon), several of which would be destroyed during the second century BCE, and the reoccupation of some (Les Baou de Saint-Marcel, Le Baou-Roux) that had been abandoned for long periods. Moreover the late third and second centuries BCE witnessed the emergence and spread of ritual practices focused on the human head and heroic statues of warriors.

GRAPHIC REPRESENTATION OF WARRIORS

One other possible indication of elevated status attributed to the arts of violence, or at least to the monumental display of the warrior body, is the presence of stone statues clearly attired in warrior garb. Indeed, the series of Iron Age statues of this type found in Provence and eastern Languedoc is the richest regional source of sculptural self-representation by Celtic-speaking peoples anywhere in Europe before the Roman conquest. It is significant that, with a few rare exceptions from Entremont, the human forms are males dressed as warriors, or severed heads. The majority of these statues date to the Late Iron Age, when both the nature of the colonial situation and indigenous sociopolitical structures had changed significantly from the initial period of the encounter. Moreover, nearly all these works were recovered from secondary contexts, as reused architectural elements. Nevertheless, there are several statues that date with high probability to the Early Iron Age. The warrior of Lattes, for example, was probably carved originally near the beginning of the fifth century BCE (fig. 6.3). Although heavily damaged during its reuse as a doorjamb during the third century BCE, it is clearly discernable as a life-size statue of a man wearing chest and dorsal armor, greaves, and probably a helmet, and in the position of an archer or spearman.[115] Similarly, the statue of Grézan, which dates probably to the end of the fifth century BCE, shows a standing male figure wearing chest and dorsal armor and a hoodlike helmet (fig. 6.4). Actual examples of this kind of equipment are extremely rare in graves or settlements of the lower Rhône basin, but numerous examples have been found in western Languedoc, as well as in Spain and Italy.[116] In the case of the statue from Lattes, it is not certain that it was actually intended as a representation of a local figure. Given the kind of dress and armor portrayed, which are virtually absent from local grave inventories, as well as the unusual crouching posture,

FIGURE 6.3
Stone warrior statue from Lattes (UFRAL; Dietler and Py 2003).

FIGURE 6.4
Stone warrior statue from Grèzan (Py 1990a).

this may well have been part of a sculptural composition showing conflict between local and foreign warriors. These figures are discussed further in chapter 8.

MERCENARIES

It is well-known that most of the major colonial powers of the Mediterranean relied on foreign mercenaries as a major component of their armies. This is abundantly clear, for example, in the cases of the Carthaginians, the Greek cities in southern Italy, and Rome. It is also clear that Gauls had a stereotypic image as fierce warriors who were willing to fight as mercenaries on any side and who were employed in all three of the cases noted above. Hence, this raises several questions of importance for understanding the situation in southern France. Did the inhabitants of this region participate in the overall recruitment of Gallic mercenaries? If so, to what extent? How was recruitment organized? When did this practice begin?

It is clear that Massalia was no exception to the general pattern of employing mercenaries. Indeed, given its small size, it was probably heavily dependent on them for its defense. But what form did this take, and from where were the soldiers drawn? The two instances known from texts have already been discussed earlier, and these sound rather different in character. Polybius referred to Celts "in the service of the Massalians" who acted as guides for Roman cavalry in their attempts to intercept Hannibal during his passage through southern France.[117] Although their origin is not specified, the fact that these Celts were acting as guides would imply that they were natives of the lower Rhône area. Later, Caesar, in his description of his siege of Massalia during the Civil War, noted that the Massalians called on the support of the Albici, "a barbarian tribe, who lived in the mountains above Massilia and had rendered allegiance to them ever since the remote past."[118] The latter case sounds perhaps more like the mobilization of an army by political allies, whereas the former sounds more like individual mercenaries in the employ of Massalia. The destruction of the site of La Cloche, twelve kilometers north of Marseille, by a Roman army at about 50 BCE may be linked to this event and may well be another indication of an indigenous ally of Massalia.[119] It is difficult to draw too much from these references, as they may simply represent different positions on a continuum of forms of military service that involved exchanges of wealth. What does seem evident, however, is that some local people were acting as mercenaries for Massalia as early as the third century BCE and that Massalia did operate through military alliances with some of its neighbors.

Other evidence indicates that Carthaginians were also recruiting mercenaries from southern France as early as the first half of the third century BCE, and perhaps earlier. Polybius mentioned that, in response to a Roman threat in Sicily leading to the outbreak of the First Punic War, the Carthaginians "recruited mercenaries from across the sea, many of them Ligurians and Celts, and even larger numbers of Iberians, and dispatched them all to Sicily."[120] This suggests a force drawn from all the major indigenous groups along the coasts of the western Mediterranean. Moreover, Herodotus listed the Elesyces people of western Languedoc among the mercenaries recruited by the Carthaginians to fight against Greeks at the battle of Himera in 480 BCE,[121] which would indicate that mercenaries were being raised in some parts of Mediterranean France by the early fifth century BCE.

SUMMARY

In brief, both archaeological and textual evidence combine to indicate that the history of the colonial encounter in Mediterranean France was marked by several kinds of inter-linked violence: both periodic episodes of conflict between colonists and natives and a gradual increase in violence or insecurity within native societies beyond the zone of immediate contact. Moreover, this regional history of violence took place within the broader context of Mediterranean geopolitics that involved military conflicts on land and sea between shifting coalitions of various city-states, the gradual emergence of two impe-rialistic powers (Punic and Roman) vying for dominance on multiple fronts, and the even-tual Roman conquest of the entire Mediterranean periphery. Although Mediterranean France was not directly involved as a significant player in much of this broader history of geopolitical struggles that would ultimately engulf it, many of the conflicts between states in the Central Mediterranean did spill over into the region in various ways: for example, through the recruitment of mercenaries by diverse agents for conflicts in other theaters, through the alliances formed by Massalia that implicated Rome in local conflicts between Massalia and its neighbors, and through the ways that the internal politics of the Roman state fueled its expansion and appetite for colonization of the region.

Within the Rhône basin, the evidence for the progressive expansion of the practice of surrounding settlements with massive stone fortifications (and their frequent recon-struction) indicates that the installation of Massalia had an important impact on regional patterns of violence. The fact that these appeared first at Massalia and on indigenous sites in its immediate periphery, in combination with the textual references to periodic conflict with Massalia's neighbors and the fact that archaeological evidence of the violent destruction of settlements is heavily concentrated in Provence throughout the Iron Age, speaks to the fact that Massalia remained an epicenter of conflict over many centuries. This does not mean that it was in a continual state of warfare, but rather that tensions periodically erupted in violence. Whether these outbreaks of violence were provoked by Massalia (for example, in attempting to expand its small chora) or by its neighbors, or both, is unclear and of less importance than the fact that the colonial encounter pro-duced a heightened level of recurrent conflict in western Provence that, until the Roman conquest, remained unresolved through either expansion of Massalian territorial control or destruction of the colony.

The pattern of expansion of these fortifications beyond the area around Marseille from the late sixth through the fourth centuries BCE, first along the coast and then inland until they became a standard feature of virtually all settlements, is an indication that the effects of the colonial encounter were not limited to direct conflict between Massalia and indigenous peoples. It is probable that Massalians (whether traders or soldiers) never had much contact with peoples beyond the immediate coastal zone, and the fact that ramparts were constructed at interior sites such as Le Marduel and Le Pègue is a sign of changes in patterns of violence and insecurity radiating out from the zone of direct colonial encounter as an unintended consequence.

Several kinds of evidence combine to suggest that the second century BCE marked a time of significant escalation in the tensions between Massalia and its neighbors. This is the period from which most of our archaeological evidence of settlement destruction by violence comes, and also the period during which texts indicate Massalia appealed to Rome several times for help in conflicts with native peoples of the region. This is a period that also saw an expansion in the size of a number of indigenous settlements quite near Marseille (Entremont and Le Baou-Roux, for instance) and the reconstruction of a number of ramparts in even more monumental form (as at Saint-Blaise, Entremont, and Constantine), as well as the reoccupation of some sites that had previously been abandoned (such as Les Baou de Saint-Marcel only seven kilometers away) and the foundation of new ones (such as Entremont, Tête-de-l'Ost, and Baou Rouge). It is also a period that saw the spread of ritual practices marked by heroic warrior statues and an emphasis on severed heads (see chapter 8) that may represent both an aggressive assertion of indigenous religious culture with a militarized tone (something like a revitalization movement, perhaps) and the emergence of new political structures.

7

CULINARY ENCOUNTERS

Food is a domain of social life that presents what should be an obvious target for investigation in seeking to understand the operation of colonialism. After all, contemporary foodways around the world are in large measure the product of a long history of colonial encounters. Moreover, food has been a consistently prominent material medium for the enactment of colonialism.[1] In other words, food is not simply a convenient index of change in colonial situations; it is an agent of change as well. And the changes produced are not confined to the semiotics of consumption: they have had a major impact on the political economy of all the societies engaged in these encounters, creating a web of profound entanglements.

This relationship between food and colonialism derives from the fact that the intimate links between food practices and the embodiment of identity and between commensality and politics have made food an important arena for the working out of colonial struggles over consciousness and identity and strategies of appropriation and resistance. Hence, a focus on food holds great analytic promise for archaeologists in their attempts to penetrate and understand ancient colonial situations and their transformative effects.[2] However, while full of promise, this relationship is by no means simple or straightforward. Progressing beyond banal generalizations to the generation of useful interpretive insights requires both methodological ingenuity and a rigorous attention to the contextualization of food issues within a broader theoretical framework.

FOOD AND COLONIALISM: THEORETICAL CONCERNS

In making the theoretical case for the significance of food and its links to colonialism, let me start by making clear that I use the word *food* in the broad sense to also include things like alcoholic beverages. These are, after all, merely special forms of food with psychoactive properties resulting from alternative techniques of culinary treatment: the same grain can become porridge, bread, beer, or whisky, depending simply on the techniques applied to it.[3] Ethnographic studies indicate that in some societies people receive substantial nutrition and as much as a third of their caloric intake in the form of beer.[4] Moreover, as much as 15 to 30 percent of the family grain supply is commonly dedicated to the production of alcoholic beverages in agrarian societies.[5] Given these facts, it is logically untenable to exclude alcohol from a consideration of food simply because beverages containing ethanol have been constructed as a "drug" in Western discourse under the influence of the nineteenth-century temperance movement.

I must begin by stating something that should be obvious but that nonetheless bears repetition. Although the consumption of food is essential for maintaining human life, such consumption is never simply a matter of taking on fuel. People do not ingest calories or protein: they eat *food*, a form of material culture subject to almost unlimited possibilities for variation in terms of ingredients, techniques of preparation, patterns of association and exclusion, preferences and prohibitions, modes of serving and consumption, aesthetic and moral evaluations, and so forth. Moreover, food is what may be called "embodied material culture"—that is, a special kind of material culture created specifically for destruction through the transformative process of ingestion into the human body. Hence, it has an unusually close relationship to the person and to both the inculcation and the symbolization of concepts of identity. Indeed, although I am usually wary of psychoanalytical explanations, the sociologist Pasi Falk has made an interesting observation on the ontogenic significance of food that is worth considering. He noted that the infant's first perception of difference—of the boundary between subject and object that defines the self—is experienced through the mouth at the mother's breast long before the development of sight. Hence, according to Falk, the mouth acts as both the model for all subsequent sensory reception and as the gateway regulating the incorporation of alien matter into the body through the culturally coded sense of taste.[6] Moreover, given that eating is a social act that must be repeated virtually every day for biological survival, it occupies a salient place among the various routinized practices that, as Pierre Bourdieu has explored at length, serve to inculcate habitus—the set of embodied dispositions that structure action in the world and that unconsciously instantiate perceptions of identity and difference.[7]

All of this goes to emphasize why food is both so intimately connected to the formation and expression of identity and is such a versatile and highly charged symbolic medium.[8] However, it should also serve to underline an important caveat: food is a sign system, but it is not *only* a sign system. Eating is more than the consumption of signs.

It is also a material construction of the self in much more than a metaphorical sense. Hence, it must be acknowledged that an exclusive focus on consumption, particularly the vision of consumption exemplified in some of the forms of analysis of a more narrowly semiotic orientation stemming from the early work of Jean Baudrillard, may risk isolating food from the crucial commodity chains that enable its existence and decoupling it from those more traditional, but still important, domains of analysis: production and exchange.[9] As noted in chapter 3, this would be particularly dangerous in a colonial context, where the issues of entanglement and exploitation should mandate that the articulation of production and consumption should be an ever-present concern.

It is certainly true that, in many ways, consumption is analytically prior to production (although temporally posterior). One need only recall Marshall Sahlins' percipient statement that "[t]he exploitation of the American environment, the mode of relation to the landscape, depends on the model of a meal that includes a central meat element with the peripheral support of carbohydrates and vegetables." As he pointed out, the entire structure of agricultural production and articulation to world markets would change dramatically if Americans ate dogs or horses, both of which are entirely edible in other cultures.[10] It is the cultural construction of proper consumption, with its symbolic prohibitions and valuations, that determines production, not vice versa. Hence, focusing on consumption is clearly crucial for comprehending the social and cultural significance of food and its role in colonialism. Moreover, given the emphasis in this book on the importance of developing an archaeology of consumption, this point is certainly fundamental to my analysis of food. What I am cautioning against is an *abstract* treatment of consumption as the circulation of pure signs that is divorced from consideration of the relations of power in which they are embedded, or that ignores the crucial material properties and effects of the food being consumed.

Hence, let us acknowledge that food is a basic and continual human physiological need that is simultaneously a form of highly condensed social fact embodying relations of production and exchange and linking the domestic and political economies in a highly personalized way. Furthermore, although eating and drinking are among the few biologically essential acts, they are never simply biological acts. Rather, they are learned, culturally patterned techniques of bodily comportment (*techniques du corps* in the sense of Marcel Mauss[11]) that are expressive of identity and difference in a fundamental way.

At this point, it becomes necessary to pose two basic questions that will structure the rest of this discussion that prepares the ground for an analysis of Mediterranean France. In the first place, given the close links between food and identity, why do people sometimes change their food habits in situations of colonial contact—in particular, why do they adopt alien foods and food practices? And when they do, what consequences does this entail, and what implications does it have for understanding colonialism?

It is often said that foodways are among the most conservative and persistent aspects of culture. Like most truisms, this turns out to be not entirely true but not entirely false, either. Examples of the avid adoption of exotic foods are legion and most cuisines of the world include many nonindigenous ingredients. Often alien foods become "indigenized" to the point that they come to be considered a fundamental marker of *local* ethnic cuisine. The tomato in Italian cooking, maize polenta in north Italian cuisine, tea in England, coffee in Italy, the potato in Ireland, the sweet potato in Highland New Guinea, mint tea in North Africa, rice in Indonesia, the banana in Central America, peanuts in West Africa, maize and cassava among the Luo in Kenya, and (as we shall see) wine in France—all of these are examples of thoroughly indigenized foods with exotic origins. Not coincidentally, most of them are also products of colonial encounters—and examples demonstrating that borrowings flow in both directions in these situations. But if foodways are so stable, and food is so closely tied to identity, then how is this possible?

In part, it can be explained by the fact that what we may, for convenience, call "ethnic" cuisine is more than simply a matter of food *ingredients*. It is true that some specific individual food items and flavoring agents do *sometimes* become marked as salient symbols of group identity. The Luo people of Kenya, for example, distinguish themselves from the neighboring Kisii by the fact that the Luo love fish, which the Kisii abhor.[12] Likewise, Americans have their hamburgers and apple pie, Bavarians their bratwurst, Scots their haggis, Valencians their paella, and so forth. And in the proscriptive sense, Muslims and Jews do not eat pork, most Hindus do not eat beef, Americans do not eat horses, dogs, or insects, and so on. Such preferences and prohibitions are the classic stuff of group boundary-marking practices. However, single items do not make an ethnic diet. Ethnic cuisines are constituted by permutations of distinctive sets of staple and secondary foods, flavoring agents, techniques of culinary processing, beliefs about kinds of food combinations that are appropriate for daily and festive consumption, and social contexts of consumption.[13] Moreover, as Mary Douglas has shown, the patterning of a whole cycle of combinations is important—in other words, a series of menus and the rhythms that structure their consumption, or what are sometimes called "meal formats."[14]

It is this complexity that allows the incorporation of alien foods into a routinized set of practices without altering the perception of continuity or threatening identity. For example, among the Luo, the central dish of any main meal—indeed, what defines a main meal—is a polenta-like starch called *kuon*. Different kinds of meat, vegetable, or fish dishes serve essentially as a relish for kuon. In the precolonial era, kuon was made from sorghum. But, following the incorporation of the Luo into the British empire at the end of the nineteenth century, maize was introduced and it became acceptable to substitute maize for sorghum in part or in whole. What is essential for a Luo meal is that kuon be present, whatever it is made from. And, whatever else is consumed, unless there is kuon, a Luo will say he or she has not eaten.

In fact, this persistence of identity and cultural integrity in the face of experimentation and incorporation of alien foods should not be surprising. As explained in chapter 3, it only becomes a problem if we have an unrealistically static conception of culture as a bundle of traits or an isolated organic whole. Rather, we need to understand it as a creative project of structured improvisation grounded in sets of embodied categorical perceptions, analogical understandings, aesthetic dispositions, and values that structure ways of reasoning, solving problems, and acting on opportunities. And, to repeat what was said before, among those problems/opportunities to be resolved is the ever-present one of dealing with exogenous peoples and objects through a process of selective domestication, or indigenization, of formerly foreign foods, tastes, and foodways, and the rejection of others. Such selective incorporation operates according to a specific cultural logic, but it also has a continual transformative effect in the reproduction of culture. Moreover, this process occurs through the often contradictory actions of individual human beings and social groups located differentially within complex relational fields of power and interest. There may be anxieties, tensions, and factional disagreements about the initial incorporation of particular exotic ingredients or recipes, but people can also see such introductions as improving the established cuisine, even making it "more traditional."[15] It is the playing out of these struggles over taste on the battlefield of conflicting social interests that determines which ingredients or practices become accepted as "traditional" and which ones are rejected.

Three major questions emerge from this discussion for an archaeologist interested in food and colonialism. First, why and how do some specific alien foods and food practices get appropriated in colonial contexts while others are ignored, rejected, or turned into points of contestation or symbols of difference? Second, what are the often unintended consequences of such cross-cultural borrowings in terms of identity, politics, and social relations? Third, how can archaeologists approach these issues in the material record of the past and use them to understand colonialism? As I noted earlier, there are no simple a priori rules that will enable us to predict these things universally. However, an improved theoretical grounding of the questions will allow a better formulation of interpretive arguments and assessment of plausibility.

Why Are Alien Foods Desired?   First to the "why" question. In this context, it is important to reiterate that such transfers occur not through the action of cultures, but through the often contradictory actions of individuals and social groups. Similarly, identity is not something that resides solely, or even primarily, at the level of ethnic groups, nations, or other large-scale imagined communities. It is lodged in intersecting networks of kinship affiliations, social categories (such as gender and age), class and status group memberships, and other such things that may be situationally relevant. And the process of cross-cultural appropriation of foods usually has much more to do with relational politics at these levels than it does with broader "ethnic" consciousness. For example, class dynamics and the creation of internal distinctions and boundaries often lie behind such adoptions, with items potentially becoming a salient marker of ethnicity only much later. This can be in the form of what Arjun Appadurai called an elite "turnstile effect," with an upper class continually adopting exotic foods that must be shifted as the process of emulation by lower classes reduces their diacritical symbolic value.[16] However, as the history of the spread of tobacco in Europe shows, goods and practices can be introduced through either lower or upper classes and trickle up or down the social hierarchy.[17] Similarly, generational struggles over authority can create powerful incentives for exotic introductions, as can the challenges of shifting gender relations.

Demand for alien foods is a product of the variable interplay of embodied categories and tastes, strategic decisions about the potential deployment of foods in particular social roles, creative analogical interpretations of new instrumental or social uses, semiotic understandings about the relationship among foods in "systems of objects,"[18] and other such factors. Demand is not a uniform property or product of cultures. It is socially situated and constructed; that is, although it clearly follows a specific cultural logic, it varies among classes and categories of people as a result of the interplay of the factors noted above in the internal improvisational politics of social life. In ancient Greek societies, for instance, food was a salient marker of a whole series of nested distinctions: Greeks versus barbarians, urban sophisticates versus country rustics, rich versus poor, men versus women, and so forth. And, as Peter Garnsey has pointed out, the Greek *nouveaux riches* imitated the elite, thus propelling the spread of certain food practices.[19]

Hence, demand for foreign foods and food practices may vary according to social position or category, and the differences may be generated largely by the relational dynamics among social groups or fields. In fact, paradoxically, the maintenance of stable systems of distinction may come to rely on a constant shifting of the specific symbols of distinction. Obviously, in archaeological contexts we will usually not be able to discern the relative operation of all these factors in great detail. But, as discussed in chapter 3, we can distinguish demand as a selective force structuring consumption within a specific world of options and attempt to discern as completely as possible the logic of patterns of choices made.

How Are Alien Foods Indigenized?   Given some partial indications of the reasons why exotic foods may be appropriated, it is also important to ask how this happens—that is, precisely what are the practices and contexts that are responsible for not simply introducing an innovation but, more importantly, producing the social validation that is necessary to make it more generally accepted? In this vein, it becomes important to make a distinction in the analysis of foodways between the routinized practices of daily consumption that we may call meals and the more self-consciously performative rituals of consumption that are called feasts. Both of these exist in a complex semiotic relationship to each other and form part of a common semiotic field that gives them both meaning.[20] The ways in which feasts are symbolically marked as ritual performances (such as through temporal eccentricity, spatial or architectonic framing, the use of unusual kinds or quantities of foods, the use of special service vessels, theatrical devices, etc.) will depend on a relationship to patterns and practices of mundane daily meals. But what is important to emphasize here is that, in addition to the various political roles that feasts serve,[21] they are also prime arenas for the construction and transformation of values and the validation of exotic novelties. And this is especially true of new foods. Polly Wiessner has provided an exemplary analysis of this phenomenon in New Guinea, where local bigmen used feasts to promote their interests by introducing and valorizing new kinds of foods (such as pigs) and objects.[22] Foods and consumption practices introduced and validated in this way can then be transferred to daily meals and eventually become indigenized standard practices; or they may remain special ritual foods that become indexical markers of ritual. Other avenues for introduction may come in the opposite direction through, for instance, the common colonial practice of intermarriage and the gradual insertion of exotic foods into daily meal formats by the alien spouse.

The introduction of the potato in Finland nicely illustrates the complexity of the relationship between these daily and ritual spheres, and between ingredients and techniques. The potato was introduced in the eighteenth century from Sweden as part of a state-sponsored campaign to have available a surrogate for bread in times of scarcity among the peasantry, but it did not catch on until people gradually adapted it to the local food system. It was first assimilated to the traditional turnip and rutabaga and cooked in the same ways (boiled potatoes, porridge, and soup), and in these forms it has become firmly established in the everyday food system. However, potatoes cooked by novel culinary techniques (baked or in salads) never became part of the daily meal cycle but were incorporated into feasts and holiday meals.[23]

The Consequences of Consumption   This discussion inevitably leads us to consider the subject of the significance of edible material culture in strategies of colonialism. Given the importance of consumption in constructing social relationships, it should not be surprising that goods, including especially food, have not only been appropriated and indigenized, they have also been used by both parties in colonial situations to attempt to control the other—"making subjects by means of objects."[24] As discussed in chapter 3, this involves attempts not only to create novel desires for new goods but also to get people to use imported objects in particular ways, as well as the (usually erroneous) belief that the use of particular goods or technologies will inherently induce certain kinds of desired behavior. Such strategies to use material objects as vectors of control always have unintended consequences for all the parties concerned.

This clearly has been true of food. For example, the Luo recount tales of, as they put it, "being chased with tea." This is a reference to attempts by colonial missionaries to instill concepts of English bourgeois domesticity and sobriety by getting the Luo to substitute tea for beer as a social lubricant. The Luo now drink tea only rarely, but Luo *women* consider it the appropriate drink for receiving certain kinds of visitors in the home, usually served with slices of white bread—another alien delicacy that is not otherwise consumed. Tea also requires the purchase of refined sugar (something that the Luo do not use for anything else) and the use of fresh milk (another unique usage, as they generally prefer soured milk). Hence, contrary to the desires of the missionaries, tea has certainly not replaced beer: it is not used in major rituals or in male commensality. Nor has it had much impact on Luo domestic habits. What it has done is help to tie women to the national cash economy by creating a periodic need for the purchase of a set of ingredients (tea leaves, sugar, bread) and specialized objects (a teapot and cups) of nonlocal origin.

Smoking tobacco was an alien practice that was not encouraged by the missionaries but that had much greater success. However, it resulted in a gender-marking pattern of consumption in which women smoke cigarettes using an unusual technique in which they hold the burning end inside the mouth, while men smoke with the burning end out. Both men and women also smoke clay pipes, an alien form that was introduced into the repertoire of potters but that is largely giving way to cigarettes. Smoking is now a thoroughly indigenized consumption practice that also serves to tie people to the broader cash economy. However, government attempts to get the Luo to raise tobacco as a cash crop have been more ambivalent. The Luo consider money gained from the sale of tobacco to be "bitter money," a substance that is dangerous to use in transactions that are socially important, such as bridewealth or cattle purchases.[25]

As these cases again underline, despite the beliefs and desires of many agents of colonialism, when an object crosses cultural frontiers, it rarely arrives with the same meanings and practices associated with it in its context of origin. Objects that traverse different "regimes of value" are, in effect, transformed into different objects. Hence, not only is the consumption of foreign foods an inadequate measure of a purported process (or degree) of what used to be called the "acculturation" of a society, but, paradoxically, imported foods or food practices may even become salient symbolic markers of the boundaries of identity between consumers and the society of origin because of subtle but symbolically important perceived differences in preparation or styles or contexts of consumption. The English adoption of tea drinking from the Chinese, the Italian adoption of coffee from Muslim North Africa, the Viennese adoption of coffee from Turks after the battle of Vienna, and the Etruscan and Roman adaptations of the Greek symposion discussed in chapter 3 are all illustrative cases.

As these various examples suggest, the consequences of the appropriation and assimilation of foods and food practices in colonial or other cross-cultural situations are difficult to predict, but the unintended consequences are often quite profound. This can be especially true when such appropriation produces an increasing entanglement of societies in a broader colonial political economy. For example, in the case of English consumption of the alien beverage of tea that has come to be regarded as a quintessentially English practice, Marshall Sahlins has shown how increasing demand for tea forced English merchants to trade with the Hawaiian kings to acquire sandalwood, the one commodity that the Chinese would accept for their tea leaves—which led to the complete destruction of all the sandalwood on the Hawaiian islands within about thirty-five years, and eventually to the opium trade as the English sought desperately to find another product desired by the Chinese to assure their supply of tea.[26] Similarly, Sidney Mintz has shown how the escalating demand for sugar among the British working class was intimately connected to the establishment of sugar plantations in the Americas and the growth of the trans-Atlantic slave trade to supply the plantations with labor.[27] Global colonial relations can also have tertiary effects on the adoption of foods: for example, the introduction of the New World domesticates the potato in Ireland and maize in Kenya were the result of parallel English colonial ventures in the New World, Ireland, and Africa. These adoptions of alien foods ultimately had significant consequences for nutrition, engendered economic entanglements that led to various forms of systemic dependency, produced major ecological and demographic transformations, and generated new regimes of production and labor. The rapid population increase in the highlands of New Guinea following the adoption of the sweet potato; the deforestation of many areas of the world to create sugar, coffee, tea, and tobacco plantations to feed new international tastes; the slave trade, the coercive regimes of mass labor migration in many European colonies, and the shifting of smallholder production from subsistence to cash crops to supply an international trade in food were all spawned by the indigenization of exotic food items.[28]

A consideration of alcohol in Africa offers perhaps an even more specifically relevant demonstration of these points.[29] As in many other colonial situations, the roles of alcohol were extremely complicated and even contradictory, ranging (often simultaneously) from an intended implement of seduction and control, to an imagined vector of disorder, a major source of colonial and postcolonial state revenue, and a central component of a subversive alternative economy (bootleg production, smuggling, etc.). In West Africa, distilled spirits (brandy, rum, and gin) played a major role in the Atlantic slave trade from its origins, serving as a commodity, a currency, and a lubricant for establishing exchange relationships.[30] Every bit as much as sugar, liquor became a key trade item in the triangle that linked Europe, Africa, and the Americas: it was traded to African rulers for slaves who worked the American sugar plantations that provided the raw material for rum that was used to obtain more slaves. Moreover, the growing slave-sugar economy also made cheap rum readily available to the working classes of England and Holland for the first time during the seventeenth century.[31]

After the incorporation of Africa into various European empires in the nineteenth century (and earlier in South Africa), alcohol became an object of ambivalence, conflicting discourses, and shifting policies and alliances—but always of major concern. On the one hand, the colonial states in most regions began to rely on taxes on alcohol for a substantial part of their operating revenues.[32] French West Africa, for example, derived about 70 percent of its revenues from alcohol duties in the early twentieth century.[33] These states also depended on alcohol for the recruitment and pacification of a native labor force.[34] At the same time, anxiety about the effects of alcohol in aggravating the unruliness of an already suspect subject population and in disrupting attempts to instill capitalist work discipline also became pervasive. Moreover, the prevalence of a strong temperance ideology among Protestant missionaries led to both political agitation for state limitations on alcohol and direct attempts to influence African drinking practices and beliefs through religious conversion.

The result of these conflicting forces was that alcohol became a constant subject of colonial legislation and (usually unsuccessful) attempts to control native consumption and production of alcohol while promoting the sale of revenue-producing imported varieties or state monopolies. Not surprisingly, alcohol also became a central object of contestation between the colonial state and both African leaders and local brewers; and this is a struggle that has continued in postcolonial African states.[35] Increasing commoditization of alcohol in these colonial contexts also frequently set off conflict between generations and genders (as senior men felt their power challenged by liberalized access to a potent political symbol and tool) and, for example, between traditionalists and Christian converts. It sometimes has produced curious alliances of interest as well, as in the case of senior women and young male drinkers uniting in opposition to official alcohol restrictions,[36] or in the case of colonial officials enacting restrictive liquor laws in Ghana, despite the loss of considerable revenues, in an effort to support the desire of local chiefs for selective access to alcohol in order to shore up the social control of these senior men on whom the state depended.[37]

CULINARY ENCOUNTERS IN MEDITERRANEAN FRANCE

Given this general theoretical perspective on the relationship between food and colonialism, what can we discern about the role food played in this series of colonial encounters in Mediterranean France? Unlike some modern colonial situations, the possibilities for major transfers of basic foods ingredients were limited in ancient Mediterranean France. That is because well before the colonial encounter the basic global repertoires of cereal crops and domestic animals were already quite similar for indigenous societies and Greeks, Etruscans, and Romans. There were, of course, significant local variations in the *relative importance* of different elements in the diet as well as in the culinary techniques used to prepare food and the ways of consuming it—precisely the kinds of things that distinguish cuisine from simple ingredients. But most of the basic staple food components were already shared by all parties to the encounter.

Given the fact that Greeks commonly saw cuisine as an index of the gulf separating them from "barbarians," we should not be surprised to learn that, despite this high degree of similarity in most of the basic food elements, Greek texts found the foodways of Gauls to be profoundly alien. No doubt the opposite was true as well, although we do not have the benefit of texts that preserve the impressions local peoples had of Greek and Etruscan cuisine. Among the few distinctive basic components of the diet at the moment of the first encounter, the preferred forms of alcohol and fat were the most salient:

Greeks and Etruscans preferred wine and olive oil while local peoples used beer and animal fats. Let us begin the discussion with the issue of alcohol before moving on to explore other aspects of food ingredients, culinary techniques, and consumption practices to see what they reveal about the role of food in the long history of colonial encounters in the region.

THE SOCIAL LIFE OF ALCOHOL: WINE, ENTANGLEMENT, AND THE COLONIAL POLITICAL ECONOMY

Not only did wine constitute the overwhelmingly dominant form of alien food desired by native peoples of Mediterranean France in their exchanges with Etruscans, Greeks, and Romans, but it was the primary object of colonial exchange *tout court* for about six centuries. Archaeological evidence compiled over the past several decades shows that, despite the fact that wild grapes were indigenous to Mediterranean France, wine was first introduced to the region by Etruscans in the late seventh century BCE; and from the very beginning of the encounter, it played a central role in articulating colonial relations.[38] Indeed, one of the most striking features that emerges from a consumption-oriented analysis of the encounter is that indigenous peoples of the lower Rhône basin initially were interested in virtually nothing else that Etruscans and Greeks had to offer. They demonstrated an immediate and avid desire for imported wine and drinking ceramics yet were largely indifferent to other goods, and this pattern persisted for generations.[39]

Demand versus Supply   This highly selective, focused, and consistent pattern of consumption will be examined in more detail later. But, for the moment, a crucial preliminary empirical question must be addressed: can we determine that this was really a product of selective demand rather than a question of restricted supply or of taphonomic factors in the differential preservation of archaeological evidence?

Even on purely theoretical grounds one can dismiss the fantasy that native peoples would be eager to acquire whatever goods Greek and Etruscan merchants deigned to present to them, and that wine and drinking ceramics were the only things merchants were willing to offer or had available. As explained in chapter 3, decades of anthropological and historical work on consumption have made it clear that demand is never an automatic response to the availability of goods.[40] Merchants and explorers in modern colonial situations frequently had great difficulty inducing peoples they encountered to take an interest in the objects they sought to exchange. It was not until they had developed some understanding of local desires and tastes that they were able to offer goods that local peoples would accept. Once exchange relationships developed, desires often expanded or shifted, but it was local demand that determined the possibility and the terms of engagement. The success of traders depends on their ability to discern local demand and respond to it, and there is no reason to assume that ancient Greek or Etruscan merchants were any less attuned to these issues than other traders. Indeed, the discussion in chapter 5 made clear the risks that traders in the ancient Mediterranean faced from weather, pirates, and uncertainty about supply and demand conditions because of slow information flows. As pointed out, two alternative strategies were generally used to counteract these risks: either carrying very mixed cargoes in the hope that one item or another would find a match with local tastes and be saleable in one place or another, or cultivating regular routes and contacts, developing a knowledge of the preferences of customers, and specializing in particular goods that were in high demand in the places they frequented.[41] It is clear that merchants peddling Etruscan and Massalian goods turned fairly quickly toward the second strategy. The cargoes of most ships during the early phase of the encounter settled quickly on wine and a limited range of drinking ceramics, and this pattern varied little in this region for centuries. The wine and ceramics were from a variety of geographic origins, but, functionally, this was an extremely narrowly targeted range of goods.

The point is that merchants typically sought to ascertain and respond to demand, and this was true throughout the Mediterranean. As was demonstrated in chapter 5, merchants were the flexible mediators in the segmented commodity networks that flowed through the ancient Mediterranean; they were not the loyal agents of manufacturers seeking to establish markets for the export production of firms. Their livelihood depended on finding goods to match the tastes of consumers, not cultivating tastes to create a market for the output of producers. There are many contemporary examples of obvious catering to local tastes, even by producers, as in the manufacture of certain kinds of Attic pottery catering to the Etruscan market[42] or Massalian production of forms of Gray-monochrome ceramics tailored to indigenous tastes in different regions of Mediterranean France (discussed later in this chapter). It is simply not credible that, had there existed an appetite for other kinds of goods, some traders would not have responded to it. A comparative analysis of what Greek and Etruscan merchants were trading in other regions shows that they certainly did so elsewhere. Wine was a common component of many early cross-cultural trade situations in the western and central Mediterranean, but the pattern was not so exclusively focused on wine in many other regions, nor was the range of accompanying ceramics the same. For example, Jean-Paul Morel has pointed out that, for the Etruscan material, comparison between southern France and contemporary patterns of Etruscan trade in North Africa and Sardinia shows a quite different range of imports in the latter areas. The trade with Carthage was dominated by perfumed oils, which are virtually nonexistent in indigenous southern French contexts, while Etruscan wine amphorae are extremely rare at Carthage. Among the Etruscan tableware ceramics imported, *kantharos* drinking cups constituted about 95 percent of this ware consumed in southern France, but less than 20 percent at Carthage and about 56 percent at the site of Tharros on Sardinia. Moreover, drinking forms constitute less than 33 percent of all Etruscan fineware ceramics found at Carthage as opposed to nearly 100 percent at sites in southern France.[43] This strongly suggests that, as one would expect, merchants were responding to local demand in each case.

The same conclusion is indicated by comparing the range of Attic ceramics (black-figure and red-figure) and Massalian Cream-ware ceramics in use at Massalia and those consumed at nearby indigenous settlements during the early centuries of the encounter. At Massalia one finds the full elaborate repertoire of Greek tableware forms, but at early Iron Age settlements in the Rhône basin forms are largely confined to drinking cups (for both Attic and Cream-ware), along with smaller quantities of Cream-ware wine pitchers and small bowls (probably also used for drinking). Again, it is difficult to imagine that local peoples were never exposed to the other forms in common use at Massalia (indeed, one does find the odd isolated example of other forms), or that merchants would not have responded had they shown any interest. Similarly, among the forms of Gray-monochrome ware consumed at indigenous sites, the only Greek forms of any quantitative significance were, again, drinking cups and wine pitchers. Moreover, the most popular form of Gray-monochrome ware in the lower Rhône basin was actually a carenated bowl (Type 3 of Pradelle) made by Greek potters after an indigenous form. In contrast, this type was far less common in the Hérault valley where the most popular form was a bowl with a flat horizontal lip (Type 4) that was uncommon in the Rhône basin.[44] All of this indicates that both merchants and producers were paying attention to the local tastes of native peoples and that the pattern of consumption we see was the result of choices made by consumers to which traders responded.

Aside from amphorae and drinking gear, virtually the only other Greek or Etruscan ceramics found in even remotely significant quantities during the early centuries of the encounter are mortars. Even these, which may have been assimilated to local *jattes* forms, could have been associated with drinking, as Greeks often used them for grinding up additives to flavor wines. Again, this would seem to point toward highly selective demand: why else would heavy mortars have been traded and not other less bulky cooking pots?

The influence of archaeological preservation factors in shaping our vision of consumption patterns is harder to assess, but important to consider. Is it simply that the durable shards we find mislead us into thinking that amphorae constituted the bulk of a trade that actually included something more perishable that has disappeared? This seems doubtful for several reasons. As shown in chapter 5, the cargoes of the shipwrecks found off the coast of southern France are composed overwhelmingly of amphorae and tableware ceramics, with little place for large quantities of other products. The only plausible candidate for a major perishable consumption object that could have disappeared without a trace is cloth. However, unlike wine, there is not a single textual reference indicating a trade in Greek or Etruscan cloth in the Rhône basin. Nor is there any archaeological evidence of such a trade; although, given its perishable nature, there is very little evidence of cloth of any kind. The ubiquity of clay spindle whorls and loom weights on native sites demonstrates that indigenous peoples were weaving their own cloth. They could, of course, have been importing other fabrics in addition to making their own (for example, as an exotic luxury item). However, other elements of clothing and bodily adornment (such as bronze and iron fibulae; bronze, glass, and lignite bracelets;

glass beads, and bronze and lignite rings) show a strong preference for local and more northerly La Tène styles, and a complete indifference to Greek and Etruscan styles.[45] Furthermore, descriptions of the dress of "Celts" or "Gauls" by Greek and Roman authors emphasize how very different the styles of clothing were from their own as late as the second and first centuries BCE. For example, Posidonius noted, "They [Gauls] wear a striking kind of clothing—tunics dyed and stained in various colours, and trousers, which they call by the name of bracae; and they wear striped cloaks, fastened with buckles, thick in winter and light in summer, picked out with a variegated small check pattern."[46] We cannot be certain where in Gaul the people so described actually lived, but Posidonius's observations likely came predominantly from Mediterranean France, the region he actually visited. He certainly made no mention of any Gauls dressed in Greek or Roman fashion. Such anecdotal information, of course, proves nothing. But, although a trade in cloth cannot be entirely ruled out, all the evidence we do have argues against rather than for it.

One final issue needs to be addressed: is it certain that all these amphorae consumed in Mediterranean France contained wine? While this cannot be demonstrated with absolute certainty, the preponderance of evidence certainly points toward wine as being the primary, if not the sole, product distributed in these containers. Wine was the most common product transported in amphorae in the ancient Mediterranean in general. But olive oil and garum fish sauce were two other main products that circulated commonly in amphorae, although usually in distinctive vessel forms.[47] Michel Gras has argued that the Etruscan amphorae found in France were almost certainly containers for wine, given that the Etruscans imported olive oil from Athens during this period and modeled their own oil amphorae (which were not exported to southern France) after the Attic type, while their wine amphorae were derived from Phoenician models.[48] The Massalian amphorae were also modeled after a Greek form of wine amphora, rather than known olive oil forms such as the Attic SOS or Corinthian A types.[49] A few specimens recovered in the excavations at Marseille do show that some Massalian amphorae contained grapes, olives, fruit, nuts, shellfish, and fish,[50] although these were found in an intentional dump zone and may have been secondary functions for reused containers. Only a small number of chemical analyses of residues have been performed on the amphorae of interest in Mediterranean France, but these have almost invariably confirmed the presence of wine.[51] Moreover, traces of pitch on the interior surface are a nearly sure sign of wine (salted fish are another, more remote possibility) because pitch is soluble in oil and could not have been used for olive oil or goods containing oil (such as garum). Amphorae with a long, narrow neck (such as the Greco-Italic and Dressel 1 types) could have been used only for a liquid, and amphorae of this shape with a pitch lining exclude virtually any possibility except wine. A relatively large number of amphorae (Etruscan, Massalian, and Italian) found in conditions favoring good preservation on consumption sites and shipwrecks in France show such preserved traces of pitch.[52] Finally, the close association at consumption sites and on ships between these Etruscan and Massalian amphorae and the ceramic drinking cups that constituted the only other imports of major interest, would also seem to argue strongly for wine.

For all these reasons, the consensus among amphora specialists is that the types of Etruscan, Massalian, and Italian amphorae found on consumption sites of Mediterranean France before the Augustan period were primarily, if not exclusively, intended to transport wine.[53] More chemical analysis of content residues clearly needs to be done to confirm this conclusion, but it seems well grounded in several intersecting lines of evidence.

Commodity Chains It is important to emphasize that this overall pattern of consumption remained strikingly consistent despite several shifts in the commodity chains supplying this wine over the centuries (fig. 7.1). In the lower Rhône basin, the first wine to arrive in the region came from southern Etruria, most probably from Vulci and Caere.[54] From the late seventh century BCE until the mid–sixth century BCE, Etruscan wine was virtually the only kind consumed in the region (along with small quantities of East Greek and Punic wine), including at Massalia.

By about 540 BCE, wine from Massalian vintners was being produced and exported on a relatively small scale in a form of amphora (Bertucchi Type 1) with a characteristic feldspathic fabric that is virtually indistinguishable in form from some contemporary types from Greek southern Italy: these are often collectively called "*Ionio-Massaliète.*" During the last quarter of the sixth century BCE, exportation of Massalian wine began on a much larger scale in distinctive amphorae with a heavily micaceous fabric that remained characteristic of subsequent Massalian amphora types until the second century BCE (fig. 7.2).[55] This was the first and only case of a Greek colony in the western Mediterranean producing wine for export.[56] Consumption of Etruscan wine declined fairly rapidly in Provence to the extent that it was a minor contributor in a mix of Massalian, other Greek, and Punic wines consumed in the region by the end of the sixth century BCE, and Massalian wine expanded to constitute over 90 percent of amphorae at most sites in this region by the mid–fifth century BCE. Etruscan wine continued to be imported in significant quantities in parts of eastern Languedoc (especially at Lattes) into the first half of the fifth century BCE, but by midcentury Massalian wine was the dominant type in this area as well.

It is uncertain to what extent the decline in Etruscan imports was due to disruption of production caused by political problems in Etruria, or a gradual realignment of local trade networks toward the closer source at Massalia (perhaps influenced by a growing danger from the notorious Ligurian pirates along the coast between Massalia and Etruria). Both factors may have played a role. As Michel Gras has noted, the mid–sixth century BCE was a period of serious internal tensions in Etruria that may have affected the ability of vintners to produce large surpluses for export among the southern cities.[57] It was also about 530 BCE that bucchero nero pottery ceased to be exported outside Etruria. In any case, the fact that Etruscan wine imports declined rapidly at Massalia well before Massalia's own export production began suggests that disruptions to Etruscan production or distribution may have provoked the debut of Massalian wine

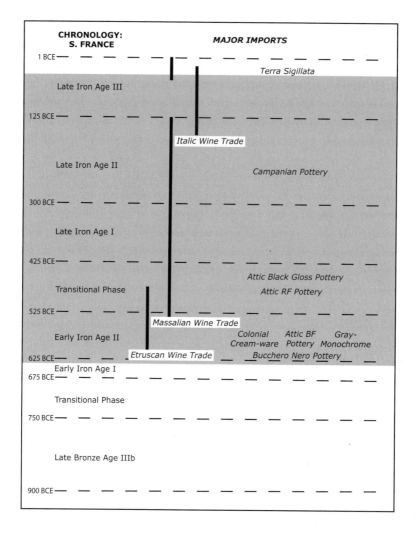

FIGURE 7.1

Chronological succession of major producers of wine consumed in the Rhône basin and corresponding major tableware import series. Gray area represents the period covered in the book.

production rather than the frequently assumed inverse scenario of competition from Massalian production forcing Etruscan wine out of the market.[58]

Whatever the precise reasons for this shift, once local vineyards achieved large-scale production in the last quarter of the sixth century BCE, Massalian vintners remained the overwhelmingly dominant source of wine in the Rhône basin for nearly four centuries. Based on abundant shipwreck data, Luc Long has estimated a minimum annual production of about 9,300 hectoliters (or approximately 46,500 amphorae) of Massalian wine during the fifth and fourth centuries BCE to feed this trade, with the proviso that it may have been two or three times this amount.[59] By way of comparison, Massalian wine was much less significant beyond the Hérault River in western Languedoc and Roussillon,

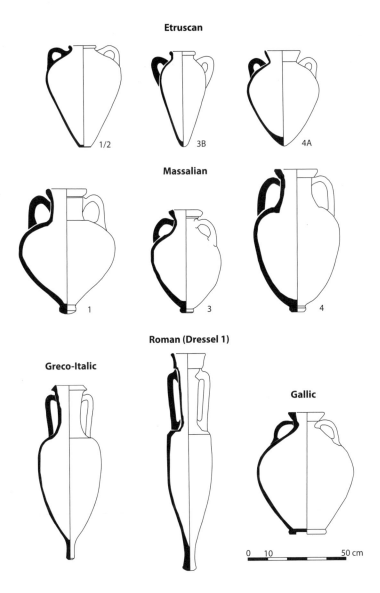

Etruscan

1/2   3B   4A

Massalian

1   3   4

Roman (Dressel 1)

Greco-Italic

Gallic

0   10   50 cm

FIGURE 7.2

Examples of major amphora types for wine consumed in the lower Rhône basin: Etruscan, Massalian, Greco-Italic, Roman Dressel 1, and Gallic. Numbers refer to variant types according to the classification in *Dicocer* (Py 1993b).

where a comparable pattern of sequential dominance did not occur and where a more diversified array of wines remained the common pattern, with relative percentages varying by site. Among these, Massalian wine constituted an important part, but Ibero-Punic wines were consistently more abundant.[60] This was true to an even greater extent at Emporion, where Massalian amphorae never constituted more than about 15 percent of the total amphorae and Ibero-Punic amphorae were consistently between 50 and 75 percent.[61]

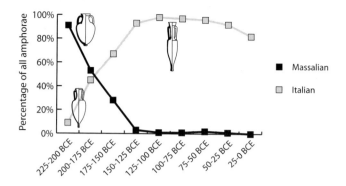

FIGURE 7.3

Sources of wine imported at Lattes from the late third through first centuries BCE: Massalian and Italian amphorae as a percentage of all amphorae from zone 30-35, N = 11,943 shards (data from Sanchez and Adroher 2004).

The second century BCE witnessed another dramatic fluctuation in commodity chains, as Italian wine rapidly displaced Massalian wine as the leading import consumed in the Rhône basin. It was accompanied by Campanian tableware, an Italian black-gloss ware of industrial-scale production that circulated widely throughout the western Mediterranean.[62] Italian wine arrived first in modest quantities during the last half of the third century BCE in the so-called Greco-Italic amphorae of southern Italy, and these increased dramatically in number during the second century BCE (fig. 7.3). Then, from about 125 BCE, Italian wine arrived in even more impressive quantities in the Roman Dressel 1 type of amphorae. At Lattes, for example, Greco-Italic amphorae had already risen from 67 percent of all the wine consumed between 175 and 150 BC to about 93 percent between 150 and 125 BC, thereby displacing Massalian wine in this dominant role a good fifty years before the conquest (fig. 7.3). During the century following the conquest, the figure for Dressel 1 amphorae rose to as high as 98 percent of all the amphorae at the site.[63]

It should be noted that Italian wine also replaced Massalian wine at Massalia.[64] As Michel Bats put it, "Paradoxically, the first people to stop drinking the wine of Marseille were the Marseillais themselves, because the earliest and most rapid decline was at Marseille and Olbia."[65] A handful of imitations of Greco-Italic and Dressel 1 amphorae in Massalian fabric have been found.[66] But, judging by the almost complete lack of Massalian amphorae anywhere in the region between about 125 and 40 BCE among the hundreds of thousands of sherds of Italian amphorae, it appears that export wine production virtually ceased for a couple of generations before restarting again in the last few decades of the first century BCE in the new "Gallic amphora" type *(amphore gauloise)*, for which a production site has been identified on the butte des Carmes.[67] It is difficult to imagine that Massalian vintners voluntarily ceased all wine production en masse during

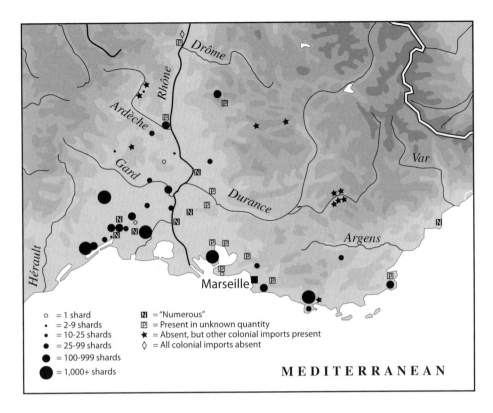

FIGURE 7.4

Quantitative distribution of Massalian amphorae at settlements of the lower Rhône basin, late sixth and early fifth centuries BCE (after Dietler 2005a).

this period simply because of Italian competition. Hence, possible explanations range from a problem of disease in the vineyards to farmers turning temporarily toward some more profitable crops, or Massalian wine continuing to be made but with consumption in bulk in the city's taverns without being transferred to amphorae for export. In the latter case, it would have continued as a local complement to the large quantity of imported Italian wine consumed in the city. When export production resumed, it was part of a general surge of production in Gaul under the Roman Empire.

Prior to the influx of Italian amphorae, wine consumption in Gaul was primarily limited to Mediterranean France (fig. 7.4). Very small quantities were consumed farther north during the late sixth and fifth centuries BCE,[68] but even this trickle had disappeared by the beginning of the fourth century BCE. The trade in Greco-Italic amphorae reintroduced the consumption of wine to temperate Gaul. But it was the Roman conquest of Mediterranean France that set off a major transformation of wine consumption and production patterns that dwarfed anything that had come before.[69]

During a period of about a century, from roughly 125 to 25 BCE, enormous quantities of Roman wine began to flow into Gaul in the ubiquitous Dressel 1 amphorae

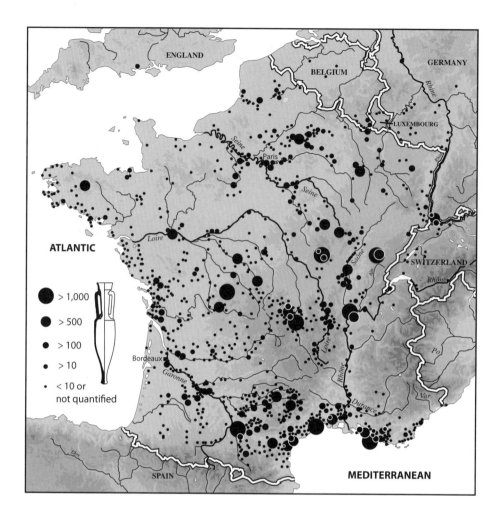

ATLANTIC

> 1,000

> 500

> 100

> 10

< 10 or
not quantified

FIGURE 7.5

Quantitative distribution of Roman Dressel 1 amphorae imports (adapted by author from Poux 2004;
courtesy of Matthieu Poux).

(fig. 7.5). André Tchernia, using evidence from shipwrecks, has offered the conservative estimate that during this hundred-year period at least fifty-five to sixty-five million
of these amphorae (containing twenty to twenty-five liters of wine each) may have
been imported into Gaul. That translates into 550,000 to 650,000 amphorae per year,
which equals twelve to seventeen times the previous estimated total annual production
of Massalia (fig. 7.6).[70] There was also a clear transformation in the scale and nature of
trade. As discussed in chapter 5, aggregate data from shipwrecks of the western Mediterranean indicate that the maximum cargo capacity of merchant ships increased at
least tenfold during this period and average capacity by at least twentyfold. The Roman
wine trade shifted the nature of the enterprise to a direct long-distance, large-scale
monofocal commerce.

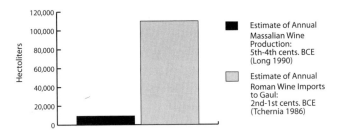

FIGURE 7.6
Estimated annual production of Massalian wine in the fifth to fourth centuries BCE vs. estimated annual Roman wine imports to Gaul from 125 to 25 BCE (these are very rough figures).

Throughout six centuries of colonial encounters, wine remained an imported commodity for indigenous societies of Mediterranean France. Massalia was the only place in Gaul producing wine for trade. Evidence for some limited wine production in indigenous contexts has been found at Lattes beginning in the late third century BCE. This includes a sudden dramatic increase in the quantity of domesticated grape pips found in third century levels of the site and well-preserved traces of vineyards a short distance from the town dating to the late second and first centuries BCE.[71] The grape pip evidence is correlated with a decline in the importation of amphorae at the site, although Massalian wine continued to be consumed in significant quantities.[72] Given that this production at Lattes was not linked to local amphora production, it appears to have been geared toward small-scale local consumption rather than trade. Moreover, this remains a rare instance of even this level of production,[73] and the general absence of indigenous wine making in Mediterranean France is striking, especially given the contrast with Spain where local production of wine and amphorae began at a number of sites within a few generations after the foundation of Phoenician colonies.[74] It was not until after the Roman conquest, and particularly the Augustan period, that significant wine production began in the rest of Gaul.

Massalian Wine Consumption: from the Symposion to the Kapeleion   Before discussing indigenous drinking practices, let us turn to Massalia. By the time Phocaean colonists arrived in southern France, wine had already long replaced other forms of alcoholic beverages as the drink of all social classes in most Greek city-states (except Sparta). This is something that happened in Etruria and Rome as well, but virtually nowhere else: in Mesopotamia and Egypt, for example, beer remained the drink of the common masses and wine consumption was reserved for the elite.[75] Within Greek and Roman societies, status came to be marked not by wine itself, but by the *kinds* of wine consumed, the vessels used, and the contexts of consumption.[76] Wine was already consumed by the elite class in Early Bronze Age Greece and was of major concern in the accounting records of the palaces, although it is not known precisely how early this practice became more generalized.[77] In any case, Greek texts of the last few centuries BCE clearly betray a thoroughly oenophilic cultural attitude in describing other forms of alcohol, such as beer and mead, with curiosity and occasional revulsion. Dionysius of Halicarnassus, for example, described Celtic beer as "a foul-smelling liquor made from barley rotted in water."[78] Greeks were aware that their ancestors had consumed mead, but by the period of the Phocaean settlement in southern France, drinking anything but wine was considered a sign of barbarism.

By this time, Greeks had also developed the practice of separating food and wine consumption, with the *deipnon* (meal) preceding the more heavily ritualized *symposion* (literally, "drinking together"). As noted in chapter 3, the Greek symposion was a male ritual at which the only females permitted were courtesans called *hetaerai*, who provided various forms of entertainment for the men. Drinking took place in a special room called the *andron* (men's room), with the drinkers reclining on *klinai* (couches) placed along three walls on slightly raised platforms in the floor. Depending on the specific occasion, drinking was accompanied by conversation, poetry, music, games, and sexual activity. The symposion was the preeminent ritual space for the construction of male civic community and status. The symposion also evolved over time in its social significance. It was originally a ceremony exclusive to and symbolic of a wealthy landed aristocracy, and this was still largely the case as late as the fifth century BCE. But it was gradually emulated by members of other social orders and eventually became simply a common ritual of urban Greek society, at least among the more affluent citizen class.[79] The diffusion of this practice beyond the aristocracy resulted in a gradual devaluation of its aristocratic aura and its association with male citizen status in general.[80]

Social distinctions were, however, still signaled by the quality and expense of the wine consumed, which were largely dependent on its place of origin and age.[81] Wine was considered valuable property: cellars were often listed in the inventory of an estate and wine was among the property confiscated from wealthy men condemned to death.[82] Initially, during the first half of the sixth century BCE, about 80 to 90 percent of the wine consumed at Massalia was imported from Etruria, with the remaining amount coming from Chios, Klazomenai, Lesbos, Milet, Samos, Athens, Corinth, southern Italy, and Punic Spain.[83] From the late sixth century BCE on, Massalia's own vineyards began to furnish an increasing percentage of its consumption, although at the end of the century imported Greek wines (especially from southern Italy in the so-called Corinthian B amphorae) had risen to constitute about 40 percent of all amphorae. But even after Massalian amphorae grew to constitute over 60 percent of the amphorae found during the fifth century BCE, wines continued to be imported from a variety of Greek cities, particularly from regions with a reputation for quality (such as Chios, Lesbos, Thasos, and parts of southern Italy), as well as from Etruria and Punic Spain.[84] The contribution of Massalian wine may actually have been higher than 60 percent, if one assumes that some lower-quality wine may have been sold in bulk in the city. But the point is that Massalia continued to import substantial quantities of wine even once it had become a major exporter.

FIGURE 7.7
Attic red-figure pottery painting showing symposium equipment (from Sparkes 1991; courtesy of the British Museum).

The symposion was not only framed architectonically in a particular space, but it required a standardized set of equipment centered on a large mixing vessel, either a *crater* or *lebes* (fig. 7.7). Wine and water were mixed in the crater by the master of the symposion *(symposiarch)*, then a ladle was used to fill a pitcher *(oinochoe)* with the mixture, and it was poured into the individual drinking cups by attendant slaves. Hence, the mixture was a communal affair rather than an individual one. Mixing water with wine was more than a question of taste to the Greeks. It was intimately tied up with the meaning and philosophy of drinking.[85] Failure to observe this practice was a certain distinguishing mark of the barbarian or the deviant and was even considered dangerous.[86] Disapproving Greek references to the practice of Celtic peoples drinking wine neat offer clear evidence of their failure to accept one of the essential features of Greek wine-drinking custom.[87]

Of course not all (or even most) of the wine in a Greek city was consumed at symposia. Another common location was the neighborhood tavern *(kapeleion)*. These establishments are well attested in ancient literature, but they have generally been neglected by modern scholars, who have devoted much more attention to the ritualized symposion (although one tavern has been identified archaeologically at the Athenian agora).[88] These shops sold both wine in bulk and individual portions of wine mixed with water for consumption in-house, and sometimes accompanying food as well. From at least the fifth century BCE, and probably earlier, they appear to have been a prevalent feature of the urban landscape, catering generally, though not exclusively, to common people, foreigners, and slaves. Both tavern keepers *(kapeloi)* and barmaids *(kapelides)* were often slaves. Drinking in these establishments was far more informal than at symposia and the wine was a commodity with a price rather than a sign of commensal hospitality and generosity.[89] We have no specific evidence of such taverns in Massalia, but given their ubiquity at other Greek cities, Massalia's character as a merchant port, and the social hierarchies known to have existed in the city, it is reasonable to assume that they would have been there to serve the needs of those who were excluded from the symposia of wealthy citizens (foreign merchants, resident metics, freedmen, slaves, poorer citizens, etc.). It is also reasonable to speculate that local Gauls who were trading or working at Massalia would have been drawn to these establishments.

Aside from recreational/social consumption, wine was also commonly used for both medicinal and religious functions in Greek society. Libations of various kinds (over altars, at the symposion, for the departure of warriors, etc.) were an important part of religious life.[90] Moreover, wine was shot through with religious significance, being particularly associated with Dionysus, who was celebrated by various annual festivals. Wine was employed for many medicinal purposes, including digestives, antiseptics, tonics, fever reducers, and the like. These were discussed in some detail by Hippocrates in the fifth century BCE and later by the Roman author Pliny.[91]

Indigenous Consumption Patterns: The Logic of Choice Having argued earlier that the patterns of consumption one sees in the archaeological record are a genuine reflection of consumer choices, the question then becomes how can we explain this highly selective set of choices? What was the social and cultural logic underlying this demand for wine? Why would indigenous societies of the region, despite their general lack of interest in Etruscan and Greek goods and culture, have developed such a rapid and avid thirst for this alien beverage? Answering this question requires us to undertake a closer contextual examination of the consumption data, as well as to explore the specific properties of wine and approach it comparatively as a particular form of the more general food category of alcoholic beverages.[92]

From the earliest period when a wine trade is visible at archaeological sites in the Rhône basin, the quantities of imported amphorae at settlements are significant. The figures vary between regions and sites, and there are changes over time that mark fluctuations in trade, but a significant flow of wine was one of the most consistent features of the colonial situation. Interpreting the details of these wine consumption data, however, requires a brief word about methods. Given the discrepancies in the sizes of excavated areas at different sites and the resultant ceramic samples, comparison of raw counts of shards or minimum number of vessels among sites are not sufficiently informative for the kind of analysis attempted here. Far more useful are *relative* measures such as the ratio of amphora shards to all ceramic shards, and the relative percentages of different types of amphorae found together. No method is without problems, but as long as one bases the analysis on sites with large samples from good stratigraphic contexts, these measures give a better indication of the importance of different classes of ceramics in contemporary situations and a better image of consumption.[93]

Aggregate data from eastern Languedoc show that Etruscan amphorae constituted about 8 to 10 percent of all ceramics on most of the limited number of settlements where they are found in the late seventh and early sixth century BCE.[94] These have been recovered from both small settlements along the coastal lagoons (such as La Rallongue, Tonnerre I, Camp Redon, and Forton) and sites on the edge of the garrigue zone (La Liquière) as much as thirty kilometers from the sea. Some Etruscan amphorae are also found at the site of Le Marduel, about fifty kilometers from the sea, but they constitute less than 2 percent of the ceramics. Etruscan amphorae gradually spread to several other sites in this zone (such as Les Gardies, Font de la Coucou, etc.) during the rest of the sixth century BCE. These were essentially the only amphorae found at sites of the region until the influx of Massalian amphorae during the last quarter of the sixth century BCE. They were originally accompanied by much smaller quantities of Etruscan bucchero nero tableware, almost exclusively kantharos drinking cups (about 97 percent). These, and a few other drinking cups (Etrusco-Corinthian, Ionian) constituted at most about 1 or 2 percent of the ceramics at these sites in the very early phase of trade.[95] During the fifth century BCE, the number of sites with Etruscan amphorae expanded to include nearly all settlements within about forty kilometers of the coast, but the relative quantities of Etruscan amphorae declined steadily at most sites of this region in favor of Massalian amphorae, such that they generally constituted less than 1 to 3 percent of all ceramics and less than 10 percent of all amphorae.[96] Lattes, and a few settlements in its vicinity, however, continued to receive Etruscan wine in significant amounts, with Lattes clearly serving as a major trade center for these imports. The fact that Etruscan amphorae constitute over 80 percent of all ceramics at Lattes during the first quarter of the fifth century BCE, as opposed to less than 2 percent at the nearby site of Espeyran, gives a proper sense of the stark contrast between these two sites, but is slightly misleading in the overwhelming dominance of amphorae in the Lattes assemblage. This is because the levels from this period excavated so far at the site consist predominantly of the house of Etruscan traders, with their storeroom full of amphorae. Espeyran, in contrast, was a trade center on the vanguard of the wave of Massalian imports.[97] A few other sites of the region show a diminished but still relatively strong continuation of Etruscan wine imports, though with a concurrent rising quantity of Massalian wine. At these settlements, including Les Gardies, Nîmes, Villevieille, Mauressip, and La Jouffe, Etruscan amphorae now represents about 15 to 35 percent of the total amphorae, with most of the rest being from Massalia.[98] Even at Lattes the figures eventually show a rapid decline, with Etruscan amphorae representing less than 6 percent of ceramics by the mid–fifth century BCE.

A similar pattern emerges from the data in Provence, albeit with even greater initial quantities of Etruscan wine. At coastal sites of the late seventh and early sixth century BCE, such as Saint-Blaise, L'Arquet, and Tamaris, roughly 20 to 35 percent of all ceramic shards are Etruscan amphorae, and these are overwhelmingly the most common type of amphora (small quantities of East Greek and Punic wine were also consumed, especially at Saint-Blaise).[99] Farther east at Mont Garou, however, Etruscan amphorae were only about 3 percent of ceramics during this period, despite being near the coast. At Saint-Pierre-les-Martigues, the levels of the second half of the sixth century BCE show a pattern of decline of Etruscan amphorae to about 12.6 percent of all shards and a rise of Massalian amphorae to about 11.2 percent, with a mix of smaller quantities of Greek and Punic amphorae.[100]

In both regions, from the early sixth century BCE on, the bucchero nero kantharoi were quickly supplemented in the range of imported drinking ceramics by Cream-ware and Gray-monochrome ware produced at Massalia and, within a couple of decades, at various indigenous workshops as well. Attic black-figure drinking cups also began to be consumed in small, but significant, quantities.[101]

The increase in Massalian amphorae in the Rhône basin was not only relative to declining Etruscan wine, but in many cases (especially west of the Rhône) represents a significant increase in absolute terms as well. In eastern Languedoc, at the presumed native emporium sites of Lattes and Espeyran, Massalian amphorae had grown to constitute around 50 and 64 percent of all ceramics, respectively, during the late fifth and early fourth centuries BCE.[102] Even at sites of the Vaunage basin (thirty kilometers from the sea) and at Le Marduel (fifty kilometers from the sea), the figure reached about 24 percent during this period. Moreover, Massalian amphorae constituted well over 90 percent of all the amphorae found. On the other side of the Rhône in western Provence, consumption of Massalian wine was increasing steadily, but until the mid–fifth century BCE it was still only one of a mix of types (Etruscan, other Greek, Punic) that were well represented at sites south of the Durance. At Saint-Blaise, Massalian amphorae constituted about 10.8 percent of the total amphorae around 540 to 520 BCE and about 37.1 percent by the end of the century, while the relative quantities of amphorae to all ceramics actually declined somewhat from 21.5 to 16.5 percent for the two periods. At Les Baou de Saint-Marcel (only eight kilometers from Marseille), Massalian amphorae were only about 23.4 percent of all amphorae during the late sixth century BCE, and amphorae in general were about 11.8 percent of all ceramics. At the emporium site of Arles, Massalian amphorae reached about 50 percent of the total amphorae by 500 BCE.[103] By the mid–fifth century BCE, however, Massalian amphorae were overwhelmingly dominant numerically: they constituted about 93 percent of the amphorae at Arles and nearly 100 percent at l'Île de Martigues. Even at Le Pègue, 130 kilometers north of Marseille, Massalian amphorae had risen to about 42.7 percent of all ceramics by the late fifth century BCE and were the only type present. They subsequently declined during the first half of the fourth century BCE to about 25.4 percent of all ceramics and were down to a mere 5 percent in the following phase.[104]

A period of retraction in the volume and geographic reach of the Massalian wine trade (though certainly not its near exclusivity among types of wine consumed) has also been signaled for sites in eastern Languedoc beginning in the fourth century BCE.[105] After a period of expansion from the late sixth to the end of the fifth century BCE, the

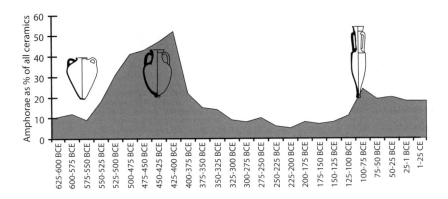

FIGURE 7.8

Regional changes in wine consumption: wine amphorae as a percentage of all ceramics at settlements of eastern Languedoc (after Py 1990a). Amphora drawings represent the changing principle sources of this wine: Etruscan, Massalian, and Italic.

quantities (that is, the relative quantities of amphorae as a percentage of all ceramics at sites) began to drop off fairly quickly from about 400 to 375 BCE at sites of the interior (Le Marduel, the Vaunage basin, etc.) (fig. 7.8). At Gailhan, for example, amphorae (over 98 percent Massalian) declined from about 24 percent of all ceramics in the last quarter of the fifth century BCE to about 9 percent during the first half of the fourth century BCE.[106] However, this seems to have been a phenomenon related to the distribution links between the coast and the interior, as consumption at the coastal emporia such as Lattes and Espeyran remained brisk and fairly steady for another century or so. It was not until the mid–third century BCE that one sees signs of a decline in consumption of Massalian wine at the coastal sites.[107]

Despite the gradual decline in the overall volume of consumption of Massalian wine at sites of the interior and, eventually, along the coast, it continued to be the nearly exclusive type consumed until the huge influx of Italian wine in the second century BCE (or late third century BCE at Massalia itself). For example, 90 percent of the amphorae at l'Île de Martigues were Massalian as late as 250 BCE, and a nearly identical percentage of those at Arles, Nîmes, Lattes, Espeyran, and many other sites were Massalian as late as the early second century BCE.[108] As noted, that situation changed radically from about 175 to 150 BCE with a rapid increase in Greco-Italic amphorae, and then from 125 BCE with the flood of Roman Dressel 1 amphorae and the disappearance of Massalian amphorae altogether.

These figures give some sense of the shifting quantitative dimensions of wine consumption over the course of the six centuries of colonial encounters, suggesting regional patterns and variations among sites. But what do these patterns mean in terms of the role of wine in the daily lives of people of the region? This is a question best answered by shifting scales and looking more closely at the microlevel of individual settlements.

Let us begin with the observation that throughout the region wine consumption appears to have rapidly become a generalized practice. That is, it was not restricted to particular kinds of settlements or particular houses within settlements. As noted, much more wine was consumed at some coastal sites (Lattes, Cailar, Espeyran, etc.) than at settlements of the interior, but within a few generations after the beginning of the wine trade virtually every town, village, and hamlet shows evidence of access to some quantities of wine.[109] Moreover, as sites from La Liquière to l'Île de Martigues, to Lattes demonstrate, from the earliest period of the wine trade through the end of the Iron Age, amphorae are found abundantly in all houses on these sites: there are no exclusive patterns of distribution within settlements that would indicate restricted access by some households.

The significance of this consumption pattern is highlighted by contrasting it with the highly restrictive pattern for imported wine and Greek and Etruscan drinking gear in Early Iron Age contexts in the western Hallstatt zone of Burgundy and southwestern Germany.[110] There, the imported objects were also centered on drinking, but the nature of the objects and the contexts in which they are found were quite different. The extremely limited number of wine amphorae and somewhat more abundant Attic drinking ceramics that have been found (with a much higher percentage of craters than in southern France) are largely confined to the so-called *Fürstensitze*, settlements that were seats of highly centralized regional political power (such as Mont Lassois and the Heuneburg). Similarly, the ostentatiously large Greek bronze drinking gear (such as the famous Vix crater and the Hochdorf *lebes*) were confined to a small number of the largest and most lavishly furnished tumulus burials with a standardized iconography of elite status, the so-called *Fürstengräber*, that were clustered around these settlements (fig. 7.9).[111] These goods clearly did not circulate among the population at large: they were appropriated by the ruling elite and incorporated into a set of "diacritical feasting" practices that were used to symbolically mark class boundaries.[112]

In contemporary Mediterranean France, the imports were far more numerous, far more widely consumed on settlements, and far less spectacular: there is no equivalent to the Vix crater or Hochdorf lebes, even though these objects probably arrived in the Hallstatt region by passing up the Rhône valley from Massalia. Nor is there any equivalent to the ostentatious Hallstatt Fürstengräber in which these items were interred. Moreover, Greek and Etruscan imports did not play a very significant role in Early Iron Age funerary practices in the Rhône basin. They certainly did west of the Hérault River, in western Languedoc, where, for example, amphorae were used as ossuaries at the cemetery of Saint-Julien at Pézenas. But in the Early Iron Age Rhône basin, amphorae are generally absent from graves and other objects are only sporadically found. Aside from a series of modest Etruscan boss-rimmed bronze basins that are known from several funerary contexts in the Rhône basin and the Alpine region, Greek and Etruscan objects were unusual in graves, few in number, and not associated in any discernable way with a consistent iconography of status distinction.[113] The contrast can be nicely summed up by

FIGURE 7.9
The Vix crater, a 1.63 m tall Greek wine-mixing vessel of bronze found in a late Hallstatt tumulus burial in Burgundy.

noting that more amphorae have been recovered from individual small villages in the interior of the Rhône basin (Gailhan, for example) than have been recovered from all the Hallstatt Fürstensitze combined. The difference is between a trade in a standardized commodity (amphorae of wine) that supplied widespread open consumption at settlements throughout a region and the highly restricted use of a few "singular"[114] exotic drinking vessels that framed elite diacritical feasting practices without an importation of wine sufficient to constitute genuine trade.

But what more can we say about the specific nature of wine consumption in the Rhône basin and about its consequences? Let us look more closely at the data from Lattes. In rapid general summary terms, initial imports at Lattes consisted, as elsewhere, primarily of Etruscan wine amphorae, and these were rapidly replaced by Massalian amphorae during the second quarter of the fifth century BCE. Massalian amphorae then constituted over 95 percent of the amphorae at the site until the second century BCE, when these were replaced by Italian amphorae: first Greco-Italic and then Roman Dressel 1 types. By the late third century BCE, wine imports were augmented to some degree by local wine production at Lattes. This flow of different wines was accompanied by the consumption of some imported tableware as well: initially Etruscan bucchero nero drinking cups and pitchers, Attic drinking cups, and drinking ceramics made at Massalia in two series known as Cream-ware and Gray-monochrome. These imported drinking ceramics were integrated into the existing ceramic repertoire as a complementary function-specific set that had no influence on the rest of the range of indigenous CNT forms, which continued to be produced and used in the traditional style. Gray-monochrome ceramics dropped out of the mix by the fourth century BCE, but Cream-ware continued to be imported for centuries. Attic ceramics changed from black-figure to red-figure to black-gloss types, and these were eventually replaced during the third century BCE by Campanian black-gloss ceramics (along with other derivative wares).

As noted earlier, in quantitative terms, the amphorae are particularly impressive. By the fourth century BCE, Massalian amphorae constituted as much as 50 percent of the total ceramic assemblage at the site. Moreover, the shards of these amphorae are ubiquitous throughout the town. As with the imported drinking cups and pitchers, they are found in abundance in all houses during every period at the site, indicating that consumption was not restricted to a particular class, category, or group of people. Although amphorae were occasionally reused as containers for ash (and perhaps other storage purposes as well), the shards are commonly found as domestic debris in houses and streets, they are found ubiquitously on house floors and in rubble levels, and they were used for various purposes such as constructing the foundations of hearths and ovens, solidifying zones of passage, providing support for walls, and so forth (fig. 7.10). This would seem to indicate that, once the contents were consumed, the amphorae were not highly valued objects in and of themselves. Rather, they were considered disposable containers that could be broken up and used for a variety of mundane household projects.

Based on the number of amphorae found per area excavated, Py has estimated that more than 111,000 Massalian amphorae, representing over 22,000 hectoliters of wine, may have been consumed at the site during the fourth century BCE alone.[115] However, these figures need to be put in perspective. The average cargo size for the rather small trading ships of this period was about sixty amphorae, and (given an average volume of about twenty liters per Massalian amphora for the types used during the fourth century BCE), these Lattarian consumption totals would represent the discharging of about nineteen ships per year at the port of Lattara (if the entire cargo was unloaded). That would mean that the arrival of wine would have been sufficient to be a regularly anticipated occurrence about every 2.5 to 3 weeks, although such voyages would almost certainly have been clustered in certain seasons that favored sailing without risk rather than spread evenly over the year. However, given an estimated population of about 1,400 people, the average annual consumption of wine would have been in the range of only about 33 liters per adult, or about 4 amphorae per household per year.[116]

In comparison to the typical alcohol consumption figures for small-scale societies found in ethnographic studies, that amount is relatively little, especially if one gives credence to the ubiquitous stereotypic image of "Celts" as heavy drinkers in classical texts. Plato, for example, writing in the fourth century BCE, included the Celts among a group of six barbarian peoples noted for drunkenness.[117] And Diodorus Siculus, writing during the first century BCE about imported wine among the Celts, noted that they drank it unmixed and voraciously, after which they "fall into a stupor or into a maniacal

FIGURE 7.10

Remains of (a) a Massalian amphora crushed in place and (b) a collapsed storage vase of minimally fired daub on the floor of a room against the west wall of house 52101 at Lattes. Fragments of charcoal and ash dot the floor (UFRAL).

disposition."[118] Both Polybius and Plutarch also noted an excessive Celtic fondness for drink that sometimes brought disaster after a battle.[119] Granted, these accounts, much like those of European colonial officials in Africa, were a product of cultural misunderstanding of alien drinking practices and anxiety about uncontrollable disorder among the colonial Other. Granted also that these generalizations about "Celts" are based on a rather vague ethnic categorization of peoples who were actually quite heterogeneous. But the point is that there is no reason to expect the inhabitants of the Rhône basin (including the people of Lattes) to have been unusually modest in their consumption of alcohol. That would surely have struck Greeks and Romans, for whom robust drinking was a central part of their own social life, as even more curious than drunkenness.

As ethnographic research has shown, alcohol is a fundamentally important part of the social, economic and political life of most societies around the world, and this is a social fact with a deep antiquity.[120] What is more, the amount of alcohol consumed and the quantities of crops generally devoted to the production of drink are significant.[121] Where such things have been measured, estimates of a minimum of 15 to 30 percent of the total yearly grain or root crop devoted to the production of alcohol are common for ethnographic studies of small-scale societies.[122] In terms of per capita consumption, estimates range from 150 liters of millet beer per year among the Kofyar of Nigeria[123] to 236 liters of traditional beer per year in the city of Ouagadougou in Burkina Faso, with half the annual grain consumption for a family being in the form of beer (fig. 7.11).[124] Similarly, among the Koma of Cameroon sorghum beer provides about one-third of the total calories consumed during the year; and hosting an age grade ceremony requires

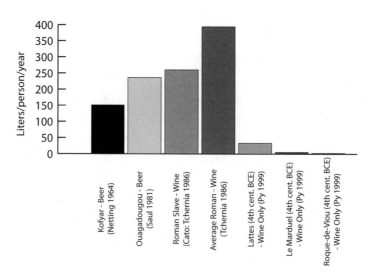

FIGURE 7.11

Comparison of annual per capita alcohol consumption figures from several sources.

about 490 liters of beer made from about 100 kilograms of cereal, a cattle dance requires 525 liters of beer, and a woman's funeral requires about 260 liters of beer.[125] In Manga, a Mossi town of about seven thousand inhabitants in Burkina Faso, memorial ceremonies called *kuure* are the occasions for the most lavish beer feasts. In one week, five kuure were held in one ward, consuming 1,900 kilograms of red sorghum (with seven cartloads of wood—1,400 kilograms—required for brewing and cooking for one of these feasts alone). During a single dry season, within the town as a whole about ten tons of sorghum were converted into beer for these memorial feasts alone, with a total annual festive consumption estimated at fourteen tons of grain brewed for beer.[126]

If these impressive figures can be taken as even crudely representative, then the average wine consumption figure at Lattara of thirty-three liters per adult per year would be miniscule in comparison. This would equal only about 20 percent of the average household needs among the Kofyar and only 14 percent of the average consumption at Ouagadougou. Moreover, the four amphorae of wine an average Lattarian household would acquire in a year would not even provide a third of the drink needed to host a single Koma woman's funeral and only 16 percent of the requirements for a Koma cattle dance. We can also compare these consumption figures to those estimated by André Tchernia for ancient Romans. Cato, who had a reputation for being stingy, believed that one needed to allot 10 amphorae (or about 260 liters) of wine per slave per year. Tchernia noted that a very frugal Roman might consume one *setier* (0.54 liter) per day, or 197 liters per year, and average consumption for adult males in general was probably double that amount.[127] The average wine consumption figures for Lattara again pale in comparison: about 13 percent of the quantity considered minimally necessary for a slave.

Hence, although the overall quantities of wine consumed at Lattes had grown to significant proportions during the fourth century BCE, these comparative data suggest that, even a couple of centuries after the beginning of the wine trade, it is highly unlikely that wine was more than a supplement to other indigenous forms of alcohol, such as beer and mead. It is important also to remember that Lattara was one of a class of coastal towns that were privileged in their consumption of wine: settlements farther toward the interior drank far less of it. For example, the wine consumption figures that Michel Py has calculated for Le Marduel and Roque de Viou, two settlements about fifty and thirty kilometers inland from the sea, are only 15 percent and 7 percent, respectively, of that for Lattara, although one can safely assume that their total consumption rates for all forms of alcohol would have been relatively similar.[128] This does not mean that wine was not a *symbolically* important element of commensality for indigenous peoples of southern Gaul, or that it had not become in some sense a social "necessity." But it is highly unlikely that traders in Massalian wine had anything like a monopoly on the alcohol consumed in the region. Hence, any dependence on Massalian wine would not have been attributable to its having become the sole source of alcohol. Rather, it would have relied on the culturally defined significance attributed to its being a *particular kind* of alcohol.

Wine continued to be only a complement to native drinks even during the period of the massive influx of Italian wine into Gaul during the century following the Roman conquest of Mediterranean France. What is striking to realize is that the ratio of amphorae as a percentage of all ceramics at the site actually was somewhat less following the Roman conquest than during the fourth century BCE, the period for which a quantitative assessment was given above (fig. 7.12). During the period from 125 to 25 BCE amphorae ranged from about 28 percent to a high of 46 percent of all ceramics, depending on the quarter century period considered, whereas during the fourth century BCE, they ranged from about 45 to 63 percent of all ceramics, again depending on the quarter century period.

What this means is that, although the overall quantity of wine being imported into Gaul as a whole had increased dramatically during this period of the Roman wine trade, this was not necessarily the case for individual towns in the Mediterranean zone. In other words, imported wine had still by no means replaced indigenous drinks in these contexts, and certainly not in the northern regions of Gaul either. To be sure, Lattes had begun to produce some wine for its own consumption by the late third century BCE, and this fact should be brought into the equation as well. But contemporary Greek and Roman texts confirm the continued consumption of native drinks in the region. Diodorus Siculus, for example, noted a drink called *zythos* (a barley beer) and mead made from honeycombs, Pliny recorded the name of *cervesia* for the Celtic grain beer, and Posidonius described a wheat beer with honey called *corma*.[129] Although these authors were not very specific about the precise region within Gaul that these observations describe, southern France is the most likely area. It is known, for example, that Posidonius traveled there, while he is unlikely to have been able to venture much farther north into

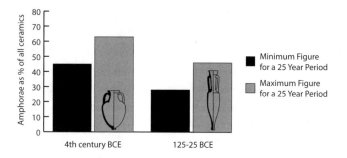

Massalian wine imports (fourth century BCE) versus Roman wine imports (second to first centuries BCE) at Lattes. Wine amphorae as a percentage of all ceramics, with figures calculated by quarter-century periods over a hundred-year span and lowest and highest periods shown for each.

free Gaul during the early first century BCE. This tends to confirm the idea that, as with Etruscan and Greek wine, the consumption of Roman wine in Gaul before Augustus was not an index or vector of something called "Romanization." Rather, in Mediterranean France it was the substitution of one alien source of wine for another—a shift in the commodity chain—but a shift in which the new wine continued to be consumed according to local practices rather than in Roman fashion. In Gaul north of the Mediterranean zone, it was the addition of an exotic form of alcohol to an existing repertoire and its incorporation, again, into traditional feasting practices. Both classical descriptions of Celtic drinking events and recent excavations of feasting sites by Matthieu Poux in central Gaul,[130] demonstrate clearly two things: (1) that Gallic drinking rituals continued local practices and bore little resemblance to what took place in the Roman *cena* or *triclinium*, and (2) that Romans and Greeks themselves saw the Gallic consumption of wine as a marker of cultural distinctiveness rather than convergence.

Why Wine? Distinctive Properties of an Alien Beverage Several features of wine could have made it desirable for the native peoples of Mediterranean France and could help to explain both its initial acceptance and the persistently single-minded demand for it over time. First is the fact that wine would have had a much better "shelf life" and transport possibilities than grain beer and mead. Without modern bottling and preservation techniques, these latter forms of alcohol generally degrade within a few days of fermentation.[131] Wine, in contrast, can be kept for years in a sealed amphora (as much as a quarter century for the best wines of antiquity[132]). Hence, wine could be stockpiled in consumable form for use at feasts in a way that other forms of alcohol could not. Wine could also be transported over long distances and traded more easily than other forms of alcohol, giving it a potential value outside of consumption contexts as a form of gift or commodity. This is one reason that ancient wineries have been identified in many archaeological contexts, while very few large-scale breweries have been found. Brewing was generally a ubiquitous practice performed on a domestic level because transport was not possible. It also had to be performed many times throughout the year as the need arose, because beer could not be stored. Where one has found large beer production sites, as in Egypt and Peru, these are state facilities designed for hosting large-scale feasts, where the beer was consumed immediately by a large crowd assembled at an adjacent site.[133] Wine, on the other hand, is made once a year from a seasonal crop, and it is stored in a fermented, ready-to-consume form. Wineries are specialized-commodity production facilities separated from consumption sites, and tend to be more archaeologically visible because of this feature.[134] These properties, as with distilled spirits in modern contexts, would have assured that wine would tend to produce more complex economic linkages than other forms of alcohol in antiquity, with geographically and temporally extended commodity chains that traversed different regimes of value.

Wine also undoubtedly had a higher alcohol content than indigenous drinks (part of the reason for its better preservation qualities). This quality increased its psychoactive effects and, potentially, its value in ritual contexts where the consciousness-transforming properties of inebriation are important. Another feature of attraction is that wine could be acquired by means other than agricultural production and culinary labor—that is, through exchange transactions with people outside the local community. This feature could be particularly important where the traditional means of access to participation in the commensal politics of feasting and labor mobilization depended on controlling a large agricultural surplus and culinary labor base.[135] In effect, wine would enlarge the field of political competition by allowing acquisition and accumulation of alcohol through exchange of goods and labor with strangers, much as happened in many modern colonial contexts with the advent of wage labor and the introduction of distilled spirits. Finally, the exotic origin of wine may have been of symbolic significance, despite the fact that, in terms of consumption, it had become a thoroughly "indigenized" beverage in southern France already by the fifth century BCE. That is, although it had become a ubiquitous element of indigenous feasting rituals, by virtue of its alien production, it was a commodity that demonstrated the power to extract benefits from an external world.

These features suggest why wine may have been singularly attractive to native peoples of Mediterranean France who were otherwise indifferent to Etruscan and Greek goods and culture. But to understand the ways in which wine was adapted to local consumption practices, and the ultimate consequences of consumption, it is necessary to consider the practice of feasting that provided the mechanism for the social acceptance of, and desire for, wine. In the ethnographic examples cited, despite the impressive quantities of resources devoted to the production of alcohol, such drink was not usually a part of daily consumption in the household. It was generally something reserved for the ritual festive events that are crucial for social reproduction and political action. Indeed, the presence of alcohol is often one of the prominent indexical signs that mark feasts off from quotidian meals as ritual events.[136] As Ivan Karp noted for the Iteso of East Africa, "Beer drinking is a social mechanism for indicating that situations are special, and Iteso conceptions of festivity are defined in terms of beer drinking."[137] Or as one Tanzanian informant succinctly summed it up to Justin Willis, "If there's no beer, it's not a ritual."[138]

Without reiterating in detail what I have published elsewhere on this theme, it is crucial to emphasize how ubiquitous and important feasts are in the social, political, and economic life of small-scale societies.[139] These are ritual consumption events in which social relationships are formed and maintained; events that both create and define a sense of community and establish relationships between individuals, as well as defining boundaries and social categories. They are also arenas in which individuals operate politically to define their social position by building prestige and a reputation for generosity. In some contexts, this can involve overt agonistic competition, but more often it involves a more subtle process of keeping up responsibilities and demonstrating the expected spirit of generosity. Feasts also frequently serve as the nodal contexts that articulate regional exchange systems: commensal hospitality establishes relationships between exchange partners, affines, or political leaders and provides the social ambiance for the exchange of valuables, bridewealth, and other goods that circulate through a region. Feasts may also provide the main context for the arbitration of disputes, the passing of legal judgments, and the public acting out of sanctions that maintain social control within a community. In the important religious sphere, feasts also serve to provide links to the gods or ancestors that can also be used to define the structure of relations between social groups or categories within a region or community and to shape conceptions of value. In the form of work-feasts, they also provide a crucial mechanism for the process of collective labor mobilization that underlies the political economy.[140]

Given these considerations, it is possible to imagine how and why wine was assimilated into the feasting rituals of the peoples of Mediterranean France. It would have served as a complement to existing forms of alcohol, bolstering the potential scale of generosity of influential individuals who were already adept operators of commensal politics, and opening the field of play to others (for example, younger men) who had previously been at a competitive disadvantage. Wine never completely replaced traditional beers and other drinks in this domain, but it may have been viewed as a special form that became appropriate (or even necessary) for certain kinds of feasts. It may have become an indexical sign of certain categories of ritual, or it may have been simply a part of all feasting rituals. Given the generally nonhierarchical structure of societies of the Rhône basin, at least during the early centuries of the encounter (see chapter 4), and the evidence of widespread consumption of wine within settlements, it did not become something that marked classes in a restrictive "diacritical" feasting pattern. Rather, it seems to have been employed in the kinds of "empowering" feasting mode that would have been used by all households in community politics and labor mobilization. Where somewhat more concentrated forms of power emerged, it may also have shifted in relative scale into a "patron-role" mode of asymmetrical hospitality obligations, but its use never became monopolized.[141]

Consequences What were the consequences of appropriating this foreign beverage and assimilating it into local institutions and practices? First, let me reiterate that, for native peoples of the Rhône basin, throughout roughly the first six centuries of the evolving colonial situation, wine remained largely an imported commodity produced in Italy or at Massalia. Wine was only a complement to indigenous drinks, but it was consumed regularly in impressive quantities and it constituted the principle substance articulating relations between Massalia and the indigenous peoples of the region. Wine consumption certainly did not produce anything like the kind of emulative "Hellenization" or imitation of the symposion sometimes imagined by earlier scholars. But it did draw indigenous peoples, Etruscans, Massalians, and Italians into ever more entangled economic and political relationships.

For its part, Massalia was essentially a consumer of imported wine for about two generations after its founding. But when its principal supply from southern Etruria declined rapidly, Massalian vintners began expanding local production and even began to export wine on a growing scale. Hence, over a period of about 150 years, Massalia's situation shifted from being a dependent consumer of imported wine to the dominant supplier of wine to the regional market. Moreover, as the population of the city grew, it became increasingly dependent on its vineyards to provide the means of acquiring its staple grain supply through trade. The limited, poor, and arid soils of Massalia's chora were better suited for vines than grain, and as vineyards expanded to meet the thriving demand for trade provided by the thirst of native peoples, they would have diminished further the meager capacity for grain production, thereby further increasing the demand for imported grain within the city.

The consequences of this situation for Massalia's increasing entanglement in an evolving regional political economy with a set of complex mutual dependencies are clear. But the situation is yet more complicated. During the four centuries that its wines dominated the indigenous market in the Rhône basin, Massalia was still simultaneously importing some fine wines from elsewhere in the Mediterranean, a demand created by the importance of wine in the competition over internal status distinctions that was played out in the evolving ritual of the symposion. For reasons that are still not entirely clear, Massalian tastes turned dramatically toward Italian wine at the end of the third century BCE, and its own vineyards ceased to supply the city (at least in higher-quality wine in amphorae—the taverns may still have been flowing with Massalian bulk wine). Shortly thereafter, the export production of its vintners declined in the face of an expanding consumption of Italian wine at other settlements of the region. And they stopped exporting wine altogether after the Roman conquest of Mediterranean France, only to resume again as the vanguard of a surge of production throughout Mediterranean France and then the rest of Gaul under the Roman Empire (discussed later). The potentially disastrous decline of exports from Massalian vintners may have been ameliorated by the fact that the Roman conquest suddenly enlarged the Massalian chora considerably. For the first time it reached to the Rhône delta, thus allowing Massalian farmers to spread over an expanded territory with soils better suited to growing grain. The fact that Massalia began exporting wine again around 40 BCE may, conversely, be linked to the loss of some or all of this territory following its defeat by Caesar in the Roman Civil War of 49 BCE. This would help to explain the rather puzzling disappearance of Massalian wine exports for a period of about eighty-five years, between 125 and 40 BCE, a seemingly curious phenomenon for a city whose economy had previously depended to such an extent on its vintners. The timing, in any case, seems highly suggestive.

Let us now shift the focus to consequences for indigenous societies. Given the earlier discussion, one can understand that wine was first seized on as an artifact that could be deployed in traditional feasting rituals that served as arenas for commensal politics and labor mobilization, most probably initiated by influential individuals seeking to increase the scale of their largesse. An introduction through this socially valued institution would have served to validate this foreign beverage as an acceptable complement to native drinks used in these roles (much as happened with pigs in the New Guinea Highlands[142]). However, once the value of wine had been established in this domain, in the absence of an effective monopoly on access to the sources of wine, it could soon have become a threat to the base of the social power of the informal leaders responsible for its introduction. It would allow those who had previously been relatively disadvantaged in their ability to engage in commensal politics on a significant scale (young men, for example, and minor managers) to obtain the means to do so and to mobilize large work parties. Access to effectively operating in this arena of social competition would no longer be limited by the traditional system of slowly building up the requisite support base and agricultural surplus. Rather, drink could be obtained by furnishing goods sought by Mediterranean traders or by providing labor services for them in exchange for amphorae of wine, thus circumventing the traditional route to engaging as a significant player in this theater of political competition by stepping outside the local system. This broadening of the recruitment base for leadership contestants would have resulted in an escalation of competition carried out through the institution of feasting, with increasing demand for both Mediterranean wine and native drinks and food. Competition would have continued to be focused especially in the arena of feasting because this was the domain through which the colonial encounter was first articulated and in which challenges to status claims were first made.

Further support for this scenario may be derived from a consideration of the two new styles of pottery that began production during the sixth century BCE, and that involved one of the few cross-cultural borrowings of technical practices. These are the Colonial Cream-ware *(Céramique claire)* and Gray-monochrome *(Céramique grise-monochrome)* ceramics that were produced in indigenous workshops using the adopted technique of throwing on a potter's wheel. These two series were produced originally at Massalia in the early sixth century BCE (and later at Agde), and they were both used at Massalia and traded to native peoples of Mediterranean France. Versions of these also began to be produced in several indigenous workshops by the end of the first quarter of the sixth century BCE. The indigenous versions are hybrid wares, combining imported production techniques (the wheel and controlled draught kilns), imported decorative concepts, and some imported forms with native forms and motifs.[143]

This phenomenon of borrowing was, once again, first explained simply as a case of imitation through "Hellenization."[144] However, the suggestion that this stems from a desire to imitate Greeks misses the point entirely, especially when one considers the adoption of the potter's wheel. The use of this technique was not as simple a matter as importing Greek objects or copying Greek forms or decoration: it involved significant material investments. These include permanent workshop equipment (such as the wheel, closed kilns, clay purification tanks, and storage facilities) as well as new specialized knowledge and completely new motor skills. In brief, it involved a change in the basic organization of part of the ceramic industry from what is called a "household industry" to a "workshop industry."[145] I emphasize that this is a change in *part* of the industry only, because (as is demonstrated in the later discussion of foodways) almost all domestic cooking and storage pots continued to be made by the same methods as before, and this remained the case for six centuries.[146] The indigenous Cream-ware and Gray-monochrome workshops were an extremely discrete and circumscribed phenomenon that ceased production by the mid–fourth century BCE and had no impact on the rest of the ceramic repertoire. Such a development implies, by its very nature, a significant increase in demand for the specific range of ceramics produced by the new workshops, because an increased volume of production is the only advantage that the use of the wheel confers. Considering that the range of prevalent forms produced in the new wares is almost entirely confined to Greek-style drinking cups and pitchers and native-derived tableware (see the later discussion of dining practices), including probable beer pots,[147] it seems highly likely that this increase in demand is linked to an inflation in the scale of feasting activities, which is also indicated by the evidence of the amphorae. The quantities of these two wares (in both their Massalian and indigenous versions) consumed at indigenous settlements climbed to impressive proportions that paralleled the increasing quantities of amphorae during the late sixth and fifth centuries BCE. The eventual disappearance of the indigenous workshops also corresponds temporally with the decline in amphorae at sites of the interior during the fourth century BCE. This is probably an index of the inflation in feasting activity set off by the disruptive impact of imported wine in the arena of political competition and its subsequent stabilization after several generations.

But the consequences of this escalating thirst for wine involved more than the development of new ceramic workshops. Indigenous peoples also became entangled in an increasing demand for the surplus production of grain and other materials (such as timber, livestock, pitch, salt, stone, fish, etc.) to trade for wine and exotic drinking ceramics. This relationship is well illustrated by the parallel trend between the escalating consumption of Massalian wine at indigenous sites around Nîmes in eastern Languedoc and the increasing presence of huge grain storage jars called *dolia* during the fifth century BCE (fig. 7.13). As figure 7.14 shows, there was a striking correspondence between the growing quantity of wine consumed and the capacity for grain storage in the region, as well as a parallel decline in both during the fourth century BCE.[148] While there were regional fluctuations in wine consumption, it never fell below a significant level. Once Massalia and native societies became linked by these commodity chains, they were entangled in economic relationships that had complex ramifications for internal social and political relations and that produced new alignments of interest of the kind that Marshal Sahlins has described as "structures of the conjuncture."[149] Merchants were dependent for their existence on understanding and feeding the demand of consumers in all parts of the commodity networks they constructed. And the various consumers and producers linked by merchants relied on these traders to furnish information that would organize their production activities and satisfy their desires.

Imperial Aftermath   Greg Woolf has pointed to a dramatic transformation in the post-Augustan period and suggested that wine consumption then became part of a broader "consumer revolution" that marked a shift toward Roman consumption practices and tastes linked to the formation of a Gallic provincial culture and identity, albeit one marked by a certain fusion of practices.[150] Unfortunately, this argument has not always been supported by detailed contextual studies of archaeological evidence of changes in daily life at particular places. It would be important to know, for example, to what extent there was a gradually complete substitution of wine for beer at this point, and what regionally specific patterns this might have followed. But not much solid evidence on this matter has been published yet.

What is clear is that there was a major shift in *production* such that various regions in Gaul became important production centers, some of which even began exporting wine back to Rome. The evidence for this comes primarily from the proliferating production in Gaul of amphorae, including especially a new flat-based, footed type known as the Gallic amphora *(amphore gauloise)* that was turned out in multiple regions of France beginning in the first century CE (see fig. 7.2).[151] But evidence also comes from the excavation of several vineyards and multiple wineries with fermentation vats and buildings full of huge storage jars *(dolia)*, as well as from a few texts.[152] The site of Molard at Donzère in the Drôme region, for example, shows a second-century CE winery with presses, fermentation vats and a warehouse holding 204 dolia with a total capacity of about 255,000 liters.[153]

The first viticultural regions to be established were in Gallia Narbonensis, and these emerged as early as the Augustan period; but production really escalated only during the late first century CE. The earliest traces are found at places as diverse as the hinterland of Fréjus, Arles, and Aix-en-Provence. During the first century CE, the wine of Béziers, in Languedoc, became highly thought of in Rome. Even more esteemed was the wine of

FIGURE 7.13
House floor at Lattes with the base of a dolium in situ, zone 52. Note also the amphora shards used as chinking in the adjacent wall (UFRAL).

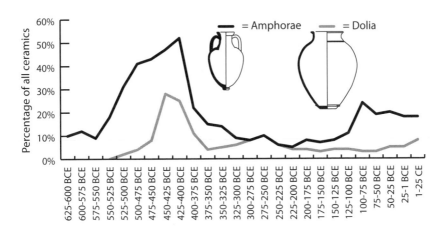

FIGURE 7.14
Amphorae and dolia as a percentage of all ceramics at settlements of eastern Languedoc (data from Py 1990a).

the Allobrogai, the people who occupied the northern Rhône region below Lyon. According to Pliny, the Allobrogai had developed a new variety of grape (a black variety called the *Allobrogica*) that was adapted to colder climates beyond the Mediterranean zone. The wine they produced was called "*picatum*" (literally "the resinous"), and it appears to have had a resinated flavor similar to that of modern Retsina.[154] In the rest of Gaul, production of amphorae began at Lyon, Augst, and the Loire before 50 CE, and near the end of the first century and during the second century in Burgundy, the Bordeaux region, the Loir-et-Cher, Normandy, and the Mosel valley.[155]

Some of the amphoric evidence should be qualified by the fact that wooden barrels, a Celtic invention, had also begun to be used for both vinification and transport from the end of the first century BCE. During the German campaigns, the Roman army adopted barrels for transporting large amounts of wine for the troops along the Rhine, and numerous barrels have been found in Roman army camps of the Rhine dating to this period.[156] According to André Tchernia, this wine for the troops was produced in Italy and Spain, then transported to Lyon in cistern boats equipped with large dolia. It was then off-loaded into warehouses equipped with dolia, and then loaded into barrels and transported by riverboats to their destinations.[157]

Hence, Gaul was both continuing to import wine and to produce large quantities of its own. While some of this Gallic wine was, as noted, exported to Rome, most of it appears to have circulated within Gaul. The Roman army was a large market, but consumption was widespread throughout Gaul. There also developed a rich and respected association of *negotiatores vinarii* at Lugdunum (modern Lyon) who controlled this trade in the Rhône region. This was an elaboration of the practice of middleman wine traders that was common for both Greeks and Romans.[158]

Near the end of the first century CE, the emperor Domitian issued an edict ordering half the vineyards in Gaul to be pulled up and planted in wheat, and forbidding the planting of vines in new regions. The idea that this was caused by Gallic wine having become serious competition for Roman wine producers has been much disputed. In any case, this edict was not actually enforced to any real extent, as is clear from the fact that it was precisely the second century CE that witnessed the greatest expansion of wine production in Gaul. Moreover the edict was later officially revoked by the emperor Probus in 281 in an attempt to gain support in Gaul for his campaigns against the Germanic tribes by granting to all Gauls the right to plant vines and make wine.

It is clear that by the second century, wine had become an extremely important part of the economy of nearly all regions of Gaul. The extent to which it had come to dominate or completely displace other forms of alcohol, in a thoroughly Roman pattern of consumption, is uncertain. But the sheer quantities in circulation certainly argue for at least a major presence of wine in daily life throughout most of Gaul in a way that had not occurred before.

OTHER FOODS AND FOODWAYS

Having examined the adoption of wine and the complex role this had in articulating and entangling colonial relations, what other appropriations can we detect, and what can we say about cuisine in general through the long history of this colonial situation?

Basic Food Ingredients   From a broad-scale view, both plant and faunal remains varied little among indigenous settlements of Mediterranean France, except in relative quantitative terms, from the Bronze Age through the end of the Iron Age. The relative differences were, of course, often important and characteristic of, for example, coastal and interior agrarian strategies and local cultural preferences.[159] Barley and several species of wheat (especially *Triticum aestivo compactum* and *Triticum dicoccum*) were the most common cereals for Iron Age settlements throughout Mediterranean France. These are found in archaeological contexts with variable remains of other varieties of wheat, millet, oats, lentils, chickpeas, vetch, and a few wild plants. Cattle, pigs, and ovicaprids were the basic sources of meat from domesticates, with horses, dogs, wild game, and fish also eaten.

Within the ubiquitous main trio of domesticates, ovicaprids are nearly always present and often dominant in archaeological faunal samples in terms of number of individuals, but cattle represent a much greater meat weight. Indeed, cattle generally constituted at least half of the meat consumed, and this was a consistent pattern throughout the Iron Age.[160] Horse and dog represent a relatively minor proportion of the food remains at sites where they are found: dog contributed less than 1.5 percent of the meat weight, although horse contributed more than 20 percent in some periods (it was least popular during the fifth and first centuries BCE).[161] Wild fauna (primarily deer, boar, rabbit, and birds) were also commonly eaten, and deer in particular sometimes constituted a significant proportion of the meat consumed: as much as 20 percent at a number of sites in the Rhône basin. The relative popularity of pork provides a distinctive marker of difference between the foodways of western Languedoc-Roussillon and those of the Rhône basin: it was generally much more significant in the diet of the former region.[162] These patterns changed very slowly, even after the Roman conquest when there was a general increase in the popularity of pork. At Ambrussum, for example, cattle remained the dominant meat (between 50 and 60 percent of the meat weight) until near the end of the second century CE, when it was replaced by pork in that role. Pork had previously been consistently the second most popular meat (at between 28 and 38 percent), with ovicaprids a distant third (about 4 to 7 percent). At Nîmes, the balance between beef and pork switched somewhat earlier, during the first century CE.[163]

But these general statements can hide a good deal of complexity at the level of individual settlements and obscure regional variation between sites. At Lattes, for example, an increase in the consumption of pork arose earlier than elsewhere in eastern Languedoc (to about 30 percent of meat weight by the mid–third century BCE). During the fifth and first half of the fourth centuries BCE, the faunal mix at Lattes was rich and abundant, with a contribution of wild game (essentially deer and rabbit) that was even higher than the already substantial average for sites of the region. Although the contribution of wild game to the diet declined from the third century BCE on, the exploitation of wild animals remained characteristic of the town even during the Roman period, with the relative importance of deer and rabbit fluctuating significantly. A wide variety of wild birds was also eaten (ducks, herons, swans, flamingoes, partridges, pigeons, etc.).[164] But, as elsewhere, beef was the most significant meat contribution to the diet, and its importance rose over time (from about 50 percent of the meat weight to almost 70 percent during the first century CE). Pork and sheep remains show a marked tendency to select young animals for consumption, although the percentage varied over time (there was a sharp regional decline in the percentage of young animals during the third century BCE, and a sharp decline that was specific to Lattes in the mid–second century BCE, before both increased again during the first century BCE).[165] Cattle, on the other hand, were slaughtered when they were old, once their utility for milk production and traction had declined. This was a pattern common to the region in general, although the people of Lattes ate even less veal than most other sites. Horses and dogs were also eaten, though less frequently (butchery marks on the bones show that these were clearly food remains).[166] Judging by the body parts represented and cut marks, it appears that butchery was performed in a domestic context rather than having cuts of meat sold from a specialized butchers' area.[167]

The data from the fifth century BCE at l'Île de Martigues are quite similar to Lattes except that dog was eaten less than at Lattes and ovicaprids provided slightly more meat weight than pigs. Beef, again, constituted about 70 percent of the meat weight and deer were a significant contributor as well. Over the centuries, the consumption of beef oscillated from a little under 50 percent to nearly 80 percent of the meat weight, with ovicaprids, deer, and pork constituting most of the rest.

Chickens make an appearance at l'Île de Martigues in the late fifth century BCE, but they constituted a minuscule 0.01 percent of the meat weight even as late as the second century BCE.[168] Chicken bones have also been found at other sites such as Lattes and La Cloche, but never in more than relatively minute quantities. Chickens are of interest because they were originally domesticated in South or Southeast Asia, and they are presumed to have been introduced to the western Mediterranean by Greek colonists. However, they constitute such a tiny fraction of faunal assemblages in the region (where they are found at all) that they can be assumed to have been little more than a curiosity for most peoples before the Roman Empire. They certainly had no appreciable impact on native cuisine, although the data from Lattes suggest that they gradually increased in importance in the diet in comparison to wild birds (chickens constitute about 11.3 percent of all bird bones recovered, and over 20 percent of bird bones between the mid–third and late first centuries BCE).[169]

It is not possible to estimate even roughly what portion of the overall diet was contributed by meat. But one may reasonably assume that, like most premodern Mediterranean societies, starches (especially wheat and barley) constituted the overwhelmingly dominant element of meals and that meat was a small, occasional, and probably highly prized complement to the staple starch dishes. Much like wine or beer, meat (especially beef, which required the slaughter of a large, valuable animal that would have to be consumed fairly quickly) may have been an indexical sign of the special festive status of a consumption event. As John Wilkins and Shaun Hill have pointed out, both meat and fish were treated as luxuries in ancient texts, and meat in particular was a symbol of wealth and power that was most often consumed on ritual occasions.[170] Greek texts noted that Celts cooked meat by both boiling and roasting, and Posidonius described large amounts of meat being eaten at what was almost certainly a feast: "And they eat their meat in a cleanly manner enough, but like lions, taking up whole joints in both hands, and gnawing them; and if there is any part which they cannot easily tear it away, they cut it off with a small sword which they have in a sheath."[171] In any case, although meat was unlikely to have been anything like a staple, the faunal data do indicate that indigenous towns maintained a stable mix of beef, pork, and mutton supplemented by other domesticates and wild game. Judging by finds of ceramic strainers, cheese was also eaten. Coastal sites also consumed a supply of protein from fish and shellfish.

The faunal data from Marseille are patchy, but samples from the Bourse excavations show that during the sixth and fifth centuries BCE cattle provided the bulk of the meat eaten (around 70 percent of the meat weight), with horse also providing a significant contribution. Among the smaller animals, pork was the most significant (at about 15 percent of the meat weight), while ovicaprids (mostly sheep) furnished only a marginal 6 percent of the meat. As at indigenous sites, cattle were generally slaughtered when old; but the average age of pigs and ovicaprids was also considerably older than at indigenous sites. Wild game was far less significant than at native settlements. Unfortunately, the sample of bones with cut marks is too small to provide an adequate comparison of butchery patterns with indigenous sites, such as the well-studied sample from Lattes,[172] as this would have furnished valuable information about cuisine.[173] By way of comparison, at Emporion, the relative contribution of beef was less than at Marseille, but still the most significant meat. Horse had a similar elevated position, and pork was also consumed far more than ovicaprids. The contribution of wild animals was similarly marginal.[174] Greeks in general also consumed cheese, yogurt, and eggs, and these were probably part of the Massalian diet as well.

Fish and shellfish were another important source of protein for both colonists and indigenous societies, at least those living along the coast. One can detect specific cultural preferences in this culinary domain. For example, Massalians were avid consumers of fish but showed a general aversion to most shellfish, whereas native settlements near the coast showed a taste for both fish and shellfish, with selective preferences for particular species varying by site and period. Excavations at Marseille and Olbia have unearthed significant amounts of fish remains, but only minute quantities of shellfish in comparison to the massive quantities found at other coastal sites such as Lattes, Saint-Blaise, Castellan, and l'Île de Martigues. Inhabitants of the latter site, for example, consumed oysters in such quantity during the second century BCE that a huge collective midden of these shells was allowed to take over the middle of the lower town.[175] The site of Castellan had a similar midden of oyster shells against the rampart during the second half of the first century BCE.[176] In contrast, for the first century BCE at Olbia and Marseille, the vast majority of the small amounts of shellfish that have been found are cockles *(cerastoderma edule)*. L'Île de Martigues in the levels of the second century BCE produced huge amounts of shell-fish, with oysters, scallops, and mussels the dominant varieties. Both l'Île de Martigues and Saint-Blaise during the second century BCE, and Castellan during the first century BCE, show a shift from a previously dominant taste for mussels to oysters. This taste for oysters is a pattern that would come to characterize most Gallo-Roman settlements, but not Marseille and Olbia, in the Roman period. The levels dated from 75 to 1 BCE at Lattes again show impressive quantities of shellfish, with a decline in the taste for mussels and cockles in favor of tellines *(donax trunculus)*. Other small hillforts in the Provence, such as La Cloche and Castellas de Rognac, show a continued preference for mussels at the same period.[177] This indicates very local patterns of taste in shellfish consumption, all of them contrasting with a general lack of interest in shellfish at Massalia and Olbia.

There was also a shift in culinary techniques for shellfish. Throughout most of the Iron Age they were usually eaten raw: this is shown by traces of cut marks on the shells indicating that they were opened by cutting the adductor muscle with a blade. However, beginning in the second century BCE, shellfish were generally opened by applying heat, and they were then either cooked or eaten raw. The excavation of a large clay oven of the second century BCE at Castellan showed that it was being used to grill mussels and oysters (perhaps in addition to the normal function of making bread), and ash samples from composite ovens at l'Île de Martigues showed tiny fragments of mussel shells, indicating that this practice was already used in some areas by the fourth century BCE.[178]

Posidonius noted that the Celts who lived near rivers or the Mediterranean coast ate fish and that they roasted it with salt, vinegar, and cumin.[179] They undoubtedly also boiled it: some fish bones show deformations linked to boiling.[180] The varieties of fish bones found at archaeological sites such as Lattes, Saint-Pierre-les-Martigues, l'Île de Martigues, Cailar, and Arles indicate that species from the coastal lagoons and littoral waters (primarily sea perch and sea bream, but also red mullet, mullet, and eel) comprised the bulk of the fish menu, at least until the first century BCE. Sweet water river fish are rare at these sites, although significant quantities of sturgeon were recovered at Arles. At Lattes, eels increased rapidly in quantity during the second century BCE, and from the mid–first century BCE there was a sudden rise in the quantity of deep-sea species (sardines, anchovies, and mackerel). The latter species do enter the coastal lagoons, but are not common there. Their sudden presence in large quantities is an indication of the development of deep-sea fishing alongside the traditional exploitation of coastal lagoons.[181] At Marseille, although much of the fish from the pre-Roman period were coastal species such as red mullet, sea perch, mullets, turbot, and eels, significant amounts of deep sea fish have been found from as early as the sixth century BCE. During the Roman period, large quantities of these deep-sea species such as mackerel, anchovies, sardines, and especially tuna were consumed.[182] Hence, the range of fish species eaten at Massalia and at indigenous coastal sites was roughly similar except that the Massalian fish repertoire was augmented by deep-sea fishing from the beginning, some five and a half centuries before the practice contributed significantly to the diet of native towns. Moreover, tuna are rare at native sites even after the emergence of deep-sea fishing, while they were especially abundant at Massalia from the third century BCE on. Fresh fish were eaten at all these sites, but we do not know to what extent indigenous peoples also used different techniques of preservation common in the Greek world such as salting, drying, smoking, pickling, or the production of garum fish sauce.[183] One fragment of a reused Massalian amphora has been found in the third century BCE levels at Lattes with sea bream bones inside and another undated fragment had traces of sardines: presumably both were the remains of preserved fish.[184] However, this is scant evidence of such practices. The importance of garum to Massalia, and Greek cuisine in general, is well known from literary references and the trade in garum amphorae. Moreover, amphorae containing preserved fish (probably salted) have been found at excavations in the port zone of Marseille.[185]

As noted, however, meat and fish were not staples, even for the wealthy: the bulk of the diet for everyone in Mediterranean France was undoubtedly composed of starches and pulses. As Peter Garnsey noted, cereals were always at the top of the list in ancient agricultural texts on food. Moreover, provisions to soldiers and slaves and handouts to citizens were almost entirely of grain (in large quantities), and when there were discussions of state intervention in the food supply it was almost invariably grain that was the subject.[186] Many ancient texts explicitly make a distinction between the cereal base of the Greek diet (*sitos*), and the accompanying meat, vegetable, or fish relishes (*opsa*; or *pulmentaria* for Romans) that provided flavor, with a clear expectation (and even moral judgment) that the former should dominate.[187] Estimates have been made of 70 to 75 percent of the Greek diet being provided by cereals, although there were undoubtedly significant variations around this figure according to class and location.[188] Posidonius offered the observation that the food of the Celts consisted of "a few loaves of bread, and a good deal of meat brought up floating in water, and roasted on the coals or on spits."[189] However, insofar as we can rely on such anecdotal evidence, this passage clearly describes a feast (the kind of event that a foreign visitor would likely have been able to observe) rather than daily meals. Like Greeks and Romans, Gauls almost certainly subsisted primarily on grain and pulses.

The abundant archaeobotanical finds at Lattes show that seven different grains were eaten, but barley and wheat were always the most common.[190] These constituted the staple foundation of the diet throughout the history of the settlement. Barley (*Hordeum vulgare*) was the most frequent cereal during all periods, and it was particularly abundant during the early centuries of the town's history. Wheat of the *Triticum aestivum/durum* variety was second in abundance, and seems to have been stored in a cleaned, ready to eat form. Other wheats are present in much smaller quantities: *Triticum dicoccum* and *Triticum monococcum*. Millet (both *Panicum miliaceum* and *Setaria italica*) has been found only in levels prior to the second century BCE. Domesticated oats have not been found at Lattes, but wild oats (*Avena* sp.) have been identified in levels prior to the first century BCE. These cereals are accompanied by frequent remains of lentils, peas, and fava beans, and less frequent chickpeas, vetch, and bitter vetch. Cultivated fruits present from the earliest levels include figs, grapes, and olives. Plums, peaches, hackberries, and walnuts appeared only during the first century CE. A number of wild plants were also consumed (berries, nuts, cherries, pine nuts, acorns, etc.). The range of common Greek legumes was very similar, including especially lentils, chickpeas, peas, fava beans, and lupine. Olives were a common accompaniment of Greek meals.

Olive Oil Aside from wine, the most significant initial difference in diet between indigenous peoples and colonial newcomers to the region was the central importance of olive oil to Etruscans, Greeks, and Romans. Although olives were indigenous to the Mediterranean regions of France and Spain,[191] the concept of olive oil as a processed foodstuff, as well as the techniques of its production, were introduced to the western Mediterranean by Greeks and Phoenicians. Native societies in both France and Spain immediately developed a taste for wine, but olive oil appears to have met with general indifference or resistance, at least in France, for over two centuries, and probably much longer. Reciprocally, Greeks appear to have been equally resistant to the use of animal fats for cooking.

Stone olive presses have been discovered at Lattes and a number of sites in the hinterland of Marseille dating from as early as the fourth century BCE (figs. 7.15 and 7.16).[192] Olive pits are present in levels at Lattes dating back to the beginning of the fifth century BCE, but in minute quantities throughout the history of the site. Moreover, no olive wood has been identified among the charcoal remains at the site before the Roman period.[193] It is uncertain how much oil was being produced with these presses or to what extent it was consumed locally. It is possible that it was made specifically for trade to Massalia or used in the production of fish sauce that was traded to Massalia (a lead tablet with Greek writing recently found at Lattes offers some suggestive, if ambiguous, hints in this direction). It is also possible that resident Greek merchants may have consumed the oil, or that it was used by local people for illumination rather than cooking: imported ceramic lamps, although rare until the first century BCE, are found as early as the sixth century BCE at Lattes and other coastal sites, and olive oil could have been burned in local illumination devices as well. We know that the vessel Greeks used for frying with olive oil was extremely rare on indigenous settlements of the Rhône basin, although oil could have been used instead as a flavoring agent. However, Posidonius offered the observation that "they [Celts] use no oil, on account of its scarcity; and because they are not used to it, it seems disagreeable to them."[194] This comment was written in the early first century BCE and seems to be referring explicitly to Mediterranean and southwestern France. However, given the ambiguity of existing data, the extent of olive oil consumption beyond Massalia cannot really be determined until a program of chemical analysis of lipid residues in ceramics has been carried out. What we do know is that it was being produced at a number of settlements by the fourth century BCE, and the proximity to Massalia or the coast of examples before the Roman conquest suggests that this may have been primarily oriented toward Massalian consumers.

FIGURE 7.15
Stone base of an olive oil press from Lattes, zone 27 (UFRAL).

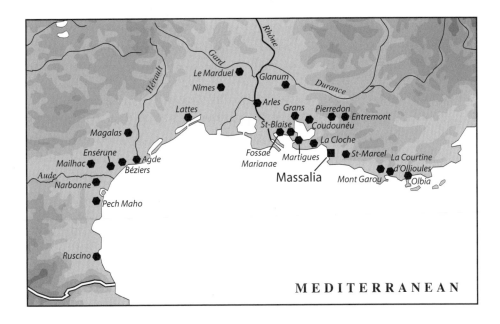

FIGURE 7.16
Map of settlements with evidence of olive oil presses in Mediterranean France (after Brun 2004:205; courtesy of Jean-Pierre Brun). A few cases (e.g. Coudounéu) may be wine presses. Dates range from the fourth century BCE to the second century CE.

Cooking Techniques   Precise recipes are elusive outside of Greek, Etruscan, and Roman contexts.[195] However, archaeological data do provide a good deal of information about techniques of food preparation and cooking at native settlements in Gaul. In the former cases, numerous depictions of cooking scenes on vase paintings and frescoes, as well as clay models, provide an additional aid in interpreting archaeological objects.[196] We do not have much specific textual information about cuisine at Massalia and its colonies, and one must be wary of using uncritically other Greeks as a model. It is clear that there were many regional differences in Greek foodways and that judgments about cuisine and dining practices were often used to differentiate among Greek cities as well as distinguishing Greeks from barbarians: Spartans, for instance were disdained for their preferred "black gruel" pork stew, Syracusans were ridiculed for cooking fish with cheese, Boeotians were stereotypically prone to gluttony, and so forth.[197] But, aside from the shared centrality of wine and olive oil, there were other foods and food practices that seem to have been more widespread among Greeks (at least Greeks in coastal zones and major cities) and were probably a part of Massalian cuisine as well.

It is clear from abundant textual evidence that the primary staple dish throughout most of the Greek world was a barley cake or porridge called *maza*, which was made from grain that had been soaked in water, parched, and ground. Maza could be prepared in various degrees of liquidity—as a thick porridge, a flatbread, or even a thin gruel—and ingredients such as honey, salt, and oil could be added. As the most basic daily fare, maza also became a symbol of frugality or poverty.[198] The importance of barley in the Greek diet resembled the situation in native societies of Mediterranean France but was in marked contrast to Rome, where barley was never popular and wheat was the overwhelmingly dominant cereal, eaten as either gruel *(puls)* or bread *(panis)*. The Greeks also used wheat of several varieties to make bread loaves (including leavened bread) or gruel.[199] Flour was ground on a stone quern in the house. Bread *(artos)* was baked in the house in small mobile, footed clay ovens *(ipnos)* or clay domes *(pnigeus)* placed over coals on the floor. Examples of these exist both on vase paintings and as archaeological specimens.[200] By the late fifth century BCE, and possibly earlier, bread was also available in the market from specialist bakers in Athens and other large cities (possibly including Massalia). Rome, in contrast, did not have specialist bakers making panis for sale until the early second century BCE. Meat, fish, vegetables, beans, lentils, cheese, and other foods served essentially as a relish for maza or bread. Seasonings included garum (a liquefied fish sauce), vinegar *(oxus)*, garlic, herbs (especially cumin, thyme, and oregano), salt, capers, cheese, and olive oil. Honey was used as a sweetening agent, and figs, dates, and apples were eaten. For Marseille, specifically, we have few archaeobotanical data published to date. However, Caesar noted that the Masslians had stored large quantities of wheat in a public granary in anticipation of his siege, and they had passed on to eating stocks of old millet and spoiled barley by the end of the siege.[201]

Greek cooking techniques included the application of dry heat *(optan)*, in the form of grilling, frying, and roasting, as well as wet-heat cooking *(hepsein)*, such as boiling or stewing. Vegetables and pulses were roasted, boiled, or, especially, made into soups and purees. Both fresh and salted fish were eaten: they were prepared by boiling, stewing, or frying. Meats were cooked by grilling or stewing, and sausages were commonly eaten by all classes. Cooking was accomplished with ceramic braziers and cooking stands in a variety of forms that supported clay grills or that held pots over coals. As B. A. Sparkes has noted, the portability of clay ovens, braziers, and grills and the lack of fixed hearths have made the identification of kitchens in Greek houses difficult before the fourth century BCE, although evidence from Olynthos indicates that kitchens with fixed cooking structures were becoming common from that period on.[202]

In terms of other equipment, at a minimum, a Greek kitchen needed storage jars for grain, water, olive oil, garum, vinegar, salted fish, and olives, in addition to amphorae of wine.[203] Some of these (such as the *hydria* used to fetch and store water, and the *pithos* for storage of large quantities of grain or other products) had specialized shapes, but there were also large pots with a flat or ring-base, and often a fitted lid, that served as generalized short-term containers and mixing bowls (*lekane*, pl. *lekanai*). Greek and Latin literary sources indicate that mortars were of two kinds: those used for pounding grain (the *olmos* or *pila*) and those used for cooking and medicines (the *thueia*, *igdis*, or *moratorium*). Ceramic mortars with a spout were of the latter type, and they were used for crushing, grinding, mixing, and making emulsions. Texts also very frequently mention grinding vegetables, herbs, and spices in a mortar, and sometimes meat, fish, and cheese. Medicines were also commonly prepared with a mortar, grinding roots, herbs, salt, minerals, and other such things.[204] Barley had to be parched to remove the husks (which do not separate easily by threshing), and a special barley parching pan *(phrygetron)*, a shallow dish with a loop handle, was a common implement: a law of Solon required every Athenian bride to take one to her wedding.[205] The *chytra*, a round-bottomed pot with a restricted mouth and one or two handles, was the most common cooking pot in the Greek world, as it served as a saucepan for boiling meat and soups, and as a kettle (fig. 7.17). The *caccabe* was a more squat form of chytra with a wider mouth (and a lid) that was used for braising or stewing.[206] The *lopas* was a wide, low covered pan that served for stewing or steaming fish. It appeared only in the mid–fifth century BCE but persisted into the Roman period.[207] The *tagenon* was a flat, low pan with a long handle used for frying, generally fish. Bats has suggested that the relatively limited number of ceramic examples found indicates that it was more often made of metal and that its appearance in the late fifth century BCE marks the first emergence of this technique in the Greek culinary repertoire.[208] From this period until the Roman Empire, the basic range of cooking pots and techniques remained unchanged except for the addition of a low baking dish with a flat bottom near the end of the second century BCE, a borrowing from the Roman repertoire.

The cooking ceramics from excavations at Marseille have not yet been analyzed sufficiently to yield a comprehensive quantitative picture of the extent to which these general Greek patterns were characteristic of practices at Massalia. However, it appears that, in contrast to tablewares, for most of the first century or so of the city's history the bulk of the cooking ceramics were hand-modeled pots from the indigenous repertoire.[209] Massalia began to produce its own cooking wares (in a micaceous fabric) only at the beginning of the fourth century BCE, about two hundred years after it began producing

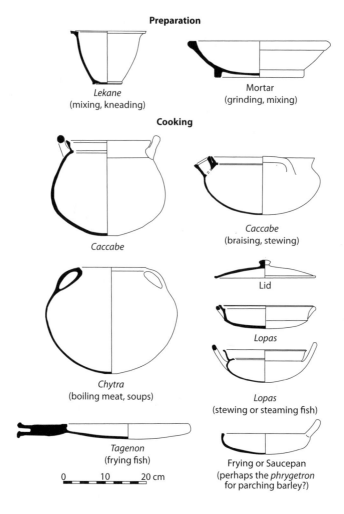

Preparation

Lekane
(mixing, kneading)

Mortar
(grinding, mixing)

Cooking

Caccabe

Caccabe
(braising, stewing)

Lid

Lopas

Chytra
(boiling meat, soups)

Lopas
(stewing or steaming fish)

Tagenon
(frying fish)

0   10   20 cm

Frying or Saucepan
(perhaps the *phrygetron*
for parching barley?)

FIGURE 7.17

Some common Greek cooking pots (drawings after *Dicocer* : Py 1993b; information from Bats 1988a and Sparkes 1962, 1991).

tablewares. These were in the standard Greek forms, such as the *caccabe* and, from the mid–fourth century BCE, the *lopas*.[210]

Bats's detailed analysis of the data from the Massalian colony of Olbia provides a more nuanced view of cooking and dining practices within the Massalian domain from the mid–fourth to the mid–first centuries BCE.[211] That analysis shows that the general forms of cooking pots at Olbia were, in fact, both remarkably stable and generally reflective of broader Greek patterns, but with some interesting twists. From the mid–fourth to the mid–second centuries BCE, these cooking ceramics included wheel-made caccabai and lopades, with lopades being more numerous: this is probably a reflection of an elevated importance of fish in the diet at Olbia, a settlement with little or no chora for raising stock.[212] The fabric of these vessels does not appear to be either Massalian or Attic, and they must have been imported from somewhere else (Bats suggests perhaps southern Italy or Sicily).[213] But the cooking ceramics also include a series of hand-modeled vessels in a nonmicaceous fabric that is very close to the ceramics of nearby indigenous sites such as Mont Garou. These were predominantly "urn" forms used for boiling and stewing at native sites, and they appear to have substituted for the role of the Greek *chytra*. They constituted as much as 37 percent of the cooking ware during the late third and early second century BCE.[214] Interestingly, in this period there is a complete absence of forms for frying fish in olive oil, as was typical in the Attic repertoire, something that Bats suggests may have been due to the use of metal frying pans.[215] Around the middle of the second century BCE, wheel–made cooking pots disappeared at Olbia and were replaced by a hand-modeled series made in indigenous workshops in the neighborhood of Massalia, probably in the area on the north flank of the Étoile mountain range. This is the distinctive cooking ware known as *"céramique non tournée des ateliers de la region de Marseille"* (or CNT-MAR for short) that was produced primarily in Greek forms and consumed almost exclusively at Massalia and its colonies during the second and first centuries BCE. It ceased production around the time that Massalia was defeated by Caesar in the Roman Civil War.[216] At Olbia, pots in this ware continued exactly the same forms as before (*caccabe, lopas*, and indigenous urn), with the addition of a frying pan and Italic–style low baking dish. Once again, the *lopades* constitute about 50 percent of the cooking ceramics, highlighting the importance of fish at the site.[217]

Hence, despite a change in the commodity chains supplying cooking pots, the general repertoire of forms remained constant over three centuries, with a few minor Italic additions in the first century BCE. The repertoire also conforms closely to broader Greek patterns, with the exception of the substitution of indigenous urns for the Greek chytra (presumably serving the same function). The flat-bottomed urns are meant to be used by placing them directly on the hearth with the fuel gathered around the pot, in contrast to the round-bottomed chytra that was set in a holder over coals. However, it is quite possible that Olbians simply placed these urns in their traditional braziers as they would a chytra (the inverse would be more difficult). In any case the ceramic data do not indicate in any convincing fashion a fusion of Greek and indigenous culinary practices, but they do show a growing dependence on native workshops for the cooking ceramics of the colony.

The cooking pot repertoire of indigenous societies was roughly similar throughout the Rhône basin, although with some regionally distinctive stylistic elements. An analytical division is usually made between two main variants, *céramique non tournée du Languedoc Oriental* (CNT-LOR) and *céramique non tournée de la Provence* (CNT-PRO), although they share many elements.[218] This repertoire remained remarkably stable throughout the Iron Age, with some gradual stylistic shifts and occasional experiments with new forms: essentially the repertoire of forms developed during the Early Iron Age was closely derived from forms of the Late Bronze Age and continued with only subtle changes until the late first century BCE. As the name suggests, these pots were hand modeled, and this continued to be the practice even after the wheel was adopted to produce some tableware. The pots were monochrome, fired in a moderately reducing atmosphere, tempered usually with crushed limestone or calcite, and decorated with comb incision or punctate impressions, if at all. The repertoire of indigenous ceramics as a whole is usually divided into five broad categories of forms: urns (*urnes* in the French typologies), *jattes*, bowls (called *coupes*), lids, and miscellaneous special forms such as strainers and exotic imitations (fig. 7.18). Of these, the *coupes* were tableware and the rest were cooking and storage forms.

The basic cooking pot was a tall "urn" form with a flat bottom. These usually had a tall neck that restricted the opening only slightly from the width of the body. They were meant to be placed directly on the surface of the hearth with the fuel placed around the body, and they were clearly pots for boiling or stewing. The category "urn" also covers some vessels that were not meant to be used for cooking over the fire, but rather for storing grain, cooling and storing water, and probably brewing and serving beer. This latter inference needs to be tested with chemical analysis of residues. It seems especially likely in the case of the Early Iron Age large urns with narrow ring bases, carenated shoulders, and very tall flaring necks that were closest to Late Bronze Age forms, but it was undoubtedly true of later urns as well, especially those with more restricted mouths.[219] The large storage urns were gradually replaced from the end of the sixth century BCE on by a new class of much larger storage jar that archaeologists call by the Latin name *dolium* (pl. *dolia*). These have very thick walls and a very coarse fabric, and they increased gradually in size.[220] The jattes label covers a range of pots of a low basin form with a flat bottom (roughly similar to a modern casserole dish). They often have a pouring spout, and occasionally small handles. These are presumed to have served as mixing basins, mortars, and cooking pots for simmering or stewing. Many of the varieties of this type of pot remained identical in form from the seventh, sixth, and fifth centuries to the end of the first century BCE. The bowl category includes a range of sizes and shapes. Some have a flat bottom, some have a ring foot, and some have a concave indented base. Some have an everted or straight rim, some have a slightly inverted rim, and some have a carenated lip. The larger examples are presumed to have been serving dishes, while smaller examples were for eating and drinking. Again, many of the varieties of this category are virtually indistinguishable over a period of seven centuries. Other kitchen ceramics included conical lids (another form that dates back to the Bronze Age) and strainers for making cheese. Of the cooking pots, urns were always the numerically dominant category: at Lattes they constituted 30 to 60 percent of the CNT wares. Lids were a relatively constant 10 to 20 percent of the CNT wares, and the importance of jattes declined over time from over 20 to under 10 percent by the mid–fourth century BCE (fig. 7.19).[221]

In general, Etruscan, Greek, and Roman ceramics had little impact on the repertoire of CNT forms made by native potters of the Rhône basin. There were a few scattered imitations of imported vessels, such as pitchers, mortars, and lopades, but these are quite rare. None became anything like a standard or popular form, and they appear to

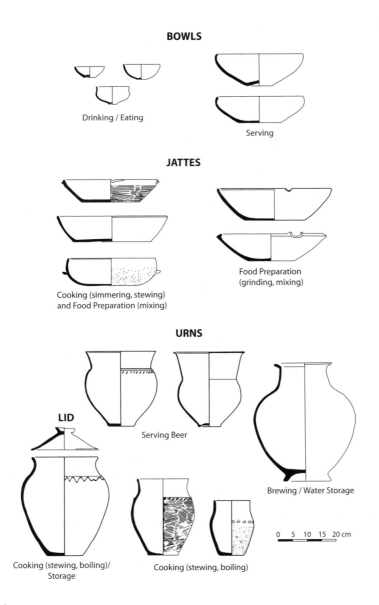

BOWLS

Drinking / Eating

Serving

JATTES

Cooking (simmering, stewing)
and Food Preparation (mixing)

Food Preparation
(grinding, mixing)

URNS

Serving Beer

Brewing / Water Storage

LID

Cooking (stewing, boiling)/
Storage

Cooking (stewing, boiling)

0   5   10   15   20 cm

FIGURE 7.18

Examples of major indigenous CNT (*céramique non tournée*) forms of the lower Rhône basin: showing bowl, *jattes*, urn, and lid categories and suggested functions (drawings after *Dicocer*: Py 1993b).

have been isolated experiments that did not catch on. Nor is there the development of something that resembles a hybrid fusion of native and exotic elements in the cooking repertoire (in contrast to the tablewares produced in Cream-ware and Gray-monochrome—discussed later). CNT cooking ceramics are a domain of remarkable conservatism in the Rhône basin, in terms of forms, fabrics, and modes of production.

Imported Etruscan, Greek, and Roman cooking ceramics also failed to penetrate native kitchens to any significant extent. During the Early Iron Age, mortars were

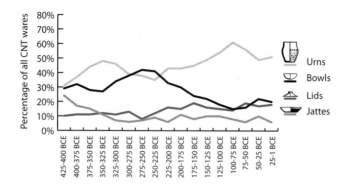

FIGURE 7.19

Changes in relative quantities of cooking and storage ceramics (urns, *jattes*, and lids) versus serving ceramics (bowls) among CNT wares at Lattes, calculated as a percentage of total CNT wares (data derived from Py et al. 2001:833).

virtually the only exotic pottery items not obviously related to drinking wine that attracted the interest of indigenous peoples of Mediterranean France, and they continued to be the only quantitatively significant form of Greek or Roman cooking ceramics found at indigenous sites until after the Roman conquest.[222] Even these may have had a wine connection, as it was common in Greece to grind up various herbs and other substances to add flavors to wine. But, as noted earlier, they were also used in the Greek world for crushing, grinding, mixing, and making emulsions. Such implements have been a standard feature of many cuisines, but they were a crucial element of Greek cooking.[223] Although most cuisines involve some kind of grinding or crushing techniques, not all cultures use ceramic mortars. The continental "Celtic" world, for example, did not have ceramic or stone mortars, although the former became relatively frequent in Mediterranean France. At Lattes, mortars constitute about 14.7 percent (by a minimum number of vessels count) of the cooking ceramics during the fourth century BCE. They are almost entirely of Massalian origin, with a few Etruscan and other types. This relative quantity of mortars is significantly less than at some sites of western Languedoc such as Agde, La Monédière, Béziers, and Sauvian, where figures around 25 percent are common, but comparable to other sites of that region such as Salses and Monfau. Eric Gomez has used these differences as an index of the relative degree of "Hellenization" of these sites.[224] However, aside from the theoretical objections to this concept in general, this seems a risky assumption without exploring how these vessels may have functioned in relation to other elements of native cuisine. In fact, they closely resemble certain native forms of jattes and were probably assimilated to the same functions, such as grinding and mixing food ingredients, if they were not used exclusively for drinking rituals.

Aside from Lattes, with its unusual collection of Etruscan ceramics in the merchants' house, only a handful of other Etruscan cooking pots have been found at other sites of the Rhône basin.[225] This is true despite the fact that the basic Etruscan pot for boiling

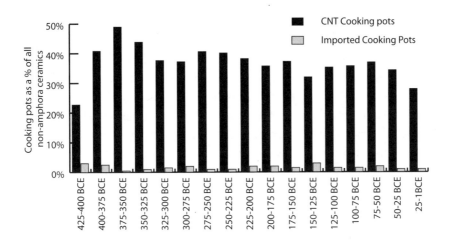

FIGURE 7.20
Relative quantities of CNT cooking pots and imported cooking pots as a percentage of all non-amphora ceramics at Lattes (data derived from Py et al. 2001:381–383).

food was very similar in form to the flat-bottomed indigenous urn (as was the Roman form for the same function since the Bronze Age, the *olla*), and it could have been easily assimilated had there been any desire to do so. Over the following centuries, a few other types of Greek cooking pots (*chytra, caccabe, lopas,* etc.) were occasionally imported at indigenous sites on the coast or in the immediate vicinity of Massalia (such as Lattes, Saint-Blaise, and La Cloche), but always in very small quantities.[226] At Lattes, for example, excluding mortars, Greek cooking pots never amounted to more than about 1.5 percent of the nonamphora ceramics, and even that figure was only for a period in the late fourth and early third century BCE; otherwise, the figure generally hovered around 0.5 percent or less (fig. 7.20). These include only nine *chytra,* one *tagenon,* about sixty *caccabai,* seventy-seven *lopades,* and fifty-nine lids spread over four hundred years.[227] And these vessels were similarly rare, if present at all, at other indigenous settlements of the Rhône basin. At Lattes, they were not concentrated in one sector of the site, as one might expect if they belonged to the house of a Greek merchant, for example. Rather, they were scattered over time and space, although, as noted, with somewhat greater frequency during the mid–fourth to early third centuries BCE. Clearly, they were not part of the accepted cooking repertoire and were more likely an occasional curiosity item left by visiting ships. Roman cooking pots had marginally better success, beginning in the mid second century BCE, but these also did not exceed about 2.8 percent of the non-amphora ceramics until the Augustan period (and these were predominantly mortars and lids).[228]

Aside from ceramics, information about indigenous culinary practices can be derived from other domestic archaeological data. Cooking was done primarily on large square, flat "platform" hearths (constructed on house floors, of clay over a foundation bed of ceramic shards) that were usually placed in the center of rooms and were often decorated (fig. 7.21). The flat-bottomed urns and jattes were placed on this surface for cooking, with embers gathered around them. But there were other common forms of hearth as well, including trench hearths dug into the floor with the embers placed in the depression. These were probably used for grilling. Patches of burned earth (called *lenticular hearths*) are also very common on house floors, especially along walls or in corners. These are the traces of smaller fires, perhaps often under a clay pot holder or grill, of which many remains have been found.[229] In addition to hearths, circular clay ovens were also common, presumably for baking bread and/or smoking meat. These include both fixed ovens (with a clay floor laid over a foundation bed of shards and a bell shaped dome) and portable clay dome ovens (fig. 7.22). Most examples are of small size (about 40 to 60 centimeters in diameter) and were probably for familial use; but much larger ones up to a meter in diameter are known (especially at Lattes during the fourth and third centuries BCE), and these may have been communal ovens for several houses, especially those located outside in open areas. The site of l'Île de Martigues has furnished especially well-preserved examples of a variety of portable clay ovens and braziers that would have been used for cooking and for parching grain.[230]

Grain was ground into flour in domestic contexts on small-capacity implements. Querns, usually of basalt, were a subject of widespread regional trade.[231] There was a shift in types over the centuries. Initially flat saddle querns were used. These were replaced progressively from the late fifth century BCE on by a Greek rectangular "hopper rubber" or "pushing mill" form with a central slit (called the "Olynthus" type in France), and these were in turn supplanted by a disk-shaped Iberian rotary hand mill during the third century BCE in eastern Languedoc and the second and first centuries BCE in Provence.[232]

Both the preponderance of urns in the cooking repertoire and bowls in the tableware indicate a cuisine largely based on liquid preparations such as soups, gruels, and stews but also complemented by grilled meat. The clay ovens also indicate that bread (flatbreads and perhaps leavened bread) alternated with cereal porridge as a staple starch. The basic food ingredients and techniques changed little over the centuries, except for shifts in preferred types of shellfish and the relative balance of different kinds of meat. Indeed, a kitchen of the sixth century BCE would have been almost identical to one of the early first century BCE, except for some stylistic changes in the pots, the increased size of storage jars, and the type of grindstone used. Moreover, the Greek technique of frying in oil seems to have made no impact on native cuisine, at least insofar as one can judge by the virtual absence of ceramic implements used for this. It is possible that olive oil began to be used for other things (flavoring porridge, for instance), but there is no evidence of such uses, and oil clearly was not used for frying. Nor does it seem that the garum fish sauce that was so prized by Greeks and Romans found any favor until the Augustan period.

As late as the first half of the first century BCE, at the small fortified site of La Cloche only twelve kilometers from the port of Marseille, the non-amphora ceramics were still

FIGURE 7.21
A decorated platform hearth at Lattes, zone 52, with a section excavation revealing the underlying foundation bed of amphora shards. The original decorated surface is preserved only in the smooth central area (UFRAL).

FIGURE 7.22
Remains of a clay oven at Lattes, with the fired clay floor partially excavated to reveal a foundation of amphora shards (UFRAL).

about 60 percent local CNT, and cooking vessels were about 99 percent CNT. Furthermore, the cuisine was still based heavily on traditional boiling techniques. This is shown by the fact that 83 percent of the cooking ware consisted of urns.[233] In stark contrast, the Greek town of Olbia had only 15 percent pots for boiled food (urns or *chytrai*).[234] To be sure, the inhabitants of La Cloche were drinking and eating primarily with Campanian bowls and plates, and pouring wine with Cream-ware and local CNT pitchers, as well as using a number of imported mortars and experimenting with a few Greek cooking forms that could easily be assimilated to native types. But their basic foodways were still quite different from their Greek neighbors: at Olbia, 69 percent of the cooking vessels were lopades, a form that Bats has suggested was used for stewing fish, and, as noted, very few pots were devoted to boiling. What is more, as is shown by the presence of only one example of a *patina* (a Roman form) at La Cloche, they were completely indifferent to Roman culinary models. Greek frying forms are also almost nonexistent at the site. As Frédéric Marty has demonstrated, these patterns are very similar to other contemporary sites along the coast of the Rhône basin, such as Lattes and Les Baux.[235]

Dining Practices As with nearly everything else, our information about Greek dining practices is heavily weighted toward Athens and toward the wealthier class of Athenians; but it may be used to serve as a rough basis for approaching Massalia, at least in very general terms. Greeks generally divided the daily eating cycle into three meals. A morning meal *(akratismos)* usually consisted of *maza* dipped in wine and accompanied by olives or figs. A midday meal *(ariston)* was also relatively light. The evening meal *(deipnon)* was the most important and was followed by the symposion when dining with guests. A light snack *(hesperisma)* might also be eaten in the afternoon. Men and women ate separately or, if the house was small, successively. For daily meals one ate while seated on a chair; for banquets one reclined on a couch.[236] The food was placed on small low tables, and people ate with their fingers.[237] This was sometimes aided by spoons for soups, although the lack of wear on bowls at Olbia indicates that spoons were probably used only rarely there.[238] Pieces of bread *(apomagdalia)* were used as napkins to wipe the fingers and then tossed to dogs.[239] For Romans, *iantacula* was the term for breakfast, *prandium* was the midday meal, and *cena* was the evening dinner. Unlike Greeks, Roman men commonly ate with women and children.[240]

As Bats has noted, the development of Greek ceramic tableware indicates a style of dining based on individualized portions (held by bowls and cups) served from larger communal vessels.[241] In contrast to the long stability of the cooking ceramics, styles of tableware changed much more rapidly and frequently (fig. 7.23). This was especially true of drinking cups.[242] The common serving vessels included platters and plates *(pinakes)*, including special fish plates, and one-handled pitchers of several kinds for water and wine *(olpai* and *oinochoai*, or collectively *choes)*. The individual vessels include small bowls for soups and stews and drinking cups. The latter come in several characteristic shapes that changed in popularity over time as tastes shifted. From the seventh through the fifth century BCE, drinking cups with a tall stemmed foot and two handles were popular. These included the *kylix*, with a broad shallow bowl and horizontal handles and the *kantharos*, an Etruscan form with a deeper bowl and tall vertical handles. In southern France, the kylix forms used included versions made in Ionia, Athens, Etruria, southern Italy, and Massalia (in both the Cream-ware and Gray-monochrome styles).

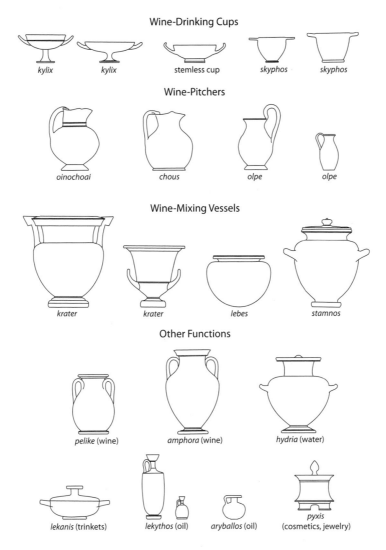

Wine-Drinking Cups

kylix kylix stemless cup skyphos skyphos

Wine-Pitchers

oinochoai chous olpe olpe

Wine-Mixing Vessels

krater krater lebes stamnos

Other Functions

pelike (wine) amphora (wine) hydria (water)

lekanis (trinkets) lekythos (oil) aryballos (oil) pyxis (cosmetics, jewelry)

FIGURE 7.23

Some common Greek tableware forms (drawings after Bats 1988a and Sparkes 1991). The range is far from complete and is intended simply to indicate the variety of specialized forms. See also figure 7.25 for plate and bowl forms.

Also popular was the *skyphos* (or *kotyle*), a form with a tall narrow bowl, a ring foot, and parallel handles. The popularity of the high-stemmed forms waned during the late fifth century BCE, and they were replaced by the skyphos and a form of the kylix with a simple ring foot (the so-called *bolsal* of Beazley). At the end of the fourth century BCE, the skyphos was replaced by a form that resembled a miniature version of a column crater. This in turn was replaced in the last quarter of the third century BCE by Athenian black-gloss deep bowls with relief imitating metal forms, and this was followed by the mass production of black-gloss deep bowls with a ring foot that served as the standard drinking vessel into the Roman period. These bowls were first produced at Athens but were soon imitated in southern Italy as the most popular form of the Campanian ware that became ubiquitous in the western Mediterranean.[243] They were also imitated at several other workshops, including the Greek colony of Rhode in Spain. The symposion also required several other vessels, including a large wine-mixing vessel of several possible shapes (a deep *crater* or spherical *lebes*), a *hydria* for the water, an *oinochoe* pitcher for pouring into cups, and a *psykter* for cooling the wine in summer.

All of these forms were consumed in quantity at Massalia, Olbia, Emporion, and other Phocaean sites of the western Mediterranean. However, once again, Bats's analysis at Olbia provides the most detailed quantitative perspective on trends for the entire range of tableware. This analysis shows that Massalian Cream-ware constituted the bulk of the tableware at Olbia (and nearly all the pitchers) until its production virtually ceased during the first half of the second century BCE. The rest consisted of Attic and then Campanian black-gloss wares. From that point on, Campanian ceramics constituted nearly all the tableware, with the occasional addition of some Ampuritan Gray ware and some Italic common ware. All the main forms in use at Athens were also used at Olbia, and the temporal trends (changes in the size and relative quantities of plates, disappearance of handles on cups, etc.) were also similar, with a few minor variations.[244]

We know relatively little about the dining practices of native peoples of Gaul. We do not know, for example, how many times a day nor at what times Gauls ate. There are a few Greco-Roman texts that offer descriptions of dining, but these are not very specific in terms of region. Insofar as they are based on firsthand observations, then they undoubtedly describe feasts rather than daily meals (with special hospitality for strangers). Posidonius, in an obvious description of a feast written in the early first century BCE, noted that Celts used grass for seats and put food before their guests on small wooden tables raised just slightly above the ground. He also noted that when many dined together, they sat in a circle, and the man with the highest prestige (derived from either military prowess, ancestry, or wealth) was seated in the middle, with the host next to him. Others were then seated in descending order of distinction on both sides. Their armor bearers stood behind them with each man's shield, and the spear bearers sat in another circle opposite and feasted like their masters. Cup bearers would serve wine from ceramic or silver pitchers, and copious supplies of meat were served on ceramic or silver platters, although wooden and basketry platters are also mentioned. The drink was Italian or Massalian wine (usually consumed unmixed with water) for the wealthy and wheat and honey beer for the poorer classes. A cup was passed around the circle in a clockwise rotation, with each man drinking a little at a time.[245] This description offers several salient contrasts with Greek dining, including the fact that drinking and dining were done together, that the wine was unmixed, that diners sat on the ground, that people drank from a common cup, and that servants ate with masters (albeit in a separate circle). Of course, as an anecdotal account, it is of uncertain value, and may be largely a stereotypic image. But it does show that foodways were an especially salient domain for Greeks in making cultural contrasts.

Abundant ceramic tableware offers the best evidence available for understanding in-digenous dining practices. This material shows that the local repertoire of CNT table-ware in Mediterranean France lacked plates: neither serving plates nor individual plates were used. Instead, bowls of various sizes constitute the sole eating vessel, thus confirm-ing the impression of the importance of boiled liquid foods (soups, stews, porridge) in the diet. These bowls have often been divided by French archaeologists into two types: *écuelles* and *coupes*, although more recent classifications tend to place all bowls within the *coupe* category and use codes to differentiate formal distinctions within the category (fig. 7.18).[246] *Écuelles* (or series CNT-LOR C2 in the now broadly used DICOCER classifi-cation) are distinguished by having a lip that turns inward, tending to limit the splashing of liquids. The angle of the lip with the body can be either rounded or carenated. *Cou-pes*, in the old sense (or CNT-LOR C1 for rounded forms and CNT-LOR C3 for conical shapes), have an open form with a rim that remains straight or everted. The term *coupelles* (or CNT-LOR C5) is also sometimes used to describe small bowls of the coupe type.

Most examples of all these bowls have well-finished surfaces, often polished, and a small minority (primarily Early Iron Age examples) have incised decoration or pattern burnishing. The bases are of several types: flat, a ring foot, or a concave depression. The écuelles forms are generally of a large diameter (often twenty-five to thirty centimeters or more, too large for individual servings) and frequently show traces of use-wear on the interior. They are interpreted as serving or communal eating bowls. The *coupelles* are in the range of seven to ten centimeters diameter and were undoubtedly for drinking. The coupes of CNT-LOR C2 form are usually in the range of fifteen to twenty-two cen-timeters, although larger examples exist. These are also seen as vessels for serving and/ or eating food, or for drinking (especially smaller examples with a ring foot). Whether the different variations in form correspond to precise distinctions in food to be served in them (for example, fish versus meat, stews versus soups) is not clear, but there was eventually a clear pattern of selective replacement with imports.

This CNT repertoire was augmented from the early days of the encounter by a range of imported tableware. As discussed earlier, initially, this was primarily limited to drink-ing cups and pitchers that accompanied the influx of wine: Etruscan bucchero nero kantharoi, "Ionian," Etrusco-Corinthian, and Attic kylikes, and especially Massalian Cream-ware and Gray-monochrome kylikes and pitchers. Whereas the cups were sim-ply substituting for long established bowl forms for drinking, Cream-ware and Gray-monochrome pitchers represented an entirely new functional addition to the repertoire, but one equally centered on drinking ritual. Aside from these drinking ceramics and some small bowls, other exotic forms of tableware failed to make much of an impact on native dining practices for several centuries. For example, in the Cream-ware and Gray-monochrome series that began to be consumed in the sixth century BCE, the only exotic forms that had much popularity in native contexts were drinking cups and pitchers.

But after several centuries the range of forms admitted to the table (if tables were used) did gradually begin to expand in interesting ways, including the use of Massalian and,

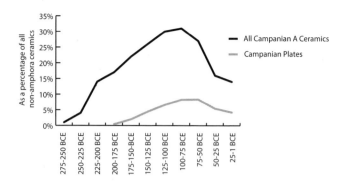

FIGURE 7.24

Campanian A ware as a percentage of all non-amphora ceramics; and Campanian A plates as a percentage of all non-amphora ceramics at Lattes (data derived from Py et al. 2001:435, 441).

especially, Campanian plates, representing the adoption of a novel function for pottery, by the mid–third century BCE. Plates were only a tiny fraction of the tableware at indigenous sites before about 175 BCE, but from that point on they constituted an escalating percentage of Campanian ware imports that, at Lattes, reached about 28 to 34 percent of Campanian ceramics imported during the early first century BCE (this figure still represents less than 10 percent of the non-amphora ceramics).[247] This increase in the relative popularity of plates occurred in the context of an increasing consumption of Campanian tableware in general, such that by the late second century BCE these ceramics constituted about 30 percent of the non-amphora ceramics at Lattes, and a major portion of all of the tableware (fig. 7.24).[248] If Posidonius is right, these plates may have been used to serve grilled meat at feasts, and it is possible that they were a substitution for basketry or wooden platters. Bowls, however, were the earliest popular form imported in Campanian ware, and they continued to be the most popular component of the range of Campanian imports. The bowl form 27a-b, for example, constituted over 70 percent of the Campanian ceramics during the last half of the third century BCE, and this was gradually replaced in popularity by form 31b and 33a bowls.[249] All of these are relatively small (generally less than fifteen centimeters diameter) hemispherical bowls with a ring foot and they undoubtedly served for eating and, in the smaller range, drinking (fig. 7.25).

That these Campanian bowls largely replaced most native CNT bowls (especially the CNT-LOR C1 form) rather than serving as an addition is evident from the fact that the decline of the popularity of CNT bowls matches precisely in time the increase in popularity of Campanian bowls. CNT bowls did not completely disappear, but the figures from Lattes show that they gradually declined to around 15 percent of CNT ceramics during the early first century BCE from a height of over 40 percent in the mid–third century BCE (fig. 7.26).[250] This means that by the first century BCE, CNT wares were about 85 percent cooking wares, and tablewares were largely imported. The Campanian bowls that were imported were remarkably similar in form to indigenous CNT bowls, again indicating a selective consumption pattern.

Campanian A Bowls

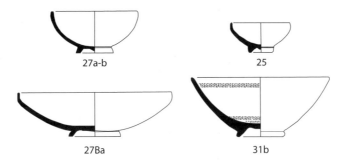

27a-b

25

27Ba

31b

Campanian A Plates

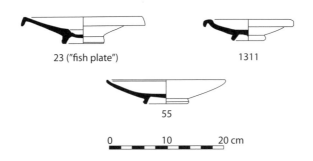

23 ("fish plate")

1311

55

0   10   20 cm

FIGURE 7.25
Examples of Campanian A ware bowls and plates consumed in Mediterranean France. Type 27a–b and 31b bowls were especially popular. Numbers refer to classification in *Dicocer* (Py 1993b).

No consideration of dining practices and ceramics can pass without returning briefly to a subject opened in the earlier discussion of drinking: Colonial Cream-ware *(Céramique claire)* and Gray-monochrome ware *(Céramique grise monochrome)*.[251] These two ceramic series represent simultaneously one of the few clearly hybrid products of the colonial encounter and the major early element of change in indigenous tablewares. Both of these were initiated by Massalian potters in the early sixth century BCE, within about twenty-five years after the colony was founded. They were destined for consumption at Massalia (especially the Cream-ware, which became the standard tableware of the city), but also for export to indigenous peoples of the region. Versions of both were also produced soon after their Massalian debuts in workshops in indigenous territory using the adopted technique of wheel throwing and firing in controlled-draft kilns. As noted earlier, the indigenous versions mark a shift in the mode of production exclusively for these tablewares to a workshop industry that was linked to an escalation of demand undoubtedly stimulated by increased feasting activity. It is uncertain precisely how these techniques spread to areas outside Massalia. But given Thucydides' observation about

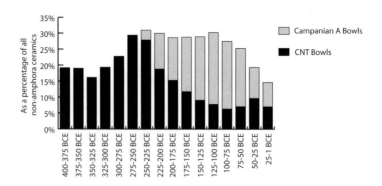

FIGURE 7.26

Relative quantities of CNT bowls and Campanian A bowls as a percentage of all non-amphora ceramics at Lattes (data derived from Py et al. 2001:435–528, 833).

the desertion of slaves from fifth century BCE Athens being primarily those engaged in craft industries, it is possible that escaped Massalian slaves from pottery workshops may have been responsible rather than Massalian workshop owners, for whom it would have made little sense.[252] Alternatively, some local peoples may have worked for a time in Massalian pottery workshops before returning home.

Production of Massalian Cream-ware lasted from about 575 BCE until the end of the second century BCE, when its place was overtaken by what is called Late Cream-ware (*Céramique à pâte claire récente*), a ware oriented toward Italic forms with multiple centers of production (including Massalia).[253] Massalia was always the major source of Cream-ware in the region. These are all ceramics with a fine, purified calcareous clay fired in an oxidizing atmosphere to produce a cream-white, light yellow, beige, or pinkish fabric. Some vessels had painted decoration in a dark brown or reddish paint and others were monochrome. At least two main indigenous centers of production have been identified in the Rhône basin, in the area around Le Pègue in the Drôme and around Nîmes in eastern Languedoc; while other centers were also active in eastern Provence and western Languedoc. The Rhône basin productions are characterized particularly by a distinctive style of painted decoration called "Rhodanian subgeometric," as well as by certain distinctive forms such as the indigenous urn (a noncooking form that was probably meant as a beer pot). The range of forms produced in Massalian Cream-ware (drinking cups, bowls, pitchers, plates, lekanai, lekythoi, lekanides, etc.) was initially inspired primarily by Ionian models, then Attic models (in the fifth and fourth centuries BCE), and finally by Campanian ceramics from the third century BCE on, although with many hybrid Ionio-Attic forms and some distinctive Massalian inventions (especially the pitchers). The indigenous productions included Greek-style drinking cups, Etruscan and Massalian shaped pitchers, and a range of indigenous forms (urns, carenated bowls, dimple-base bowls); and these represent a hybrid fusion of local and exotic forms, and local and exotic techniques, and local and exotic decorative motifs (fig. 7.27).[254]

Some Common Forms: Massalian Cream Ware

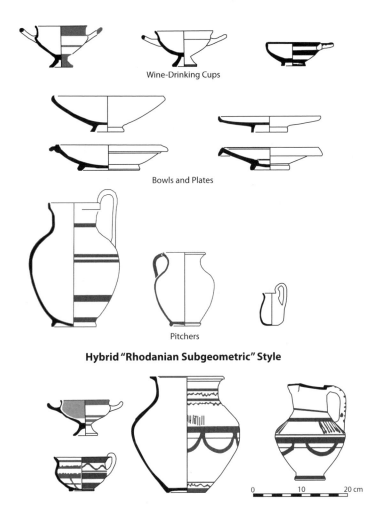

Wine-Drinking Cups

Bowls and Plates

Pitchers

Hybrid "Rhodanian Subgeometric" Style

0   10   20 cm

FIGURE 7.27

Examples of some common Massalian Cream-ware drinking cups, plates, pitchers; and indigenous hybrid Cream-ware with Rhodanian Subgeometric decoration (after Dicocer: Py 1993b).

Production of Gray-monochrome tableware also began in Massalian workshops by about 575 BCE, and this style was very quickly picked up by indigenous potters as well as by the Massalian colony of Agde. However, Gray-monochrome had a shorter life span than Cream-ware, with its popularity declining over the course of the fifth century BCE and production ending by about 375 BCE. The work of Charlette Arcelin-Pradelle was instrumental in identifying and localizing a number of workshops at Marseille and in the Rhône basin and subsequent work has added to that list (fig. 7.28).[255] At least fourteen different production groups have now been identified, representing workshops at Massalia (four), Agde (three), and the rest in the Rhône basin, western Languedoc, and Roussillon.

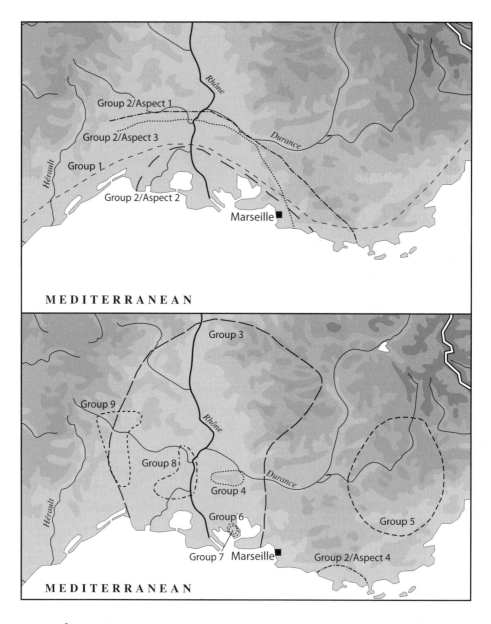

FIGURE 7.28

Gray-monochrome pottery distribution zones for different workshop centers: Massalian productions (top) and indigenous productions (bottom)(after Dietler 2005a).

These are all wheel-thrown pots with a highly purified clay fired in a reducing atmosphere to produce a light to dark gray color. Decoration is generally limited to channeling and comb incisions in a wavy pattern. But what is especially interesting about them is that from the beginning they represent a hybrid production geared toward the indigenous market and tastes specific to each region. That is, they combine Greek production

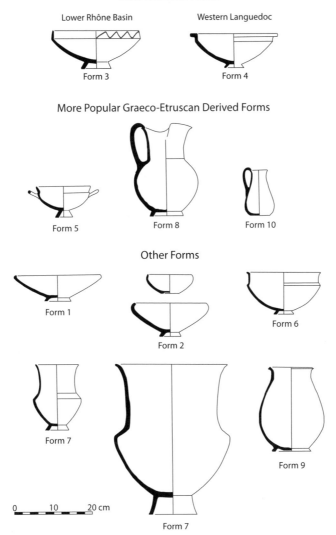

Most Common Forms

Lower Rhône Basin   Western Languedoc

Form 3   Form 4

More Popular Graeco-Etruscan Derived Forms

Form 5   Form 8   Form 10

Other Forms

Form 1

Form 2

Form 6

Form 7

0   10   20 cm

Form 7

Form 9

FIGURE 7.29

Examples of some of the common forms of Gray-monochrome ceramics (after Arcelin-Pradelle 1984; courtesy of De Boccard Editions).

techniques with a range of forms drawn from both the Greek (drinking cups, pitchers, bowls) and local (carenated bowls, urns, dimple-base bowls) repertoires (fig. 7.29). In fact, indigenous-derived forms account for over three quarters of all Gray-monochrome shards of recognizable forms found in the Rhône basin.[256] Moreover, by far the most popular form in the Rhône basin is a carenated bowl of indigenous type (Form 3 of Arcelin-Pradelle, or GR-MONO 3 of DICOCER) that resembles the CNT-LOR C4 form that extends back to the Bronze Age: in Provence it represents over 52 percent of all the

Gray-monochrome shards of identifiable forms found in the region, and it is the most common form for all but two of the production groups (in some cases constituting up to 95 percent of the production of a group).[257] This form is considerably less dominant in eastern Languedoc, but at Lattes it also represents about 56 percent of the Gray-monochrome ceramics.[258] The five Greek-derived forms combined (Arcelin-Pradelle Forms 1, 4, 5, 8, and 10) account for only about 14 percent of the total production in the Rhône basin, and among these, only the *oinochoe* pitcher (Form 8) and drinking cups (Forms 5 and 5a) have any numerical significance outside the immediate area of Marseille.[259] The Rhône basin situation is in marked contrast to the productions across the Hérault River in western Languedoc and Roussillon, where a Greek-derived form of wide, low bowl with a flat protruding lip (*"plat à marli"*: Arcelin-Pradelle Form 4; GR-MONO 4) is the predominant type. Thousands of examples have been found in this region as opposed to the approximately eighteen examples known from Provence.[260]

Initially, these wares were largely confined to sites within about thirty kilometers from the coast. However, by the late sixth and early fifth centuries BCE both Cream-ware and Gray-monochrome were found at virtually every settlement in the lower Rhône basin (including hillforts, villages, and farmsteads), and they were vastly better represented than any other non-CNT ceramics except amphorae until the influx of Campanian tableware in the second century BCE. The quantities of Attic fineware, for example, were miniscule in comparison. However, a quantitative discrepancy in the importance of imported tablewares persisted between coastal and interior sites. Moreover, preferences for one or the other of these two wares varied widely, as did their quantitative significance, although a taste for Gray-monochrome predominated at about two-thirds of indigenous sites before the mid–fifth century BCE.[261] Lattes was somewhat unusual (along with Tonnerre 1, Le Pègue, and Mont Garou) in that the taste was largely for Cream-ware rather than Gray-monochrome. Cream-wear averaged between 25 and 35 percent of the non-amphora ceramics from the mid–fifth through the mid–third centuries BCE, before Cream-ware cups and bowls began to decline in favor of Campanian versions; whereas Gray-monochrome never rose above about 13 percent and was usually in the range of 6 percent or less. Moreover, most of the Cream-ware at Lattes seems to have come from Massalia, with very few examples from indigenous workshops, and it consists predominantly of pitchers, with cups (especially one-handled cups) and a variety of bowls making up most of the rest.[262] Although sites toward the interior were receiving amphorae and some fineware from Massalia, most of the Gray-monochrome ware used at these sites was locally produced and distributed through indigenous exchange networks. What is more, tableware pottery was not only moving inland from the coast: sites such as Espeyran on the Rhône delta show that by the late sixth century Gray-monochrome pottery was also moving south from indigenous production sites at the same time that imports were arriving from the coast. Moreover, in a number of coastal locations, small-scale indigenous productions began to augment or replace Massalian Gray-monochrome imports.[263]

The regional data concerning various aspects of foodways are extremely complex. But what emerges fairly clearly from this analysis of changing food practices over the course of the colonial encounter is, in the first place, a curious inversion. Native Gauls remained almost completely indifferent to Etruscan, Greek, and Roman cooking ceramics, yet they enthusiastically adopted selected elements of exotic tableware. Indeed, it is safe to say that by the late sixth century BCE most inhabitants of the Rhône basin were consuming alcohol (both local and imported) from imported drinking cups or hybrid colonial wares. For several centuries this interest was largely confined to the realm of drinking vessels (and a highly selected range within this category), but by the mid–third century BCE demand had begun to expand to other eating vessels such as bowls and plates. Greek colonists, on the other hand, remained remarkably resistant to any Gallic penetration of their tableware, but initially relied heavily on native cooking ceramics (at least as far as the limited evidence from early levels indicates). It was only several generations after the founding of the colony that Massalians began to demand a more orthodox Greek repertoire in the kitchen. Ironically, by the second and first centuries BCE, this Greek repertoire of cooking pots was produced for them in indigenous workshops catering to Massalian tastes. It is important to point out that this easy initial acceptance of local cooking pots in Greek kitchens cannot be explained by an inability of early settlers to produce their own. After all, Massalian potters began producing tablewares (Cream-ware and Gray-monochrome) almost immediately: within a few decades after the foundation of the colony, they were making these ceramics in sufficient quantities to export them widely, all the while importing additional tableware from Athens and elsewhere. This emphasizes even more acutely the almost obsessive adherence to Greek models in the performative domain of consumption in the *andron*, with an apparent indifference to how meals were produced in the kitchen (at least initially).

One tempting possible explanation for this pattern is that it may represent the importance of native wives in the households of early settlers. It provides possible additional evidence for the pattern of intermarriage suspected on other grounds, as discussed in chapter 4. In the rigidly structured division of labor and gender relations in Greek households, wives did the cooking and did not eat with their husbands. It is not unreasonable to imagine that native women married to Massalian husbands would have preferred using the pots they best knew how manipulate in the kitchen to produce the new recipes expected by their husbands, and that husbands would not have spent much time observing cooking procedures as long as food of the proper type arrived on the table. This would, in any case, have been performatively constituted as proper Massalian food by being consumed in the appropriate vessels in the arena of male commensality at the *deipnon*. In wealthier households, one might imagine the same scenario, only with slaves or local people hired as cooks performing the duties that wives fulfilled in other households. The choice of ceramics used might be much the same in either case.

How, then, can we explain the eventual replacement of indigenous cooking pots with imported Greek cooking vessels and the Massalian production of such ceramics beginning in the fourth century BCE? If the intermarriage hypothesis is correct, then this could be the result of an increasing "Hellenization" (the one time this word may be admissible) of subsequent generations of Massalian wives and daughters, perhaps abetted by an influx of women from Phocaea with the large-scale flight from the mother city to the western Mediterranean in the late sixth century BCE. It corresponds roughly with the development of an increasingly conservative and rigid social ethos among the upper classes and a constitution that preserved Ionian laws and a rather archaic, closed form of aristocratic government. This sociopolitical hierarchy emphasized three-generation descent from a family of citizens as a condition of eligibility for access to power and was, therefore, obviously an archaizing construction that dates to a period after the sixth century BCE when this condition would be possible for the first time. One can imagine a new orthodoxy in the material equipment of the kitchen as being one manifestation of a new general concern to construct a sense of Hellenic identity during the period when this idea was emerging in the broader Greek diaspora, and as a product of an anxiety about the possibility of "going native"— a Massalian version of the colonial angst behind the Statutes of Kilkenny in fourteenth-century Ireland. Unfortunately, the state of the archaeology of domestic structures at Massalia and most of its colonies is not yet sufficient to judge with any subtlety the extent of these patterns and changes among different social groups and orders, and interpretive statements must be treated with caution. Nevertheless, preliminary analysis has certainly opened questions that should direct the attention of researchers in future excavations and publications.

On the indigenous side, the colonial encounter was initially articulated through the performative ritual domain of feasting, with an alien imported alcoholic beverage, wine, adapted to native practices along with a selected set of ceramic vessels for its consumption. This domain of ritual commensality continued to be the primary venue for the introduction of other exotic culinary items, although for several centuries these were primarily limited to items associated with drinking. The consequences of these introductions to the realm of commensal politics stimulated an escalating demand for a function-specific set of tablewares that was met by both imports and the emergence of a new indigenous hybrid ceramic industry. These special wares were a parallel ceramic domain most probably associated for a long period with feasting; but by the second century BCE, Campanian bowls were actually beginning to largely replace native bowls in general—strongly suggesting that imported ceramics had invaded the domain of daily meals as well. The taste for new forms, such as plates beginning in the third century BCE, has been suggested by some scholars as part of a shift to a more individualized pattern of dining. The scenario envisaged is one of people generally eating boiled foods out of individual bowls filled from an urn, but consuming stewed foods directly out of a large communal jatte (forty to seventy centimeters in diameter) until the second century BCE, when these large jattes essentially passed out of the indigenous CNT repertoire.

Individual service on plates and in small bowls would have replaced this practice and become the norm, an interpretation supported by pointing to the multiplication of small low bowls in CNT ware and the increasing popularity of Campanian plates.[264] However, it is also possible that ceramic plates are something that simply began to gradually replace basketry or wooden platters for serving grilled meats at feasts during the third century BCE, and then entered more quotidian realms of dining along with Campanian bowls during the second century BCE without signaling a major transformation of dining customs.

Whatever the case, these exotic appropriations may have originally served as indexical markers of the status of events, but they do not appear to have served as markers of the status of social classes or groups. From the beginning, they were consumed in all homes at settlements without any signs of restrictive access. For example, even the large central-courtyard houses at Lattes showed inventories of cooking and tableware ceramics that were identical to those of other contemporary small houses at the site.[265] The role food played in competition for prestige and power within indigenous societies would have been in terms of quantity rather than style of consumption. One gets little sense of the use of cuisine in patterns of diacritical symbolic segregation of classes, something that corresponds to other indications of a lack of strong hierarchical class formation in the Rhône basin before the Augustan period. In the midst of these changing tablewares, the repertoire of cooking ware remained impervious to outside influences, with the sole exception of mortars. And this remained true until nearly a century after the Roman conquest. Urns continued to remain the overwhelmingly most popular cooking vessel, implying a continued preference for boiled foods. Jattes experienced a slight decline in popularity during the fourth century BCE, but they remained the only other popular cooking pot. Lids were in constant demand, and were presumably used to seal both of these pot types. Imported cooking wares, however, remained at best a novelty item present in miniscule proportions, even at coastal sites in the most direct contact with Greek and Roman traders. Moreover, there was no move toward hybrid forms in the native CNT repertoire. All indications are that native peoples saw little use for foreign cooking pots and remained indifferent to them for over six centuries, as they did also for garum and, probably, olive oil.

On a broader level, it should also be noted that the diets of both sides in the encounter came to depend heavily on foods imported from the other. The staple foundation of the Massalian diet, maza and bread, would have increasingly depended on importing barley and wheat from native peoples of Mediterranean France. Reciprocally, once a taste had developed for Etruscan wine, local peoples became accustomed to a substantial flow of wine imported from Massalia, and then Italy, to fuel the cycles of feasting that were crucial to the operation of commensal politics and labor mobilization. Wine did not replace beer, but it would have become a valued and symbolically important complement that was consumed in substantial (if variable) quantities. This large-scale exchange of basic foodstuffs had a variety of entangling consequences that were significant for the regional political economy, but it did not lead to either emulation of culinary practices or hybrid fusions of such practices on a significant scale. Rather, one gets a sense of culturally distinctive domains of consumption in which selective alien goods were periodically appropriated and "indigenized" according to local aesthetic and technical dispositions that evolved on a microregional basis in locally discrete ways. This means that foodways of the various parties to the encounter were neither isolated nor static: they were interconnected in complex ways and undergoing constant transformations. But rather than leading to regional "acculturation," homogenization, or hybridity, these processes of consumption and transformation in the culinary realm followed different local social and cultural logics and produced different chains of unintended consequences.

8

CONSTRUCTED SPACES: LANDSCAPES OF EVERYDAY LIFE AND RITUAL

The colonial encounter unfolded within an evolving set of interrelated material and conceptual spaces that both organized the flow of interactions and were reconfigured by the colonial experience. This chapter examines two dimensions of that set of spaces—landscapes of everyday life and ritual—and asks what these features can tell us about the nature and consequences of the encounter. Obviously, the distinction between the two is, to a large extent artificial, and these terms do not necessarily describe separate physical spaces: many ritual practices were carried out within urban settings, and many aspects of the built environment of towns were imbued with sacred significance.[1] But this provisional analytic separation does have some heuristic merit. In both Greek and indigenous societies, most sites of funerary ritual (aside from infant burials) were located outside urban contexts. On the other hand, the location of other kinds of ritual places, or at least the architectonic marking of such places, offers an interesting contrast between Greek and indigenous societies. Greek settlements were generally centered on monumental buildings dedicated to religious ritual, while indigenous settlements generally had no monumental public buildings within the city walls. Instead, traces of ritual structures are found in the countryside or reincorporated into ramparts. However, this pattern changed at a few Provençal sites during the third and second centuries BCE with the first traces of clear ritual structures inside settlements. Hence, it is useful to examine both the separations and intersections of these two domains in order to see what they can reveal about the changing nature of daily life. Obviously, a complete description of the history of urban and sacred landscapes is beyond the possibilities or purpose of this chapter.[2] Instead, it offers a selective exploration of some major transformations that are related to the colonial encounter.

URBAN LANDSCAPES

The everyday lives of people in Mediterranean France were structured by the civic and domestic environments that they constructed for themselves and inhabited; and these built environments were, reciprocally, an accretionary materialization of the cultural dispositions and life experiences of their inhabitants.[3] Urban landscapes of the region changed gradually but significantly during the course of the pre-Roman Iron Age, and these changes frequently have been linked by scholars to the evolving colonial situation. However, the relationship of such changes to the colonial encounter is by no means simple or straightforward, such as the emulation of Greek houses or the Greek *polis* imagined by earlier scholars under the rubric of Hellenization. Rather, the transformation of both indigenous and Greek settlements must be seen as an historical social process with a great deal of local variation, in which entanglement with the broader Mediterranean colonial world played variable and complicated roles. Changes in urban landscapes were in part a response to changes in the regional political economy under conditions of colonial interaction, but they took place within the framework of local cultural structures and cosmologies and of evolving local social and political relations. This was the case even with the further, and more dramatic, transformations that occurred during the period of Roman domination, when a more direct and pervasive colonial hand was operative.

The process of change in indigenous settlements of the region is frequently described in the aggregate as one of "urbanization" or "urbanism," and a subtle tendency toward evolutionist teleology sometimes underlies discussions of this phenomenon, with the Greco-Roman city as the tacitly accepted end point of evolutionary development. For instance, various factors are credited with "hindering" or "slowing" the evolution of societies of the interior in comparison to those along the coast that had direct contact with Greeks and Etruscans. However, the towns that developed in Mediterranean France were quite different from both Greek colonies in the region and the large urban settlements called *oppida* that developed farther north in continental "Celtic" Europe during the late phases of the Iron Age. In contrast to the latter, indigenous Mediterranean towns were both small and very densely occupied. They were usually less than five to ten hectares in size and exceeded 20 hectares only in a few exceptional cases, whereas the continental oppida ranged from about 20 to over 1,500 hectares and had much more dispersed arrangements of domestic units organized in quite different ways, with radically different architecture and fortifications.[4] As will be shown, indigenous Mediterranean towns also differed from Greek colonial settlements in terms of most of their basic characteristics, including the organization of the urban landscape (especially the general absence of monumental public buildings or open public spaces in indigenous towns) and the basic form and internal organization of houses. Of course, there were also important regional and individual differences among the settlements within each of these broad categories that can be obscured while trying to describe general trends. It is the interplay between contrasts and commonalities, examined on a variety of shifting scales, that offers the best potential for understanding the relationship between colonial encounters and urban landscapes.

The possibilities for examining transformations in urban landscapes and the experience of daily life are unusually good in Mediterranean France because of the extraordinary quantity and quality of settlement data, and these data are especially good in the lower Rhône area (figs. 8.1 and 8.2). For example, in Provence, sites such as Le Mont Garou, Saint-Blaise, l'Île de Martigues, Saint-Pierre-les-Martigues, and Marseille offer stratigraphic sequences stretching over many centuries (in some cases, virtually the entire Iron Age); and eastern Languedoc offers sites of comparable duration, such as Le Marduel, Lattes, and Espeyran. Moreover, excavations at many sites have uncovered areas of sufficient extent (with preserved house walls, living floors, streets, and fortifications) to yield a good grasp of the overall organization of urban landscapes rather than simply small windows of stratigraphy. A number of recent excavations have also yielded extraordinarily good possibilities for reconstructing the details of daily life, including the organization of domestic space, the repertoire of household equipment, the range of cooking and storage features, and the performance of craft activities in and around dwellings.[5]

In general, such data are much richer and more complete for Late Iron Age levels at sites (from the mid–fifth century BCE on). The small, fortified town of l'Île de Martigues, for instance, offers a near Pompeii-like surface of abandonment after an episode of destruction by fire with complete inventories of ceramics left in place and hearths preserved in the streets.[6] And the extensive, long-term excavations at Lattes are gradually revealing a detailed picture of the evolution of urban life on a large scale and with remarkable chronological precision.[7] Finally, recent programs of intensive regional survey and rescue excavation are beginning to yield a more detailed understanding of the relations between towns, villages, and farmsteads and their location within changing social and natural ecologies.[8] The very wealth of data available and the consequent recognition of local variability make generalizations subject to various caveats. However, it is possible to identify some trends in the transformation of urban landscapes during the Iron Age.[9]

VERNACULAR EXPERIMENTATION

As noted, settlements in Mediterranean France show a history of significant transformations in several aspects during the colonial period, including especially spatial organization, defensive structures, and construction materials and techniques. When viewed on a very general scale, and with a chronology based on crude phases encompassing several generations each, this can give the impression of sudden uniform regional change, lending credence to the idea of a dramatic colonial impact. However, when these elements

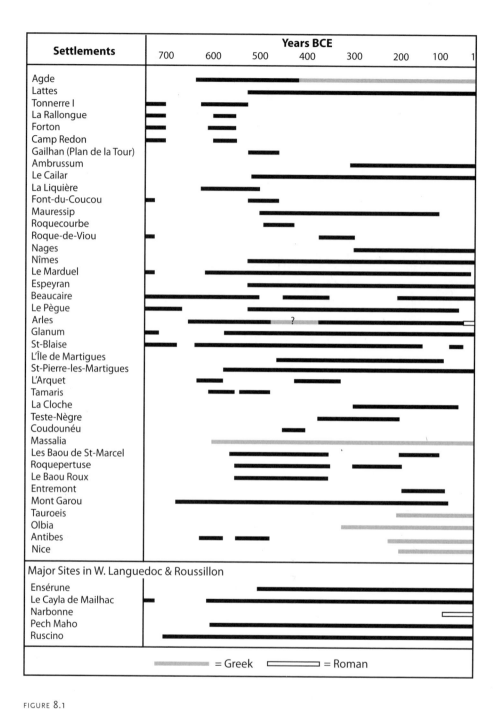

Settlements	Years BCE						
	700	600	500 400	300	200	100	1

Agde
Lattes
Tonnerre I
La Rallongue
Forton
Camp Redon
Gailhan (Plan de la Tour)
Ambrussum
Le Cailar
La Liquière
Font-du-Coucou
Mauressip
Roquecourbe
Roque-de-Viou
Nages
Nîmes
Le Marduel
Espeyran
Beaucaire
Le Pègue
Arles
Glanum
St-Blaise
L'Île de Martigues
St-Pierre-les-Martigues
L'Arquet
Tamaris
La Cloche
Teste-Nègre
Coudounéu
Massalia
Les Baou de St-Marcel
Roquepertuse
Le Baou Roux
Entremont
Mont Garou
Tauroeis
Olbia
Antibes
Nice

Major Sites in W. Languedoc & Roussillon

Ensérune
Le Cayla de Mailhac
Narbonne
Pech Maho
Ruscino

= Greek   = Roman

FIGURE 8.1

Chronological chart of the periods of occupation of the principal settlements in the lower Rhône basin discussed in the book.

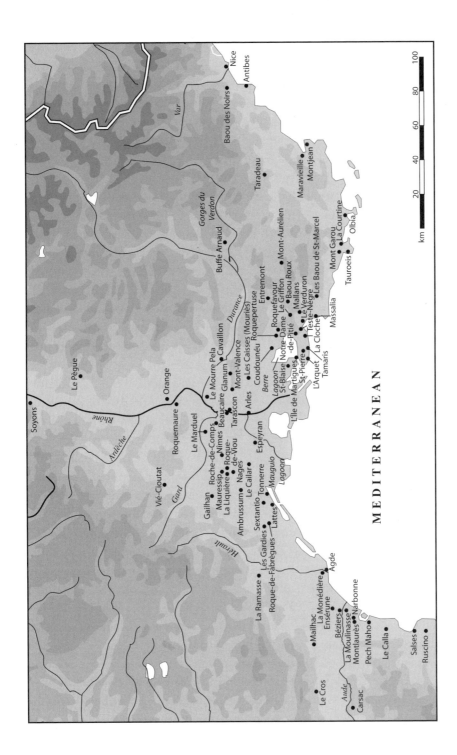

FIGURE 8.2

Map of settlements in Mediterranean France discussed in the book.

are unpacked and examined on a detailed comparative scale within and between sites, the picture that emerges resembles much more a complex mix of local conservatism and experimentation that eventually resulted in a limited set of vernacular adaptations to a range of shared social challenges and opportunities structured by similar cultural dispositions. Ethnographic research has shown that there is very good reason to examine independently such things as changes in settlement organization, house form, and building materials and techniques, as these often respond to quite different problems and opportunities and can have radically different social implications and consequences.[10]

As explained in more detail later, it is clear that, although innovations such as stone fortification walls, mud-brick or stone architecture, and rectilinear settlement organization eventually came to characterize most of the lower Rhône basin, the process by which these elements became culturally established as defining the customary urban landscape—that is, the process by which they spread and were transformed from innovation to tradition—took several hundred years. In addition, although ultimately during the Late Iron Age these features were usually associated together, they frequently spread independently, in different permutations with variable regional chronologies and patterns.[11] In general, settlements in the coastal zone were the earliest innovators, but the pattern was far from uniform even within the coastal area. Many settlements of the region remained indifferent to certain innovations for over a couple of centuries after the beginning of the colonial encounter. This was especially true of sites of the interior, but many settlements of the littoral showed a similar conservatism. For instance, inhabitants of the site of Le Baou Roux, only seventeen kilometers from Massalia, were still using wattle-and-daub houses until near the end of the fifth century BCE, almost two centuries after some of their neighbors had changed to mud brick.[12] Moreover, some elements, such as mud-brick architecture, never had much success in penetrating very far beyond the littoral zone despite the deep proliferation of stone fortifications.

What is more, innovation certainly did not cease once these features became common. Throughout the Iron Age there was a continual process of experimentation with such things as the size, form, and furnishing of houses and with the appropriation and adaptation of alien models.[13] The appearance of central courtyard style houses at a few settlements in the third and second centuries BCE, discussed later, is an illuminating case in point, as it nicely illustrates the process of creative vernacular experimentation with a new form within an evolving tradition.[14] It should also be emphasized that the colonial encounter occurred in the context of indigenous societies already in a continual process of experimentation and change. Etruscans and Greeks were not the sudden catalyst for provoking dynamic transformations in previously static societies, but rather an occasional source for creative appropriation of some elements and a contributing agent in the emerging regional structure of economic and political relations that shaped the social challenges and opportunities to which local groups responded. Nor did architecture and urban organization at Massalia and its colonies provide a stable uniform "Greek" model for emulation. They were the product of a similar process of local experimentation played out through a different set of cultural dispositions toward civic and domestic space and form and a different structure of social relations.

COLONIAL PERIOD INNOVATIONS

For the period of the precolonial transition from the Late Bronze Age to the Early Iron Age, evidence is less abundant than for later periods, but traces of both local continuity and experimentation within regionally diverse traditions of settlement types are evident throughout Mediterranean France. In the mountainous areas of eastern Provence, there was a persistence of scattered small settlements in rock shelters and caves, as exemplified in the Gorges du Verdon.[15] The coastal lowland areas of the Lower Rhône basin and western Languedoc were dotted with scattered hamlets and small villages. Often, as around the Mauguio lagoon, these were on the edges of coastal lagoons. The interior areas of the Rhône basin began to witness the establishment of hilltop villages, along with the persistence of some cave and rock shelter occupations. The domestic units at these small sites were generally one-room structures of wattle-and-daub construction on a post frame. They were arranged in noncontiguous formations according to organizational criteria that are often difficult to discern.[16]

From the late seventh century BCE on, a number of innovations began to occur at scattered sites along the coast that, as noted, would gradually become more generalized throughout the region over the course of about two centuries, resulting in a set of patterns that Michel Py has grouped under the heading of the *oppidum-cité*.[17] These changes involved several features, including (1) the construction of monumental stone ramparts marking the boundaries of settlements, (2) a shift in house construction materials and techniques, (3) an alteration in the form of houses, and (4) a transformation of settlement organization. The change in construction techniques consisted of the replacement of post frames by stone foundations with load-bearing walls and the replacement of wattle-and-daub by stone or mud-brick construction. The change in the form of domestic structures was from irregular oval or rectangular single room constructions to neatly rectangular units, and, eventually (during the Late Iron Age), to domestic units composed of multiple rooms of this type. The arrangement of these houses also changed from detached units with variable intervening spaces and orientations to tight alignment in contiguous clusters, in rectilinear fashion, separated by streets onto which the domestic units opened. Let us examine each of these features in turn, as well as explore the relationships among them.

Fortifications   The history of the appearance and spread of defensive ramparts at indigenous settlements has already been treated in the examination of violence in chapter 6. Without repeating that discussion in detail, let me simply summarize that history briefly and discuss a few additional features that are relevant to the theme of urban landscapes. In the lower Rhône basin, ramparts appeared first at Massalia and in the area in close proximity to Massalia. Before the mid–sixth century BCE, only four sites are known to have such defensive structures in the lower Rhône basin: Massalia, Les Baou de Saint-Marcel (only seven kilometers east of Massalia), Tamaris (twenty-three kilometers north-west of Massalia), and Saint-Blaise (about sixteen kilometers north of Tamaris).[18] Both the number and geographic range of defended sites expanded slowly, and first along the coast, during the succeeding century and a half until, by the fourth century BCE, ramparts had become a standard feature of most settlements throughout the region, even as far north as sites such as Le Pègue in the Drôme (about 130 kilometers north of Marseille). They surrounded sites ranging in area from as little as 0.1 hectare to as much as 20 to 30 hectares, although examples of the latter are very rare and late—essentially Nîmes and Glanum (and perhaps Arles). More usually the upper limits were in the range of about four to seven hectares, depending on the region.

Against the naive suggestion that these ramparts were simply imitations of Massalia stands the fact of the considerable diversity in the form and construction techniques of early indigenous ramparts.[19] In the first place, there are several types of arrangements that represent different topographic strategies. At the minimal end of the scale, in terms of effort invested in construction, is the so-called *éperon barré* (or defended spur), which takes advantage of natural defenses by simply closing off one side of a plateau spur or promontory.[20] At the maximal end of the scale, there are entirely closed ramparts encircling settlements. The latter are relatively uncommon and confined to sites such as Lattes with no natural topographic protection. A middle-range strategy involved either blocking vulnerable areas of terrain with discontinuous sections of fortifications or enclosing two or three sides of a plateau or hill with fortifications and relying on cliffs or other elements of relief to provide natural defenses or the other sides (the latter is often called *appui sur à-pic*, or pincer enclosure).[21] But beyond this diversity in strategic layouts, the basic wall and tower arrangements and techniques also exhibit great variation. Many were simple dry-stone walls, sometimes with earth fill, sometimes of double or triple construction, but almost always made of undressed stones (with the exception of a couple of second-century BCE ramparts at Saint-Blaise and Glanum). In a few cases (Baou Roux, Lattes, and Agde), mud brick was also used in rampart walls. Sometimes the rampart was also accompanied by fronting walls (for instance, at Nages, Lattes, and Taradeau) or ditches (for example, at Roquefavour).

As Py has observed, these were not designed and built by architects or specialist masons and stone cutters: they show various signs of learning on the job and experimentation, such as rebuilding of walls and sporadic doubling (as older walls were incorporated within new thicker walls; fig. 8.3).[22] Most probably they were built by communal labor organized through work parties.[23] When towers or bastions were included, they were generally few in number, and there were regional differences in their form. Interestingly, in Provence, the area closest to the potential model of Massalia, the Greek pattern of regularly spaced rectangular towers was not followed; local peoples initially preferred instead a small number of towers of ovoid or rounded form.[24] This pattern persisted

FIGURE 8.3
The rampart at Saint-Blaise showing three phases of construction: the "Hellenistic" wall (left), the archaic rampart (center), and a Medieval construction (upper right).

in Provence until rectangular towers became more common during the fourth century BCE. In Languedoc, the trajectory was the inverse, with an initial preference for rectangular towers shifting to a dominance of rounded towers in the third century BCE. In both cases, regularly spaced series of towers along the curtain walls did not become common until the mid–third century BCE; and by the late second century BCE, towers were more or less abandoned, except at gates and corners, in favor of simple straight walls. In the second century BCE, Saint-Blaise and Glanum did adopt walls that were not only of Greek style but show evidence of probable Greek craftsmen involved in their construction (based on the technique of dressing stone, the wall assemblage, and the presence of Greek letters on many blocks[25]). However, at Saint-Blaise, this impressive new rampart of carefully dressed limestone blocks faithfully followed the trace of the prior rampart (fig. 8.3).

Construction Materials Changes in house form and construction materials also occurred first along the coast, although not necessarily always at the sites with the earliest ramparts. The Late Bronze Age technique of wattle-and-daub construction on a wood frame continued to characterize nearly all domestic architecture in the region during the Early Iron Age (that is, at least five generations after the founding of Massalia). The earliest deviations from this pattern occurred during the first half of the sixth century BCE at a group of three sites located within about fifteen kilometers of each other in an area along the Provençal coast about twenty-five kilometers west of Massalia: L'Arquet, Tamaris, and Saint-Blaise.[26] The first two are small settlements built on spurs of land jutting into the sea and the last is a hilltop settlement. This new building technique consisted of solid load-bearing walls (stone, mud brick, or rammed earth) constructed on foundations of stone.[27] In some cases, as at Tamaris, one can see transitional experiments with first wattle-and-daub houses and then houses with mixed stone and wattle-and-daub walls. Two of the settlements with these architectural innovations (Saint-Blaise and Tamaris) had a contemporary rampart, while L'Arquet did not. Another site that shared the distinction of having an early rampart (Les Baou de Saint-Marcel) continued the traditional wattle-and-daub domestic architecture during this early period, as did the settlement inside the first (late seventh century BCE) rampart at Saint-Blaise.

During the second half of the sixth and early fifth centuries BCE, several other settlements along the coast or the near coastal hinterland began to employ the stone foundation construction technique. They include Les Baou de Saint-Marcel, only seven kilometers from the city gates of Massalia, but also settlements as far away as Montjean, Antibes, Saint-Pierre-les-Martigues, and Arles in Provence; and Lattes, Sextantio, Les Gardies, Agde, and La Monédière in Languedoc. However, many sites in this coastal region continued to build houses in the traditional style for several generations. At Le Baou Roux, only seventeen kilometers north of Marseille, for instance, wattle-and-daub houses remained the norm until the end of the fifth century BCE, or roughly two hundred years after the change to the new technique at Saint-Blaise, a mere thirty-five kilometers away. A very few sites with stone construction techniques also appeared during this period farther to the interior of the lower Rhône basin, such as Le Marduel, Plan-de-la-Tour, Le Mourre Pela, and Le Pègue, but wattle-and-daub was still used at sites such as Gaujac and Vié-Cioutat in the fourth century BCE.[28] All of the littoral sites noted except Arles and Antibes had a contemporary rampart, as did the interior sites of Le Marduel and Le Mourre Pela. However, at Les Gardies the rampart preceded the stone-built houses, and there are several other sites with initial ramparts without contemporary stone or mud-brick house construction (for example, Les Baou des Noirs, Roquecourbe, Maravielle, Soyons, and Le Baou Roux). Inversely, neither of the interior sites of Le Pègue and Plan de la Tour had ramparts contemporary with the earliest stone structures there. Moreover, house construction techniques were not always uniform over an entire site: some settlements show evidence of contemporary structures of both post support and stone foundation types (for example, Plan de la Tour, Les Gardies, Lattes, and Marseille). Moreover, although rectangular house forms, stone-foundation support wall construction, and rectilinear compact settlement plans tend to be associated at several sites, this is not a necessarily coterminous relationship. The contrast between the geographically close and similarly situated coastal settlements of L'Arquet and Tamaris illustrates this well: L'Arquet has all of these features together (but no rampart), while at Tamaris the rectangular house form with stone foundation construction existed first in a nonrectilinear settlement organization (with a rampart) before developing a rectilinear pattern later.[29]

In the littoral zone, mud brick eventually became the most common material employed for wall elevations above the stone foundation in this kind of construction.[30] However, stone was generally preferred for load-bearing walls at interior sites beyond about thirty kilometers from the coast, and wattle-and-daub remained the most common general technique in the deep interior (for example, in the Cevennes and the Ardèche),[31] as it did for the rest of France beyond the Mediterranean throughout the Iron Age.[32] Examples of mud-brick architecture (in the form of walls still preserved in elevation, walls that have fallen into rooms during periods of abandon or reconstruction, and fragments in rubble levels) are known from at least forty-four sites in Mediterranean France dating to before the end of the first century BCE (figs. 8.4 and 8.5).[33] Aside from Marseille, Agde, Olbia, and the Roman colony of Narbonne, this includes twenty-six indigenous sites in the lower Rhône region and another fourteen in western Languedoc-Roussillon. Only six of those in the Rhône basin are more than about thirty kilometers from the sea, and only two of those are more than fifty kilometers distant.[34] In other words, about 76 percent are within thirty kilometers of the sea, and all but one of those dating to the Early Iron Age fall within this zone.

As it happens, southern France was the last region in the western Mediterranean to develop a tradition of mud-brick architecture, and, as the previous discussion makes

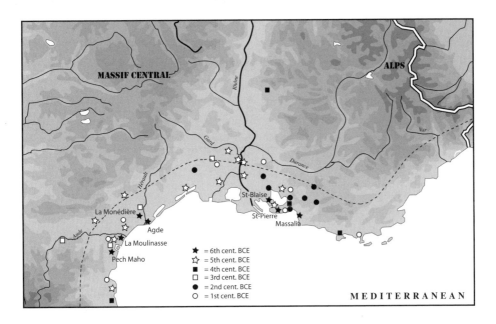

FIGURE 8.4

Map showing the spread of mud-brick architecture in Mediterranean France. Symbols indicate the different centuries of the first traces of mud brick at settlements of the region. Sites with sixth-century BCE evidence are named. Hatched line indicates zone within approximately thirty kilometers from the sea (data from Chazelles-Gazzal 1997, with updated additions).

FIGURE 8.5

Mud bricks of different colors from a rubble level composed of a third-century BCE wall that has fallen
into a room of house 52101 at Lattes; scale in centimeters (UFRAL).

clear, it remained predominantly a phenomenon of the Mediterranean littoral before
the Roman conquest.[35] Aside from the curious appearance of a mud-brick rampart at the
Heuneburg hillfort in southwestern Germany in the late sixth century BCE,[36] and one
example of mud-brick architecture in the Limousin during the first century BCE,[37] the
technique did not penetrate beyond the lower Rhône basin until the period of Augustus;
and it was little used in southern France beyond the coastal plain until that period. Mud-
brick construction on a stone foundation was a long-established Near Eastern and Greek
technique, dating back several millennia in both areas. It had been adopted along the
coasts of North Africa, Sicily, and southern Spain by the eighth century BCE following
Phoenician colonial encounters in those areas, and it was in use in Etruria by the seventh century as well. Moreover, northeastern Spain had an ancient indigenous tradition
of such architecture dating back to the Late Bronze Age that extended far inland.[38]

In France, traces of mud-brick walls on a stone foundation dating to the beginning
decades of the sixth century BCE have been identified at Marseille (although wattle-and-
daub architecture was also used contemporaneously).[39] The earliest clearly attested example of mud-brick construction in the Rhône basin outside Marseille was at Saint-Blaise
during the second quarter of the sixth century. Only five other indigenous sites in Mediterranean France have clear evidence for mud-brick construction before the last quarter
of the sixth century BCE, and none of these was in the lower Rhône basin: they were Agde
and La Monédière in the lower Hérault valley,[40] Le Cros at Caunes-Minervois in the Aude
basin,[41] and Pech Maho and La Moulinasse on the coast of western Languedoc.[42]

A connection between the use of mud brick at Marseille and Saint-Blaise seems highly probable given their close proximity and contemporary evidence of intensive trading contact. The early use of mud brick at Agde and La Monédière has also been interpreted as being linked to Greek models, and it has even been used by André Nickels to propose a resident Greek presence at these sites (which disappeared several generations before a genuine Greek colony was subsequently founded at Agde at the end of the fifth century BCE).[43] However, given the geographic proximity of Pech Maho and La Moulinasse to Spain and its indigenous tradition of mud-brick architecture, the earthen architecture expert Claire-Anne de Chazelles has suggested that traders from Iberia may have been a more likely catalyst for the precocity of the use of mud brick in this region.[44] The same argument would presumably pertain in the even earlier case of Le Cros as well.

By the late sixth and early fifth centuries BCE, the mud-brick technique had become more widespread at a number of settlements along the Mediterranean littoral, such as Saint-Pierre-les-Martigues and Lattes. Sometimes, as at Lattes, mud brick was used in combination with rammed earth construction.[45] By the end of the fifth century BCE, the mud-brick technique was used at many littoral sites ranging from Le Mont Garou,[46] Espeyran,[47] Le Coudounéu, and Arles in the Rhône basin to Le Port at Salses,[48] Le Calla de Durban[49] and Montlaurès in western Languedoc-Roussillon, although at Roquepertuse[50] and some other coastal sites, mud brick did not replace wattle-and-daub until the fourth century BCE. The technique had also been tried at a small number of sites of the interior, such Le Marduel, Beaucaire, and Tarascon by the end of the fifth century BCE. But it remained a minority taste north of the coastal plain, where walls of stone were preferred. For example, the people of Nages (only twenty-eight kilometers from the sea) were still building stone houses in the third and second centuries BCE, continuing a tradition in the Vaunage valley seen at the earlier nearby sites of Roque-de-Viou and Mauressip, when mud brick had been in use for over two hundred years at the site of Espeyran only twenty kilometers away.[51]

There is a common tendency among scholars working in the region to associate wattle-and-daub construction, often tellingly referred to as "*construction en matériaux périssables*," with temporary occupation of settlements and stone foundation load-bearing walls (of stone or mud brick), called "*construction en dur*," with permanent occupation, and to see the spread of the latter as a sign of an historical/evolutionary process of increasing "sedentarization."[52] However, it is not clear why one or the other type of construction technique should be necessarily associated with the mobility of the people occupying the structures, or especially with their conceptions of permanence. As the ethnographic record makes clear, wattle-and-daub houses are perfectly capable of lasting for a generation and forming the basis for a stable, long-term settlement that is considered "permanent" by its occupants.[53] This was certainly the case in non-Mediterranean France where Late Iron Age major urban centers much larger than anything in Mediterranean France were composed entirely of wattle-and-daub structures. In fact, the differences between these construction techniques, including relative labor and material investment (which need not be markedly different), offer little clue by themselves to the degree of "sedent-ism" at a site. This inference must be drawn from other evidence, such as faunal and floral indications of seasonality, density and nature of occupation debris, and patterns of repeated reconstruction. Judging from the quantities and range of ceramics (including large storage jars) and other domestic debris found at most Early Iron Age sites with wattle-and-daub houses and the complex mixed agropastoral subsistence base, it seems reasonable to posit that these were, in fact, occupied year-round on a basis that could be described as permanent from the viewpoint of residents of the settlement.[54] It can at least be said that this kind of evidence does not differ systematically from those sites with mud-brick or stone structures. Moreover, people at a number of settlements with wattle-and-daub houses invested enormous energy in the construction of monumental stone ramparts, which hardly implies a vision of impermanence. And mud-brick houses were constantly being leveled and rebuilt (albeit usually on the same spot), sometimes yielding multiple levels of rubble and reconstruction within a twenty-five-year period, which calls into question the conception of construction en dur and its aura of perma-nence. It is difficult to see how the periodic rearrangements, refurbishing, and room-to-room residence shifts found in mud-brick "permanent" settlements such as Saint-Pierre-les-Martigues or Lattes differ greatly from settlements such as La Liquière, which was occupied for over a century with wattle-and-daub houses.[55]

The concept of mobility seems to derive largely from a preconceived ethnocentric association of wattle-and-daub architecture with impermanence in a general evolution-ary scheme that does not take account of the time frame of the actual inhabitants (for whom a house designed to last twenty-five years would be "permanent"). As noted, one suspects that an implicit economizing argument underlies this evolutionary assump-tion: that this kind of building en dur involves more labor and therefore indicates an investment that would not have been made unless it could be maximized through longer use, although the precise calculation of relative labor and material costs between the two techniques has not been offered. The fact that mud brick was a technique used by Greeks has certainly played a role in the uncritical acceptance of this evolutionary logic (and in imbuing mud brick with an aura of technological sophistication and permanence), even though evidence of wattle-and-daub construction has also been found at Massalia. This feature is clearly reflected in the vocabulary commonly used to describe dwellings: those of indigenous peoples are generally called "huts" (cases or cabanes), whereas Greek dwell-ings are always referred to as houses (maisons). This dichotomy between native huts and the houses of colonists was also, of course, part of the standard system of hierarchical binarisms of modern European colonialism, and its use in this context should raise flags of alarm. It is a striking example of the dangers warned about at the beginning of this book.

This is more than semantic quibbling: such implicit attitudes can lead to some curi-ous paradoxes, such as the characterization of a period of over a century at La Liquière as a "fairly short occupation,"[56] while the settlement of L'Arquet, with its stone wall houses, lasted for less than half this time. It is also questionable that one can deduce a sudden increase in sedentism at settlements that were originally built in wattle-and-daub and later adopted mud-brick architecture, such as Le Baou-Roux, which continued the wattle-and-daub tradition until the end of the fifth century BCE. And what does one make of the case of Lattes, where the mid–fifth and mid–fourth centuries BCE marks (at least in one part of the site) a shift back to wattle-and-daub structures on top of a level of houses with stone foundations and earthen walls?[57]

To be sure, the broader argument made by Michel Py and others, that some indigenous sites were engaging in more intensive agricultural production to meet the demands of an expanding trade with Massalia, leading to greater concern with stable land tenure boundaries,[58] may well have merit. But this view does not explain the gradual adoption of mud-brick or stone wall construction techniques, a shortcoming that is especially evident with settlements of the interior that do not appear to have been receiving vast stocks of Greek or Etruscan goods sufficient to fuel such a process of major economic reorientation. As ethnographic research has shown, the reasons for experimenting with such new building techniques can be extremely complex, as are the cultural criteria for evaluating their acceptability.[59]

In this case, one more plausible factor may be a response to the gradual process of deforestation around settlements that had been occurring in the region since the Neolithic and that accelerated during the Iron Age.[60] Charcoal analysis at Lattes, for instance, shows that large trees such as ash and elm had disappeared by 350 BCE, to be replaced by green oak and briar until these, too, declined and were replaced by tamarix and pistachio around the mid–first century BCE.[61] Walls of mud brick or stone solve this problem by greatly reducing the amount of wood, particularly large posts, necessary to build and repair houses. Producing mud brick is actually a fairly simple and rapid technique that takes advantage of an abundant renewable resource that is ubiquitous on the coastal plain and river valleys. Ethnographic and experimental studies have shown that bricks can be produced by hand at a rate of 250 per hour working alone or 3,000 per day by a team of two, and even novice workers can master the technique quickly.[62] Once a few molds are made, the need for wood has been eliminated almost entirely, except for roofs and doors. Stone wall construction offers the same advantage in reducing the need for wood, and it does not even require the preliminary step of producing bricks. In the arid limestone hills of the lower Rhône basin, the raw material is easily available everywhere on the surface, more so even than the earth appropriate for the production of mud brick. It must be pointed out, however, that the building of stone foundations for walls at a site such as Lattes, located on the coastal plain at the edge of a lagoon in terrain devoid of natural stone resources, required an enormous amount of labor to import stones from several sources that were three to eleven kilometers away.[63] Clearly, this effort was deemed acceptable, as the practice persisted for several centuries, although, as noted, there were some fluctuations between techniques in the early history of the site.

One must also consider the role of aesthetic criteria. Walls of both wattle-and-daub and mud-brick houses were plastered with a clay covering, so the external appearance of walls would have remained nearly identical. However, as the taste for more precisely rectangular house forms with straight walls grew (and especially rectangular houses aligned in contiguous rows with common party walls; see the later discussion), this could have provided another incentive for the use of mud brick and stone. It is, of course, perfectly possible to construct rectangular houses with the wattle-and-daub technique,[64] but this form becomes even easier with mud brick. The question is whether the growing preference for rectangular forms led to experimentation with mud brick or vice versa. That is, although it is certainly possible to build elliptical structures with mud brick, it is somewhat more complicated than using them to build rectangular forms. Hence, it is conceivable that the adoption of mud brick may have been one factor influencing the emergence of an aesthetic preference for rectangular forms.

Finally, let us also dispose of another idea about the adoption of mud-brick architecture that is rarely voiced explicitly anymore but lingers on as an implicit sentiment behind many interpretations: that the technique was adopted as part of a general admiration for, and imitation of, Greek culture. In the first place, as already noted, because the walls of both wattle-and-daub and mud-brick houses were plastered with a clay covering, the underlying structure would not have been visible once houses were built. The two kinds of house walls were intentionally rendered indistinguishable. Second, although the early adopters in the Rhône basin may have first observed the technique at Massalia, as it spread beyond the immediate hinterland of the Greek colony, indigenous peoples were more likely adopting a technical novelty that they saw at other indigenous sites rather than something they associated with Greeks or a Greek city they may never have seen. Remember that this regional spread took several hundred years, during which time the technique became thoroughly indigenized. After a generation or two, and a territory or two of distance from Marseille, the construction technique, even if it were visible (which it was not), would no longer have been considered distinctively Massalian. Hence, insofar as we can invoke the concept of imitation, it would rapidly have become a process of natives imitating other natives, and the aura of "Greekness" idea moves from the realm of the implausible to the absurd.

All of this indicates that the cultural dispositions that govern the ways new techniques and materials are experimented with to solve problems, and the criteria of evaluation that determine their ultimate acceptability or rejection, cannot be reduced simply to a purported evolutionary force, such as sedentarization, or to a supposed admiration for a "superior" culture. Experimental adoptions of this kind are determined by a variety of technical, aesthetic, and social evaluations that include such factors as possible changes in the social relations entailed in the construction and maintenance of houses. And these tend to be very local in terms of the sets of dispositions, the problems and opportunities being addressed, and the trajectories of change that result. For instance, the logic of adopting load-bearing walls at Lattes (with its lack of stone) will have been different from that at Le Marduel, Plan-de-la-Tour, or Tamaris.

A number of sites actually offer possibilities for observing in detail the process of experimentation being worked out in different contexts. Plan-de-la-Tour, for example, shows three successive phases of construction moving from wattle-and-daub to stone structures, with an intermediary example with a stone base and wattle-and-daub elevation, and a concurrent shift in form from apsidal to rectangular.[65] At Tamaris as well, one can see a shift over three phases from wattle-and-daub houses to mixed stone and wattle-and-daub, to stone walls, with a concurrent shift to detached rectangular house forms and then to conjoined rectangular houses organized in a rectilinear pattern.[66] Lattes offers a comparative view from two neighborhoods (zones 1 and 27) of shifting architectural experiments with wattle-and-daub, mud brick, and rammed earth walls and shifting organizational arrangements during the fifth century BCE prior to working out a stable set of techniques and forms that would remain remarkably consistent over the entire site for the following several centuries.[67]

Within houses, a relatively narrow range of techniques for earthen floors was shared throughout the region, although there is a range of variability even within the same settlement (tamped earth, clay, pebble-foundation beds, etc.). A number of instances of floors paved with mud brick are also known, notably six cases from the third and second centuries BCE at Lattes and earlier examples at Saint-Pierre-les-Martigues and l'Île de Martigues.[68] Preserved decoration on floors is rare, but there is sporadic evidence for the practice at a few sites, all in late contexts of the third to first centuries BCE. For instance, at Lattes eleven different examples have been found of decorations composed of small delicate *telline* (*Donax trunculus* L.) shells embedded in the surface of a number of house floors dating from the late second to mid–first centuries BCE (fig. 8.6). The patterns range from a clearly defined mule or horse to more fanciful creations of unidentifiable form, to simple geometric rectangles. All of these examples come from houses in very close proximity in the same neighborhood (zone 30-35), and this precise technique is unknown elsewhere on the site or in the region. However, a couple of similar decorations made with other kinds of shells are known from other second and first century BCE contexts at Lattes.[69] Another even more rare technique of floor decoration consists of embedding small stones of different colors in the floor surface. One of these with a simple geometric motif in a lime concrete floor has been found at Lattes, in an unusual late third-century BCE house,[70] and other examples come from Entremont and Glanum in late second- to first-century BCE contexts.[71] Another with a complex motif and Gallo-Greek writing (the name of the house's owner?) was found in an early first-century BCE context at Cavaillon.[72] These have been compared to the *opus signinum* type of mosaic floor decorations that were favored in Greek homes of the Hellenistic period and that have been found at Marseille, Olbia, and Emporion.[73] Other forms of floor decoration include different brightly colored clay surfaces (white, gray, yellow) that were reapplied several times, and a wash painting of a red color found at Lattes.[74] These various kinds of decorations correspond to a period when a notable change in domestic habitus can be observed in practices of refuse disposal and cleanliness at the site: from the third

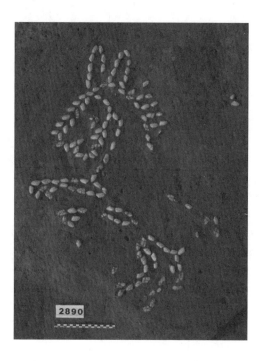

FIGURE 8.6

Floor decoration made from *telline* (*Donax trunculus*) shells in the form of a horse or donkey from the end of the second century BCE: Lattes, zone 35 (UFRAL). (Scale in centimeters.)

century BCE on, floors are generally very clean, with an obvious effort having been made to sweep them regularly and dispose of most refuse elsewhere.[75]

Hearths are the most consistently identifiable feature on these floors, and, as noted earlier, these were of several types: "lenticular" (*foyer lenticulaire*, with the fire simply arranged directly on the floor and recognized as a patch of burned earth), "platform" (*foyer construit*, a flat platform modeled in clay over a supporting bed of shards or stones, with the upper surface sometimes decorated), or "trench" (*fosse-foyer*, with the fire placed in a small linear trench dug into the floor).[76] All three types were used at the same settlements, and even within the same structure, and both lenticular and platform hearths are found in houses of wattle-and-daub, stone, and mud brick.[77] This is a continuation of types dating back to the Late Bronze Age.[78] Hearths have also been found commonly in courtyards and occasionally in the street outside houses (such as at l'Île de Martigues and Notre-Dame-de-Pitié).[79]

A tradition of decorating the surface of platform hearths with incisions and impressions in a variety of geometric patterns is especially characteristic of eastern Languedoc, but cases are known from western Provence and western Languedoc as well. The earliest known example (from Sextantio, near Lattes) dates to the late sixth century BCE and others have been found as late as the early first century BCE in Provence; but the period of greatest popularity occurred from the late fifth through the early third centuries BCE.

FIGURE 8.7
Decorated platform hearth of the third quarter of the 4th century BCE: Lattes, zone 1. Scale in ten-centimeter units (UFRAL).

These hearths tend to be nearly square in form and range from about 0.7 to 1 square meter in area on average (fig. 8.7).[80]

Benchlike platforms *(banquettes)* constructed of stone or mud brick covered with clay are found along one or more walls of many mud-brick or stone houses (especially well-preserved examples have been found at Lattes and l'Île de Martigues). The majority of these are too narrow to have been beds, and it is assumed that they were more likely used as platforms for holding pots and other objects, for performing culinary activities, for sitting, and for carrying out a range of other functions.[81] Traces of bed furniture have not been found, and it is not clear where people slept, although it is probable that they slept on hides or woven mats on the floor. Posidonius offered the observation "Their [Gauls'] custom is to sleep on the ground on the skins of wild animals," although precisely which Gauls he was describing or where he observed this is not clear.[82] Other typical constructed features in houses include the remains of clay ovens and perforated clay grill floors.[83] Shallow pits (often filled with sand, and often along the walls or in the corners of rooms) were used to support large storage jars *(dolia)*, and preserved dolia have sometimes been found partially buried in floors. In addition to dolia, earthen storage vessels that were built in place and lightly fired *(vases mal cuit)* are also common.

Roofs on indigenous houses were generally of thatch or of daub covering a foundation of boards, branches, and reeds. Traces of the remains of such roofs, consisting of fragments of daub with impressions of reeds and branches have been found at many sites, especially in levels with evidence of burning.[84] The basic technique of constructing roofs seems to have changed very little over many centuries, although there were experiments with the use of support poles and perhaps different species of trees used in the roof platform.[85] It is noteworthy that ceramic tiles, the preferred roofing material in the Etruscan, Greek, and Roman worlds (although not to the same extent at Massalia), were ignored for centuries.[86] They are found sporadically from the late second century BCE but are extremely rare at most indigenous sites until the Augustan period.[87] A few ceramic architectural ornaments in a Massalian fabric have been recovered from contexts dating from the mid–third to mid–second centuries BCE at Lattes, and sawn limestone shingles (a technique used at Massalia) were employed on monumental buildings at Glanum in the late second and first centuries BCE, but these are rare exceptions to the general pattern.[88]

Whether roofs were used as additional work and/or storage spaces in these crowded settlements is not always known, although some sites show indications of this. A few houses at l'Île de Martigues, for instance, have broken storage vessels and amphorae lying on top of the thick remains of the collapsed roof of houses destroyed by fire, indicating that these pots were on top of the roof when it fell.[89] Second stories are attested by the remains of stairs at several sites in Provence, such as Entremont, La Cloche, les Caisses-de-Saint-Jean, and Roquefavour.[90] In contrast, the extensive excavations at Lattes have yielded no traces of stairs. This is perhaps not surprising at this coastal lagoon site: given the unstable ground and the frequent evidence of subsidence and leaning walls, second floors of mud brick would have been risky if not impossible to construct. But traces of stairs are extremely rare throughout eastern Languedoc, being confined essentially to one example associated with an odd building at Nages.[91]

House Form and Domestic Space   Wattle-and-daub houses of the Iron Age ranged in form from elliptical to rectangular, and they were often somewhat uneven in plan. Most structures with stone walls were of rectangular (or at least rectilinear) form, though not of consistent dimensions, and those with mud-brick elevations appear to have been almost universally rectangular and, again, not of consistent dimensions. One interesting exception consists of several early sixth-century BCE structures at Saint-Blaise, which have been suggested as apsidal houses, a form also duplicated during the second half of the sixth century BCE at the site of La Monédière, near Agde. In both cases this house form has been used to suggest a Greek presence at the site because apsidal structures are known in Greece.[92] However, in combination with other evidence, the discovery of a similar house form in the mid-fifth-century BCE levels at Plan-de-la-Tour at Gailhan, in the garrigues zone, calls this interpretation into question and suggests that this may have been simply a variation on a traditional indigenous house form.[93] As far as can be determined, nearly all native houses of the Early Iron Age, whatever the construction material and form, appear to have been single room, multifunctional units (sleeping, cooking, eating, craft production, etc.); although structures with a common wall are found at the rectilinear settlements (for example, Saint-Blaise and L'Arquet), and Tamaris appears to offer a few cases of houses with two rooms connected by a common door.[94] But for the most part, clear multiple-room domestic units do not appear until the late fifth century BCE.[95]

Only a few dozen Early Iron Age structures excavated in the lower Rhône basin are sufficiently complete to accurately determine their dimensions, although information for the Late Iron Age is much more abundant. Several analysts have noted a slight trend toward larger structures from the Late Bronze Age through the fifth century BCE, but with the reservation that this is a weak trend rather than a uniform rule.[96] In fact, Early Iron Age house dimensions range from about 6 square meters to about 25 square meters, with an average size of about 14.5 ± 5 square meters. House form and construction technique do not appear to be correlated significantly with size: both wattle-and-daub and stone foundation structures are represented in the below-10 and above-20 square meter ranges, and rectangular and oval houses are both spread over the entire range of sizes. In brief, the size of domestic units did not change with the initial switch from wattle-and-daub to mud brick and stone structures, either regionally or at individual sites where both types are found. Py has, quite reasonably, suggested that this represents a basic continuity in the composition of the family unit, which he sees as being independent nuclear families occupying one-room houses.[97]

From the late fifth century BCE on, although single room domestic units remained the norm at most sites, there was a gradual increase in the size of some houses through the addition of one or more connecting rooms or courtyard spaces. Before the second century BCE, these houses were generally created not by building a new multiroom structure but by a process of piecemeal *bricolage* with existing units. That is, a door was opened between previously separate adjacent rooms forming part of long linear blocks, or an interior curtain wall with a door was built to divide a previous single room, or new additional rooms were added on. All three practices could be employed at the same site.

Rather than indicating an increase in family size, these larger houses mark a functionally specialized separation of space. The main residential/kitchen room remained roughly the same size (or smaller) and had much of the same functional equipment, but it was now connected to a storeroom or courtyard area, and sometimes to other types of rooms. The residential/kitchen rooms typically have one large platform hearth (either plain or decorated) in the center along with perhaps a few other traces of lenticular and trench hearths towards the walls, often a bench/platform along one or more walls, one or more large storage jars, and shards of cooking pots and tableware. Storerooms are identifiable by the presence of multiple pits that supported large storage vessels, sometimes with portions of the vessels still intact, and the absence of hearths, ash, charcoal, and other typical kitchen signatures. Lattes and l'Île de Martigues offer the largest sample of well-preserved rooms with furniture and equipment (described later), but such remains are found in small quantities at many sites.

There was a remarkable continuity in the placement of houses over the centuries at many sites, with structures being rebuilt in the same space multiple times, although frequently with significant changes in internal walls. In Provence, people remained attached to the custom of single-room domestic units at most sites until the late second century BCE even when sites were rebuilt after an episode of destruction, as at l'Île de Martigues, or when settlements were newly founded or expanded.[98] There might be a slight increase in size of the interior space, but the unit type remained basically the same. There were a few early exceptions. Tamaris had a few two-room and even three-room structures already in the sixth century BCE, but this was exceptional.[99] In the fifth century BCE, Arles had a block composed of multiple large-room structures separated by courtyards; during the fourth century BCE, these were subdivided into several four and five-room structures (see chapter 4). Saint-Blaise also had several blocks of multiple-room houses beginning in the third century BCE in the lower town, as did Glanum and Entremont in the second century BCE.

In eastern Languedoc as well, the small single-room house remained the norm at most sites throughout the Iron Age, although with a little more variation than in Provence. Py has estimated that roughly 80 percent of the houses were of this type in both older towns and newly founded settlements.[100] At Nages, for example, the settlement phase of the mid–third century BCE was composed entirely of these single-room houses arranged in long linear blocks, and it was only during the second century BCE that one begins to see experimentation with multiple-room structures. At Lattes, where the appearance of multiple-room structures began much earlier and where two- and three-room structures became the most frequent types, single-room houses were, nevertheless, still a common type into the first century BCE. Although isolated examples appeared as early as the fifth century BCE at Gailhan,[101] in general, it was during the fourth century BCE that more widespread experiments with multiple-room houses began in this region. The earliest evidence comes from Lattes and Roque-de-Fabrègues, both near Montpellier, with later examples (third and second centuries BCE) from sites as diverse as Le Marduel, Roque-de-Viou, and Nages.[102]

In what must be considered the fundamental publication on domestic structures of the region, Py has produced the most thorough analysis of these multiple-room houses and their functional signatures based on the very large sample available at Lattes.[103] He developed a typology of forms for houses of one, two, three, four, and five or more rooms (fig. 8.8) and analyzed the ceramics and other contents and features (hearths, bench-platforms, pits, etc.) within each room for patterning that would yield clues about function, as well as examining changes over time. A classification of thirteen different functional room types was developed: kitchen, food storeroom, equipment storeroom, kitchen and storeroom, kitchen and dining room, kitchen and living room, boutique,[104] undifferentiated living room, living and dining room, exterior space, polyvalent space,[105] specialized work space, and unknown. This study, published in 1996,

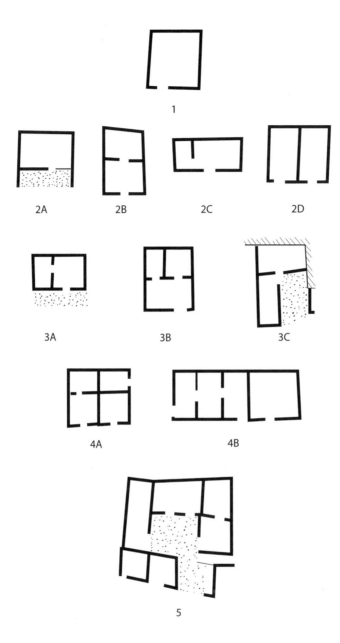

FIGURE 8.8

Typology of house forms at Lattes. Speckled area indicates courtyard (after Py 1996a).

was based on an analysis of seventy-six examples of houses (or "functional units," as Py preferred to call them). Dozens of additional units from subsequent excavations have confirmed and expanded his observations, which are summarized in highly schematic and selective form here.[106]

The single-room houses (type 1) are always of polyvalent function and are present throughout the history of the site, ranging in form from square to rectangular to trapezoidal, and in size from thirty-four to seventy-five square meters in area. Two-room structures can be composed of a room and an open front courtyard (type 2A) or various configurations of two connected rooms: with only one room having an external door and the second room reached by passage through the first (types 2B and 2C), or two rooms connected by passing through the street (2D).[107] For blocks that are two rooms deep, one can find either parallel linear two-room houses separated by a common wall and with doors opening onto parallel streets or, more commonly, houses that are two rooms deep (that is, traversing the width of the block). Type 2 houses range in size from thirty-five to eighty square meters (in other words, basically the same size range as one-room houses). With type 2A houses, either the closed room is a polyvalent functional space and the courtyard serves as an equipment storage area or the closed room serves as a living and dining room and the courtyard as a kitchen and food storeroom. For types 2B and 2C, the front room is most often a kitchen (or some combination kitchen-living room, kitchen-storeroom, etc.), and the backroom was used for other functions (storage, dining, living, polyvalent), although sometimes this arrangement is reversed. Three-unit houses consist of either a frontal courtyard flanked by two connecting rooms (type 3A), or a house of similar form where the courtyard is replaced by an enclosed room (type 3B), or houses of various forms in which two rooms form a right angle around an open courtyard (3C). These range in size from thirty-three to ninety-six square meters (that is, still roughly the same range as one-room structures, with a few examples up to 28 percent larger at the upper end). The functional organization of these houses is quite regular, with back rooms almost always serving as living, dining, and food storerooms while the kitchen was in the courtyard or front enclosed room. Four-room houses are usually of nearly square form with right angle walls dividing the internal space (type 4A). These range in size from 77 to 129 square meters, and, whereas the other three types were built during all periods, type 4 houses all date between the mid–third century and the beginning of the second century BCE. The room functions are typically quite discrete: a kitchen, a storeroom, a dining room, and a general living room. A couple of eccentric four-room houses have been grouped into a special category (type 4B). One of these is the unusual house with an *opus signinum* floor decoration that has been suggested as the possible residence of a Greek merchant (see chapter 4).[108] Type 5 houses constitute a special class of houses with a central courtyard, and they are discussed later.

According to the statistical figures provided by Py, the average overall size of the two-room and most three-room houses is roughly equivalent to that of one-room structures, especially if one considers the "utilizable space" (that is, excluding the space taken up by walls): about two thirds of all cases fall within the range of twenty to fifty square meters for this measure. Moreover, about 80 percent of all houses from all periods cluster fairly closely around a mean of sixty-four square meters of total space, indicating that there was a standard module that could be divided in a variety of ways.[109] Only the houses of four rooms or larger diverge significantly, being generally quite a bit larger.

In general, within what might be called the "grammar" of built forms outlined by Py, there was an impressive multiplicity of individual house arrangements. This patterned variety and the ways houses changed over time (the "biographies" of blocks and houses[110]) demonstrate a constant process of vernacular experimentation operating according to a set of local cultural dispositions governing social space and architectural forms.

Suggestions about the influence of Greek or Etruscan models on native housing have been frequent, but generally unconvincing. For example, it has been claimed that Py's house forms 3A, 2B, and 2A may represent simplified forms of 3B, which, in turn, may be derived from Etruscan or Greek "pastas" type houses.[111] However, both the pastas-type house and the Lattes 3B are, in fact, fairly elementary configurations of space (fig. 8.9). Moreover, in looking at the cultural logic of the spatial patterning of indigenous houses, one can easily see the 3B pattern as resulting from a process of structured improvisation in solving the problem of creating a third room division while adhering to a coherent approach to domestic space represented by several other common patterns (1, 2A, 2B, 2C, and 3A).[112]

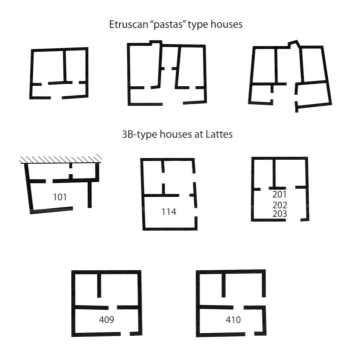

FIGURE 8.9
Examples of some simple Etruscan "pastas" style houses compared to some typical 3B-type houses from Lattes (after Py 1996a).

In all these cases, the common feature is a single point of entry to the structure as a whole, with access to all domestic space and all other rooms flowing directly through that single entry space. In other words, single-room structures at Lattes almost always have only one entry door. When a second room is added to the plan, it typically became secluded space that could only be reached through the entry room. When a third room was to be added, the most common solution at Lattes is that the third room also became a secluded room that also leads directly off the entry room. This pattern implies a binary division of space, with an entry area and one or more subsidiary areas that lead directly off from it. In outlining a spatial grammar, one might designate this arrangement as a "Y form." An alternative solution is what may be called an "I form" in which successive rooms became increasingly secluded, with access to the deepest room requiring passage through all of the others in a tripartite division of space. A different logic from either of the others is a "U form," in which there are two points of access to the exterior and all rooms fall along the path of a U and have two access doors.

Given a conceptual model of a house of 2B or 2C type, if one wanted to create a third room, either a Y form or an I form would be alternative solutions consistent with the prior logic of spatial penetration of the domestic space, although one would end up with either a binary or tripartite spatial division. The U form (or some similar bidirectional penetration model) would be a significant departure. In fact, the U pattern does not appear to be represented in the fourth-century BCE repertoire when the 3A form was established,[113] and seems to be a much later, and never popular, innovation of the late third century BCE due to subsequent experimentation.[114] Hence, the elaboration of triple-room structures at Lattes can be more plausibly attributed to the working out of structured improvisations guided by a basic local habitus generating dispositions toward the organization of space. This produced forms with vague similarities to the Greek and Etruscan pastas-style house (itself a rather fluid category) that are more plausibly interpreted as resulting simply from similar solutions to a common problem of adding a third room division.

It is not that the idea of adopting foreign models is inherently impossible, but approaching the encounter from the kind of critical reflexive perspective introduced at the beginning of this book should force us to reframe our analysis: to question the standards of plausibility by which we judge alternative interpretations and to ask new questions of the data. Why, for example, should the inhabitants of Lattes have been attracted by an alien house form, and why would it have become so popular that its derivatives would come to constitute the majority of the residential structures? Where would Lattarians have observed this model in the first place—where would they have penetrated the recesses of Etruscan or Greek homes to even be aware of the internal structure that is not visible from the street, and why would they have thought this was such a clever idea (especially considering that they do not seem to have faithfully reproduced the *functions* of the rooms of pastas houses)? Why would they have imitated this largely invisible interior form yet rejected the highly visible use of roof tiles that were a common part of contemporary household architecture in the Etruscan and Greek world by this time? Granted, there were probably some Etruscan merchants resident at the site, but the houses they were living in do not appear to have been of the pastas type. Moreover, part of the argument for identifying the presence of these merchants is precisely that their houses were *so different* from other houses at the site. This, to say the least, complicates the argument for imitation. But if, instead of crediting Greek or Etruscan models with an inherent attractiveness, one focuses on the logic of vernacular experimentation and normalization of architectural forms, then transformations of domestic space become more comprehensible.

This experimentation was driven by a desire to create functional separation of space within the dwelling that was formerly a single polyfunctional space, and the forms that experimentation took were channeled by embodied cultural dispositions toward social space, movement, privacy, proxemics, and other such things. Why a desire for functional separation of space occurred and spread (and why it occurred when it did, and to the extent that it did, in different areas) is still an open question. In the context of the modern Euro-American "consumer society", this trend appears to be linked, at least in part, to an ever-increasing accumulation of goods. But this seems an unlikely explanation for Iron Age France, especially given that, unlike the modern case, these internal divisions were initially made by subdividing the same area of space rather than increasing the overall size of the dwelling. Given that specialized storerooms seem to be the most common first division, it is possible that it may be connected to increasing demands for storage of grain and wine that were, in turn, linked to both surplus production for trade and stockpiling of provisions for feasting. Single-room houses with furnishings that have been preserved more or less intact after fires, as at l'Île de Martigues, certainly give the impression of having been extremely crowded with such storage vessels (fig. 8.10). But the desire for spatial separation could also be linked to other subtle cultural factors such as changes in concepts of privacy, concerns about the penetration of magic or the evil eye into the home, increasing secrecy about accumulating wealth or foodstuffs, or a host of other factors that ethnographic studies have shown can affect the arrangement of domestic space. We may never be able to understand precisely what caused this emerging desire for the segregation of space within the house, but it is clear that this, rather than some longing to imitate Greek or Etruscan houses, is what drove the complex process of vernacular architectural experimentation we see reflected in the archaeological data.

Central Courtyard Houses Another aspect of house form that has frequently raised the interpretation of Greek influence (with perhaps more plausibility) is the appearance during the third and second centuries BCE of a small number of multiple-room houses of another kind: houses formed around a central un-roofed courtyard (*maisons à cour*, or type 5 in the classification of Py).[115] These houses merit examination in somewhat greater detail, as they provide an excellent platform for exploring the nature of creative adaptation and vernacular experimentation that characterized the history of the colonial encounter.

FIGURE 8.10

Reconstruction of the interior of a one-room house at l'Île de Martigues (watercolor by Denis Delpalillo, from Chausserie-Laprée 2005; courtesy of Denis Delpalillo).

It is not the presence of a courtyard per se that makes these houses distinctive: small open courtyards in front of houses that served as locations for domestic activities are known from sites of the region, including Lattes, as early as the fifth century BCE.[116] What is distinctive is a house form that encloses an interior courtyard within wings of rooms and where the rooms open inward onto the courtyard rather than outward onto a street. Although courtyard houses of a clearly Roman type became fairly widespread during the Roman Empire (from the late first century BCE on), when dramatic urban and rural landscape transformations occurred throughout Mediterranean France, these early courtyard houses are quite different. On the one hand, they represent a significant departure in form from the traditional local norm of houses arranged in linear blocks (see below), and they are generally much larger than other types of houses at native sites. On the other hand, they also exhibit a range of important differences from contemporary Greek and Roman houses.

Lattes offers the largest sample of such pre-Augustan courtyard houses in the region: six have now been identified and subjected to extensive excavation, and another is suspected on the basis of surface remains. A few other courtyard houses have been identified in other parts of Mediterranean France, although none is as early as several examples at Lattes. In Provence, Glanum has yielded one example, the "Maison des antes," which is of comparable size to the largest house at Lattes but dates to the second century BCE.[117] A much smaller example from Entremont[118] and possible examples at Saint-Blaise[119] and Nîmes[120] are also of second century BCE date. In western Languedoc, Ensérune has produced a still later example, house A of Insula X, that dates to about 40/30 BCE.[121] The only other examples documented with convincing evidence are from Greek colonial sites, such as Marseille[122] and the possible Greek quarter at Arles.[123]

At Lattes, these houses can be roughly divided into two categories: those that exhibit a more symmetrical form and appear to have been conceived originally as courtyard houses, and those of more irregular form that were assembled in a piecemeal fashion by blocking off a street between two formerly separate linear blocks of houses to create a courtyard and joining rooms from the two blocks as a single house.[124] The former include the oldest (early third century BCE) and largest (eight to ten rooms) of these structures and are concentrated in a neighborhood in the southeastern part of the town near the gate to the port, along the rampart and the main southern street. The others are smaller (two to six rooms) and more recent (second and first century BCE), and they are located in several different neighborhoods (fig. 8.11). For the earliest examples, excavation is still in progress and conclusions must be regarded as provisional, but enough is known to establish a working understanding of the structures and their histories and to date their origin to at least the early third century BCE.[125]

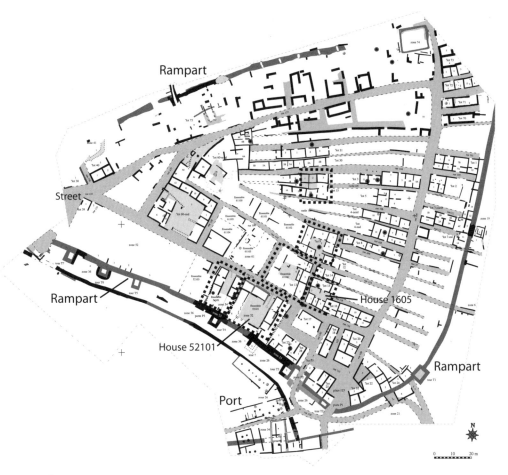

FIGURE 8.11

Map of Lattes showing location of central courtyard houses (marked in dashed lines) (after Dietler et al. 2008).

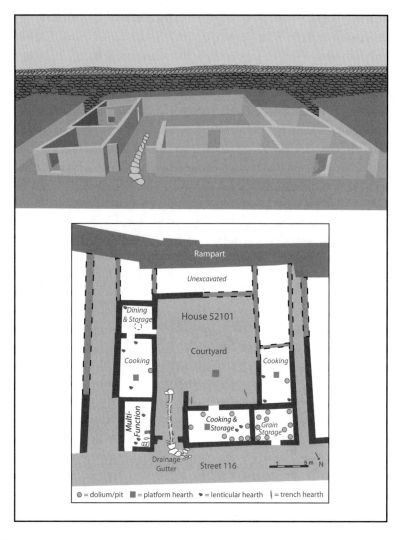

FIGURE 8.12

Plan and reconstructed elevation drawing of the largest central-courtyard house (52101) at Lattes. Roofs are shown only on unexcavated portions of the house, although all rooms were originally roofed. Only clearly identified doors are shown, although others must have existed.

House 52101 (fig. 8.12), built near the beginning of the third century BCE, is an example of the early type and is the largest yet found. It is roughly square in shape, composed of about ten rooms, and occupies an area of approximately 550 square meters, of which about one-third consists of a large open courtyard around which the rooms are arranged and a passageway that leads from the courtyard to the street. This house is roughly nine times the size of the average one- to three-room house at Lattes and over three and a half times the size of the largest non-courtyard-style house. It is also one of the largest pre-Roman houses found in the region to date, exceeding even the largest house yet excavated at Marseille by about 150 square meters.[126] This is also the house in which the torso of a limestone statue of a warrior was found reutilized as a doorjamb.[127]

The stratigraphy of the courtyard shows two major phases. In the most recent phase, during the first quarter of the second century BCE, the entire surface was paved with several successive floors of large pebbles. During the earlier phase, before the second century BCE, the courtyard was not paved and one finds instead a series of occupation surfaces and sedimentation levels between thick beds of rubble. These beds are richly littered with charcoal, ash, shards, animal bones, shellfish and other domestic debris and they resemble the beds that are typical for earlier open courtyards found in front of houses. There is also abundant evidence of hearths of all three types described earlier. During the most recent level preserved, the courtyard was drained by a substantial stone-lined gutter (capped by huge flagstones) that runs through the middle of the passage and empties into the street. A large stone wheel guard located at the juncture of the passage and the street suggests that the passage was designed to accommodate the entry of wagons into the courtyard. Each wing of the house contains one room that served as a kitchen, with a large platform hearth, numerous traces of lenticular hearths, platforms along walls, some storage vessels, and abundant shards of cooking and tableware. The rooms in the corners of the house had other specialized functions. The room in the northwest corner, which opened onto the street, was entirely dedicated to grain storage: through several levels it was completely filled with shallow pits for dolia (as many as ten in a room of about twenty square meters) without any traces of hearths. The functions of two other corner rooms are less clear, but they were certainly not kitchens.[128]

House 1605, dated to the first half of the second century BCE, is an example of the more recent and irregular type of courtyard house (fig. 8.13).[129] It consists of five rooms from two blocks (zones 16 and 15) that were previously separated by street 119. This street was blocked off by a wall at its west end, where it formerly intersected with street 115, to form a central courtyard between two rooms to the north and three to the south. The house occupies about 148 square meters, of which about 27 percent consists of the courtyard that was drained by a stone-lined gutter that emptied into street 115. The courtyard also showed traces of a large platform hearth and two clay ovens, indicating that it served as a space for cooking. The room in the southwestern corner of the house, which opens onto street 116 rather than into the other rooms, contained nine pits, at least eight of which were designed to support large storage jars (dolia), and it appears to have had a specialized function as a granary. The adjacent small room to the east showed traces of two hearths and faunal remains and it has been interpreted as a kitchen. The function of the other three rooms is more difficult to discern, as their floors of this period were largely devoid of features or objects.

These brief descriptions are sufficient to convey a general sense of the nature of these houses and some of the differences among them. As noted, it has frequently been suggested that these courtyard houses represent the adoption of a model of Greco-Italic origin. In the highly unusual and very late case of Glanum, where there are other elements that closely resemble Greco-Italic architecture, this seems quite true; but it is less evident what this might mean at Lattes. Moreover, simply pointing to an ultimate source

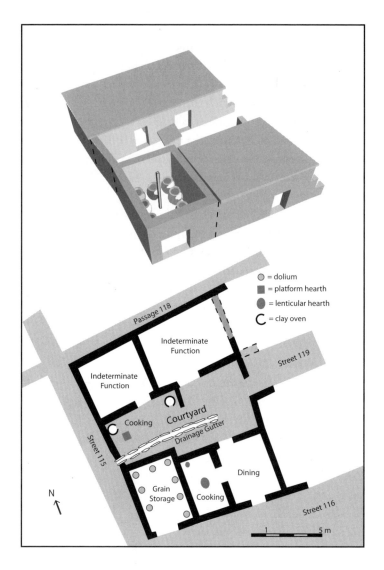

FIGURE 8.13

Plan and reconstructed elevation drawing of courtyard house 1605 at Lattes (after Py 1996a).

of "influence" does little to explain why such a process of adoption happened, why it happened when and where it did, and what significance these houses may have had for the indigenous peoples of the region. In assessing these questions, it is important to point out that, while the model of the *interior* courtyard is clearly a departure from earlier indigenous house forms at Lattes and elsewhere in the region, the organization of space and features within rooms, the dimensions of those rooms, and the techniques of construction remained resolutely consistent with prior (and contemporary) indigenous cultural models. In other words, the interior living spaces of rooms within a house such as

52101 were identical to those in the traditional houses arranged in linear blocks, as were the techniques of forming floors, building walls, constructing hearths, and so forth. There were no mosaic floors, painted plaster, roof tiles, columns, or other elements that one would expect in a contemporary Greek or Roman house. In fact, standing inside a given room, one would not be able to say whether it belonged to a courtyard house or a more traditional house. Moreover, the courtyards, with their abundant domestic debris and hearths, were clearly neither a Roman *atrium* or *peristylum* with a pool of water and ordered garden, nor a copy of a typical Greek house courtyard, such as that in Marseille with its central well and terrazzo paving. Rather, they appear to have been spaces used for a multitude of activities, including cooking, craft work, and refuse disposal, much like the open courtyards found in front of houses in earlier periods. Hence, to the extent that the idea of the central courtyard house may be considered of foreign origin, its appearance at Lattes represents the appropriation of a general form and its creative adaptation to indigenous social units, domestic practices, and cultural models of residential space rather than a simple imitation of Greek or Roman houses. Life inside the rooms continued much as it had before and was much the same as in the contemporary houses of the traditional types in linear blocks described earlier, which remained the norm.

What, then, is the significance of these houses? In addition to the suggestion of Hellenic models, their appearance is also frequently interpreted as signaling the emergence of new relations of social hierarchy and the formation of an indigenous elite or "aristocratic" class in the region. While possible, this proposition requires some scrutiny. In the first place, this is not necessarily a sign of the first emergence of social differentiation in the settlement, but rather a sign of the emergence of the desire to use the urban landscape to mark *some kind* of social distinction—and, most importantly, a sign of the social acceptability of that practice.[130] It is important to remember that the construction of these houses involved not only experimentation with a new architectural form, but perhaps more important, the appropriation of civic space (that is, a street) and its enclosure within a domestic building. As the history of house 3501 (where the courtyard was ultimately reduced to half its size in order to reestablish the flow of the street it had blocked) shows, this practice of appropriation was not always successful.[131] But most of these houses did last for at least a couple of generations, which implies that the ability to enclose civic space was accepted for relatively long periods in some cases.

Granted that this spatial fact implies a form of authority (or at least acquiescence to some form of power), the question remains of precisely what kind of social differentiation was being evoked by these houses. Are they the material signs of a new elite class, the homes of wealthy and powerful individuals? Or, for instance, are we seeing the material reflection of political relations between competing clans, lineages, or other corporate groups within the settlement, as each group built a courtyard house (or a large four-room house) for its leading or most genealogically senior family? In this case, there need not be any class differences between residents of the different kinds of neighboring houses: the large house would be a symbol of the collective identity of the group as a whole and perhaps an expression of its aspirations for influence within the competitive politics of the town. Or might we be witnessing the gradual emergence of "traditionalist" and "cosmopolitan" factions within the settlement, as certain groups or individuals saw their fortunes and identity increasingly tied to contacts with the broader world of Mediterranean trade connections and employed more eclectically mimetic symbolic strategies while others saw this as threatening and adhered to a reactionary orthodoxy of "tradition" in their lifeways? In the last case, distinctions might have fallen along family or generational cleavages without the formation of classes. Distinguishing between these and other possible forms of social differentiation is difficult, but the preliminary data available can give us some clues about relative plausibility.

It is important to note that social distinctions seem to have depended on manipulation of space and architectural form alone. The material culture found in the houses does not indicate any marked differences in patterns of consumption between the structures. The range and quantities of ceramics, metal objects, foods, coins, and other goods found within rooms do not appear to be significantly different between the courtyard houses and other contemporary houses at the site. There are no obvious differences in wealth and no patterns of restricted consumption of objects that might have served as diacritical sumptuary markers of status (for example, exotic imports). Nor do the interior furnishings of the houses, the size of the rooms, or materials of construction differ significantly from other houses. The manipulation of civic space alone could be quite a significant symbolic statement in the context of a densely packed urban environment such as Lattes. But if this is linked to a shift in relations of power, it appears to be a subtle one that took place within a context constrained by a generally egalitarian cultural ethos rather than one marked by the emergence of an elite class or aristocracy with a diacritical life style.

It is also highly unlikely that the large early courtyard houses were the stately residences of individual wealthy men, unless they were polygynous. House 52101, for example, shows a repetition at least three times (once in the middle of each wing) of precisely the same functional indicators of kitchens. The house also has one well-packed storeroom and rooms of other, undetermined function in the other corners. In other words, it appears this house was not the residence of a single nuclear family, with each room having a distinct specialized function—on the model of, for example, the Roman *domus* with its *triclinium, tablinium, cubiculae, culina,* and so forth. Rather, it appears that the house as a whole represents a multiplication of similar domestic units. How these units were related is still uncertain. Whether we are faced, for example, with a house containing a large extended family with individual monogamous nuclear units housed in different rooms, or with a large polygynous family with co-wives and their children housed in different rooms, or even with unrelated nuclear families housed in different rooms, is difficult to determine on the basis of current evidence.

These houses were also clearly not built as a single project by a specialized crew of craftsmen directed by an architect. Like all other pre-Augustan houses at the site, they are the product of unspecialized vernacular construction. This is abundantly clear in the later piecemeal houses that block off and incorporate streets. But even the more symmetrical early examples show clear signs of this. House 52101, for example, exhibits a great deal of internal variety in the stonework for wall foundations of different rooms and in the size and history of those rooms (shifts in wall positions, changes in doors, etc.) that indicate that it was probably constructed (and remodeled) by numerous small work groups, with a common general idea of an overall form, but a wide range of particular techniques and ideas about appropriate size for rooms. They may well have incorporated existing structures into the building as well, while leveling others to make way for the courtyard.

In brief, during the third and second centuries BCE we see the development at Lattes of a small set of houses that are considerably larger than other previous or contemporary forms. Some of these (the courtyard houses) have an alien form that bears a general resemblance to common Greek models, while others (Py's type 4) do not. While it might be reasonable to speculate that the earliest central courtyard houses may have played creatively on an exotic model of house form, the later courtyard houses are more likely simply piecemeal imitations of the large early courtyard houses at Lattes itself. The latter had, after all, been a part of the urban landscape for over a century before the more modestly sized and irregular houses were cobbled together through a process of *bricolage*. Moreover, even the houses possibly based on a Greek form were very un-Greek in every way except the single feature of having rooms arranged around a central courtyard. Calling this Greek "influence" does nothing to explain the social and cultural significance of these houses or the way they came into being. Far more important is what they illustrate in terms of vernacular improvisation and what they represent in terms of the appropriation of civic space and the use of the urban landscape to mark social distinctions.

Settlement Organization   One of the most visually striking developments in the history of urban landscapes in Mediterranean France is the emergence of densely packed rectilinear forms of settlement organization based on blocks composed of attached rectangular houses and parallel streets. This phenomenon is sometimes described in vaguely evolutionist terms as a change to settlements having an "organized plan" from one in which the placement of structures was, by implication, fairly haphazard. That purportedly novel "organization" has also been linked frequently to the necessity of the emergence of a centralized political authority capable of planning and implementing such an organized scheme. But this is a misconception. As ethnographic research has demonstrated, all settlements have a coherent structural organization that is integrally connected to the structuring of social relations and daily practice, although this organization may be inscrutably opaque to an outsider not familiar with the cultural codes and conceptions of space-time that generated the placement of houses and other features.[132] Saying that some settlements have no organization is equivalent to saying that some languages have no grammar. What this change actually represents is simply the development of a rectilinear form of organization that is more easily identified by the archaeologist. One should not mistake the inability to recognize the organizing principles of a settlement for the absence of such principles. Nor should one imagine that the ability to recognize a certain order in rectilinear forms indicates the sudden emergence of centralized urban planning. The construction of these rectilinear housing blocks with common walls does indicate an ability to coordinate collective labor within the community, as does the maintenance of streets, and the construction and maintenance of ramparts. But this does not require centralized authority directing a unified urban plan: such work is frequently undertaken in acephalous societies through work feasts.[133] To cite one ethnographic example, thousands of Luo settlements in western Kenya manage to reproduce the same spatial structure and architectural forms without any direction from a central authority.[134] Moreover, Native American pueblos of the American Southwest, such as Taos and Acoma, offer an example of densely occupied rectilinear settlements of attached mud-brick houses that have existed for centuries without any necessity of direction from highly centralized political authorities.[135]

To be sure, as with any change, this transformation could potentially indicate a significant alteration of social relations precisely because the spatial configuration of residence units is so intimately implicated in the structuring of personal interaction and the inculcation of "habitus" (the axiomatic dispositions that structure practice) in the domain of social space.[136] But that evaluation depends on a close analysis of the biography of individual settlements. How radical a departure really is this rectilinear landscape from prior forms, and how did it develop?

One other tempting point of reference has been the so-called Hippodamian regular orthogonal plan that is seen to lie behind the layout of many Greek cities, particularly colonial ones, founded or rebuilt from the fifth century BCE on, and especially during the Hellenistic period. Miletus and Olynthos are two examples used frequently to illustrate this system of urban organization. The Massalian colony of Olbia, founded around 400 BCE, is an example (the only clearly known one) of such a Hippodamian plan in Mediterranean France (fig. 8.14). The assumption has been that this plan must have in some way influenced native settlements, even though native sites with rectilinear organization predate the earliest Greek example in the region by over one hundred years. Massalia and Emporion did not follow such a plan, but rather were typical of cities founded in the Archaic period in having the kind of organization that Henri Tréziny has called "heterogeneously regular"—that is, irregular when considered as a whole, but regular within the details of specific neighborhoods.[137] These two cities had vaguely orthogonal systems of streets and quasi-rectangular blocks within neighborhoods, but with far less homogeneity in the size, arrangement, or orientation of the parts than a site like Olbia. Moreover, Greeks are not the only people capable of inventing regular geometric forms of settlement: sites such as Biskupin in Poland exhibited a perfectly orthogonal grid layout in the seventh century BCE a couple of centuries before any Greek city exhibited comparable regularity. Furthermore, closer inspection reveals that native

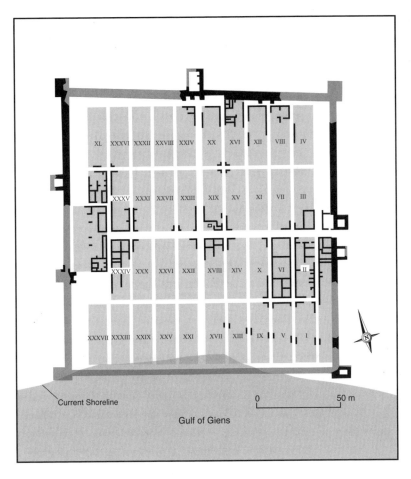

XL XXXVI XXXII XXVIII XXIV XX XVI XII VIII IV

XXXV XXXI XXVII XXIII XIX XV XI VII III

XXXIV XXX XXVI XXII XVIII XIV X VI II

XXXVII XXXIII XXIX XXV XXI XVII XIII IX V I

Current Shoreline

0   50 m

Gulf of Giens

FIGURE 8.14

Plan of the Massalian colony of Olbia (after Bats 2004; courtesy of Michel Bats).

French sites are actually quite different from Hippodamian Greek colonies and other less regular Greek grid arrangements: they do not use the same modules, they generally have far more linear conceptions of blocks without intersecting cross streets (that is, they are linear rather than orthogonal), and they do not have central open spaces for an agora. Finally, given all that one knows ethnographically about the social significance of space, it is simply not credible to imagine that large numbers of people across a region would change their settlement patterns voluntarily because they had been exposed to a clever Greek idea (and where would they have seen this?). This kind of thing happens in colonial situations only under conditions of extensive colonization and accompanying major transformation of consciousness, sometimes accompanied by forcible resettlement: conditions that certainly have no relevance to the pre-Roman Iron Age in Mediterranean France. Even if one were to accept the implausible suggestion of Greek influence in this case, one would still have to provide a sociologically credible explanation of why people thought this was such a good idea? What would have made this Greek model both attractive and compatible with local cultural dispositions toward social space, and how would it have been translated into organizing thousands of vernacular dwellings?

What a comparative analysis of these native rectilinear settlements shows is that, in the first place, there were both important differences and commonalities in the urban landscapes of the region that are grouped under the general descriptive label of *rectilinear*. Moreover, these arrangements did not appear suddenly as a fully formed system. That impression can only occur if one collapses six centuries of settlements into an ahistorical category and juxtaposes it against a prior static idea of "unplanned" settlements. Once again, close analysis of the "settlement biography" of Early Iron Age sites such as Lattes, Tamaris, Gailhan, or Saint-Pierre-les-Martigues shows that early forms of rectilinear organization were not the result of a preconceived urban plan, but rather the eventual order that gradually emerged over several generations out of a series of experiments within the compact space delimited by a rampart. Regionally, this process of local experimentation led to a set of related, but not identical, solutions to similar problems, and these gradually became normalized as part of the collective spatial habitus.[138] This kind of habitus governing the production and habitation of urban landscapes is not a set of rigid, static rules, but rather a "generative principle of regulated improvisations"[139] that allows the solution of daily technical and social problems through a process of culturally structured analogical reasoning; and the solutions to these problems, in turn, reflexively influence the development of the generative dispositions. In the case of sites such as Nages or Entremont, founded during the third and second centuries BCE, after this kind of rectilinear settlement organization had become worked out and widely normalized (although certainly not frozen) in previous centuries, the initial division of space (streets and housing blocks) laid out for a new settlement could be extremely regular and uniform, to the point of seeming almost authoritarian in conception. However, subsequent expansions of these sites and reconstructions of the existing neighborhoods showed much more variability and experimentation, although always structured by this locally evolving set of cultural dispositions toward social space and architectural form.

To illustrate this more concretely, let us look briefly at a few sites that exemplify some of these points: Lattes, l'Île de Martigues, Nages, Entremont, and others.

At Lattes, the first century or so of occupation after its foundation in the late sixth century BCE was a period that saw a variety of experiments with different construction techniques and spatial arrangements. Both zones 1 and 27, where the excavations have been targeted on the early history of the site, have shown phases of continual reconstruction during the fifth century BCE with alternating materials (wattle-and-daub, mud brick, and rammed earth) and varying kinds of spatial organization that include attached houses with common walls, detached houses separated by broad open spaces, and adjacent houses separated by narrow passages.[140] Out of this emerged, by the late fifth century BCE, an organization of streets and housing blocks that would remain remarkably stable down to the late first century BCE, although with continuing experimentation in the internal structure of houses within these blocks (fig. 8.11).[141] There was also a continuing increase in the density of occupation during the fourth century BCE such that the open areas in front of houses and in parts of some blocks were gradually filled in. There was also the growth of an extra-muros settlement that, by the third century BCE, would expand the 3.3-hectare core contained within the rampart to an area of over 20 hectares.

The basic pattern for the old core of the town within the rampart involved a combination of two principles that Py has identified as being common elements of many indigenous urban landscapes of the Rhône basin: what he called the "concentric" and the "linear strip" (en lanières) patterns.[142] The concentric element at Lattes consists of a ring of house blocks (consistently about twenty-five meters wide) abutting against the interior face of the rampart around its entire roughly triangular circumference. These houses were bordered by a triangle of three main streets (averaging 4 to 4.5 m in width) that formed a ring road running parallel to the triangular course of the fortifications.[143] Within the central core space delimited by the concentric ring road, the contrasting linear strip principle resulted in a series of long (from about 110 to 150 meters) parallel linear blocks of houses oriented roughly east-west and separated by a set of narrower streets (averaging about 2.5 to 3.5 meters in width) and even narrower alleyways (less than 1 m to about 1.6 meters in average width). The latter were essentially for drainage, as no doors opened onto them. These blocks converged and narrowed somewhat toward the point of the triangle in the west. There were a few short north-south streets cutting perpendicularly through small portions of this parallel series of east-west streets in a few spots, but the organization was resolutely linear rather than gridlike. Most streets had no possibility of accessing a parallel street except by going all the way to the ring road or the point of convergence in the west. These central linear housing blocks were of two widths: either one room (about 4.6 to 5 meters) or two rooms (about 9 meters), with the former being the most common arrangement. The backs of the narrow blocks would be separated by a very narrow alley and the houses of each would open onto wider streets. This system carved the site up into a series of tunnel-like communities composed of the houses opening onto a common street, with access to those living behind requiring a trip all the way back to the ring road and then down into the next tunnel. The blocks that compose the perimeter ring either follow this same east-west strip orientation (as they tend to do on the eastern side) or are of broader rectangular form with intervening passages oriented perpendicular to the main ring road (as they tend to be on the north and south).

Several points need to be raised here. First, these linear blocks are far longer and narrower than those found in the Greek Hippodamian system or other Greek grids. The blocks at Olbia are uniformly 11 meters wide by 34.5 meters long (or roughly 1 to 3 in proportion),[144] which is a starkly different conception than blocks of 5 or 9 meters wide by over 110 meters long (at least 1 to 22 or 1 to 12 in proportions).[145] Furthermore, although blocks at Olbia and at other Hippodamian plan sites are generally elongated rectangles rather than squares, the conception is decidedly an orthogonal grid system, with regular perpendicular cross-streets. This is profoundly different in conception than the adamantly linear world that was created at the center of Lattes.

It is also important to point out that, although a casual glance at the map of the settlement might give the impression of a project designed and executed on a large scale, there was actually an impressive variety of creative solutions adopted in the internal structuring of each block and in the biographies of the component houses. There were numerous variations in room configurations and sizes of the houses, resulting in narrow blocks with a row of single-room houses, wide blocks with a double row of houses of single-room depth separated by an axial wall, an open courtyard area in front of a house, multiple-room houses of various configurations, multiple-room houses with a transversal orientation, and so forth.[146] During the second century BCE, some streets were even blocked to join formerly separate blocks into single large houses. All of this indicates a certain liberty of action by the families inhabiting this urban landscape, although, of course, one constrained by the spatial habitus that generated the range of improvisations considered possible and appropriate. As with the original phases of the settlement when the rectilinear organization was being gradually worked out, the subsequent history shows an unending process of experimentation operating within an overarching framework of structuring dispositions.

The result of this process was the creation of an urban landscape that, in terms of its phenomenological aspect, would have been oppressively claustrophobic by modern Western sensibilities. For someone entering the interior of the town for the first time through one of the gates in the rampart, the experience would have been rather disorienting. It would have seemed like a densely packed, introverted maze with few open lines of sight (apart from the relative expanse of the ring road) and no external landmarks for navigation that would be visible from street level above the rampart or the roof line of the houses. Nor, on present evidence, would there have been any broad open public spaces, monumental temples, or distinctive administrative buildings to provide internal landmarks until the first century BCE. Of course, unlike the stranger, a native Lattarian would have been intimately familiar with the social and physical geography of the site constituted by the system of parallel tunnel-like narrow streets and rows of houses encircled by the ring road that ran parallel to the rampart. In general terms, a citizen of Lattara of the fourth century BC would have felt quite at home on these streets two hundred or three hundred years later. This is as true of the techniques of construction and aesthetic appearance of buildings as it is of the organization of space. Although there was an increase in the use of nails in construction during the first century BCE,[147] the general practice of mud-brick walls constructed on stone foundations with daub covered wood roofs continued unchanged until the Augustan period.[148] A few changes had occurred over the centuries, to be sure, such as the appearance of some courtyard houses. But aside from blocking a few streets, these did not fundamentally alter the grammar or aesthetics of the built environment. In the Augustan period, this all changed dramatically in a wave of landscape transformations that emphasizes all the more the remarkable stability during the preceding centuries.

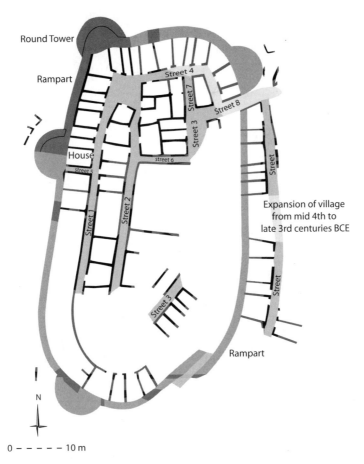

Round Tower

Rampart

Street 4

Street 7

Street 8

Street 3

House

street 6

street 5

Street 1

Street 2

Street

Expansion of village
from mid 4th to
late 3rd centuries BCE

Street 3

Rampart

N

0 – – – – – 10 m

FIGURE 8.15

Plan of l'Île de Martigues: the settlement of the early fourth century BCE, with the mid-fourth- to late
third-century BCE expansion shown outside the early rampart to the east (after Chausserie-Laprée
2005, courtesy of Jean Chausserie-Laprée).

The site of l'Île de Martigues, founded during the third quarter of the fifth century
BCE, offers, initially, an example of the same combination of concentric and linear strip
principles on a smaller scale, as well as illustrating a later change to an entirely linear
logic (fig. 8.15). The first settlement there, of only 0.4 hectare, offers a continuous elliptical ring of one-room mud-brick houses built against the interior wall of the rampart.
These open onto a narrow ring road that follows the outline of the rampart and the outer
ring of houses. Within the core delimited by this street is a series of parallel linear blocks
of one- and two-room widths oriented in a north-south direction separated by narrow
parallel streets. Given the very narrow width of the streets (including the ring road) and
the dense packing of structures, this site gives an even more claustrophobic impression
than Lattes (fig. 8.16). This overall structure was reproduced several times after violent
episodes of destruction, but during the four periods of this "first village" there were

numerous shifts in the internal walls of houses: first subdividing the one-room houses with walls to make smaller units and then, in the late third century BCE, tearing out the subdivision walls and joining rooms to make larger houses. There was also an expansion of the settlement outside the rampart.

After another episode of destruction at the beginning of the second century BCE, the site (now designated the "second village") was enlarged to slightly more than one hectare and restructured. The settlement was actually divided into two distinct sectors, one built on top of the ruins of the old village, and one two meters below it to the east. Still composed of linear blocks, their orientation now shifted to an east-west direction and they were now uniformly of two-room width composed of a double row of one-room houses with an axial wall. In the newer, eastern part of the site, these blocks were extremely regular and without perpendicular cross-streets, while in the west they were more irregular. The organization of this period seems to be entirely linear, without a trace of the concentric principle of a block of houses and a ring road following the contours of the rampart. This state of the town lasted for less than a century before being destroyed again and finally abandoned at the end of the second century BCE.[149]

The hillfort of Nages, on one of the hills ringing the Vaunage basin, offers an illustration of another variation on a strong, almost purely linear logic (fig. 8.17).[150] It was founded about 300 BCE, but, aside from the initial rampart (fig. 8.17-A), most traces of the initial settlement (Nages I) have been obliterated by later occupations. The settlement of the last half of the third and early second centuries (Nages II ancien) was built inside

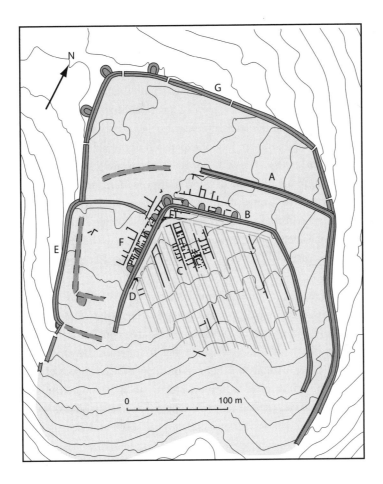

FIGURE 8.17

Plan of Nages showing the organization of the urban landscape with multiple phases of rampart construction (after Py 1990a; courtesy of Michel Py).

a new rampart with round towers (fig. 8.17-B) and was composed of very regular parallel linear blocks of stone houses (fig. 8.17-C). These blocks are uniformly of about 4.5-meter width and separated by unusually wide streets of about 5-meter width. The blocks are composed of one-room rectangular houses about 7.5-meter length and about 25 square meters in area. The concentric pattern in this case is reduced (except for one small row of identical houses built against the rampart in its northwestern corner) to a ring road that runs along the interior wall of the rampart (fig. 8.17-D). The linear strip blocks flow downhill and are oriented towards the corner of the rampart; in other words, they form about a 45-degree angle with the rampart walls rather than running parallel or perpendicular to any wall. Or as the excavator, Michel Py, put it, the orientation of the blocks is independent of the rampart.[151] At about 175 BCE, the settlement expanded to the west and a new section of rampart (fig. 8.17-E) was added to the first (Nages II récent). In this new area (fig. 8.17-F), the linear blocks run parallel to the old rampart (that is, at a 45-degree angle to the blocks of the older settlement). The blocks of the older settlement also were widened at this time to about 7 meters by encroaching on the streets, reducing them by half to 2.5 meters in width. The expansion was uniform, but the interior arrangements of the larger houses that resulted were quite varied. During the third quarter of the second century BCE, a new rampart (fig. 8.17-G) was built that completely enclosed the old one (Nages III), and the settlement expanded again, although, because of preservation factors, less is known about the later settlement. Py saw both the impressive regularity of the first layout and the uniform line of expansion of the older blocks into the streets during Nages II *récent* as evidence of a coordinated communal action directed by a central authority, although the diversity of interior arrangements indicates that communal action and consensus was limited to the realm of apportioning civic space.[152] However one evaluates the assertion of the need for centralized political authority in this case, what must be emphasized for the present discussion is that this spatial organization is rigidly linear, rather than orthogonal, in its logic and the concentric element seems little in evidence as well.

The hillfort of Entremont, three kilometers north of Aix-en-Provence, offers yet another variation on these patterns: in this case orthogonal (figs. 8.18 and 8.19).[153] As at Nages, there are distinct phases of expansion, with an extension of the rampart to enclose the new neighborhood. The settlement was founded in the early second century BCE with a small town of about 0.9 hectare in the southeast corner of a plateau, and it expanded over the entire plateau around 150 to 130 BCE to enclose a total area of about 3.5 hectares. The early settlement (the Upper Town, or habitat 1) is protected by a rampart on the north and east sides and cliffs on the south and west sides. Within this parallelogram area is a concentric element consisting of a row of single-room houses built against the interior face of the rampart and a ring road following the same perimeter. Within the ring road is a series of an estimated 18 fairly regular blocks (only a few of these have been entirely excavated) of parallelogram shape, each composed of two rows of one-room houses abutting along a median wall. This plan is somewhat less

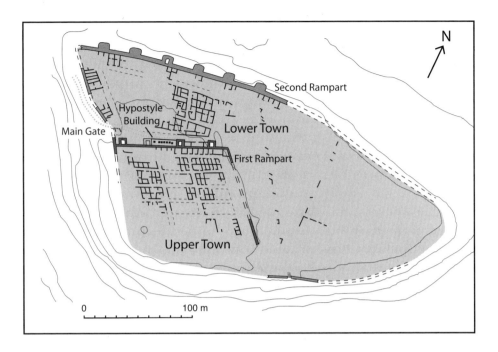

FIGURE 8.18

Plan of Entremont showing two phases of settlement construction and enlargement of the rampart (after Arcelin 1993; courtesy of Patrice Arcelin).

FIGURE 8.19

Reconstruction of Entremont showing the dense urban landscape: view from the north (watercolor by Jean-Claude Golvin © editions-errance.fr: from Goudineau 1996).

regular than was originally thought: the early excavations were in quite regular blocks but subsequent excavations have revealed various irregularities, including blocks with four rows of houses and connections between rooms.[154] These blocks are separated by a uniform grid of cross-streets of two to three meters width meeting at oblique angles. The corners of a few blocks are rounded in order to allow the turning of wagons. The houses are usually only thirteen to fifteen square meters in area, but numerous traces of stairs have been identified and it is presumed that second stories were common. The blocks are generally roughly ten to eleven meters wide and twenty-four meters long.

The Lower Town (or habitat 2) has been excavated predominantly in the area north of the Upper Town. It shows a quite different, and less regular, orthogonal organization with larger blocks of a more square form (roughly twenty by twenty-four meters), and others of narrower and more elongated form. The internal arrangement of rooms is also much more complicated, with some isolated single rooms of highly variable size and other houses of two or three connected rooms, and in one case perhaps an internal courtyard. The orientation of streets, now three to four meters in width, is also slightly different, as the old rampart had been razed and was no longer the reference for the grid: a new rampart to the north now served this function. In the area between two towers of the old rampart was constructed a hypostyle building with an *opus signinum* floor that has been interpreted as a ritual structure, not least because about twenty skulls, some with clear traces of having been affixed, were found in the wide street in front of this structure, which is often referred to as a *voie sacrée*. This is one of the few instances known of a monumental ritual structure found inside a settlement (discussed later).

A number of settlements also exhibit what Dominique Garcia has called a "loose order" *(ordre lâche)*—that is, without any easily definable pattern (streets of multiple orientations, irregular clusters of houses) or with some cross-streets and vaguely rectangular blocks of different sizes and shapes, but without a regular grid pattern or clear linear strips.[155] In the lower Rhône basin, sites such as Roque-de-Viou and the early phases of Ambrussum are prime examples.[156] One could continue presenting a series of further distinctive variations of such urban landscape organizations at sites such as Saint-Blaise, Le Baou Roux, Le Marduel, or the highly variable arrangements of settlements of eastern Provence. But the point seems clear. In the first place, we are not looking at a single model of rectilinear settlement organization. These were not reproductions of a uniform plan, and certainly not one that derived from a Greek conception. Rather, they were different local experimentations with a few common dispositions toward space (concentric, linear, orthogonal, and some unknown principles) that show different permutations and trajectories in different areas. Second, they did not arrive on the scene as fully formed urban plans, but rather were the product of experimentation that occurred while adapting to increasing populations within the confines of a rampart. This fact is well demonstrated at settlements such as Lattes where the Early Iron Age levels have been adequately explored, and other sites will undoubtedly throw more light on this process as their early levels are more extensively excavated. What is also urgently needed is more extensive excavation at sites that predate this transformation (for example, at the coastal villages near the Mauguio lagoon or La Liquière) to determine how radical a difference there really is. One may well find that dispositions toward linear and concentric arrangements of houses, for example, were an existing feature of settlements with detached wattle-and-daub houses, but that these have been less easy to detect when the houses are not forced up against each other. More excavation and close analysis may reveal that even the highly regular rectilinear settlements, which at first glance seem so different, are following an experimental development of the logic of earlier spatial dispositions. Aside from the issue of the origins of these rectilinear patterns, the histories of sites also show a continual process of experimentation with the rectilinear systems involved. Expansions of sites always show significant variations from the older core, and even when the basic layout of streets and blocks remains stable within a settlement, there is considerable experimentation with the internal structure.

One hypothetical developmental model has been proposed by Dominique Garcia to explain the ontology of some aspects of these different patterns. He sees the settlements with stone or mud-brick architecture that exhibit a loose order as descending directly from the organization of earlier settlements of wattle-and-daub houses, sometimes through a simple replacement of one house by another of the new technique. The concentric pattern he sees as stemming from either (1) the building of a rampart (and a row of new stone or mud-brick houses against it) around an existing settlement and the subsequent progressive abandonment of wattle-and-daub houses in the center, or (2) the building of refuge sites occupied permanently by a small population living in houses against the rampart and only an occasional occupation by a larger population. Finally, the linear pattern he sees as resulting from either (1) the progressive infilling of the center of a concentric arrangement of type 1, or (2) the founding of a new settlement where the rampart was constructed first and then blocks of houses set up within it.[157] In some of these cases, the oldest houses would be on the periphery rather than the center, while in others the pattern would be reversed. At the moment, this remains a set of plausible scenarios with implications for excavation strategies rather than a demonstrated fact. But what such models emphasize is the necessity of treating urban landscapes as dynamic social phenomena rather than synchronic structures (or simple products of an urban plan), and the consequent need to explore the "settlement biography" of different sites in a comparative fashion.[158]

SUMMARY: INNOVATION AND NORMALIZATION

It has long been recognized that these various transformations in urban landscapes, which are often jointly described as "urbanism," are linked to the colonial experience. As the previous discussion makes clear, the temporal and spatial pattern of their occurrence is too closely correlated with the expansion of early trade with Etruscans and Massalians to be entirely coincidental. However, earlier interpretations that saw these changes as simple imitation of Greek civilization or the diffusion of Greek ideas with trade contacts have gradually given way to more sophisticated explanations. For example, Py proposed a complex economic model in which native societies that entered into trade relations with these alien merchants were gradually constrained to abandon certain traditional subsistence practices (such as transhumant pastoralism between the coast and interior) and focus on others that would produce the surpluses necessary for trade. This necessitated more sedentary settlements with a need to control a productive territory and defend surpluses with ramparts. This emphasis on long-term stability also fostered greater "rationalization" of both agricultural territory and urban structure.[159] This model, which is presented here in a telegraphic form that does not do justice to its multiple nuances, has the virtue of being much more sociologically plausible than prior interpretations and of addressing both the role of unintended consequences and microregional diversity. Moreover, Py carefully documented the evidence for a relationship between increasing trade followed by evidence of increasing storage at a range of coastal sites across several regions, and correlated this with differences in the chronology of changes in urban landscapes between the coast and interior. However, in its primary focus on economic causation, this interpretive model risks flirting with a kind of economic functionalism in which the systemic needs of economic processes determine individual motivations and actions: choices are explained on the basis of a systemic logic of which people could not themselves have been aware. This kind of explanation tends to neglect the cultural dimension of such historical processes: that is, for instance, the way in which cultural dispositions toward space affect the patterns of choice in solving problems of creating and inhabiting the built environment. Why, for example, would an increase in surplus production lead to *this particular pattern* of settlement from among many other possibilities? Moreover, it leaves certain key questions unasked. For example, how does one explain the initial demand for alien goods that set off this spiral of surplus production and urban consolidation? Why would native societies have had an initial interest in Etruscan or Greek goods sufficient to engage in trade and to expand that trade to the point that it necessitated a change in structures of production? Why was there a demand for particular kinds of goods and not others, and what implications did this selective desire have for the nature of the entanglement that followed? These latter questions have already been addressed in previous chapters, and here I want to focus more on discussion of the landscape issues.

Individual sites were founded, expanded, contracted, abandoned, and reoccupied for a variety of local historical reasons that are often difficult to discern. The Vaunage basin, for example, had a series of settlements on the various hills that rim the basin over the centuries. Some of these seem to have been abandoned as others were founded, as if there were a transfer of population, while others persisted in place for long periods of time and overlapped in their chronologies.[160] Such changes in settlements can occur because of disease, exhaustion of agricultural land, natural disasters such as floods or earthquakes, internal political conflict, violent destruction inflicted from outside, or shifts in residential preference from dispersed rural to concentrated urban (or the reverse). It is not an event itself that causes a shift (except in the unusual event of an entire population being destroyed), but people's collective reaction to an event: some sites continue to be rebuilt multiple times after disasters (such as l'Île de Martigues and Roquepertuse), while others are abandoned. And some sites simply dwindle away after centuries of occupation without any apparent signs of a dramatic cause. This means that, as the previous discussion has indicated, attempting to understand individual site histories requires several scales of analysis. Regional patterns may point to broader forces at play, but this level of analysis alone will not provide adequate explanations because the inhabitants of different sites will often react differently to the same vector. Comparative analysis of individual site histories, within a regional framework, is crucial.

Given the patterns outlined here, it is abundantly clear that the initial appearance of fortifications at indigenous settlements cannot be explained as an imitation of Massalia, but rather was a reaction to the effects of Massalia's insertion into the landscape—that is, a response to increased levels of insecurity in the neighborhood of the Greek colony. The subsequent spread of fortifications along the coast follows the general expansion of maritime merchant activity and may be related to attempts to control this trade (its agents, benefits, and disruptive effects), as certain towns (Lattes, Cailar, Espeyran, Arles) emerged as privileged, circumscribed spaces of commercial interaction. The gradual spread of fortifications throughout the rest of the Rhône basin over the next couple of centuries may plausibly be attributed to gradual alterations in indigenous networks of political alliance and shifting strategies of defense (from social buffers to physical barriers). This may have been, in part, a result of changes in the social landscape stemming from this trading activity along the coast, but also, perhaps, as Py has suggested, of a growing concern to symbolically mark territory by small polities that were increasingly constrained in terms of mobility.[161] In any case, the spread of fortifications was not a uniform phenomenon explicable by a single cause. Rather, it followed somewhat different logics in different areas (close to Massalia, along the coast, and towards the interior, for instance) as solutions to distinctive, but interrelated, problems. However, once established, these massive stone barriers resulting from communal labor had some similar effects. For one thing, they tended to constrain the population within a relatively small space and shape a movement toward increasing density of the urban landscape. This may have been one of the pressures that led to the forms of densely packed rectilinear settlement organization that one sees emerging over the course of the sixth and fifth centuries BCE. Here again, these arrangements of dwellings and streets do not resemble Greek settlements, and the idea of imitation must be rejected. Rather, they may be seen as responses to, among other things, the artificial confinement of monumental enclosures worked out through cultural dispositions toward social space. The spatial constraints imposed by ramparts were by no means absolute: they were the materialized expression of culturally organized preferences and perceptions of the possible. Sometimes solutions involved experiments in other directions as well. For example, extra-mural settlements seem to have sprung up as early as the fifth century BCE at a number of sites, such as

Lattes, Beaucaire, and Roche de Comps.[162] Others tried expanding the fortifications to enable the construction of new neighborhoods within an enclosed space (for example, Nages and Entremont). But both of these initiatives seem to have occurred as secondary maneuvers, or subsequent adaptations, after the custom of dense rectilinear settlement within a delimiting fortification had already been established. In some cases, such as at Roquepertuse, extra-mural settlement expansion was followed by a retreat back within the walls that enclosed the early settlement.[163]

One case of an unmistakable adoption of Greco-Italic models does exist: the site of Glanum (or *Glanon*) in the mid–second century BCE. The clarity of this whole-sale importation of alien architectural models emphasizes by stark contrast its difference from the transformations seen at other sites. Founded in the Bronze Age near Saint-Remy-de-Provence on the north side of a narrow valley cutting through the Alpilles hills, it has become famous for its well-preserved complex of monumental buildings dating to the mid–second century BCE through the Roman period. Until quite recently, the pre-Roman settlement had been subjected to little excavation, and much still remains to be published of recent work.[164] However, during most of the Iron Age it appears to have been a fairly typical small settlement located on the upper slopes of a hill near a sacred spring associated with the Celtic god Glanis. It had a rampart already in the sixth century BCE, but it was around the second quarter of the second century BCE that the settlement expanded onto the lower slopes and plain below and was surrounded by a new rampart running over the surrounding hills and enclosing about thirty hectares (although only about half of the interior was inhabitable space). This move was accompanied around 150 BCE by the construction of an extensive town with a monumental center of about two hectares size built around the sacred spring. During the late second or early first century BC, areas on the periphery of this new town that had previously been occupied were restructured. A neighborhood of large new two-story houses of a clearly Greco-Italic style (with peristyle courtyards) built of large Greek-type dressed stone blocks was established on both sides of a main road leading into the monumental center (fig. 8.20).[165] The building of the monumental center itself has a complicated chronology, but the various structures were erected sequentially from about 150 to 75 BCE. These included first a Tuscan style temple and a rectangular courtyard building next to the spring, followed by a huge trapezoidal peristyle building with an *opus signinum* floor, a monumental gate, a portico, a rectangular structure with bench platforms that resembles a Greek *bouleuterion* (a citizens' council meeting place), and several other structures. One is no longer in the realm of vernacular architecture here: these are buildings constructed by skilled stonemasons working from complex architectural models. But in the midst of this monumental complex of assertively Greco-Italic style was also found a small area housing stone stelae painted in a style typical of other indigenous sites of the region as well as several stone statues of warriors in the typical cross-legged position known from sites such as Roquepertuse and Entremont.[166]

FIGURE 8.20
Photograph of Glanum showing Greco-Italic style houses lining the road to the sanctuary.

Not only is the architecture of an alien style, but the very conception of a city constructed around a center composed of monumental public buildings of a ritual nature fronted by a neighborhood of ostentatiously large houses is a marked departure from the indigenous traditions of the region. Glanum is one of a handful of sites in Provence to witness the incorporation of ritual buildings within the settlement in the last few centuries BCE, but it is the only one to do this with flamboyant alien architecture and to create an entire monumental district.

How does one explain this curious phenomenon? Interpretation would undoubtedly be easier if one had available more than the patchy existing excavation data from areas outside the monumental center. But several possible hypotheses can at least be raised. In the first place, it should be remembered that this development began at the height of the period of tensions between Massalia and the Salyen confederation that led soon after to the Roman conquest, and much of the building actually postdates the conquest. One might reasonably surmise that Glanum is in part the reflection of a Massalian strategy to diffuse the Salyen threat by trying to secure alliances with some groups in the Salyen domain. In this way, Glanum may have been showered with special political and economic favors, perhaps including sending teams of masons, architects, and workers to offer buildings honoring a site of religious significance as a way of cementing an alliance. It is even possible that some Massalians (merchants and others) may have resided at Glanum and vice versa. After the conquest, which followed very quickly after the first

Greco-Italic buildings, a former ally would have continued to enjoy a special relationship with Massalia and Rome, perhaps as one of the "Massalian cities" *(poleis Massalias)* mentioned by Artemidorus. The position of Glanum alongside the newly established Via Domitia, as well as its reputation as a ritual center (perhaps attracting pilgrimages), may also have aided its fortunes. Whatever the case, by the mid–second century BCE Glanum clearly had established a relationship of a very different kind with Massalia than any other indigenous town—one that involved a rapid transformation of the landscape and, at least for an elite group living adjacent to the ritual center, a transformation of tastes that greatly accelerated after the conquest of the Salyes. Glanum is of great interest not only because it provides a dramatic contrast with developments at other contemporary sites of the region, but also because it prefigures in many ways lifestyle changes that would occur at other sites nearly a century later under the different political conditions of the Augustan period.

MASSALIA AND ITS COLONIES

The urban landscapes of Massalia and its colonies experienced transformations that were no less dynamic than indigenous settlements, and the "biographies" of these colonial sites deserve a symmetrical analysis. Julius Caesar, in his siege of Massalia in 49 BCE during the Roman Civil War, described the city as "washed by the sea on three sides" and defended by a rampart on the landward side,[167] a description that makes sense in the light of recent excavations and studies of changes in the shoreline since the first century BCE.[168] In effect, Massalia was a defended promontory much like Tamaris but larger. Although it had expanded over an area of about fifty hectares by the time Caesar was writing, initially it occupied only the western end of the peninsula and was comparable in size to many native sites. That this small precarious settlement would eventually become the largest city in the region was by no means obvious or inevitable at the beginning.

Until recently Marseille was often sardonically referred to as "the antique city without antiquities." This was a reflection of the fact that, although the early city was known from ancient texts, no visible remains of monumental architecture had survived the 2,600 years of continuous occupation and landscape transformations, and archaeological documentation was limited.[169] However, archaeological exploration of Massalia has seen a dramatic improvement in the four decades since François Villard and Fernand Benoit published their interpretations, and this has particularly accelerated since the 1980s. This is the result of several grand-scale excavations along the edge of the ancient port (at the Centre Bourse, Place Jules-Verne, and Place Villeneuve-Bargemon sites) and a very active program of smaller rescue excavations throughout the interior portion of the city and its northern perimeter (fig. 8.21).[170] These have revealed the ancient ramparts and gates of the city (fig. 8.22), docks, domestic, commercial, and monumental structures, cemeteries, craft production areas, massive quantities of ceramics, and extremely

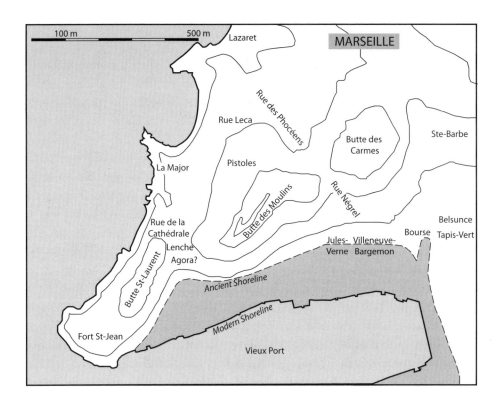

FIGURE 8.21
Map of locations of major excavations at Marseille.

FIGURE 8.22
Remains of the city wall and gate of Massalia and the edge of the Roman period dock at the Centre Bourse shopping mall, Marseille.

well-preserved organic material (including cordage, baskets, leather, food, and a series of wooden ships dating back to the sixth century BCE). [171] The evidence still consists of scattered patches and there are many unresolved questions; but it is beginning to illuminate a bustling port city that expanded rapidly and at its maximum size was considerably larger than any other settlement in Mediterranean France until the Roman period: only Nîmes reached much more than about half the size of Massalia, and that was not until the second century BCE.

Massalia was founded in an area that had no existing indigenous settlement. [172] The city eventually extended over three large hills (the buttes Saint-Laurent, des Moulins, and des Carmes) separated by narrow depressions: these formed the central spine of a triangular peninsula overlooking a harbor to the south. But the initial settlement was in the area of the Fort Saint-Jean, on the western tip of the peninsula overlooking the narrow entrance to the harbor, and the adjacent butte Saint-Laurent (and perhaps also the butte des Moulins).

The earliest traces of a rampart date only to about 510 BCE and are found in the Bourse area at the eastern end of the harbor, constructed in the middle of what was formerly an extra-muros industrial zone (fig. 8.23). There are traces of two later ramparts as well. Although no evidence has yet been found, it is assumed that an earlier rampart existed farther to the west protecting the original settlement. Henri Tréziny has provided a hypothetical reconstruction of two phases of this early rampart based on traces of settlement: initially it would have enclosed the buttes Saint-Laurent and des Moulins in the early sixth century BCE, before expanding northward to include the Panier area. [173] The later ramparts are known only in sporadic sections, and there has been much debate about their precise courses. It seems clear, however, that the defenses were expanded to include the butte des Carmes by the end of the sixth century BCE, and expanded again to include the descending slopes northwest of the butte des Carmes (the *vallon des Phocéens*) during the second quarter of the second century BCE. [174]

The only city gate clearly defined by archaeological remains is the eastern gate at the Bourse, which, at least in the Hellenistic period, was flanked by monumental towers. This would have been breached by an east-west road running along the southern flanks of the city's hills close to the port. Outside the gate to the east was a swampy wetland zone, and various attempts were made to stabilize roads leading through it by laying down beds of pebbles, clay, and hundreds of empty amphorae. [175] Another major road is suspected to have run northward along the western part of the city, breaching the early walls near the current Place du Séminaire and the Hellenistic wall near the Tour Sainte-Paule. A third major route is suspected to have run in a northeastern direction from the northern slope of the butte des Carmes, exiting through a gate somewhere between the Accoules church and the rue de la Roquette. [176]

The early sixth-century BCE rampart, assuming one existed, may have been of mud brick, although no traces have yet been identified. The late sixth century BCE rampart

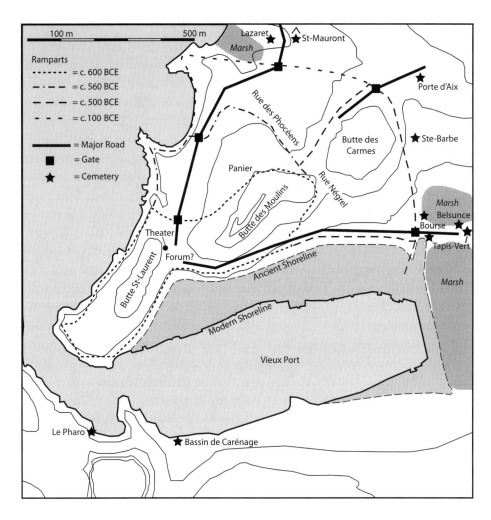

Ramparts
· · · · · · · = c. 600 BCE
—·—·— = c. 560 BCE
— — — = c. 500 BCE
- - - - = c. 100 BCE

——— = Major Road
■ = Gate
★ = Cemetery

FIGURE 8.23
Map of the successive rampart expansions at Massalia, major roads and gates leading out of the city, and location of major pre-Roman cemeteries (information from Bouiron and Tréziny 2001).

and its refurbished version of the second half of the fourth century BCE were both composed of a foundation of several courses of large rectangular blocks of white limestone from the nearby quarry of Saint-Victor. The superstructure was composed of large blocks of tufa, or perhaps mud brick in the case of the sixth-century BCE version.[177] The second-century BCE rampart, the one seen by Caesar, was constructed of large rectangular blocks of pink limestone quarried from Cap Couronne, near the site of L'Arquet (about twenty-six kilometers west of Marseille). This rampart (fig. 8.22) was built in a style typical of Hellenistic period Greek fortifications (standard block module, inner and outer stone facings, square towers, etc.), and one quite similar to the contemporary ramparts at Saint-Blaise and Glanum.[178]

The massive dressed-stone wharf that one now sees at the *corne du port* (fig. 8.22) is a fairly late feature of the Roman period (first to third centuries CE), and its construction created such disturbance that possible earlier dock constructions in this area are impossible to detect. However, the excavations farther east at the Place Jules-Verne and Place Villeneuve-Bargemon have revealed the presence of a substantial wharf construction of large stone blocks in this area already in the early sixth century BC. At that time, the shoreline was located over 150 meters north of the current edge of the Vieux Port, at the foot of the steep slope of the buttes des Moulins and Saint-Laurent. Over the centuries the shoreline continued to shift as a result of silting and changes in water level, and dock installations were repeatedly reconstructed. During the fourth century BCE, this area was apparently used for shipbuilding; and for the last few centuries BCE, the shore is littered with the remains of wooden hoists (poles, ropes, etc.) for maneuvering ships into drydock. From the first century CE on, a series of more substantial wharfs of wood and stone construction and warehouses filled with large storage jars (dolia) were built.[179]

The combined rampart and settlement data document a rapid expansion of the city.[180] The original settlement covered only about ten or twelve hectares, if one credits the actual concentrations of early sixth century BCE material found in the Fort Saint-Jean and butte Saint-Laurent areas and analysis of the spatial and temporal patterns of street and building orientations.[181] But it may have been as large as twenty-five hectares, if one follows Henri Tréziny's debatable argument that the butte des Moulins was probably the acropolis and would have been part of the city from the beginning.[182] The addition of the Panier neighborhood would have pushed this total to around thirty hectares during the second quarter of the sixth century BCE, and the addition of the butte des Carmes would have expanded it to about forty hectares by the end of the century. Finally, the second century BCE would have seen an ultimate expansion to about fifty hectares, which remained fairly constant until the post-Roman period. Assuming a relative stability of population density, this indicates a remarkably rapid demographic expansion during the sixth century BCE, followed by a slower but sustained growth afterward. Such an expansion is beyond the bounds of normal demographic processes, particularly for ancient cities, and could have resulted only from the arrival of additional settlers or the inclusion of native peoples and foreign merchants within the city.

Inside the city walls there is not yet enough evidence to reconstruct a detailed overall plan of streets, quarters and public buildings. However, what is visible from the scattered patches of evidence indicates rapid expansion and continual transformations of the urban landscape, including changes in the structure of domestic units, the organization and orientation of housing blocks and streets, and the function of particular neighborhoods. For example, the Rue Leca site, at the northern foot of the butte des Moulins, served as a rubbish dump for houses on top of the hill during the late sixth and early fifth centuries BCE. During the early fifth century BCE, it became a potters' area, with the installation of a very large circular kiln for amphorae and a basin, perhaps for clay preparation. Near the end of the century it was replaced by a building with another large amphora kiln, and during the mid–fourth century BCE this was replaced by an impressive public bath complex with a large circular room. This building in turn was destroyed in the mid–third century BCE and replaced by a large U-form courtyard house with a central well and a workshop for metallurgy. In the mid–first century BCE, this house was replaced by an even larger pastas-style house with a courtyard and enclosed garden.[183] Similarly, the butte des Carmes appears to have had only a few structures with artisanal functions during the sixth century BCE, after which it became a quarry for potters' clay during the mid–fifth century BCE, changed to a residential neighborhood at the end of the third century BCE, and then became a potters' area again (with kilns for amphorae and clay purification tanks) in the mid–first century BCE.[184]

From the beginning, there was no single orientation of a general orthogonal grid that organized the city. Rather, the diversity of orientations of buildings and streets (up to five different systems identified by Manuel Moliner already in the Archaic period) indicates a local adaptation to the diverse topography. Particular neighborhoods developed coherent structures extending over areas up to a couple of hectares, but the overall situation was heterogeneous, with a tendency toward the emergence of functional zones (industrial, ritual, residential, port, etc.) that shifted over time as the city expanded. The least coherently discernable pattern (Moliner's System 1) was that found in the western part of the peninsula in levels dating to the early sixth century BCE, and this was replaced during the second quarter of the century by a new set of orientations that also guided the first orthogonal settlement in the Panier area.[185] Henri Trèziny has argued tentatively for the emergence of two modules for blocks within these systems: a narrow one of about twenty-two meters in width in the sixth century BCE, as in the Panier, and a wider one of about thirty-five meters during the Hellenistic period, as in the rue Leca area.[186] During the Classical period, the main axes of the center of the city became increasingly fixed and newly settled areas to the north were oriented by main streets and public spaces that were definitively established in the fabric of the grid. From this period on the general organization of the different neighborhoods was largely set, using four main patterns, and further developments were worked out within these systems.[187]

Patches of evidence of domestic architecture have been recovered from several parts of the city and from a variety of different periods, but these represent a miniscule sample in a city of Massalia's size. It is risky to generalize on the basis of the scant evidence available, but for the period covering the first few generations of the settlement, the picture seems to be one of modest structures with small rooms of mud-brick, stone, or wattle-and-daub construction. For example, a small section of a housing block was excavated near the Saint-Laurent church in the late 1980s exposing parts of several irregular rectangular structures with mud-brick walls on a stone foundation. The rooms are quite small: one room of only 4.25 square meters had a tamped earth floor but few other signs of interior features. Ceramics included an urn of indigenous CNT ware, an Etruscan amphora, and several fragments of Colonial Cream-ware (a lid and some cup bowls), and Corinthian and other imported ceramics were found in other rooms.[188] Another excavation in the Panier area yielded a small wattle-and-daub structure with traces of ironworking (trench hearths and slag) that was replaced by a larger (about seventy square meters) two-room rectangular domestic structure around 580 to 570 BCE. The Place des Pistoles in the Panier area has provided rectangular rooms with stone walls, circular hearths on tamped earth floors, and a bench platform in one room. For the fifth century BCE, a post-built wattle-and-daub structure of 5 by 11 meters was found at the Îlot des Phocéens site under an early second-century BCE rectangular two-room house (5.5 by 9 meters) that had an opus signinum floor with the word XAIPE ("welcome") in the larger room and a large quantity of drinking cups and pitchers. Domestic structures of the Hellenistic period are poorly known because of the large amount of reconstruction performed during the Roman period and the extensive damage this did to the buildings existing at the time. House foundations of white limestone are known from several areas and the elevations are presumed to have been of mud brick, but few floors have been preserved. One Hellenistic domestic structure that has been recovered is a courtyard house at the Rue Leca dating to the second half of the third century BCE. This two-story mud-brick house of about four hundred square meters is composed of three wings of rooms around a central courtyard that constitutes about a third of the total space. The courtyard had a terrazzo floor, a circular well (or perhaps an *impluvium*), and a drainage gutter lined with fragments of roof tiles in a lime cement, as well as a gallery with pillars along the south side. The southwestern wing had four rooms with numerous traces of iron working, a terrazzo lined vat, hearths, and basalt grindstones: it was probably an artisanal area. The southeastern wing consisted of two rooms of residential space with a terrazzo floor and another floor of opus signinum decoration. The northwestern wing had stairs leading to a second floor and three rooms, the function of which is unknown.[189]

While the port, the fortifications, some industrial areas (especially pottery production), and a few residential structures have been at least reasonably well documented by archaeological excavations, the same is not true of monumental public buildings and spaces, especially religious ones. In fact, very few have even been positively identified. Strabo noted the presence of two large temples dedicated to Ephesian Artemis and Delphinian Apollo, and a sanctuary to Athena Polias;[190] however, archaeological evidence of these and the other public structures that were normal for a major Greek city is still meager. The acropolis (in the sense of a promontory citadel of refuge) is generally assumed to have been located on the heights of the butte des Moulins, but the lower butte Saint-Laurent is considered a more likely place for the major temples noted above, especially given that Strabo situated them on the "headland" of the peninsula.[191] Unfortunately, no evidence has been found to confirm this hypothesis aside from a massive Ionic capital of white limestone that was found reused in another building at the foot of the butte Saint-Laurent. This architectural fragment is of uncertain and much disputed date, with recent opinions ranging from the late sixth to post–fourth century BCE.[192] Evidence of other public structures from recent excavations includes a fourth-century BCE bath complex at the Rue Leca mentioned earlier, a much larger bath complex of the first century CE located next to the port in the Villeneuve-Bargemon area,[193] a few traces of water control facilities (wells, cisterns, aqueducts, sweet-water basins for replenishing ships, etc. of various dates),[194] and a probable small sanctuary of the fourth century BCE and later discovered at the northeast foot of the Butte des Moulins, at the Parc des Phocéens site.[195] The oldest (possibly) ritual structure known is a small circular building (about 4 m in diameter) of mud brick dating to 575 to 500 BCE found in the Place des Pistoles in the Panier. It contained a rare ceramic "lantern" in the form of a house model, and this structure is located next to a rectangular building that contained a mixture of imported ceramics and Massalian Cream-ware shards. Because of the very high percentage (about 78 percent) of tableware (and especially drinking forms), it has been interpreted as the scene of feasting.[196] Aside from the Ionic capital, earlier discoveries are limited to a Greek-type theater of Roman period date at the rue des Martégalles (on the southeastern slope of the Butte Saint-Laurent) and a series of forty-eight limestone stelae (or *naïskoi*) found without good stratigraphic context at the rue Négrel, representing a woman seated inside a building with a hipped roof (thought to be a sanctuary).[197] These naïskoi range in size from about thirty to sixty-six centimeters tall and probably date to the second half of the sixth century BCE. They may have been part of a sanctuary for a cult of Cybele, Athena, or Artemis on the butte des Moulins, or a small cult site dedicated to a water goddess or nymph located outside the city wall.[198]

The *agora*, the market and meeting place that was the central civic space of a Greek city, is assumed to have been located at the Place de Lenche, in the depression between the buttes Saint-Laurent and des Moulins because of its central topographic position. There are some possible indications of the Roman period *forum* in this general area (for example, two areas paved with flagstones),[199] but for the pre-Roman period this is simply an hypothesis unconfirmed by archaeological evidence. Suggestions have also been made of a shift of the agora to the area of the Place Villeneuve-Bargemon, near the port, during the early expansion of the city.[200] The remains of a theater of the Roman period (noted earlier) were also located just to the southwest of the Place de Lenche. During the late second century or early first century BCE, an impressive structure of pink limestone blocks from La Couronne was erected at the Saint-Sauveur site, on the southern edge of the Place de Lenche. This building, consisting of a row of seven uniform rooms of 5 by 10.4 meters each (and at least 7.5-meter height) surrounded by a 4.1-meters-wide gallery, was probably a facility for grain storage.[201] A stadium is also mentioned in an inscription of the first to third centuries CE found in the Vieille-Major area, but there are no convincing indications of where this might have been located or whether the pre-Roman city had one.[202]

In brief, the result of the past several decades of intensive archaeological research have failed to reveal much evidence of monumental buildings at Massalia before the Hellenistic period. That is certainly not to say that there were not any: the limestone Ionic capital clearly belonged to a monumental structure perhaps as old as the sixth century BCE, and the bath complex at the Rue Leca dates to the mid–fourth century BCE. These surely were not the only structures of their kind. Traces of earlier monumental buildings were undoubtedly severely disturbed by the wave of constructions of the Hellenistic and, especially, the Roman period; and the late sixth-century BCE rampart demonstrates the use of construction techniques involving large dressed stone blocks at least for defensive edifices within a century after the founding of the colony. But it may well be the case that the monumental quality of the urban landscape was considerably less impressive in the early centuries of the city's growth than it came to be in the Hellenistic and Roman periods. It is significant, for example, that there is an almost complete lack of architectural terra cottas in the early levels of Marseille. In the Greek colonies of southern Italy and Sicily, the roofs of temples were usually of wood covered with polychrome terra cottas (tiles, cornices, gutters, etc.) to such an extent that these objects are a handy archaeological marker of religious buildings. Their absence at Marseille during the sixth century BCE is surprising, and probably an indication that such structures had wooden or thatch roofs.[203] Moreover, finds of roof tiles from later periods are far less common at Marseille than at most other Greek cities. Excavations at the Bourse have shown that they were present from the fourth century BCE on, and perhaps a little earlier, but they were not in common usage. Shingles of sawn limestone were often used for public buildings, but most domestic structures probably had roofs of thatch or wood covered with earth, as did houses at indigenous settlements. As late as the first century BCE, Vitruvius, in outlining a theory about the evolution of architecture, singled out Massalia as a city where one could still find roofs made of "earth mixed with straw" rather than tiles, a technique he associated with the primitive stages of architectural development.[204]

It is undoubtedly wrong to push this image to the extreme, but in thinking about Massalia before the second century BCE it is equally wrong to envision it as a smaller version of Classical Athens with its gleaming marble temples. In many ways it would have been not terribly more impressive than indigenous towns of the region such as Saint-Blaise or Lattes; much larger and differently structured, to be sure, but not necessarily greatly more spectacular. It is also important not to project the image of Hellenistic or Roman Massalia back in time. One must recognize that, just like indigenous towns, it has a distinctive biography of development and transformation that occurred over the course of the colonial encounter in conjunction with developments and transformations at other sites in the region. When neighboring peoples of the sixth or fifth centuries BCE looked down on Massalia from the surrounding hills, they did not see either Classical Athens or Hellenistic Massalia, but rather a fortified town of mostly mud-brick structures with thatch and daub roofs experimenting with the organization of the urban landscape and the erection of some monumental structures as it grew. But there is little reason for them to have been terribly impressed by the appearance of the city, except by its size.

Of Massalia's colonies, only Olbia and Agde present much useful information about urban landscapes. Agde was founded on a low basalt plateau on the banks of the Hérault river 3.5 kilometers north of the current seacoast at the site of a previous indigenous settlement. Only small areas of the site's 4.25-hectare settlement have been subjected to excavation, but André Nickels placed the date of the transition from native to colonial town at the end of the fifth century BCE. The fortifications of the indigenous site were razed and the first colonial rampart was built in the fourth century BCE. This had an elevation of mud bricks on a foundation of undressed basalt blocks and formed a rectangle of 200 by 270 meters. This was replaced by a rampart built on a foundation of rectangular dressed stone blocks, probably during the second century BCE. Within the ramparts the tentative traces of an orthogonal urban grid have been identified on a rectangular module of about 200 by 257 meters, and this is still visible in the alignment of current streets in the old town center.[205]

Olbia, benefitting from the absence of a current city on top of it, has been more thoroughly excavated, although the early levels are the least well documented.[206] It was founded about 325 BCE on the edge of a small plateau abutting the sea near Hyères. There are no traces of a prior indigenous settlement, but the small hillfort of Costebelle, about one kilometer away, was abandoned at roughly the same date. The layout of the small site (only 2.5 hectares) of Olbia is extremely regular: a 3.5-meter-thick rampart with towers at each corner and one main gate to the east encloses a square area of 160 meters per side divided into an orthogonal grid of four quarters of ten blocks each (fig. 8.24). The quarters are divided by two main streets (of 4.2 and 5.2 meters width) meeting at a right angle in the center, and the rectangular blocks (11 by 34.2 meters) are separated by

smaller streets of 2.2-meter width. An unusual feature is the absence of any open space for an agora, although there was a small square with public wells at the main crossroads in the center. This fact, along with the exceptional homogeneity of the layout and the designation of the site by Strabo as an *epiteichisma* (fortress), has favored the interpretation of the site as a military garrison. One of the very few departures from the extreme regularity of the grid is along the western wall of the rampart, where two half-blocks on both sides of the main east-west street were joined to form a single building that, because of its unusual form and the presence of clay figurines, has been interpreted as a sanctuary, probably to Artemis. Another religious structure has been identified in a regular block along the north wall of the rampart by the presence of a large stone inscribed to Aphrodite, but all other buildings appear to have been residential. The initial rampart, with rectangular towers, was built of large undressed blocks of sandstone. During the second or first century BCE, this was rebuilt in parts with dressed rectangular blocks.

The basic room module appears to be a near square of 4.8 by 5.2 meters, with blocks composed of two rows of rooms abutting along a central axial wall that served as the support for a roof sloping down on both sides. No stairs or other indications of second stories have been found. Excavations to date have not furnished sufficient information to know if houses originally had more than one room, but there was a dramatic alteration in the early second century BCE in which multiple rooms were connected with internal doorways to create larger houses and some rooms were enlarged. Other periods of significant modification occurred in the late second century BCE and around 40 to 30 BCE.[207] The houses had mud-brick walls on stone foundations and tamped earth floors, although a few had concrete floors. Roofs were of reeds or thatch covered with daub until the first century BCE, when tiles appeared. There is little evidence of specialized functions for rooms, and no traces of commercial or artisanal sectors have been found before the Roman period. Michel Bats noted the uniform "mediocrity" of the architecture, with no dwelling appearing to be better built or more impressively outfitted than another. The ceramics give the same impression of uniformity and ordinariness.[208] This has reinforced the idea of a dependent defensive garrison, similar in nature to the Athenian *cleruchy*, inhabited by common Massalian citizens with few social distinctions: soldier-fishermen-farmers resembling Athenian *cleruchs*.[209]

In brief, Massalia and its two colonies with available settlement data were structured by a general orthogonal conception of civic organization, but one that resulted in quite different physical manifestations in the process of constructing and inhabiting specific built environments.

RITUAL LANDSCAPES

Let me emphasize again that use of the term *ritual landscapes* in this chapter is not intended to signal that ritual activity occupied a separate space or was excluded from urban landscapes. Rather, this category offers a way of talking about a particular *dimension* of social life that took place both inside and outside the civic and domestic spaces of settlements. In some cases there were specially constructed spatial domains for certain kinds of ritual activity that were intentionally placed outside the boundaries of towns, while in others monumental ritual sites actually structured the flow of urban life within town walls. And rituals of various kinds clearly formed an important part of social life within domestic contexts, even if these are not always as easy to detect as ritual activities that were spatially or architectonically marked.

MASSALIAN RITUAL LANDSCAPES

Evidence for reconstructing and interpreting religious practices and other forms of ritual consists of both textual and archaeological data. For indigenous societies of the region the texts are limited to sporadic observations by alien Greek and Roman authors, mostly from the last two centuries BCE, and these are subject to the same interpretive caveats voiced earlier concerning situated perspective, distortion, ignorance, and contextual ambiguity. These documents are both more abundant and more reliable for Greek and Roman practices, although certainly not without problems and gaps. Archaeological evidence consists primarily of the material remnants of funerary ritual, communal civic spaces with traces of ritual activity, and traces of domestic practices that stand out in some symbolically marked way from daily activity.

With the emergence of the polis in the eighth century BCE, many Greek cities developed a common conception of the city as a landscape structured around three kinds of communal spaces that were symbolically marked as public domains: (1) an open place for communal assembly and economic exchange (the agora), (2) a series of monumental religious structures, and (3) cemeteries to preserve the memory of the dead.[210] As Tonio Hölsher has remarked, these spaces evoke and encapsulate three dimensions of temporality: "(1) the unstable political present of the agora, (2) the timeless eternity of the gods in the sanctuaries; and (3) the normative memory of the past in the burial grounds."[211] The first two elements, with their spatiotemporal complementary opposition between political center and cult center,[212] came to define the core of the city proper, whereas, by the second half of the eighth century BCE, the city of the ancestors (the *necropolis*) had been separated from the city of the living in Athens, Corinth, and Argos in a pattern that would become standard for most Greek cities.[213]

Greek religious structures (and Etruscan and Roman ones) are often discussed in terms of two categories: sanctuaries and temples. Temples are a particular form of sanctuary marked by monumental architecture and usually dedicated to gods (often the communal gods of the city). Sanctuaries could also be far more modest, consisting of an altar *(bomos)*, a ritual enclosure *(temenos)*, or simply a collection of votive objects deposited at a natural site; and they might be dedicated to a god or a hero cult of an *oikos, deme,* or tribe. Sanctuaries were found not only within the city: they were an important part of the rural landscape outside the city walls, marking the territory of the city and its boundaries.

They are found just outside the city gates, at crossroads, on hilltops, on the coast, and on the edges of the chora, but the main temples to the gods of the polis were always within the urban center. Many of these extraurban sanctuaries were treated to processions coming out of the city during festivals. Others were used mainly by farmers who lived on the land of the chora rather than in the city.[214]

During the eighth century BCE, the number of cult sites multiplied rapidly in Greece, and the form of sacred space that defined the Greek sanctuary emerged. The role of these sanctuaries in the developmental history of the polis is a subject of debate.[215] But one thing is clear in the colonial context: so important were religious structures that they were among the first things established by new colonists.[216] The specific evolutions of these general dispositions toward urban landscape produced cities that often looked quite different: in some cases the agora and main temples were separated, while in others they were placed together. But the basic common conception is still discernible within the variety of particular configurations. Moreover, these arrangements evolved among cities in conversation with each other. For example, the spread of temple architecture through the Greek world was rapid, and probably involved a form of competition between city-states. Sacred architecture became an expression of civic identity, an index of prestige, and a focus of competitive display.[217] The experience of colonial expansion also had a decided influence on the evolution of models of urban landscape and the placement of temples and agora, as the foundation of new cities in new lands enabled an experimentation that was unconstrained by the accretionary material palimpsests of older cities. There were also phases of broad historical transformation, as during the Classical period when the agora became increasingly marked by monumental buildings with specific political functions (law courts, magistrates' offices, public assembly structures, etc.) and statuary with political implications, and the self-conscious visual monumentalization of cityscapes during the Hellenistic period.[218]

The Phocaeans who settled at Marseille were no exception to these broad movements within the Greek world. They arrived with some common cultural conceptions of "natural" urban structure involving shared dispositions toward space and aesthetics, and these informed the organization of the colony as it expanded over the three hills, at least as far as the somewhat meager evidence allows us to tell. The evidence for major temples and smaller sanctuaries at Marseille has already been discussed. In brief, material traces of such structures are limited (because of poor preservation), but they are spread in various parts of the city. Large temples to Ephesian Artemis and Delphinian Apollo noted by Strabo are presumed to have been located on the butte Saint-Laurent, overlooking the port. Both of these gods were pan-Ionian favorites, although Phocaea did not have a cult of Ephesian Artemis. A temple to Athena was also mentioned by Strabo, who noted that the statue of the goddess was in a seated position but without indicating its location. Pompeius Trogus's recounting of the attack of Catamandus against Massalia also mentions this statue and places it on the acropolis, which Henri Tréziny has argued was the butte des Moulins.[219] The naïskoi of the Rue Négrel are evidence of a smaller sanctuary located either on an eastern extension of the crest of that same hill (the butte de la Roquette) or farther down the slope, perhaps just outside the city walls before they expanded eastward near the end of the sixth century BCE.[220] Yet smaller ritual sites are perhaps represented by the round structure and adjacent feasting site at the Place des Pistoles in the Panier.[221] Sites such as this mark the ambiguous boundary between civic and domestic (or familial) ritual spaces and the difficulty of discerning the latter. As Tréziny has suggested, the finds of a few later terra cotta architectural ornaments (normally a sign of monumental religious buildings) at the Place des Pistoles may indicate the transformation of a sixth-century BCE familial cult site into a more imposing civic sanctuary during the fourth century BCE.[222] A number of other objects such as small clay human statues (predominantly female) also attest to religious practices, but these are much more rare at Marseille than at other Greek sites of the central and western Mediterranean. They are mostly concentrated at the Centre Bourse site, and mostly of second century BCE date or later.[223]

The pre-Roman cemeteries of Massalia are still poorly known, and funerary evidence is clearly underrepresented in terms of the population known to have inhabited the city. However, over 150 different sites with premodern funerary evidence have been identified in seven major zones, of which only about 17 percent date to the pre-Roman period (fig. 8.23).[224] The pre-Roman cemeteries are always on the exterior of the city, a practice common to the larger Greek world, and they are generally very modest in the elaboration of grave goods and structure.

RITUAL PLACES AND PRACTICES IN INDIGENOUS SOCIETIES

Indigenous settlements of the Rhône basin shared with Massalia the idea of the separation of cities of the living and the dead, with cemeteries located well away from settlements. Burials under a tumulus mound became the most popular practice during the Early Iron Age,[225] but these were far from uniform in terms of either structure of the mound, burial rite, or inventories of grave goods. The various patterns represented in the Rhône basin are not only internally variable: they are radically different from tumulus burials in other regions, such as the Alps or the Hallstatt area.[226] In comparison to the latter (where mounds of fifty to one hundred meters diameter are known), those of the lower Rhône basin are all quite small, ranging in diameter from about two to twenty-four meters, with examples above fifteen meters being uncommon. Burial patterns in the Rhône basin are also quite different than those in western Languedoc-Roussillon, which favored large cemeteries of pit graves with cremations accompanied by large quantities of ceramics.[227] Because of a change to less visible burial practices, evidence is extremely meager in the Rhône basin from the fifth to the end of the third centuries BCE. During the last two centuries BCE, the evidence is slightly better, and it shows that funerary ritual at that time appears to have followed a relatively similar range of practices throughout Mediterranean France.[228]

For the purposes of this chapter, perhaps the most important point to make is that throughout the first several centuries of the colonial encounter there was little direct influence on local funerary customs from Etruscan and Greek practices, and certainly nothing remotely like a "Hellenization" of funerary customs. Etruscan and Greek objects played a minimal role in the local funerary domain. Indeed, in view of their relative abundance on contemporary settlements of the region and in graves in the neighboring lower Hérault valley, such imports are remarkably rare in Rhône basin graves before the second century BCE. During the last two centuries BCE, Mediterranean imports (especially Campanian ceramics) became common grave goods throughout Mediterranean France.[229] But the almost complete absence of imports in graves in the hinterland of Massalia during the period of major trade expansion in the later sixth century BCE is particularly noteworthy. Moreover, when present, these objects appear to have been simply incorporated into a few typical local graves, indicating an adaptation of the objects to native customs rather than a transformation of funerary practices. The absence of any consistently distinctive structure, mode of treatment of the body, or class of grave goods with burials incorporating Etruscan or Greek goods during this period argues strongly for this conclusion.

Sanctuaries and Other Nonfunerary Ritual Sites   Native urban landscapes differed radically from Massalia by a striking absence of specialized religious structures and communal spaces: as noted earlier, with a few late exceptions, nearly all Late Iron Age settlements show a dense clustering of domestic structures and narrow streets within the defensive walls with little space allotted to communal gatherings even at crossroads and no traces of architectural monumentality or buildings with a specifically ritual function.[230] This is not to say that ritual was excluded from the interior of settlements. Quite the contrary: there is much evidence for a variety of ritual practices in domestic contexts and one may presume that they were a pervasive feature of social life. Moreover, Dominique Garcia has even made the intriguing suggestion that many towns may have been established on sacred places that previously had ritual structures.[231] But for many centuries religious and political rituals were not architectonically framed in specialized civic buildings as part of the urban landscape. That pattern changed at a handful of sites that integrated ritual structures within settlements beginning in the third century BCE (most examples date to the second and first centuries BCE); nearly all are located in Provence, and even more specifically in the territory of the Salyes. The third century BCE case, Roquepertuse, had the "sanctuary" still outside the rampart but within the extra-muros settlement.[232] It was not until the second century BCE that such structures are found inside the fortifications. Here, again, this is clearly not the adoption of Greek models, as these new structures demonstrate a radically different conception of ritual practices than those of Massalia.

Let us first briefly consider the evidence for domestic ritual before discussing the communal ritual sites. Such evidence is abundant, if often difficult to interpret. Among the acts that would fall under this category is the widespread practice of burying newborn babies or very young infants in house walls or floors.[233] This kind of burial was already practiced in the Late Bronze Age and it was common well into the Roman period, although it became less common in Provence after the fourth century BCE. It was originally thought to be some kind of foundational or votive ritual. While this is possible, the twin facts that this age class is not represented in cemeteries and it is so common on settlements throughout the region may indicate that it was a standard form of burial for this social category of person, although the number found is clearly not commensurate with the demographic representation expected. Other common practices include the burial of whole ceramic vessels in the floor, often upside down, often with a perforation in the bottom, sometimes containing the skeleton of a snake or bird. In many cases these are empty and are presumed to have contained food or alcohol. Skeletons of animals (especially dogs, sheep, pig, and birds) were also frequently buried in house floors, perhaps as foundational sacrifices.[234] In general, these practices were both widespread and fairly consistent over the entire Iron Age. They demonstrate a persistence of at least certain types of domestic ritual over long periods of time, and despite other transformations. For example, infant burials, animal interments, and pottery deposits are all found in both wattle-and-daub houses at undefended settlements of the Early Iron Age and densely packed mud-brick houses at fortified sites in the Late Iron Age.

In the case of communal ritual, as noted above, before the third century BCE (and in most cases before the late first century BCE), such practices were performed outside settlements. This conclusion, drawn from archaeological evidence, is reinforced by the few descriptions of such sites preserved in Greek and Roman texts. Lucan, for example, described druids practicing their "mysteries strange and hateful rites" in "secluded groves . . . and forests far remote,"[235] and he further described such a site near Massalia, a dark stagnant grove where "savage rites and barbarous worship" took place on "altars horrible on massive stones upreared" in the midst of rudely fashioned wooden effigies of gods near a spring.[236] Pomponius Mela also mentioned druid training taking place in caves or hidden forests.[237] These observations must, of course, be treated with proper caution, especially given that they were written after druids had become a target of Roman suppression. But they do point vaguely in the same direction as the archaeological evidence.

That evidence consists, firstly, of diverse collections of ceramic and metal objects found at a number of open-air sites such as hilltops, caves, and springs. Although often ambiguous, these are interpreted as votive deposits at sacred places, a practice that was already common in the Bronze Age.[238] In one late case, a 120-meter-long ditch at Aix-en-Provence filled with large quantities of Italic amphorae and a few other ceramics and grindstones may have been part of a feasting site such as those found in the Auvergne.[239] Another form of evidence consists of several types of stone monuments: stelae, statues, and carved architectural elements.[240] By the latest count, more than seventy sites with such evidence of public ritual places have been identified in Mediterranean France, of which sixty-five are in the lower Rhône basin.[241]

FIGURE 8.25
A stone stela from Le Pègue, in the Drôme.

The most numerous of the stone objects are stelae; and these are also the oldest, as the tradition dates back to the Late Bronze Age. They are quite heterogeneous in form, treatment, and size, ranging from about twenty centimeters to one meter in height.[242] They are often somewhat rough in workmanship, and some were virtually undressed raw stones. The forms were generally rectangular and tops could be rounded or flat. They are often plain, but sometimes have sculpted, engraved or painted decoration (fig. 8.25). The decoration is usually geometric, but at the Provençal sites of Les Caisses at Mouriès and Glanum, there was a range of anthropomorphic and zoomorphic engraved figures, including horses and some mounted warriors.[243] Almost five hundred of these have now been found at sites in Mediterranean France, predominantly in the lower Rhône basin and especially in Provence. Nearly all of them have been found in secondary contexts, reused in the foundations of ramparts or, occasionally, houses. The largest collections come from the sites of Saint-Blaise, Les Caisses at Mouriès, Glanum, and La Ramasse, but they have been identified in many ramparts ranging from Lattes on the coast to Le Pègue in the deep interior.[244] These anepigraphic stelae should be distinguished from monuments of a roughly similar form with Gallo-Greek inscriptions that date to after the Roman conquest. The latter stelae with inscriptions are primarily funerary markers, whereas the stelae that have been found *in situ* in contexts dating before the second century BCE suggest a probably nonfunerary ritual context in most cases, and a few have been found in association with statuary. As noted, the vast majority of these anepigraphic stelae have been found reused in the foundations of the ramparts of settlements, and the date of these ramparts indicates that most of the stelae must have been originally in use from the seventh to the fifth centuries BCE, if not earlier.[245]

The statuary consists predominantly of life-sized human figures or busts set on pedestals or pillars, and often painted with a polychrome decoration. The busts are found only in eastern Languedoc. Full statues are more widely distributed, but with a predominant concentration in western Provence. The statues are overwhelmingly representations of male warriors, with the full figures usually sitting in a cross-legged pose (fig. 8.26). A few female figures, human heads, a bird, and horses have also been found. The majority of these statues come from contexts dating to the second and first centuries BCE, and they were originally suggested to be a fourth–century BCE development.[246] But the excavation of the remains of a ritual complex dating to the mid–sixth century BCE at Le Marduel, in eastern Languedoc, with associated stelae, pillars and a (probably

FIGURE 8.26
Reconstruction of the warrior statue from Glanum with polychrome painting (after Barbet 1992, courtesy of Alix Barbet).

bicephalic) sculptural bust of a warrior pushes the date back by two centuries.[247] Lattes has also yielded a warrior statue reused as a doorjamb in a mid–third century BCE house, but which can be dated on the basis of the belt buckle and other objects depicted to the fifth century BCE (fig. 6.3).[248] Moreover, stylistic and iconographic reanalysis of some of the statues from second- and first-century BCE contexts suggests that many may be several centuries older than the contexts in which they were found (hence in use as relics), although this remains controversial.[249] A number of these statues (for example, those from Grézan, Corconne, and Saint-Anastasie in eastern Languedoc) have been found in contexts completely isolated from settlements, and they probably mark the location of ritual sites in the countryside.[250] Whether such sites might have resembled the rectangular ritual enclosures with statues found in other regions, such as the recently discovered Herbues enclosure at Vix, in Burgundy, is unknown.[251] Others, such as the statue from Lattes, were reused in later buildings and their original context is unknown. But a large number come from the settlements with internal ritual structures (Roquepertuse, Glanum, Entremont, and La Cloche).

Finally, there are the architectural elements, including stone lintels and pillars with carved representations of human heads, cephaliform niches for human skulls, and engraved animals (fig. 8.27). Many of these were also painted with polychrome decorations. They are assumed to have been part of roofed portico structures with a ritual function

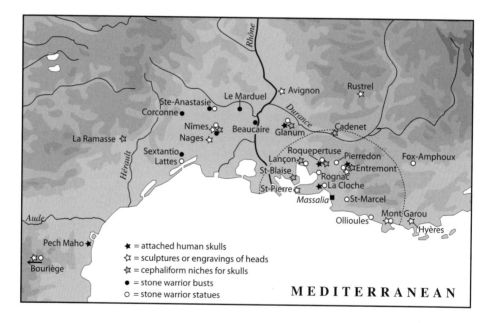

FIGURE 8.27

Evidence of ritual practices in Mediterranean France centering on the human head and heroic representations of warriors. Sites with attached skulls, carved heads, cephaliform-niche pillars and lintels, and stone warrior statues. Hatched line indicates the area within a fifty-kilometer radius from Massalia (data from Arcelin et al. 1992, Arcelin et al. 2003, updated with more recent finds).

that appear to have been erected on the periphery of settlements, such as at Mouriès and La Ramasse, as early as the fifth century BCE.[252] During the second and first centuries BCE these also are found inside settlements such as Entremont and Glanum. The interpretation as elements of ritual structures is supported by the fact that many are associated with stelae, warrior statues, or human skulls.[253]

In terms of the historical development of the relationship between communal ritual spaces and urban landscapes, several alternative trajectories are suggested. Dominique Garcia has argued that the fact that numerous settlements have older stelae reused in the foundations of their ramparts indicates that many of the fortified towns of the Late Iron Age were founded on the site of earlier open air sanctuaries that were dismantled and incorporated into the one monumental aspect of these new towns. Whether this was an act of desacralization or an attempt to embed the protective sacred power of these objects into the civic walls is uncertain, although Garcia favors the latter given that they are incorporated consistently into ramparts rather than domestic structures.[254] The result, however, is that the sacred site was razed and no longer existed within the town. This was the most common relationship between prior ritual structures and later towns where these two were brought into direct contact (although many towns show no traces of having been founded on ritual sites and had no immediately proximal relationship to ritual sites). Some settlements, however, took a different path: building near (rather than on) a sacred site and gradually expanding until the sacred space was integrated within the fabric of the urban landscape.[255] At Glanum, for example, a sacred spring in a valley existed originally outside the boundaries of a small sixth-century BCE town on the adjacent hills. The spring was marked off by a monumental gate that had numerous reused stelae and fragments of painted pillars in its wall. During the second century BCE, the town expanded to surround the spring and a monumental ritual complex was erected around the spring that became the center of the large fortified city.[256] A third alternative was followed by a few other sites that either reconstructed an existing ritual structure within the new settlement or erected a new ritual structure to house relics from an older ritual site and display new ones.[257] Entremont is the best example of this scenario, assuming that at least some of the statues are older than the second century BCE settlement (as has been suggested on stylistic grounds). These latter two processes were also marked by a trend toward architectural monumentality in the construction of the portico and statuary complexes. Wooden supports were replaced by dressed stone and there was a general amplification of the spectacular dimensions of these ritual sites as they entered the urban sphere.[258]

The eventual integration of ritual structures within the urban landscape in these few cases constitutes a *convergence* with Greek and Roman practices, but it is not an *imitation* of those practices. Glanum, beginning in the mid–second century BCE, is the only case (aside from a few elements at Nîmes) in which Greco-Italic architecture was clearly employed in the elaboration of a religious complex before the Augustan period.[259] But given the persistence of the cult of the local god Glanis and finds of statuary

of a cross-legged warrior, a stone lintel with carved heads in niches, and head motifs
worked into Greco-Italic columns, one can plausibly argue for the emergence of a hybrid
colonial phenomenon, a syncretic incorporation of elements of Greco-Italic architectural
ornamentation into what were clearly local ritual contexts, due perhaps to a special political relationship with Massalia discussed earlier. And even here, this involved the incorporation of a traditional religious site within the town rather than the adoption of Greek
religious practices. A closer look at a few of these ritual sites emphasizes how dramatically different from the Greek world the religious practices of native peoples remained
even within a few kilometers of Massalia after five hundred years of interaction.

At Roquepertuse in Provence, four statues of cross-legged warriors were found in the
late nineteenth century, and subsequent excavations have yielded fragments of at least
six more statues. These were associated with stone pillars and lintels with niches carved
to accommodate human skulls, a two-faced stone head and a statue of a bird.[260] Recent
research has demonstrated that the statues, pillars, and lintels were also decorated with
elaborate polychrome painting depicting horses, birds, serpentiform creatures, and geometric designs (fig. 8.28).[261] Early interpretations of the site saw it as an isolated sanctuary, but recent excavations have revealed that the statuary and architectural elements
were part of a ritual portico structure erected just outside the massive rampart of
a small (0.5-hectare) village on a terrace in the midst of an extra-muros domestic
neighborhood.[262]

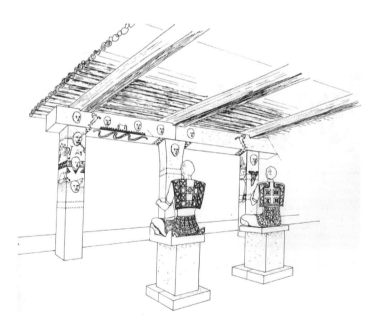

FIGURE 8.28

Reconstruction of the sanctuary at Roquepertuse showing polychrome painting and skulls in niches
(after Barbet 1992, courtesy of Alix Barbet).

At Entremont a prior fortified village was expanded into a town around 150 BCE. The main entrance road into the town was enlarged and (according to hypothetical reconstructions) was bordered by a structure housing numerous stone sculptures of heroized male warriors (seated cross-legged and standing), many with their hands placed on top of carved-stone severed heads (figs. 8.29 and 8.30). There are also a few statues of women and even two horse statues. All these statues were found smashed in the street outside the gate. Nearby, along the external face of the rampart of the earlier site (now inside the walls of the larger settlement), was constructed a hypostyle hall with a second story. This structure dates probably to the last quarter of the second century BCE, and it contained reused fragments from an earlier portico structure including a stone pillar and lintel with engraved representations of severed human heads and carved niches for skulls (fig. 8.31). Twenty-two human skulls were also found in the street near this structure, of which six had traces of having been affixed.[263]

A statue of a cross-legged warrior like those of Entremont and Roquepertuse was also excavated at the small fortified town of La Cloche, only twelve kilometers from Marseille in a context dating to the first half of the first century BCE.[264] This was found smashed on a spot outside the gate of the town, according to Louis Chabot as a result of the sacking of the town by the Romans about 50 BCE. The site also had human skulls fixed by iron clamps found near the entry gate to the main street of the town. There was also a ritual site established during the early phases of the settlement in the third century BCE near a secondary gate opened in the southern rampart. This is identified by a collection of votive or magic offerings (perforated coins and bronze plaques, rings, twisted strips of bronze, etc.). This site was subsequently covered over and a new collection of the same type was deposited on this spot during the first century BCE. At another location in the middle of the upper part of the town was an unusual building that Chabot interprets as equivalent to a *heroon* (a Greek shrine to a hero, often containing bones). This structure,

FIGURE 8.29
Stone sculpture of a hand holding a severed head, from Entremont.

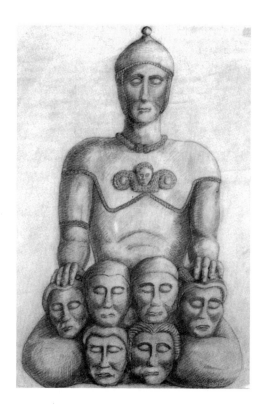

FIGURE 8.30

Reconstruction of the original state of a warrior statue with a pile of carved severed heads, from Entremont (drawing by R. Ambard, from Salviat 1993; courtesy of the Association des Amis du Musée Granet).

built about 100 BCE, consisted of three connected rooms (at a site composed otherwise of one-room houses) in which were found superimposed hearths with ash and human bone, silver jewelry, blocks of pine resin, broken ceramics (including twelve amphorae), and other objects. Chabot interpreted this as a structure dedicated to the veneration of an important deceased person of the community—a woman, judging by the type of jewelry.[265]

Two interrelated elements of these sites stand out: the heroized warrior statues and the dramatic emphasis on severed heads and skulls. The proliferation of warrior statues at sites of the third and second century BCE has generally been linked to changes in the sociopolitical structure of indigenous societies, particularly in the lower Rhône basin. The process of increasing monumentalization of ritual spaces and the emphasis on heroic warrior statuary is seen as part of an ideological strategy of a developing elite class in some areas to transform traditional communal ritual practices into a symbolic device intended to promote personal glorification and naturalize the increasingly asymmetrical structure of social relations.[266] Skulls with evidence of having been nailed up or otherwise suspended for display have been found at five sites, all but Pech Maho being in the

FIGURE 8.31
Reconstruction of the hypostyle structure at Entremont with head-adorned pillars and lintels (watercolor by Jean-Claude Golvin © Editions Errance: from Goudineau 1996).

region around Massalia in western Provence. Additionally, eight sites have turned up architectural elements with cephaliform niches and six sites have sculptural representations of severed heads, all but two being in the lower Rhône basin.[267] Seventy percent of these sites are in Provence, and the heaviest concentration is found within a radius of less than fifty kilometers from Marseille. This evidence is tantalizing because Posidonius (who actually visited the hinterland of Marseille at the beginning of the first century BCE) described in lurid detail the local practice of taking, preserving, and displaying the heads of vanquished enemies. He noted with disgust that the heads were nailed to the entrances of houses, while those of enemies of high repute were embalmed in cedar oil and shown proudly to visitors.[268] The archaeological finds have often been interpreted in the light of these documents as trophies of war, a view supported by, for example, the motif of the piling up of heads on pillars and statuary at Entremont. Ian Armit has even suggested that the undifferentiated stylized representation of heads on a pillar may represent an emphasis on quantitative success in battle by the community, whereas the pile of distinctively individualized heads under the hands of an individual warrior statue may represent either particular individuals killed or stereotypic icons of particular tribes vanquished by the Salyes.[269] But, as Patrice Arcelin has argued, the practice of ancestral veneration is also possible, especially as many of the skulls may have been adorned with clay masks.[270] Such decoration, however, is not incompatible with the idea of war trophies, particularly given Posidonius's observation about the way the heads of notable enemies were preserved, treasured, and displayed. In fact, both practices are possible, and there is no reason to assume regional homogeneity.

Whatever the precise origin of these skulls, the human head clearly had a very pronounced symbolic significance in practices that took place at these public ritual sites. Moreover, although there is scattered evidence for various kinds of special funerary treatment of skulls extending back to the Bronze Age, and although the human head was a central symbolic element of La Tène artwork in temperate Europe, the archaeological data indicate that the practice of ritually displaying heads or their simulacra was a rather late development of the third and second centuries BCE, and that this was also a fairly localized phenomenon largely confined to the lower Rhône basin. The fact that in the first century BCE at a site such as La Cloche, only twelve kilometers from Marseille, ritual was focused on practices involving skulls that Greek authors considered a repulsive sign of barbarism is a strong indication of what little effect Greek religious practices had on surrounding native peoples even after five centuries of close interaction.

This is not to say that indigenous religious practices remained unaffected by the colonial encounter, adhering to static tradition over the centuries. The fact that these ritual sites centered on heroic warrior statues and severed heads were heavily concentrated in the hinterland of Massalia and emerged precisely during a period of increasing violence between Massalia and its neighbors is an indication of a connection to *hostility* toward the Greek colony. This may have been a gradual coalescing of ritual symbolism around forms of power capable of opposing more violent types of Massalian colonialism, perhaps in conjunction with the emergence of institutionalized forms of authority lodged in military leadership. Or it may have been something akin to what Anthony Wallace described as a "revitalization movement": a self-conscious effort by charismatic leaders to construct new cultural forms by playing on and reinterpreting strands of traditional practice.[271] Movements of the latter type, such as the Native American ghost dance or the Mumbo cult of Kenya, often assume a predominantly religious form and can spread rapidly.[272] They do not, of course, provide a precise analogy, because such movements usually arise under conditions that correspond more to Roman colonization than Massalian colonialism. But one can imagine something along these lines developing in response to increasing Massalian aggression. We may never be able to discern the precise meaning of these communal ritual sites, but two things are clear: they developed in relation to transformations in the colonial situation and they show the dynamism and resilient cultural inventiveness of indigenous peoples. There is perhaps no clearer demonstration of the absurdity of Pompeius Trogus's assertion that Gaul "seemed to have been transplanted into Greece."[273]

9

CONCLUSION AND IMPERIAL EPILOGUE

This book began with a passage by the Gallo-Roman historian Pompeius Trogus extolling the radiant civilizing influence of Massalia and claiming that the progress of the surrounding barbarians was so brilliant that it seemed as though Gaul had essentially been transformed into Greece (fig. 9.1). In subsequent chapters, analysis of archaeological data covering the six centuries of colonial encounters that preceded the account of Pompeius Trogus have shown how wildly inaccurate his statement was. As late as the end of the second century BCE, five hundred years after the foundation of the Greek colony, the inhabitants of Entremont, a mere twenty-six kilometers to the north, were cooking their meals in pots that had changed little since the Bronze Age, were affixing human skulls to the walls of a sanctuary in a practice that Greeks found repugnant, and were engaged in a violent struggle with Massalia that threatened its very existence. Clearly, Entremont had not been transported to Greece; nor did its citizens have any desire to be like Greeks. Yet neither is this a story of the parallel persistence of two static cultures through the ages. The evidence shows that centuries of colonial encounter had entangled colonists and natives in complex relationships that had far reaching unintended cultural, social, economic, and political consequences for both.

The goal of the book is not simply to expose the fiction of Pompeius Trogus's self-serving observations. Rather, the objective is to apprehend the complex processes of entanglement and transformation that transpired in ancient Mediterranean France and to use this colonial situation to engage a broader set of theoretical issues central to the

FIGURE 9.1

Poster of the Gyptis legend from the twenty-fifth centenary celebration of the city of Marseille (courtesy of the Musée d'Histoire de Marseille).

comparative study of colonialism in anthropology and postcolonial studies. The point is to move beyond the well-known event history of the expansion of Etruscans, Greeks, and Romans into the western Mediterranean toward a more subtle understanding of the implications of this history of encounter and interaction for the daily lives of people who were experiencing and fashioning this process. The book is designed to reveal and comprehend agents and agency, the martial and the material, the contradictions and contingencies, the social and cultural logic of desire and indifference, and the entangling consequences of consumption—in brief, the messy multifaceted workings of colonialism. Achieving this goal requires first understanding why a perspective very similar to that of Pompeius Trogus had come to exert such a powerful influence in the formation of modern European cultural identity and colonial ideology, and how the legacy of that perspective has come to constrain the ability of archaeologists to approach this ancient encounter. It also requires developing an analytic strategy that would enable one to circumvent some of the difficulties posed by these intellectual constraints.

I have suggested that these ancient colonial encounters in the western Mediterranean pose some particular challenges for us because of the traditions of European cultural ancestry invented during the Renaissance and the Romantic Hellenist movement of the eighteenth century. Those movements constructed these ancient encounters as a seminal event in the history of the nations that were in the process of becoming the major colonial powers of the modern world: the moment of the spreading of "civilization" to the western barbarians by Greeks and Romans. This vision of ancestral enlightenment enabled European nations to imagine themselves both as models of the success of the civilizing process and as heirs to the civilizing mission of Greece and Rome; their own colonial ventures were thereby construed as a duty imposed by history. The ancient colonial encounters, known exclusively through the texts of colonists, were seen as prototypes of modern colonial ventures and they furnished the symbolic raw material for the development of modern colonial discourse and practices. Even as archaeologists in the postcolonial era have gradually distanced themselves from older notions of emulative "Hellenization" and "Romanization" as explanatory frameworks, many of the alternative perspectives they have turned to, such as acculturation and world-systems theory, rely on very similar problematic assumptions concerning agency and unidirectionality of influence and causation. Similarly, it has been shown that even analyses that eschew an overt theoretical orientation often have operated under an implicit evolutionary model structured by a hierarchical telos pointing toward Greek and Roman "civilization," in which different native societies are "privileged," "hindered," or "slowed" by various factors in achieving some evolutionary state linked to Greek or Roman contact.

All of this goes to explain why a critical reexamination of these ancient colonial encounters in the western Mediterranean that lie at the heart of "Western" constructions of identity is both so important and so difficult. Dealing with this predicament requires archaeologists to exercise a constant critical reflexivity that is mindful of the history of recursive entanglements between ancient and modern colonialisms and attuned to the resultant problems of anachronism, semantic fusion, and presentism. This critical alertness cannot, of course, produce a position of stable objectivity for the analyst; but it can expose hidden assumptions, enable new questions, and shift the standards of plausibility in evaluating interpretations.

I also suggested that understanding the complexities of colonial encounters in general requires a multidimensional analytical strategy employing several different paths of entry, scalar shifts, and narrative structures. Although it is intended to be a fully freestanding statement on its own, this book is one of a set of such approaches targeting the colonial encounter in Mediterranean France. It employed a "vertical" exploration of the long-term history of colonial engagements and entanglements between the first encounter with Etruscan merchants and the end of the first century of Roman occupation of the region six centuries later, and it focused on several selected strands in the colonial fabric (trade, violence, foodways, and urban and ritual landscapes), using shifting scales of analysis to illuminate the interplay of local and global processes. Hence, it was not intended as a comprehensive treatment of the encounter, but as a means of revealing certain facets of the colonial situation and opening new questions.

The book also has made the case for the utility of an approach to colonialism that focuses on consumption as a way of reframing the actions of people engaged in colonial encounters: by revealing choices made, restoring an appreciation of the role of agency by indigenous peoples in colonial situations, and provoking a realization of the contingent historicity of colonialism. But it also argues for a vision of consumption that treats this process as more than the consumption of pure signs in an abstract semiotic system. This symbolic action and meaning must also be grounded in a careful examination of the material world of colonial situations and of the unintended consequences of consumption. Cross-cultural consumption, as a material social process, generally entangles people in complex webs of social and economic relationships that can have a profound impact on the development of structures of power and the transformation of culture. The importance of the material dimension of colonialism is clearly a prominent theme of the book: both the role of material objects in the enactment of colonialism and the material conditions that structure relations of power. But it argues against approaches that simply fetishize objects by treating colonialism as a relationship between people and objects rather than understanding it as a relationship between people that is mediated by objects. Hence, the approach deployed here emphasizes exploring the social and cultural logic of choices made in cross-cultural consumption (including both appropriations and rejections, patterns of desire and indifference), as well as examining the shifting commodity chains that link consumers to producers through intermediary agents. This approach also involves a symmetrical analysis of developments among colonists and native peoples. Realizing that all parties to colonial encounters are transformed by the process, it seeks to approach the history of such engagements without presupposing directions of influence or causality. It tries to understand the interlinked history of transformations and to understand how asymmetrical relations of power can often develop out of situations that did not initially entail such asymmetries. This is why I feel it is appropriate, in fact essential, to include this long sequence of interactions in the history of colonialism even though one may legitimately question whether many of the early forms of encounter can legitimately be called colonialism.

Approaching the history of ancient colonial encounters in the Rhône basin of France with these strategies and considerations has revealed a complex process of entanglement and transformation in the region. Throughout most of this history, Massalia and the various indigenous societies of the region remained politically autonomous and in control of the conditions of their own cultural reproduction. But they were simultaneously entangled in relationships of various kinds that had subtle but profound consequences beyond their immediate control. That entanglement was the product not of major actions by polities or societies, but of little decisions made by small groups of actors with different, often contradictory, socially situated interests. These are the people who encountered each other on beaches, at markets, in homes, and on borders, and who struggled to comprehend the alien values and customs of the other enough to effect exchanges of goods that were seen as potentially useful in their own social projects according to their own cultural dispositions. The consumption driving these transactions involved creative appropriation and reinterpretation of selected alien objects (wine, tableware ceramics, coinage) and techniques and practices (the potter's wheel, mudbrick architecture, writing)—sometimes quickly, sometimes after long periods of indifference—as well as a much longer list of rejections of other goods and practices (garum, dress, weapons, religious practices, etc.) that were seen to have little value or utility. Each of these appropriations had its own complicated consequences, as did the more straightforward trade of some goods that required no radical cultural reinterpretation (grain, stone, metals, etc.). These exchanges were mediated by merchants who became cultural brokers between consumers and producers who had no knowledge of each other, and they involved composite commodity chains that underwent multiple shifts over time. But the encounter involved raiding as well as trading. At the same time that Massalia was entangled in a series of broader Mediterranean conflicts and alliances among Etruscans, Carthaginians, Romans, and other Greeks, it was also sporadically fighting with its neighbors. Warfare and piracy were a significant part of the regional picture, and there were shifts in the patterns and intensity of violence, as well as the networks of alliance. However, over most of the history of the colonial situation, until the Romans entered the picture, the balance of power was such that no party was capable of imposing its will over the other or colonizing the other. Neither was it possible to ignore the other. The changing concatenations of these patterns of exchange and violence had important ramifications for social and political relations and they resulted in transformations of the cultural and political landscape of the region.

The details of various strands of this colonial situation have been analyzed at considerable length in the previous chapters, and there is no need to reiterate that analysis here. However, some attempt at a highly compressed summary that briefly weaves these strands back together seems mandatory for a chapter that dares to call itself a conclusion. Among the several possible ways to undertake such a summary, I have opted for a chronological phase presentation despite the obvious problems with representing complex continuous processes in the form of schematic periodization. For example, as I have tried to emphasize throughout the book, developments were always different between societies along the coast and those in the interior, and relations with Massalia were different for societies living in direct proximity to the city in Provence and those living at a greater distance, where contact was mediated by traders. One could also have drawn the phase boundaries at other points in time, depending on what aspects of the encounter one chose to emphasize.

PHASE 1: FLOATER TRADE, ENGAGEMENT, AND ACCOMMODATION (625–600 BCE)

The initial phase of the encounter involved the first appearance of Etruscan traders (or traders with Etruscan goods) along the coast of France in small ships and the development of a periodic "floater" trade. It is characterized by the mutual working out of systems of value, taste, and demand, and the terms and procedures of exchange between indigenous people and foreign merchants. It is characterized especially by the local recognition of the social utility of an exotic alcoholic beverage and indifference to other goods by native peoples, and the recognition and targeting by merchants of a local demand for wine. It is also characterized by the rapid establishment of commodity chains between the Rhône basin and vintners and potters in southern Etruscan cities mediated by these merchants.

The demand for wine was created by its perceived utility in traditional feasting rituals, and wine was quickly adapted to local practices. The attraction of wine was undoubtedly linked to its properties as a storable and tradable commodity, properties that native forms of alcohol did not posses, and to its higher alcohol content and exotic origin.

PHASE 2: COLONIAL SETTLEMENT AND EMERGING EMPORIA (600–450 BCE)

This period is marked by the establishment of the first colonial settlement in the region (Massalia), by the emergence of several indigenous settlements as privileged centers of trade, and by the installation of small enclaves of foreign traders at some of these native emporia. It also saw the first episodes of violence between Massalia and its neighbors.

When Phocaean colonists settled at Massalia around 600 BCE, they at first became another ready market for Etruscan wine, along with wine from Greek and Phoenician cities, and the port of Massalia became an active center for merchants plying their wares along the shores of Mediterranean France. When the supply of Etruscan wine began to diminish around the mid–sixth century BCE, Massalian farmers began to produce their own wine; and by the last quarter of the century they were exporting this on a large scale to indigenous societies of the region, becoming the nearly exclusive source of wine throughout the area by the mid–fifth century BCE. Despite this shift in commodity chains, the nature of demand by native societies remained exactly the same: wine and drinking ceramics were the nearly exclusive objects of interest.

With the growth of several towns (Lattes, Cailar, Espeyran, Arles) along rivers leading to the interior of eastern Languedoc and western Provence and their emergence as native emporia, these centers of exchange attracted foreign merchants and became large consumers of imported wine, as well as trading some of that wine to towns farther toward the interior. The amounts of wine imported during this period grew substantially over the previous phase as a result of an escalation of feasting provoked by the introduction of wine into commensal politics and the consequent broadening of the field of social competition. Wine never replaced beer in indigenous drinking practices, but it was consumed in substantial quantities and had become established as a widespread social necessity, especially along the coast. Although there would be significant fluctuations in the amounts imported over subsequent centuries and another major change in commodity chains, from this point on wine remained the dominant exotic item of interest to native consumers. Reciprocally, Massalians were not able to feed themselves entirely from their own small agricultural territory, nor were they powerful enough to expand that territory militarily. As the size of the city grew, Massalia became increasingly dependent on trade with native societies to supply the cereals that constituted the bulk of the staple diet of its citizens. The entangled economic forces that resulted from these separate sources of demand are reflected in the parallel escalation of wine imports and the production of large ceramic jars for grain storage at indigenous sites during the late sixth and early fifth centuries BCE, as the requirements of an escalation of the scale of commensal politics stimulated by the introduction of wine required a commensurate increasing production of grain for export. All of these commodity chains were mediated by independent merchants, many of whom were transient or resident foreigners of various kinds. Indigenous peoples of the region also undoubtedly played a role in maritime trade networks as both merchants and pirates, and they controlled interior terrestrial networks.

Massalia, while a major wine exporter, also continued to be a significant consumer of foreign wines, as well as of imported tableware from Athens and Italy. However, the basic tableware of the city was made by local potters who began production of two new series (Colonial Cream-ware and Gray-monochrome) within a couple of decades after the foundation of the colony. Both of these ceramic wares were also exported to native peoples of the region, and one series was even tailored to indigenous tastes. Hybrid versions of these two series were also soon produced in indigenous workshops, mixing borrowed Greek techniques and Greek forms with native forms and decorations. Throughout this period, the only Greek pottery forms popular with native peoples were drinking cups and pitchers, although ceramic mortars were also consumed in small quantities. Massalians were very resistant to any borrowing of native tableware and would remain so throughout the centuries. However, the evidence shows that their kitchens were initially stocked with a good deal of indigenous cooking pottery. This and other factors are a possible indication of widespread intermarriage with native women among the first generation or so of colonists.

This period also saw the rapid expansion of the city of Massalia and the first signs of conflict with its neighbors. From the first years of the encounter, Massalia was protected by a substantial fortification wall, which was expanded to encompass the city as it grew. Several native towns in the vicinity of Massalia also erected fortifications almost immediately. This practice gradually spread along the coast and then throughout the region until, by the beginning of the fourth century BCE, virtually every town and village of the Rhône basin was fortified with an imposing stone wall—a sign of growing regional insecurity in relations among indigenous societies. This may have been exacerbated by Massalian interventions in local political struggles, as it is known to have made alliances with some groups, as well as employing mercenaries.

The period also witnessed a gradual transformation of urban landscapes throughout the region. One of the few technical practices adopted from Massalia was the use of mud brick in the construction of dwellings. This appropriation was limited to towns of the coastal zone, but it took place in the context of a broader series of experiments with new building materials, house forms, and kinds of spatial organization that transformed indigenous urban landscapes from the sixth through the fourth centuries BCE. These innovations involved the delimitation of settlement boundaries with stone defensive ramparts, the substitution of mud-brick or stone architecture for wattle-and-daub, the use of rectangular house plans, and the emergence of several kinds of rectilinear settlement organization with contiguous houses arranged along narrow streets. It also involved the gradual development of multiple-room houses, although traditional single-room houses remained popular until well after the Roman conquest. These features were not an imitation of Greek or Etruscan dwellings or settlement plans, nor did they spread as a uniform package. Rather, they represent a complex process of vernacular experimentation that eventually resulted in a limited set of adaptations to a range of shared social challenges and opportunities structured by similar cultural dispositions. This process took place over several hundred years, with variable microregional chronologies and patterns.

Nor was Massalia a static homogeneous model of "Greek" architecture and urban organization. It was a city in a constant state of expansion and experimentation in which the character of neighborhoods changed radically over the centuries. Before the flurry of monumental building in the Hellenistic and Roman periods, Massalia was probably not a terribly impressive place. Most buildings were made of mud brick and, in comparison to many other Greek cities, roofing tiles were relatively rare. Both Massalia and native settlements were products of experimentation in the service of solving social problems, but according to different cultural dispositions toward social space. One of the most persistently distinctive elements is that, like Greek cities in general, Massalia was conceptually centered on an open political and economic space, the agora, and a series of monumental religious temples; whereas native cities, as they emerged in their compact rectilinear forms during this period, were densely packed with dwellings but left no open public squares and contained no public ritual buildings within their walls.

PHASE 3: URBAN STABILITY, FLUCTUATING TRADE, AND NEW COLONIAL SETTLEMENTS (450–300 BCE)

This phase is marked by a decline in the consumption of Massalian wine on sites of the interior, but a continued robust consumption at coastal sites, particularly at the native emporia such as Lattes. One also sees a relative stability in urban landscapes in which the systems of streets and blocks that had emerged by the end of the fifth century BCE were continued with a remarkable degree of stability, albeit with shifts in the interior arrangements of houses within the blocks.

Evidence of periodic violence between Massalia and its neighbors comes from archaeological traces of settlement burning and destruction during this phase. This evidence concerns Provence rather than the region west of the Rhône, and such traces are sporadic before the end of the third century BCE. This is also the period when Massalia, although still confined to a meager chora, launched the first efforts at establishing small settler colonies (essentially garrisons) along the coast of France. The earliest of these was at Agde (around 400 BCE) just beyond eastern Languedoc, and this was followed by Olbia (late fourth century BCE) on the Ligurian coast of Provence. All subsequent colonies in the succeeding phase would also be along the Ligurian coast.

On the domestic front, by the fourth century BCE Massalia was no longer using indigenous cooking pots, but was making its own in typically Greek forms as well as importing Greek pots from elsewhere. This was probably part of a growing concern to construct an orthodox sense of Massalian, and more broadly Hellenic, identity within a colonial society, particularly among its ruling elite. It is reflected by the emergence sometime before the mid–fourth century BCE of an archaic, highly conservative form of constitution supporting a rigid hierarchical, aristocratic form of government; and it constitutes a very different direction than the Phocaean colony of Emporion, founded within a few decades of Massalia about three hundred kilometers farther west on the Catalan coast.

PHASE 4: INCREASING CONFLICT AND SOCIAL TRANSFORMATION (300–125 BCE)

The third century BCE was a period of social and cultural transformations in native societies that witnessed the first evident use of the built environment to mark social distinctions at a few settlements, in the form of central-courtyard houses built on a much larger scale than anything before. In the second century BCE, additional versions of such houses appropriated civic space by blocking streets to create domestic courtyards. This phase also saw the growing popularity of sanctuaries containing heroized warrior statues along with the display of human heads and carved stone representations of heads, especially in Provence. These phenomena are thought to be linked to increasing social differentiation and the emergence of larger regional political confederations, particularly in the area around Massalia. One of these confederations, led by the Salyes, was sufficiently threatening that Massalia required military aid from Rome in 125 BCE. The late third century BCE also witnessed the first adoption of the practice of writing after centuries of indifference, as Greek letters were used to mark personal property (largely drinking cups) with Celtic names. This is also the period with the first sporadic traces of wine production in the region outside Massalia, although apparently still not on a large-scale export basis. By the mid–second century BCE, another shift occurred in the commodity chain supplying wine, with Italian wine in Greco-Italic amphorae rapidly replacing Massalia as the principal source, including at Massalia.

The use of imported tableware commonly used in indigenous homes also expanded beyond drinking vessels for the first time to include plates and bowls: increasingly this consisted of Campanian ware imported from Italy. By the second century BCE, Campanain bowls had largely replaced native-made bowls and indigenous people were eating and drinking primarily from imported ceramics. However, foreign cooking wares still had made no impact in native kitchens; local hand-modeled ceramics continued to be used in forms that had changed little since the Bronze Age, and this practice persisted for nearly a century after the Roman conquest. These ceramics show that indigenous cuisine was based heavily on boiled foods (much more so than Greek cuisine), with the addition of some grilled meat. Massalia was continuing to use typical Greek cooking pots, but by the second century BCE, these were now manufactured in indigenous workshops catering to Massalian tastes. Massalian tableware was also increasingly imported from Italy, as Campanian ware grew in popularity in the city. Aside from the large-scale exchange of wine and grain, and the various selective appropriations of imported tableware, the Massalian and native cuisines appear to have had little impact on each other. Native diners, for example, were indifferent to the charms of garum fish sauce, which was an important condiment in Greek cuisine, and they appear to have been largely indifferent to olive oil as well for several centuries. They also ignored the popular Greek technique of frying food (or at least the implements for cooking with this technique).

During this phase, the urban landscape of Massalia underwent a major transformation, with a surge of monumental construction that obliterated archaeological traces of many earlier structures. Massalia also continued to expand the foundation of garrison colonies along the Ligurian coast of Provence: at least three more are known (Antibes, Nice, and Tauroeis). It also made alliances with some native groups, and the Hellenistic style limestone rampart built at Saint-Blaise as well as various Greek architectural features at Glanum are undoubtedly testimony to the operation of Massalian masons at these sites. However, despite these ventures, it appears that Massalia was still not able to expand its territorial control much beyond the meager chora it had established centuries earlier or to subdue pirates along the Ligurian coast. Evidence of periodic outbreaks of violence between Massalia and its neighbors in Provence continued during this phase, and the second century BCE seems to have marked a crescendo in the escalation of conflict to the extent that Massalia was repeatedly forced to solicit aid from its ally, Rome. The last of these appeals resulted in a Roman military conquest of the entire region of Mediterranean France and at least the nominal end of independent sovereignty for indigenous societies that were now incorporated into a Roman province.

PHASE 5: ROMAN CONQUEST AND COLONIZATION (125–25 BCE)

The scale of violence Roman armies brought to the region far exceeded anything that had occurred before, and the entire region of Mediterranean France was conquered within a few years. Pacification was a more gradual process that required the suppression of a series of revolts and incursions around the new province over the following sixty years. However, by the time of Caesar's war of conquest against the rest of Gaul in 58 BCE, the Gauls of Mediterranean France had ceased to be a threat. They offered support rather than resistance, for which many of the major towns of the south were granted Latin rights by Caesar at the end of his campaigns. Rome also immediately established a military base at Aix-en-Provence and a colony of Italian settlers at Narbonne (Narbo Martius) in 118 BCE. Narbo, which was situated on the Aude River and along the newly constructed Via Domitia linking Spain and Italy, soon began to rival Massalia as the major port in Mediterranean France. About 46 BCE, Caesar settled veterans of his Tenth Legion at Narbo with grants of land in the newly restructured territory of the city. Other colonies of Roman veterans were established soon after at Béziers, Arles, Orange, and Fréjus.

It was due to this Roman intervention that Massalia was, for the first time, able to expand territorially outside its small chora, as it was left as an autonomous city and awarded land between the city and the Rhône delta. However, Massalia would soon be exposed to the force of Roman violence as well when the civil war between Caesar and Pompey spilled over into Mediterranean France and Massalia was besieged and captured by Caesar in 49 BCE, after which it apparently lost much of the territory it had been given about seventy years earlier. Massalian wine exports essentially disappeared around the time of the conquest and resumed again soon after its defeat by Caesar, a phenomenon probably linked to its acquisition and subsequent loss of new agricultural territory capable of providing grain for the city.

The effects of the Roman conquest on daily life in indigenous towns of the region were neither sudden nor dramatic: for nearly a century after the initial military intrusion, life continued much as it had before. Roman wine in Dressel 1 amphorae had replaced Greco-Italic and Massalian imports, but the quantities consumed were not greatly different than before. With a few exceptions (such as Glanum), most urban landscapes of the region were not affected significantly by the Roman occupation until the reign of Augustus. At the same time, however, the sudden proliferation of coins on native sites during the first century BCE constitutes one of the few striking changes during this early Roman period. It marks a sudden monetization of the economy with a large-scale circulation of low-value coins after centuries of relative indifference to coinage, and it is probably an unintended consequence of the imposition of Roman taxation.

IMPERIAL EPILOGUE

An inhabitant of the port town of Lattara of the fourth century BCE would have felt very much at home on the streets of the settlement even a couple of generations after the Roman conquest of the region. Despite the establishment of a Roman colony only 85 km away in the late second century BCE, little had changed at Lattara nearly a hundred years after the conquest. The settlement outside the rampart was now more extensive, but inside the fortifications the same streets were lined by the same blocks of mud-brick houses, still roofed with thatch and daub. Kitchens were still stocked with cooking pots that had changed little and gradually since the Bronze Age. The port was still thriving. Ships that arrived were now laden with amphorae of Italian wine and Campanian tableware rather than Massalian wine, but that had been the case since at least the mid–second century BCE. Coins were now used commonly for economic transactions, but these tended to be Massalian rather than Roman coins. A few changes had occurred since the fourth century BCE, to be sure, including the appearance of a few central-courtyard houses in the third and second centuries; but these did not look radically different from other houses, and they were still in the minority. There had even been a few buildings with modest monumental features constructed after the conquest, but these respected the traditional orientation of the city. The quantity of weapons at the site increased during the late third century BCE, but it had diminished again by the mid–second century BCE, and there is no evidence of Roman military violence directed at Lattara.[1]

This does not, of course, mean that the Roman presence in the region had no effect on the inhabitants of Lattara (and other settlements), but rather that the initial effects were complex and subtle. And they were not in the direction of an imitation of Roman tastes and lifeways. Given the material evidence, it seems highly probable that, whatever the view from Rome or Narbo, the residents of Lattara had not yet begun to envisage themselves as part of an imperial world with Rome as its center. They were still first and foremost Lattarians. That is, they had not yet become little fish in a big pond but were still the big fish in their own little pond.[2] This seems especially evident from the continuity in bodily adornment and the absence of any indication of a mimetic appropriation of Roman attire. For example, weapons were predominantly of "Celtic" type and fibulae and other jewelry show continuity with previous local forms.[3]

All of that began to change rapidly in the last quarter of the first century BCE, during the reign of Augustus and the emergence of the Roman Empire out of the Republic. The lifeways and urban landscape of Lattara underwent a sudden and dramatic transformation that indicates a new relationship with the Roman colonial enterprise. Lattara was not alone in this: it exemplifies a regional pattern of such dramatic changes. New buildings were erected in a clearly Roman style and according to a new orientation that disregarded completely the previous rectilinear system that had channeled the flow of social life for centuries. Wells were dug in various parts of the site in locations (the middle of former rooms and streets) that indicate that the old system was no longer relevant or even visible.[4] This new order included very large courtyard houses on a Roman model (a house in zone 60 was about 725 square meters and had opus signinum floors) as well as monumental buildings with foundations that cut across previous housing blocks and new specialized production facilities. The interior walls of houses were decorated with polychrome painted frescoes. People were eating from the same *terra sigillata* dishes as people in other parts of the empire. Garum fish sauce was not only imported for the first time but actually produced at the site. A kiln began firing the new Gallic amphorae as wine production for export began.[5] There are a few indications of the appearance of some monumental architecture in the initial phase after the Roman conquest (the period from 125 to about 25 BCE), in the form of fragments of stone pillars and other architectural ornaments that are found as reused elements in later structures. However, these traces of architectural monumentality were apparently incorporated into the existing settlement structure rather than disrupting it, and they were soon demolished by the Augustan wave of transformation. These changes did not all happen at once, but they were part of a series of dramatic cultural and social modifications that occurred throughout the region and throughout Gaul in general.

The formation of this new imperial world with its provincial cultures that, while maintaining some regional distinctiveness, show broad similarities over many different provinces, involved restructuring of rural landscapes with cadastral systems, the building of roads and aqueducts, the mass production and consumption of tableware ceramics and other goods on a scale not seen before, the construction of monumental civic buildings sponsored by the *eurgetism* (philanthropy) of local elites, an escalation of gaps in wealth and social divisions, and various processes of ethnogenesis produced by administrative divisions of the landscape with juridical implications. This was accomplished by an imperial bureaucracy that was quite small by modern standards and that had severe limitations on communication, finance, and surveillance. But, despite the radically different relations of power structuring the colonial situation, much of what happened can also be linked to processes of consumption and could benefit from the kind of analysis of consumption proposed here. Indeed, Greg Woolf has argued that a "consumer revolution" occurred at this time simultaneously at Rome and in the provinces, which was both a sign and an agent of this broader cultural transformation.[6] A fundamental avenue for understanding the transformation of consciousness in this period remains understanding how and why some objects and practices were incorporated into the daily lives of people, why others were rejected, and what the entangling consequences of this process were. It is not obvious, for example, that the same type of mass-produced terra sigillata bowl was used for the same things or had the same meanings in households in southern France, Britain, Spain, and Italy. Instead of treating such items simply as an index of "Romanization," one needs to examine the patterns of association of the entire repertoire of objects from household and ritual contexts, as well as the spaces in which they were used, in order to understand how these items were consumed locally and what they meant to people. To date, little of the kind of close contextual analysis of household consumption that is necessary to resolve these questions has been undertaken in Roman provincial contexts.

The analysis of these various transformations under the Roman Empire lies beyond the scope of this book. I briefly introduce them here simply to give a dramatically contrastive sense of the differences in the colonial experience before and after Augustus. But I also raise them to emphasize that these transformations were not inevitable. This book has attempted to present a method for understanding the colonial history of Mediterranean France that sees the actions of Etruscan merchants in the seventh century BCE as linked to the imposition of an imperial administration six hundred years later, but in a way that does not present those links as having an ineluctable evolutionary telos or as resulting from the articulation of global structures of economic and political power. Rather, the goal was to understand colonialism as a highly contingent process of entanglement in which asymmetries of power emerge from the unintended consequences of the actions of individuals and small social groups operating on the basis of socially situated interests and local cultural dispositions. Cross-cultural consumption is a creative act of appropriation and reinterpretation within different regimes of value and fields of social competition. But even the apparently benign act of developing a taste for an alien alcoholic beverage or importing a staple grain can entangle whole societies in complex webs of economic dependencies, political alliances, and violence that can have far reaching ramifications for the transformation of culture, identity, and sovereignty. The other imperative goal of the book was, of course, to wrest this ancient colonial encounter free from its deeply embedded place in the construction of Western ancestral mythology and colonial ideology (to the extent this is possible) and subject it to critical scrutiny from a new analytical perspective. Because of the powerful and pervasive legacy of the civilizing discourse of Pompeius Trogus, the success of this mission is of major concern to the comparative understanding of colonialism in general.

NOTES

1. Greeks generally preferred to use the name Celts *(Keltoi)* and Romans preferred the name Gauls *(Galli, Gallati)* to designate rather broadly the same set of peoples living north of the Mediterranean and the Alps in Western Europe (see chapter 4). The word *Gaul (Gallia)* was also used by the Romans to designate a geographic region (roughly modern France and northern Italy) that was smaller than the overall distribution of Celtic languages. Following the Roman conquest of this region, it was divided up into administrative provinces (Gallia Narbonensis, Gallia Lugdunensis, Gallia Aquitania, Gallia Belgica, Gallia Cisalpina). The term *Celtic* has been further complicated by its use in modern identity politics (see Chapman 1992; Collis 2003; Dietler 1994; James 1999).

2. For pragmatic rhetorical purposes, I use the term *colonial encounter* in this book to represent collectively what was a complex series of diverse encounters between a range of actors from different societies over a long period of time.

3. The earliest version of the tale is from a fragment (Frag. 549 Rose) attributed by Athenaeus (XIII.576) to a now missing *Constitution of Massalia* written by Aristotle. In Aristotle's version, the Greek wayfarer was named Euxenos (meaning "good guest"), and the daughter of Nannos was called Petta. In Aristotle's version, the proffered cup contained wine mixed with water, whereas in the other version it held water. Pompeius Trogus was a Roman historian of Gallic ancestry who recorded his more complete version of the tale in the late first century BCE. Unfortunately, his original text has also disappeared and survives only in a later epitome by Justin (XLIII.3). In interpreting the remarks of Pompeius Trogus concerning the consequences of the colonial experience, it is important to note

that he was a colonial subject writing in Latin with an interest in assimilating his own ancestry to Roman values. His standing as a Roman citizen derived from the conferral of this status on his grandfather by the Roman consul Pompey in exchange for mercenary service leading a troop of cavalry in the army Pompey raised to suppress a rebellion in Spain, and his father had served as a secretary for Julius Caesar (Justin XLIII.5). Establishing a deep pedigree of Greek civilizing influence, however spurious, for his own cultural roots would have served him well within the Hellenophilic world of elite Roman culture.

4. See Abu El-Haj 2001; Anderson 1991; Cohn 1996; Trigger 1984.

5. For example, see Chatterjee 1993; Prakash 1995; Young 2001.

6. For example, Bourdieu 2004; Lenoir 1997.

7. Bourdieu 2004; Bourdieu and Wacquant 1992.

8. See Aubet 1993; Dietler 1997, 2005a, 2007a; Dietler and López-Ruiz 2009; Lomas 2004a; Hodos 2006.

9. See Aubet 1993; Boardman 1980; Carratelli 1996; Dietler and López-Ruiz 2009; Graham 1983; Gras et al. 1995; Lomas 2004a; Tsetskhladze and De Angelis 1994.

10. Brun 1987; Dietler 1989, 1990a, 1995, 1999a, 2005a; Frankenstein and Rowlands 1978; Kimmig 1983; Wells 1980.

11. *Punic* is the Roman version of *Phoenician*, but the term is now conventionally used to differentiate things associated with Carthage rather than the original Phoenician city-states.

12. Cohn 1996.

13. See Derks 1998; Dietler 2004; Dondin-Peyre and Raepsaet-Charlier 1999; Roymans 2004; Wells 1999; Woolf 1998.

14. Dietler 1990b, 2005a.

15. For example, Dietler 1990b; Garcia 2004; Hodge 1998; Py 1993a.

16. For example, see Comaroff and Comaroff 1997; Cooper and Stoler 1997.

17. See Dietler 1990b, 2005a.

18. Two different systems of historical periodization are brought to bear on the colonial encounter in this region. The Early/Late Iron Age system, with multiple subdivisions based on changes in regional material culture styles, is used by archaeologists studying indigenous societies. Although several variants exist (see Dietler 1997, 2005a), the framework adopted here is based on the widely used scheme developed for southern France by Michel Py (1993a). Archaeologists studying Greeks and Etruscans generally employ the Archaic/Classical/Hellenistic temporal terminology developed in the eastern Mediterranean. Although the two systems do not coincide neatly, chronometric dating within the indigenous system is based largely on stylistic distinctions within Greek, Etruscan, and Roman ceramics that have been tied to historical events.

19. Ballantyne and Burton 2005; Comaroff 1985; Stoler 2002; Stoller 1994; Young 1995.

20. Dening 1980.

21. Pratt 1992.

22. Ferguson and Whitehead 1992.

23. White 1991.

24. Sahlins 1985.

25. White 1991.

26. For example, Bhabha 1994; Young 1995.

27. For example, Brun 1987; Cunliffe 1988; Frankenstein and Rowlands 1978; Sherratt 1993; Wells 1980.

28. Foucault 1972.

29. Said 1993:9.

30. Fieldhouse 1981.

31. For example, Bartel 1985 and Hovarth 1972.

32. Young 2001:19, 27.

33. Lenin 1996.

34. See Kohn 1958.

35. Osterhammel 1997:4.

36. Osterhammel 1997:16.

37. Finley 1976:173.

38. Osterhammel 1997:21.

39. Ho 2004:211, 225.

40. Hobson 1965[1902]; Lenin 1996[1916]; see also the historical discussions of terminology in Finley 1976; Koebner and Schmidt 1964; and Pagden 1995.

41. See chapter 4. Greek *apoikiai* were usually independent city-states that maintained only cultural, religious, or vaguely sentimental ties to the mother city. The meaning of the term *colonia* changed over the course of Roman history, but these were originally settlements of Roman or Latin citizens (often military veterans) established in conquered territories as a tool of control. See Bresson and Rouillard 1993; Dondin-Payre and Raepsaet-Charlier 1999; Finley 1976; Graham 1983; and note 43.

42. Young 1995:163.

43. The meanings of the term *colonia* were already complicated in the Roman context, and there was a significant change between the Roman Republic and the Roman Empire. Originally, *coloniae* were settlements established within conquered territory in Italy for strategic reasons, and there was a difference between "Latin colonies," in which settlers gave up their original citizenship and became citizens of the colony, and "colonies of Roman citizens," which were small outposts of strategic importance. Later, citizen colonies on a larger scale became a means for politicians to reward supporters and army veterans with grants of land in conquered provinces (e.g., in southern France). Finally, from the mid–second century CE, the term was transformed to designate the highest status that could

be granted to a *civitas* within the administrative structure of the Empire, whatever the foundational history of that settlement. See Dondin-Payre and Raepsaet-
Charlier 1999; Finley 1976; Keppie 1983; Salmon 1969.

44. For example, Ahmad 1992; Comaroff 1997; Cooper 2005; Dirks 1992a; Thomas 1994.
45. Girault 1921, cited in Osterhammel 1997:25.
46. See Klor de Alva 1995; McClintock 1992.
47. Braudel 1992; Wallerstein 1974; Wolf 1982.
48. See Sahlins 1995.
49. Trouillot 1995.
50. Spivak 1988.
51. For example, see Burke 1996; Cohn 1996; Comaroff and Comaroff 1991, 1997; Hansen 1992; Howes 1996b; Thomas 1991; Turgeon 1998, 2002.
52. Gosden 2004:3–4.
53. Appadurai 1986:5.
54. See Chakrabarty 2000; Cooper 2005; Dietler 2005b; Stoler et al. 2007.
55. Stoler et al. 2007.
56. For example, Alcock et al. 2001; Cusick 1998b; Dietler 1990b, 1997, 2002, 2005a; Dyson 1985; Gosden 2004; Hodos 2006; Hurst and Owen 2005; Lightfoot 2005; Lyons and Papadopolous 2002; Rowlands 1998; Rowlands et al. 1987; Schreiber 1992; Stein 2005; Van Dommelen 1998; Wells 1999.
57. Braudel 1992; Frank 1993; Wallerstein 1974, 1991.
58. For example, see Kirch and Sahlins 1992.
59. For example, see Boardman 1980; Tsetskhladze and De Angelis 1994.
60. Thomas 1991:84.
61. Justin XLIII.3 and 4.
62. Justin XLIII.3 and 4.
63. Dougherty 1993. See also Dietler 1995.
64. Dougherty 1993:9.

CHAPTER 2

1. See Mignolo 1995; Quinn 1976.
2. Bourdieu 1990.
3. Trouillot 1995:31.
4. See Pagden 1995; Quinn 1976.
5. For example, see Auslander 1996; Haskell and Penny 1981; Kostof 1995; Mukerji 1997.
6. See Butler 1935; Marchand 1996; Wohlleben 1992.
7. Winckelmann 1987 [1755]:3.
8. Wohlleben 1992.

9. See Webb 1982; Zuber 1992.
10. Shelley 1822.
11. See Grafton 1992; Jenkyns 1980; Marchand 1996; Turner 1981.
12. Marchand 1996:xviii–xix.
13. See Koebner and Schmidt 1964; Vance 1997.
14. Murray 1953:13.
15. See Bourdieu 1984, 1990.
16. *Gymnasium* was the public sports ground associated with a school in ancient Athens and other Greek cities, while the *Lyseum* was the ancient Greek school associated with Aristotle and the Peripatetic scholars. Similarly, the term *academia* employed in English to refer to modern universities derives from the name of the philosophical school founded by Plato in Athens.
17. Ringer 1979, 1992.
18. Gérard 1982:357.
19. Bowen 1989:183.
20. Vance 1997:13.
21. James 1994:206–207.
22. Vance 1997:15; see also Grafton 1992.
23. Bourdieu 1984.
24. Constantine 1984; Fox 1978.
25. Dr. Johnson, in Boswell 1887 (vol. 3):36.456.
26. Bowen 1992; W. B. Cohen 1971; Marchand 1996.
27. Gladstone 1858.
28. Quoted in Livingstone 1935:43.
29. Napoléon III 1866.
30. See Macarthur 1943; Morris 1994.
31. Kostof 1995:624.
32. Kostof 1995:625.
33. See Scott 1998:40–51.
34. On the implantation of cadastral systems in southern France, see Clavel-Lévêque 1983.
35. Pagden 1995:11–12.
36. For example, Machiavelli 1980.
37. See Quinn 1976; Seed 1995; Tulard 1997.
38. Seed 1995:180.
39. Jenkyns 1980.
40. Marchand 1996:24.
41. For example, Bryce 1901; Cromer 1910; Lucas 1912.
42. Vance 1997.
43. See Cohn 1996 and Scott 1998 for analyses of these practices designed to make subject peoples and territory "legible" and governable.

44. Quoted in Jenkyns 1980:337.
45. MacArthur 1943.
46. Ferrero 1914.
47. Murray 1953:58. See also de Sismondi 1837: 8–9.
48. Livingstone 1935:117–118.
49. Hall 1993:193.
50. Jenkyns 1980:333.
51. Hautecoeur 1953.
52. For example, de Sismondi 1937.
53. Kipling 1899: 323–324; Murray 1953:59.
54. Galton 1869.
55. Mitchell 1947:3.
56. Lugard 1922:618.
57. Napoléon III 1866:397.
58. Napoléon III 1866:397.
59. On the "Ancients and Moderns" debate, see Perrault 1979.
60. Marchand 1996:6.
61. For example, see de Sismondi 1837; Hobson 1965 [1902].
62. Koebner and Schmidt 1964:244.
63. Jenkyns 1980:333.
64. Bowen 1989:183.
65. Marchand 1996; Ringer 1979.
66. See Dietler 1994, 2005b; Dyson 1989; Hingley 2000; Marchand 1996; Mattingly 1996; Morris 1994; Shanks 1996; van Dommelen 1997, 1998; Vasunia 2005; Webster 1996.
67. Murray 1953:6.
68. Murray 1953:7.
69. Livingstone 1935:14.
70. Goudineau 1990:17–18.
71. Marchand 1996; Morris 1994; Schnapp 1996.
72. Ridley 1992.
73. Bourdieu 1984.
74. Marchand 1996.
75. For example, Dunbabin 1948.
76. See Comaroff and Comaroff 1991:xiii.
77. Clavel-Lévêque 1974.
78. See Cougny 1892; Rankin 1987.
79. Webster 1995.
80. Momigliano 1975:50–64.
81. Momigliano 1975:57.
82. I am by no means rejecting the importance of Greek and Roman texts for the analysis of the ancient colonial encounter in the western Mediterranean. Quite

the opposite. They are clearly essential for understanding Greek and Roman institutions, attitudes, agents, and historical events. But, as with any colonial document, they must be interpreted with proper "against the grain" skepticism and be put in dialectical conversation with archaeological data.

83. For example, see Pelloutier 1740.
84. For example, Eggert 1991.
85. See Dietler 1990b, 2005a:25–38.
86. Déchelette 1913:581.
87. For example, Benoit 1965; Boardman 1980; Bouloumié 1981; Jacobsthal and Neuffer 1933. For a more detailed discussion of the history of research under the Hellenization perspective, see Dietler 1990b, 2005a.
88. Morel 1983; see also Dietler 1989, 1990b; Morris 1994; Whitehouse and Wilkins 1989.
89. See, for example, Ando 2000; Keay and Terrenato 2001; Le Roux 2004; Millet 1990; Paunier 2006; Wood and Queiroga 1992; Woolf 1998.
90. See Collingwood 1934 and Haverfield 1905; and see Bénabou 1976; Hingley 2000; and Mattingly 2005 for critical historical discussion.
91. For example, Herskovits 1938; Redfield et al. 1936; Social Science Research Council 1954; Spicer 1962.
92. Wolf 1982.
93. Social Science Research Council 1954.
94. See Cusick 1998a and Ervin 1980 for a more detailed critique and some attempts to revive aspects of acculturation theory.
95. For example, Amin 1976; Frank 1967.
96. Braudel 1992; Frank 1993; Wallerstein 1974, 1991.
97. See Roseberry 1988; Sahlins 1985; Wolf 1982.
98. For example, Champion 1989; Chase-Dunn and Hall 1991; Rowlands et al. 1987.
99. See Brun 1987; Cunliffe 1988; Frankenstein and Rowlands 1978; Sherratt 1993.
100. See Arafat and Morgan 1994; Bintliff 1984; Dietler 1989, 1990b, 1995, 1998; Eggert 1991; Pare 1991; Woolf 1990.
101. In Kirch and Sahlins 1992:2.
102. See Comaroff and Comaroff 1991; Roseberry 1988; Sahlins 1985, 1994; Stoler 1992; Stoler and Cooper 1997; Thomas 1991; Wolf 1982.
103. For example, Chakrabarty 2000.
104. Archaeologists working on colonialism in the ancient Mediterranean have engaged increasingly with postcolonial theory in recent years, and somewhat less so with the historical anthropology of colonialism, but (with the exception of my own work) these approaches have so far had limited appeal in France. See Dietler 1990b, 1998, 2002, 2005a; Hodos 2006; Owen 2005; van Dommelen 1998, 2005; Vives-Ferrándiz 2005, 2008.
105. Césaire 1972; Fanon 1967; Memmi 1965.

106. Bhabha 1994; Young 1995.
107. Bernabé et al. 1993; Brathwaite 1971; Hannerz 1992.
108. Amselle 1998; Turgeon 2002.
109. In the case of creolization, this was first a linguistic concept that was then extended to race before becoming a term of cultural analysis. See Dawdy 2000; Palmié 2006.
110. Young 1995.
111. Bakhtin 1981.
112. Bhabha 1994.
113. For example, Young 1995.
114. Césaire 1972:83.
115. See Palmié 2006 for an astute anthropological critique of creolization.
116. For example, Cohn 1996; Comaroff and Comaroff 1991, 1997; Cooper and Stoler 1997; Dietler 1990b, 1998, 2002, 2005a; Dirks 1992; Sahlins 1985; Thomas 1991.
117. For example, Bhabha 1984, 1994; Said 1978, 1993; Young 1995, 2001.
118. For example, Ashcroft 1996; Mishra and Hodge 1991.
119. For example, Ahmad 1992; Slemon 1994; Young 1995, 2001.
120. For example, Ahmad 1992; Parry 1987.
121. van Dommelen 1998.
122. Amselle 1998.
123. I am not convinced that using the term *hybridization* instead of *hybridity*, as some archaeologists working in the Mediterranean have advocated (e.g., Knapp 2008; van Dommelen 2005), avoids the problems discussed. It is sometimes claimed that this emphasizes a more active, agent-oriented understanding of colonial processes, but, as noted, the notion of hybridity of Bhabha (from Bakhtin) was already a pointedly active definition.
124. Several other concepts that have also raised some interest recently among scholars working on the ancient Mediterranean I mention only in passing, as their analytical utility in this case seems limited. These include Richard White's (1991) "middle ground" (see Gosden 2004; Malkin 2004), the notion of "connectivity" popularized by Horden and Purcell (2000), and Malkin's (2004) turn toward network analysis. As White (2006) himself has noted, the idea of the middle ground is not really a theoretical tool but a description of a frequent colonial situation in which a relative balance of power in a region creates the conditions for working out creative cultural misunderstandings that have transformative effects. The power of White's book lies in the brilliance of his detailed and subtle analysis of a specific colonial context, rather than the concept itself. Network analysis, which was briefly popular in anthropology during the 1950s to 1970s, was largely abandoned because of the complexity of the mathematical modeling required and the ponderous data requirements relative to the limited explanatory yield (see Boissevain 1979; Sanjek 1974).

Although it has had a somewhat longer life in sociology (Scott 1991), the severe data limitations of archaeology preclude it from serving as a feasible analytical technique and render it at best a possibly heuristic metaphor.

125. Dirks 1992:7.

CHAPTER 3

1. Sahlins 1999:vi.
2. For example, see Baudrillard 1998; Bourdieu 1984; Dietler 2010; Douglas and Isherwood 1979; Miller 1987, 1995.
3. For example, Appadurai 1986; Haugerud et al. 2000; Hoskins 1998; Miller 1987, 2005; Myers 2001; Warnier 1999.
4. For example, Appadurai 1996; Burke 1996; Cohn 1996; Comaroff and Comaroff 1997; Dietler 1990a, 1990b, 1998; Howes 1996a; Mintz 1985; Rogers 1990; Sahlins 1985, 1992; Thomas 1991; Turgeon 2002.
5. Harvey 1990; Miller 1987.
6. For example, see Appadurai 1996; Friedman 1994; Hannerz 1992; Haugerud et al. 2000.
7. Comaroff and Comaroff 1997.
8. Baudrillard 1998; Bourdieu 1984; Douglas and Isherwood 1978.
9. Bourdieu 1984.
10. Howes 1996b.
11. Sahlins 1999.
12. Amselle 1998:x; Ricouer 1992.
13. Sahlins 1999:xi.
14. Sahlins 1993:2.
15. Comaroff and Comaroff 1997; Cooper and Stoler 1997; Thomas 1991.
16. Comaroff and Comaroff 1997.
17. Dietler 2007b.
18. Howes 1996b:6; Pendergrast 1993:245–247.
19. James 1993.
20. Hannerz 1992: 217.
21. Thomas 2002:182.
22. Comaroff and Comaroff 1997:218.
23. Thomas 2002.
24. Comaroff and Comaroff 1997.
25. Appadurai 1996:90.
26. Appadurai 1996; Kelly 1997.
27. Dentzer 1982; Murray 1990.
28. Dunbabin 1998; Haynes 2000:96–97.
29. Davidson 1997; Kurke 1999.

30. Cicero *Against Verres* 2.1.26.66.
31. Bradley 1998; D'Arms 1990; Dunbabin 1995, 1998.
32. Bhabha 1994.
33. Sahlins 1985.
34. Bourdieu 1984.
35. A consumption approach places some stringent demands on archaeological research strategies that cannot always be met by past and current excavations. See Dietler 2005b:66–67; 2010.
36. Shlasko 1992.
37. Thomas 1991:95–97.
38. Sahlins 1999:xiv.
39. Meadows 1847:235 quoted in Sahlins 1999:xiv.
40. See also Dietler 1990b.
41. See Caesar *Gallic War* IV.2; II.15; Dietler 1990a, 2006; Fitzpatrick 1989:311–312.
42. Mintz 1985.
43. See Appadurai 1986; Kopytoff 1986.
44. Turgeon 1997.
45. Lohse 1988.
46. See Dietler 2005b:66–67; 2010.
47. Sahlins 1999:xii.
48. Guha 1997.
49. The book originally contained a chapter examining these features in detail, but the economics of publishing required that this be cut. See Dietler 1997, 2004, 2007a.
50. Bats 1988c.
51. Bats 1988b, 1988c; Dietler et al. 2008:203.
52. Bats 1988b.
53. Bats 1988b; Lambert 1994; Panosa Domingo 1993; Untermann 1969.
54. Lambert 1992, 1994:81–89; Lejeune 1983.
55. de Hoz 1993.
56. Untermann 1969.
57. Bats 1988b.
58. de Hoz 1983; Solier and Barbouteau 1988.
59. Campmajo 1993.
60. Richard and Villaronga 1973.
61. Py 2006; Richard 1992.
62. Martos 2000.
63. Martos 2000.
64. Py 2006.
65. Py 2006.

66. See Kurke 1999; Meadows and Shipton 2001.

67. Lejeune et al. 1988.

68. See Py 2006.

69. See Dietler 2004; Luley 2008; Py 2006.

70. Py 2006.

71. See Barth 1967; Bloch and Parry 1989; Bohannan 1959; Dietler 2004; Salisbury 1962:210.

72. See Dietler 1997, 1998.

CHAPTER 4

1. See Gómez Espelosin 2009 on the western Mediterranean in the Greek imagination.

2. For example, see de Hoz 2004.

3. Baslez 1984; Whitehead 1977.

4. Lambert 1994; Whatmough 1970.

5. Strabo IV.1.14.

6. See Barruol 1975:146.

7. Jacoby 1957: Hecataeus of Miletus fragments 55 and 57.

8. Herodotus V.9.3. On the basis of a few textual references and some arguable interpretations of linguistic data, some scholars have supported the idea of an indigenous Ligurian-speaking substratum for the whole of Mediterranean France (e.g., Benoit 1965, Untermann 1969, 1980). However, names identified as linguistically Ligurian in western Languedoc-Roussillon are very rare in the Iberian script (about ten cases); and the other cases are all late examples in the Latin script from two sites (Narbonne and Béziers) with a marked Roman influence (Panosa Domingo 1993).

9. See Braun 2004:291–292.

10. Strabo III.4.19. See Dominguez Monedero 1983 for an interesting hypothesis about the possible origin of this term in the context of Greek colonies in the Black Sea and its symbolic significance in Greek thought. The original meaning of the term *Ligurian* may also have its origin outside the western Mediterranean (Barruol 1975).

11. Roth Congès 2001.

12. See Dietler 1990b, 2005a; Pralon 1992.

13. Untermann 1992.

14. On the Hérault material culture boundary, see Dietler 1990b, 1997, 2005a; Garcia 1993a, 2004; Py 1993a. On the alphabetic boundary, see Untermann 1992.

15. Bats 1989:124.

16. Strabo IV.6.3.

17. For example, Hatt 1959; Jannoray 1955.

18. For example, see Py 1974, 1990a, 1993a.

19. See Dietler and Herbich 1998; Jones 1997.

20. Bonfante and Bonfante 1983; Rix 1991.

21. Nurse and Hinnebusch 1993; Samarin 1990.

22. See especially Dietler 1990b, 1997, 2005a; Garcia 1993a, 2004; Janin 2006; Lagrand 1968; Py 1990a, 1993a.

23. For the Mailhac sequence, see Taffanel and Janin 1998. The "Suspendian" material culture complex is named after the site of the Grotte Suspendue at Collias, in eastern Languedoc. See Py 1990a, 1993a.

24. See especially Py 1990a, 1993a.

25. See Gailledrat 1997; Garcia 1993b; Panosa Domingo 1993; Py 1993a; Ugolini 1993.

26. Panosa Domingo 1993; Ugolini 1993.

27. Compare Panosa Domingo 1993; Gailledrat 1997; Py 1993a; Rouillard 1991:63–71; Ruiz and Molinos 1998; Solier 1976–1978; Ugolini 1993.

28. See, for example, Jones 1997.

29. On the dangers, see Dietler 1994; Kohl and Fawcett 1996. On ethnogenesis in colonial contexts, see Comaroff and Comaroff 1991; Hill 1996; Vail 1989b.

30. Compare Barth 1969; Hutchinson and Smith 1996; Nash 1989.

31. For other examples, see Harries 1989; Ranger 1989.

32. Cohn 1996; Vail 1989a.

33. Bilby 1996; Sattler 1996; White 1991:1–49.

34. Comaroff and Comaroff 1991:167–169; Ferguson and Whitehead 1992; White 1991:1–49.

35. Hickerson 1996.

36. For more complete reviews of this information, see especially Barruol 1975; Bats 1988b; Lambert 1994; and Untermann 1969.

37. See Hall 1997, 2002.

38. See especially Barruol 1973, 1975, 1980; Gayraud 1981.

39. Py 2006:398–405.

40. Py 1981, 1990a:178, 605; 2006:447–474.

41. The *civitates* were bounded territories organized around a principal town according to a standardized administrative model.

42. Sahlins 1985.

43. Shipton 1984.

44. The *Ora Maritima* of Avienus (v. 585–589) mentions the "fierce realm" of a group called the Elesyces, with their chief city of Naro, near the river Attagus (Aude). This is thought to have been derived from a *periplus* written by a Massalian sailor of the sixth or fourth century BCE; see the introduction by Murphy in Avienus 1977. They were again mentioned by Polybius (*Histories* I.17) as a group from whom the Carthaginians recruited mercenaries to fight at the battle of Himera in 480 BCE, but they then pass out of the historical record.

45. Strabo IV.1.12.

46. Although Livy XXI.26, writing in the early first century CE, mentioned the Volcae in connection with the earlier passage of Hannibal through the lower Rhône basin in the late third century BCE, in describing the same events, Polybius III.41–46, writing in the late second century BCE, made no mention of this name.

47. See Dietler 1990b, 2005a; Py 1990a:170–177, 1993a.

48. See Py 1993a.

49. Arcelin 1999; Arcelin and Gruat 2003:191.

50. Py 1990a:117–199.

51. Garcia 2004:172.

52. Pliny H.N. III.37; Strabo IV.1.12.

53. See Christol 1999; Christol and Goudineau 1988.

54. See Clavel 1975 in favor of an early date, and the critical assessment of Christol and Goudineau 1988; Monteil 1999:489–499 and Py 1974, 1990a:179–181.

55. For example, Bats 1992, who saw Nîmes as a dominant "central place" linked to Massalian trade.

56. Monteil 1999:490; Py 1981.

57. Monteil 1999:490–491.

58. Py 1990a:177–179.

59. Monteil 1999:491.

60. The mid–second century BCE rampart at Glanum enclosed an area of about thirty hectares, but only half of this land was inhabitable; Agusta-Boularot et al. 2000. A settlement of thirty hectares has been claimed (Arcelin 1995:331) for fifth-century BCE Arles, but excavations are still far too limited to verify this observation, and it must be treated with caution.

61. Py 2006:447–498.

62. Py 2006.

63. The Volcae Arecomici were probably first officially recognized, or defined, by Rome as an entity around 75 BCE. Around 70 BCE, Pompey apparently ceded some Arecomici land to Massalia but did not, as some have claimed, place the Arecomici under the domination of Massalia; see Christol and Goudineau 1988:89.

64. An inscription on a column base found at Nîmes lists the names of eleven of these towns: Andusia (modern Anduze), Briginn (modern Brignon), Brugetia (perhaps modern Bruyès or Brouzet?), Segusion (modrn Suzon), Sextant (modern Substantion/Castelnau-le-Lez), Statumae (modern Seynes), Tedusia (Théziers), Uatrute (Vié Cioutat), Ucetiae (modern Uzès), Ugerni (modern Beaucaire), and Uirinn (modern Védrines). See Hirschfeld 1888:3362; Rivet 1988:168–176.

65. See Christol 1999; Christol and Goudineau 1987–1988; Monteil 1999:493–496; Py 1974, 1990a:170–193.

66. Py 1974, 2006:474–492.

67. Strabo IV.6.3.

68. See Barruol 1975, who provides a thorough analysis and lists the Anatilii, Avatici, Camactulici, Comani, Ceciates, Dexivates, Libii, Liguani, Nearchi, Oxybii, Reii, Segobrigii, Suelteri, Tricori, and Tritolli among the tribes of the Salyes confederation.
69. Strabo IV.6.4.
70. Arcelin 1993; Arcelin and Tréziny 1990.
71. The first episode is generally assumed to be linked to the Roman defeat of the Salluvii directed by Gaius Sextius Calvinus around 123–122 BCE. He subsequently founded the Roman garrison of Aquae Sextius (Aix-en-Provence) on the plain just south of Entremont (see Livy *Perichorae*, Epit. 61).
72. Arcelin 1993:94.
73. Salviat 1993.
74. Livy *Perichorae*, Epit. 61.
75. Earlier texts refer simply to "Ligurians" *(Ligyes)* or "Celto-ligurians" in this region. The mention of the Salyes by Avienus in his *Ora Maritima* (v. 701) can hardly be used as evidence of the earlier presence of this name. This text was composed in the fourth century CE from a bricolage of much earlier Greek *periplus* accounts, but with many anachronisms and errors. See Berthelot's introduction to Avienus 1934.
76. Polybius *Histories* XXXIII, 5.8–14; Strabo IV.6.4.
77. Strabo IV.6.4.
78. Barruol 1975:278–294.
79. Caesar *Gallic War* I.10; Livy XXI.31; Strabo IV.1 and IV.6.
80. Pliny N.H. III.37; Strabo IV.6.4.
81. Goudineau 1979; Goudineau and de Kisch 1984.
82. Goudineau and de Kisch 1984.
83. Strabo IV.1.11.
84. See Barruol 1975:231–272.
85. Barruol 1975:234.
86. Such as the Albici, who were allies of Massalia; see Barruol 1975.
87. See Bonfante and Bonfante 1983; Pallottino 1986; Rix 1991.
88. See Dedet and Py 2006; Dedet et al. 2006; Gras 1985a, 1985b; Morel 1981b, 2006; Py 1995; and see Bats 1998, 2000 for the skeptical position.
89. Gras 1985a, 1985b; Morel 1981b, 2006.
90. Dietler 1989, 1990b, 1997, 2005a; Hérubel 2000; Hérubel and Gailledrat 2006; Morel 1981b.
91. Dietler 2005a:41–47; Gras 1985a; Py 1995; Py and Py 1974.
92. Bouloumié 1985; Dietler 2005a:50–52; Morel 1981b; Py 1979.
93. Dietler 1990b, 2005a:59–61; Gras 1985a, 2000; Hérubel 2000; Hérubel and Gailledrat 2006; Morel 1981b; Py 1993a, 1995.
94. Py 1993b; Gomez 2000.
95. Bouloumié 1985; Bouloumié and Lagrand 1977; Dietler 1990b, 2005a:61–65; Hérubel 2000; Hérubel and Gailledrat 2006; Tendille 1982.

96. Hérubel 2000; Hérubel and Gailledrat 2006.

97. Bats 1998, 2000.

98. Dietler 1990b, 2005a; Hérubel 2000; Hérubel and Gailledrat 2006; Morel 1981b; Py 1995.

99. See Colonna 1986.

100. See A. Cohen 1971; Curtin 1984; and Fitzhugh 1985 on this distinction.

101. Bouloumié 1987; Py 1995.

102. Lebeaupin and Séjalon 2008; Py et al. 2006.

103. Bats 1988c.

104. Lebeaupin and Séjalon 2008:54.

105. Colonna 1980; Cristofani 1983 sees it instead as the name of an Etruscan woman: Morel 2006:40.

106. Py 1988.

107. As noted in the text, CNT stands for *céramique non tournée*, the designation given to indigenous hand-modeled ceramics in the standard classification used for the region; see Py 1993b and chapter 7.

108. Py 1995; Py et al. 2006.

109. Lebeaupin and Séjalon 2008; Barruol and Py 1978.

110. Barker and Rasmussen 1998; Cristofani 1986; D'Agostino 1990; Haynes 2000; Torelli 2000.

111. Cristofani et al. 1985; Cristofani 1986; Sestini 1981; Tanelli 1989.

112. Gras 1985a:326–328; Py 1995.

113. Barker and Rasmussen 1998; D'Agostino 1990; Haynes 2000; Menichetti 2000.

114. D'Agostino 1990.

115. Morley 1996:38.

116. For example, Boardman 1980.

117. See Dietler 1989, 1990b, 2005a.

118. See Dietler and López-Ruiz 2009; Rouillard 1991, 2009.

119. Arnaud 2005.

120. Strabo IV.1.8.

121. For example, Aristotle in Atheneus XIII.576a; Justin XLIII.3; Strabo IV.1, 4; Thucydides I.13.6.

122. See Trèziny 2000:84. It is also possible that local peoples formed part of the original mix of inhabitants of the settlement, as may have happened in some cases in southern Italy (see Osborne 1998 and several cases in Lomas 2004a), but the empirical evidence tends to suggest otherwise, aside from the possible incorporation of native women.

123. Hall 2002.

124. Hall 2002: 172–228.

125. Morel 1992; Özyigit 1995.

126. Herodotus 1.163.

127. See Dietler and López-Ruiz 2009; Rouillard 1991.

128. It amounts to a scattering of Greek pottery and a few other objects dating to the seventh century BCE in southern France and Spain. See Gras 2000; Morel 1992; Rouillard 1991.

129. See Morel 1992. Most of the ancient texts mention only Alalia and Velia as receiving Phocaean refugees, although a brief passage from Aristoxenus of Tarentum (frag. 23) speaks of Massalia instead.

130. Hyginus in Aulus Gellius X.16.4; Lucan III.301; Pausanias X.8.6. Given that all these texts date to at least 6 centuries after the foundation, it is probable that their perception of the original chronology was a little confused.

131. See Graham 1983.

132. Morel 2000:34.

133. Robert 1968.

134. Hermary and Tréziny 2000.

135. Morel 1995:23.

136. Furtwängler 2000; Pournot 2000; Py 2006:11–61.

137. See chapter 7. Bats 1986:23; Py 1993a; Tréziny 2005.

138. Strabo III.4.8; Livy XXXIV.9.

139. Sanmartí-Grego 1992:29.

140. Aquilué et al. 2002.

141. Strabo III.4.8; Livy XXXIV.9.

142. Strabo III.4.8.

143. Herodotus IV.17.1, IV108.2; Thucydides IV.109.3–4.

144. See Dominguez 2004; Sanmartí-Grego 1992.

145. See chapter 8.

146. See chapter 5.

147. Aristotle, *Politics* 7.7.4 and 8.6.2–3; Cicero *Pro Flacco* 25.63; Strabo IV.1.5.

148. Strabo IV.1.5.

149. Cicero *Pro Fronteio* 5.13, Strabo IV.1.5.

150. Callaway 1992.

151. Livy XXXVII.54.

152. Strabo III.4.8.

153. Athenaeus 12.25. See Hodge 1998:4.

154. Hodge (1998:128–130) attributes these differences to correlated differences in chronology and perspective: post-Hellenistic Roman texts emphasize conservative aristocratic virtue, while earlier Greek texts offer a less flattering picture. These were undoubtedly important factors. As Strabo (IV.1.5) noted, the reputation of the city as a center of learning for Romans dates to a relatively late period. But things do not line up quite that simply. For example, a description of the conservative constitution comes from Aristotle, while disparaging comments by Athenaeus, although relying partly on earlier texts, were written in the second

century CE. More likely, they are also reflecting a continuing internal diversity in Massalian society. See also Lomas 2004b.

155. Momigliano 1975:55.
156. See Morley 1996:40–43.
157. See Grmek 1989:177–197, 245–283.
158. Dougherty 1993.
159. For examples, see Coldstream 1993; Graham 2001; Hodos 1999.
160. Strabo IV.1.4.
161. Akyeampong 1996:xviii.
162. Solon's role may be apocryphal: see Kurke 1999:196.
163. Pomeroy 1975:91.
164. Davidson 1997; Kurke 1999; Pomeroy 1975. Male prostitutes also existed, though probably in smaller numbers; see Davidson 1997.
165. Davidson 1997:73.
166. Herodotus I.146.2–3.
167. Buchner 1979; Coldstream 1993; de la Genière 1995; Rougé 1970; van Compernolle 1981.
168. Hodos 1999.
169. Graham 2001:327–348.
170. Herodotus IV.186.
171. Boissinot 2005:131.
172. Gantès 1990a, 1992.
173. Boissinot 2005:131.
174. Moliner et al. 2003:159.
175. Herodotus I.164.3–167.
176. Strabo VI.1.1.
177. See especially Bats and Tréziny 1986.
178. See Bats 1986; Garcia 1995; Morel 1995; Tréziny 1986.
179. For the earlier maximal view, see Clavel-Lévêque 1977; de Wever 1966; Villard 1960. For the more recent view, see Arcelin 1986; 1992b; Bats 1986; Sternberg and Tréziny 2005.
180. Strabo IV.1.8.
181. Bats 1989:204–205.
182. For example, Lepore 1970; see Bresson and Rouillard 1993 on the issue of emporia.
183. Villard 1992.
184. Tréziny 1986.
185. Bats 1986:23; Py 1993a.
186. Gras 1995a:95.
187. Isager and Skydsgaard 1992.
188. Garcia 1995:155.

189. Strabo IV.1.5.

190. Bats 2004.

191. Pseudo-Scymnus v. 206–216; Strabo IV.1.5, IV.1.9.

192. Nickels 1982, 1995.

193. Bats 1989:216–220, 1994, 2004, 2006; Coupry 1973.

194. Arnaud and Moréna 2004; Bats 1990, 2004; Ducat 1982.

195. Brien-Poitevin 1990.

196. See Morel 1992.

197. Strabo IV.1.5, IV.1.9.

198. Bats 1989:220, 2004.

199. Garcia 1995.

200. Rouillard 1991:258.

201. Arcelin 1995, Bats 1992:272, Nickels 1976, 1983, Py 1990a:112–113.

202. See Nickels 1983, 1995, Ugolini et al. 1991 for claims of Greek foundation, and Dedet 1990b and Py 1990a:112–113, 1993a for the indigenous interpretation.

203. Arcelin 1990, 1992b.

204. Nickels 1981, 1982.

205. Nickels 1989.

206. Bats 1988b, 1988c.

207. Lebeaupin and Séjalon 2008:63.

208. Hermary et al. 1999:75; Marcet and Sanmartí 1989:109. Examples have also been found at Entremont (late second century BCE), and at Glanum and Cavaillon (first century BCE): Arcelin 1993; Dufraigne 2000:200–201.

209. Chazelles 1990:142–143; Py 1996a:234.

210. Arcelin 1990; Bouloumié 1992; Py 1993a:115.

211. Arcelin et al. 1983.

212. Arcelin and Tréziny 1990; Tréziny 2004; Tréziny and Trousset 1992.

213. Bertucchi 1992a.

214. Boissinot 2001.

215. Bats 1990; Bertucchi 1992a; Dietler 1990b.

216. *Céramique Claire* and *Grise Monochrome* in the current French typology.

217. Benoit 1965; Bertucchi 1982; Bertucchi et al. 1995; Conche 2001.

218. Bouloumié 1989:879.

219. See Cartledge 2001; Garnsey 1980a.

220. Finley 1981; Westermann 1955; Wood 1983; see Jameson 1977–78 for a position attributing a greater importance to slave labor in Greek agriculture than others have.

221. Wood 1983:23–24.

222. Garnsey 1980b; Whittaker 1980.

223. Garlan 1980:8; Garnsey 1980b:4.

224. Strabo III.4.17.

225. Justin 43.4.
226. Livy XL.18.
227. Polybius *Fragments* XXXIII. 5, 8–10; Livy *Periocha* 47.
228. Livy *Epitome* 40; Florus 3.2.3.
229. Nicolet 1991.
230. Comaroff and Comaroff 1997.
231. Cicero *Pro Fonteio* 27f.
232. Dio XXXVII.47–9; see also Livy *Epitome* 73; Sallust *Hist.* II.98.9; Cicero *Pro Fonteio* 6.
233. Lintott 1993:23.
234. Dio Cassius XXVII, fr. 90.
235. Livy *Periocha* LXXIII.
236. Cicero *Pro Fonteio* 9.20.
237. Dio XXXVII.47–49; see also Livy *Epitome* 73; Sallust *Hist.* 2.98.9; Cicero *Pro Fonteio* 6.
238. Gayraud 1981:149–153; Rivet 1988:131.
239. Christol 1999; Clavel-Lévêque 1983.
240. Christol 1999:4. Latin Right *(ius Latii)* was a status somewhere between Roman citizenship and noncitizenship. It was originally the status of the people of Italy outside Rome, before universal Roman citizenship was granted in Italy following the Social War of 91–87 BCE. It was subsequently applied to cities in the provinces outside Italy, and it entailed the granting of Roman citizenship to local city magistrates, but not to the whole population.
241. Dietler 2004.
242. Garnsey and Saller 1987:20–21.
243. Grain was the only item of consumption in which the Roman state had an active concern during the Republic and the Early Empire. This intervention was motivated by a desire to pacify the poor and avoid food riots in Rome. Most of the grain was produced privately and the state had little role except the exaction of grain taxes, the purchase of grain in the market with tax money, and paying private merchant ships to transport the grain to Rome (see Garnsey and Saller 1987:83–88).
244. Garnsey and Saller 1987:21.
245. Garnsey and Saller 1987:34.
246. Cicero *Pro Fonteio* 5.12.
247. For information on the *publicani* and the Roman tax system, see especially Lintott 1993: 70–96; Garnsey and Saller 1987.
248. Lintott 1993:90.
249. Suetonius *Divus Julius* XXIV.2.
250. Rivet 1988:78.
251. Chastagnol 1995.
252. Chastagnol 1995.

CHAPTER 5

1. Including perhaps the eventual use of coinage as a specialized token for effecting larger exchanges between merchants and locals. See Py 2006.
2. Morley 2007a:31.
3. For example, see Bohannan 1955; Dalton 1978:158–159; Humphrey and Hugh-Jones 1992; Piot 1991; Robbins 1973.
4. Compare Bouloumié 1982b; Hesnard 1992; Long et al. 1992, 2002; Pomey and Long 1992; Tchernia et al. 1978.
5. Hesnard 1992.
6. Hesnard 1992; Pomey and Long 1992.
7. Long et al. 2002, 2006.
8. Hesnard 1992; Long 1990:58–60.
9. Long et al. 2006; Sourisseau 2007.
10. Long et al. 1992.
11. Bouscaras 1964; Bouscaras and Hugues 1967.
12. Garcia 1987; Soutou and Arnal 1963.
13. Py 1993a:108.
14. Liou and Rouquette 1983.
15. Long 1988.
16. Long 1987.
17. Baudoin et al. 1994.
18. http://www.culture.gouv.fr/culture/archeosm/fr/fr-medit.htm.
19. Colls 1977.
20. See Long et al. 1992.
21. Arribas 1987; Panosa Domingo 1993.
22. Long et al. 1992.
23. In the original nineteenth-century meaning of the term, derived from the French (which still maintains this sense).
24. See also Morel 1981:487–488, 1983.
25. Pomey and Long 1992; Pomey and Tchernia 1978; Tchernia 1986; Tchernia et al. 1978.
26. Larger ships are known from earlier periods in the Eastern Mediterranean, such as the twenty-oared ship carrying three thousand amphorae of Medaean wine mentioned in an Athenian court case of the fourth century BCE (Demosthenes, *Against Lacritus*). But there is little evidence for such ships in the western Mediterranean until later centuries.
27. Blot 1995.
28. Morley 2007b:585.
29. Harris 2007:553, see also Morley 2007b:572–573.
30. See Knorringa 1987 and Reed 2003; and see Bravo 1977 for the argument for dependent traders.

31. Brun 2003:103.
32. Cato *Agr.* 146, 154.
33. Brun 2003:103; Tchernia 2000:199–209.
34. Brun 2003:107; Hesnard and Gianfrotta 1989:393–449.
35. For example, Demoththenes *Against Zenothemis*, 32.7–8.
36. For example, Demosthenes *Against Apatourius* 33.10–11.
37. Bravo 1977.
38. For example, Bats 2000.
39. For a critique, see Dietler 1990b, 2005a, 2007a and Gras 2000.
40. Möller 2007:370; Morley 2007a:57.
41. Baslez 1984; Möller 2007; Morley 2007a; Reed 2003.
42. The records of court cases arising from such disputes are a prime source of information about the conduct of trade and the identities of merchants, ship owners, and lenders.
43. As at Athens, state-owned brothels were established in many cities in large part to make them attractive places for foreign merchants. See Davidson 1998; Kurke 1999.
44. Reed 2003:44, 54–61. There were a few Athenian citizens among the known emporoi and naukleroi (Möller 2007:369), but they were a small minority.
45. Reed 2003:45.
46. Colonna 1985; Ridgway 1990.
47. Morel 2006.
48. Briquel et al. 2006; Sourisseau 2002:95.
49. Sourisseau 1997:95; see Morel 2006:43.
50. See Bats 2000 and Mele 1979 for examples of works that attribute a major significance to this battle in changing trade patterns.
51. See Long et al. 1992:230–231.
52. de Hoz 1987.
53. Colona 2006; Long et al. 2006.
54. Rouillard 1991.
55. Chadwick 1990; Gailledrat and Solier 2004; Lejeune et al. 1988.
56. Demosthenes, *Against Lacritus*, 35.10, 35.20, 35.33. Among other complaints, Demosthenes found it absurdly implausible that anyone would return with a cargo of wine from the Black Sea, as this was a region that imported wine. Mende was a city on the coast of Macedonia, Kos is an island off the western coast of Turkey.
57. Baslez 1984; Knorringa 1987; Morley 2007a; Reed 2003.
58. Mele 1979.
59. Humphreys 1978:214.
60. See Humphreys 1978; Mele 1979; Osborne 2007; Reed 2003; Tandy 1997.
61. Gras 2000. In contrast, Mele (1979) rather unconvincingly argued that the battle of Alalia in 540 BCE marked the end of the aristocratic *prexis* trade.

62. Humphreys 1978:70. Bravo 1977 argued for the participation of impoverished nobles as well during the Archaic period.

63. Reed 2003:74. Humphreys (1978:70) also pointed out that even in the Homeric texts, traders were depicted as foreigners.

64. Morley 2007b:585.

65. See D'Arms 1981.

66. D'Arms 1981.

67. Morley 2007b:584–585.

68. D'Arms 1981:41.

69. Diodorus Siculus V.26.

70. de Izarra 1993.

71. See Dietler 1989.

72. For rare exceptions, see Gailledrat and Solier 2004:437–439 and Py 1993a:92 concerning Iberians; and Gazenbeek 2004:272–273 for Ligurians.

73. Livy XL.18 and 25–28.

74. Polybius III.42.

75. Diodorus Siculus V.39.

76. Sternberg 1995, 2006.

77. Cleyet-Merle 1990.

78. Sternberg 1995:133.

79. Py 1993a:92.

80. Garcia 2008; Garcia and Vallet 2002.

81. Fitzhugh 1985b.

82. Kaplan 1985.

83. Grumet 1984:28–29.

84. Curtin 1984.

85. Curtin 1984:5–6.

86. See Gras 2000; Morel 2006:24–25.

87. Py 1995; Py et al. 1984.

88. See Aubet 1993; Azuar et al. 1998; Dietler 2007a; González Prats et al. 1997.

89. Arcelin 1995.

90. Garcia 1995; Nickels 1983.

91. Ugolini et al. 1991.

92. Gailledrat and Rouillard 2003; Gailledrat and Solier 2004.

93. Badie et al. 2000; Rouillard 2009.

94. For example, Pseudo-Scymnus v. 201–216.

95. Contrast Barruol and Py 1978 with Bats 1988a and Py 1990a:112–113.

96. On the Greek side, see Arcelin 1995; Nickels 1983; Ugolini et al. 1991; against the Greek interpretation, see Dedet 1990b; Py 1990a, 1993a.

97. Garcia 2008; Garcia and Vallet 2002.

98. Py and Roure 2002.

99. Py and Roure 2002:210.
100. Barruol and Py 1978; Dietler 2005a:207.
101. Arcelin 1995; Bats 1992.
102. Caesar *Civil War* IV.1.219; Strabo IV.1.6. Strabo noted Arelate as one of the two major emporia of Narbonensis, along with Narbo.
103. Arcelin 1995:326; Avienus *Ora Maritima* 689–691; Polybius III.42; Pseudo-Scymnus v. 201–216; Strabo IV.1.6, IV.1.9.
104. Arcelin 1995:331.
105. Arcelin 1995.
106. Arcelin 1986:83.
107. Dedet and Py 2006.
108. Py 1990a, 1993a.
109. de Souza 1999:2–13. These terms were often used to designate banditry on land as well, and the same people were sometimes involved in both activities.
110. Braund 1993; de Souza 1999; Garlan 1978.
111. Strabo I.3.2, V.1–2, V.3.5, VI.2.2.
112. Herodotus *Histories* I.166.1.
113. Livy XXXVII.57.1–2, XL.18.3–4, XL.28.7; Strabo IV.1.9., IV.6.3.
114. de Souza 1999:60–65.
115. Strabo IV.6.3.

CHAPTER 6

1. See Ferguson and Whitehead 1999.
2. See Thornton 1999.
3. See White 1991.
4. For example, see Armit et al. 2006; Carman and Harding 1999; Ferguson and Whitehead 1999; Fried et al. 1968; Haas 1990; Keeley 1996; Lambert 2002; Reyna and Downs 1994; Simons 1999.
5. For example, see Hanson 1989; Hassig 1992; Raaflaub and Rosenstein 1999; Rich and Shipley 1993; Thornton 1999.
6. Justin XLIII.3.
7. Justin XLIII.4.
8. Presumably he was referring to the battle of Alalia, off Corsica, in about 540–535 BCE.
9. Justin XLIII.5.
10. Livy 40.18 and 25–28.
11. Polybius *Histories* XXXIII.5:8–14.
12. Strabo IV.5. The exact distances depend on which of two possible measures of the stadium is used.
13. Strabo IV.5.

14. These accounts could, of course, be selectively representing only native reactions to unreported acts of Massalian aggression, but it seems unlikely that significant conquests, had they occurred, would not have been celebrated in such texts.

15. Strabo IV.6.3.

16. I know of no text that reports episodes of conflict between Massalia and its neighbors dating to the third century BCE, for example, although this may be simply a feature of the differential survival of documents.

17. Polybius *Histories* III.41.

18. Caesar *Civil War* I.34. The Albici were possibly from the area around Apt (Barruol 1975:273–277).

19. If Caesar's *(Gallic War)* undoubtedly exaggerated casualty figures can be believed. The number was certainly substantial, even if far less than claimed by Caesar.

20. See Rosenstein 1999.

21. Hamilton 1999; Hanson 1989; Raaflaub 1999.

22. Livy XL.18 and 25–28.

23. Livy LXVII.

24. Livy LXVIII, Plutarch *Marius* XXI.

25. See Bats 1986:23, who noted also that the population of Marseille in the medieval and early modern period, when the city covered a roughly comparable area, varied between ten thousand and twenty-five thousand.

26. See Lo Cascio 2001; Morley 1996:33–39; and Scheidel 1996:93–138 on the estimation of Roman population and military recruitment.

27. Hodge 1998:106, for example, raises very reasonable doubts, especially in view of the fact that Massalia was unable even to beat off the attacks of Ligurian pirates without Roman help.

28. Herodotus *Histories* I.166.1.

29. Thucydides *Peloponnesian War* I.13.6.

30. From a fragment of a lost text by Sosylos of Sparta (Jacoby 176 F1).

31. Strabo IV.1.5.

32. Caesar *Civil War* I.34–36, I.56–58, II.1–16, II.22; Strabo IV.1.5.

33. Lebeaupin and Séjalon 2008; Py et al. 2006.

34. Tacitus *Histories* III.72; Pliny 34.139.

35. Diodorus Siculus XI.51; Pindar *Pythian Odes* I.72.

36. Thucydides XX, XXIII.

37. Livy V.33. See also Sassatelli 2001; Stopponi 2001.

38. Livy V.33–36. The number 12 is suspiciously formulaic, but the general pattern of expansion seems to be roughly accurate.

39. Strabo V.2.3.

40. Livy V.30.8, VII.15.9–10.

41. See Haynes 2000:327–333.

42. See Dietler 1997; Garcia 2004; Py 1993a.

43. Concerning the oppida, see Audouze and Buchsenschutz 1991; Collis 1984; Wells 1984.

44. Polybius *Histories* II.28.

45. See Caesar *Gallic War* IV.33.

46. See Bretz-Mahler 1971; Metzler 1986; Van Endert 1987.

47. Polybius *Histories* II.28; Strabo IV.4.5; Diodorus Siculus *History* V.29.4–5; see also Tierney 1960.

48. See Armit 2006.

49. Strabo IV.4.2.

50. Dedet 1992:155, 2000.

51. Dedet 1992:154–155, 184–187; Dietler 2005a:103–123.

52. See Dietler 2005a:103–104.

53. Gasco 1984.

54. Janin 2000b.

55. Py 1993a:144.

56. Passelac et al. 1981.

57. Py 1993a: 144.

58. Herodotus VII.165.

59. For example, as Robb (1997) has indicated in the case of ancient Italy, the prevalence of iconographic representations of weapons and warriors shows little relationship to the biological evidence for violence (i.e., the proportional rate of cranial injuries) from the Neolithic through the Iron Age.

60. Brunaux and Lambot 1987:15.

61. Réjane Roure, personal communication.

62. Had there been no inclusion of weapons at all, one might have been justified in entertaining the hypothesis of some sort of ritual prohibition against placing in graves weapons that individuals wore regularly in life. But their presence in some graves would seem to belie that interpretation.

63. For the Champagne case, see Stead 1983.

64. *Pace* Dedet 2000.

65. See Dietler 1990b, 2005a.

66. See Dedet 2000.

67. See Bouloumié 1978; Dietler 2005a:224–225

68. See Dedet 1992; Dietler 2005a; Gasco 1984.

69. Turner 1980.

70. Strabo IV.1.2.

71. Avienus *Ora Maritima* v. 588.

72. See Carozza 2000; Dietler 1990b, 2005a; Garcia 2004; Lagrand 1987; Py 1993a.

73. Kristiansen 1999.

74. Carozza 2000; Guilaine et al. 1986.

75. Boissinot 1985.

76. Arcelin and Dedet 1985:13, note 6.

77. Gasco 1994.

78. Dietler 1990b, 1997, 2005a; Py 1993a.

79. See Arcelin and Dedet 1985; Py 1982, 1993a.

80. Bats 1989; Bretaudeau 1996; the dating of these sites is often uncertain due to insufficient excavation and publication. Many appear to date to the third to first centuries BCE.

81. Duval 1998; Lagrand 1981, 1986.

82. Guichard and Rayssiguier 1986.

83. Lopez and Net 1996; Py et al. 2008.

84. The early rampart at Glanum is dated to the sixth century BCE without greater precision; see Agusta-Boularot et al. 2000.

85. An early fifth-century BCE rampart at a site occupied since the late sixth century BCE; Arcelin and Ferrando 2000.

86. Latour 1985.

87. Hatt 1959.

88. Gailledrat and Solier 2004.

89. Rancoule 1994.

90. Gailledrat et al. 2002.

91. Gasco 1994.

92. Passelac 1995.

93. Arcelin and Dedet 1985; Dietler 1990b, 1997, 2005a; Py 1993a.

94. See Rowlands 1972.

95. See Rowlands 1972.

96. One must be cautious with the dating of such episodes of violence in early excavation reports, as there was a tendency to link them uncritically to specific historical events (the Roman campaign of 123 BCE, the passage of the Cimbri and Teutones, the campaign during the Civil War of 49 BCE, etc.) and then to use those historical events to date levels at sites without independent verification. This pattern has subsequently been corrected for most sites by careful analysis of the material: for example, the destruction of Entremont has been readjusted downward from 123 to about 90 BCE and that at Roquepertuse upward from 123 to around 200 BCE. See Py 1990a.

97. Arcelin and Cayot 1984; Bouloumié 1990; Gateau 1990; Roth Congès 1999.

98. Boissinot 1987:84; Gateau 1990.

99. Garcia and Bernard 2000.

100. Guichard and Rayssiguier 1993.

101. Marty 1999.

102. Bernard 2000.

103. Gantès 1990a.

104. Gantès 1990b.
105. Verdin 1999.
106. Arcelin 1995:330.
107. Verdin 1996–1997.
108. Chausserie-Laprée 2005:97.
109. Chausserie-Laprée 2000.
110. Boissinot and Gantès 2000.
111. This episode of violence may be linked to Roman activity in the area associated with the war against Hannibal and the conquest of Spain. See Gailledrat and Solier 2004.
112. Lebeaupin and Séjalon 2008.
113. Buxó et al. 1996.
114. Py 1993a:161–162.
115. Dietler and Py 2003.
116. Cerdeño Serrano 1978; Jannoray 1955:396; Jehasse and Jehasse 1973; Passelac et al. 1981; Taffanel and Taffanel 1960:33.
117. Polybius *Histories* III, 41.
118. Caesar *Civil War*, I.34. Massilia is the Roman name for the city.
119. Marty 1999:210.
120. Polybius *Histories* I.17.
121. Herodotus VII.165.

CHAPTER 7

1. See Dietler 2007b, from which much of the early part of this chapter derives.
2. Dietler 1990b, 1998, 2001, 2005a, 2006, 2007b; Franke 1987; Goody 1982; Lightfoot et al. 1998; Mills 2008; Wolf 1982.
3. Dietler 1990a, 2006.
4. Platt 1955, 1964; Steinkraus 1995.
5. de Garine 1996; Dietler 2001; Jennings 2005; Platt 1964.
6. Falk 1994; much of the rest of the book is highly problematic, but this insight is usefully provocative.
7. Bourdieu 1990.
8. See also Counihan and Kaplan 1998; Douglas 1984; Twiss 2007b; Weismantel 1988.
9. For example, Baudrillard 1998. See Goody 1982 for a critique of the semiotic approach.
10. Sahlins 1976:171.
11. Mauss 1935.
12. Information on practices among the Luo is derived from ethnographic fieldwork carried out by Ingrid Herbich and me in western Kenya, some of it still

unpublished: see, for example, Dietler and Herbich 1993, 1998, 2001, 2007; Herbich 1987; Herbich and Dietler 2008, 2009.

13. Douglas 1984; Ohnuki–Tierney 1993; Rozin and Rozin 1981.
14. Douglas 1984:28.
15. See Paulson 2006:653.
16. Appadurai 1986.
17. von Gernet 1995.
18. In the sense of Baudrillard 1998.
19. Garnsey 1999:6; see also Dentzer 1982.
20. See Dietler 2001; Douglas 1984; Elias 1978.
21. See Dietler 2001; Hayden 2001.
22. Wiessner 2001.
23. Talve 1981.
24. Comaroff and Comaroff 1997:218.
25. Shipton 1989.
26. Sahlins 1994.
27. Mintz 1985.
28. Franke 1987; Weissner and Tumu 1998; Wolf 1982.
29. Dietler 2006; Pan 1975.
30. Ambler 2003; Pan 1975.
31. Matthee 1995:44.
32. Akyeampong 1996; Crush and Ambler 1992; Pan 1975.
33. Pan 1975:16.
34. Crush and Ambler 1992; Holtzman 2001; Suggs and Lewis 2003.
35. Akyeampong 1996; Colson and Scudder 1988; Crush and Ambler 1992; Dietler 2006; Gewald 2002; Partanen 1991; Willis 2002.
36. Gewald 2002.
37. Akyeampong 1996.
38. See Dietler 1990b, 2005a, 2006, 2007a, 2007b; Poux 2004; Tchernia 1983.
39. Dietler 1990a, 1990b, 2005a.
40. Dietler 1998, 2009; Howes 1996a; Miller 1995.
41. Morley 2007a:31.
42. Morel 1981b.
43. Morel 1981b: 483.
44. Dietler 2005a:90–101.
45. Paterno 2004; Py 1990a:517–521.
46. Tierney 1960:250–251. Diodorus Siculus V.30.
47. Laubenheimer 1990.
48. Gras 1987:44–46.
49. Bertucchi 1992a; Johnston and Jones 1978; Koehler 1978, 1981.
50. Bertucchi 1992a:186–191.

51. For example, Condamin and Formenti 1976; Formenti et al. 1978.

52. For example, the five hundred Greco–Italic amphorae from the shipwreck of Chétienne C, near Saint–Raphaël (Joncheray 1975), and the numerous Massalian amphorae in the marshy area near the sweet water basin at the Bourse (Bertucchi 1992a:191).

53. Bertucchi 1992a; Gras 1985a, 1985b, 1987; Tchernia 1986; van der Mersch 1994.

54. Gras 1985a; Morel 2006; Py 1995.

55. Bertucchi 1992a.

56. That is, beyond the Greek colonies of the central Mediterranean, in southern Italy and Sicily.

57. Gras 1985b:159.

58. Bats 2006a:86.

59. Long 1990:66. By way of comparison, during the sixteenth century, Marseille produced as much as 220,000 hectoliters of wine in good years, of which a little over a quarter was consumed in the city itself; see Bats 1986:25.

60. Gailledrat 1997; Kotarba and Pezin 1990; Passelac et al. 1990.

61. Sanmartí et al. 1990.

62. Morel 1981a.

63. Calculated on the basis of data from Adroher and Sanchez 2004.

64. Gantès 1990a.

65. Bats 1990b:290.

66. Bertucchi 1992a.

67. Bats 1990b; Bertucchi 1992a.

68. Dietler 1999b, 2005a.

69. Bats 1986; Fitzpatrick 1985; Loughton 2009; Poux 2004; Tchernia 1983, 1986.

70. Tchernia 1986:86.

71. Buxó 1996; Daveau 2007; Py and Buxó 2001.

72. Py and Buxó 2001:41.

73. Convincing evidence for wine–making, as opposed to simply eating grapes, is very rare in the region: essentially the data from Lattes and some remains of possible fermentation must at l'Île de Martigues; see Py and Buxó i Capdevilla 2001.

74. Buxó 2009; Dietler 2007a; Dominguez 1987; Guérin and Gómez Bellard 1999.

75. Geller 1993; Powell 1995.

76. Dentzer 1982; Murray 1990; Tchernia 1986; Vickers 1990.

77. Palmer 1995; Wright 1995.

78. Dionysius of Halicarnassus XIII.10.

79. Dentzer 1982; Murray 1990.

80. Dentzer 1982:450.

81. Such distinctions of wine connoisseurship and their association with social distinctions became even more marked in Roman society; see Tchernia 1986.

82. Davidson 1998:222.
83. Gantès 1992; Villard 1960.
84. Bats 2006; Sourisseau 1997.
85. Durand et al. 1984; P. Villard 1988.
86. See, for instance, Pliny N.H. XIV.29; Athenaeus X.427a–c, X.432a. On the dangers, Pausanias (X.23.12) claimed that Brennus, the leader of the Celtic army that attacked Delphi in 278 BC, committed suicide by drinking neat wine. See Athenaeus X.437a–b for other cautionary tales about the dangers of undiluted wine.
87. For example, Diodorus V.26.3.
88. Lawall 2000.
89. Davidson 1998:53–60.
90. Lissarrague 1995.
91. Pliny N.H. 14.
92. Dietler 1990a, 2006.
93. For a discussion of the problems with quantitative assessments of regional consumption patterns see Dietler 2005a:39–40; Py et al. 2006.
94. Dedet and Py 2006; Dietler 1990b, 2005a:41–47; Py 1990a:532; Py et al. 2001:15–44.
95. Py 1990a:529.
96. Dedet and Py 2006:124; Py et al. 2001:16.
97. Lebeaupin and Séjalon 2008; Py 1995; Py et al. 2006.
98. Dedet and Py 2006:124, 126.
99. Duval 2006. At Saint–Blaise, Etruscan amphorae rose from about 10 percent of ceramics in the late seventh century to about 20 percent in the early sixth century BCE: Arcelin 1995.
100. Duval 2006.
101. Dietler 2005a:56–59.
102. Py 1990b.
103. Arcelin 1990:202.
104. Arcelin 1990:194–198.
105. See Py 1990a, 1990c, 1993a.
106. Dedet 1990a:90.
107. See Py 1990c:76.
108. Arcelin 1990:201.
109. See Dietler 1990b, 2005a:155–163.
110. Dietler 1990a, 1999a.
111. Brun 1987; Brun and Chaume 1997; Chaume 2001; Frankenstein and Rowlands 1978; Pare 1991; Wells 1980.
112. See Dietler 1990a, 1999a, 2001, 2005a.
113. See Dietler 1990a, 2005a:103–123. A number of these basins were also found as cargo on the Grand Ribaud F shipwreck off the Provençal coast: Long et al. 2006.

114. See Kopytoff 1986.

115. Figures for wine consumption at Lattes are based on estimates by Michel Py (1999b) but adjusted on the basis of new information about the total size of the site made during the 2003 excavation season. This is obviously a crude estimate with many potential sources of error, but even if one were to double or triple the figure, the gist of the analysis would hold.

116. Py 1999b:654–655.

117. Plato *Laws* 637 d–e.

118. Diodorus Siculus V.26.3.

119. Plutarch *Camillus*, XII; Polybius II.19.

120. Dietler 1990a, 2006; Heath 1987, 2000.

121. See Dietler 2001, 2006.

122. See, for example, Haggblade 1992; Netting 1979; Richards 1939:80.

123. Netting 1979.

124. Saul 1981.

125. de Garine 1996.

126. Saul 1981.

127. Tchernia 1986.

128. Py 1999b:655.

129. Diodorus Siculus V.26; Pliny N.H. XIV.29; XXII.82; Athenaeus IV.36. See also Dionysius of Halicarnassus XIII.10.

130. Poux 2004, 2006.

131. See, for instance, Bruman 2000; Huetz de Lemps 2001.

132. Tchernia 1986.

133. For example, Geller 1993; Moore 1989.

134. For example, see Amouretti and Brun 1993; Brun 2003; Rice 1996.

135. See Dietler 2001; Dietler and Herbich 2001.

136. See Dietler 2001.

137. Karp 1980:90.

138. Willis 2002:61.

139. See Dietler 1990a, 1999a, 2001; Dietler and Hayden 2001; Hayden 2001; Mills 2004.

140. See Dietler and Herbich 2001.

141. See Dietler 2001.

142. See Wiessner 2001.

143. See Dietler 2005a:80–102.

144. For example, Benoit 1965.

145. In the terminology of Peacock 1982.

146. The only other use of the wheel was for the brief production of a local series of urns around Nîmes and Alès in eastern Languedoc during the fifth century BCE (see Py et al. 2001:585–591) and a series of monochrome tableware forms with

channeled decoration at Le Pègue in the Drôme during the fifth century BCE (Lagrand 1987; Lagrand and Thalmann 1973).

147. The large Cream–ware "urns" produced with Rhodanian subgeometric style decoration and the Form 7 urns of the Gray–monochrome series are quite probably beer pots, although this interpretation remains to be verified by chemical analysis of residues.

148. Py 1993a:124.

149. Sahlins 1985.

150. Woolf 1998.

151. Laubenheimer 1985, 1990.

152. Boissinot 2001; Brun 1993, 2001, 2003; Buffat and Pellecuer 2001; Jung et al. 2001; Laubenheimer 1990.

153. Brun 1993:325.

154. Pliny N.H. XIV.26 and 57.

155. Brun 1993:323.

156. Kühlborn and Schnurbein 1992.

157. Tchernia 1997:121–129.

158. Tchernia 1986.

159. See Alonso 1999; Alonso et al. 2008; Buxó 1997; Columeau 1978; Erroux 1976; Garcia 1993a; Py et al. 1984:317–323.

160. Compare Arcelin et al. 1982:131–137; Colomer and Gardeisen 1992; Columeau 1978, 1984, 1993, 2002, 2003; Crégut and Gagnière 1980; Gardeisen 1999a, 1999b, 2008.

161. Colomer and Gardeisen 1992:103.

162. Columeau 2003:118.

163. Columeau 2003:120–121; Forest 1994:31.

164. Garcia Petit 1999.

165. Colomer and Gardeisen 1992:97.

166. Colomer and Gardeisen 1992; Gardeisen 2008.

167. Colomer and Gardeisen 1992:97; Gardeisen 2008.

168. Columeau 2002.

169. Garcia Petit 1999.

170. Wilkins and Hill 2006:145–147.

171. Athenaeus IV.36.

172. Gardeisen 1999a, 1999b.

173. Columeau 2002, 2003.

174. Columeau 2003; Molist i Capella and Miro i Alex 1994.

175. Chausserie Laprée 2005:201.

176. Marty 2002:159.

177. Bats 1988c; Brien 2006; Brien–Poitevin 1992, 1993, 1996; Sternberg 1995, 1999b, 2006.

178. Chausserie-Laprée 2005:200.

179. Athenaeus IV.36.

180. Cleyet–Merle 1990:166.

181. Sternberg 1995, 1999a.

182. Sternberg 1998, 1999b; Sternberg and Tréziny 2005 offers an emended analysis showing new evidence of earlier deep-sea fishing.

183. Wilkins and Hill 2006:143.

184. Sternberg 1995:127–128.

185. Sternberg and Tréziny 2005.

186. See Garnsey 1999:18.

187. Wilkins and Hill 2006:112.

188. Amouretti 1986; Foxhall and Forbes 1982; Garnsey 1999; Wilkins and Hill 2006.

189. Athenaeus IV.36.

190. See Alonso et al. 2008.

191. Buxó 1997.

192. Brun 1993, 2003; Garcia 1992.

193. Alonso et al. 2008:197.

194. Athenaeus IV.36.

195. See Bats 1988a; Dalby 1996; Flacelière 1965; Garnsey 1999; Wilkins et al. 1995; Wilkins and Hill 2006; Winspeare 2005.

196. See especially Bats 1988a; Sparkes 1962; Winspeare 2005.

197. Flacelière 1965; Sparkes 1962; Wilkins and Hill 2006:20–24.

198. Amouretti 1986; Bats 1988a:33–34; Braun 1995; Sparkes 1962.

199. See Amouretti 1986; Bats 1988a:35–36.

200. Sparkes 1962.

201. Caesar *Civil War* I.36, II.22.

202. Sparkes 1962:132.

203. On Greek pot forms and functions, see Bats 1988a; Sparkes 1962, 1991.

204. Amouretti 1986; Gomez 2000.

205. Braun 1995:26.

206. Bats 1988a:46–48.

207. Bats 1988a:48–50.

208. Bats 1988a:50.

209. In contrast to amphorae and tableware, published reports on cooking ceramics at Marseille have been minimal. Nevertheless, the general impression is that CNT cooking wares dominate during at least the sixth century BCE. See Gantès 1992; Moliner 2000.

210. Bats et al. 2005:254.

211. Bats 1988a, 1995:378.

212. Bats 1988a:201.

213. Bats 1988a:202.

214. Bats 1995:378.

215. Bats 1988a:202.

216. Py 1993b: These ceramics have ground calcite temper and were fired in a reducing atmosphere.

217. Bats 1988a:202.

218. See Arcelin 1971; Py 1990a, 1993b; Py et al. 2001:831–972.

219. Such as forms CNT-LOR U1a, U1b, U1c, U5g, U5j, U5m and CNT-PRO U1a, U2a, U2c, U5b of Py 1993b. This hypothesis is based on the similarity of ethnographic examples of beer brewing pots (e.g., in Africa: see Dietler and Herbich 2007; Huetz de Lemps 2001) and the fact that, for reasons discussed earlier, we can reasonably conclude that beer was being produced.

220. Py 1993b; Py et al. 2001:835–841.

221. Py et al. 2001:833.

222. Another series of mortars was produced at Béziers beginning in the fifth century BCE, but these were not used in the lower Rhône region; see Gomez 2000.

223. Amouretti 1986; Gomez 2000.

224. Gomez 2000:141.

225. Gailledrat 2008; Lebeaupin and Séjalon 2008; Py et al. 2001:973–980.

226. Bats 1993; Marty 1999; Py et al. 2001.

227. Py et al. 2001:981–1006.

228. Py et al. 2001:981, 1007–1027.

229. See Dedet 1987:190–194; Roux and Raux 1996 for a discussion of hearths.

230. Chausserie-Laprée 2005:170–172; Marty 2002:156. See also Daumas and Laudet 1981–82:30–31; Py et al. 1992.

231. Reille 1999; Reille and Chabot 2000.

232. See Alonso i Martínez 1997, 1999; Amouretti 1986; Py 1992a.

233. Obviously, these relative percentages of ceramics need to be interpreted with some caution, as ethnoarchaeological studies have shown that small cooking pots have the most rapid breakage and accumulation rate; see Shott 1996. However, these factors should have been constant for all sites in the region and the relative differences, taken in terms of broad order of magnitude, should be significant.

234. Bats 1986:21; Marty 1999:209.

235. Marty 1999.

236. These customs describe life for the better off citizens who appear in literature or vase painting. We have very little information about the poorer classes in smaller houses; it is possible that they may have eaten seated on the floor; see Bats 1988a:51–52.

237. Dalby 1996; Flacelière 1965.

238. Bats 1988a:205.
239. Sparkes 1962:127.
240. Nielsen 1998.
241. Bats 1988a:58.
242. For the forms, names, and functions of Greek tablewares, see Bats 1988a; Sparkes 1991.
243. Morel 1981a.
244. Bats 1988a:203–210.
245. Athenaeus IV.36.
246. For example, Arcelin 1971:20–22. Py 1993b and Py et al. 2001 include all bowls under the labels *coupes* and *coupelles*.
247. In contrast to other regions such as western Languedoc, Campanian imports of the Rhône basin were heavily dominated by Campanain A fabrics that were produced at Naples and perhaps Ischia. Campanian B (from Etruria and Campania) and, especially, Campanian C (from Sicily) series were rare in this region. See Morel 1981a; Py 1993c; Py et al. 2001.
248. See Py et al. 2001:435–441.
249. Py et al. 2001:452–464, 484–494.
250. Figures for Lattes, from Py et al. 2001:833.
251. See Arcelin-Pradelle 1984; Dietler 1990b, 2005a:80–102; Py 1993b; Py et al. 2001:623–801, 1087–1115. Cream-ware was known in publications before the early 1990s as "Pseudo-Ionian" ware (e.g., Lagrand 1963) and Gray-monochrome was called "Phocaean" ware prior to the publication of Charlette Arcelin-Pradelle's revolutionary analysis in 1984.
252. Thucydides VII.27.5.
253. See Py et al. 2001:803–825.
254. See Dietler 2005:80–89 for a detailed discussion.
255. See Arcelin-Pradelle 1984; Arcelin-Pradelle et al. 1982; Dietler 1990b, 2005a:90–102; Nickels 1978, 1980; Py 1990a:544–547; Py et al. 2001:1087–1112.
256. Arcelin-Pradelle 1984:145.
257. Arcelin-Pradelle 1984:17.
258. Py et al. 2001:1091.
259. Arcelin-Pradelle 1984:13–28.
260. Arcelin-Pradelle 1984:19; Nickels 1978.
261. See Dietler 2005a:97–100.
262. Py et al. 2001:623–624, 1087.
263. See Dietler 2005a:101.
264. Py 1993a:192.
265. Dietler et al. 2008b.

CHAPTER 8

1. For example, see Dedet and Schwaller 1990; Nin 1999.
2. For attempts at synthetic treatment at various scales, see Arcelin 2004; Arcelin et al. 1992; Arcelin and Tréziny 1990; Bats 1989, 2004; Bouiron and Tréziny 2001; Chazelles 1993; Dedet 1992, 1995; Dedet and Py 1985; Dietler 1990b, 1997, 2005a; Fiches 1987, 2002; Garcia 1993a, 2002, 2003, 2004; Gasco 1984; Janin 2000b, 2005; Michelozzi 1982; Olive and Ugolini 1993; Pezin 1993; Py 1982, 1990a, 1993a; Solier 1992.
3. I use the terms *civic* and *domestic* to avoid the ethnocentric assumptions of terms like *public* and *private*. By domestic I mean simply the space inside dwellings, and by civic the space outside dwellings. Many household activities took place outside in the streets.
4. See Audouze and Buchsenschutz 1989; Buchsenschutz 1984; Collis 1984; Fichtl 2005.
5. See especially Chausserie-Laprée 2005 and Py 1996b.
6. Chausserie-Laprée 2005; see also Plan-de-la-Tour at Gailhan: Dedet 1987.
7. Dietler et al. 2008a, 2008b; Garcia 1994, 2008; Py 1990b, 1996b, 1999, 2004a, 2008.
8. For example, see Bel and Daveau 2008; Borréani et al. 1992; Chazelles 1993; Daveau 2007; Fiches 1987; Garcia 1993a; Leveau and Provansal 1993; Nuninger 2002; Olive and Ugolini 1993; Pezin 1993; Py 1990a; Solier 1992.
9. For useful broad synthetic overviews, see Dietler 1990b, 1997, 2005a; Garcia 2004a; and Py 1993a.
10. See Dietler and Herbich 1998; Herbich and Dietler 2009.
11. See Dietler 1990b, 1997, 2005a; Garcia 2004a; Py 1993a.
12. Boissinnot 1985.
13. Dietler 1997; Py 1996a.
14. Dietler et al. 2008b.
15. Lagrand 1968.
16. Dietler 1990b, 2005a; Py 1993a.
17. Py 1990a, 1993a.
18. An early rampart at Glanum has also been dated to the sixth century BCE, but without greater precision; see Agusta-Boularot et al. 2000.
19. Arcelin and Dedet 1985; Dietler 1990b, 1997, 2005a; Py 1993a.
20. Such as Roquecourbe, Test-Nègre, and Tamaris.
21. Such as Mont Garou, Roque-de-Viou, La Cloche, Entremont, etc.
22. Py 1993a:237.
23. See Dietler and Herbich 2001.
24. With the exception of Mallans, about ten kilometers north of Marseille: Py 1993a:197.
25. Tréziny 2004; Tréziny and Trousset 1992.

26. In the light of recent excavations, the appearance of this construction technique at Saint-Pierre-les-Martigues, has been readjusted from the early sixth century BCE (Lagrand 1979a, 1986) down to the first quarter of the fifth century BCE (Chausserie-Laprée 2000, 2005).

27. See Py 1990a:638–642.

28. Charmasson 1981; Dedet 1973:5.

29. Duval 1998; Lagrand 1981, 1986. La Monédière, in the lower Hérault valley is another site with early mud-brick architecture without a rectilinear settlement plan; see Nickels 1989.

30. The stone wall technique is well attested in elevation at sites such as Le Marduel, Nages, and Plan de la Tour: Dedet 1987; Py 1990a; Py et al. 1994.

31. For example, see Courbin and Gilles 1976 on Saint-Etienne-de-Dions.

32. Audouze and Buchsenschutz 1991.

33. See Chazelles-Gazzal 1997:190 and Dedet 1987.

34. Nîmes, Caissargues, Beaucaire, and Tarascon are all 30 to 40 kilometers from the sea, Le Marduel is just over 50 kilometers, and Le Pègue is about 110 kilometers.

35. Chazelles-Gazzal 1997.

36. Kimmig 1983.

37. Chazelles-Gazzal 1997:54.

38. Chazelles-Gazzal 1997:49–55.

39. Gantès and Moliner 1990:9.

40. Nickels 1995.

41. Gasco 1994.

42. Barruol 1971; Solier 1976–1978.

43. Nickels 1983, 1989.

44. Chazelles-Gazzal 1997.

45. Chazelles-Gazzal 1997; Lebeaupin and Séjalon 2008; Roux 2008.

46. Arcelin et al. 1982.

47. Barruol and Py 1978.

48. Ugolini and Pezin 1993.

49. Solier 1992.

50. Boissinot and Gantès 2000.

51. Py 1978, 1990a.

52. For example, Arcelin and Dedet 1985; Py 1982, 1990a, 1993a.

53. See Herbich and Dietler 2009; Rapaport 1969.

54. A few sites, such as those at Mont-Aurélian in the Var (Bérato et al. 1994) and Mont-Valence at Fontvieille in the Alpilles (Arcelin and Bremond 1977), do seem to have been more temporary settlements exploiting pastoralist environments; but these sites emphasize, by contrast, the similarities in the nature of the occupation of most other Early Iron Age sites whether in wattle-and-daub, stone, or mud brick.

55. Py et al. 1984a:327–330.

56. Py et al. 1984a:329.

57. Lebeaupin and Séjalon 2008; Roux and Chabal 1996. A similar phenomenon is observable at La Monédière, near Agde, in the fifth century BCE: Nickels 1989.

58. Py 1993a.

59. See Dietler and Herbich 1998; Herbich and Dietler 2009.

60. Chabal 1989; Loublier 1992.

61. Ambert and Chabal 1992:22.

62. The major time consuming factor is drying the bricks. See Chazelles-Gazzal 1997:58; Fathy 1970.

63. See Reille 1996.

64. The Luo people of Kenya have demonstrated this clearly in their partial shift from round to rectangular house forms. In this context, the more difficult adaptation was from conical to pyramidal shaped thatched roofs to accommodate the new house form. But this was also mastered quickly. See Dietler and Herbich 1998; Herbich and Dietler 2009.

65. Dedet 1987, 1990b, 1995.

66. Duval 1998, 2000; Lagrand 1963, 1986.

67. Belarte 2008; Py 1996a, 1999b, 2008.

68. Chazelles 1996:305–307; Chazelles-Gazzal 1997:135–139.

69. Belarte and Py 2004.

70. Chazelles 1990:142–143, 1996:296.

71. Arcelin 1993.

72. Dufraigne 2000:200–201.

73. Hermary et al. 1999:75; Marcet and Sanmartí 1989:109.

74. Py 1990a.

75. Dispositions toward cleanliness varied considerably among sites and between different periods at the same sites.

76. Dedet 1987:190–194; Roux and Raux 1996.

77. Dedet 1987:190.

78. Michelozzi 1982:31–32.

79. Chausserie-Laprée 2005; Gantès 1990c:74.

80. Roux and Raux 1996.

81. Chausserie-Laprée 2005; Dedet 1987:194–196; Py 1996a.

82. Tierney 1960:252. Diodorus Siculus V.32.7.

83. Chausserie-Laprée 2005:170–172; Marty 2002:156.

84. See Chazelles 1997:159–172; Dedet 1987:23–32; Dufraigne 2000:201.

85. Chazelles 1996:280–283.

86. In the post-Mycenaean world, roof tiles were developed again in the first half of the seventh century BCE around Corinth (initially for temples only) and became popular in many parts of the eastern and central Mediterranean during the last

half of that century. They had become a standard feature of domestic architecture in Etruria by the sixth century BCE, although Greece lagged behind in this regard, as private houses and even many public buildings were still not fitted with tile roofs in the sixth century BCE in much of Greece. The use of tiles seems to have become more generalized in the fifth century BCE, as at Olynthus: see Wikander 1990. But Massalia was slower to use ceramic tiles, even for temples.

87. Given the much greater weight of roof tiles, a switch to this form of roofing material would undoubtedly have involved a change in roof support construction as well.

88. Chazelles 1996:280–283.

89. Chausserie-Laprée 2005:156.

90. Arcelin 1993, 2004.

91. Py 1996a:246–247.

92. Arcelin et al. 1983; Nickels 1989.

93. Dedet 1990b.

94. Duval 2000.

95. See Dedet 1987; Michelozzi 1982; Py 1990a, 1996a.

96. Compare Dedet 1987:188; Michelozzi 1982:24; Py 1996; Py et al. 1984a:300.

97. Py 1993a:134.

98. If the apparent pattern of two-story structures being far more common in Provence than in Languedoc is accurate, then this may be one factor in the stronger adherence to one room houses in Provence: supplementary rooms may have been added vertically rather than horizontally.

99. Duval 1998.

100. Py 1993a:177.

101. Dedet 1987.

102. Larderet 1957; Py 1978, 1990a:692 and 659, 1996a.

103. Py 1996a.

104. A room with a commercial or craft function, and physically independent of other rooms, opening directly onto a street.

105. A room with multiple functions but no predominant one.

106. See Belarte 2004; Dietler et al. 2008b; Py 1999b, 2004b, 2008.

107. A type 2D house is, strictly speaking, two single units (without an internal connection), but these units are presumed to form a single unit because of the functional complementarity indicated by their contents.

108. Py 1996a.

109. Py 1996a:235–240.

110. See Herbich and Dietler 2009.

111. Together, these four house types represent about 57 percent of all houses at Lattes from the fourth to second century BCE: Py 1996a:249. For the suggestion of Etruscan influence, see Py 1996a:248–251. For "pastas" houses, see Nevett 1999:22–25, 81.

112. Dietler 1999b.

113. Except possibly for house 408, which is also unusual because of its metalworking furnace: Py 1996a:179–181.

114. For example, houses 117 and 301 are both late third century BCE, and 301 is the eccentric house suspected as a possible residence of a Greek merchant: Py 1996a:163–164, 169–171.

115. Dietler et al. 2008b.

116. See also Garcia 1994b:167–168; Lebeaupin 1999.

117. Bouet 1986; Garcia 1994b:168.

118. Arcelin 1987:63.

119. Arcelin 2004:255; Py 1993a:213.

120. Monteil 1999:260–261.

121. Garcia 1994b:168.

122. Conche 2001:134.

123. Arcelin 2004:253.

124. The former may also have incorporated prior blocks of architecture in their wings, but the courtyards are larger than any street and were not created simply by blocking off streets.

125. See Dietler et al. 2008b.

126. Hesnard et al. 1999:96.

127. Dietler and Py 2003.

128. Dietler et al. 2008b.

129. See Dietler et al. 2008b; Garcia 1994b:171–173; Py 1996a:212–215.

130. See Dietler 2004; Py 2004a.

131. See Dietler et al. 2008b; Py et al. 2004:164–223.

132. See Blier 1987; Dietler and Herbich 1998; Herbich and Dietler 2009; Lane 1994; Pearson and Richards 1994b.

133. See Dietler and Herbich 2001.

134. See Herbich and Dietler 2009.

135. For example, see Beals and Siegel 1966.

136. Bourdieu 1990; Dietler and Herbich 1998; Lefebvre 1991.

137. Tréziny 2001a.

138. See Bourdieu 1990; Dietler and Herbich 1998.

139. Bourdieu 1990.

140. See Py 2008.

141. See Dietler 2004; Dietler et al. 2008a; Garcia 1996; Lebeaupin 1996; Py 2004b, 2008.

142. Py 2008:125.

143. See especially Lebeaupin 1996 on the streets of Lattes.

144. Bats 2004:53.

145. Tréziny (2004) has shown that 1:3 is a fairly common standard in Greek orthogonal plans.

146. See Belarte 2008; Dietler 1999b; Dietler et al. 2008b; Garcia 1996; Py 1996a, 2008.
147. Paterno 2004.
148. Belarte 2004, 2008; Dietler 2004.
149. Chausserie-Laprée 2005.
150. Py 1978, 1990a.
151. Py 1978:151.
152. Py 1978:150–157.
153. Arcelin 1993.
154. See Arcelin 1993:62.
155. Garcia 2004:154.
156. Fiches 2002; Py 1990a.
157. Garcia 2004:154.
158. See Herbich and Dietler 2009.
159. Py 1990a, 1993a.
160. See Py 1990a.
161. Py 1993a:114.
162. Py 1990a; Roubaud and Michelozzi 1993; Roure 2002.
163. Boissinot and Gantès 2000.
164. Agusta-Boularot et al. 1998, 2000, 2004; Gateau and Gazenbeck 1999; Rolland 1946, 1968; Roth Congès 1985, 1992a, 1992b, 1999.
165. Van de Voort 1991.
166. Roth Congès 1992a.
167. Caesar *Civil War* II.1.1.
168. Tréziny 2001b.
169. Until the late 1960s, archaeological information was largely limited to the almost anecdotal data contained in Benoit 1965; Clerc 1927; Vasseur 1914; and Villard 1960.
170. See Bouiron and Tréziny 2001; Rothé and Tréziny 2005.
171. See Bertucchi et al. 1995; Conche 2001; Denoyelle and Hesnard 2006; Gantès 1992; Gantès and Moliner 1990; Hermary et al. 1999; Hesnard et al. 1999; Hesnard et al. 2002; Rothé and Tréziny 2005.
172. Bouiron and Gantès 2001:32–33.
173. Tréziny 2001b.
174. Tréziny 2001b.
175. Guéry 1992; Maurin and Sillano 2001.
176. Tréziny 2001b:53–54.
177. See Tréziny and Trousset 1992.
178. Tréziny 2001b; Tréziny and Trousset 1992.
179. Hesnard et al. 1999, 2001, 2002.
180. Gantès 1992; Tréziny 2001.
181. Gantès 1992:72; Moliner 2001a:115.

182. Tréziny 2001b:50.

183. Bana et al. 2005; Conche 2001.

184. Bouiron and Gantès 2001.

185. Moliner 2001a; Tréziny 2005.

186. Tréziny 2001.

187. See Moliner 2001a.

188. Bana et al. 2005:316–317.

189. Bana et al. 2005:476–477; Conche 1996, 2001.

190. Strabo IV.1.4; XII.1.41.

191. Gantès et al. 2001; Tréziny 2000.

192. Gantès and Moliner 1990:81–82; Theodorescu and Tréziny 2000; Tréziny 2005:236.

193. Hesnard et al. 1999:71–74.

194. Gantès et al. 2001:210–211.

195. Gantès 1992; Gantès and Moliner 1990.

196. Moliner 2000.

197. Benoit 1965.

198. Gantès et al. 2001:206; Hermary 2000.

199. Tréziny 2001b.

200. Gantès et al. 2001.

201. Tréziny 2001b.

202. Gantès et al. 2001:208–209.

203. Tréziny 2005:236. A piece of a fifth-century BCE wooden column found in the Jules-Verne excavations may be an indication of the use of wooden architecture for monumental buildings: Tréziny 2000:87.

204. Vitruvius II.1.5; Strabo XII.8.11.

205. Bats 2004; Nickels 1981.

206. Bats 1988a, 2004, 2006.

207. Bats 1988a, 2006b.

208. Bats 1988a:28–29.

209. Unlike other Greek colonies, a *cleruchy* was not an independent polity: *cleruchs* remained citizens of Athens. They were given plots of land (a *cleros*) in a settlement that served the strategic interests of the mother city. See Graham 1983:166–192.

210. This general conception was closely mirrored by Etruscan and Roman cities as well, albeit with distinctive cultural elaborations: see Jannot 2005; Purcell 2007; Smith 2007. Funerary ritual is largely excluded from analysis here, aside from aspects treated in previous chapters. The economics of publishing mandated cutting that discussion from the final version of this chapter.

211. Hölscher 2007:169.

212. The distinction between agora and temple should not be read in modernist terms as a separation of church and state, but rather as specialized spaces for different forms of ritual within a landscape permeated by religion.

213. Morris 1987:62–69, 183–196.
214. See Alcock and Osborne 1994; Bruit Zaidman and Schmitt Pantel 1992; de Polignac 1995; Pedley 2005.
215. See especially de Polignac 1995; Osborne 1987; Pedley 2005.
216. Graham 2001:345–348; Pedley 2005.
217. Osborne 2007.
218. Hölscher 2007.
219. Strabo XIII.601; Justin XLIII.5; Trèziny 2000:85.
220. Hermary 2000.
221. Moliner 2000.
222. Tréziny 2000:87.
223. Tréziny 2000:88–91.
224. Moliner 2001b.
225. See Dedet 1992; Dietler 1990b, 1997, 2005a:103–123; Gasco 1984.
226. See Dietler 1999a, 2005a.
227. See Janin 2000b; Janin and Chardenon 2000.
228. Bats 1989; Py 1993a.
229. Bel et al. 2008; Dedet et al. 1974; Fiches 1989.
230. Arcelin et al. 1992; Dietler 1997; Garcia 2004; Py 1990a, 1993a; Tréziny 2004.
231. Garcia 2003, 2004.
232. Only Pech Maho in western Languedoc seems to have had a ritual site inside the rampart before the second century BCE; see Arcelin and Gruat 2003:234–238.
233. Dedet and Schwaller 1990; Dedet et al. 1991; Vabre 1994.
234. Gardeisen 2008.
235. Lucan I.506–510.
236. Lucan III.453–481.
237. Pomponius Mela III.2.
238. Arcelin 2000; Arcelin and Gruat 2003:174–179; Brun and Michel 2000; Garcia 2003.
239. The ditch was filled with barrow dumps of broken amphorae of good-quality wine from Campania and Brindisi, constituting about 90 percent of the material, and then covered rapidly. See Nin 2000; and Poux 2004, 2006 for the Auvergne.
240. Arcelin et al. 1992; Arcelin and Gruat 2003; Garcia 2003, 2006.
241. Arcelin and Gruat 2003.
242. For a typology, see Bessac and Bouloumié 1985.
243. Coignard et al. 1998.
244. For instance, see Arcelin 2000; Arcelin et al. 1992; Arcelin and Gruat 2003; Bessac and Bouloumié 1985; Bessac and Chausserie-Laprée 1992; Dedet 1992; Garcia 2003; Lagrand 1981.
245. Garcia 2003:225; Arcelin and Gruat 2003:193 suggest an even earlier date range from the ninth to sixth centuries BCE.

246. Arcelin et al. 1992.
247. Py et al. 1994.
248. Dietler and Py 2003; Janin and Py 2008.
249. Garcia 2003; Guillaumet and Rapin 2000.
250. Arcelin et al. 1992; Py 1990a:816–819.
251. Chaume et al. 2000.
252. Coignard and Coignard 1991; Coignard et al. 1998.
253. Arcelin et al. 1992.
254. Garcia 2003. Arcelin and Gruat 2003:193 argue for desacralization, given the fact that some were broken or reworked.
255. Garcia 2003.
256. Roth Congès 1999.
257. Garcia 2003.
258. Arcelin et al. 1992.
259. Roth Congès 1985, 1992a, 1992c; Guillet et al. 1992.
260. Boissinot and Lescure 1998.
261. Barbet 1991, 1992.
262. Boissinot and Gantès 2000; Boissinot and Lescure 1998.
263. Arcelin 1993; Salviat 1993.
264. Marty 1999:209.
265. Chabot 2000.
266. Arcelin et al. 1992; Arcelin and Gruat 2003.
267. Arcelin et al. 1992; Arcelin and Gruat 2003; Benoit 1964.
268. Diodorus V.29; Strabo IV.4.5; see also Hermary 2003.
269. Armit 2006:9–10.
270. Arcelin et al. 2003:201–209.
271. Wallace 1965.
272. Kehoe 1989; Shadle 2002.
273. Justin XLIII.4.

CHAPTER 9

1. Paterno 2004.
2. See Dietler 2004.
3. Paterno 2004.
4. Piquès and Buxó 2005.
5. Piquès and Martínez 2008.
6. Woolf 1998.

REFERENCES

Abu El-Haj, N.

    2001 *Facts on the Ground: Archaeological Practice and Territorial Self Fashioning in Israeli Society*. University of Chicago Press, Chicago.

Adroher, A., and C. Sanchez

    2004 La céramique du quartier 30–35. Évolutions, implications historiques et économiques. In Py 2004a, pp. 319–344.

Agusta-Boularot, S., M. Christol, M. Gazenbeek, Y. Marcadal, V. Matthieu, J.-L. Paillet, A. Roth Congès, J.-C. Sourisseau, and H. Tréziny

    2004 Dix ans de fouilles et recherches à Glanum (Saint-Rémy-de-Provence): 1992–2002. *Journal of Roman Archaeology* 17:26–56.

Agusta-Boularot, S., M. Gazenbeek, Y. Marcadal, and J.-L. Paillet

    1998 Glanum, l'extension de la ville et sa périphérie. *Les Dossiers d'Archéologie* 237:20–25.

    2000 Alimentation en eau et système défensif de l'oppidum de Glanum à l'époque préromaine. In Chausserie-Laprée 2000, pp. 185–188.

Agusta-Boularot, S., and X. Lafon (editors)

    2004 *Des Ibères aux Vénètes*. École Française de Rome, Rome.

Ahmad, A.

    1992 *In Theory: Classes, Nations, Literatures*. Verso, London.

Akyeampong, E.

    1996 *Drink, Power, and Cultural Change: A Social History of Alcohol in Ghana, c. 1800 to Recent Times*. Currey, Oxford.

Alcock, S., T. N. D'Altroy, K. D. Morrison, and C. M. Sinopoli (editors)

    2001 *Empires: Perspectives from Archaeology and History*. Cambridge University Press, Cambridge.

Alcock, S., and R. Osborne (editors)

    1994 *Placing the Gods: Sanctuaries and Sacred Space in Ancient Greece*. Oxford University Press, New York.

    2007 *Classical Archaeology*. Blackwell, Oxford.

Alonso i Martínez, N.

1997 Origen y expansión del molino rotavo bajo en el Mediterráneo occidental. In Garcia and Meeks, pp. 15–19.

1999 *De la llavor a la farina: Els processos agrícoles protohistòrics a la Catalunya occidental.* Monographies d'Archéologie Méditerranéenne 4. CNRS, Lattes, France.

Alonso, N., R. Buxó, and N. Rovira

2008 Archéobotanique des semences et des fruits de *Lattara*. *Gallia* 65:193–200.

Ambert, M., and L. Chabal

1992 L'environment de Lattara (Hérault): Potentialités et contraintes. In Py 1992A, pp. 9–26.

Ambler, C.

2003 Alcohol and the slave trade in West Africa, 1400–1850. In *Drugs, Labor, and Colonial Expansion*, edited by W. Jankowiak and B. Bradburd, pp. 73–87. University of Arizona Press, Tucson.

Amin, S.

1976 *Imperialism and Unequal Development.* Monthly Review Press, New York.

Amouretti, M.-C.

1986 *Le pain et l'huile dans la Grèce antique: De l'araire au moulin.* Annales Littéraires de l'Université de Besançon 328. Les Belles Lettres, Paris.

Amouretti, M.-C., and J.-P. Brun (editors)

1993 *La production du vin et de l'huile en Méditerranée.* Boccard, Paris.

Amselle, J.-L.

1998 *Mestizo Logics: Anthropology of Identity in Africa and Elsewhere.* Stanford University Press, Stanford.

Anderson, B.

1991 *Imagined Communities: Reflections on the Origin and Spread of Nationalism.* Second ed. Verso, London.

Ando, C.

2000 *Imperial Ideology and Provincial Loyalty in the Roman Empire.* University of California Press, Berkeley.

Anonymous (editor)

2006 *Gli Etruschi de Genova ad Ampurias. Atti des XXIV Convegno de Studi Etruschi ed Italici, Marseille—Lattes, 2002.* Instituti Editoriali e Poligrafici Internazionali, Pisa.

Appadurai, A.

1986 Introduction: Commodities and the politics of value. In *The Social Life of Things: Commodities in Cultural Perspective*, edited by A. Appadurai, pp. 3–63. Cambridge University Press, Cambridge.

1996 *Modernity at Large: Cultural Dimensions of Globalization.* University of Minnesota Press, Minneapolis.

Aquilué, X., P. Castanyer, M. Santos, and J. Tremoleda

2002 Nuevos datos acerca del hábitat arcaico de la *Palaia Polis* de Ampurias. *Pallas* 58:301–328.

Arafat, K., and C. Morgan

    1994 Athens, Etruria and the Heuneburg: Mutual misconceptions in the study of Greek-barbarian relations. In Morris 1994b, pp. 108–134.

Arcelin, P.

    1971 *La céramique indigène modelée de Saint-Blaise (Saint-Mitre-les-Remparts, Bouches-du-Rhône)*. Editions Ophrys, Paris.

    1986 Le territoire de Marseille grecque dans son contexte indigène. In Bats and Tréziny 1986, pp. 43–104.

    1990 La diffusion des amphores massaliètes en Provence occidentale. In Bats 1990a, pp. 191–205.

    1992a Salles hypostyles, portiques et espaces cultuels d'Entremont et de Saint-Blaise (B.-du-Rh.). *Documents d'Archéologie Méridionale* 15:13–27.

    1992b Société indigène et propositions culturelles massaliotes en basse Provence occidentale. In Bats et al. 1992, pp. 305–336.

    1993 L'habitat d'Entremont: urbanisme et modes architecturaux. In Coutagne 1993, pp. 57–98.

    1995 Arles protohistoriques, centre d'échanges économiques et culturels. In Arcelin et al. 1995, pp. 325–338.

    1999 L'habitat dans l'image sociale des Gauois du Midi: la question des résidences aristocratiques. In *Habitat et société*, edited by F. Braemer, S. Cleuziou and A. Coudart, pp. 439–479. Actes des XIXe rencontres internationales d'archéologie et d'histoire d'Antibes 1998. APDCA, Antibes.

    2000 Arles protohistorique, agglomération et structuration urbaine. In *Espaces et urbanisme à Arles, des origines à nos jours. Actes du Colloque d'Arles, 1998*, edited by M. Baudat, pp. 7–23. Groupe Archéologique Arlésien, Arles.

    2004 Les prémices du phénomène urbain à l'Âge du Fer en Gaule méridionale: les agglomerations de la basse vallée du Rhône. *Gallia* 61:223–269.

Arcelin, P., C. Arcelin-Pradelle, and Y. Gasco

    1982 Le village protohistorique du Mont-Garou (Sanary, Var). Les premières manifestations de l'impérialisme marseillais sur la côte provençale. *Documents d'Archéologie Méridionale* 5:53–137.

Arcelin, P., and J. Bremond

    1977 Le gisement protohistorique du Mont-Valence, commune de Fontvieille (Bouches-du-Rhône). *Cypsela* 2:161–172.

Arcelin, P., and B. Dedet

    1985 Les enceintes protohistoriques du Midi méditerranéen des origines à la fin du IIe s. av. J.-C. In Dedet and Py 1985, pp. 11–37.

Arcelin, P., B. Dedet, and M. Schwaller

    1992 Espaces publics, espaces religieux protohistoriques en Gaule méridionale. *Documents d'Archéologie Méridionale* 15:181–242.

Arcelin, P., and P. Ferrando

    2000 L'habitat fortifié du Mourre Pela au premier Âge du Fer. In Chausserie-Laprée 2000, pp. 194–196.

Arcelin, P., and P. Gruat

2003 La France du Sud-Est (Languedoc-Roussillon, Midi-Pyrénées, Provence-Alpes-Côte d'Azur). *Gallia* 60:1–268.

Arcelin, P., C. Pradelle, J. Rigoir, and Y. Rigoir

1983 Note sur des structures primitives de l'habitat protohistorique de Saint-Blaise (Saint-Mitre-les-Remparts, B.-du-Rh.). *Documents d'Archéologie Méridionale* 6:138–143.

Arcelin, P., and H. Tréziny

1990 Les habitats indigènes des environs de Marseille grecque. In *Voyage en Massalie: 100 ans d'archéologie en Gaule du Sud*, pp. 26–31. Edisud, Marseille.

Arcelin-Pradelle, C.

1984 *La céramique grise monochrome en Provence.* Supplement 10 of the Révue Archéologique de Narbonnaise. Boccard, Paris.

Arcelin-Pradelle, C., B. Dedet, and M. Py

1982 La céramique grise monochrome en Languedoc oriental. *Documents d'Archéologie Méridionale* 15:19–67.

Aristotle

1943 *Aristotle's Politics.* Translated by B. Jowett. Modern Library, New York.

Armit, I.

2006 Inside Kurtz's compound: Headhunting and the human body in prehistoric Europe. In *Skull Collection, Modification and Decoration*, edited by M. Bonogofsky, pp. 1–13. BAR International Series 1539, Oxford.

Armit, I., C. Knüsel, J. Robb, and R. Schulting

2006 Warfare and violence in prehistoric Europe: An introduction. *Journal of Conflict Archaeology* 2(1):1–11.

Arnaud, P.

2005 *Les routes de la navigation antiques. Itinéraires en Méditerranée.* Errance, Paris.

Arnaud, P., and M. Moréna

2004 À la recherche d'Antipolis grecque: l'apport des opérations récentes. In Agusta-Boularot and Lafon 2004, pp. 227–250.

Arribas, A.

1987 El Sec: presentación. *Revue des Études Anciennes* 89(3–4):15–20.

Ashcroft, B.

1996 On the hyphen in post-colonial. *New Literatures Review* 32:23–32.

Athenaeus

1927–1941 *The Deipnosophists.* Translated by C. B. Gulick. Loeb Classical Library. 7 vols. Heinemann, London.

Aubet, M. E.

1993 *The Phoenicians and the West: Politics, Colonies and Trade.* Cambridge University Press, Cambridge.

Audouze, F., and O. Buchsenschutz

1991 *Towns, Villages and Countryside of Celtic Europe.* Batsford, London.

Auslander, L.

1996 *Taste and Power: Furnishing Modern France.* University of California Press, Berkeley.

Avienus

   1977   *Ora Maritima or Description of the Seacoast [From Brittany Round to Massilia].* Translated by J. P. Murphy. Ares Publishers, Chicago.

Azuar, R., P. Rouillard, E. Gailledrat, P. Moret, F. Sala, and A. Badie

   1998   El asentamiento orientalizante e ibérico antiguo de "La Rabita," Guardamar del Segura (Alicante). Avance de las excavaciones 1996–1998. *Trabajos de Prehistoria* 55(2):111–126.

Badie, A., E. Gailledrat, P. Moret, P. Rouillard, M. J. Sánchez, and P. Sillières

   2000   *Le site antique de La Picola à Santa Pola (Alicante, Espagne).* Casa de Velázquez, Madrid.

Bakhtin, M. I.

   1981   *The Dialogic Imagination: Four Essays.* Translated by C. Emerson and M. Holquist. University of Texas Press, Austin.

Ballantyne, T., and A. Burton (editors)

   2005   *Bodies in Contact: Rethinking Colonial Encounters in World History.* Duke University Press, Durham, NC.

Bana, C., S. Bien, J.-L. Bizot, et al.

   2005   Pré-inventaire archéologique de Marseille: Marseille centre. In Rothé and Tréziny 2005, pp. 308–601.

Barbet, A.

   1991   Roquepertuse et la polychromie en Gaule méridionale à l'époque préromaine. *Documents d'Archéologie Méridionale* 14:53–82.

   1992   Polychromie des nouvelles sculptures préromaines de Nîmes (Gard). *Documents d'Archéologie Méridionale* 15:96–102.

Barker, G., and T. Rasmussen

   1986   *The Etruscans.* Blackwell Publishers, Oxford.

Barruol, G.

   1973   Les Elisyques et leur capitale Naro/Narbo. In *Narbonne. Archéologie et Histoire. XLVe Congrès de la Féderation Historique du Languedoc méditerranéen et du Roussillon (Narbonne, 14–16 avril 1972),* pp. 49–55. Fédération historique du Languedoc méditerranéen et du Roussillon, Montpellier.

   1975   *Les peuples préromains du sud-est de la Gaule. Étude de géographie historique.* Revue Archéologique de Narbonnaise Supplément 1. Boccard, Paris.

   1980   Le pays des Sordes. In *Ruscino. Château-Roussillon, Perpignan (Pyrénées-Orientales). I. État de travaux et recherches en 1975,* edited by G. Barruol, pp. 29–35. Supplement 7 of the Revue Archéologique de Narbonnaise. Boccard, Paris.

Barruol, G., and M. Py

   1978   Recherches récentes sur la ville antique d'Espeyran à Saint-Gilles-du-Gard. *Revue Archéologique de Narbonnaise* 11:19–100.

Bartel, B.

   1985   Comparative historical archaeology and archaeological theory. In Dyson 1985, pp. 8–37.

Barth, F.

   1967   Economic spheres in Darfur. In *Themes in Economic Anthropology,* edited by R. Firth, pp. 149–174. Tavistock, London.

1969 Introduction. In *Ethnic Groups and Boundaries*, edited by F. Barth, pp. 9–38. Little, Brown and Co., Boston, MA.

Baslez, M. F.

1984 *L'étranger dans la Grèce antique*. Les Belles Lettres, Paris.

Bats, M.

1986 Le territoire de Marseille grecque: réflexions et problèmes. In Bats and Tréziny 1986, pp. 17–42.

1988a *Vaiselle et alimentation à Olbia de Provence (v. 350–v. 50 av. JC.): modèles culturels et catégories céramiques*. Revue Archéologique de Narbonnaise, Supplément 18. CNRS, Paris.

1988b La logique de l'écriture d'une société à l'autre en Gaule méridionale protohistorique. *Revue Archéologique de Narbonnaise* 21:121–148.

1988c Les inscriptions et grafittes sur vases céramiques de Lattara protohistorique (Lattes, Hérault). In *Lattara 1*, edited by M. Py, pp. 147–160. ARALO, Lattes, France.

1989 La Provence protohistorique. In *La Provence des origines à l'an mil: histoire et archéologie*, edited by P.-A. Février, pp. 169–256. Editions Ouest-France, Évreux.

1990a (editor) *Les amphores de Marseille grecque. Chonologie et diffusion (VIe–Ier s. av. J.-C.)*. ADAM, Collection Études Massaliètes, 2, Lattes.

1990b La diffusion des amphores massaliètes en Provence orientale. In Bats 1990a, pp. 207–213.

1992 Marseille, les colonies massaliètes et les relais indigènes dans le trafic le long du littoral méditerranéen gaulois (VIe–Ier s. av. J.-C.). In Bats et al. 1992, pp. 263–278.

1998 Marseille archaïque: Étrusques et Phocéens en Méditerranée nord-occidentale. *Mélanges de l'École Française de Rome, Antiquité* 110:609–633.

2000 Les Grecs en Gaule au Premier Âge du fer et le commerce emporique en Méditerranée occidentale. In Janin 2000a, pp. 243–248.

2004 Les colonies massaliètes de Gaule méridionale. Sources et modèles d'un urbanisme militaire aux IVe-IIIe s. av. J.-C. In Agusta-Boularot and Lafon 2004, pp. 51–64.

2006 *Olbia de Provence (Hyères, Var) à l'époque romaine (Ier s. av. J.-C.–VIIe s. ap. J.-C.)*. Études Massaliètes 9, Edisud, Aix-en-Provence.

Bats, M., G. Bertucchi, G. Congès, and H. Tréziny (editors)

1992 *Marseille grecque et la Gaule*. ADAM, Lattes, France.

Bats, M., M. Bonifay, D. Foy, L.-F. Gantès, T. Mukai, M. Pasqualini, J.-P. Pelletier, and Y. Rigoir

2005 Les productions artisanales de Marseille: les céramiques et le verre. In Rothé and Tréziny 2005, pp. 252–268.

Bats, M., B. Dedet, P. Garmy, T. Janin, C. Raynaud, and M. Schwaller (editors)

2003 *Peuples et territoires en Gaule méditerranéenne. Hommages à Guy Barruol*. Revue Archéologique de Narbonnaise, Supplément 35, Montpellier.

Bats, M., L.-F. Gantès, and S. T. Loseby

2005 Regards sur l'économie de Marseille antique. In Rothé and Tréziny 2005, pp. 269–278.

Bats, M., and H. Tréziny (editors)

1986 *Le territoire de Marseille grecque*. Université de Provence, Aix-en-Provence.

Baudoin, C., L. Long, and B. Liou

1994 Une cargaison de bronzes hellénistiques: l'épave Fourmigue C à Golfe-Juan. *Archaeonautica* 12:142.

Baudrillard, J.

1998[1970] *The Consumer Society: Myths and Structures.* Sage, London.

Beals, A. R., and B. J. Siegel

1966 *Divisiveness and Social Conflict: An Anthropological Approach.* Stanford University Press, Stanford.

Bel, V., and I. Daveau

2008 L'occupation du territoire autour de Lattara. Quelques aspects mis en lumière par les fouilles récentes. *Gallia* 65:23–44.

Bel, V., S. Barberan, N. Chardenon, V. Forest, I. Rodet-Bélarbi, and L. Vidal

2008 *Tombes et espaces funéraires de la fin de l'âge du Fer et du début de l'époque romaine à Nîmes (Gard).* Monographies d'Archéologie Méditerranéenne, 24. CNRS, Lattes, France.

Belarte, C.

2004 Les maisons du quartier 30–35. Plans, techniques de construction et aménagements intérieurs. In Py 2004, pp. 361–384.

2008 Habitat et pratiques domestiques des Ve-IVe s. av. n. è. dans la ville de Lattes. *Gallia* 65.

Belarte, C., and M. Py

2004 Les décors de sol à base de coquillages du quartier 30–35 de Lattara. In Py 2004, pp. 385–394.

Bénabou, M.

1976 *La résistance africaine à la romanisation.* François Maspero, Paris.

Benoit, F.

1959 L'économie du littoral de la Narbonnaise à l'epoque antique: le commerce du sel et les pêcheries. *Revue d'Etudes Ligures* 25:87–110.

1964 Les "têtes sans bouche" d'Entremont. *Cahiers Ligures de Préhistoire et d'Archéologie* 13:68–81.

1965 *Recherches sur l'hellénisation du Midi de la Gaule.* Publications des Annales de la Faculté des Lettres, 43, Aix-en-Provence.

Bérato, J.

2002 Territoire et faciès culturel à l'âge du Fer dans le Var: bilan de vingt ans de recherches. In Garcia and Verdin 2002, pp. 160–172.

Bernabé, J., P. Chamoiseau, and R. Confiant

1993 *Eloge de la créolité. In Praise of Creoleness.* Bilingual edition. Gallimard, Paris.

Bernard, L.

2000 L'habitat préromain du Verduron. In Chausserie-Laprée 2000, pp. 158–160.

Bertucchi, G.

1992a *Les amphores et le vin de Marseille, VIe s. avant J.-C.–IIe s. après J.-C.* Supplément 25 de la Révue Archéologique de Narbonnaise. CNRS, Paris.

1992b Nécropoles et terrasses funéraires à l'époque grecque. Bilan sommaire des recherches. In Bats et al. 1992, pp. 123–137.

Bertucchi, G., L.-F. Gantès, and H. Tréziny

    1995 Un atelier de coupes ioniennes à Marseille. In Arcelin et al. 1995, pp. 367–370.

Bessac, J.-C., and B. Bouloumié

    1985 Les stèles de *Glanum* et de Saint-Blaise et les sanctuaires préromains du Midi de la Gaule. *Revue Archéologique de Narbonnaise* 18:127–187.

Bessac, J.-C., and J. Chausserie-Laprée

    1992 Documents de la vie spirituelle et publique des habitats de Saint-Pierre et de l'Ile à Martigues (B.-du-Rh.). *Documents d'Archéologie Méridionale* 15:134–157.

Bhabha, H. K.

    1984 Representation and the colonial text: A critical exploration of some forms of mimeticism. In *The Theory of Reading*, edited by F. Gloversmith. Barnes and Noble, Totowa, NJ.

    1994 *The Location of Culture.* Routledge, London.

Bilby, K.

    1996 Ethnogenesis in the Guianas and Jamaica: Two Maroon cases. In *History, Power, and Identity: Ethnogenesis in the Americas*, edited by J. D. Hill, pp. 119–141. University of Iowa Press, Iowa City.

Bintliff, J.

    1984 Iron Age Europe in the context of social evolution from the Bronze Age through to historic times. In *European Social Evolution: Archaeological Perspectives*, edited by J. Bintliff, pp. 157–226. University of Bradford Press, Bradford.

Blier, S. P.

    1994 *The Anatomy of Architecture: Ontology and Metaphor in Batammaliba Architectural Expression.* University of Chicago Press, Chicago.

Bloch, M., and J. Parry

    1989 Introduction: Money and the morality of exchange. In *Money and the Morality of Exchange*, edited by J. Parry and M. Bloch, pp. 1–32. Cambridge University Press, Cambridge.

Blot, J.-Y.

    1995 *L'histoire engloutie ou l'archéologie sous-marine.* Gallimard, Paris.

Boardman, J.

    1980 *The Greeks Overseas.* Thames and Hudson, London.

Bohannan, P.

    1955 Some principles of exchange and investment among the Tiv. *American Anthropologist* 57:60–70.

    1959 The impact of money on an African subsistence economy. *Journal of Economic History* 19:491–503.

Boissevain, J.

    1979 Network analysis: A reappraisal. *Curent Anthropology* 20:392–394.

Boissinot, P.

    1985 Le Baou-Roux, Bouc-Bel-Air, Bouches-du-Rhône. In Dedet and Py 1985, pp. 123–125.

    2001 Archéologie des vignobles antiques du Sud de la Gaule. *Gallia* 58:45–68.

    2005 Le pays des Ségobriges? La protohistoire du bassin de Marseille. In Rothé and Tréziny 2005, pp. 117–140.

Boissinot, P., and L.-F. Gantès

2000 La chronologie de Roquepertuse. Propositions préliminaire à l'issue des campagnes 1994–1999. *Documents d'Archéologie Méridionale* 23:249–271.

Boissinot, P., and B. Lescure

1998 Nouvelle recherches sur le "sanctuaire" de Roquepertuse à Velaux (IIIe s. av. J.-C.). Premiers résultats. *Documents d'Archéologie Méridionale* 21:84–89.

Bonfante, G., and L. Bonfante

1983 *The Etruscan Language: An Introduction.* Manchester University Press, Manchester.

Borréani, M., L. Chabal, L. Mathieu, J.-M. Michel, M. Pasqualini, and M. Provansal-Lippmann

1992 Peuplement et histoire de l'environement sur les îles d'Hyères (Var). *Documents d'Archéologie Méridionale* 15:391–416.

Boswell, J.

1887 *Boswell's Life of Johnson: Including Boswell's Journal of a Tour to the Hebrides and Johnson's Diary of a Journey into Nort Wales.* George Birkbeck Hill ed. 6 vols. Clarendon, Oxford.

Bouiron, M., and L.-F. Gantès

2001 La topographie initiale de Marseille. In Bouiron and Tréziny 2001, pp. 23–34.

Bouiron, M., and H. Tréziny (editors)

2001 *Marseille: trames et paysages urbains de Gyptis au Roi René.* Edisud, Aix-en-Provence.

Bouloumié, B.

1978 Les tumulus de Pertuis (Vaucluse) et les oenochoés "rhodiennes" hors d'Etrurie. *Gallia* 36:219–241.

1981 Le vin étrusque et la première hellénisation du Midi de la Gaule. *Revue Archéologique de l'Est* 32:75–81.

1982a Saint-Blaise et Marseille au VIe siècle avant J.-C.: l'hypothèse étrusque. *Latomus* 41:74–91.

1982b *L'épave étrusque d'Antibes et le commerce en Méditerranée occidentale au VIe siècle av. J.-C.* Kleine Schriften aus dem Vorgeschichtlichen Seminar Marburg 10. Marburg University, Marburg.

1985 Les vases de bronze étrusques et leur diffusion hors d'Italie. In Cristofani et al. 1985, pp. 167–178.

1987 Le rôle des Etrusques dans la diffusion des produits étrusques et grecs en milieu préceltique et celtique. In *Hallstatt-Studien (Tübinger Kolloquium zur westeuropäischen Hallstatt-Zeit, 1980)*, pp. 20–43. VCH Acta humaniora, Weinheim.

1989 L'Étrurie et les ressources de la Gaule. In *Atti: Secondo Congresso Internazionale Etrusco, Firenze 26 Maggio-2 Giugno 1985*, pp. 813–892. Giorgio Bretschneider, Rome.

1992 *Saint-Blaise (fouilles H. Rolland). L'habitat protohistorique, les céramiques grecques.* Publications de l'Université de Provence, Aix-en-Provence.

Bouloumié, B., and C. Lagrand

1977 Les bassins à rebord perlé et autres bassins de Provence. *Revue Archéologique de Narbonnaise* 10:1–31.

Bourdieu, P.

1984 *Distinction: A Social Critique of the Judgement of Taste.* Harvard University Press, Cambridge, MA.

1990 *The Logic of Practice*. Stanford University Press, Stanford.

2004 *Science of Science and Reflexivity*. Translated by R. Nice. University of Chicago Press, Chicago.

Bourdieu, P., and L. J. D. Wacquant

1992 *An Invitation to Reflexive Sociology*. University of Chicago Press, Chicago.

Bouscaras, A.

1964 Notes sur les recherches sous-marines d'Agde. *Revue d'Etudes Ligures* 30:267–294.

Bouscaras, A., and C. Hugues

1967 La cargaison des bronzes de Rochelongue, Agde, Hérault. *Revue d'Etudes Ligures* 33:173–84.

Bowen, J.

1989 Education, ideology and the ruling class: Hellenism and English public schools in the nineteenth century. In *Rediscovering Hellenism: The Hellenic Inheritance and the English Imagination*, edited by G. W. Clarke, pp. 161–186. Cambridge University Press, Cambridge.

Bradley, K.

1998 The Roman family at dinner. In *Meals in a Social Context: Aspects of the Communal Meal in the Hellenistic and Roman World*, edited by I. Nielsen and H. S. Nielsen, pp. 36–55. Aarhus University Press, Aarhus.

Braithwaite, E. K.

1971 *The Development of Creole Society in Jamaica, 1770–1820*. Oxford University Press, Oxford.

Braudel, F.

1992 [1984] *The Perspective of the World. (Civilization and Capitalism 15th–18th Century, Vol. 3)*. University of California Press, Berkeley.

Braun, T.

1995 Barley cakes and emmer bread. In *Food in Antiquity*, edited by J. Wilkins, D. Harvey and M. Dobson, pp. 25–37. University of Exeter Press, Exeter.

2004 Hecataeus' knowledge of the western Mediterranean. In Lomas 2004a, pp. 287–350.

Braund, D.

1993 Piracy under the Principate and the ideology of eradication. In Rich and Shipley 1993, pp. 195–212.

Bravo, B.

1977 Remarques sur les assises sociales, les formes d'organisation et la terminologie du commerce maritime grec à l'époque archaïque. *Dialogues d'histoire ancienne* 3(1):1–59.

Bresson, A., and P. Rouillard (editors)

1993 *L'emporion*. Boccard, Paris.

Bretaudeau, G.

1996 *Les enceintes des Alpes-Maritimes*. Institut de Préhistoire et d'Archéologie Alpes Méditerrannée, Nice.

Bretz-Mahler, D.

1971 *La civilisation de la Tène I en Champagne: le faciès marnien*. Supplément á *Gallia* 23. CNRS, Paris.

Brien, F.

2006 Les coquillages marins. In Bats 2006, pp. 451–455.

Brien-Poitevin, F.

1990 Tauroeis. In *Voyage en Massalie: 100 ans d'archéologie en Gaule du Sud*, pp. 202–205. Edisud, Marseille.

1992 Collecte, consommation et réutilisation des coquillages marins sur le site de Lattes (IVe s. av. n.è.–IIe s. de n.è.). In Py 1992a, pp. 125–138.

1993 Etudes conchyliologiques de quelques sites. L'étang de Berre et la vallée de l'Arc. In Leveau and Provansal, pp. 285–300.

1996 Consommation des coquillages marins en Provence à l'époque romaine. In *Carte archéologique de la Gaule: 13/1. Étang-de-Berre*, edited by F. Gateau and M. Provost, pp. 137–142. Editions MSH, Paris.

Briquel, D., L.-F. Gantes, J. Gran-Aymerich, and P. Mellinand

2006 Marseille, nouvelles découvertes grecques et étrusques. *Archéologia* 432:36–43.

Bruit Zaidman, L., and P. Schmitt Pantel

1992 *Religion in the Ancient Greek City*. Translated by P. Cartledge. Cambridge University Press, Cambridge.

Bruman, J. H.

2000 *Alcohol in Ancient Mexico*. University of Utah Press, Salt Lake City.

Brun, J.-P.

1993 L'oléiculture et la viticulture antique en Gaule: instruments et installations de production. In Amouretti and Brun 1993, pp. 307–341.

2001 La viticulture antique en Provence. *Gallia* 58:69–89.

2003 *Le vin et l'huile dans la Méditerranée antique. Viticulture, oléiculture et procédés de fabrication*. Errance, Paris.

Brun, J.-P., and J.-M. Michel

2000 Sanctuaires de l'Âge du Fer dans le Var. In Chausserie-Laprée 2000, pp. 260–263.

Brun, P.

1987 *Princes et princesses de la Celtique: le Premier Age du Fer en Europe, 850 - 450 av. J.-C.* Errance, Paris.

Brun, P., and B. Chaume (editors)

1997 *Vix et les éphémères principautés celtique. Les VIe et Ve siècles avant J.-C. en Europe centre-occidentale. Actes du colloque de Châtillon-sur-Seine (27–29 octobre 1993)*, Paris.

Brunaux, J.-L., and B. Lambot

1987 *Guerre et armement chez les Gaulois, 450–52 av. J.-C.* Errance, Paris.

Bryce, J.

1901 The Roman Empire and the British Empire in India. In *Studies in History and Jurisprudence* pp. 1–71. vol. 1. Oxford University Press, London.

Buchner, G.

1979 Early Orientalizing: Aspects of the Euboean connection. In *Italy Before the Romans: The Iron Age, Orientalizing, and Etruscan periods*, edited by D. Ridgway and F. R. S. Ridgway, pp. 129–144. Academic Press, New York.

Buchsenschutz, O.

    1984 *Structures d'habitats et fortifications de l'Age du Fer en France septentrionale.* Société Préhistorique Française, Paris.

Buffat, L., and C. Pellecuer

    2001 La viticulture antique en Languedoc-Rousillon. *Gallia* 58:91–111.

Burke, T.

    1996 *Lifeboy Men, Lux Women: Commodification, Consumption, and Cleanliness in Modern Zimbabwe.* Duke University Press, Durham, NC.

Butler, E. M.

    1935 *The Tyrrany of Greece over Germany.* Cambridge University Press, Cambridge.

Buxó, R.

    1996 Evidence for vines and ancient cultivation from an urban area, Lattes (Hérault), southern France. *Antiquity* 70:393–407.

    1997 *Arqueología de las Plantas. La explotación económica de las semillas y los frutos en el marco mediterráneo de la Península Ibérica,* Barcelona.

    2009 Botanical and archaeological dimensions of the colonial encounter. In Dietler and López-Ruiz 2009, pp. 155–168.

Caesar, J.

    1961 *Caesar's Civil Wars.* Loeb Classical Library. Heinemann, London.

    1962 *Caesar's Gallic War.* Translated by F. P. Long. Clarendon, Oxford.

Callaway, H.

    1992 Dressing for dinner in the bush: Rituals of self-definition and British Imperial authority. In *Dress and Gender: Making and Meaning in Cultural Contexts,* edited by R. Barnes and J. B. Eicher, pp. 232–247. Berg, New York.

Campmajo, P.

    1993 Témoignages écrits de la présence d'Ibères en Cerdagne. *Documents d'Archéologie Méridionale* 16:104–110.

Carman, J., and A. Harding (editors)

    1999 *Ancient Warfare: Archaeological Perspectives.* Sutton, Thrupp.

Carozza, L.

    2000 A la source du Premier Âge du fer languedocien. In Janin 2000a, pp. 9–23.

Carratelli, G. P. (editor)

    1996 *The Greek World: Art and Civilization in Magna Graecia and Sicily.* Rizzoli, New York.

Cartledge, P.

    2001 *Money, Labour and Land in Ancient Greece: Approaches to the Economics of Ancient Greece.* Routledge, London.

Cato (the Elder)

    1998 *On Farming/De Agri Cultura.* Translated by A. Dalby. Prospect Books, Totnes, UK.

Cerdeño Serrano, L.

    1978 Los broches de cinturon peninsulares de tipo celtico. *Trabajos de Prehistoria* 35:279–306.

Césaire, A.

    1972 *Discourse on Colonialism.* Monthly Review Press, New York.

Chabal, L.

1989 Perspectives anthracologiques sur le site de Lattes (Hérault). In *Introduction à l'étude de l'environnement de Lattes antique*, edited by M. Py, pp. 53–72. Lattara 2. ARALO, Lattes, France.

Chabot, L.

2000 L'oppidum de La Cloche. In Chausserie-Laprée 2000, pp. 161–166.

Chadwick, J.

1990 The Pech Maho lead. *Zeitschrift für Papyrologie und Epigraphik* 82:161–166.

Chakrabarty, D.

2000 *Provincializing Europe.* Princeton University Press, Princeton.

Champion, T. (editor)

1989 *Centre and Periphery: Comparative Studies in Archaeology.* Unwin Hyman, London.

Chapman, M.

1992 *The Celts: The Construction of a Myth.* St. Martin's Press, New York.

Charmasson, J.

1981 L'oppidum de Saint-Vincent à Gaujac (Gard). Découvertes protohistoriques. *Archéologie en Languedoc* 4:77–84.

Chase-Dunn, C., and T. D. Hall (editors)

1991 *Core/Periphery Relations in Precapitalist Worlds.* Westview Press, Boulder, CO.

Chastagnol, A.

1995 *La Gaule romaine et le droit latin. Recherches sur l'histoire administrative et sur la romainisation des habitants.* Collection du Centre d'études romaines et gallo-romaines, nouvelle série 14. Boccard, Lyon.

Chatterjee, P.

1993 *The Nation and its Fragments: Colonial and Postcolonial Histories.* Princeton University Press, Princeton.

Chaume, B.

2001 *Vix et son territoire à l'Age du Fer. Fouilles du Mont Lassois et environnement du site princier.* Errance, Paris.

Chaume, B., L. Olivier, and W. Reinhard

2000 L'enclos hallstattien de Vix 3 Les Herbues 2: un lieu cultuel de type aristocratique? In Janin 2000a, pp. 311–327.

Chausserie-Laprée, J.

2000 (editor) *Le temps des Gaulois en Provence.* Musée Ziem, Martigues, France.

2005 *Martigues, terre gauloise entre Celtique et Méditerranée.* Errance, Paris.

Chazelles, C.-A. de

1990 Histoire de l'îlot 3. Stratigraphie, architecture et aménagements (IIIe s av. n. è.–Ier s de n. è.). In Py 1990a, pp. 113–150.

1993 Les habitats du bassin de l'Aude et des Corbières orientales. *Documents d'Archéologie Méridionale* 16:57–60.

1996 Les techniques de construction de l'habitat antique de Lattes. In Py 1996b, pp. 259–328.

Chazelles-Gazzal, C.-A. de

1997 *Les maisons en terre de la Gaule méridionale.* Éditions Monique Mergoil, Montagnac.

Christol, M.

1999 La municipalisation de la Gaule Narbonnaise. In Dondin-Payre and Raepsaet-Charlier 1999, pp. 1–27.

Christol, M., and C. Goudineau

1988 Nîmes et les Volques Arécomiques au Ier siècle avant J.-C. *Gallia* 45:87–103.

Cicero

1928 *The Verrine Orations: Against Caecilius. Against Verres, Part 1; Part 2, Books 1–2.* Translated by L. H. G. Greenwood. Loeb Classical Library. Harvard University Press, Cambridge, MA.

1931 *Orations: Pro Milone. In Pisonem. Pro Scauro. Pro Fonteio. Pro Rabirio Postumo. Pro Marcello. Pro Ligario. Pro Rege Deiotaro.* Translated by N. H. Watts. Loeb Classical Library. Harvard University Press, Cambridge, MA.

1976 *Orations: In Catilinam 1–4. Pro Murena. Pro Sulla. Pro Flacco.* Translated by C. Mac-Donald. Loeb Classical Library. Harvard University Press, Cambridge, MA.

Clavel, M.

1975 Pour une problématique des conditions économiques de l'exploitation romaine dans le Midi gaulois. *Cahiers Ligures de Préhistoire et d'Archéologie* 24:35–75.

Clavel-Lévêque, M.

1977 *Marseille grecque: la dynamique d'un impérialisme marchand.* Jeanne Laffitte, Marseille.

1983 Pratiques impérialistes et implantations cadastrales. *KTEMA* 8:185–251.

Clerc, M.

1927 *Massalia: histoire de Marseille dans l'antiquité, des origines à la fin de l'empire romain d'Occident. Vol. 1.* Librairie A. Tacussel, Marseille.

Cleyet-Merle, J.-J.

1990 *La préhistoire de la pêche.* Errance, Paris.

Cohen, A.

1971 Cultural strategies in the organization of trading diasporas. In *The Development of Indigenous Trade and Markets in West Africa,* edited by C. Meillassoux, pp. 266–281. Oxford University Press, Glasgow.

Cohen, W. B.

1971 *Rulers of Empire: The French Colonial Service in Africa.* Hoover Institution Press, Stanford.

Cohn, B.

1996 *Colonialism and Its Forms of Knowledge: The British in India.* Princeton University Press, Princeton.

Coignard, O., R. Coignard, N. Marcadal, and Y. Marcadal

1998 Nouveau regard sur le sanctuaire et les gravures de l'âge du Fer de l'oppidum des Caisses (Mouriès, B.-du-Rh.). *Documents d'Archéologie Méridionale* 21(1998):7108.

Coignard, R., and O. Coignard

1991 L'ensemble lapidaire de Roquepertuse: nouvelle approche. *Documents d'Archéologie Méridionale* 14:27–42.

Coldstream, J. N.

1993 Mixed marriages at the frontiers of the early Greek world. *Oxford Journal of Archaeology* 12(1):89–107.

Collingwood, R. G.

1934 *Roman Britain.* Clarendon Press, Oxford.

Collis, J.

1984 *Oppida: Earliest Towns North of the Alps.* Sheffield University Press, Sheffield.

2003 *The Celts: Origins, Myths and Inventions.* Tempus, Stroud, England.

Colls, D.

1977 L'épave Port-Vendres II et le commerce de la Bétique à l'époque de Claude. *Archéonautica* 1.

Colomer, A., and A. Gardeisen

1992 La consommation des animaux d'élevage et de chasse dans la ville de Lattara. In Py 1992a, pp. 91–110.

Colonna, G.

1980 Graffiti etruschi in Linguadoca. *Studi Etruschi* 48:181–185.

1985 (editor) *Santuari d'Etruria.* Electa, Milan.

1986 Urbanistica e architettura. In *Rasenna. Storia e civiltà degli Etruschi,* pp. 369–530. Libri Scheiwiller, Milan.

2006 A proposita della prezensa etrusca nella Gallia meridionale. In Anonymous 2006, pp. 657–678.

Colson, E., and T. Scudder

1988 *For Prayer and Profit: The Ritual, Economic, and Social Importance of Beer in Gwembe District, Zambia, 1950–1982.* Stanford University Press, Stanford.

Columeau, P.

1978 La faune de la Vaunage pendant l'Age du Fer. *Revue Archéologique de Narbonnaise* 11:215–242.

1984 Etude de la faune. In Py et al. 1984, pp. 335–348.

1993 Le ravitaillement en viande, la chasse et l'élevage sur les rives de l'Etang de Berre (essaie d'une synthèse). In Leveau and Provansal 1993, pp. 301–314.

2002 *Alimentation carnée en Gaule du sud (VIIe s. av. J.-C.–XIVe s.).* Université de Provence, Aix-en-Provence.

2003 Production et consommation de la viande: approche de quelques singularités du littoral méditerranéen, de l'âge du Fer à l'Antiquité romaine. In *Agriculture méditerranéenne. Variété des techniques anciennes,* edited by M.-C. Amouretti and G. Comet, pp. 109–125. Presses de l'Université de Provence, Aix-en-Provence.

Comaroff, J.

1985 *Body of Power, Spirit of Resistance: The Culture and History of a South African People.* University of Chicago Press, Chicago.

Comaroff, J., and J. L. Comaroff

1991 *Of Revelation and Revolution, Vol. 1: Christianity, Colonialism, and Consciousness in South Africa.* University of Chicago Press, Chicago.

Comaroff, J. L.

1997 Images of empire, contests of conscience: models of colonial domination in South Africa. In *Tensions of Empire: Colonial Cultures in a Bourgeois World,* edited by F. Cooper and A. L. Stoler, pp. 163–197. University of California Press, Berkeley.

Comaroff, J. L., and J. Comaroff

    1997 *Of Revelation and Revolution. Vol. 2. The Dialectics of Modernity on a South African Frontier.* University of Chicago Press, Chicago.

Conche, F.

    2001 Les fouilles du 9, rue Jean-François Leca. In Bouiron and Tréziny 2001, pp. 131–136.

Condamin, J., and F. Formenti

    1976 Recherches de traces d'huile d'olive et de vin dans les amphores antiques. *Figlina* 1:143–158.

Constantine, D.

    1984 *Early Greek Travellers and the Hellenic Ideal.* Cambridge University Press, Cambridge.

Cooper, F.

    2005 *Colonialism in Question: Theory, Knowledge, History.* University of California Press, Berkeley.

Cooper, F., and A. L. Stoler (editors)

    1997 *Tensions of Empire: Colonial Cultures in a Bourgeois World.* University of California Press, Berkeley.

Corcoran, T. H.

    1963 Roman fish sauces. *The Classical Journal* 58(5):204–210.

Cougny, E.

    1892 *Extraits des auteurs Grecs concernant la géographie et l'histoire des Gaules.* Renouard, Paris.

Coulon, G., and J.-C. Golvin

    2002 *Voyages en Gaule romaine.* Errance, Paris.

Counihan, C. M., and S. L. Kaplan (editors)

    1998 *Food and Gender: Identity and Power.* Gordon and Breach, Newark, NJ.

Courbin, P., and R. Gilles

    1976 L'oppidum de Saint-Etienne-de-Dions, Saint-Marcel-d'Ardèche (Ardèche). In *Néolithique et Ages des Métaux dans les Alpes françaises,* edited by A. Bocquet and C. Lagrand, pp. 59–63. Louis Jean, Gap, France.

Coutagne, D. (editor)

    1993 *Archéologie d'Entremont au Musée Granet.* Association des Amis du Musée Granet, Aix-en-Provence.

Crégut, E., and S. Gagnière

    1980 Les sondages 1b-Nord des Baou de Saint-Marcel à Marseille, IV Etude préliminaire de la faune. *Documents d'Archéologie Méridionale* 3:91–92.

Cristofani, M.

    1983 *Gli Etruschi del mare.* Longanesi, Milan.

    1986 Economia e società. In *Rasenna. Storia e civiltà degli Etruschi,* edited by C. Belli, P. Orlandini, and P. Carratelli, pp. 77–156. Libri Scheiwiller, Milan.

Cristofani, M., S. Moscati, G. Nardi, and M. Pandolfini (editors)

    1985 *Il commercio etrusco arcaico. Atti dell'incontro di studio, 5–7 dicembre, 1983.* Quaderni del Centro di Studio per l'Archeologia Etrusco-Italica 9. Consiglio Nazionale delle Ricerche, Rome.

Cromer, Earl of

    1910 *Ancient and Modern Imperialism.* Longmans, Green and Co., New York.

Crush, J., and C. Ambler (editors)

    1992 *Liquor and Labor in Southern Africa.* Ohio Univiversity Press, Athens, OH.

Cunliffe, B. W.

    1988 *Greeks, Romans and Barbarians: Spheres of Interaction.* Batsford, London.

Curtin, P. D.

    1984 *Cross-Cultural Trade in World History.* Cambridge University Press, Cambridge.

Curtis, R. I.

    1991 *Garum and Salsamenta: Production and Commerce in Materia Medica.* E.J. Brill, Leiden.

Cusick, J.

    1998a Historiography of acculturation: An evaluation of concepts and their application in archaeology. In Cusick 1998b, pp. 126–145.

    1998b (editor) *Studies in Culture Contact: Interaction, Culture Change, and Archaeology.* Southern Illinois University Press, Center for Archaeological Investigations, Carbondale.

D'Agostino, B.

    1990 Military organization and social structure in Archaic Etruria. In *The Greek City: From Homer to Alexander*, edited by O. Murray and S. Price, pp. 59–82. Clarendon Press, Oxford.

D'Arms, J. H.

    1981 *Commerce and Social Standing in Ancient Rome.* Harvard University Press, Cambridge, MA.

    1990 The Roman *convivium* and the idea of equality. In *Sympotica: A Symposium on the Symposion*, edited by O. Murray, pp. 308–320. Clarendon Press, Oxford.

Dalby, A.

    1996 *Siren Feasts: A History of Food and Gastronomy in Greece.* Routledge, London.

Dalton, G.

    1978 The impact of colonization on aboriginal economies in stateless societies. *Research in Economic Anthropology* 1:131–184.

Daumas, J.-C., and R. Laudet

    1981–1983 L'habitat du Bronze Final des Gandus à Saint-Ferréol-Trente-Pas (Drôme). *Etudes Préhistorique* 16:1–32.

Daveau, I. (editor)

    2007 *Port Ariane (Lattes, Hérault). Construction deltaïque et utilisation d'une zone humide lors des six derniers millénaires.* Lattara 20. ARALO, Lattes, France.

Davidson, J. N.

    1997 *Courtesans and Fishcakes: The Consuming Passions of Classical Athens.* Harper Collins, London.

Dawdy, S.

    2000 Understanding cultural change through the vernacular: Creolization in Louisiana. *Historical Archaeology* 34(3):107–123.

de Garine, I.

    1996 Food and the status quest in five African cultures. In *Food and the Status Quest: An Interdisciplinary Perspective*, edited by P. W. Wiessner and W. Schiefenhövel, pp. 193–218. Berghahn Books, Oxford.

de Hoz, J.

1987 El Sec: les graffites mercantiles en Occident et l'épave d'El Sec. *Revue des Études Anciennes* 89(3–4):117–130.

1993 La lengua y la escritura Ibéricas, y las lenguas de los íberos. In *Lengua y cultura en la hispania prerromana: actas del V coloquio sobre lenguas y culturas de la peninsula iberica*, pp. 635–666. Universidad de Salamanca, Salamanca.

2004 The Greek man in the Iberian street: Non-colonial Greek identity in Spain and southern France. In Lomas 2004a, pp. 411–428.

de Izarra, F.

1993 *Hommes et fleuves en Gaule romaine*. Errance, Paris.

de La Genière, J.

1995 Les Grecs et les autres. Quelques aspects de leurs relations en Italie du Sud à l'époque archaïque. In *Les Grecs et l'Occident. Actes du Colloque de la Villa "Kérylos" (1991)*, pp. 29–39. Boccard, Paris.

2006 (editor) *Les clients de la céramique grecque. Actes du Colloque de l'A.I.B.L., Paris, 30–31 janvier 2004*. Boccard, Paris.

de Polignac, F.

1995 *Cults, Territory, and the Origins of the Greek City-State*. University of Chicago Press, Chicago.

de Sismondi, J.-C.-L.

1837 *Les colonies des anciens comparées à celles des modernes, sous le rapport de leur influence sur le bonheur du genre humain*. Imprimérie de Lador et Ramboz, Geneva.

de Souza, P.

1999 *Piracy in the Graeco-Roman World*. Cambridge University Press, Cambridge.

de Wever, J.

1966 La XΩPA massaliote d'après les fouilles récentes. *L'Antiquité classique* 35:71–117.

Déchelette, J.

1913 *Manuel d'archéologie préhistorique, celtique et gallo-romaine*. 8 vols. Picard, Paris.

Dedet, B.

1987 *Habitat et vie quotidienne en Languedoc au milieu de l'Age du Fer: l'unité domestique no. 1 de Gailhan, Gard*. Supplement 17 of the Revue Archéologique de Narbonnaise. CNRS, Paris.

1990a La diffusion des amphores massaliètes dans les Garrigues du Languedoc oriental, les Cévennes et la Lozère. In Bats 1990a, pp. 87–97.

1990b Une maison à absides sur l'oppidum de Gailhan (Gard) au milieu du Ve siècle av. J.-C. La question du plan absidal en Gaule du Sud. *Gallia* 47:29–55.

1992 *Rites funéraires protohistoriques dans les garrigues languedociennes: approche ethno-archéologique*. CNRS, Paris.

1995 Etrusques, Grecs et indigènes dans les Garrigues du Languedoc oriental au premier Age du fer. Habitats et sépultures. In Arcelin et al. 1995, pp. 277–307.

Dedet, B., H. Duday, and A.-M. Tillier

1991 Inhumations de foetus, nouveau-nés et nourrissons dans les habitats protohistoriques du Languedoc: l'example de Gailhan (Gard). *Gallia* 48:59–108.

Dedet, B., T. Janin, G. Marchand, and M. Schwaller

    2006 Les Étrusques en Languedoc central: des premiers contacts au commerce. In Anonymous 2006, pp. 145–158.

Dedet, B., A. Michelozzi, and M. Py

    1974 La nécropole des Colombes à Beaucaire, Gard. *Revue Archéologique de Narbonnaise* 7:59–117.

Dedet, B., and M. Py

    1985 (editors) *Les enceintes protohistoriques de Gaule méridionale.* ARALO, Caveirac.

    2006 Chronologie et diffusion des importations étrusques en Languedoc oriental. In Anonymous 2006, pp. 121–144.

Dedet, B., and M. Schwaller

    1990 Pratiques cultuelles et funéraires en milieu domestique sur les oppida languedociens. *Documents d'Archéologie Méridionale* 13:137–161.

Demosthenes

    1939 *Demosthenes.* Translated by A. T. Murray. Heinemann, London.

Dening, G.

    1980 *Islands and Beaches: Discourse on a Silent Land: Marquesas, 1774–1880.* University of Hawaii Press, Honalulu.

Denoyelle, M., and A. Hesnard

    2006 La céramique grecque du port de Marseille (places Jules Verne et Villeneuve-Bargemon). In *Les clients de la céramique grecque,* edited by J. de La Genière, pp. 133–140. Cahiers du Corpus Vasorum Antiquorum, France 1. De Boccard, Paris.

Dentzer, J.-M.

    1982 *Le motif du banquet couché dans le Proche-Orient et dans le monde grec du VIIe au IVe siècle avant J.-C.* Bibliothèque des Ecoles Françaises d'Athènes et de Rome 246. Boccard, Paris.

Derks, T.

    1998 *Gods, Temples, and Ritual Practices: The Transformation of Religious Ideas and Values in Roman Gaul* Amsterdam University Press, Amsterdam.

Dietler, M.

    1989 Greeks, Etruscans and thirsty barbarians: Early Iron Age interaction in the Rhône Basin of France. In Champion 1989, pp. 127–141.

    1990a Driven by drink: The role of drinking in the political economy and the case of Early Iron Age France. *Journal of Anthropological Archaeology* 9:352–406.

    1990b *Exchange, Consumption, and Colonial Interaction in the Rhône Basin of France: A Study of Early Iron Age Political Economy.* 2 vols. Ph.D. Dissertation, Anthropology, University of California, Berkeley.

    1994 "Our ancestors the Gauls": Archaeology, ethnic nationalism, and the manipulation of Celtic identity in modern Europe. *American Anthropologist* 96:584–605.

    1995 The cup of Gyptis: rethinking the colonial encounter in Early Iron Age Western Europe and the relevance of world-systems models. *Journal of European Archaeology* 3(2):89–111.

    1997 The Iron Age in Mediterranean France: Colonial encounters, entanglements, and transformations. *Journal of World Prehistory* 11:269–357.

1998 Consumption, agency, and cultural entanglement: Theoretical implications of a Mediterranean colonial encounter. In Cusick 1998b, pp. 288–315.

1999a Rituals of commensality and the politics of state formation in the "princely" societies of Early Iron Age Europe. In *Les princes de la Protohistoire et l'émergence de l'état*, edited by P. Ruby, pp. 135–152. Collection de l'École Française de Rome 252, Naples.

1999b Reflections on Lattois society during the 4th century BC. In Py 1999, pp. 663–680.

2001 Theorizing the feast: Rituals of consumption, commensal politics, and power in African contexts. In Dietler and Hayden 2001, pp. 65–114.

2002 L'Archéologie du colonialisme: consommation, emmêlement culturel, et rencontres coloniales en Méditerranée. In Turgeon 2002, pp. 135–184.

2004 La société lattoise à l'aube de la conquête romaine: réflexions sur le colonialisme et la vie quotidienne dans une ville portuaire indigène. In Py 2004a, pp. 403–412.

2005a *Consumption and Colonial Encounters in the Rhône Basin of France: A Study of Early Iron Age Political Economy.* Monographies d'Archéologie Méditerranéenne 21. CNRS, Lattes, France.

2005b The archaeology of colonization and the colonization of archaeology: Theoretical challenges from an ancient Mediterranean encounter. In Stein 2005, pp. 33–68.

2006 Alcohol: Anthropological/archaeological perspectives. *Annual Review of Anthropology* 35:229–249.

2007a The Iron Age in the western Mediterranean. In Scheidel et al. 2007, pp. 242–276.

2007b Culinary encounters: Food, identity, and colonialism. In Twiss 2007a, pp. 218–242.

2010 Consumption. In *The Oxford Handbook of Material Culture Studies*, edited by D. Hicks and M. Beaudry, pp. 207–226. Oxford University Press, Oxford.

Dietler, M., and B. Hayden (editors)

2001 *Feasts: Archaeological and Ethnographic Perspectives on Food, Politics, and Power.* Smithsonian Institution Press, Washington, DC.

Dietler, M., and I. Herbich

1993 Living on Luo time: Reckoning sequence, duration, history, and biography in a rural African Society. *World Archaeology* 25:248–260.

1998 Habitus, techniques, style: An integrated approach to the social understanding of material culture and boundaries. In *The Archaeology of Social Boundaries*, edited by M. T. Stark, pp. 232–263. Smithsonian Institution Press, Washington, DC.

2001 Feasts and labor mobilization: Dissecting a fundamental economic practice. In Dietler and Hayden 2001 pp. 240–264.

2007 Liquid material culture: Following the flow of beer among the Luo of Kenya. In *Grundlegungen. Beiträge zur europäischen und afrikanischen Archäologie für Manfred K.H. Eggert*, edited by H.-P. Wotzka, pp. 395–408. Francke Verlag, Tübingen.

Dietler, M., T. Janin, J. López, and M. Py

2008 Conclusion. *Gallia* 65:201–209.

Dietler, M., A. Kohn, A. Moya i Garra, and A. Rivalan

2008 Les maisons à cour des IIIe-IIe s. av. n. è. à Lattes: émergence d'une différentiation dans l'habitat indigène. *Gallia* 65:111–122.

Dietler, M., and C. López-Ruiz (editors)

    2009 *Colonial Encounters in Ancient Iberia: Phoenician, Greek, and Indigenous Relations.* University of Chicago Press, Chicago.

Dietler, M., and M. Py

    2003 The warrior of Lattes: An Iron Age statue discovered in Mediterranean France. *Antiquity* 77:780–795.

Dio Cassius

    1914 *Roman History.* Vol. 2. Translated by E. Cary and H. B. Foster. Loeb Classical Library. St Edmundsbury Press, Bury St Edmunds, UK.

Diodorus Siculus

    1939 *The Library of History, Volume III, Books 4.59-8.* Translated by C. H. Oldfather. Loeb Classical Library. Harvard University Press, Cambridge, MA.

Dionysius of Halicarnassus

    1950 *Roman Antiquities, Vol. 7, Books 11–20.* Translated by E. Cary. Loeb Classical Library. Harvard University Press, Cambridge, MA.

Dirks, N. B.

    1992a Introduction: Colonialism and culture. In Dirks 1992b, pp. 1–25.

    1992b (editor) *Colonialism and Culture.* University of Michigan Press, Ann Arbor.

Domínguez, A. J.

    1987 El vino y los pueblos del Norte de la Peninsula Iberica: aproximación historico-arqueológica. In *El vi a l'Antiguitat, economia, producció i comerç al Mediterrani Occidental*, pp. 376–382. Museu de Badalona, Badalona.

    2004 Greek identity in the Phocaean colonies. In Lomas 2004a, pp. 429–456.

Dominguez Monedero, A.

    1983 Los terminos "Iberia" e "Iberos" en las fuentes greco-latinas: Estudio acerca de su origen y ambito de aplication. *Lucentum* 2:203–224.

Dondin-Payre, M., and M.-T. Raepsaet-Charlier (editors)

    1999 *Cités, municipes, colonies. Le processus de municipalisation en Gaule et en Germanie sous le Haut Empire romain.* Publications de la Sorbonne, Paris.

Dougherty, C.

    1993 *The Poetics of Colonization: From City to Text in Archaic Greece.* Oxford University Press, Oxford.

Douglas, M.

    1984 Standard social uses of food: Introduction. In *Food in the Social Order*, edited by M. Douglas, pp. 1–39. Russell Sage Foundation, New York.

Douglas, M., and B. Isherwood

    1979 *The World of Goods: Towards an Anthropology of Consumption.* Norton, New York.

Ducat, J.

    1982 *Antipolis* et *Nikaia*: implantations et activités économiques. *KTEMA* 7:89–99.

Dufraigne, J.-J.

    2000 L'habitat préromain de la place du Cloître à Cavaillon. In *Le temps des Gaulois en Provence*, edited by J. Chausserie-Laprée, pp. 199–202. Musée Ziem, Martigues, France.

Dunbabin, K. M. D.

  1995 Scenes from the Roman *Convivium*: Frigida non derit, non derit calda petenti (Matial xiv.105). In Murray and Tecusan 1995, pp. 252–265.

  1998 Ut Graeco more biberetur: Greeks and Romans on the dining couch. In *Meals in a Social Context: Aspects of the Communal Meal in the Hellenistic and Roman World*, edited by I. Nielsen and H. S. Nielsen, pp. 81–101. Aarhus University Press, Aarhus.

Dunbabin, T. J.

  1948 *The Western Greeks: The History of Sicily and South Italy from the Foundations of the Greek Colonies to 480 BC.* Oxford University Press, Oxford.

Durand, J. L., F. Frontisi-Ducroux, and F. Lissarrague

  1984 L'entre-deux-vins. In *La cité des images: religion et société en Grèce antique*, pp. 117–126. Fernand Nathan, Lausanne.

Duval, S.

  1998 L'habitat côtier de Tamaris (B.-du-Rh.). Bilan des recherches et étude du mobilier des fouilles de Ch. Lagrand. *Documents d'Archéologie Méridionale* 21:133–180.

  2006 Mobilier céramique et commerce à destination d'habitats indigènes en Provence occidentale, du VIe s. au début du Ve s. av. J.-C. In Anonymous 2006, pp. 103–120.

Dyson, S. L.

  1985 (editor) *Comparative Studies in the Archaeology of Colonialism.* 233. BAR International Series, Oxford.

  1989 The role of ideology and institutions in shaping classical archaeology in the nineteenth and twentieth centuries. In *Tracing Archaeology's Past*, edited by A. L. Christenson, pp. 127–135. Southern Illinois University Press, Carbondale.

Eggert, M. K. H.

  1991 Prestigegüter und Sozialstruktur in der Späthallstattzeit: Eine kulturanthropologische Perspektive. *Saeculum* 42:1–28.

Elias, N.

  1978 *The History of Manners.* Pantheon Books, New York.

Erroux, J.

  1976 Les débuts de l'agriculture en France: les céréales. In *La Préhistoire française*, edited by J. Guilaine, pp. 187–191. vol. 2. CNRS, Paris.

Ervin, A. M.

  1980 A review of the acculturation approach in anthropology with special reference to recent change in native Alaska. *Journal of Anthropological Research* 36:49–70.

Falk, P.

  1994 *The Consuming Body.* Sage, London.

Fanon, F.

  1967 [1952] *Black Skin, White Masks.* Grove Press, New York.

Fathy, H.

  1970 *Construire avec le peuple. Histoire d'un village d'Egypte.* Gourna, Paris.

Ferguson, R. B., and D. Whitehead

  1992 The violent edge of empire. In *War in the Tribal Zone: Expanding States and Indigenous Warfare*, edited by R. B. Ferguson and D. Whitehead, pp. 1–30. SAR Press, Santa Fe.

Ferrero, G.

1914 *Ancient Rome and Modern America: A Comparative Study of Morals and Manners.* G.P. Putnam's Sons, New York.

Fiches, J.-L.

1987 L'espace rural antique dans le sud-est de la France: ambitions et réalités archéologiques. *Annales, Économies, Sociétés, Civilisations* 1987(1):219–238.

1989 *L'Oppidum d'Ambrussum et son territoire. Fouilles au quartier du Sablas (Villetelle, Hérault): 1979–1985.* CNRS, Paris.

2002 Volques Arécomiques et cité de Nîmes: évolution des idées, évolution des territoires. In Garcia and Verdin 2002, pp. 119–128.

Fichtl, S.

2005 *La ville celtique. Les oppida de 150 av. J.-C. à 15 ap. J.-C.* Errance, Paris.

Fieldhouse, D. K.

1981 *Colonialism 1870–1945: An Introduction.* Weidenfeld and Nicolson, London.

Finley, M. I.

1976 Colonies—An attempt at a typology. *Transactions of the Royal Historical Society* 26:167–188.

1981 *Economy and Society in Ancient Greece.* Chato & Windus, London.

Fitzhugh, W. W.

1985a (editor) *Cultures in Contact: The Impact of European Contacts on Native American Cultural Institutions, A.D. 1000–1800.* Smithsonian Institution Press, Washington, DC.

1985b Early contacts north of Newfound land before A.D. 1600: a review. In Fitzhugh 1985a, pp. 23–43.

Fitzpatrick, A. P.

1989 The uses of Roman imperialism by the Celtic barbarians in the later Republic. In *Barbarians and Romans in North-West Europe*, edited by J. Barrett, A. P. Fitzpatrick and L. Macinnes, pp. 27–54. BAR International Series 471, Oxford.

Flacelière, R.

1965 *Daily Life in Greece at the Time of Pericles.* Translated by P. Green. Weidenfeld and Nicolson, London.

Forest, V.

1994 Nombre de restes déterminés des principales espèces animales consommées en milieu urban en France durant les périodes historiques. Essai de synthèse. *Anthropozoologica* 19:29–57.

Formenti, F., A. Hesnard, and A. Tchernia

1978 Note sur le contenu d'une amphore Lamboglia 2 de l'épave de la Madrague de Giens. *Archaeonautica* 2:95–100.

Foucault, M.

1972 *The Archaeology of Knowledge and the Discourse on Language.* Pantheon Books, New York.

Fox, D. S.

1978 *Mediterranean Heritage.* Routledge and Kegan Paul, London.

Foxhall, L., and H. A. Forbes

1982 *Sitometreia*: The role of grain as a staple food in classical antiquity. *Chiron* 12:41–90.

Frank, A. G.

    1967 *Capitalism and Underdevelopment in Latin America.* Monthly Review Press, New York.

    1993 Bronze Age world system cycles. *Current Anthropology* 34(4):383–429.

Franke, R. W.

    1987 The effects of colonialism and neocolonialism on the gastronomic patterns of the third world. In *Food and Evolution: Toward a Theory of Human Food Habits,* edited by M. Harris and E. B. Ross, pp. 455–479. Temple University Press, Philadelphia.

Frankenstein, S., and M. J. Rowlands

    1978 The internal structure and regional context of Early Iron Age society in southwestern Germany. *Bulletin of the Institute of Archaeology, London* 15:73–112.

Fried, M., M. Harris, and R. Murphy (editors)

    1968 *War: The Anthropology of Armed Conflict and Aggression.* Natural History Press, Garden City, NY.

Friedman, J.

    1994 *Cultural Identity and Global Process.* Sage, London.

Furtwängler, A.

    2000 Le trésor d'Auriol et les types monétaires phocéens. In Hermary and Tréziny 2000, pp. 175–181.

Gailledrat, E.

    1997 *Les Ibères de l'Ebre à l'Hérault.* Monographies d'Archéologie Méditerranéenne 1. CNRS, Lattes, France.

    2008 Faciès commerciaux et usages de la céramique à Lattes durant la protohistoire. *Gallia* 65:151–168.

Gailledrat, É., and P. Rouillard

    2003 Pech Maho aux VIe-Ve s. av. J.-C. Une place d'échange en territoire élysique. In Bats et al. 2003, pp. 401–410.

Gailledrat, É., and Y. Solier

    2004 *L'etablissement côtier de Pech Maho (Sigean, Aude) aux VIe–Ve s. av. J.-C. (fouilles 1959–1976).* Monographies d'Archéologie Méditerranéenne 19. CNRS, Lattes, France.

Galton, F.

    1869 *Hereditary Genius: An Inquiry into Its Laws and Consequences.* Macmillan, London.

Gantès, L.-F.

    1990a Les amphores massaliètes à Marseille: approche quantitative. In Bats 1990a, pp. 21–23.

    1990b Teste-Nègre. In *Voyage en Massalie. 100 ans d'archéologie en Gaule du Sud,* pp. 78–83. Edisud, Marseille.

    1990c Notre-Dame-de-Pitié. In *Voyage en Massalie. 100 ans d'archéologie en Gaule du Sud,* pp. 72–77. Édisud, Marseille.

    1992 L'apport des fouilles récentes à l'étude quantitative de l'économie massaliète. In Bats et al. 1992, pp. 171–178.

Gantès, L.-F., and M. Moliner

    1990 *Marseille, itinéraire d'une mémoire. Cinq années d'archéologie municipale,* Marseille.

Gantès, L.-F., M. Moliner, and H. Tréziny

    2001 Lieux et monuments publics de Marseille antique. In Bouiron and Tréziny 2001, pp. 205–212.

Gantès, L.-F., and G. Rayssiguier

    1980 Les sondages 1b-Nord des Baou de Saint-Marcel à Marseille. I Étude archéologique. *Documents d'Archéologie Méridionale* 3:65–85.

Garcia, D.

    1987 Le dépôt de bronzes launacien de Roque-Courbe (Saint-Saturnin, Hérault). *Documents d'Archéologie Méridionale* 10:9–29.

    1992 Du grain et du vin, à propos des structures de stockage de l'agglomération portuaire de Lattes. In Py 1992a, pp. 165–182.

    1993a *Entre Ibères et Ligures. Lodévois et moyenne vallée de l'Hérault protohistorique.* CNRS, Paris.

    1993b La place de la vallée de l'Hérault dans "l'ibérisation" du Languedoc méditerranéen. *Documents d'Archéologie Méridionale* 16:47–56.

    1994a (editor) *Exploration de la ville portuaire de Lattes. Les îlots 2, 4–sud, 5, 7–est, 7–ouest, 8, 9. et 16 du quartier Saint-Sauveur.* Lattara 7. ARALO, Lattes, France.

    1994b Une maison à cour de plan méditerranéen de la fin de l'Age du fer à Lattes (l'îlot 9 au IIe s. av. n. è.). In Garcia 1994a, pp. 155–169.

    1995 Le territoire d'Agde grecque et l'occupation du sol en Languedoc central durant l'Age du fer. In Arcelin et al. 1995, pp. 137–167.

    1996 Dynamique de développement de la ville de Lattara, implantation, urbanisme et métrologie (VIe s. av. n. è.–II s. e n. è.). In Py 1996b, pp. 7–24.

    2002 Dynamiques territoriales en Gaule méridionale durant l'âge du Fer. In Garcia and Verdin 2002, pp. 88–103.

    2003 Espaces sacrés et genèse urbaine chez les Gaulois du Midi. In Bats et al. 2003, pp. 223–234.

    2004 *La Celtique méditerranéenne.* Errance, Paris.

    2006 Religion et société: la Gaule méridionale. In Goudineau 2006, pp. 135–164.

    2008 Le port de Lattara. Premiers acquis sur les phases préromaines et romaines. *Gallia* 65:131–149.

Garcia, D., and L. Bernard

    2000 L'oppidum de Buffe Arnaud. In Chausserie-Laprée 2000, pp. 126–129.

Garcia, D., and D. Meeks (editors)

    1997 *Techniques et économie antiques et médiévales. Le temps de l'innovation.* Errance, Paris.

Garcia, D., and L. Vallet (editors)

    2002 *L'espace portuaire de Lattes antique.* Lattara 15. ARALO, Lattes, France.

Garcia, D. and F. Verdin (editors)

    2002 *Territoires celtiques: espaces ethniques et territoires des agglomérations protohistoriques d'Europe occidentale.* Errance, Paris.

Garcia Petit, L.

    1999 Les oiseaux de Lattes et leur exploitation pendant l'Antiquité. In Py 1999, pp. 635–640.

Gardeisen, A.

1999a Découpe et consommation de viande au début du IVe siècle avant notre ère. Quelques éléments de boucherie gauloise. In Py 1999, pp. 569–588.

1999b Économie de production animale et exploitation du milieu à Lattes au cours du IVe siècle avant notre ère. In Py 1999, pp. 537–568.

2008 Terrestres ou volants: les animaux dans la ville antique de Lattes. *Gallia* 65: 185–192.

Garlan, Y.

1978 Signification de la piraterie grecque. *Dialogues d'histoire ancienne* 4:1–16.

1980 Le travail libre en Grèce ancienne. In Garnsey 1980a, pp. 6–22.

1988 *Slavery in Ancient Greece*. Cornell University Press, Ithaca, NY.

Garmy, P.

1974 Cinq ans de recherches sur l'oppidum protohistorique de Roque-de-Viou (Communes de Nages-et-Solorgues et de Saint-Dionisy, Gard). *Revue Archéologique de Narbonnaise* 7:1–24.

Garnsey, P.

1980a (editor) *Non-slave Labour in the Greco-Roman World*. Cambridge Philological Society, Cambridge.

1980b Introduction. In Garnsey 1980a, pp. 1–5.

1999 *Food and Society in Classical Antiquity*. Cambridge University Press, Cambridge.

Garnsey, P., and R. Saller

1987 *The Roman Empire: Economy, Society, and Culture*. University of California Press, Berkeley.

Garnsey, P., and C. R. Whittaker (editors)

1978 *Imperialism in the Ancient World*. Cambridge University Press, Cambridge.

Gasco, J.

1994 Caunes-Minervois, l'enceinte du Cros. In *Aude des origines*, edited by J. Guilaine, D. Sacchi, and J. Vaquer, pp. 142–143. Archéologie en Terre d'Aude, Carcassonne.

Gasco, Y.

1984 Les tumulus du Premier Age du Fer en Languedoc Oriental. *Archéologie en Languedoc* 9:1–246.

Gateau, F.

1990 Amphores importées durant le IIe s. av. J.-C. dans trois habitats de Provence occidentale: Entremont, Le Baou-Roux, Saint-Blaise. *Documents d'Archéologie Méridionale* 13:163–183.

Gayraud, M.

1981 *Narbonne antique des origines à la fin du IIIe siècle*. Boccard, Paris.

Gazenbeek, M.

2004 Les oppida de la ligurie occidentale: état de la question. *Collection de l'École Française de Rome* 328:251–275.

Geller, J.

1993 Bread and beer in fourth-millennium Egypt. *Food and Foodways* 5(3):255–267.

Gellius, A.

1927 *Attic Nights*. Translated by J. Rolfe. Loeb Classical Library. 3 vols. Heinemann, London.

Gérard, A.

1982 La vision de la défaite gauloise dans l'enseignement secondaire (particulièrement entre 1870 et 1914). In *Nos ancêtres les Gaulois*, edited by P. Viallaneix and J. Ehrard, pp. 357–365. Faculté des Lettres et Sciences Humaines de l'Université de Clermont-Ferrand II, Clermont-Ferrand, France.

Gewald, J.-B.

2002 Diluting drinks and deepening discontent: colonial liquor controls and public resistance in Windhoek, Namibia. In *Alcohol in Africa: Mixing Business, Pleasure, and Politics*, edited by D. F. Bryceson, pp. 117–138. Heinemann, Portsmouth, N.H.

Girault, A.

1921 *Principes de colonisation et de législation coloniale.* Larose, Paris.

Giry, J.

1965 La nécropole pre-romaine de Saint-Julien (Cne de Pézenas–Hérault). *Revue d'Etudes Ligures* 31:117–238.

Gladstone, W. E.

1858 *Studies in Homer and the Homeric Age.* Oxford University Press, Oxford.

Gomez, E.

2000 Contribution à l'étude des mortiers de cuisine: les mortiers du Languedoc occidental du VIe au IVe s. av. J.-C. *Documents d'Archéologie Méridionale* 23:113–143.

Gómez Espelosin, J.

2009 Iberia in the Greek geographical imagination. In Dietler and López-Ruiz 2009.

González Prats, A., A. Garcia Menárguez, and E. Ruiz Segura

1997 La Fonteta, una ciudad fenicia en occidente. *Revista de Arqueología* 190:8–13.

Goody, J.

1982 *Cooking, Cuisine and Class: A Study in Comparative Sociology.* Cambridge University Press, Cambridge.

Gosden, C.

2004 *Archaeology and Colonialism: Cultural Contact from 5000 BC to the Present* Cambridge University Press, Cambridge.

Goudineau, C.

1979 *Les fouilles de la Maison au Dauphin. Recherches sur la romanisation de Vaison-la-Romaine.* CNRS, Paris.

1983 Marseilles, Rome and Gaul from the third to the first century B.C. In *Trade in the Ancient Economy*, edited by P. Garnsey and C. R. Whittaker, pp. 76–86. Chatto and Windus, London.

1990 *César et la Gaule.* Errance, Paris.

1996 Voyage dans la Provence antique. *L'Archéologue: Archéologie Nouvelle* 23:5–50.

2006 (editor) *Religion et société en Gaule.* Errance, Paris.

Goudineau, C., and Y. de Kisch

1984 *Vaison La Romaine.* Ministère de la Culture, Office du Tourisme de Vaison, Vaison.

Grafton, A.

1992 Germany and the West 1830–1900. In *Perceptions of the Ancient Greeks*, edited by K. J. Dover, pp. 225–244. Blackwell Publishers, Oxford.

Graham, A. J.

　1983 *Colony and Mother City in Ancient Greece.* Second ed. Ares Publishers, Chicago.

　2001 *Collected Papers on Greek Colonization.* Brill, Leiden.

Gras, M.

　1985a *Trafics tyrrhéniens archaïques.* Bibliothèque des Écoles Françaises d'Athènes et de Rome 258. École Française de Rome, Rome.

　1985b Aspects de l'économie maritime étrusque. *KTEMA* 10:149–159.

　1987 Amphores commerciales et histoire archaïque. *Dialoghi di Archeologia* 5:41–50.

　2000 Les Étrusques et la Gaule méditerranéenne. In Janin 2000a, pp. 229–241.

Gras, M., P. Rouillard, and J. Teixidor

　1995 *L'univers phénicien.* Hachette, Paris.

Grmek, M. D.

　1989 *Diseases in the Ancient Greek World.* Translated by M. Muellner and L. Muellner. Johns Hopkins University Press, Baltimore.

Grottanelli, C., and L. Milano (editors)

　2004 *Food and Identity in the Ancient World.* SARGON, Padua.

Grumet, R. S.

　1984 Managing the fur trade: The Coast Tsimshian to 1862. In *Affluence and Cultural Survival,* edited by R. F. Salisbury and E. Tooker, pp. 26–39. American Ethnological Society, Washington, DC.

Guérin, P., and C. Gómez Bellard

　1999 La production du vin dans l'Espagne préromaine. In *Els productes alimentaris d'origen vegetal a l'etat del Ferro de l'Europa Occidental: de la producció al consum,* edited by R. Buxó and E. Pons, pp. 379–388, Girona.

Guha, R.

　1997 *Dominance without Hegemony: History and Power in Colonial India.* Harvard University Press, Cambridge, MA.

Guichard, C., and G. Rayssiguier

　1993 Les Baou de Saint-Marcel à Marseille. Étude stratigraphique du secteur III (VIe–IIe siècles avant J.-C.). *Documents d'Archéologie Méridionale* 16:231–256.

Guillaumet, J.-P., and A. Rapin

　2000 L'art des Gaulois du Midi. In Chausserie-Laprée 2000, pp. 79–84.

Guillet, E., V. Lelièvre, J.-L. Paillet, M. Piskorz, A. Recolin, and F. Souq

　1992 Un monument à portique tardo-hellénistique près de la source de la Fontaine, à Nîmes (Gard). *Documents d'Archéologie Méridionale* 15:57–89.

Guizot, F. P. G.

　1869 *A Popular History of France from the Earliest Times* 1. Estes and Lauriat, Boston, MA.

Haas, J. (editor)

　1990 *The Anthropology of War.* School of American Research Press, Santa Fe, NM.

Haggblade, S.

　1992 The shebeen queen and the evolution of Botswana's sorghum beer industry. In *Liquor and Labor in Southern Africa,* edited by J. Crush and C. Ambler, pp. 395–412. Ohio University Press, Athens, OH.

Hall, J. M.

   1997 *Ethnic Identity in Greek Antiquity*. Cambridge University Press, Cambridge.

   2002 *Hellenicity: Between Ethnicity and Culture*. University of Chicago Press, Chicago.

Hall, M.

   1993 The archaeology of colonial settlement in southern Africa. *Annual Review of Anthropology* 22:177–200.

Hamilton, C. D.

   1999 The Hellenistic world. In Raaflaub and Rosenstein 1999, pp. 163–191.

Hannerz, U.

   1992 *Cultural Complexity: Studies in the Social Organization of Meaning*. Columbia University Press, New York.

Hansen, K. T. (editor)

   1992 *African Encounters with Domesticity*. Rutgers University Press, New Brunswick, NJ.

Hanson, V. D.

   1989 *The Western Way of War: Infantry Battle in Classical Greece*. Knopf, New York.

Harries, P.

   1989 Exclusion, classification, and internal colonialism: The emergence of ethnicity among the Tsonga-speakers of South Africa. In Vail 1989b, pp. 82–117.

Harris, W. V.

   2007 The Late Republic. In Scheidel et al. 2007, pp. 511–539.

   2008 (editor) *The Monetary Systems of the Greeks and Romans*. Oxford University Press, Oxford.

Harvey, D.

   1990 *The Condition of Post-modernity: An Inquiry into the Origins of Cultural Change*. Blackwell Publishers, Oxford.

Haskell, F., and N. Penny

   1981 *Taste and the Antique: The Lure of Classical Sculpture, 1500–1900*. Yale University Press, New Haven, CT.

Hassig, R.

   1992 *War and Society in Ancient Mesoamerica*. University of California Press, Berkeley.

Hatt, J.-J.

   1959 Fouilles du Pègue (Drôme) et de Malpas (Ardèche) et leur signification pour la chronologie des invasions celtiques. *Comptes rendus de l'Academie des Inscriptions et Belles-Lettres* 1959:86–92.

Haugerud, A., M. P. Stone, and P. D. Little (editors)

   2000 *Commodities and Globalization: Anthropological Perspectives*. Rowman and Littlefield, Boulder, CO.

Hautecoeur, L.

   1953 *Histoire de l'architecture classique en France 5: Révolution et Empire*. Picard, Paris.

Haverfield, F.

   1905 *The Romanization of Roman Britain*. British Academy, London.

Hayden, B.

   2001 Fabulous feasts: Prolegomenon to the importance of feasting. In Dietler and Hayden, pp. 23–64.

Haynes, S.

2000 *Etruscan Civilization: A Cultural History.* British Museum Press, London.

Heath, D. B.

1987 Anthropology and alcohol studies: current issues. *Annual Review of Anthropology* 16:99–120.

2000 *Drinking Occasions: Comparative Perspectives on Alcohol and Culture.* Brunner/Mazel, Philadelphia.

Herbich, I.

1987 Learning patterns, potter interaction and ceramic style among the Luo of Kenya. *The African Archaeological Review* 5:193–204.

Herbich, I., and M. Dietler

2008 The long arm of the mother-in-law: Post-marital resocialization, cultural transmission, and material style. In *Cultural Transmission and Material Culture: Breaking Down Boundaries,* edited by M. T. Stark, B. J. Bowser and L. Horne, pp. 223–244. University of Arizona Press, Tuscon.

2009 Domestic space, social life, and settlement biography: Theoretical reflections from the ethnography of a rural African landscape. In *L'espai domestic i l'organizació de la societat a la protohistòria de la Mediterrània occidental (Ier mil·leni aC),* edited by Carme Belarte, pp. 11–23. Arqueo Mediterrània, 10, Barcelona.

Hermary, A.

2000 Les naïskoi votifs de Marseille. In Hermary and Tréziny 2000, pp. 119–133.

2003 Grecs et barbares cloueurs de têtes: compléments au témoignages de Poseidonios. In Bats et al. 2003, pp. 525–530.

Hermary, A., A. Hesnard, and H. Tréziny (editors)

1999 *Marseille grecque: la cité phocéenne (600–49 av. J.-C.).* Errance, Paris.

Hermary, A. and H. Tréziny (editors)

2000 *Les cultes des cités phocéennes.* Édisud, Études Massaliètes 6, Aix-en-Provence.

Herodotus

2003 *The Histories.* Translated by A. de Selincourt. Penguin Classics, London.

Herskovits, M.

1938 *Acculturation: The Study of Culture Contact.* Augustin, New York.

Hérubel, F.

2000 Mobilier étrusque en Languedoc occidental (VIe–Ve s. av. J.-C.). *Documents d'Archéologie Méridionale* 23:87–112.

Hérubel, F., and É. Gailledrat

2006 Répartition et chronologie du mobilier étrusque en Languedoc occidental et en Roussillon (VIe–IVe s. av. J.-C.). In Anonymous 2006, pp. 159–174.

Hesnard, A.

1992 Nouvelles recherches sur les épaves préromaines en baie de Marseille. In Bats et al. 1992, pp. 235–243.

1995 Les ports antiques de Marseille, Place Jules-Verne. *Journal of Roman Archaeology* 8:65–77.

Hesnard, A., P. Bernardi, and C. Maurel

2001 La topographie du port de Marseille de la fondation de la cité à la fin du Moyen Âge. In Bouiron and Tréziny 2001, pp. 159–202.

Hesnard, A., M. Moliner, F. Conche, and M. Bouiron (editors)

    1999 *Parcours de Villes. Marseille: 10 ans d'archéologie, 2600 ans d'histoire.* Edisud, Aix-en-Provence.

Hesnard, A., J.-C. Sourisseau, and F. Marchand

    2002 Le port de Marseille. In Long et al. 2002, pp. 81–105.

Hickerson, N. P.

    1996 Ethnogenesis in the South Plains: Jumano to Kiowa? In Hill 1996, pp. 70–89.

Hill, J. D.

    1996 (editor) *History, Power, and Identity: Ethnogenesis in the Americas, 1492–1992.* University of Iowa Press, Iowa City.

Hingley, R.

    2000 *Roman Officers and English Gentlemen: The Imperial Origins of Roman Archaeology.* Routledge, London.

Hirschfeld, O. (editor)

    1888 *Inscriptiones Galliae Narbonensis Latinae. Corpus Inscriptionum Latinarum, Vol. 12.* G. Reimerum, Berlin.

Ho, E.

    2004 Empire through diasporic eyes: A view from the other boat. *Journal of Comparative Studies in Society and History* 46(2):210–246.

Hobson, J. A.

    1902 *Imperialism.* University of Michigan Press, Ann Arbor.

Hodge, A. T.

    1998 *Ancient Greek France.* University of Pennsylvania Press, Philadelphia.

Hodos, T.

    1999 Intermarriage in the Western Greek colonies. *Oxford Journal of Archaeology* 18(1): 61–78.

    2006 *Local Responses to Colonization in the Iron Age Mediterranean.* Routledge, London.

Hölscher, T.

    2007 Urban spaces and central places: The Greek world. In Alcock and Osborne 2007, pp. 164–181.

Holtzman, J.

    2001 The food of the elders, the "ration" of women: Brewing, gender, and domestic processes among the Samburu of northern Kenya. *American Anthropologist* 103:1041–1058.

Horden, P., and N. Purcell

    2000 *The Corrupting Sea: A Study of Mediterranean History.* Blackwell Publishers, Oxford.

Hoskins, J.

    1998 *Biographical Objects: How Things Tell the Stories of People's Lives.* Routledge, New York.

Hovarth, R. J.

    1972 A definition of colonialism. *Current Anthropology* 13:45–57.

Howes, D.

    1996a (editor) *Cross-Cultural Consumption.* Routledge, London.

    1996b Introduction: Commodities and cultural borders. In Howes 1996a, pp. 1–16.

Huetz de Lemps, A.

    2001 *Boissons et civilsations en Afrique.* Presses Universitaires de Bordeaux, Bordeaux.

Humphrey, C., and S. Hugh-Jones

    1992 Introduction: barter, exchange and value. In *Barter, Exchange and Value: An Anthropological Approach,* edited by C. Humphrey and S. Hugh-Jones, pp. 1–20. Cambridge University Press, Cambridge.

Humphreys, S. C.

    1978 *Anthropology and the Greeks.* Routledge, London.

Hurst, H., and S. Owen (editors)

    2005 *Ancient Colonizations: Analogy, Similarity and Difference.* Duckworth, London.

Hutchinson, J., and A. D. Smith (editors)

    1996 *Ethnicity.* Oxford University Press, Oxford.

Isager, S., and J. E. Skydsgaard

    1992 *Ancient Greek Agriculture: An Introduction.* Routledge, London.

Jacobsthal, P., and E. Neuffer

    1933 Gallia Graeca. Recherches sur l'hellénisation de la Provence. *Préhistoire* 2:1–64.

Jacoby, F.

    1957 *Die Fragmente der griechischen Historiker.* Brill, Leiden.

James, J.

    1993 *Consumption and Development.* St. Martin's Press, New York.

James, L.

    1994 *The Rise and Fall of the British Empire.* Little, Brown, London.

James, S.

    1999 *The Atlantic Celts: Ancient People or Modern Invention?* British Museum Press, London.

Jameson, M. H.

    1977–1978 Agriculture and slavery in Classical Athens. *Classical Journal* 73(2):122–145.

Janin, T.

    2000a (editor) *Mailhac et le Premier Âge du fer en Europe occidentale: hommages à Odette et Jean Taffanel.* Monographies d'Archéologie Méditerranéenne 7. CNRS, Lattes, France.

    2000b Nécropoles et sociétés Élysiques: les communautés du Premier Âge du fer en Languedoc occidental. In Janin 2000a, pp. 117–132.

    2006 Systèmes chronologiques et groupes culturels dans le Midi de la France de la fin de l'âge du Bronze à la fondation de Marseille: communautés indigènes et premières importations. In Anonymous 2006, pp. 93–102.

Jannoray, J.

    1955 *Ensérune. Contribution à l'étude des civilisations préromaines de la Gaule méridionale.* Boccard, Paris.

Jannot, J.-R.

    2005 *Religion in Ancient Etruria.* Translated by J. Whitehead. University of Wisconsin Press, Madison, WI.

Jehasse, J., and L. Jehasse

    1973 *La nécropole préromaine d'Aléria.* Supplement 25 of Gallia. CNRS, Paris.

Jenkyns, R.

    1980 *The Victorians and Ancient Greece*. Harvard University Press, Cambridge, MA.

Jennings, J.

    2005 La chichera y el patrón: Chicha and the energetics of feasting in the prehistoric Andes. *Archaeological Papers of the American Anthropological Association* 14:241–259.

Johnston, A. W., and R. E. Jones

    1978 The 'SOS' amphora. *Bulletin of the Society of Antiquaries* 73:103–141.

Joncheray, J.-P.

    1975 *L'épave C de la Chrétienne*. Cahiers d'Archéologie Subaquatique, Supplement 1, Fréjus, France.

Jones, S.

    1997 *The Archaeology of Ethnicity: Constructing Identities in the Past and Present*. Routledge, London.

Jung, C., T. Odiot, J.-F. Berger, and D. Seris

    2001 La viticulture antique dans le Tricastin (Moyenne vallée du Rhône). *Gallia* 58:113–128.

Justin, M. J. J.

    1853 *Epitome of the Philippic History of Pompeius Trogus*. Translated by J. S. Watson. Henry G. Bohn, London.

Kaplan, S.

    1985 European goods and socio-economic change in early Labrador Inuit society. In Fitzhugh 1985a, pp. 45–69.

Karp, I.

    1980 Beer drinking and social experience in an African society. In *Explorations in African Systems of Thought*, edited by I. Karp and C. Bird, pp. 83–119. Indiana University Press, Bloomington.

Keay, S. J., and N. Terrenato (editors)

    2001 *Italy and the West: Comparative Issues in Romanization*. Oxbow, Oxford.

Keeley, L. H.

    1996 *War Before Civilization: The Myth of the Peaceful Savage*. Oxford University Press, New York.

Kehoe, A. B.

    1989 *The Ghost Dance: Ethnohistory and Revitalization*. Holt, Rinehart, and Winston, New York.

Kelly, W. W.

    1997 An anthropologist in the bleachers: Cheering a Japanese baseball team. *Japan Quarterly* 44:66–79.

Keppie, L. J. F.

    1983 *Colonisation and Veteran Settlement in Italy, 47–14 B.C.* British School at Rome, London.

Kimmig, W.

    1983 Die griechische Kolonisation im westlichen Mittelmeergebiet und ihre Wirkung auf die Landschaften des Westlichen Mitteleuropa. *Jahrbuch des Römisch-Germanischen Zentralmuseums Mainz* 30:5–78.

Kipling, R.

  1899 The White Man's Burden. In *McClure's Magazine*. vol. 12 (Feb. 1899).

Kirch, P. V., and M. Sahlins

  1992 *Anahulu: The Anthropology of History in the Kingdom of Hawaii*. 2 vols. University of Chicago Press, Chicago.

Klor de Alva, J. J.

  1995 The postcolonization of the (Latin) American experience: a reconsideration of "colonialism", "postcolonialism", and "mestizaje". In *After Colonialism: Imperial Histories and Postcolonial Displacements*, edited by G. Prakash, pp. 241–275. Princeton University Press, Princeton.

Knapp, A. B.

  2008 *Prehistoric and Protohistoric Cyprus*. Oxford University Press, Oxford.

Knorringa, H.

  1987 [1926] *Emporos: Data on Trade and Trader in Greek Literature from Homer to Aristotle*. Ares Publishers, Chicago.

Koebner, R., and H. D. Schmidt

  1964 *Imperialism: The Story and Significance of a Political Word, 1840–1960*. Cambridge University Press, Cambridge.

Koehler, C. G.

  1978 *Corinthian A and B Transport Amphoras*. Ph.D. Dissertation, Princeton University, Princeton.

  1981 Corinthian developments in the study of trade in the Fifth Century. *Hesperia* 50(4):449–458.

Kohl, P., and C. Fawcett (editors)

  1998 *Nationalism, Politics and the Practice of Archaeology*. Cambridge University Press, Cambridge.

Kohn, H.

  1958 Reflections on colonialism. In *The Idea of Colonialism*, edited by R. Strausz-Hupé and H. Hazard. Praeger, New York.

Kopytoff, I.

  1986 The cultural biography of things: Commoditization as process. In *The Social Life of Things: Commodities in Cultural Perspective*, edited by A. Appadurai, pp. 64–91. Cambridge University Press, Cambridge.

Kostof, S.

  1995 *A History of Architecture: Settings and Rituals*. Oxford University Press, Oxford.

Kotarba, J., and A. Pezin

  1990 Les amphores massaliètes en Roussillon. In Bats 1990a, pp. 155–158.

Kristiansen, K.

  1999 The emergence of warrior aristocracies in later European prehistory and their long-term history. In Carman and Harding 1999, pp. 175–789.

Kühlborn, J. S., and S. von Schnurbein

  1992 *Das Römerlager in Oberaden, III: die Ausgrabungen im nordwestlichen Lagerbereich und weitere Baustellenuntersuchungen der Jahre 1962–1988*. Aschendorff, Münster.

Kurke, L.

   1999   *Coins, Bodies, Games, and Gold: The Politics of Meaning in Archaic Greece*. Princeton University Press, Princeton.

Lagrand, C.

   1963   La céramique "pseudo-ionienne" dans la vallée du Rhône. *Cahiers Rhodaniens* 10:37–82.

   1968   *Recherches sur le Bronze final en Provence méridionale*, Université d'Aix-en-Provence.

   1979a   Un nouvel habitat de la période de colonisation grecque: Saint-Pierre-les-Martigues (Bouches-du-Rhône) (VIème s. av. J.-C.–Ier s. ap. J.-C.). *Documents d'Archéologie Méridionale* 2:81–106.

   1981   Le territoire de Martigues au Bronze final et à l'Age du Fer. In *Quatrième centenaire de l'union des trois quartiers de Martigues*, pp. 39–54. Provence Historique, Marseille.

   1986   Les habitats de Tamaris, l'Arquet et Saint-Pierre à Martigues. In *Le territoire de Marseille grecque (Actes de la Table-Ronde d'Aix-en-Provence, mars 1985)*, edited by M. Bats and H. Tréziny, pp. 127–135. Etudes Massaliètes 1. Université de Provence, Aix-en-Provence.

   1987   Le Premier Age du Fer dans le Sud-Est de la France. In *Hallstatt-Studien (Tübinger Kolloquium zur westeuropäischen Hallstatt-Zeit, 1980)*, pp. 44–88. VCH Acta humaniora, Weinheim.

Lagrand, C., and J.-P. Thalmann

   1973   *Les habitats protohistoriques du Pègue (Drôme), le sondage no. 8 (1957–1971)*. Centre de Documentation de la Préhistoire Alpine, Cahier 2, Grenoble.

Lambert, P.-Y.

   1992   Diffusion de l'écriture gallo-grecque en milieu indigène. In Bats et al. 1992, pp. 289–294.

   1994   *La langue gauloise. Description linguistique, commentaire d'inscriptions choisies*. Errance, Paris.

Lambert, P. M.

   2002   The archaeology of war: a North American perspective. *Journal of Archaeological Research* 10(3):207–241.

Lane, P. J.

   1994   The temporal structuring of settlement space among the Dogon of Mali: an ethnoarchaeological study. In Pearson and Richards 1994a, pp. 196–216.

Lang, F.

   2002   Housing and settlement in Archaic Greece. *Pallas* 58:13–32.

Latour, J.

   1985   L'oppidum du Baou-des-Noirs à Vence (A.-M.). *Documents d'Archéologie Méridionale* 8:9–24.

Laubenheimer, F.

   1985   *La production des amphores en Gaule narbonnaise*. Les Belles Lettres, Paris.

   1990   *Le temps des amphores en Gaule. Vins, huiles et sauces*. Errance, Paris.

Lawall, M. L.

   2000   Graffiti, wine selling, and the reuse of amphoras in the Athenian Agora, CA. 430 to 400 B.C. *Hesperia* 69(1):3–90.

Le Roux, P.

2004 La romanisation en question. *Annales, Histoire, Sciences Sociales* 59:287–311.

2006 Regarder vers Rome aujourd'hui. *Mélanges de l'École Française de Rome, Antiquité* 118(1):159–166.

Lebeaupin, D.

1996 Les rues et places de Lattes. Stratigraphie, fonction et évolution des voies publiques. In Py 1996b, pp. 103–139.

1999 Évolution d'un groupe d'habitations du IVe siècle dans l'îlot 27. In Py 1999, pp. 129–170.

Lebeaupin, D., and P. Séjalon

2008 Lattara et l'Étrurie: nouvelles données sur l'installation d'un comptoir aux environs de 500 av. n. è. *Gallia* 65.

Lefebvre

1991 *The Production of Space.* Blackwell Publishers, Oxford.

Lejeune, M.

1983 Rencontre de l'alphabet grec avec les langues barbares au cours du Ier millénaire avant J.-C. In *Modes de contacts et processus de transformation dans les sociétés anciennes*, pp. 731–743. École Française de Rome, Rome.

1988 *Textes gallo-étrusques, textes gallo-latins sur pierre (Recueil des Inscriptions Gauloises, Vol. 2, fasc. 1).* CNRS, Paris.

Lejeune, M., J. Pouilloux, and Y. Solier

1988 Étrusque et ionien archaïques sur un plomb de Pech Maho (Aude). *Revue Archéologique de Narbonnaise* 21:19–59.

Lenin, V. I.

1996[1916] *Imperialism: The Highest Stage of Capitalism. A Popular Outline.* Pluto Press, London.

Lenoir, T.

1997 *Instituting Science: The Cultural Production of Scientific Disciplines.* Stanford University Press, Stanford.

Lepore, E.

1970 Strutture della colonizzazione focea in Occidente. *La Parola del Passato* 130–133: 19–54.

Leveau, P., and M. Provansal (editors)

1993 *Archéologie et environnement: de la Sainte-Victoire aux Alpilles.* Publications de l'Université de Provence, Aix-en-Provence.

Lightfoot, K.

2005 *Indians, Missionaries, and Merchants: The Legacy of Colonial Encounters on the California Frontiers.* University of California Press, Berkeley.

Lightfoot, K., A. Martinez, and A. M. Schiff

1998 Daily practice and material culture in pluralistic social settings: An archaeological study of culture change and persistence from Fort Ross, California. *American Antiquity* 63(2):199–222.

Lintott, A. W.

1993 *Imperium Romanum: Politics and Administration.* Routledge, London.

Liou, B., and J.-M. Rouquette

    1983 *Archéologie sous-marine. Exposition: Arles, salles romanes du cloître Saint-Trophime, juillet–octobre 1983*. City of Arles, Arles.

Lissarrague, F.

    1995 Un rituel du vin: la libation. In Murray and Tecusan 1995, pp. 126–144.

Livingstone, R. W.

    1935 *Greek Ideals and Modern Life*. Harvard University Press, Cambridge, MA.

Livy (Titus Livius)

    1929 *History of Rome, Volume V, Books 21–22*. Translated by B. O. Foster. Loeb Classical Library. Harvard University Press, Cambridge, MA.

    1959 *History of Rome, Volume XIV, Summaries. Fragments. Julius Obsequens*. Translated by A. C. Schlesinger. Loeb Classical Library. Harvard University Press, Cambridge, MA.

    1976 *Rome and the Mediterranean: Books XXXI–XLV of the History of Rome from its Foundations*. Translated by A. H. McDonald. Penguin Classics, London.

Lo Cascio, E.

    2001 Recruitment and the size of the Roman population from the third to the first century BCE. In *Debating Roman Demography*, edited by W. Scheidel, pp. 111–137. Brill, Leiden.

Lohse, E. S.

    1988 Trade goods: History of Indian-White relations. In *Handbook of North American Indians*, Volume 4, edited by W. E. Washburn, pp. 396–403. Smithsonian Institution Press, Washington, DC.

Lomas, K.

    2004a (editor) *Greek Identity in the Western Mediterranean: Papers in Honour of Brian Shefton*. Brill, Leiden.

    2004b Hellenization, Romanization and cultural identity in Massalia. In Lomas 2004a, pp. 475–498.

Long, L.

    1987 Quelques précisions sur le conditionnement des lingots de l'épave antique Bagaud 2. In *Mines et métallurgie en Gaule et dans les provinces voisines*, pp. 149–163. Caesarodunum, 22, Paris.

    1988 The ancient wreck of Carry-le-Rouet: Evidence of sea transport of stone in the 2nd or 1st century B.C. In *Archaeology in Solution. Proceedings of the 17th Annual Conference on Underwater Archaeology, Sacramento, 1986*, edited by J. W. Forster and S. O. Smith, pp. 22–27. Coyote Press, Salinas, CA.

    1990 Amphores massaliètes: objets isolés et gisements sous-marins du littoral français méditerranéen. In Bats 1990a, pp. 27–70.

Long, L., L.-F. Gantès, and M. Rival

    2006 L'épave Grand Ribaud F. Un chargement de produits étrusques du début du Ve s. av. J.-C. In Anonymous 2006, pp. 455–495.

Long, L., J. Miro, and G. Volpe

    1992 Les épaves archaïques de la pointe Lequin (Porquerolles, Hyères, Var). Des données nouvelles sur le commerce de Marseille à la fin du VIe s. et dans la première moitié du Ve s. av. J.-C. In Bats et al. 1992, pp. 199–234.

Long, L., P. Pomey, and J.-C. Sourisseau (editors)

    2002 *Les Étrusques en mer. Épaves d'Antibes à Marseille.* Édisud, Aix-en-Provence.

Loublier, Y.

    1992 Premiers résultats d'analyses polliniques effectués sur cinq prélèvements de Lattes. In Py 1992a, pp. 35–42.

Loughton, M. E.

    2009 Getting smashed: The deposition of amphorae and the drinking of wine in Gaul during the Late Irone Age. *Oxford Journal of Archaeology* 28(1):77–110.

Lucan

    1993 *Pharsalia.* Translated by J. W. Joyce. Cornell University Press, Ithaca, NY.

Lucas, C. P.

    1912 *Greater Rome and Greater Britain.* Clarendon Press, Oxford.

Lugard, F. J. D.

    1922 *The Dual Mandate in British Tropical Africa.* Blackwood, Edinburgh.

Luley, B. P.

    2008 Coinage at Lattara. Using archaeological context to understand ancient coins. *Archaeological Dialogues* 15(2):174–195.

Lyons, C. L., and J. K. Papadopoulos (editors)

    2002 *The Archaeology of Colonialism.* Getty Research Institute, Los Angeles, CA.

Macarthur, J. R.

    1943 *Ancient Greece in Modern America.* Caxton Printers, Caldwell, ID.

Machiavelli, N.

    1980 *The Prince.* Translated by L.P.S. de Alvarez. University of Dallas Press, Irving, TX.

Malkin, I.

    2004 Postcolonial concepts and ancient Greek colonzation. *Modern Language Quarterly* 65(3):341–364.

Marcet, R., and E. Sanmartí

    1989 *Empúries.* Diputación de Barcelona, Barcelona.

Marchand, S. L.

    1996 *Down from Olympus: Archaeology and Philhellenism in Germany, 1750–1970.* Princeton University Press, Princeton.

Marty, F.

    1999 Vaisselle et organisation sociale du village de La Cloche (Les Pennes-Mirabeau, B.-du-Rh.) au Ier siècle avant notre ère. *Documents d'Archéologie Méridionale* 22:139–220.

    2002 L'habitat de hauteur du Castellan (Istres, B.-du-Rh.) à l'âge du Fer. Étude des collections anciennes et recherches récentes. *Documents d'Archéologie Méridionale* 25:129–169.

Matthee, R.

    1995 Exotic substances: The introduction and global spread of tobacco, coffee, cocoa, tea, and distilled liquor, sixteenth to eighteenth centuries. In *Drugs and Narcotics in History*, edited by R. Porter and M. Teich, pp. 24–51. Cambridge University Press, Cambridge.

Mattingly, D. J.

1996 From one Colonialism to Another: Imperialism and the Maghreb. In *Roman Imperialism: Post-colonial Perspectives*, edited by J. Webster and N. Cooper, pp. 49–69. Leicester University Press, Leicester.

2005 Vulgar and weak "Romanization," or time for a paradigm shift? *Journal of Roman Archaeology* 15:535–540.

Maunier, R.

1949 *The Sociology of Colonies*. 2 vols. Routledge and Kegan Paul, London.

Maurin, M., and B. Sillano

2001 Transformations de la frange littorale de l'âge du Bronze au haut Moyen Âge. In *Marseille, du Lacydon au faubourg Sainte-Catherine. Les fouilles de la place du Général-de-Gaulle*, edited by M. Bouiron, pp. 17–42. Documents d'Archéologie Française 87. Maison des Sciences de l'Homme, Paris.

Mauss, M.

1935 Les techniques du corps. *Journal de Psychologie* 32:271–293.

McCartney, M.

2006 Finding fear in the Iron Age of southern France. *Journal of Conflict Archaeology* 2(1):99–118.

McClintock, A.

1992 The angel of progress: Pitfalls of the term "post-colonialism." *Social Text* 31/32: 84–98.

Meadows, A., and K. Shipton (editors)

2004 *Money and its Uses in the Ancient Greek World*. Oxford University Press, Oxford.

Meadows, T. T.

1847 *Desultory Notes on the Government and People of China, and on the Chinese Language: Illustrated with a Scetch of the Province of Kwang-Tûng, Shewing Its Division into Departments and Districts*. W. H. Allen, London.

Mela, P.

1998 *Pomponius Mela's Description of the World*. Translated by F. E. Romer. University of Michigan Press, Ann Arbor.

Mele, A.

1979 *Il commercio greco arcaico. Prexis ed emporie*. Institut Français de Naples, Cahiers du Centre Jean Bérard, 4, Naples.

Memmi, A.

1965 *The Colonizer and the Colonized*. Orion Press, New York.

Menichetti, M.

1994 *Archeologia del potere: re, immagini e miti a Roma e in Etruria in età arcaica*. Longanesi, Milan.

Metzler, J.

1986 Ein frühlatènezeitliches Gräberfeld mit Wagenbestattung bei Grosbous-Vichten. *Archäologisches Korrespondenzblatt* 16:161–177.

Michelozzi, A.

1982 *L'habitation protohistorique en Languedoc Oriental*. ARALO, Caveirac.

Mignolo, W. D.

 1995 *The Darker Side of the Renaissance: Literacy, Territoriality, and Colonization.* University of Michigan Press, Ann Arbor.

Miller, D.

 1987 *Material Culture and Mass Consumption.* Blackwell Publishers, Oxford.

 1995 (editor) *Acknowledging Consumption: A Review of New Studies.* Routledge, London.

 2005 (editor) *Materiality.* Duke University Press, Durham, NC.

Millett, M.

 1990 *The Romanization of Britain: An Essay in Archaeological Interpretation.* Cambridge University Press, Cambridge.

Mills, B. J.

 2004 (editor) *Identity, Feasting, and the Archaeology of the Greater Southwest.* University of Colorado Press, Boulder, CO.

 2008 Colonialism and cuisine: Cultural transmission, agency, and history at Zuni Pueblo. In *Cultural Transmission and Material Culture: Breaking Down Boundaries,* edited by M. T. Stark, B. J. Bowser and L. Horne, pp. 245–262. University of Arizona Press, Tucson.

Mintz, S.

 1985 *Sweetness and Power: The Place of Sugar in Modern History.* Viking, New York.

Mishra, V., and B. Hodge

 1991 What is Post(-)colonialism? *Textual Practice* 5(3):399–414.

Mitchell, P. E.

 1947 *The Agrarian Problem in Kenya.* Government Printer, Nairobi.

Moliner, M.

 2000 Les niveaux archaïques de la place des Pistoles à Marseille: un espace cultuel? In Hermary and Tréziny 2000, pp. 101–117.

 2001a Orientations urbaines dans Marseille antique. In Bouiron and Tréziny 2001, pp. 101–120.

 2001b Les nécropoles grecques et romaines de Marseille. In Bouiron and Tréziny 2001, pp. 337–354.

Moliner, M., P. Mellinand, L. Naggiar, A. Richier, and I. Villemeur

 2003 *La nécropole de Sainte-Barbe à Marseille (IVe s. av. J-C. - IIe s. ap. J.-C.).* Études Massaliètes 8. Edisud, Aix-en-Provence.

Molist i Capella, N., and C. Miro i Alex

 1986 Estudio de la macrofauna. In *Las estructuras griegas de los siglos V y IV a. de J.-C. Halladas en el sector sur de la neapolis de Ampurias (Campana de excavaciones del ano 1986),* edited by E. Sanmartí-Greco, I. Castaner, J. Tremoleda and I. Barbera, pp. 142–217. Cuadernos de la Prehistoria y Arqueologia Castellonenses.

Möller, A.

 2007 Classical Greece: Distribution. In Scheidel et al. 2007, pp. 362–384.

Momigliano, A.

 1975 *Alien Wisdom: The Limits of Hellenization.* Cambridge University Press, Cambridge.

Monteil, M.

 1999 *Nîmes antique et sa proche campagne.* Monographies d'Archéologie Méditerranéenne 3. CNRS, Lattes, France.

Moore, J. D.

   1989 Pre-Hispanic beer in coastal Peru: technology and social context of prehistoric pro-duction. *American Anthropologist* 91:682–695.

Morel, J.-P.

   1981a *Céramique campanienne: les formes.* 2 vols. École Française de Rome, Rome.

   1981b Le commerce étrusque en France, en Espagne et en Afrique. In *L'Etruria mineraria: Atti del XII Covegno di Studi Etruschi e Italici, Firenze 1979*, pp. 463–508. Olshki, Florence.

   1983 Greek colonization in Italy and in the West (problems of evidence and interpreta-tion). In *Crossroads of the Mediterranean*, edited by T. Hackens, N. D. Holloway and R. R. Holloway, pp. 123–161. Collège Erasme, Louvain-la-Neuve.

   1992 Marseille dans la colonisation phocéenne. In Bats et al. 1992, pp. 15–25.

   1995 Les Grecs et la Gaule. In *Les Grecs et l'Occident. Actes du Colloque de la Villa "Kérylos" (1991)*, pp. 41–69. Boccard, Paris.

   2000 Observations sur les cultes de Velia. In Hermary and Tréziny 2000, pp. 33–49.

   2006 Les Étrusques en Méditerranée nord-occidentale: résultats et tendances des recher-ches récentes. In Anonymous 2006, pp. 23–45.

Morley, N.

   1996 *Metropolis and Hinterland: The City of Rome and the Italian Economy, 200 B.C.–A.D. 200.* Cambridge University Press, Cambridge.

   2007a *Trade in Classical Antiquity.* Cambridge University Press, Cambridge.

   2007b The early Roman Empire: Distribution. In Scheidel et al. 2007, pp. 570–591.

Morris, I.

   1987 *Burial and Ancient Society: The Rise of the Greek City-state.* Cambridge University Press, Cambridge.

   1994 Archaeologies of Greece. In *Classical Greece: Ancient Histories and Modern Archae-ologies*, edited by I. Morris, pp. 8–47. Cambridge University Press, Cambridge.

   2006 The growth of Greek cities in the first millennium BC. In *Urbanism in the Preindus-trial World: Cross-Cultural Approaches*, edited by G. R. Storey, pp. 27–51. University of Alabama Press, Tuscaloosa, AL.

Moscati, S., and P. Amiet (editors)

   1988 *Les Phéniciens.* Bompiani, Milan.

Mukerji, C.

   1997 *Territorial Ambitions and the Gardens of Versailles.* Cambridge University Press, Cambridge.

Mullins, P. R.

   1999 *Race and Affluence: An Archaeology of African America and Consumer Culture.* Kluwer Academic/Plenum Publishers, New York.

Murray, G.

   1953 *Hellenism and the Modern World.* Allen and Unwin, London.

Murray, O.

   1990 Sympotic history. In *Sympotica: A Symposium on the Symposion*, edited by O. Mur-ray, pp. 3–13. Clarendon Press, Oxford.

Murray, O., and M. Tecusan (editors)

   1995 *In Vino Veritas.* British School at Rome, London.

Myers, F. (editor)

2001 *The Empire of Things: Regimes of Value and Material Culture.* SAR Press, Santa Fe.

Napoléon III

1866 *Histoire de Jules Césare, 2.* 2 vols. Imprimerie Impériale, Paris.

Nash, M.

1989 *The Cauldron of Ethnicity in the Modern World.* University of Chicago Press, Chicago.

Netting, R.

1979 Beer as a locus of value among the West African Kofyar. *American Anthropologist* 66:375–384.

Nevett, L. C.

1994 Separation or seclusion? Towards an archaeological approach to investigating women in the Greek household in the fifth to third centuries BC. In Pearson and Richards 1994a, pp. 98–112.

1999 *House and Society in the Ancient Greek World.* Cambridge University Press, Cambridge.

Nickels, A.

1978 Contribution à l'étude de la céramique grise archaïque en Languedoc-Roussillon. In *Les céramiques de la Grèce de l'Est et leur diffusion en Occident (Actes du Colloque International du CNRS, 569, Naples, 1976)*, pp. 248–267. Bibliothèque de l'Institut Français de Naples, Naples.

1980 Les plats à marli en céramique grise monochrome de type roussillonnais. In *Ruscino. Château-Roussillon, Perpignan (Pyrénées-Orientales). I-État de travaux et recherches en 1975*, edited by G. Barruol, pp. 155–162. Boccard, Paris.

1981 Recherches sur la topographie de la ville antique d'Agde (Hérault). *Documents d'Archéologie Méridionale* 4:29–50.

1982 Agde grecque, les recherches récentes. *La Parola del Passato* 204–207:269–279.

1983 Les Grecs en Gaule: l'example du Languedoc. In *Modes de contacts et processus de transformation dans les sociétés anciennes*, pp. 409–428. École Française de Rome, Rome.

1989 La Monédière à Bessan (Hérault). Le bilan des recherches. *Documents d'Archéologie Méridionale* 12:51–120.

1995 Les sondages de la rue Perben à Agde (Hérault). In Arcelin et al. 1995, pp. 59–98.

Nicolet, C.

1991 *Space, Geography, and Politics in the Early Roman Empire.* University of Michigan Press, Ann Arbor.

Nielsen, H. S.

1998 Roman children at mealtimes. In Nielsen and Nielsen 1998, pp. 56–66.

Nielsen, I., and H. S. Nielsen (editors)

1998 *Meals in a Social Context: Aspects of the Communal Meal in the Hellenistic and Roman World.* Aarhus University Press, Aarhus.

Nin, N.

1999 Les espaces domestiques en Provence durant la Protohistoire. Aménagements et pratiques rituelles du VIe s. av. n. è. à l'epoque augustéenne. *Documents d'Archéologie Méridionale* 22:221–278.

2000 Un fossé rituel à Aix-en-Provence? In Chausserie-Laprée 2000, pp. 266–269.

Nuninger, L.

2002 Pôles de peuplement et organisation territoriale au second âge du Fer en Vaunage, Vidourlenque et Vistrenque (Gard). In Garcia and Verdin 2002, pp. 129–138.

Nurse, D., and T. J. Hinnebusch

1993 *Swahili and Sabaki: A Linguistic History*. University of California Publications in Linguistics, 121, Berkeley.

Ohunki-Tierney, E.

1993 *Rice as Self: Japanese Identities through Time*. Princeton University Press, Princeton.

Olive, C., and D. Ugolini

1993 Les habitats de l'Orb et l'Hérault (VIe–IVe siècles avant J.-C.). *Documents d'Archéologie Méridionale* 16:80–87.

Osborne, R.

1987 *Classical Landscape with Figures: The Ancient Greek City and Its Countryside*. Sheridan House, Dobbs Ferry, NY.

1998 Early Greek colonization? The nature of Greek settlement in the West. In *Archaic Greece: New Approaches and New Evidence*, edited by N. Fisher and H. van Wees, pp. 251–269. Duckworth, London.

2007 Cult and ritual: The Greek world. In Alcock and Osborne 2007, pp. 246–262.

Osborne, R., and B. W. Cunliffe (editors)

2005 *Mediterranean urbanization 800–600 BC*. Oxford University Press, Oxford.

Osterhammel, J.

1997 *Colonialism: A Theoretical Overview*. Marcus Wiener Publishers, Princeton.

Owen, S.

2005 Analogy, archaeology and Archaic Greek colonization. In Hurst and Owen 2005, pp. 5–22.

Özyigit, Ö.

1995 Les dernières fouilles de Phocée. In *Phocée et la fondation de Marseille*, pp. 47–59. Musée de Marseille, Marseille.

Pagden, A.

1995 *Lords of All the World: Ideologies of Empire in Spain, Britain and France, c. 1500–c. 1800*. Yale University Press, New Haven, CT.

Pallottino, M.

1986 I documenti scritti e la lingua. In *Rasenna. Storia e civiltà degli Etruschi*, edited by C. Belli, P. Orlandini, and P. Carratelli, pp. 309–367. Libri Scheiwiller, Milan.

Palmer, R.

1995 Wine and viticulture in the Linear A and B texts of the Bronze Age Aegean. In *The Origin and Ancient History of Wine*, edited by P. E. McGovern, S. J. Fleming, and S. H. Katz, pp. 269–286. Gordon and Breach, Amsterdam.

Palmié, S.

2006 Creolization and its discontents. *Annual Review of Anthropology* 35:433–456.

Pan, L.

1975 *Alcohol in Colonial Africa*. Finnish Foundation for Alcohol Studies, 22, Helsinki.

Panosa Domingo, I.

1993 Approche comparée de l'écriture ibérique en Languedoc-Roussillon et en Catalogne. *Documents d'Archéologie Méridionale* 16:93–103.

Pare, C.

1991 Fürstensitze, Celts and the Mediterranean world: Developments in the West Hallstatt Culture in the 6th and 5th centuries BC. *Proceedings of the Prehistoric Society* 57:183–202.

Parkins, H., and C. Smith (editors)

1998 *Trade, Traders, and the Ancient City.* Routledge, London.

Parry, B.

1987 Problems in current discourse theory. *Oxford Literary Review* 9:27–58.

Partanen, J.

1991 *Sociability and Intoxication: Alcohol and Drinking in Kenya, Africa, and the Modern World.* Finnish Foundation for Alcohol Studies, Helsinki.

Passelac, M., G. Rancoule, and Y. Solier

1981 La nécropole de "Las Peyros" à Couffoulens, Aude, découverte d'un second groupe de tombes. *Revue Archéologique de Narbonnaise* 14:1–53.

1990 La diffusion des amphores massaliètes en Languedoc occidental et sur l'axe Aude-Garonne et ses abords. In Bats 1990a, pp. 131–152.

Paterno, L.

2004 Les petits objets du quartier 30–35 dans leur contexte lattois. In Py 2004, pp. 345–360.

Paterson, J.

1998 Trade and traders in the Roman world: Scale, structure, and organization. In *Trade, Traders, and the Ancient City,* edited by H. Parkins and J. Smith, pp. 149–167. Routledge, London.

Paulson, S.

2006 Body, nation, and consubstantiation in Bolivian ritual meals. *American Ethnologist* 33(4):650–664.

Paunier, D. (editor)

2006 *Celtes et Gaulois, l'archéologie face à l'histoire: La romanisation et la question de l'héritage celtique.* Bibracte, Centre Archéologique Européen, Glux-en-Glenne.

Pausanias

1965 *Description of Greece.* Translated by J. G. Frazer. 6 vols. Biblo and Tannen, New York.

Peacock, D. P. S.

1982 *Pottery in the Roman World: An Ethnoarchaeological Approach.* Longman London.

Pearson, M. P., and C. Richards

1994a (editors) *Architecture and Order: Approaches to Social Space.* Routledge, London.

1994b Ordering the world: Perceptions of architecture, space and time. In Pearson and Richards 1994a, pp. 1–37.

Pedley, J. G.

2005 *Sanctuaries and the Sacred in the Ancient Greek World.* Cambridge University Press, Cambridge.

Pelloutier, S.

    1740 *Histoire des Celtes et particuliarement des Gaulois et des Germains depuis les temps fabuleux jusqu'à la prise de Rome par les Gaulois* I. 2 vols. Isaac Beauregard, The Hague.

Pendergrast, M.

    1993 *For God, Country and Coca-Cola: The Unauthorized History of the Great American Soft Drink and the Company That Makes It.* Scribner's, New York.

Perrault, C.

    1979 [1692] *Parallèle des Anciens et des Modernes.* Slatkin Reprints, Geneva.

Pezin, A.

    1993 Les habitats de Roussillon. *Documents d'Archéologie Méridionale* 16:53–56.

Pindar

    1997 *Olympian Odes. Pythian Odes.* Translated by W. H. Race. Loeb Classical Library. Harvard University Press, Cambridge, MA.

Piot, C.

    1991 Of persons and things: Some reflections on African spheres of exchange. *Man* 26:405–424.

Piquès, G. and R. Buxó (editors)

    2005 *Onze puits gallo-romains de Lattara (Ier s. av. n.è.-IIe s. de n. è.). Fouilles programmées 1986–2000.* Lattara 18. ARALO, Lattes, France.

Piquès, G., and V. Martínez

    2008 Nouvelles données sur *Lattara* romaine. *Gallia* 65:175–184.

Platt, B. S.

    1955 Some traditional alcoholic beverages and their importance in indigenous African communities. *Proceedings of the Nutrition Society* 14:115–124.

    1964 Biological ennoblement: Improvement of the nutritive value of foods and dietary regimens by biological agencies. *Food Technology* 18:662–670.

Plutarch

    1932 *Plutarch's Lives: Complete and Unabridged in One Volume.* Translated by J. Dryden. Modern Library, New York.

Polybius

    1922–1927 *The Histories.* Translated by W. R. Paton. 6 vols. Heinemann, London.

Pomeroy, S. B.

    1975 *Goddesses, Whores, Wives, and Slaves: Women in Classical Antiquity.* Schocken Books, New York.

Pomey, P., and L. Long

    1992 Les premiers échanges maritimes du Midi de la Gaule du VIe au IIIe s. av. J.-C. à travers les épaves. In Bats et al. 1992, pp. 189–198.

Pomey, P. and A. Tchernia

    1978 Le tonnage maximum des navires de commerce romain. *Archaeonautica* 2: 233–251.

Pournot, J.

    2000 Les cultes phocéens et le monnayage massaliète de la deuxième moitié du Ve s. In Hermary and Tréziny 2000, pp. 183–189.

Poux, M.

2004 *L'âge du vin. Rites de boisson, festins et libations en Gaule indépendante.* Éditions Monique Mergoil, Montagnac.

2006 Religion et société: le sanctuaire arverne de Corent. In Goudineau 2006, pp. 117–134.

Powell, M.

1995 Wine and the vine in ancient Mesopotamia. In *The Origin and Ancient History of Wine*, edited by P. E. McGovern, S. J. Fleming, and S. H. Katz, pp. 97–122. Gordon and Breach, Amsterdam.

Prakash, G. (editor)

1995 *After Colonialism: Imperial Histories and Postcolonial Displacements.* Princeton University Press, Princeton.

Pralon, D.

1992 La légende de la fondation de Marseille. In Bats et al. 1992, pp. 51–56.

Pratt, M. L.

1992 *Imperial Eyes: Travel Writing and Transculturation.* Routledge, London.

Pseudo-Scymnus

2003 *Orbis Descriptio: Die Welt-Rundreise eines anonymen griechischen Autors.* Translated by M. Korenjak. G. Olms, Hildesheim, NY.

Purcell, N.

2007 Urban spaces and central places: The Roman world. In Alcock and Osborne 2007, pp. 182–198.

Py, F., and M. Py

1974 Les amphores étrusques de Vaunage et de Villevieille (Gard). *Mélanges de l'École Française de Rome, Antiquité* 86:141–254.

Py, M.

1974 Le problème des Volques Arécomiques à la lumière des résultats actuels de la recherche archéologique. In *Miscelánea Arqueológica*, Volume 2, pp. 209–253, Barcelona.

1978 *L'oppidum des Castels à Nages, Gard, fouilles 1958–1978.* Supplement 35 of Gallia. CNRS, Paris.

1981 *Recherches sur Nîmes préromain, habitats et sépultures.* Supplement 41 of Gallia. CNRS, Paris.

1982 Civilisation indigène et urbanisation durant la Protohistoire en Languedoc-Roussillon. *KTEMA* 7:101–119.

1985 Les amphores étrusques de Gaule méridionale. In Cristofani et al. 1985, pp. 73–94.

1988 Sondages dans l'habitat antique de Lattes: les fouilles d'Henri Prades et du Groupe Archéologique Painlevé (1963–1985). In *Lattara 1*, pp. 65–146. ARALO, Lattes, France.

1990a *Culture, économie et société protohistorique dans la région nimoise.* Collection de l'École Française de Rome 131. Boccard, Paris.

1990b (editor) *Fouilles dans la ville antique de Lattes. Les îlots 1, 3 et 4–nord du quartier Saint-Sauveur.* Lattara 3. ARALO, Lattes, France.

1990c La diffusion des amphores massaliètes sur le littoral du Languedoc oriental. In Bats 1990a, pp. 73–86.

1992a (editor) *Recherches sur l'économie vivrière des Lattarenses.* Lattara 5, ARALO, Lattes, France.

1992b Stèles anépigraphes du Marduel à Saint-Bonnet-du-Gard. *Documents d'Archéologie Méridionale* 15:131–133.

1993a *Les Gaulois du Midi: de la fin de l'Age du Bronze à la conquête romaine.* Hachette, Paris.

1993b (editor) *DICOCER: dictionnaire des céramiques antiques (VIIème s. av. n. è.–VIIème s. de n. è.) en Méditerranée nord-occidentale.* Lattara 6. ARALO, Lattes, France.

1995 Les Etrusques, les Grecs et la fondation de Lattes. In Arcelin et al. 1995, pp. 261–276.

1996a Les maisons protohistoriques de Lattara (IVe–Ier s. av. n.è.), approche typologique et fonctionelle. In Py 1996b, pp. 141–258.

1996b (editor) *Urbanisme et architecture dans la ville antique de Lattes.* Lattara 9. ARALO, Lattes, France.

1999 (editor) *Recherches sur le quatrième siècle avant notre ère à Lattes.* Lattara 12. ARALO, Lattes, France.

2004a (editor) *Le quartier 30–35 de la ville de Lattara (fin IIIe–Ier siècles av. n. è.). Regards sur la vie urbaine à la fin de la Protohistoire.* Lattara 17. ARALO, Lattes, France.

2004b Le quartier 30–35 de Lattara dans son contexte urbanistique. In Py 2004a, pp. 395–402.

2006 *Les monnaies préaugustéennes de Lattes et la circulation monétaire protohistorique en Gaule méridionale.* Lattara 19. 2 vols. ARALO, Lattes, France.

2008 Nouvelles données, nouvelles questions sur l'urbanisme et la société de *Lattara* protohistorique. *Gallia* 65:123–129.

Py, M., A. Adroher, C. Belarte, M. Dietler, M. Gomis, L. Paterno, P. Pinto, S. Raux, C. Sanchez, and A. Vidal

2004 Le dossier de fouille du quartier 30–35: structures, stratigraphies et mobiliers. In Py 2004a, pp. 7–318.

Py, M., A. Adroher Aroux, and C. Sanchez

2001 *Corpus des céramiques de l'Âge du Fer de Lattes (fouilles 1963–1999).* 2 vols. Lattara 14. ARALO, Lattes, France.

Py, M., and R. Buxó i Capdevila

2001 La viticulture en Gaule à l'âge du Fer. *Gallia* 58:29–43.

Py, M., D. Lebeaupin, and J.-C. Bessac

1994 Stratigraphie du Marduel (Saint-Bonnet-du-Gard). VI—Les niveaux du Bronze final au milieu du Ve s. av. n.è. sur le Chantier Central. *Documents d'Archéologie Méridionale* 17:201–267.

Py, M., D. Lebeaupin, and C.-A. d. Chazelles

1992 Stratigraphie du Marduel (Saint-Bonnet-du-Gard). V. Les niveaux de la deuxième moitié du Ve s. av. n.è. sur le Chantier Central. *Documents d'Archéologie Méridionale* 15:261–326.

Py, M., D. Lebeaupin, P. Séjalon, and R. Roure

2006 Les Étrusques et *Lattara*: nouvelles données. In Anonymous 2006, pp. 583–608.

Py, M., J. B. López and D. Asensio

    2008 L'enceinte protohistorique de Lattes. *Gallia* 65.

Py, M., F. Py, P. Sauzet, and C. Tendille

    1984 *La Liquière, Calvisson, Gard: Village du Premier Age du Fer en Languedoc Oriental.* Supplement 11 of the Revue Archéologique de Narbonnaise. CNRS, Paris.

Py, M., and R. Roure

    2002 Le Cailar (Gard). Un nouveau comptoir lagunaire protohistorique au confluent du Rhôny et du Vistre. *Documents d'Archéologie Méridionale* 25:171–214.

Quinn, D. B.

    1976 Renaissance influences in English colonization. *Transactions of the Royal Historical Society* 26:73–93.

Raaflaub, K.

    1999 Archaic and Classical Greece. In Raaflaub and Rosenstein 1999, pp. 129–161.

Raaflaub, K., and N. Rosenstein (editors)

    1999 *War and Society in the Ancient and Medieval Worlds.* Center for Hellenic Studies and Harvard University, Cambridge, MA.

Ranger, T.

    1989 Missionaries, migrants and the Manyika: The invention of ethnicity in Zimbabwe. In Vail 1989, pp. 118–150.

Rankin

    1987 *Celts and the Classical World.* Routledge, London.

Rapoport, A.

    1969 *House Form and Culture.* Prentice Hall, Englewood Cliffs, NJ.

Rayssiguier, G.

    1983 Le sondage IIIa des Baou de Saint-Marcel à Marseille. *Documents d'Archéologie Méridionale* 8:101–112.

Redfield, R., R. Linton, and M. Herskovits

    1936 Memorandum for the study of acculturation. *American Anthropologist* 38:149–152.

Reed, C. M.

    2003 *Maritime Traders in the Ancient Greek World.* Cambridge University Press, Cambridge.

Reille, J.-L.

    1996 Les murs de pierre dans la ville antique de Lattes, composition lithologique, signification. In Py 1996b, pp. 329–336.

    1999 Détermination pétrographique de l'origine des meules de Lattes au IVe siècle avant notre ère. Changements et contrastes dans les importations. In Py 1999, pp. 519–524.

Reille, J.-L., and L. Chabot

    2000 L'origine et l'importation des meules à grains dans un village de la chôra marseillaise aux IIe et Ier s. av. J.-C. (oppidum de La Cloche, Les Pennes-Mirabeau, B.-du-Rh.). *Documents d'Archéologie Méridionale* 23:279–282.

Rétif, M.

    2000 Le mobilier métallique de l'habitat protohistorique de l'Île de Martigues, B.-du-Rh. (Ve-IIe s. av. J.-C.). *Documents d'Archéologie Méridionale* 23:157–208.

Reyna, S. P., and R. E. Downs (editors)

1994 *Studying War: Anthropological Perspectives.* Gordon and Breach, Langhorne, PA.

Rice, P. M.

1996 The archaeology of wine: The wine and brandy haciendas of Moquegua, Peru. *Journal of Field Archaeology* 23:187–204.

Rich, J., and G. Shipley (editors)

1993 *War and Society in the Roman World.* Routledge, London.

Richard, J.-C.

1992 La diffusion des monnayages massaliètes au-delà du territoire de Marseille. In Bats et al. 1992, pp. 255–260.

Richard, J.-C., and L. Villaronga

1973 Recherches sur les étalons monétaires en Espagne et en Gaule du Sud antérieurement à l'époque d'Auguste. *Mélanges de la Casa Velasquez* 9:81–131.

Richards, A. I.

1939 *Land, Labour and Diet in Northern Rhodesia.* Oxford University Press, London.

Ricoeur, P.

1992 *Oneself as Another.* University of Chicago Press, Chicago.

Ridgway, F. R. S.

1990 Etruscans, Greeks, Carthaginians: The sanctuary at Pyrgi. In Greek Colonists and Native Populations, edited by J.P. Descoeudres, pp. 511–530. Clarendon Press, Oxford.

Ridley, R. T.

1992 *The Eagle and the Spade: Archaeology in Rome during the Napoleonic Era.* Cambridge University Press, Cambridge.

Ringer, F. K.

1979 *Education and Society in Modern Europe.* Indiana University Press, Bloomington, IN.

1992 *Fields of Knowledge: French Academic Culture in Comparative Perspective, 1890–1920.* Cambridge University Press, Cambridge.

Rivet, A. L. F.

1988 *Gallia Narbonensis: Southern Gaul in Roman Times.* Batsford, London.

Rix, H.

1991 *Etruskische Texte.* 2 vols. G. Marr, Tübingen.

Robb, J.

1997 Violence and gender in early Italy. In *Troubled Times: Violence and Warfare in the Past*, edited by D. L. Martin and D. W. Frayer, pp. 111–144. Gordon and Breach, Amsterdam.

Robbins, R. H.

1973 Alcohol and the identity struggle: Some effects of economic change on interpersonal relations. *American Anthropologist* 75:99–122.

Robert, L.

1968 Noms de personnes et civilisation grecque, I. Noms de personnes dans Marseille grecque. *Journal des Savants*:197–213.

Rogers, J. D.

1990 *Objects of Change: The Archaeology and History of Arikara Contact with Europeans.* Smithsonian Institution Press, Washington, DC.

Rolland, H.

    1946 *Fouilles de Glanum (Saint-Rémy de Provence)*. Supplement 1 to Gallia. CNRS, Paris.

    1968 Nouvelles fouilles du sanctuaire des Glaniques. *Revue d'Etudes Ligures* 34:7–34.

Roseberry, W.

    1988 Poltical economy. *Annual Review of Anthropology* 17:161–185.

Roth Congès, A.

    1985 Glanum préromaine: recherche sur la métrologie et ses applications dans l'urbanisme et l'architecture. *Revue Archéologique de Narbonnaise* 18:189–220.

    1992a Le centre monumental de *Glanon* ou les derniers feu de la civilisation salyenne. In Bats et al. 1992, pp. 351–367.

    1992b Nouvelles fouilles à Glanum (1982–1990). *Journal of Roman Archaeology* 5:39–55.

    1992c Monuments publics d'époque tardo-hellénistique à Glanon (B.-du-Rh.). *Documents d'Archéologie Méridionale* 15:50–56.

    1999 Glanum, les recherches actuelles. *Archéologia* September:41–47.

    2001 *Glanum, de l'oppidum salyen à la cité latine*. Editions du Patrimoine, Paris.

    2004 Le contexte archéologique de la statuaire de *Glanon* (Saint-Rémy-de-Provence, Bouches-du-Rhône). *Documents d'Archéologie Méridionale* 27:23–43.

Rothé, M.-P., and H. Tréziny (editors)

    2005 *Marseille et ses alentours*. Carte Archéologique de la Gaule 13/3, C.I.D., Paris.

Roubaud, M.-P., and A. Michelozzi

    1993 Un quartier de l'oppidum de la Roche-de-Comps (Gard) au milieu de l'âge du Fer. *Documents d'Archéologie Méridionale* 16:257–278.

Rougé, J.

    1970 La colonisation grecque et les femmes. *Cahiers d'Histoire* 15:307–317.

Rouillard, P.

    1991 *Les Grecs et la péninsule ibérique du VIIIe au IVe siècle avant Jésus-Christ*. Boccard, Paris.

    2009 Greeks and the Iberian Peninsula: Forms of exchange and settlements. In Dietler and López-Ruiz 2009, pp. 131–151.

Roure, R.

    2002 Nouvelles données sur l'occupation protohistorique de Beaucaire (Gard). *Documents d'Archéologie Méridionale* 25:215–223.

Roux, J.-C., and L. Chabal

    1996 Une maison à torchis de Lattes au deuxième quart du IVe s. av. n. è. In Py 1996b, pp. 337–362.

Roux, J.-C.,and S. Raux

    1996 Les foyers domestiques dans l'habitat lattois du IIe Age du fer (IVe-Ier s. av. n.è.). In Py 1996b, pp. 401–432.

Rowlands, M. J.

    1972 Defence: A factor in the organization of settlements. In *Man, Settlement and Urbanism*, edited by P. J. Ucko, R. Tringham, and G. W. Dimbleby, pp. 447–462. Duckworth, London.

    1998 The archaeology of colonialism. In *Social Transformations in Archaeology: Global and Local Perspectives*, edited by K. Kristiansen and M. J. Rowlands, pp. 327–333. Routledge, London.

Rowlands, M. J., M. T. Larsen, and K. Kristiansen (editors)

   1987 *Centre and Periphery in the Ancient World*. Cambridge University Press, Cambridge.

Roymans, N.

   2004 *Ethnic Identity and Imperial Power: The Batavians in the Early Roman Empire*. Amsterdam University Press, Amsterdam.

Rozin, E., and P. Rozin

   1981 Some surprisingly unique characteristics of human food preferences. In *Food in Perspective*, edited by A. Fenton and T. M. Owen, pp. 243–252. John Donald, Edinburgh.

Ruiz, A., and M. Molinos

   1998 *The Archaeology of the Iberians*. Cambridge University Press, Cambridge.

Sahlins, M.

   1976 *Culture and Practical Reason*. University of Chicago Press, Chicago.

   1985 *Islands of History*. University of Chicago Press, Chicago.

   1992 The economics of develop-man in the Pacific. *Res* 21:12–25.

   1993 Goodbye to tristes tropes: Ethnography in the context of modern world history. *Journal of Modern History* 65:1–25.

   1994 Cosmologies of Capitalism: The trans-Pacific sector of "the World System." In *Culture/Power/History: A Reader in Contemporary Social Theory*, edited by N. B. Dirks, G. Eley, and S. B. Ortner, pp. 412–455. Princeton University Press, Princeton.

   1995 *How "Natives" Think: About Captain Cook, For Example*. University of Chicago Press, Chicago.

   1999 What is anthropological enlightenment? Some lessons of the twentieth century. *Annual Review of Anthropology* 28:i–xxiii.

Said, E.

   1978 *Orientalism: Western Representations of the Orient*. Penguin, Harmondsworth.

   1993 *Culture and Imperialism*. Vintage Books, New York.

Salisbury, R. F.

   1962 *From Stone to Steel: Economic Consequences of a Technological Change in New Guinea*. Melbourne University Press, Melbourne.

Sallares, R.

   1991 *The Ecology of the Ancient Greek World*. Cornell University Press, Ithaca, NY.

   2002 *Malaria and Rome: A History of Malaria in Ancient Italy*. Oxford University Press, Oxford.

Sallust

   1992 *The Histories, Volume I, Books 1–2*. Translated by P. McGushin. Clarendon, Oxford.

Salmon, E. T.

   1969 *Roman Colonization under the Republic*. Thames and Hudson, London.

Salviat, F.

   1993 La sculpture d'Entremont. In Coutagne 1993, pp. 165–239.

Samarin, W. J.

   1990 The origins of Kituba and Lingala. *Journal of African Languages and Linguistics* 12:47–77.

Sanjek, R.

    1974 What is network analysis, and what is it good for? *Reviews in Anthropology* 1: 588–597.

Sanmartí, E., P. Castanyer and, J. Tremoleda

    1990 Les amphores massaliètes d'*Emporion* du milieu du VIe au milieu du IVe s. av. J.-C. In Bats 1990a, pp. 165–170.

Sanmartí-Grego, E.

    1992 *Massalia* et *Emporion*: une origine commune, deux destins différents. In Bats et al. 1992, pp. 27–41.

Sanmartí-Grego, E., P. Castanyer, J. Tremoleda, and M. Santos

    1995 Amphores grecques et trafics commerciaux en Méditerranée occidentale au IVe s. av. J.-C.: nouvelles données issues d'Emporion. In Arcelin et al. 1995, pp. 325–338.

Sattler, R. A.

    1996 Remnants, renegades, and runaways: Seminole ethnogenesis reconsidered. In Hill 1996, pp. 36–69.

Saul, M.

    1981 Beer, sorghum, and women: Production for the market in rural Upper Volta. *Africa* 51:746–764.

Scheidel, W.

    1996 *Measuring Sex, Age and Death in the Roman Empire: Explorations in Ancient Demography*. Journal of Roman Archaeology, Supplementary Series 21, Ann Arbor, MI.

    2001a (editor) *Debating Roman Demography*. Brill, Leiden.

    2001b Progress and problems in Roman demography. In Scheidel 2001a, pp. 1–81.

Scheidel, W., I. Morris, and R. Saller (editors)

    2007 *The Cambridge Economic History of the Greco-Roman World*. Cambridge University Press, Cambridge.

Schmitt Pantel, P.

    1995 Rite cultuel et rituel social: à propos des manières de boire le vin dans les cités grecques. In Murray and Tecusan 1995, pp. 93–105.

Schnapp, A.

    1996 *The Discovery of the Past: The Origins of Archaeology*. British Museum Press, London.

Schreiber, K. J.

    1992 *Wari Imperialism in Middle Horizon Peru*. Museum of Anthropology, University of Michigan (Anthropological Papers, No. 87), Ann Arbor.

Scott, J.

    1991 *Social Network Analysis: A Handbook*. Sage, Newbury Park, CA.

Scott, J. C.

    1998 *Seeing Like a State: How Certain Schemes to Improve the Human Condition Have Failed*. Yale University Press, New Haven, CT.

Seed, P.

    1995 *Ceremonies of Possession in Europe's Conquest of the New World, 1492–1640*. Cambridge University Press, Cambridge.

Sestini, A.

1981 Introduzione all'Etruria mineraria. Il quadro naturale e ambientale. In *L'Etruria mineraria. Atti del XII Convegno di Studi Etruschi e Italici, Firenze-Populonia-Piombino, 1979*, pp. 3–21. Leo. S. Olschki, Florence.

Shadle, B. L.

2002 Patronage, millennialism and the serpent god Mumbo in South-West Kenya, 1912–34. *Africa: Journal of the International African Institute* 72(1):29–54.

Shanks, M.

1996 *Classical Archaeology of Greece: Experiences of the Discipline*. Routledge, London.

Shelley, P. B.

1822 *Hellas: A Lyrical Drama*. C. and J. Ollier, London.

Sherratt, A.

1993 What would a Bronze-Age world system look like? Relations between temperate Europe and the Mediterranean in later prehistory. *Journal of European Archaeology* 1(2):1–57.

Shipton, P. M.

1984 Strips and patches: A demographic dimension in some African land-holding and political systems. *Man* New Series 19(4):613–634.

1989 *Bitter Money: Cultural Economy and Some African Meanings of Forbidden Commodities*. American Ethnological Society, Washington, DC.

Shlasko, E.

1992 The roles of wampum in seventeenth century North America. *Yale Graduate Journal of Anthropology* 4:56–63.

Shott, M.

1996 Mortal pots: On use life and vessel size in the formation of ceramic assemblages. *American Antiquity* 61(3):463–482.

Simons, A.

1999 War: back to the future. *Annual Review of Anthropology* 28:73–108.

Slemon, S.

1994 The scramble for post-colonialism. In *De-scribing Empire: Postcolonialism and Textuality*, edited by C. Tiffin and A. Lawson, pp. 15–32. Routledge, London.

Smith, C.

1998 Traders and artisans in archaic central Italy. In *Trade, Traders, and the Ancient City*, edited by H. Parkins and J. Smith, pp. 31–51. Routledge, London.

2007 Cult and ritual: the Roman world. In Alcock and Osborne 2007, pp. 263–280.

Social Science Research Council

1954 Acculturation: An exploratory formulation. Social Science Research Council Summer Seminar on Acculturation, 1953. *American Anthropologist* 56:973–1000.

Solier, Y.

1976–78 La culture ibéro-languedocienne aux VIe–Ve siècles. *Ampurias* 38–40:211–264.

1992 L'occupation des Corbières à l'Age du fer. Habitats et mobiliers. *Documents d'Archéologie Méridionale* 15:327–390.

Solier, Y., and H. Barbouteau

 1988 Découverte de nouveaux plombs inscrits en Ibère, dans la région de Narbonne. *Revue Archéologique de Narbonnaise* 21:61–94.

Sourisseau, J.-C.

 1990 Le Jardin d'Hiver à Arles. In Bats 1990a, pp. 197.

 1997 *Recherches sur les amphores de Provence et de la basse vallée du Rhône aux époques archaïque et classique (fin VIIe-début IVe s. av. J.-C.).* Unpublished Thèse de doctorat, Aix-en-Provence.

 1998 Marseille et la production d'amphores "ionio-massaliètes" en Occident: les problèmes de fabrication. In *Artisanat et matériaux. La place des matériaux dans l'histoire des techniques,* edited by M.-C. Amouretti and G. Comet, pp. 127–152. Publications de l'Université de Provence, Aix-en-Provence.

 2002 Les importations étrusques à Marseille, de Gaston Vasseur aux grandes interventions d'archéologie préventive: une découverte progressive, des problematiques renouvellées. In Long et al. 2002, pp. 89–103.

 2007 Les épaves de Méditerranée occidentale et le commerce maritime étrusque. *Les Dossiers d'Archéologie* 322:118–121.

Soutou, A., and J. Arnal

 1963 Le dépôt de la Croix-de-Mus, Murviel-lès-Béziers (Hérault) et la datation du Launacien. *Bulletin du Musée d'Anthropologie Préhistorique de Monaco* 10:173–210.

Sparkes, B. A.

 1962 The Greek kitchen. *Journal of Hellenic Studies* 82:121–137.

 1991 *Greek Pottery: An Introduction.* Manchester University Press, Manchester.

Spicer, E.

 1962 *Cycles of Conquest: The Impact of Spain, Mexico and the United States on the Indians of the Southwest, 1533–1960.* Arizona University Press, Tucson.

Spivack, G. C.

 1988 Can the subaltern speak? In *Marxism and the Interpretation of Culture,* edited by C. Nelson and L. Grossberg, pp. 271–313. University of Illinois Press, Champaign-Urbana.

Spivey, N., and S. Stoddart

 1990 *Etruscan Italy.* Batsford, London.

Stead, I. M.

 1983 La Tène swords and scabbards in Champagne. *Germania* 61:487–510.

Stein, G. (editor)

 2005 *The Archaeology of Colonial Encounters: Comparative Perspectives.* School of American Research Press, Santa Fe, N.M.

Steinkraus, K. H. (editor)

 1995 *Handbook of Indigenous Fermented Foods.* Marcel Dekker, New York.

Sternberg, M.

 1995 *La pêche à Lattes dans l'Antiquité à travers l'analyse de l'ichtyofaune.* Lattara 8, ARALO, Lattes, France.

 1998 Les produits de la pêche et la modifications des structures halieutiques en Gaule Narbonnaise du IIe siècle av. J.-C. au Ier siècle ap. J.-C. *Mélanges de l'École Française de Rome, Antiquité* 110:81–109.

1999a La pêche et la consommation du poisson à Marseille dans l'Antiquité. In Hesnard et al. 1999, pp. 70.

1999b Les caractéristiques de la pêche à Lattes au IVe siècle avant notre ère. In Py 1999, pp. 589–608.

2006 Les poissons. In Bats 2006, pp. 431–449.

Sternberg, M. and H. Tréziny

2005 Le terroir marseillais et les ressources naturelles. In Rothé and Tréziny 2005, pp. 244–251.

Stoler, A. L.

1992 Rethinking colonial categories: European communities and the boundaries of rule. In Dirks 1992b, pp. 319–352.

2002 *Carnal Knowledge and Imperial Power: Race and the Intimate in Colonial Rule.* University of California Press, Berkeley.

Stoler, A. L., and F. Cooper (editors)

1997 *Tensions of Empire: Colonial Cultures in a Bourgeois World.* University of California Press, Berkeley.

Stoler, A. L., C. McGranahan, and P. C. Perdue (editors)

2007 *Imperial Formations.* SAR Press, Santa Fe.

Stoller, P.

1994 Embodying colonial memories. *American Anthropologist* 96(3):634–648.

Strabo

1923 *Geography, Volume II, Books 3–5.* Translated by H. L. Jones. Loeb Classical Library. Harvard University Press, Cambridge, MA.

Suetonius

1914 *The Lives of the Caesars, I: Julius, Augustus, Tiberius, Gaius, Caligula.* Translated by J. C. Rolfe and K. R. Bradley. Loeb Classical Library. Harvard University Press, Cambridge, MA.

Suggs, D. N., and S. A. Lewis

2003 Alcohol as a direct and indirect labor enhancer in the mixed economy of the Ba-Tswana, 1800–1900. In *Drugs, Labor, and Colonial Expansion,* edited by W. Jankowiak and B. Bradburd, pp. 135–149. University of Arizona Press, Tucson.

Swanepoel, N.

2005 Socio-political change on a slave-raiding frontier: war, trade and "Big Men" in nineteenth century Sisalaland, Northern Ghana. *Journal of Conflict Archaeology* 1:265–293.

Symonds, J. A.

1880 *Studies of the Greek Poets* 1. Harper, New York.

Tacitus

2009 *The Histories.* Translated by K. Wellesley. Penguin Classics, London.

Taffanel, O., and J. Taffanel

1960 Deux tombes de chefs à Mailhac (Aude). *Gallia* 18:1–37.

Taffanel, O., J. Taffanel, and T. Janin

1998 *La nécropole du Moulin à Mailhac (Aude).* Monographies d'Archéologie Méditerranéenne 2. ARALO, Lattes, France.

Talve, I.

1981 The potato in Finnish food economy. In *Food in Perspective*, edited by A. Fenton and T. M. Owen, pp. 277–282. John Donald, Edinburgh.

Tandy, D. W.

1997 *Warriors into Traders: The Power of the Market in Early Greece*. University of California Press, Berkeley.

Tanelli, G.

1989 I depositi metaliferi dell'Etruria e la attività estrattive degli Etruschi. In *Secondo Congresso Internazionale Etrusco, Firenze 1985. Atti*, Volume 3, pp. 1409–1417. Giorgio Bretschneider, Florence.

Tchernia, A.

1983 Italian wine in Gaul at the end of the Republic. In *Trade in the Ancient Economy*, edited by P. Garnsey and C. R. Whittaker, pp. 87–104. Chatto and Windus, London.

1986 *Le vin de l'Italie romaine: essai d'histoire économique d'après les amphores*. Bibliothèque des Écoles Françaises d'Athènes et de Rome 261. Boccard, Paris.

1997 Le tonneau, de la bière au vin. In Garcia and Meeks 1997, pp. 121–129.

Tchernia, A., P. Pomey, A. Hesnard, et al.

1978 *L'épave romaine de la Madrague de Giens (Var)*. Supplement 34 of Gallia. CNRS, Paris.

Tendille, C.

1982 Mobiliers métalliques protohistoriques de la région nîmoise: instruments et outils divers (v). *Documents d'Archéologie Méridionale* 5:33–52.

Tennevin, J.-P.

1972 *Le Baou-Roux, oppidum celto-ligure*. Cahier 1 de l'Association "Les Amis d'Entremont et du Pays d'Aix Antique," Aix-en-Provence.

Theodorescu, D., and H. Tréziny

2000 Le chapiteau ionique archaïque de Marseille. In Hermary and Tréziny 2000, pp. 135–146.

Thinon, M.

1980 Les sondages 1b-Nord des Baou de Saint-Marcel à Marseille, V Etude du matériel anthracologique. *Documents d'Archéologie Méridionale* 3:93–94.

Thomas, N.

1991 *Entangled Objects: Exchange, Material Culture, and Colonialism in the Pacific*. Harvard University Press, Cambridge, MA.

1994 *Colonialism's Culture: Anthropology, Travel and Government*. Princeton University Press, Princeton.

2002 Colonizing cloth: Interpreting the material culture of nineteenth-century Oceania. In Lyons and Papadopoulos 2002, pp. 182–198.

Thornton, J. K.

1999 *Warfare in Atlantic Africa, 1500–1800*. University College London Press, London.

Thucydides

2009 *The Peloponnesian War*. Translated by M. Hammond. Oxford University Press, Oxford.

Tierney, J.

  1960 The Celtic ethnography of Posidonius. *Proceedings of the Royal Irish Academy* 60:189–275.

Torelli, M. (editor)

  2000 *The Etruscans.* Bompiani, Milan.

Tréziny, H.

  1986 Cité et territoire: quelques problèmes. In Bats and Tréziny 1986, pp. 7–15.

  2000 Les lieux de culte dans Marseille grecque. In Hermary and Tréziny 2000, pp. 81–99.

  2001a Urbanisme et voirie dans les colonies grecques archaïques de Sicile Orientale. *Pallas* 58:267–282.

  2001b Les fortifications de Marseille dans l'Antiquité. In Bouiron and Tréziny 2001, pp. 45–57.

  2001c Trames et orientations dans la ville antique: lots et îlots. In Bouiron and Tréziny 2001, pp. 137–145.

  2004 Urbanisme grec, urbanisme indigène dans le Midi de la Gaule. In Agusta-Boularot and Lafon 2004, pp. 65–77.

  2005 Topographie, urbanisme et architecture de Marseille pendant l'Antiquité. In Rothé and Tréziny 2005, pp. 320–244.

Tréziny, H., and P. Trousset

  1992 Les fortifications de Marseille grecque. In Bats et al. 1992, pp. 89–107.

Trigger, B.

  1984 Alternative archaeologies: Nationalist, colonialist, imperialist. *Man* 19:355–370.

Trouillot, M.-R.

  1995 *Silencing the Past: Power and the Production of History.* Beacon Press, Boston, MA.

Tsetskhladze, G. R., and F. De Angelis (editors)

  1994 *The Archaeology of Greek Colonisation.* Oxford University Committee for Archaeology, Oxford.

Tulard, J.

  1997 Introduction. In *Les empires occidentaux de Rome à Berlin*, edited by J. Tulard, pp. 9–16. Presses Universitaires de France, Paris.

Turgeon, L.

  1997 The tale of the kettle: Odyssey of an intercultural object. *Ethnohistory* 44(1):1–29.

  1998 (editor) *Les entre-lieux de la culture.* Presses de l'Université Laval, Quebec.

  2002 (editor) *Regards croisés sur le métissage.* Presses de l'Université Laval, Québec.

Turner, F. M.

  1981 *The Greek Heritage in Victorian Britain.* Yale University Press, New Haven, CT.

Turner, T.

  1980 The social skin. In *Not Work Alone: A Cross-Cultural View of Activities Superfluous to Survival*, edited by J. Cherfas and R. Lewin, Beverly Hills, CA.

Twiss, K. C.

  2007a (editor) *The Archaeology of Food and Identity.* Center for Archaeological Investigations, Southern Illinois University, Carbondale.

  2007b We are what we eat. In Twiss 2007a, pp. 1–15.

Ugolini, D.

1993 Civilisation languedocienne et ibérisme: un bilan de la question (VIIe–IVe siècles avant J.-C.). *Documents d'Archéologie Méridionale* 16:26–40.

Ugolini, D., C. Olive, G. Marchand, and P. Columeau

1991 Béziers au Ve s. av. J.-C.: Étude d'un ensemble de mobilier représentatif at essai de caractérisation du site. *Documents d'Archéologie Méridionale* 14:141–203.

Untermann, J.

1969 Lengua gala y lengua ibérica en la Galia Narbonensis. *Archivo de Prehistoria Levantina* 12:99–161.

1980 Les inscriptions préromaines et la langue indigène du Roussillon. In *Ruscino. Château-Roussillon, Perpignan (Pyrénées-Orientales). I-État de travaux et recherches en 1975*, edited by G. Barruol, pp. 103–106, Paris.

1992 Quelle langue parlait-on dans l'Hérault pendant l'antiquité? *Revue Archéologique de Narbonnaise* 25:19–27.

Vail, L.

1989a Introduction: ethnicity in Southern African history. In *The Creation of Tribalism in Southern Africa*, edited by L. Vail, pp. 1–19. University of California Press, Berkeley.

1989b (editor) *The Creation of Tribalism in Southern Africa*. University of California Press, Berkeley.

van Compernolle, R.

1981 Femmes indigènes et colonisateurs. In *Modes de contact et processus de transformation dans les sociétés anciennes*, pp. 1033–1049. École Française de Rome, Rome.

Van de Voort, J.-F.

1991 La maison des Antes de Glanum (B.-du-Rh.): analyse métrologique d'une maison à péristyle hellénistique. *Revue Archéologique de Narbonnaise* 24:1–17.

van der Mersch, C.

1994 *Vins et amphores de Grande Grèce et de Sicile: IVe–IIIe s. avant J.-C.* Boccard, Paris.

van Dommelen, P. A. R.

1997 Colonial constructs: Colonialism and archaeology in the Mediterranean. *World Archaeology* 28:305–323.

1998 *On Colonial Grounds: A Comparative Study of Colonialism and Rural Settlement in First Millennium BC West Central Sardinia*. Doctoral thesis, Faculty of Archaeology, Rijksuniversiteit of Leiden.

2005 Colonial interactions and hybrid practices: Phoenician and Carthaginian settlement in the ancient Mediterranean. In Stein 2005.

Van Endert, D.

1987 *Die Wagenbestattungen der späten Hallstattzeit und der Latènezeit westlich des Rheins.* BAR International Series 355, Oxford.

Vance, N.

1997 *The Victorians and Ancient Rome*. Blackwell Publishers, Oxford.

Vasseur, G.

1914 *L'origine de Marseille. Fondations des premiers comptoirs ioniens de Massalia vers le milieu du VIIe siècle. Résultats de fouilles archéologique exécutées à Marseille dans le Fort*

Saint-Jean. Annales du Musée d'Histoire Naturelle de Marseille 13. Moullot Fils Ainé, Marseille.

Vasunia, P.

2005 Greater Rome and Greater Britain. In *Classics and Colonialism*, edited by B. Goff, pp. 38–64. Duckworth, London.

Verdin, F.

1996–1997 Coudounèu (Lançon de Provence, Bouches-du-Rhône): une ferme-grenier et son terroir au Ve s. av. J.-C. *Documents d'Archéologie Méridionale* 19–20:165–198.

1999 Diagnostique archéologique sur le site du Griffon (Vitrolles, B.-du-Rh.). *Documents d'Archéologie Méridionale* 22:278–289.

2002 Les Salyens, les Cavares et les villes du Rhône. In Garcia and Verdin 2002, pp. 139–149.

Vickers, M.

1990 Attic *symposia* after the Persian Wars. In *Sympotica: A Symposium on the Symposion*, edited by O. Murray, pp. 105–121. Clarendon Press, Oxford.

Villard, F.

1960 *La céramique grecque de Marseille (VIe–IVe siècle), essai d'histoire économique.* Bibliothèque des Ecoles Françaises d'Athènes et de Rome 195. Boccard, Paris.

1988 Des vases grecs chez les Celtes. In *Les princes celtes et la Méditerranée*, pp. 333–341. La Documentation Française, Paris.

1992 La céramique archaïque de Marseille. In Bats et al. 1992, pp. 163-170.

Villard, P.

1988 Ivresses dans l'antiquité classique. *Mélanges de l'École Française de Rome, Antiquité* 65:7–34.

Vitruvius

1999 *Ten Books on Architecture.* Translated by I. Rowland. Cambridge University Press, Cambridge.

Vives-Ferrándiz, J.

2005 *Negociando encuentros. Situaciones coloniales e intercambios en la costa oriental de la península ibérica (ss. VIII–VI a.C.).* Cuadernos de Arqueología Mediterránea, 12. Universidad Pompeu Fabra de Barcelona, Barcelona.

2008 Negotiating colonial encounters: Hybrid practices and consumption in Eastern Iberia (8th–6th centuries BC). *Journal of Mediterranean Archaeology* 21(2):241–272.

von Gernet, A.

1995 Nicotian dreams: The prehistory and early history of tobacco in eastern North America. In *Consuming Habits: Drugs in History and Anthropology*, edited by J. Goodman, P. E. Lovejoy, and A. Sherratt, pp. 67–87. Routledge, London.

Wallace, A. F. C.

1956 Revitalization movements. *American Anthropologist* 58:264–281.

Wallerstein, I.

1974 *The Modern World System: Capitalist Agriculture and the Origin of the European World-Economy in the Sixteenth Century.* Academic Press, New York.

1991 World System versus world-systems: a critique. *Critique of Anthropology* 11:189–194.

Warnier, J.-P.

    Construire la culture materielle. L'homme qui pensait avec ses doigts. Presses Universitaires de France, Paris.

Webb, T.

    1982 *English Romantic Hellenism, 1700–1824.* Barnes and Noble, New York.

Webster, J.

    1995 The just war: Graeco-Roman texts as colonial discourse. In *TRAC 1994 Proceedings of the Fourth Theoretical Roman Archaeology Conference, Durham 1994,* edited by S. Cottam, D. Dungworth, S. Scott, and J. Taylor, pp. 1–10, Oxford.

    1996 Roman imperialism in the post-imperial age. In *Roman Imperialism: Post-colonial Perspectives,* edited by J. Webster and N. Cooper. Leicester University Press, Leicester.

    2001 Creolizing the Roman provinces. *American Journal of Archaeology* 105(2):209–225.

Weismantel, M. J.

    1988 *Food, Gender and Poverty in the Ecuadorian Andes.* Cambridge University Press, Cambridge.

Wells, P. S.

    1980 *Culture Contact and Culture Change: Early Iron Age Central Europe and the Mediterranean World.* Cambridge University Press, Cambridge.

    1984 *Farms, Villages, and Cities: Commerce and Urban Origins in Late Prehistoric Europe.* Cornell University Press, Ithaca, NY.

    1999 *The Barbarians Speak: How the Conquered Peoples Shaped Roman Europe.* Princeton University Press, Princeton.

Westermann, W. L.

    1955 *The Slave Systems of Greek and Roman Antiquity.* American Philosophical Society, Philadelphia.

Whatmough, J.

    1970 *The Dialects of Ancient Gaul.* Harvard University Press, Cambridge, MA.

White, R.

    1991 *The Middle Ground: Indians, Empires, and Republics in the Great Lakes Region, 1650–1815.* Cambridge University Press, Cambridge.

    2006 Creative misunderstandings and new understandings. *William and Mary Quarterly* 63(1):9–14.

Whitehead, D.

    1977 *The Ideology of the Athenian Metic.* Cambridge Philological Society, Cambridge.

Whitehouse, R. D., and J. B. Wilkins

    1989 Greeks and natives in south-east Italy: Approaches to the archaeological evidence. In Champion 1989, pp. 102–126.

Whittaker, C. R.

    1980 Rural labour in three Roman provinces. In Garnsey 1980a, pp. 73–99.

Wiessner, P.

    2001 Of feasting and value: Enga feasts in a historical perspective (Papua New Guinea). In Dietler and Hayden, pp. 115–143.

Wiessner, P., and A. Tumu

    1998 *Historical Vines: Enga Networks of Exchange, Ritual, and Warfare in Papua New Guinea.* Smithsonian Institution Press, Washington, DC.

Wikander, O.

1990 Archaic roof tiles: The first generations. *Hesperia* 59(1):285–290.

Wilkins, J., D. Harvey, and M. Dobson (editors)

1995 *Food in Antiquity*. University of Exeter Press, Exeter.

Wilkins, J. M., and S. Hill

2006 *Food in the Ancient World*. Blackwell Publishers, Oxford.

Will, E. L.

1982 Greco-Italic amphoras. *Hesperia* 51(3):338–356.

Willis, J.

2002 *Potent Brews: A Social History of Alcohol in East Africa, 1850–1999*. British Institute in Eastern Africa, Nairobi.

Winckelmann, J. J.

1987 [1755] *Reflections on the Imitation of Greek Works in Painting and Sculpture (Gedanken über die Nachahmung der griechischen Werke in der Malerei und Bildhauerkunst)*. Translated by E. Heyer and R. C. Norton. Open Court, La-Salle, IL.

Winspeare, M. P. (editor)

2005 *Cibi e sapori nel mondo antico*. Sillabe, Livorno, Italy.

Wohlleben, J.

1992 Germany 1750–1830. In *Perceptions of the Ancient Greeks*, edited by K. J. Dover, pp. 170–202. Blackwell Publishers, Oxford.

Wolf, E.

1982 *Europe and the People without History*. University of California Press, Berkeley.

Wood, E. M.

1983 Agriculture and slavery in Classical Athens. *American Journal of Ancient History* 8(1):1–47.

Wood, M., and F. Queiroga (editors)

1992 *Current Research on the Romanization of the Western Provinces*. BAR International Series S575, Oxford.

Woolf, G.

1990 World-systems analysis and the Roman Empire. *Journal of Roman Archaeology* 3:44–58.

1998 *Becoming Roman: The Origins of Provincial Civilization in Gaul*. Cambridge University Press, Cambridge.

Wright, J. C.

1995 Empty cups and empty jugs: the social role of wine in Minoan and Mycenaean societies. In *The Origin and Ancient History of Wine*, edited by P. E. McGovern, S. J. Fleming, and S. H. Katz, pp. 287–310. Gordon and Breach, Amsterdam.

Young, R. J. C.

1995 *Colonial Desire: Hybridity in Theory, Culture and Race*. Routledge, London.

2001 *Postcolonialism: An Historical Introduction*. Blackwell Publishers, Oxford.

Zuber, R.

1992 France, 1640–1790. In *Perceptions of the Ancient Greeks*, edited by K. J. Dover, pp. 147–169. Blackwell Publishers, Oxford.

INDEX

Phocaeans
  as pirates, 141, 155–156, 163
  as traders, 104, 108
Phoenicians, 4–7, 71, 139–140, 144, 147, 203,
  268, 348 n.12
Phoenician trade goods, 7, 136, 141, 196,
  230, 338
Pindar, 370 n.35
pirates/piracy, 8, 122, 132, 140–141, 143–144,
  155–156, 159, 161, 163, 176–177, 194, 197,
  337, 339, 342, 370 n.27
Plane 2 (shipwreck), 134–135
Pliny, 89–90, 206, 215, 223, 359 n.52,
  360 n.80, 370 n.34, 376 n.86, 376 n.91,
  377 n.129, 378 n.154,
Pointe de Lequin 1A (shipwreck), 134–135, 141
Polybius, 85, 92, 144, 151, 159–160, 165,
  180, 213, 358 n.44, 359 n.46, 360 n.76,
  365 n.227, 368 n.74, 369 n.103, 369 n.11,
  370 n.17, 371 n.44, 371 n.47, 373 n.117,
  373 n.120, 377 n.119
PompeiusTrogus, 1–2, 14, 24, 43–44, 93,
  158–159, 168, 320, 332–333, 335, 346,
  347 n.4
Port Vendres II (shipwreck), 136
Posidonius, 85, 91, 121, 165, 196, 215, 227–230,
  244, 246, 275, 331–332
postcolonial theory/studies, 13, 15, 17, 19–22, 46,
  49–53, 57, 64–65, 334, 353 n.104
potter's wheel, 220–221, 236, 247, 337,
  377 n.146
prostitutes(pornai), 111–113, 363 n.164
Protis, 1, 77, 104, 111
Pseudo-Scymnus, 118, 151, 364 n.191, 368 n.94,
  369 n.103
public school (English), 31–32
Punic Wars, 5, 7, 122, 163, 180
Pyrgi, 101, 140

querns/grindstones, 120, 138, 232, 240, 314, 323

Rallongue, La, 154, 207, 260
Ramasse, La, 261, 324, 326–327
ramparts/fortifications, 89–91, 97–98,
  118–120, 135, 150, 160, 166, 169–174,
  176–177, 181–182, 227, 257–259,
  262–266, 268, 270, 285, 292, 294–306,
  308, 310–312, 314, 316–318, 322,
  324–325, 327–329, 340, 342, 344, 359

n.60, 372 n.84, 372 n.85, 382 n.18,
  389 n.232
Rasenna (see Etruscans)
Renaissance, 28–29, 39–41, 44, 61, 76, 335
revitalization movements, 70, 182, 332
Rhodanousia, 110, 118, 149
Rhode/Rosas, 5, 72, 244
ritual/rituals (see also cemeteries, feasts,
  sanctuaries/temples, symposion)
  and identity, 64, 166–167, 182, 204–205, 216,
    218–219, 227
  domestic/familial, 321–323
  drinking, 64–65, 204–205, 216–217, 238,
    244–245
  funerary, 166–167, 257, 319, 321–322,
    388 n.210
  landscapes, 318–332, 336, 388 n.212
  practices, 64, 166–167, 178, 182, 188–190,
    205, 217–218, 220, 227, 245, 254, 302,
    321–323, 326–332, 371 n.62
  of colonialism, 35–36
  sites, 71–72, 92, 151, 167, 257, 307–308, 313,
    319, 323, 325–332, 389 n.232
  structures, 92, 257, 302, 315, 319–320, 322,
    325–330, 341
Roche-de-Comps, 261, 306
Rochelongue (shipwreck), 134–135
Roman conquest (of Gaul), 1, 5, 7–8, 12, 39, 41,
  57, 71–72, 78, 80, 82, 86, 88, 90–91, 94,
  104, 122–123, 128, 159, 178, 181, 201, 203,
  215, 219–220, 230, 238, 255, 268, 307, 325,
  340, 342–345
Roman Empire(Principate), 19, 22, 35–36, 46,
  125, 139, 201, 219, 226, 284, 344, 346,
  349 n.44
  effects on language, 8, 22, 79, 81–82, 95
  provincial administration, 73, 86, 89–90,
    93–94, 123–129, 345, 347 n.2, 349 n.44,
    365 n.247
Roman Republic, 7, 34, 36, 43, 139, 344,
  349 n.44
Romanization, 13, 32, 45–47, 123, 216, 335, 346
Rome
  demography of, 104, 123–124, 162, 370 n.26
  colonial practices, 8, 34–37, 43, 73, 89–90,
    93–94, 123–129, 343–345, 323, 344
  colonies, 8, 17, 117–119, 125–126, 128–129,
    149, 151, 260–261, 267, 343–344,
    349 n.42, 349 n.44

taxes/taxation, 36, 73, 112, 124–128, 140, 191, 344, 365 n.243, 365 n.247

tea, 61, 186, 189, 190–191

temples (see sanctuaries)

Teste-Nègre, 116, 174–175, 178, 260–261

Tête-de-l'Ost, 116, 174, 182

Theline (see also Arles), 117–119, 151–152

Thucydides, 163, 248, 361 n.121, 362 n.143, 370 n.29, 370 n.36, 381 n.252

Timouchoi, 109

Titan (shipwreck), 134, 138

tobacco, 188, 190–191

Tonnerre I, 154, 207, 252, 260–261

Tourelle de la Fourmigue, La (shipwreck), 134–135

trade (see also *cabotage*, *collegio*, emporion, Etruscans, Greeks, Massalia, piracy, Rome, Phoenician trade goods, *societatesprivatae*, *societatespublicanorum*)
shipcargoes, 62, 68, 101, 132–141, 194–195, 202, 212, 367 n.56, 376 n.113
emporic vsprexis trade distinction, 142
floater, 96–97, 145–146, 337–338
state involvement in, 140–141, 365 n.243

traders/merchants (see also *emporoi*, Iberian merchants, *mercatores*, metics,, *naukleroi*, *nautae*, *nautes*, *navicularii*, *negociatores*, *xenoi*)
enclaves/diaspora, 97–101, 117–119, 132, 139–140, 145–149, 150, 153, 206, 230, 269, 283, 338–339
ethnic identities of, 7, 80, 94, 119, 139–142, 144–146, 367 n.42
social identities of, 103, 139, 142–143, 147

tryclinium, 119

Tyrrhenoi (see Etruscans)

urban structure/settlement organization
concentric pattern, 295, 297, 299–300, 302–303
"heterogeneously regular" pattern, 292
"Hippodamian", 292–293, 295
linear strip pattern, 295–302
"loose order" (*ordre lâche*) pattern, 302–303
orthogonal, 292–293, 296, 300, 302, 313, 317–318, 386 n.145
rectilinear, 262–263, 266, 273, 277–278, 291–306, 340–341, 345, 383 n.29

Varro, 111

Vaunage basin, 149–150, 154, 208–209, 269, 299, 304

Verduron, Le, 116, 174–175, 178, 261

Via Domitia, 7, 90, 123, 126, 308

Vié-Cioutat, 261, 266, 359 n.64

Villevieille, 207

Vix/Mont Lassois, 210–211, 326

Vocontii, 1, 87–88, 93, 126, 161

VolcaeArecomici, 87–93, 359 n.63

VolcaeTectosages, 87, 125, 161, 359 n.46

Vulci, 100–101, 103, 197

warfare/violence (see also ramparts, mercenaries, pirates)
among indigenous polities, 165–166, 177, 181
and colonialism, 18, 85, 157–158
Etruscan, 141, 156, 162–164
evidence of, 158, 165–166, 173–180
Massalian, 7, 122–123, 151, 156, 158–165, 168, 175–178, 180–182, 235, 307–308, 332–333, 337–338, 340, 342–343, 359 n.55, 370 n.14, 370 n.16, 370 n.27
revolts/resistance to Rome, 93, 124–126, 175, 343, 347–348 n.4
Roman, 7–8, 91–92, 94, 115–116, 122–123, 125–126, 156–157, 159–163, 164, 174–176, 178, 180–181, 329, 342–343, 360 n.71, 372 n.111
scale of, 105, 161–162, 165, 169, 177, 337
settlement destruction, 156, 163, 167, 169, 173–178, 180–182, 259, 278, 297–298, 304, 341, 372 n.96
warrior statues, 72, 92, 178–180, 182, 286, 306, 324–332, 341–342
weapons, 70, 81, 151, 158, 166–169, 173–176, 244, 337, 344, 371 n.59, 371 n.62

wattle-and-daub, 89, 262–263, 265–274, 276–277, 294, 303, 313–314, 323, 340, 383 n.54

wild game, 225–227

wine (see also alcohol, amphorae, symposion, taverns)
consumption, 64, 96, 149, 153–155, 195, 197, 199–212, 214–222, 232–233, 238, 242, 244, 254–255, 337, 339, 344, 347 n.4, 375 n.81, 376 n.86, 377 n.115, 389 n.239

wine (*continued*)

    demand for, 61–62, 68–69, 132, 135, 186, 193–194, 204, 206, 210, 213, 215–218, 220–221, 255, 338

    production, 100, 118, 120, 122, 138, 197–201, 203, 217, 222–223, 255, 283, 342, 345, 375 n.59, 375 n.73

    trade, 5, 7, 94–96, 98, 103–105, 120, 122, 131–132, 135–139, 141, 144–145, 154–155, 193–203, 208–210, 212, 216–217, 219–221, 224, 338–339, 342, 344, 366 n.26, 367 n.56

vineyards, 114, 117, 120–121, 138, 198, 201, 203–204, 219, 222, 224

Winckelmann, Johann Joachim, 29–30, 68, 350 n.7

world system/world-systems, 20, 22, 42, 45, 48–50, 58, 335

writing/inscriptions (see also graffiti)

    Gallo-Greek, 71, 80, 90–91, 109, 273, 342

    Greek, 70–71, 95, 107, 119, 145, 150, 230

    Etruscan, 70–71, 95

    Iberian, 71, 80, 82, 83, 109, 144, 356 n.8

xenoi, 140

COMPOSITION: Michael Bass Associates
TEXT: 9.5/14 Scala
DISPLAY: Scala Sans
PRINTER AND BINDER: Thomson Shore, Inc.